THE
GOLFING UNION
OF IRELAND

1891–1991

THE
GOLFING UNION
OF IRELAND

1891–1991

William A. Menton

Gill and Macmillan

In gratitude

To the memory of my wife, Claire
for her unwavering support,
and to the Pioneers of Golf in Ireland,
and the many other absent friends
whose names and achievements
are recorded.

CONTENTS

ACKNOWLEDGMENTS

I must first express my grateful thanks to the Council of the Union for inviting me to undertake this most interesting task. The invitation came some time after I had retired as General Secretary and was most welcome not only because of my extensive knowledge of the subject acquired over the years but it also helped to fill the inevitable void after so many years of active participation in the affairs of golf in Ireland.

In 1988 a book entitled *Early Irish Golf* was published. Its author was William H. Gibson, an Irish Army Officer. The concept for the publication is best explained by quoting from the introduction to the book.

Early Irish Golf began as a research project into the formative years of golf in the Curragh, Co. Kildare. At an early stage the author found that there was no definitive account of the development of the game in Ireland itself. This book represents five years' research into the influences which led to the spread of this ever popular game in this country. The author does not claim to have discovered every fact of early golf history. However, many Club historians and members will find key material concerning the formative years of their own Clubs.

The period extends up to the end of 1922 and it contains authenticated information which will prove invaluable to the many affiliated Clubs whose origins were hitherto unknown or unsubstantiated.

I first met Bill Gibson in the National Library, Dublin when commencing research into this book. During the intervening years he was always available with advice and guidance as to sources and I am most grateful for his help.

As my brief was to trace the progress of the Golfing Union of Ireland from its foundation in 1891, I decided to research from 1886 because, like so many of our affiliated Clubs, there was no evidence of the inaugural meeting to found the Union. I immediately came across results of competitions in Royal Belfast (1881) and Dublin (1885) (later Royal Dublin) Golf Clubs. Later I discovered reports of meetings to found other Clubs and all have been listed in some of the earlier chapters. I was also able, with the help of the Union minute books, to ascertain the year of affiliation of these Clubs. More importantly, I discovered the date and venue of the meeting to found the Union together with the names of those in attendance and the resolutions passed.

Bill Gibson's self-imposed research project was to trace the game from its beginnings in Ireland. He has shown that as early as 1606 the game of 'goff' was mentioned in Ulster and that the first golf Club in Ireland was active in Bray, Co. Wicklow in 1762 almost 140 years before our Union, the first such Union in the world, was founded.

Other Clubs which were not located in my research and which are recorded in *Early Irish Golf* are:

1891   *The Grove (Belfast, Co. Down)*
1894   *Fonthill (Chapelizod, Co. Dublin); Kilwaughter Castle Park (Larne, Co. Antrim); Rathconey (Co. Cork)*
1895   *Claremont (Howth, Co. Dublin); Dromana (Rush, Co. Dublin)*
1897   *Castlegregory (Tralee, Co. Kerry); Killorglin (Co. Kerry)*
1898   *Augher (Co. Tyrone)*
1900   *Royal Hospital (Kilmainham, Co. Dublin)*
1903   *Stewartstown (Co. Tyrone)*
1906   *St James Gate (Co. Dublin)*
1910   *Mohill (Co. Leitrim)*
1911   *Knocklofty (Clonmel, Co. Tipperary)*
1923   *Dunmanway (Co. Cork); Rossnowlagh (Co. Donegal)*

Regrettably, as in the case of many other early Clubs, the above sixteen are no longer in existence.

In the chapters on the development of Club golf I have recorded the year of foundation and the year of affiliation of all Irish Clubs which I could trace. As a first step I contacted all existing Clubs to obtain this information. In a great number of cases there were no records and my research had to be extended to obtain accurate and factual data. I wish to acknowledge the many sources from which I was able to obtain most valuable information and without which my task would have proved impossible: The National Library of Ireland; the Library of Trinity College Dublin; the Library of the Royal and Ancient Golf Club; the British Museum Library; the *Belfast Newsletter*; *Golfing Annual* 1888–1903; the Golfing Union of Ireland Minute Books from 1891 to date; *The Derry Journal* 1891; *The Irish Sportsman* 1891–1892; the *Irish Independent*; *The Irish Times*; *The Irish Field*; *The Irish Golfers' Annual* 1897 (courtesy P. McDonald, Lisburn Golf Club); *Sportman's Holiday Guide* 1897; *Riverside Press Golfers' Guide* Volume IV, 1897; *The Irish Golfer 1899–1905*; *The Golfers' Handbook* 1902; *Nisbet's Golf Yearbook* 1907; *Nisbet's Golf Guide* 1908; *The Irish Golfers' Guide* 1910 (published by *The Irish Field*); *The Irish Golfing Guide* 1911–1916 (published by *Irish Life*); The Golfing Union of Ireland Yearbooks 1927 to date; *Irish Golf 1927–1971*; *The Irish Golfers' Blue Book* (incorporating the *Irish Golfers' Guide)* 1939–1940.

My special thanks are extended to: John Burgess and his staff of Lafayette Photography for providing the majority of photographs which are used to illustrate this book. Whilst he was provided with all the Union trophies and medals from which he produced colour photographs, on many occasions only newspaper, periodical or yearbook photographs of many earlier players, teams and officials were obtainable and this inevitably resulted a loss of quality; the Provincial Branches for photographs of trophies awarded in Provincial tournaments; the many Clubs and individuals for kindly providing photographs for reproduction; Robert A.L. Burnet, Historian and Librarian of the Royal & Ancient Golf Club of St Andrews for photographs and other material on many of our earlier golfers; Desmond Rea O'Kelly, the long serving Union Honorary Secretary and the Convenor of the Centenary Committee, for his advice and support at all times; Ivan E.R. Dickson, General Secretary of the Union, for making me a welcome visitor to Union headquarters to inspect minute books, yearbooks and other records to obtain the factual information necessary for my task; the staff at Union Headquarters, Betty Brophy, Florence Greene, Cora Harris and Pamela Carroll for their ever cheerful and willing co-operation with research, typing and photocopying. I want to pay a special tribute to Betty Brophy who, in the days before the installation of word processors in the office, not only typed every word of text and the appendices but, on many occasions had to re-type amended text when further information came to light. The Union is most fortunate in having such an efficient and dedicated staff. Michael Gill is the son of the late Willie Gill who had been my guide and mentor for over twenty-five years. Michael, through his firm, Gill and Macmillan, undertook the onerous task of publishing this volume which has been so meticulously edited by his colleague Kathleen Nealon. As a literary novice I welcomed her expertise. Denis Baker of The Unlimited Design Company designed the entire book.

Each and everyone has contributed to this work. I must also commend the Centenary Committee for inaugurating a Patronage scheme to assist in offsetting the printing and publication costs. To all these friends whose names are included at the end of the book I express thanks.

Recording one hundred years of development tends to result in a series of dates, decisions and events. I have sought to lighten the story by occasionally introducing items of interest somewhat outside the Union's field of influence but which I consider important in the context of the main subject.

W.A.M.
February 1991

FOREWORD

Having been founded in Portrush, Co. Antrim, on 12 October 1891, the Golfing Union of Ireland acquired the unique distinction of being the first Golf Union or Federation to be established in the world. Now, as we celebrate the Centenary Year, it is appropriate that this history has been written as a record of the growth of the Union and of the achievements of the golfers of Ireland.

I have been greatly honoured by being chosen as President of the Union for 1991, and I am particularly pleased that this position affords me the opportunity of commending this history and of praising its author, who has produced this very comprehensive record of the development of the Union over its first one hundred years.

The vitality of the Union was assured initially by the energy of the members of the founding clubs who, in the first decade, inaugurated two championships and two inter-club tournaments. As interest in the game increased with the formation of more clubs, the Union produced a handicap system and established further championships and tournaments to cater for the growing demand for competitive golf.

By the second decade — with 155 clubs affiliated to the Union — the Constitution was amended to enable four Provincial Branches, based in the historic provinces of Ireland, to be formed. Inter-provincial rivalry enhanced further the competitive spirit of the game.

For the next four to five decades growth, although positive, was less spectacular perhaps due to the affects of two world wars and an intervening period of economic recession.

About 35 years ago, the Union initiated a programme to promote Junior Golf, as a result of which Irish youths and boys can compete annually in twenty championships and tournaments. Junior teams represent Ireland in six international events, thus enhancing our international involvement at adult level.

The growth of the Union is entirely due to the enthusiastic support which it receives from its affiliated clubs and from the dedicated officials which they have elected to administer the affairs of the Union since its foundation. Without that loyal support the Union could not progress. Spaced throughout this history are the records of the dates of their formation and affiliation to the Union.

In 1949, because of the ever-increasing demand for daily administration of the Union, William A. Menton was appointed as General Secretary. He held this position until 1983 when illness compelled him to retire after thirty-five years of dedicated service, in recognition of which he was elected Honorary Delegate to the Central Council. Fortunately his health recovered and, because of his knowledge and personal involvement in the administration of the Union over such an extended period, the Central Council invited him to research and recount our history.

Endowed with a prodigious memory, Bill Menton entered into this mammoth task with remarkable persistence, patience and attention to detail. It is perhaps due to these qualities that we now owe him grateful acknowledgment for tracking down the very large number of photographs used to illustrate the book. His list of acknowledgments will give some insight into the extraordinary amount of research required. His decision to include, in a series of appendices, complete details of the winners of championships and inter-club tournaments together with the records of International and Inter-Provincial representatives at all levels over the century provides a permanent record, in one volume, of the players who have contributed to our development as a golfing nation.

I have read the history and I feel sure that, when you have done so, you will be grateful to the Scottish pioneers, who introduced the game to our shores, and to our historian, Bill Menton, for recounting the story to date.

Finally, I wish to express our sincere gratitude for the support which we have received from the many Patrons who so generously contributed to the cost of the publication of this book.

Desmond Rea O'Kelly
President, Golfing Union of Ireland, 1991

PRINCIPAL ABBREVIATIONS USED

CONGU	Council of National Golf Unions
EABGTC	European Amateur Boys' Golf Team Championship
EAGTC	European Amateur Golf Team Championship
EAYGTC	European Amateur Youths' Golf Team Championship
EGA	European Golf Association
EGU	English Golf Union
GUI	Golfing Union of Ireland
IAGA	Irish Artisan Golfers' Association
IGA	International Golf Association
ILGU	Irish Ladies' Golf Union
IPGA	Irish Professional Golfers' Association
JAC	Joint Advisory Council
NIFC	Northern Ireland Football Club
PGA	Professional Golfers' Association
PTC	Panel Training Committee
R&A	Royal and Ancient Golf Club of St Andrews
RCD	Royal County Down
SGU	Scottish Golf Union
SSS	Standard Scratch Score
STRI	Sports Turf Research Institute
TOC	Tournament Organising Committee
WGU	Welsh Golfing Union

THE CENTRAL AND PROVINCIAL COUNCILS OF THE GOLFING UNION OF IRELAND

The Central Council

PRESIDENT
Desmond Rea O'Kelly
(Howth)

President-Elect Liam Reidy (Kilkenny)
Honorary Secretary J. Gerard O'Brien (Clontarf)
Honorary Treasurer David M. McAuley (Royal
County Down)

Vice-Presidents (Branch Chairmen)
J.L. (Ian) Bamford
(Royal Portrush)
Declan J. Howley
(County Sligo)
Eamon Curran
(Woodbrook)
John F. O'Reilly
(Monkstown)

HONORARY VICE-PRESIDENTS *(Past Presidents)*
David L. Baine
(Belvoir Park)
John P. McInerney
(Lahinch)
Francis W. Bowen
(Douglas)
Thomas Montgomery
(Shandon Park)
Barry T. Crymble
(Royal County Down)
Michael J. Murphy
(Ballina)
Michael P. Fitzpatrick
(Sutton)
J. Gerard O'Brien
Patrick J. Foley
(Muskerry)
William O'Sullivan
(Killarney)
Gerard D. Golden
(Westport)
Gerald H. Owens
(Skerries)
H. Max Hadden
(Royal Belfast)
Frederick W. Perry
(Boyle)
Michael J. Hennelly
(Galway)
Joseph M. Quinlan
(Tralee)
Peter V. Lyons
(County Louth)
Thomas J. Rogers
(Roscommon)
Michael C. McAuley
(Royal County Down)
Brendan J. Scannell
(Woodbrook)
John G. McErvel
(Royal County Down)

HONORARY DELEGATES
Charles H. Adams
(Royal County Down)
Val Harte
(Strandhill)
Robert Bell (Greencastle)
William Flynn (Shannon)
Joseph B. Carr (Sutton)
William A. Menton
(Milltown)

GENERAL SECRETARY
Ivan E.R. Dickson (Grange)

PROVINCIAL OFFICERS AND DELEGATES
CONNACHT
Chairman Declan J. Howley
Honorary Secretary/Treasurer Thomas Grealy
(Roscommon)

Delegates
Ken Cunningham (County
Sligo)
Michael P. O'Donoghue
(Galway)

Secretary Sean Hosty
(Galway)

LEINSTER
Chairman Eamon Curran
Honorary Secretary Paul Smyth (Lucan)
Honorary Treasurer William Rossiter
(Tullamore)

Delegates
Joseph Furlong (Royal Tara) Martin McDonald (Elm
Park)
John McKiernan (Newlands)
Secretary Kenneth W. Haughton
(Greystones)

MUNSTER
Chairman John F. O'Reilly
Honorary Secretary/Treasurer Richard Barry (Mallow)
Honorary Match Secretary J. Percy Shannon (Mallow)
Delegates
John V. Lynch (Limerick) John F. O' Grady (Thurles)

ULSTER
Chairman J.L. (Ian) Bamford
Honorary Secretary Peter J.O'Hara (Massereene)
Honorary Treasurer Harold E. Richardson
(Carrickfergus)

Honorary Match Secretary William G. Black (Malone)
Delegates
Brendan G. Edwards
(Shandon Park)
Vincent J. O'Connor
(County Cavan)
Secretary Alfred J.C. Collis
(Holywood)

The Provincial Councils

CONNACHT

Chairman	Declan J. Howley
Honorary Secretary/Treasurer	Thomas Grealy
Delegates	
Ken Cunningham	Paddy Lanigan
Patrick Curley	(Tuam)
(Ballyhaunis)	Tommy Larkin
Eugene Fayne	(Ballinasloe)
(Athlone)	Michael P. O'Donoghue
Padraig Flanagan	Liam Walsh
(County Sligo)	(Westport)
Val Harte	
Honorary Delegates	
Gerard D. Golden	Frederick W. Perry
Michael J. Hennelly	J. Harry Rice
Frank Kelly	(Athlone)
(County Sligo)	Thomas J. Rogers
Secretary	Sean Hosty (Galway)

LEINSTER

Chairman	Eamon Curran
Honorary Secretary	Paul Smyth
Honorary Treasurer	William Rossiter
Delegates	
Tom Bishop	Albert Lee
(Hermitage)	(Mullingar)
Michael Craddock	Martin McDonald
(Malahide)	Michael McGinley
William F. Deegan	(Naas)
(New Ross)	John McKernan
Barry Doyle	Colm Madigan
(Carlow)	(Curragh)
Joseph Furlong	Walter H. Skelton
Jim Greene	(The Island)
(Grange)	
Honorary Delegates	
Michael P. Fitzpatrick	Gerald H. Owens
Con Harnett	Brendan J. Scannell
(Portmarnock)	
H. Breifne O'Reilly	
(Grange)	
Secretary	Ken W. Haughton

MUNSTER

Chairman	John F. O'Reilly
Honorary Secretary/	
Treasurer	Richard Barry
Honorary Match	
Secretary	J. Percy Shannon
Delegates	
Bernard J. Carroll	Michael Minihan
(Cork)	(Dunmore)
Michael J. Cashman	John Molyneaux
(East Cork)	(Ballybunion)
Bernard Hynes	Seamus Norton
(Carrick-on-Suir)	(Lahinch)
John V. Lynch	J. Kieran O'Connor
Alan McIlraith	(Killarney)
(Tramore)	John F. O'Grady
James J. McKenna	Philip O'Sullivan
(Muskerry)	(Monkstown)
Sean McMahon	John Scanlon
(Adare Manor)	(Douglas)
Michael Meehan	
(Castletroy)	
Honorary Delegate	Austin Slattery
	(Lahinch)

ULSTER

Chairman	J.L. (Ian) Bamford
Honorary Secretary	Peter J. O'Hara
Honorary Treasurer	Harold E. Richardson
Honorary Match	
Secretary	William G. Black
Delegates	
D. Brian Blaikie	Cecil Lindsay
(Bangor)	(Ballyclare)
Anthony P. Campbell	Sam McBurney
(Warrenpoint)	(Massereene)
P.J. Collins	Frank E. McCarroll
(County Armagh)	(City of Derry)
Brendan G. Edwards	Eamon J. O'Connor
John Graham	(Donegal)
(Castlerock)	Vincent O'Connor
Tom Jones	J. Lindsay Shanks
(Belvoir Park)	(Bushfoot)
Immediate Past	
Chairman	Robert Bell
Immediate Past	
President GUI	
(Ulster)	Barry T. Crymble
Honorary Delegates	
H. Max Hadden	John G. McErvel
Rt Hon. Lord Lowry	Tom Montgomery
(Royal Portrush)	J. Harold Pyper
Michael C. McAuley	(Clandeboye)
Secretary	Alfred J.C. Collis

Desmond Rea O'Kelly

President 1991

THE IRISH AMATEUR OPEN CHAMPIONSHIP

(Chapter 5 Appendix I Section 4)

Year	Venue	Winner and Club	Year	Venue	Winner and Club
1892	Portrush	A. Stuart, Hon. Co. Edinburgh Golfers	1924	Dollymount	E.F. Spiller, North West
			1925	Portrush	T.A. Torrance, Sandy Lodge
1893	Newcastle	J. Ball Jr, Royal Liverpool	1926	Portmarnock	C.O. Hezlet, Royal Portrush
1894	Dollymount	J. Ball Jr, Royal Liverpool	1927	Newcastle	R.M. McConnell, Royal Portrush
1895	Portrush	W.B. Taylor, Carlton			
1896	Newcastle	W.B. Taylor, Carlton	1928	Dollymount	G.S. Noon, Edinburgh Burgess
1897	Dollymount	H.H. Hilton, Royal Liverpool			
1898	Portrush	W.B. Taylor, Carlton	1929	Portrush	C.O. Hezlet, Royal Portrush
1899	Portmarnock	J. Ball Jr, Royal Liverpool	1930	Portmarnock	William Sutton, Timperley
1900	Newcastle	H.H. Hilton, Royal Liverpool	1931	Newcastle	E.A. McRuvie, Leven Thistle
1901	Dollymount	H.H. Hilton, Royal Liverpool	1932	Dollymount	J. McLean, Hayston
1902	Portrush	H.H. Hilton, Royal Liverpool	1933	Newcastle	J. McLean, Hayston
1903	Portmarnock	Geo. Wilkie, Leven Thistle	1934	Portmarnock	H. Thomson, Williamwood
1904	Newcastle	J.S. Worthington, Royal Mid-Surrey	1935	Portrush	H. Thomson, Williamwood
			1936	Portmarnock	J.C. Brown, Waterford
1905	Dollymount	H.A. Boyd, Portmarnock	1937	Dollymount	J. Fitzsimmons, Bushfoot
1906	Portrush	H.H. Barker, Huddersfield	1938	Newcastle	J. Bruen Jr, Cork
1907	Portmarnock	J. Douglas Brown, Murrayfield	1939	Portmarnock	Championship cancelled
			1940-45	No Championship	
1908	Newcastle	J.F. Mitchell, Royal Musselburgh	1946	Portrush	J.B. Carr, Sutton
			1947	Dollymount	J. Burke, Limerick
1909	Dollymount	L.O. Munn, North-West	1948	Newcastle	Cecil Ewing, Co. Sligo
1910	Portrush	L.O. Munn, North-West	1949	Killarney	W.M. O'Sullivan, Killarney
1911	Portmarnock	L.O. Munn, North-West	1950	Rosses Point	J.B. Carr, Sutton
1912	Newcastle	Gordon Lockhart, Prestwick St Nicholas	1951	Portmarnock	Cecil Ewing, Co. Sligo
			1952	Portrush	N.V. Drew, Bangor
1913	Dollymount	C.A. Palmer, Handsworth	1953	Killarney	N.V. Drew, Bangor
1914-18	No Championship		1954	Dollymount	J.B. Carr, Sutton
1919	Portrush	C. Bretherton, Handsworth	1955	Newcastle	J.F. Fitzgibbon, Cork
1920	Portmarnock	G.N.C. Martin, Royal Portrush	1956	Portmarnock	J.B. Carr, Sutton
			1957	Portrush	J.L. Bamford, Royal Portrush
1921	Newcastle	D. Wilson Smyth, Royal Co. Down	1958	Dollymount	T. Craddock, Malahide
			1959	Newcastle	J. Duncan, Shandon Park
1922	Portrush	Alfred Lowe, Malone	1960	Championship discontinued and the Cup awarded to the winning province in the Irish Amateur Interprovincial Championship.	
1923	Newcastle	G.N.C. Martin, Royal Portrush			

Alexander Stuart — First Irish Amateur Open Champion 1892.

Taken from a portrait hanging in the Lounge of the Honorable Company of Edinburgh Golfers' Clubhouse at Muirfield, Scotland, of which he was also Club Captain in 1892. (Chapter 5)

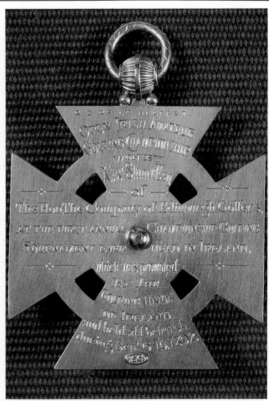

*Front and reverse side of the gold medal presented to Alexander
Stuart when he won the Inaugural Irish Amateur Open
Championship at Portrush in 1892. (Chapter 5)*

THE IRISH AMATEUR CLOSE CHAMPIONSHIP

(Chapter 6 Appendix II)

Year	Venue	Winner and Club
1893	Portrush	T. Dickson, Co. Down
1894	Newcastle	R. Magill, Co. Down
1895	Dollymount	W.H. Webb, Royal Portrush
1896	Portrush	J.S. Moore, Dublin University
1897	Newcastle	H.E. Reade, Royal Belfast
1898	Dollymount	W.H. Webb, Royal Portrush
1899	Portrush	H.E. Reade, Royal Belfast
1900	Portmarnock	R.G.N. Henry, Portmarnock
1901	Newcastle	W.H. Boyd, Portmarnock
1902	Dollymount	F.B. Newett, Malone
1903	Portrush	H.E. Reade, Royal Belfast
1904	Portmarnock	H.A. Boyd, Portmarnock
1905	Newcastle	F.B. Newett, Malone
1906	Dollymount	H.A. Boyd, Portmarnock
1907	Portrush	H.M. Cairnes, Portmarnock
1908	Portmarnock	L.O. Munn, Dublin University
1909	Newcastle	A.H. Patterson, Dublin University
1910	Dollymount	J.F. Jameson, Malahide
1911	Portrush	L.O. Munn, North-West
1912	Castlerock	A.H. Craig, Fortwilliam
1913	Portmarnock	L.O. Munn, Royal Dublin
1914	Hermitage	L.O. Munn, North-West
1915–18 No Championship		
1919	Portmarnock	E.F. Carter, Royal Portrush
1920	Castlerock	C.O. Hezlet, Royal Portrush
1921	Portmarnock	E.F. Carter, Royal Dublin
1922	Portrush	E.M. Munn, North-West
1923	Milltown	J.D. MacCormack, Hermitage
1924	Newcastle	J.D. MacCormack, Hermitage
1925	Portmarnock	C.W. Robertson, Delgany
1926	Portrush	A.C. Allison, Royal Portrush
1927	Cork	J.D. MacCormack, Hermitage
1928	Castlerock	D.E.B. Soulby, Fortwilliam
1929	Dollymount	D.E.B. Soulby, Fortwilliam
1930	Lahinch	J. Burke, Lahinch
1931	Rosses Point	J. Burke, Lahinch
1932	Portrush	J. Burke, Lahinch
1933	Cork	J. Burke, Lahinch
1934	Rosslare	J.C. Brown, Waterford
1935	Galway	R.M. MacConnell, Royal Portrush
1936	Castlerock	J. Burke, Newlands
1937	Ballybunion	J. Bruen Jr, Muskerry
1938	Castle	J. Bruen Jr, Muskerry
1939	Rosses Point	G.H. Owens, Skerries
1940	Dollymount	J. Burke, Castletroy
1941–5 No Championship		
1946	Dollymount	J. Burke, Castletroy
1947	Lahinch	J. Burke, Castletroy
1948	Portrush	C. Ewing, Co. Sligo
1949	Galway	J.P. Carroll, Sutton
1950	Baltray	B. Herlihy, Portmarnock
1951	Cork	M. Power, Muskerry
1952	Craigivad	T.W. Egan, Monkstown
1953	Rosses Point	J. Malone, Portmarnock
1954	Carlow	J.B. Carr, Sutton
1955	Lahinch	J.R. Mahon, Portmarnock
1956	Malone	A.G.H. Love, Knock
1957	Galway	J.B. Carr, Sutton
1958	Ballybunion	C. Ewing, Co. Sligo
1959	Portmarnock	T. Craddock, Malahide
1960	Portstewart	M. Edwards, Shandon Park
1961	Rosses Point	D.B. Sheahan, Grange & UCD
1962	Baltray	M. Edwards, Shandon Park
1963	Killarney	J.B. Carr, Sutton
1964	Newcastle	J.B. Carr, Sutton
1965	Rosses Point	J.B. Carr, Sutton
1966	Dollymount	D.B. Sheahan, Grange
1967	Lahinch	J.B. Carr, Sutton
1968	Portrush	M.D. O'Brien, New Ross
1969	Rosses Point	V. Nevin, Limerick
1970	Grange	D.B. Sheahan, Grange
1971	Ballybunion	R.M. Kane, Malahide
1972	Newcastle	K. Stevenson, Banbridge
1973	Rosses Point	R.K.M. Pollin, Royal Belfast
1974	Portmarnock	R.M. Kane, Ealing
1975	Cork	M.D. O'Brien, New Ross
1976	Portrush	D. Branigan, L'town & B'town
1977	Westport	M.A. Gannon, Co. Louth
1978	Carlow	M.F. Morris, Portmarnock
1979	Ballybunion	J. Harrington, Adare Manor
1980	Newcastle	R. Rafferty, Warrenpoint
1981	Rosses Point	D. Branigan, L'town & B'town
1982	Woodbrook	P. Walton, Malahide
1983	Killarney	T. Corridan, Castletroy
1984	Malone	T.B.C. Hoey, Shandon Park
1985	Westport	D.F. O'Sullivan, Cork
1986	Dollymount	J. McHenry, Douglas
1987	Tramore	E. Power, Tramore
1988	Portrush	G. McGimpsey, Bangor
1989	Rosses Point	P. McGinley, Grange
1990	Baltray	D. Clarke, Dungannon

Irish Amateur Close Championship medal designed to enable winner to have his name
& year engraved on front side. (Chapter 34)

AFFILIATED GOLF CLUBS
Total Number of Clubs – 275

The figure before the name of the club indicates the number of holes.

CONNACHT - 33

CO. GALWAY - (11)
18 Athenry
18 Ballinasloe
18 Connemara
18 Galway
9 Gort
9 Loughrea
9 Mountbellow
18 Oughterard
18 Portumna
18 Tuam
- University College

CO. LEITRIM - (2)
9 Ballinamore
9 Carrick-on-Shannon

CO. MAYO - (10)
9 Achill Island
9 Ballina
9 Ballinrobe
9 Ballyhaunis
9 Belmullet
18 Castlebar
9 Claremorris
9 Mulrany
9 Swinford
18 Westport

CO. ROSCOMMON - (5)
18 Athlone
9 Ballaghdereen
9 Boyle
9 Castlerea
9 Roscommon

CO. SLIGO - (5)
9 Ballymote
18 Co. Sligo
18 Enniscrone
18 Strandhill
9 Tubbercurry

LEINSTER - 95

CO. CARLOW - (2)
9 Borris
18 Carlow

CO. DUBLIN - (21)
18 Balbriggan
18 Ballinascorney
18 Beaverstown
18 Beech Park
18 Donabate
18 Dublin & County
18 Dun Laoghaire
18 Forrest Little
18 Hermitage
18 The Island
9 Killiney
18 Kilternan
18 Lucan
27 Malahide
18 Old Conna
27 Portmarnock
9 Rush
18 Skerries
18 Slade Valley
9 Westmanstown
18 Woodbrook

DUBLIN CITY - (20)
9 Carrickmines
18 Castle
18 Clontarf
18 Deer Park
- Dublin University
18 Edmonstown
18 Elm Park
9 Foxrock
18 Grange
9 Hazel Grove
18 Howth
18 Milltown
18 Newlands
9 Rathfarnham
- Royal College of
   Surgeons
18 Royal Dublin
18 St Anne's
18 Stackstown
9 Sutton
- University College

CO. LAOIS - (5)
9 Abbeyleix
18 Heath
9 Mountrath
18 Portarlington
9 Rathdowney

CO. KILDARE - (10)
9 Athy
36 Bodenstown
18 Castlewarden
9 Cill Dara
- Clane
9 Clongowes
18 Curragh
18 Four Lakes
18 Knockanally
9 Naas

CO. KILKENNY - (4)
9 Callan
9 Castlecomer
18 Kilkenny
18 Waterford

CO. LONGFORD - (1)
18 Co. Longford

CO. LOUTH - (4)
18 Ardee
18 Co. Louth
18 Dundalk
18 Greenore

CO. MEATH - (7)
9 Black Bush
9 Gormanston
18 Headfort
9 Kilcock
18 Laytown & Bettystown
18 Royal Tara
9 Trim

CO. OFFALY - (3)
18 Birr
9 Edenderry
18 Tullamore

CO. WESTMEATH - (2)
9 Moate
18 Mullingar

CO. WEXFORD - (5)
18 Courtown
18 Enniscorthy
9 New Ross
18 Rosslare
18 Wexford

CO. WICKLOW - (11)
18 Arklow
9 Baltinglass
18 Blainroe
9 Bray
9 Coollattin
18 Delgany
18 European
18 Greystones
9 Tulfarris
9 Wicklow
9 Woodenbridge

MUNSTER - 56

CO. CLARE - (7)
18 Dromoland Castle
18 Ennis
9 Kilkee
9 Kilrush
36 Lahinch
18 Shannon
9 Spanish Point

CO. CORK - (25)
18 Bandon
9 Bantry Park
9 Berehaven
18 Charleville
9 Cobh
18 Cork
9 Doneraile
18 Douglas
9 Dunmore
18 East Cork
18 Fermoy
9 Frankfield
9 Glengarriff
9 Kanturk
9 Kinsale
9 Macroom
18 Mahon
18 Mallow
9 Mitchelstown
18 Monkstown
18 Muskerry
9 Raffeen Creek
9 Skibbereen
- University College
18 Youghal

CO. KERRY - (8)
36 Ballybunion
9 Ceann Sibeal
18 Dooks
9 Kenmare
36 Killarney
9 Parknasilla
18 Tralee
18 Waterville

CO. LIMERICK - (4)
9 Adare Manor
18 Castletroy
18 Limerick
9 Newcastle West

CO. TIPPERARY - (9)
9 Cahir Park
9 Carrick-on-Suir
18 Clonmel
18 Nenagh
9 Rockwell
9 Roscrea
9 Templemore
18 Thurles
9 Tipperary

CO. WATERFORD - (3)
9 Dungarvan
9 Lismore
18 Tramore

ULSTER - 91

CO. ANTRIM - (16)
18 Ballycastle
18 Ballyclare
18 Ballymena
9 Bushfoot
18 Cairndhu
18 Carrickfergus
9 Cushendall
- Garron Tower
9 Greenisland
9 Lambeg
9 Larne
18 Lisburn
18 Massereene
- Rathmore
36 Royal Portrush
18 Whitehead

CO. ARMAGH - (5)
18 Co. Armagh
18 Lurgan
18 Portadown
9 Silverwood
18 Tandragee

CO. CAVAN - (5)
9 Belturbet
9 Blacklion
9 Cabra Castle
18 Co. Cavan
9 Virginia

BELFAST - (12)
18 Balmoral
18 Belvoir Park
9 Cliftonville
18 Dunmurry
18 Fortwilliam
9 Gilnahirk
18 Knock
18 Knockbracken
27 Malone
9 Ormeau
- Queen's University
18 Shandon Park

CO. LONDONDERRY - (7)
9 Brown Trout
27 Castlerock
27 City of Derry
9 Kilrea
18 Moyola Park
36 Portstewart
- University of Ulster

CO. FERMANAGH - (1)
9 Enniskillen

CO. MONAGHAN - (4)
9 Castleblayney
9 Clones
9 Nuremore
18 Rossmore

CO. TYRONE - (6)
18 Dungannon
9 Fintona
18 Killymoon
18 Newtownstewart
18 Omagh
18 Strabane

CO. DONEGAL - (16)
18 Ballybofey & Stran.
18 Ballyliffin
9 Buncrana
18 Bundoran
9 Cruit Island
18 Donegal
18 Dunfanaghy
9 Greencastle
9 Gweedore
18 Letterkenny
18 Narin & Portnoo
18 North West
9 Otway
18 Portsalon
9 Redcastle
18 Rosapenna

CO. DOWN _ (19)
18 Ardglass
12 Banbridge
18 Bangor
18 Bright Castle
18 Carnalea
36 Clandeboye
18 Donaghadee
18 Downpatrick
9 Helen's Bay
18 Holywood
9 Kilkeel
18 Kirkistown Castle
9 Mahee Island
- Mourne
18 Royal Belfast
36 Royal Co. Down
18 Scrabo
18 Spa
18 Warrenpoint

SUMMARY

9 HOLE COURSES	108
12 HOLE COURSES	1
18 HOLE COURSES	142
27 HOLE COURSES	5
36 HOLE COURSES	8
PLAYING FACILITIES	4
UNIVERSITY CLUBS	7

Chapter 1

THE
ORIGIN OF GOLF
IN
IRELAND

There can be no doubt that it is Scotland we have to thank for introducing golf to our shores. The Curragh Golf Club celebrated its centenary in 1983 and published a detailed account of its early history. It records that David Ritchie, who was a member of Musselburgh (later Royal Musselburgh) Golf Club migrated from Scotland to Ireland in 1851 and laid out the first recorded golf course in Ireland on the Curragh in 1852.[1]

The Earl of Eglinton, who was appointed Lord Lieutenant of Ireland in 1852, was an enthusiastic golfer and was a founder member of Prestwick Golf Club in 1851. He often played on the Curragh course. He was also dedicated to the promotion of the game. Not only did he play a prominent part in the origin of the Open Championship, but he presented the Championship Belt, which was won outright by Tom Morris Jr in 1870. The Belt is one of the most prized trophies in the Royal and Ancient Golf Club Museum at St Andrews. The Earl was appointed Captain of the R & A when he returned to Scotland from Ireland in 1853.

The Curragh Golf Club can rightly claim to have the earliest recorded course in Ireland. With various alterations, it is still in active use to the present time. However, no properly constituted Golf Club was founded there until 1883 and thus the Curragh can only be listed as the second oldest Golf Club in this country. The oldest Irish Golf Club is Royal Belfast which was founded on 9 November 1881, just ten years before the founding of the Golfing Union of Ireland.

Thomas Sinclair, a Scottish businessman living in Belfast, returned to Scotland for a holiday in the summer of 1881. He played golf at St Andrews and on his return to Belfast he met a fellow Scotsman, George L. Baillie, a newly appointed Master of The Royal Academy, and known to be an experienced golfer. Baillie came from Musselburgh where he had played golf since he was a boy. Captain John Harrison, the 'Laird' of Holywood, gave them permission to lay out a golf course on his land, free of rent and other charges. Royal Belfast's first home was a 6 hole course on 80 acres at the Kinnegar, Holywood. The course was laid out by George Baillie with the assistance of Walter Day of the Bruntsfield Club, Musselburgh. Walter's brother, Alexander Day, was later to become professional at the Royal Belfast Club where he remained for 22 years. Thomas Sinclair was elected the first Captain. The course was later extended to 9 holes and because of increasing membership the Club moved to Carnalea in 1890 and eventually, in 1925, to its present location at Craigavad.

George Baillie had been appointed first Honorary Secretary of the Club, a position he retained until 1888 when he resigned as he wished to direct his energies to the development of the game at other venues. He played a major part in the foundation and organisation of two golf links which were ultimately to earn world renown — Royal Portrush and Royal County Down.

John Lumsden of Banffshire, Scotland, came to Ireland in 1867 to take up an appointment with the Provincial Bank in Drogheda. A few years later he was promoted to Head Office in Dublin. Whilst on holiday in England, he was introduced to the game on Wimbledon Common. Like Thomas Sinclair, he took to the game with enthusiasm, and on his return to Dublin looked around for a suitable place to play. His attention turned to the broad acres of the Phoenix Park, where the British Military had been playing for some 30 years. Lumsden decided to form a Golf Club and called a meeting on 5 May 1885 at which the Dublin Golf Club was founded.

One of the earliest members of this new Club was a prominent Scottish golfer, Thomas Gilroy. Born in Dundee in 1852, he migrated to Ireland and acquired Mornington House at the mouth of the Boyne in the grounds of which he laid out an 11 hole course in 1886. Gilroy was possibly the one person whose influence and ability fostered golf in Ireland. (See Chapters 3 and 7). In 1885, Gilroy lent his expertise and knowledge to Lumsden in the design of an 18 hole course of 3904 yards which was laid out near the Magazine Fort. This is certainly short by today's standards, but at the time of the gutty ball and hickory shafts, it was of adequate interest to the early pioneers of the Park course. It was just 105 yards longer than the 12 hole links at Prestwick, the home of the Open Championship for the first 12 years of its existence. In 1886 the Club moved from the Park to Cush Point, Sutton, where it remained until 1889 when, having successfully negotiated with the Dublin Port and Docks Board, it moved to its present home on North Bull Island.

It left behind it a taste for the game as on 23 May 1890 a monthly tenancy agreement was entered into between the Earl of Howth and the Dublin Scottish Golf Club to use Cush Point at a rent of 1/- (now 5p) a month.[2] There is, however, no evidence as to how long the Dublin Scottish remained in possession, as in 1896 the area was acquired by a yacht club. The members elected John Lumsden the Club's first Captain, a position he held from 1885 to 1887. He was succeeded by Thomas Gilroy who was Captain for the next two years.

Two other Scotsmen, W.C. Pickman and George Ross, rowed across the estuary from Sutton in 1889 to explore the peninsula which they later developed into what now comprises the links of Portmarnock. J.P. Rooney, the golf writer, published a history of Sutton Golf Club and showed that the Sutton Yacht and Boat Club was founded on 6 September

Scottish Pioneers of Golf in Ireland

David Ritchie who laid out the first
recorded golf course at the Curragh
in 1852.

Thomas Sinclair (left) and George L. Baillie (right)
the founders of The Belfast Golf Club at the
Kinnegar, Holywood in 1881.

John Lumsden (left) founder of The Dublin Golf
Club in 1885.
Thomas Gilroy (right) who helped Lumsden lay out
the first course in the Phoenix Park.

Baillie and Gilroy visited Portrush in 1888 and were
instrumental in the formation of the County Club. Baillie is also
credited as one of the movers in the formation of the County
Down Club at Newcastle in 1889 whilst Gilroy laid out the
original links at Baltray in 1892. The title of 'Royal' was
conferred on five of the above clubs in the following years:
Belfast 1885, Dublin 1891, County 1892,
County Down 1908 and Curragh 1910.

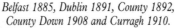

George Ross (left) and W.C. Pickman (right)
founders of Portmarnock Golf Club in 1894.

1894.[3] Portmarnock approached Sutton YBC to use the jetty at Cush Point to boat their members over to the links. A suggestion by the yacht club that their members be allowed to join Portmarnock at one-half the present entrance fee was turned down and the yacht club broke off negotiations. Some of the yacht club members acquired the former Dublin Club course at the Burrow where, on payment of a small extra subscription, the members of the yacht club could have the privilege of playing golf in the Burrow. The golfers began to oust the yachtsmen and on 20 January 1896 the yacht club elected a committee to manage the affairs of what came to be Sutton Golf Club. In his article, Rooney states that in all likelihood had the Portmarnock Club agreed to the terms of the yacht club, no Golf Club would have been started at Sutton.

A report in the *Belfast Newsletter*[4] records that a correspondent of one of the London dailies wrote that he had noticed the opening game on a course at Fota Island, Cork, in February 1883 and had observed that the ways of Scoticism had crossed the Channel and travelled as far as Cork where the game had been initiated with much success. Unfortunately, no other information regarding the game or the course can be found and Fota Island must therefore be ranked as a private course as also was the 11 hole course at Mornington, neither of which was ever developed into a members' Club.

It should be mentioned that the legendary Scottish professional, Old Tom Morris, was invited to visit County Down in July 1890 with a view to extending the links to 18 holes. Morris spent two days on the ground and 'blocked out' a long but interesting course. His fee for the work was £4. Old Tom also visited Portrush and Carnalea (Royal Belfast) to advise on how to improve their grounds.

The game introduced to Ireland by the Scots had come to stay, for between 1888 and 1891 a further 25 courses were opened for play of which all but seven eventually joined the Union.

The first clubhouse at Dollymount (above) opened in 1899 to which extensions resulted in the two storey building (below) destroyed by fire in 1948.

The Royal Dublin clubhouse erected on the same site and opened in 1954.

Chapter 2

THE
DEVELOPMENT
OF GOLF
IN IRELAND

Period: 1881 to 1891

One of the most important aspects of the GUI is the development of Club golf without which the Union would have little purpose. From time to time in this history the names of Clubs which were opened for play will be recorded. In publishing the list, the present name of each existing Club is recorded and its year of foundation is shown. Where the Club has altered its name from the name by which it was known when founded, its original name is recorded in parenthesis. Where a Club has ceased to operate, the name of the county in which it was located is recorded in parenthesis after the name of the Club.

Sometimes a Club opened for play, closed down after some years and then, many years later (and often at another location) a Club with the same name commenced activities. In these cases the existing Club has been contacted and if it wishes to be recorded as being founded at the later date, the term 'Old' is entered in parenthesis after the Club of the same name at the earlier date. 'A' denotes the affiliation of a Club to the Union and the year is shown immediately thereafter.

The nine original Clubs which formed the Union were located in Ulster, and all the 'Founding Fathers' hailed from there, but golf in Ireland at the time of the establishment of the Union was not confined to that province. In all, 28 'greens', as golf courses were then designated, had been opened for play by the time the Union was founded on 12 October 1891:

1881   *Royal Belfast (originally Belfast), A 1891.*

1883   *Curragh (originally Curragh, then Royal Curragh), A 1898; Fota Island (Co Cork).*

1885   *Royal Dublin (originally Dublin), A 1892.*

1886   *Mornington (Co. Meath).*

1888   *Aughnacloy (Co. Tyrone), A 1891; Cork, A 1900; Royal Portrush (originally County Antrim, then the County, then the Royal County), A 1891.*

1889   *Killymoon, A 1891; Queen's County Heath (Queen's County, now Co. Laois); Royal County Down (originally County Down) A 1891.*

1890   *Ballycastle, A 1891; Bushfoot, A 1906; Dublin Scottish (Sutton, Co. Dublin); Dungannon, A 1891; Shanes Park (Randalstown, Co. Antrim), A 1893; The Island, A 1901.*

1891   *Belmont (Garnerville, Co. Down) A 1894; Carrickfergus (Old) (Co. Antrim); Fortwilliam (originally Fortwilliam Park) A 1895; Leopardstown (Co. Dublin); Limerick, A 1909; Lisburn (Old) (Co. Antrim), A 1894; North West (originally Buncrana), A 1891; Omagh (originally Tyrone) (Old) (Co. Tyrone); Portsalon, A 1891; Rushbrooke (Co. Cork), A 1905; Thomastown (Co. Kilkenny) A 1923.*

It is fortunate that 21 of these greens developed into members' Clubs and became affiliated to the Union; 17 of the initial Clubs are still actively in existence.

Chapter 3

THE
FOUNDING
OF THE
UNION

In 1882, Henry Gregg, off a handicap of 50, won his first medal on the Royal Belfast links at Hollywood. He improved so rapidly that at the opening meeting of the Portrush Club in 1888, he defeated his preceptor, George Baillie, to win the Scratch Cup. Gregg became Captain of Royal Belfast in 1886 and six years later was similarly honoured with the captaincy of County Down.[5] Henry Herdman also started his golf in 1882 at the Royal Belfast links and was described as one of the quiet workers for the spread of the game despite the fact that it was regarded with ridicule by the entire community. Those associated with it were treated with contempt and sarcasm on every occasion when they had the temerity to allude to their pastime or ventured to exhibit any of its appurtenances. Other early 'converts' were William Henry Mann, George Combe, Thomas Dickson and Captain James McCalmont.

Another was James Henderson who was not only a member of the original Belfast Club, but also of the County Club at Portrush and the County Down Club at Newcastle. In 1887, he was Captain of Royal Belfast and presented the Henderson Cup for open competition in order to encourage golf in Ireland. At that time, there were only three golf Clubs: Royal Belfast, Curragh and Dublin. One of the original conditions was that the Cup would become the property of the player who won it twice, not necessarily in succession, from and after 1 April 1891. However, in 1895 Henderson found that there were then many challenge cups offered. On the advice of some experienced golfers he decided to offer the Cup for final competition that year on the Dollymount links, immediately preceding the Championship meeting.

During its short lifetime the Cup was won by the following: H.J. Cameron on the Royal Belfast links at Holywood in 1888; Thomas Gilroy on the Dublin links at Dollymount in

Some Early Prizes and Trophies

The 1881 Belfast Golf Club Monthly medals.

The Henderson Cup 1888–95.

The Aughnacloy Putter, which
was first competed for in 1889
and is still competed for at
Dungannon Golf Club.

1889; Hugh Adair on the County links at Portrush in 1890 and on the Auchnacloy links in 1891; Samuel Wilson Jr on the County Down links at Newcastle in 1892; James Dickson on the Killymoon links at Cookstown in 1893; W.R.B. West on the Dungannon links at Mullaghmore in 1894 and James Stevenson on the Royal Dublin links at Dollymount in 1895.

Another popular and much coveted trophy was the Auchnacloy Putter, the competition for which survives to this day. This extremely ornate putter was first played for at the Aughnacloy Club's spring meeting in 1889. The result was a tie between two members of Royal Belfast, Hugh Shaw playing off scratch who returned 79 and Hugh C. Kelly, the man destined some two years later to become the first Honorary Treasurer of the Union and who, playing off 25 went round in 104 strokes which also gave him a 79. Shaw, by winning the first tie hole, became the first holder of the Aughnacloy Putter. This was also the first recorded 'sudden death'. Alas the Aughnacloy Golf Club, one of the nine original Clubs forming the Union, has ceased to exist, but the competition has been continued by the Dungannon Golf Club.

Research has failed to establish who first mooted the idea of the formation of the Golfing Union of Ireland and no one name could be traced. However, in June 1891, at the conclusion of the summer meeting of the County Club at Portrush, a conference was held in the clubhouse. The Club Captain, William H. Mann, first presented the prizes. William H. Webb returned nett 73 off 14 handicap and won the Stroke competition. The monthly medal final was won by Ronald R. Gilroy with 80 nett off 15 handicap. Thomas Gilroy off plus 4 won the Silver Cup for the three lowest gross scores in competitions during the year and Dr Charles L. Magill, playing off a handicap of 25 won the Silver Cup for the three lowest nett scores in competitions during the year. Then the conference got under way. The establishment of an Irish Championship was discussed, though the vulgar ambition of record-breaking and young members attempting to do more than they could ('pressing') were abhorred. Present at this conference were members not only of the County Club but also some leading Scottish Clubs and the Royal Belfast Golf Club.

A minute of a meeting of the committee of County Down Golf Club held on 19 September 1891 records a proposal made by Dr Charles Magill, seconded by Ernest Young and passed that Captains, Secretaries and Treasurers of all recognised Golf Clubs in Ireland be asked to the Club dinner on 26 September.

The autumn meeting of County Down Club took place on Saturday, 26 September. The competition was for the Annesley Cup which had first been played for in 1890 when it was won by Thomas A. Dickson. At the dinner which followed in the clubhouse, the chair was taken by Thomas Gilroy who had also been at the Portrush conference.

It has been suggested that the proposal to form a Union may have been discussed at the dinner that evening in Newcastle but there is no evidence to support this suggestion. Whether agreement was reached at the conference held at Portrush the previous June when the Club Captain expressed the desire for the establishment of an Irish Championship, or whether discussions did take place at Newcastle in September on the subject is a matter for conjecture; nevertheless, a little more than two weeks after the Newcastle dinner, on 12 October to be precise, a meeting was held in the Northern Counties Railway Hotel, Portrush, for the purpose of forming a Golfing Union and of establishing an Irish Championship Meeting.

The attendance at this historic meeting was: Captain James L. McCalmont, J.P., (Captain Royal Belfast) (Chairman), John S. Alexander and John Patrick (County Down),

*Left: Captain James L. McCalmont
(Captain of The Royal Belfast Golf Club)
who chaired the inaugural meeting to found
the Union on 12 October 1891.*

*William H. Mann
(Captain of The County Club)
who chaired the adjourned meeting
on 11 November 1891.*

*At the inaugural meeting it was proposed by Captain
McCalmont, 'that it is desirable to establish a Golfing Union,
consisting of Representatives of all Golf Clubs in Ireland'. This
was seconded by Mr Mann and adopted.*

Hugh Adair (Killymoon), William H. Mann (Aughnacloy), John Kinley and Dr Charles L. Magill (Dungannon) and Hugh C. Kelly (County).

Apologies were received from the following Club Honorary Secretaries who were unable to attend: Henry Herdman (Royal Belfast), Ernest Young (County Down), George V. Craig (North West) and James D. Donaldson (Killymoon).

The first resolution to be adopted was 'that it is desirable to establish a Golfing Union, consisting of representatives of all Golf Clubs in Ireland'. It was also agreed that the immediate objects of the Union would be:

— to fix the dates of all competitions to avoid clashing;
— to consider the advisability of organising an Irish Championship meeting;
— to adopt some fixed principle of handicapping;
— to treat with the different railway companies with a view to obtaining railway facilities for golfers;
— generally to consider such matters as may be for the advancement of golf in Ireland.

The meeting then adjourned to resume in Belfast as soon as convenient.

The resolution to seek railway facilities for golfers may seem unusual, but at that time it was almost the exception rather than the rule for a golf course to be laid out very far from a railway station, either on a main or a branch line. Locals became used to seeing the pioneers of the game, resplendent in their red coats, meeting at the local railway station and departing to the course of their choice. Obviously the resolution was acted upon with success, as these two newspaper advertisements dated 4 February and 9 April 1892 show:[6]

'Portrush links has been pronounced by prominent players as one of the best in the United Kingdom. Friday to Monday railway and hotel tickets, fare 27s and Saturday to Monday railway and hotel tickets, fare 20s. issued from Belfast. These tickets are issued any day to members of the County Club.' 'To golfers and friends commencing on Saturday, 2 April, a fast train will leave Belfast every Saturday at 2.00 p.m. for Newcastle, return tickets 3s. first class; 2s.6d. second class and 2s. third class.'

The Great Southern and Western Railway followed suit and gave a special concession to golfers who wished to travel from Dublin to Lahinch, Co. Clare to play over the links there 'for one guinea first class return'.

Considerable activity took place in November 1891. The first office holders of the fledgling Union had to be chosen and more detailed resolutions prepared for consideration at the adjourned meeting which had been fixed for 13 November at the Royal Hotel, Belfast. The following attended this meeting: William H. Mann (Captain, County) (Chairman), Hugh C. Kelly (County Down), Henry Herdman (Royal Belfast), George Combe (County Down), Ernest Young (County Down), Dr Charles L. Magill (County Down), Hugh Adair (Killymoon), Arthur W. Gaussen (Killymoon), Robert Daniel (Dungannon), James Dickson, J.P. (Dungannon), Rev. Edward F. Campbell (Dungannon) and Richard A. Collingwood (Portsalon). The following resolutions were formally submitted and passed:

— that the Golfing Union be and is hereby established;
— that the Union be managed by a Council consisting of a President, three Vice-Presidents, a Secretary, a Treasurer and delegates from different Clubs joining the Union;
— that Lord Ranfurly be President;

— that Captain James L. McCalmont and John S. Alexander be Vice-Presidents and that a third Vice-President be not at present appointed;

— that George Combe be Honorary Secretary;

— that Hugh C. Kelly be Honorary Treasurer;

— that there be a delegate from each Club and one extra for every 150 members or part thereof over and above the first 150 members, always provided that there are not more than three delegates from any one Club;

— that the subscription from each Club to the Union be £1.1.0d for every delegate the Club is entitled to have;

— that the following be the original Clubs forming the Golfing Union of Ireland: The County Down, Royal Belfast, Killymoon, Dungannon, Aughnacloy, Ballycastle, Portsalon and Buncrana (North West);

— that any Club wishing to join the Union shall be proposed by any one member of the Council and seconded by another and may be admitted on getting a majority of votes of those members of the Council present at the next meeting;

— that all Clubs of the Union shall be entitled to have their fixtures published by the Union before 1 December and two cards of such fixtures be sent to the Secretary of each Club;

— that the Union take steps to establish an Irish Championship open to members of all recognised golf Clubs to be competed for on links appointed by the Union;

— that the Honorary Secretary be empowered to call a meeting of Council at any time he may consider necessary and shall be required to do so on receiving a requisition to do so signed by the delegates of any two Clubs.

It was also agreed that H. Herdman, G. Combe and H.C. Kelly be appointed a sub-committee to draw up rules both for the Union and Championship meetings and to submit them to a subsequent meeting of the Union. The meeting also decided to prescribe the objects of the Union as being:

> to popularise Golf,
> to arrange Championship Meetings, and
> to provide a universal system of handicapping.

Also recorded is a definition of an amateur golfer promulgated by the Royal and Ancient Golf Club of St Andrews and effective at the date of the founding of the Union:

> 'An amateur golfer is a golfer who has never made for sale golf clubs, balls, or any other article connected with the game; who has never carried clubs for hire after attaining the age of 15 years, who has not carried clubs for hire at any time within six years of the date on which the competition begins; who has never received any consideration for playing in a match, or for giving lessons in the game; and who, for a period of five years prior to 1 September 1886, has never received a money prize in any open competition.'

According to an early edition of the *Golfers' Handbook* John Ball III was born on 24 December 1861. When still only 14 years of age he competed in the Open Championship at St Andrews and finished eighth just 8 strokes behind the winner. He won a prize of 30/-. The story goes that young Ball asked Tom Morris if he should take the money and was told to "put it in your pocket, laddie".'

In 1885 John Ball III played in the first Amateur Championship at the Royal Liverpool Club, Hoylake. He was 23 years old but was still known as John Ball III as his father John

Ball Jr was also a competitor. The son defeated the father by 4 and 2 in the third round and was eventually beaten by Horace Hutchinson in the semi-final. In subsequent years the son assumed the name of John Ball Jr.[7]

On 8 August 1886 a meeting was arranged in the Windsor Hotel, Edinburgh, at which were representatives of nine British Clubs who resolved to lay down specific regulations for future amateur championships. The regulations included the above definition of an amateur golfer. The R & A confirm that this was the first such definition promulgated by them and was worded so as to include John Ball Jr who had won 30/- in the 1876 open.

At the Union meeting on 13 November 1891 the choice of officers could hardly have been more shrewd. George Combe was one of the original committee of the County Down Club in 1889 and was among the best players in the country. The Royal County Down history records that he was educated at Rugby and had his first golf tuition from Jack Burns at Warwick in 1888 and went on to become one of Ireland's finest players. An excellent all-round sportsman, he had a powerful influence on all aspects of the RCD Club affairs and indeed on golf in Ireland. One of the first plus handicap golfers in the country, he was an eager founder of the Union. He worked indefatigably, years in advance of most, in the layout, upkeep and maintenance of golf courses, and also on rules and handicapping. At Newcastle he had worked closely with Hugh Kelly, so they formed an ideal team to lay the foundation of the national body.

Hugh Kelly was another accomplished sportsman. As a rugby player he was a forward of exceptional strength and vitality and whilst a member of NIFC he was capped for Ireland six times against Scotland and England between 1876 and 1881 and was, in fact, Captain of the Irish team in 1881. He was an expert lacrosse player and brought an Irish team to America in 1886. A keen huntsman, he was a member and Honorary Treasurer of the Co. Down Staghounds for many years. A distinguished yachtsman, he represented Sir Thomas Lipton on 'Columbia' in the first America's Cup race in 1889. Having turned his mind to golf he could be described as one of the main architects of the GUI and served as Honorary Treasurer of the Union for 22 years. On his retirement, he was elected Honorary Vice-President and in 1926 at the age of 77 he was elected President of the Union and guided its affairs for three years. He also had the unique honour and distinction of being elected a Vice-President of the Ladies' Golf Union. When he died in 1944 at the age of 95 he had, for a great number of years, rightly been regarded as the Grand Old Man of Irish Golf.

In current phrasing, the 'frontman' was Uchter John Mark, 5th Earl of Ranfurly. The head of the Knox family of Dungannon, he gave the game encouragement through having a 12 hole course on his estate. At the time of the GUI foundation, he was 36 and clearly a royal favourite as from 1895 to 1897 he was Lord-in-Waiting to Queen Victoria and was Governor of New Zealand from 1897 to 1904. During his period of office there, he presented the Ranfurly Shield which is New Zealand's most important rugby trophy as it is awarded to the winners of the Provincial Championship. The noble lord was not exactly knowledgeable about the oval ball game, as a round ball was depicted on the Shield!

Thus was history made. The Golfing Union of Ireland became the first national, as distinct from Club, controlling body. The Ladies' Golf Union was founded in 1893, as was also the Irish Ladies' Golf Union. The United States Golf Association followed in 1894; the Welsh Golfing Union came next in 1895 and not until after the First World War did the Scottish Golf Union in 1920 and the English Golf Union in 1924 complete the circle.

The First Officers of the Union

Lord Ranfurly,

President 1891–1906

George Combe,

Honorary Secretary 1891–9

Hugh Cunningham Kelly,

Honorary Treasurer 1891–1912

The final quarter of the nineteenth century was a period of foundation and expansion of sport in Ireland and Britain. The Irish Rugby Football Union came into being in the season 1874–75. The tennis championships started in 1877 and the first Irish Championships were held in 1879 at Fitzwilliam Square, Dublin. The Gaelic Athletic Association was founded in 1884. As well as these important landmarks, games playing was spreading rapidly, and was therefore in need of organisation.

Golf was no exception to this, but whilst the Royal and Ancient was regarded as the controlling body, its grip on the Open and Amateur Championships appears to have been curiously loose. In fact, it was not until 1920, 60 years after the founding of the Open and 35 years after the founding of the Amateur, that the R & A was invited to take over control and management of these two prestigious Championships.

Chapter 4

THE
DEVELOPMENT
OF GOLF
IN IRELAND

Period: 1892 to 1900

Once a properly constituted organisation had been established to administer the game, golf became more popular and this, of course, was one of the main objects of the Union. Ninety-seven Clubs were started between 1892 and 1900:

1892 *Athlone (originally Athlone Garrison), A 1899; County Louth, A 1895; Greencastle, A 1896; Lahinch, A 1897; Lismore (Old) (Co. Waterford); Malahide, A 1905; Mallow, A 1948; Nenagh A 1911; Newry (Co. Down); Rostrevor (Co. Down), A 1894.*

1893 *Ballybunion, A 1909; Bandon, A 1911; Birr (originally King's County and Ormond, Parsonstown), A 1912; County Armagh, A 1894; Fermoy, A 1905; Foxrock, A 1894; Killarney, A 1909; Lurgan, A 1894; Ormeau, A 1894; Otway, A 1893; Roscrea (originally Mill Park), A 1896; Stillorgan (Co. Dublin); Warrenpoint, A 1894.*

1894 *Ballinasloe, A 1911; Banagher (Taylor's Cross, King's County, now Co. Offaly); Bundoran, A 1895; Cookstown (Co. Tyrone); County Cavan, A 1899; County Sligo, A 1902; Dublin University, A 1896; Greenisland, A 1896; Larne, A 1895; Mullingar (originally County Westmeath), A 1905; Newborough (Co. Wexford); Portadown A 1902; Portmarnock, A 1895; Portstewart, A 1895; Tramore (originally Waterford and Tramore), A 1905.*

1895 *Abbeyleix, A 1905; Ballinrobe, A 1902; Blackrock (Rochestown, Co. Cork); Clonakilty (Co. Cork), A 1916; County Monaghan (Co. Monaghan), A 1907; Dooks (originally Glenbeigh Dooks, then Glenbeigh, Caragh and Dooks), A 1903; Dromore (Co. Down); Galway, A 1899; Greystones, A 1897; Knock, A 1896; Malone, A 1895; Massereene, A 1896; Rosapenna, A 1898.*

1896 *Ardfert (Co. Kerry); Ardglass, A 1900; Coleraine (Co. Antrim); Dufferin (Killyleagh, Co. Down); Enniskillen, A 1911; Greenore, A 1896; Helen's Bay, A 1906; Kilkee, A 1908; Kilkenny, A 1910; Magilligan (Co. Derry); Naas (originally County Kildare), A 1907; Saintfield (Rowallane, Co. Down); Spanish Point (originally West Clare), A 1915;*

> *Sutton (originally Sutton Yacht and Boat Club) A 1899; Tipperary, A 1906; Toome (Co. Antrim); Trabolgan (Co.Cork); Tralee, A 1907, Tullamore, A 1899.*

1897 *Bray, A 1899; Carrick (Co. Donegal); Corick (Clogher, Co. Tyrone); Courtmacsherry (Co. Cork); Derrynane (Co. Kerry); Ennis (Old) (Claureen, Co. Clare); Kinsale (Old) (Charlesfort, Co. Cork); Lucan (originally Moor of Meath) A 1905; Muskerry, A 1910; Newmarket (Co. Cork); Scrabo (Old) (Co. Down); Woodenbridge, A 1899; Youghal, A 1912.*

1898 *Ardara (Co Donegal); Newport (Co. Tipperary); Trim (originally The Royal Meath), A 1904.*

1899 *Carlow (originally Leinster), A 1901; Donaghadee, A 1900; Garron Tower (Old) (Co. Antrim); Rathfarnham, A 1900.*

1900 *Adare Manor (originally Adare), A 1932; Berehaven (Co. Cork), A 1939; Carrickmines, A 1901; Castlerock, A 1902; County Longford, A 1910; Killaloe, (Co. Clare); Moate, A 1925.*

The early pioneers of the GUI inaugurated four competitions in this period because the demand for competitive golf increased so much during this time: The Irish Amateur Open Championship, The Irish Amateur Close Championship (both 1892) and The Irish Golf Clubs' Senior and Junior Challenge Cup Tournaments (both 1899). Moreover, they introduced a handicapping system in 1897 which was regarded as the most far-reaching advance in the promotion of the game (please see Chapter 7 for further detailed information).

On 4 March 1898 the Council decided that Ulster and Leinster interprovincial matches should be played at Newcastle on Saturday 16 April 1898. On 29 May 1900 a committee of Henry J. Daly, T.H.R. Craig and Rev. J.L. Morrow was appointed by the Council to draw up a constitution and rules of the GUI. In September of the same year, the Council decided that they should contact the Championship Committee to get the Amateur and Open Championships played in turn in Ireland (please see Chapters 00 for more on the interprovincial matches and the Union constitution).

Efforts to have some Irish golf links included on the Championship rota turned out to be an abortive excercise, 'Red Tapeism gone to seed', as the newspapers of the day described it.

A committee was appointed at the Edinburgh meeting in August 1886 to run future amateur championships. This Committee met once a year. In May 1900, three of the GUI officers travelled to St Andrews which was the venue of the 1901 Amateur, and, whilst they were received and welcomed by the R & A officials, the Championship Committee refused to allow them to attend the meeting to present Ireland's case because the item was not on the agenda. Two subsequent efforts also failed, but may have been advantageous in the long run. The Union was prepared to abandon the Irish Amateur Open if Ireland could be host to the Amateur even once in every four years. British entries in the Irish Amateur Open then increased greatly as a result of press publicity. Many leading amateurs sought to add this Championship to their list of achievements. Over the next four years a total of 330 competitors entered the Championship of which 210 were from Scotland and England. The winners were Harold Hilton (Royal Liverpool) playing off plus 7 at Portrush in 1902; T. Wilkie (Leven) off plus 4 at Portmarnock in 1903; J.S. Worthington (Mid-Surrey) off plus 4 at Newcastle in 1904 and Ireland's first winner at Dollymount in 1905 when Henry A. Boyd (Portmarnock) playing off plus 3 beat J.F. Mitchell (Royal Musselburgh) plus 4 by 3 and 2 in the 36 hole final.

Ireland was not alone in being thwarted by this Championship Committee. They refused to recognise A.F. Macfie as the first Amateur Champion, and it was not until the R & A took over control in 1920 that, in the words of Bernard Darwin, Macfie became 'retrospectively canonised'.[8]

Henry Herdman (Royal Belfast) who proposed the inauguration of the Irish Amateur Open Championship at a meeting on 25 March 1892.

Henry J. Daly (Co. Louth) Union Honorary Secretary 1899–1906. Daly helped in the inauguration of the Senior and Junior Cups Inter-Club Tournaments in 1900. He led a deputation to the Championship Committee in 1901 to seek to have the Amateur Championship played in Ireland on a rota basis.

Reverend John L. Morrow (Royal Dublin) Union Honorary Secretary 1906–20. A member of the 1901 deputation. He was also actively involved in efforts to have a public golf course in the Dublin area in 1906.

Chapter 5

THE
IRISH AMATEUR
OPEN
CHAMPIONSHIP

No time was lost in getting down to arranging Championships. The next meeting of the Officials and Delegates was held in Belfast on 25 March 1892, and the following resolutions were passed:

1. 'that an Open Amateur Championship (by holes) called the "Irish Amateur Championship" be held on the County Links, Portrush, on a date in the autumn to suit the present fixtures of the County Club.'

2. 'that a Championship Trophy be provided by the Clubs of the Union at a cost of not more than Fifty Pounds and that the members of the Clubs of the Union be requested to contribute thereto the sum of 2/6 [now 12½p] each to establish the said trophy and if a balance be required to pay for said trophy, such deficiency shall be contributed by the Clubs of the Union. The arrangements, rules and regulations for same and the prizes in connection therewith to be left in the hands of the Sub-Committee appointed at the last Meeting and to be in accordance with (as far as possible) the Rules of the Royal and Ancient Championship.'

The meeting also made the following decisions:

1. 'that Royal Dublin Golf Club be invited to join the Union.'
2. 'That the subject of the Professional Championship be put off until arrangements are completed for the Amateur Championship.'
3. 'That the subject of handicapping by the Union be deferred until the Sub-Committee appointed should ascertain from the various Clubs of the Union their respective basis of handicapping and report to the next meeting when the matter would be gone into'.

The first clubhouse (above) at Portrush built at a cost of £1,300 on a site close to the Railway Station was opened on 27 June 1892. By the end of that year the membership had reached 370 and the County Club had become 'The Royal County Club'. In 1946 the club acquired the Holyrood Hotel a few miles from the original clubhouse. Extensions added to it over the years have resulted in the present clubhouse (below).

Why was the County Club, Portrush, chosen by the Union as the venue not only for the inaugural Irish Amateur Open Championship in 1892, but also the inaugural Irish Amateur Close Championship in 1893?

The original County Club at Portrush was fortunate indeed. The terrain was naturally well suited to the game of golf, since natural bunkers and other hazards existed, the ground was capable of withstanding flood or drought and plans were underway to extend the course to one of 18 holes. Moreover, the surrounding landscape was beautiful and the presence of a nearby railway station was an obvious bonus. In 1890, 'a commodious Clubhouse' was built which was very popular with the members and in July 1890 Tom Morris was engaged 'for a couple of days . . . in taking in the capabilities of the ground and making the most of them!' Tom Morris warmly praised the links and especially admired the bunker hazards.

Unfortunately there is no description of the second nine holes laid out by Tom Morris but it would be safe to assume that they were akin to the original nine holes which became the venue for the first Irish Amateur Open Championship at Portrush on 8–10 September 1892.

Shortly after the formal resolution to inaugurate the Irish Amateur Open Championship had been approved, George Combe, Union Honorary Secretary dispatched a letter to the Secretary of the R & A:

'As we have formed a Golfing Union of Ireland and propose to hold Championship Meetings I would esteem it a great favour if you would send me a copy of the rules governing your Championship Meeting so that we may have some basis to go on in arranging ours. I should also be much obliged if you would let me know as soon as possible any dates you may have arranged or approximate dates of the larger Meetings so as to avoid clashing as we are most anxious to encourage Scotch and English Golfers to visit this distressed Country.' This was the era of Home Rule.

The advice and guidance of the R & A was obviously helpful, since the British entry comprised 40 per cent of the field. The Clubs represented were as follows:

Royal County (11) C.J. and W.H. Webb, R.R. and T. Gilroy, Dr D. Moore, J.S. Alexander, C.B. Topping, H. Adair, W.H. Mann, W.J. MacGreagh and R. Woodside; County Down (4) T.A. Dickson, G. Combe, E. Maguire and Major Alison; Royal Belfast (3) Captain J.L. McCalmont, M.P., G.M. Shaw and H.J. Johnson; Royal Dublin (1) J.H. Pigot.

King James VI Perth (3) R. Keay, R. Dunsmore and A. Jamieson; Prestwick St Nicholas (3) C.J. Randall, J.A. Andrews and A.A. Taylor; Royal Musselburgh (1) W. Tait; The Honourable Company of Edinburgh Golfers (1) A. Stuart; Troon (1) E.D. Prothero; Carnoustie (1) D. Anderson.

Cambridge (1) J. McKeown; St George's, Sandwich (1) C. Plummer; Royal Wimbledon (1) C. Clare.

The desire for a championship event in addition to the Amateur Championship was obvious. Ten players from Scotland and three players from England took part, out of a total entry of 32.

Stuart had played in the Amateur Championship at St George's, Sandwich, earlier in the year. It was a measure of his quality that while he lost in the first round his conqueror was the great John Ball Jr of Royal Liverpool who went on to win a closely contested match by

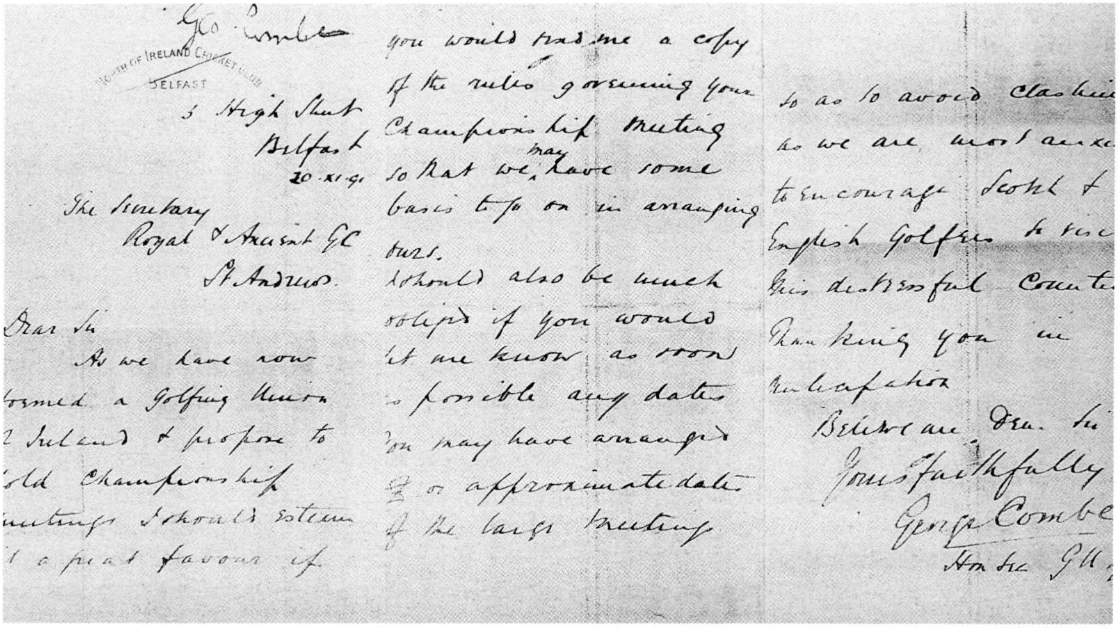

Geo. Combe

NORTH OF IRELAND CRICKET CLUB
BELFAST

5 High Street
Belfast
20.XI.91

The Secretary
Royal & Ancient G.C.
St Andrews.

Dear Sir

As we have now formed a Golfing Union of Ireland & propose to hold Championship meetings I should esteem it a great favour if you would send me a copy of the rules governing your Championship Meeting so that we may have some basis to go on in arranging ours.

I should also be much obliged if you would let me know as soon as possible any dates you may have arranged or approximate dates of the large meetings so as to avoid clashing as we are most anxious to encourage Scotch & English Golfers to visit this distressful Country.

Thanking you in anticipation

Believe me, Dear Sir
Yours faithfully
George Combe
Hon Sec G.U.I.

George Combe's letter to the R&A of 20 November 1891.

only one hole. Ball won the third of his eight titles in the event. Although Thomas Gilroy had competed each year since the start of the Amateur Championship and had reached the semi-final in 1891, he was missing from the list at Sandwich, possibly preferring to reserve his fire for Portrush.

The Championship meeting commenced with a medal competition over 18 holes under handicap open to all bona-fide amateurs who were members of recognised golf Clubs. The first prize was a gold medal valued at £4 and the second prize, a silver medal valued at £2, both of which were presented by the Royal County Club. Seventy people entered for the stroke event which was regarded as an encouraging number especially since it was the Union's first year. The detailed results of the competition are set out in Appendix I (Section 1).

Even though there was no official handicapping system at that time, in this first Championship there were four players on a handicap of plus 4, three on a handicap of plus 2 and two on a handicap of scratch. The range of handicapping varied between plus 4 and 28 (see Appendix I, Section 1).

Local interest in the Championship was maintained until the semi-final when Dr D. Moore of the home Club was defeated by Alexander Stuart by 3 and 2 and Thomas Gilroy, also of the home Club, was defeated by J.A. Andrews by 1 hole. Stuart went on to defeat Andrews by 1 hole in the final and thus became the winner of the first Irish Amateur Open Championship. The detailed results of the Championship are set out in Appendix I (Section 2).

Alexander Stuart was born in 1858 and educated at Edinburgh Academy. He had his first lesson in golf from his father at Leith, but it was really at Musselburgh where, under the tuition of old Willie Park and Bob Ferguson, he mastered the intricacies of the game and at the age of 18 he carried off the gold medal at the Royal and Ancient Club. Subsequently he won eight medals at St Andrews. His winning score of 83 for the Silver Cross in 1883 stood as the Club's record until September 1892 when it was lowered by Mr Edward R.H. Blackwell. At Prestwick he carried off the Eglinton medal five times; at Hoylake in 1883 he won the Duke of Connacht Star; at North Berwick in 1889 he won the double event of the Moncrieff Cross (scratch) and the New Club Handicap Medal; and in 1891, his greatest year, he carried off in rapid succession the St Andrews Autumn, the Tantallon Autumn and the Honourable Company of Edinburgh Golfers' Winter Medal at Musselburgh played over by the Honourable Company on that occasion for the last time. As proof of his personal popularity, it may be noted that Mr Stuart was a past Captain of the Prestwick Golf Club and at the time of his victory at Portrush was also Captain of the Honourable Company of Edinburgh Golfers. He continued to be an active member of the latter during his life-time and played a daily round at Muirfield almost up to the time of his death in 1948 at the age of 90.

The Championship attracted some of the leading cross-channel amateurs of the time. John Ball Jr of Royal Liverpool won at Newcastle in 1893, at Dollymount in 1894 and at Portmarnock in 1899. The official R & A Championship records show that he won both the Open Championship at Prestwick and the Amateur Championship at Hoylake in 1890. He had earlier won the Amateur in 1888 and he won it again in 1892, 1894, 1899, 1907, 1910 and 1912. Another member of Royal Liverpool, Harold H. Hilton, won the Championship at Dollymount in 1897 and then had a hat-trick of wins in 1900, 1901 and 1902. Hilton had joined Ball by becoming the second amateur golfer to win the Open which he achieved at

The first links at the County Club Portrush

Bunker at the first hole.

Crater bunker at the sixth hole.

Muirfield in 1892 and he again won the Open at his home Club in 1897. He had also won the Amateur in 1900, 1901, 1911 and 1913. Of the 119 Open Championships, only one other amateur golfer (the American, Robert Tyre Jones) has won golf's most prestigious trophy.

The first Irish winner was Henry A. Boyd of Portmarnock. At Dollymount in 1905 he defeated J.F. Mitchell of Royal Musselburgh who had also been runner-up at Newcastle the previous year. Mitchell had to wait until the Championship returned to Newcastle in 1908 to record his first victory — and that at the expense of another prominent Portmarnock member, H.M. Cairnes!

An Irish hat-trick was achieved in 1909, 1910 and 1911 when Lionel O. Munn of North West was victorious. Whilst a gold medal was presented to Alexander Stuart when he won the inaugural Championship at Portrush in 1892, and gold medals were awarded to winners, after the Championship was restarted in 1919, for some years prior to 1914 a silver replica of the Championship trophy was the winner's prize. The replica won by Lionel Munn in 1909 is now the Interprovincial Trophy, the story of which we will develop later (see Chapter 17).

Irish players were again successful in each of the next four years to 1924 during which period both the Scottish and English Golf Unions were founded. Possibly because of an increase in championships and other tournaments as a result of the establishment of these two administrative bodies, or due to financial considerations following the war, some leading players from these countries no longer visited Ireland. However, many first class visiting players still competed here as over the next ten years our Trophy crossed the channel on eight occasions — twice to England and six times to Scotland. These included two Walker Cup players who each successfully defended the title: Jack McLean of Hayston in 1932 and 1933 and Hector Thomson of Williamson in 1934 and 1935. Thomson went on to win the Amateur Championship at St Andrews in 1936. We then had three more Irish victories culminating with Jimmy Bruen of Cork winning his only Irish Amateur Open at Newcastle in 1938.

The Championship was suspended during the Second World War. When it was resumed in 1946 at Portrush, Joe Carr of Sutton won the first of his four Irish Amateur Open titles by defeating Alex T. Kyle of Sandmoor, the 1939 Amateur Champion.

The records show that the Cup never left our shores after Joe Brown of Waterford won it in 1936 when he defeated William M. O'Sullivan of Dooks. Billy O'Sullivan, entering from Killarney, was successful at his home Club in 1949 beating Brendan J. Scannell of Woodbrook on the last green in the 36 hole final. Apart from Joe Carr's four victories which equalled the record of individual wins set by Harold H. Hilton in 1902, only two other players won the Championship twice after its resumption in 1946: Cecil Ewing of County Sligo (1948 and 1951) and Norman Drew of Bangor (1953 and 1954).

From its inception in 1892, the Championship had been matchplay throughout, with a 36 hole final. This was preceded by an 18 hole medal competition open to all entrants in the Championship. In 1958, due to a growing lack of top class competitors from Britain, the Central Council decided to abandon the medal competition and alter the format to a 72 hole strokeplay championship. This survived for only two years and the Championship was discontinued in 1959 after John Duncan of Shandon Park won the trophy at Newcastle with a somewhat high score of 313 for the 72 holes.

By today's standards the entry fee was exceedingly small. Starting with half a guinea in 1892 it was increased to one guinea in 1919, then to one and a half guineas in 1946 and remained at this level until the format was changed to strokeplay in 1958 when the fee became two guineas.

The Championship was considered an important event on the international golfing scene because in every Walker Cup match played from 1924 to 1959 at least one member of the Britain and Ireland team was already (or subsequently became) an Irish Amateur Open Champion. The R & A Championship records show that, between them, Irish champions had received 35 'caps' during this period. This total was increased by another eight 'caps' and by two more champions after the Irish event was discontinued. The records also show that five Irish champions and three defeated finalists reached the pinnacle of amateur golf by winning the Amateur Championship. These eight players had, between them, won the Amateur on 20 occasions. The record of winners of both the Open Stroke competition and Championship are set out in Appendix I (Sections 3 and 4).

Chapter 6

THE IRISH AMATEUR CLOSE CHAMPIONSHIP

At a meeting of the Council on 25 November 1892 another decision was made, to establish what must have been the first National Amateur 'Close' Golf Championship in history. The Union decided to expend the sum of £50 on the purchase of a Perpetual Challenge Trophy for this Championship, and whilst its overall measurements are not quite as large as those for the Amateur Open Cup it is, none the less, the most coveted trophy in Irish golf.

Like that for the 'Open', the 'Close' Trophy is a magnificent solid silver hand-chased circular bowl, similar to a punch bowl. There is no record to show if, as in the case of the Open Trophy, the members of Clubs affiliated to the Union were likewise invited to subscribe for its purchase. The first Irish Amateur Close Championship was played at Portrush on 26–28 April 1893. There was an entry of 13 which included only two of the 19 players who had entered from Irish Clubs for the Irish Amateur Open at the same venue the previous September. However, it is known that a number of these 19, although residing in Ireland, were born in Scotland and were therefore not eligible for the Close.

In the first round some exceedingly tight matches were witnessed. In the matches between Hugh Adair and John Alexander, Hugh Kelly and George Shaw, the results at the end of 18 holes were both all square. The now accepted 'sudden death' format was not then in vogue and the players had to start off again and play a match over another 18 holes until a majority of holes up was reached. In the two replays, Adair beat Alexander by 4 and 3 and Kelly beat Shaw by one hole.

The R & A Championship records explain that this 're-play' was similar to the rules operating in the Calcutta Cup, a competition played in St Andrews at the time of the first

*Thomas A. Dickson (County Down), the first Irish Amateur Close
Champion. He defeated George Combe (County Down) by two holes in the
36 hole final at the County Club, Portrush in 1893.*

Winner's gold medal.

Amateur Championship in 1885. In this, when similar halved matches occurred, the two players advanced into the next round and played again. Macfie, the first Amateur Champion, halved his first round match against W. Doleman of Glasgow Golf Club and won the re-play by 5 and 4 to advance to the third round where he met and defeated Thomas Gilroy of Dublin Golf Club by 2 and 1. In the next round, Macfie met W.M. de Zoete of Royal Blackheath Golf Club and it took two 18 hole re-plays before Macfie was successful and then by just one hole. Apparently the other matches were being played at the same time and as a result of the 54 hole marathon Macfie will go down in golf legend as the only man in the history of the Amateur Championship to get a bye into the final, but by the time he got there he had played two more rounds than his opponent. Imagine the chaos which would have occurred down the years had the administrators of the game not legislated that matches should go down the 19th and continue until one or other player had gained a hole.

In the Irish Close, due possibly to a slight alteration in the Calcutta Cup rules or because of the small entry, the two players in each match who were all square after their first round were able to settle their differences by a further round on the same day and the two winners advanced to the second round.

The first winner of the native championship was Thomas A. Dickson of the County Down Club who defeated George Combe, also of the County Down Club, by two holes in the final. The detailed results of the Championship are set out in Appendix II (Section 1).

Thomas A. Dickson only took up golf in the summer of 1891 when he was 29 years of age. That autumn he visited St Andrews and holed out the links in 95 strokes which was regarded as an extraordinary achievement by one who had only been playing the game for two months. He was an accomplished tennis player, a magnificent shot, a competent cricketer and he also dabbled in training greyhounds, owning the famous Duke MacPherson which was runner-up for the Waterloo Cup. Whilst he had entered from the County Down Club in the Close he was also a member of the Royal County, Dungannon and Lurgan Golf Clubs. Having won the Close after only two years at the game, he also annexed the Annesley Cup at County Down, the McCalmont Cup at Royal County, the Ranfurly Cup and the Corbett Cup at Dungannon and the Malcolm Cup at Lurgan all within a year of his success in the Championship. He was honoured by being elected Captain of the County Down Club in 1894.

Unlike the Irish Amateur Open which was played in rotation over the same four links for the first 46 years of its existence, the Close was confined to these four links for its first 21 years only. In 1914 Hermitage became the first park course to be given the honour of hosting the native championship. Of the 89 championships held in the first 100 years, 67 have been played on links and 22 on park courses.

The Championship used to be matchplay throughout with a 36 holes final. In 1962 at Baltray the format was changed to a 36 holes stroke qualification with the leading 32 players advancing to compete by matchplay.That year a record number of holes were required to decide the final. Michael Edwards of Shandon Park and Jackie Harrington of Adare Manor had to play 42 holes before Edwards triumphed. Also in 1962 the Central Council discontinued the practice of presenting a 'replica' Cup for retention by the winner and decreed that the winner would receive a gold medal, the runner-up would receive a silver medal and the defeated semi-finalists would each receive a bronze medal. A silver medal would be awarded to the competitor who obtained the best gross score in the 36 holes of the qualifying rounds. The first stroke qualifying silver medal was won by Fergus Gallagher (County Louth) whilst the bronze semi-finalists' medals were won by David Sheahan (Grange), the winner at Rosses Point the previous year, and Michael McGuirk (County Louth).

From time to time the Council made other changes to the Championship format. In 1964, the number of qualifiers for matchplay was increased to 64 and the final was reduced from 36 to 18 holes. In the 1970 Championship at Grange, there were 242 entries. Thereafter, the Council decided to limit the entry to 192 with the proviso that should the number of entries exceed this, the higher handicapped players would be balloted out. The Council had to make further changes to the rules in 1975 when there was a record entry of 304 at Portmarnock. Anxious to allow as many as possible to compete in Ireland's premier golfing event, the Council decided to introduce a 36 hole stroke qualification per province. This would exempt the holder from having to qualify and would allow 127 of the qualifiers to go on to the matchplay stage. Provincial qualification, however, did not prove popular and so in 1978 the rules were again changed to one 36 hole stroke qualification for 182 competitors at the Championship venue, with 64 going forward for matchplay.

Again a further alteration was made in 1981. It was decided that the field would be limited to 192 competitors with handicaps of 5 and under. Should entries exceed this number balloting-out of the higher handicap players would be made. The Championship would be matchplay throughout with the 64 lowest handicap entrants receiving a bye into the second round. The remaining 128 players would play in the first round and be drawn in such a manner that the winner of each first round match would be slotted in alternatively to play one of the 64 players who had received a bye into the second round. Also, the selectors were authorised to nominate 16 seeds.

This format continued until 1987 when the Central Council accepted a proposal by the Leinster Provincial Council:

(1) each competitor must have submitted a minimum of eight returns during the 12 months prior to the date of entry into the Championship.
(2) Each competitor shall play 18 holes stroke on the first and second days of the Championship, and the 64 competitors who return the lowest gross scores over the 36 holes shall qualify for matchplay. (The Union tie break conditions to operate.)
(3) In addition to the gold, silver and bronze medals, the recipients shall also receive vouchers.

The vouchers awarded are: winner £200; runner-up £150; defeated semi-finalists £100 each; defeated quarter-finalists £75 each and defeated in last 16 £50 each. In addition, the leading qualifier will receive a voucher for £100 provided the total amount he receives in prize vouchers does not exceed the limit permitted under the amateur status rules.

An examination of the records of winners of the Irish Amateur Open and Close Championships shows that of the 20 Irish players who won the Amateur Open during its 57 years, only eight of these also won the Close, and of this group five were holders of the two Championships in the same year: Lionel Munn (North West) in 1911; Jimmy Bruen (Cork) in 1938; John Burke (Lahinch) in 1947; Cecil Ewing (County Sligo) in 1948 and Joe Carr (Sutton) in 1954.

The record of winners of the Close which are set out in Appendix II (Section 2) shows that John Burke won on eight occasions, with both four and three successive victories in these eight wins, whilst Joe Carr won six times, three of which were in succession. Lionel Munn also had three victories.

The most consistent runners-up were Frank P. McConnell of Royal Portrush and George F. Crosbie of Cork, each of whom was a defeated finalist in three successive years.

Chapter 7

THE HANDICAPPING SYSTEM

The provision of a universal system of handicapping constantly exercised the minds of the officers of the Union. They realised that it was important that a system should be designed which would allow players of different skills to compete against one another on equal terms despite the enormous variation in the greens being opened for play. Therefore, the evolution of a universal system of handicapping was, of its nature, a difficult problem.

To appreciate more fully the extent of the problem, we must examine the situation which prevailed, not only in Ireland but in other countries where golf was played during the last two decades of the nineteenth century.

Whilst the early pioneers sought out coastal links (land with natural dunes and dry springy turf) it was not always possible to find such locations in reasonably accessible areas. In Ireland, a site convenient to a railway station appears to have been the criterion and a green or links was situated in any available area where enthusiasts could congregate to play the game. Many of the landed gentry laid out a green on their own demesnes and whilst some of these remained private courses others were made available for use as members' Clubs.

Whins, bracken and other natural hazards were accepted as part of the challenge of the game. It was regarded as a measure of good fortune to find the ball in a smooth grassy lie. There was no closely mown area and the term 'fairway' was unknown. Nor were there any designated areas for putting, except what the player himself would regard as near enough to the hole to allow him to use his putting cleek. It was some years before the horsedrawn cricket mower began serving the two field sports. On many of these courses, livestock was looked on as a bonus in that the grass was kept cropped, whereas today's golfer regards the rare case of sheepgrazing as a nuisance.

Depending on its accessibility and sportiness, any new green attracted not only local players but those from further afield if the location was near a railway station. Having been opened for play, the next step was to ascertain the 'ground score' for each hole. The terms 'bogey' and 'par' had not yet entered the vocabulary of golf when Royal Belfast and other earlier Irish Clubs were founded.

Golf has always been regarded as a healthy sport and pastime but nevertheless the focal point of the game has ever been competitive, either against a particular opponent in a match or against all other competitors in a stroke competition. Because of the wide disparity between the skills of one player and another, some balance had to be achieved by giving a greater allowance of strokes to the less skilful player.

Again we turn to Scotland to ascertain how this balance was achieved. Records in the R & A show that towards the end of the nineteenth century, Clubs, Societies and Associations organised their own method of allowance of strokes or handicaps. In those days most of the golf in Scotland was played on commonages. This, incidentally, was the reason why golfers were obliged to wear red jackets in order to alert perambulating citizenry of their approach. Groups of golfers formed Societies or Associations to play with or against one another. From this grew the established golf Club as we know it today.

Finally, a group or Club selected its best player and monitored his scores over a number of rounds, then took the average for each hole and this became the 'ground score' for that hole. The total for the round became the 'ground score' or 'green score' for the course. The player became the 'backmarker' and strokes were allocated to the other members based on their ability to play a round on equal terms. Whilst this method may have proved practical within a Club, it could not prove satisfactory in away matches or in open competitions, not only from the point of view of the degree of difficulty or otherwise of the different courses; more importantly there may have been an extremely wide variation between the skills of the best player in one Club compared with the best player in another. If their backmarker was a really good player then all other members were on too low a handicap when compared with a Club with a mediocre backmarker. The converse was likewise true.

About 1890, a variation between matchplay and strokeplay was introduced in the form of a competition against 'bogey'. This became a popular form of Club competition, although since the introduction of the Stableford System in 1931, the bogey competition lost much of its popularity in favour of Stableford. But the term 'bogey' had another important meaning in the lore of golf. According to *Nisbet's Golf Year Book*, 1891, 'the bogey of a hole or round is the number of strokes in which they can be taken without serious mistakes, and may be said to represent good steady play'. Thereafter, instead of ground score, Clubs referred to the bogey of a hole or the bogey of a course.

It must be remembered too that this was the era of the hickory shaft. There was no such thing as a matched set of clubs. It was also the era of the gutty ball which had replaced the feathery ball in 1848 and was itself replaced by the rubber-cored ball in 1902. Steel shafts were not made legal by the R & A until November 1929.

In 1983 the American professionals, Jack Nicklaus and Ben Crenshaw, each playing with an amateur in a $1,000 per hole match for charity over the Old Course at St Andrews and having played up to that point with their own clubs, elected to play the 425 yards par 4 14th hole with a set of old hickory shafted clubs and gutta percha balls provided by the Scottish clubmaker, Laurie Auchterlonie. The players agreed that nobody would use a golf glove, each would build his own tee with sand on which to tee the ball and each must also use the narrow-headed driver off the tee. Crenshaw was the only one of the four to reach the green in three shots and holed out in five. His amateur partner got one in four and sank a 15 yard putt for another five. Nicklaus took six and his partner seven. Whilst the playing of one hole is perhaps an inadequate example it does, nevertheless, help to illustrate the degree of difference in equipment.

The difficulties and variety of the terrain of the ever increasing number of courses being opened for play (all of which had ground scores or bogeys in the 80's) as well as the equipment available were challenges which the Union sub-committee of George Combe (Honorary Secretary), Hugh C. Kelly (Honorary Treasurer) and Henry Herdman had to face. Following their first meeting on 25 March 1892, they asked all Clubs affiliated to the Union to submit details of the basis on which each Club handicapped its members.

By this time there were 37 greens or courses in Ireland. At a meeting of the Union on 26 May 1893 the sub-committee was able to submit a report as a result of which the Council instructed the Honorary Secretary 'to get out a scheme of, say, 50 handicaps based on T. Gilroy's St Andrews handicap and to inform all Secretaries of handicaps thus prepared. These handicaps are to apply only in Open meetings. It is also necessary to penalise local players on their own green at such meetings.'

Thomas Gilroy, the 'backmarker' selected by the Union, was born in Dundee on 2 October 1852 and, according to a biography published in *Golf* on 17 February 1893, Gilroy was to be seen knocking balls around Carnoustie with a cleek at the age of seven. He was educated at St Andrews where he received much valuable tuition from 'Old' Tom Morris and Tom Morris Jr with whom he frequently played. He had great enthusiasm for the game and became a member of Carnoustie, Dalhousie, Monifieth, St Andrews, Panmure, Royal North Devon (Westward Ho) and Worcestershire Golf Clubs. He also had the distinction of being Captain of Monifieth and Worcestershire, the latter for two years.

He came to Ireland in 1885 and took up residence at Mornington House at the mouth of the Boyne. He became acquainted with a fellow Scotsman, John Lumsden, and being involved with the lay-out of the links in the Phoenix Park, immediately became a member of the Dublin Club. A man of untiring zeal, Gilroy laid out an 11 hole green beside Mornington House.

The first Inter-City match was played on 24 October 1885. The Dublin Club, which was only five months old, was host to the Belfast Club in a ten-a-side match in the Phoenix Park. It was agreed that 'whilst each player must hole out for the eighteen holes as in a competition for a medal, the player who used the least number of strokes in propelling the ball from the tee to the hole gained that hole on his opponent'. Gilroy, playing off scratch, led for Dublin against George Baillie who was one of the founders of the Belfast Club. He also played off scratch and led for the visitors. Gilroy holed the 18 holes in 82 to Baillie's 95, with Gilroy winning 9 of the holes to Baillie's 1, the other 8 being halved. The official result was a win for Dublin by 70 holes to 58.

Just one year later, on 30 October 1886, Gilroy entertained the Belfast and Dublin Clubs at Mornington. This time the teams were 13-a-side and the match comprised two rounds (22 holes). Gilroy again faced Baillie and won 14 holes to Baillie's 2 with 6 holes halved. Dublin were victorious by 121 holes to 110. Gilroy took 52 to Baillie's 57 in the first round and was 5 holes to the good. In his second round Gilroy made a clean run away from his opponent, played a faultless game, and finished in 44 (11 holes) made up as follows: 5, 3, 4, 4, 3, 4, 5, 5, 3, 4, 4, = 44.

To complete the circle, the third match of this series was played on the Belfast course at the Kinnegar, Holywood, and on this occasion the host team was victorious by 45 holes to 11. Gilroy retained his unbeaten record by disposing of H.J. Johnson, another Belfast scratchman, by winning 5 holes with 13 halved.

Gilroy joined the Belfast Club and also became a founder member of the County Club, Portrush, near which he acquired a summer residence; he also joined County Down and later still County Louth when it was founded. He served as Captain of the Dublin Club in 1898 and 1899.

Gilroy knew George Pentland who lived at Blackhall near Drogheda, and Gilroy often rowed across the Boyne at Baltray where he was met by Pentland's groom with a pony and trap and transported to Blackhall. On one occasion Pentland drove over to meet Gilroy and the two friends went for a stroll through the sand-dunes at Baltray and Gilroy is said to have exclaimed, 'Here was I trying to make a course of poor material when less than a mile away there was one of the best pieces of golfing ground in the world.' At the instigation of Pentland he set about designing what has become one of the outstanding links in Ireland and the venue of the East of Ireland Amateur Open Championship. Gilroy was also appointed County Louth's first Captain.

Despite his business interests, Gilroy found time to maintain his cross-channel golfing activities. He competed in the first seven Amateur Championships from 1885 to 1891, entering from the Dublin Golf Club for the first six and from Royal County, Portrush, for the seventh in which he was beaten in the semi-final by J.E. Laidlay (Honourable Company of Edinburgh Golfers), the eventual winner. He also competed in the Open Championship at St Andrews in 1891 entering from Dublin Golf Club.

In the eight years between his arrival in Ireland in 1885 and the decision of the Union to base the handicapping system on his golfing skills, Gilroy's name was seldom out of reports of golf competitions. He held the course record for most Irish golf courses. The winning of the gross prize in any competition in which he played became almost automatic. His highest handicap was scratch and his lowest was plus 6. He won the Henderson Cup (Dublin 1886), the Murphy-Grimshaw Plate (Royal Belfast 1890), the Portglenone Cup (County 1890), the Murphy-Grimshaw Plate (Royal Belfast 1890), the Corry Cup (County 1890), the Lowry-Corry Cup (County Down 1891) and the Silver Cup (County 1891). This last was awarded at the summer meeting immediately prior to the conference at which the holding of an Irish Championship was first suggested. He was beaten in the semi-final of the inaugural Irish Amateur Open Championship also at the Royal County Club, Portrush, the following year.

Regarding Gilroy's St Andrews handicap at the time of the Union's decision on 26 May 1893, the Historian of the R & A has advised that Thomas Gilroy joined the R & A in 1887. He did not play in the Jubilee Vase or the Calcutta Cup in 1893, but all the main players — Laidlay, Melville Balfour, Ball — were off plus 1 and it is certain that that would have been his rating too. Laidlay won the Amateur Championship in 1889 and 1891, Balfour Melville in 1898 and Ball won it six times (1888, 1890, 1892, 1894, 1899 and 1907) in addition to winning the Open Championship in 1890. Gilroy was the obvious choice of the Union to be the backmarker of the first ever universal system of handicapping.

The sub-committee must have been constantly monitoring the various domestic schemes in order to establish the most equitable method of assessing handicaps because at a meeting of the Council on 5 October 1894 it was decided that each Club should select a green score to which the members must be handicapped. Any member returning a nett score lower than the green score shall be reduced by as many strokes as his nett score is below this green score.

The sub-committee reported its findings to the Council which decided to have an open forum discussion on the whole subject. A meeting of Club Secretaries or their delegates was arranged at the Royal Hotel, Belfast, on 6 December 1896 to consider a system of handicapping introduced by George Combe, Union Honorary Secretary. Combe was instructed to submit his scheme to the various Clubs and get their opinions of it.

As a result of that meeting only two Clubs (Royal Portrush and Killymoon) were 'on the fence' vis-à-vis Combe's handicapping system, a harsh but descriptive term for them which, whilst not being wholly against, were likewise not wholly in favour of the handicapping scheme. (Refer to Appendix III for a list of those Clubs which had adopted or approved the scheme).

At the next meeting of the Council, on 23 February 1897, the Honorary Secretary reported that the majority of Clubs in the Union either had already adopted or were prepared to adopt the system of handicapping which had been submitted to them. Adoption of the scheme was recommended as a step towards getting Clubs into line. Furthermore, the main obstacle in the way of a practically even basis of handicapping was that par scores were arranged on very varying basis, so Combe was instructed to visit, at his discretion, the various greens belonging to the Union to inspect and discuss the par scores with the local committee and, if possible, arrange all par scores on an even footing.

Whilst the sub-committee had the benefit of the many inter-Club matches which were increasing in popularity, it was not until the first Interprovincial Match between Leinster and Ulster at Portrush (before the 1896 Close Championship) that they were able to assess properly the standard of the players selected to represent each province. The teams comprised 20 a side and the match was singles and foursomes. Leinster won the singles by 37 holes to 32, whilst Ulster were victorious in the foursomes winning 21 holes to 14. However, it was not the result which was important but the examination of the handicaps allotted to the players by their Clubs of which the sub-committee obtained details. (See Appendix III for George Combe's description of his handicapping scheme).

The system propounded by George Combe was a shrewd and well devised scheme. Firstly, it set out the range of handicaps in ten classes from plus to 30; secondly, it laid down specific allowances for matchplay whereby the weaker player would not be disadvantaged by the stronger; and thirdly it prescribed, for the first time, yardage measurements for reckoning the 'par' score of a hole or a course.

This is the first mention of the term 'par' which *Nisbet's Golf Year Book* defined as 'the number of strokes in which a hole or round can be taken without mistakes. Thus if the green can be reached in two strokes, two putts are allowed on the putting green and the par of the hole is 4. In other words, par represents perfect play without flukes.' Par became the accepted standard of the genuine scratch player and still retains its original meaning whilst in the last 25 years bogey is now used to indicate one or more strokes in excess of par. In addition another term entered the vocabulary in later years, the standard scratch score (SSS).

Even when introducing the first system of handicapping, the Council was aware of a difficulty which has remained a problem and which successive legislators are still trying to solve. 'Course rating' cannot be fixed purely by a mathematical formula, although length plays a prominent part in the assessment. The 'human factor' was and still is the core of the problem. Two golfers, both enjoying the same handicap, can have widely divergent views regarding how the scratch score of a particular course should be fixed. This is why the Council considered it advisable, in 1897, that George Combe should visit all Clubs affiliated to the Union and seek to arrange all par scores on an even footing.

Although by 1897, 109 courses had been opened for play not every Club immediately applied for membership of the Union, and the records show that George Combe's brief was not overburdensome. Even though it necessitated a fair degree of travel, only 36 Clubs had by then become affiliated to the Union. However, three years later, 91 Clubs had become affiliated and the handicapping system must be afforded a large measure of the credit for this increase.

Some Clubs in Ulster, Combe's own Province, decided that his circular was more a recommendation than a directive and declined to adjust the handicaps of their members by four strokes. This created a serious anomaly in standards. There were complaints by visiting English and Scottish players that Irish handicapping was too generous. Possibly as a result of this a meeting was held on 24 September 1900 (the year our Inter-Club Cups Tournaments were inaugurated) and the Council decided to reduce the handicaps of all players in Leinster, Munster and Connacht on the following scales:

handicaps of 5 and under to be reduced by 2 strokes;
handicaps over 5 and not exceeding 10 to be reduced by 3 strokes;
handicaps over 10 and not exceeding 18 to be reduced 4 strokes;
handicaps over 18 to be reduced by 5 strokes.

It further ruled that scratch scores would, in future, be assessed from bogey as was the practice at Hoylake and other golfing centres, and not from par and fixed the length for an averagely-good drive and an averagely-good brassie shot at 160 and 140 yards respectively and determined the bogey rating of a hole as:

160 yards bogey 3;
over 160 to 300 yards bogey 4;
over 300 to 440 yards bogey 5;
over 440 yards bogey 6.

However, in 1902 a revolutionary concept happened in golf with the introduction of the 'Bounding Billy' as the rubber-cored golf ball was christened. The idea for such a ball belongs to Coburn Haskell of the Goodrich Tyre and Rubber Company of Akron, Ohio, and the ball was officially known as the 'Haskell'. The professionals did not, at first, take too kindly to the new ball and in December 1902, after Sandy Herd of Huddersfield had become the first to win the Open Championship using a rubber-cored ball, the PGA prohibited the use of this type of ball in all tournaments under its jurisdiction. (This did not include the Open which is under the jurisdiction of the R & A.)

As a result of this new advance in technology, the Council increased the length factor of drives and brassie shots to 170 and 160 yards respectively and many bogey 5 holes became 4s and a bogey 6 became almost non-existent.

Other handicapping systems were introduced. In April 1903 an American system of handicapping was devised; the Scottish Borders Association and Clubs in Northumberland also operated their own systems.

However, in 1925 the British Golf Union's Joint Advisory Committee (since named the Council of National Golf Unions) introduced a standard scratch score and handicapping scheme which was adopted by the Irish (1891), Welsh (1895), Scottish (1920) and English (1924) Golfing Unions and came into operation in the four countries on 1 March 1926.

This 'standard scratch score and handicapping scheme' superceded all the schemes in operation in these islands up to that time. The committee charged with the task of devising an acceptable and workable scheme was J.E. Turner (Scottish Golf Union), F.S. Bond (English Golf Union), T.W. Pearson (Welsh Golfing Union) and James Henderson (Golfing Union of Ireland).

Handicapping forms one of the most important aspects of Club golf and we examine it now in some detail. The committee decided that there were two separate but inseparable matters to be dealt with: to devise a method of fixing the scratch scores for all types of golf courses, and a method of providing a system which would enable players of varying degrees of skill to play on equal terms on all these courses. Fixing the scratch score was accomplished by the application of three factors: the standard par, the length adjustment and the additional course value.

The standard par represented the number of strokes a scratch player would require to reach the 18 greens in spring and autumn conditions, without wind, plus 36 putts. In 1925, a scratch player was defined as one who had attained a standard of skill 3 strokes per round worse than the standard attained by post-war amateur champions. As the length expected from a scratch player varied on different courses according to their geographical position and the nature of the soil, courses were divided into five grades ranging from grade A (where the fairways are fast and give a good run) to Grade E (where the fairways are exceptionally heavy and there is no run at all). Where the ground is flat, the 'playing length' of the hole is its actual length. In cases where the ball lands on an uphill or downhill slope, a calculation is made regarding the difference the slope makes to the length of the shot. This must be added to or subtracted from the actual length of the hole to arrive at its 'playing length'. The committee devised a table covering the five grades of courses setting out the playing length on flat ground of par 3, 4 and 5 holes by which the standard par of a course could be ascertained.

The length adjustment provided for an 'excess' or 'shortage' of the playing length of the three classes of holes. The average for a par 3 was 160 yards. Par 4 varied from 370 yards on a grade A course to 330 yards on a grade E course whilst a par 5 varied from 490 yards (grade A) to 420 yards (grade E). The committee devised a table showing the number of strokes which could be allotted for any 'excess' or 'shortage' with the average.

Finally, it provided allowances for additional course value to be based on the excellence or otherwise of the lay-out, side hazards, whether greens are well guarded or open, the width of fairways, nature of rough and, generally, the severity of the punishment for an indifferent shot. The allowances ranged from 1 to 4 strokes.

When prescribing the rules for handicapping, the committee acknowledged that they were based largely on the systems which had been used by the Golfing Union of Ireland and the Scottish Borders Association. They allocated four handicap categories and drew up a series of corresponding handicap tables to cover courses with a standard scratch score (SSS) of 66 to those with an SSS of 80. This provision allowed for an adjustment of a player's handicap when visiting a course with a different SSS to that of his home course, but was discontinued with the introduction of the Irish pilot scheme in 1971. For example, an 18 handicap player from an SSS 67 course got 4 additional shots when visiting an SSS 74 course. The committee urged that whilst handicap committees must have discretionary powers to handicap players on general form, not only the letter but the spirit of the system must also be observed; also, the lengths used in the scheme were based upon the length obtained with the balls used at the time (i.e. rubber-cored balls). If in future, balls be introduced which could be driven appreciably further than the present ball, or if a new limit of size or weight be adopted by the R & A (which would have the effect of curtailing the present length) a revised scheme may need to be issued, and scratch scores would be altered accordingly.

When the schemes had been approved by the four Unions and had received the 'imprimateur' of the R & A, a 30 page booklet was issued to all affiliated Clubs. Most of the booklet was concerned with setting out the handicap tables.

Later, revisions to the scheme were introduced and, following the 1939–45 War, the JAC (it did not become CONGU until 1959) noted a considerable improvement in the performance of the golf ball and decided to carry out tests during the 1949 international matches at Portmarnock. Professor Purcell, one of the delegates to the JAC was put in charge of the operation and selected the 9th and 10th holes. Pegs were placed at measured distances along each side of both fairways and only the length of carry of tee shots hitting the fairways was to count.

Some of the Irish players are listed here. On the 9th hole Jimmy Bruen carried 280 yards; Joe Carr 265; Billy O'Sullivan and Jimmy Carroll each 250. The other six players carried between 235 and 225 yards. Scottish players carried between 235 and 210 yards; English players between 235 and 196 and Welsh players between 230 and 215. On the 10th, where some of the players used irons, the carries were: Ireland 250 to 210 yards; Scotland 237 to 200; England 235 to 195 and Wales 230 to 190. A further revision followed.

The Irish pilot scheme came about with the approval of CONGU and radically changed the previous revision. With some modifications this scheme was adopted by CONGU and became the sixth revision operative from January 1976.

The JAC/CONGU found it necessary to revise the 1925 scheme on six occasions up to 1982. It then decided to introduce a completely new scheme based on a system in use by the Australian Golf Union, 'The Standard Scratch Score and Handicapping Scheme 1983'.

The 1983 scheme transferred control of all Category One players' handicaps back from the provincial branches to each player's Club. In addition, every Club was instructed to increase the handicap of every member by one stroke and the handicap limit was raised to 28. The scheme prescribed that a player had an exact handicap and a playing handicap. The exact handicap was adjusted by decimal points following returns in qualifying competitions; the playing handicap was the nearest round figure upwards or downwards from the exact handicap.

The automatic aspect provided fixed decimal point figures reduction for net returns below the SSS of the course in medal, par and Stableford competitions. Carefully calculated tables were included in the SSS and handicapping booklet (issued free to every Club member in Ireland) covering downwards adjustments for all ranges of handicap. Initially, a player with a net score above the SSS was credited with 0.2 of a stroke but this was changed to 0.1.

In 1977 the Union, at the request of affiliated Clubs, decided to register golfing societies, and any society applying for registration had to sign an undertaking to comply with the rules of amateur status and the regulations in the handicapping scheme. There are now 573 societies registered with the Union. In March 1983 the Union prescribed that returns in society competitions below the SSS of the course only should be returned to the player's Club for handicap adjustment. No return above the SSS could be used for an increase in handicap.

The 1983 scheme was revised in 1986 and again in 1989. Instead of all competition returns being assessed against the basic SSS of the course for handicap purposes, the latest revision introduced a competition scratch score, calculated at the conclusion of each round of a qualifying competition. This is a prescribed calculation based on the number of competitors in the different categories. Another departure from the pre-1983 scheme was the introduction of flexibility into the fixing of the par for each hole in relation to its length and playing difficulty.

As most Clubs now have access to computers, the handicaps of all playing members are adjusted as necessary after each qualifying competition and the printout posted on the Club notice board.

The long-standing method of fixing the SSS of a course purely by length will be replaced by a course rating system which is operated by the United States Golf Association and which will provide more effective uniformity and equity in handicapping. The course rating system is not yet in operation and only recently have National Unions been authorised to phase it in.

THE IRISH GOLF CLUBS SENIOR AND JUNIOR CHALLENGE CUPS TOURNAMENTS

A little more than three years after the Union was founded, a method of promoting the game and improving the standard of golf in Ireland was put into operation. At a meeting on 15 March 1895 the Council decided 'that instructions be sent to Clubs divided into districts to arrange Inter-Club matches according to the convenience of the smaller Clubs. Players are to be selected as far as possible to ensure a good match but not necessarily victory for the larger Club.' It seems that the aim was for a series of friendly sociable encounters in the truest meaning of the term. At that date 21 Clubs had become affiliated to the Union and 18 of these had been divided into four districts:

1. Royal Belfast, Lurgan, Ormeau and Armagh.
2. Royal County (Portrush), Randalstown, Killymoon, Ballycastle and North West.
3. Royal Dublin, Foxrock, County Louth, Rostrevor and Warrenpoint.
4. County Down, Dungannon, Lisburn and Belmont.

There is no explanation why the other three affiliated Clubs, (Aughnacloy, Portsalon and Otway) were not included in this list.

Over the next four years, a further 24 Clubs joined the Union and at a meeting on 23 May 1899 it was decided 'that the Union would organise Senior and Junior Challenge Cups to be competed for by teams of Clubs belonging to the Union.' It was also decided that 'G.C. May (Royal Dublin), H.S. Upton (Athlone), W.F. Todd (Portmarnock), H.E. Reade (Royal Belfast) and J.H. Richardson (Royal Dublin) with H.C. Kelly (Honorary Treasurer and Royal County Down) and H.J. Daly (Honorary Secretary and County Louth) would be appointed as a committee to draft rules and submit them to the next meeting.' By this time George Combe's handicapping system had been in operation for some years.

On 28 August 1899 the committee submitted rules for both tournaments and they were formally approved. These rules are set out in Appendix IV(Section 1). The same meeting also appointed the following delegates from the provinces to manage the two tournaments:

Leinster: F.H. Orr (Royal Dublin) and W.C. Pickman (Portmarnock);
Munster: R. Plummer (Lahinch);
Connacht: J. Meldon (Galway);
Ulster: Colonel Knox (Royal Portrush) and George Combe (Royal County Down);
Union: H.C. Kelly (Honorary Treasurer) and H.J. Daly (Honorary Secretary).

From their inception the two trophies have been known simply as 'The Senior Cup' and 'The Junior Cup' and every Club affiliated to the Union is now entitled to enter either or both tournaments; however, today's Club members may find it difficult to appreciate that the original concept of each of these events was (as the official titles then indicated) a tournament for Senior Golf Clubs and a separate tournament for Junior Golf Clubs. The 1899 meeting approved rules of 'The Irish Senior Golf Club Challenge Cup' and 'The Irish Junior Golf Club Challenge Cup'. Some time over the intervening years, when the designation of Senior or Junior Golf Club was no longer the criteria, the titles of the two events published in the Union Yearbook were changed to what they are known as today: 'The Irish Golf Clubs Senior Challenge Cup'. and 'The Irish Golf Clubs Junior Challenge Cup'.

Records are unavailable to show what entitled a Club to Senior or Junior ranking. It is certainly not the number of holes, as both 18 and 9 hole links were allocated the status of being suitable for the Senior Cup; nor, for the first few years at any rate, was a Club precluded from entering both competitions.

In the inaugural year only six Clubs (three Leinster, two Ulster and one Munster) entered for the Senior Cup, whilst 11 Clubs (eight Leinster, two Ulster and one Munster) entered for the Junior Cup. Below are listed the draws made by the Union for each event.

SENIOR CUP

Leinster

	First Round:	A	Royal Dublin	v.	Portmarnock
			Dublin University		a bye
	Second Round:		Winner of A	v.	Dublin University
Ulster			Royal County Down	v.	Royal Portrush
Munster			Lahinch		w.o.
	Semi-Final	B	Ulster	v.	Munster
			Leinster		a bye
	Final		Leinster	v.	Winner of B

JUNIOR CUP

Leinster

First Round:	A	Foxrock	v.	Bray
	B	Dublin University	v.	Malahide
	C	Portmarnock	v.	Royal Dublin
	D	County Louth	v.	Sutton
Second Round:	E	Winner of A	v.	Winner of B
	F	Winner of C	v.	Winner of D
Third Round:		Winner of E	v.	Winner of F

Connacht	Athlone	v.	Galway
Munster	Lahinch	w.o.	

Semi-Final:	G	Munster	v.	Leinster
		Connacht	a bye	
Final:		Connacht	v.	Winner of G

In the Senior Cup national final at Portmarnock in May 1900, immediately preceding the Close Championship, Dublin University defeated Royal County Down by 11 holes to 3. The Dublin University team was: C. Moore, E.K. Figgis, R.P. Meredith, H. Dodd, E. Gibson and A.C. Newett.

In the Junior Cup national final at the same venue on the same day Portmarnock defeated Athlone by 24 holes to 1. The Portmarnock team was: G.S. Kinahan, R.G.N. Henry, W.H. Roper, R.R. Boyd, W.K. Rogers and W.J. Carberry.

The sub-committee recommended and the Union agreed 'that competing Clubs should be requested to subscribe funds for the purchase of a challenge cup for each tournament and that medals and badges be presented to the winning team in each event.' A total of £49 was subscribed by the following Clubs:

Royal Dublin	£10.0.0.
Royal Portrush, Portmarnock, Royal County Down and Bray £5 each:	20.0.0.
Foxrock	3.0.0.
Malahide, Dublin University, Sutton and Lahinch £2 each:	8.0.0.
North West, Greenore, County Louth, Athlone, Ormeau, Knock, Greenisland and Malone £1 each:	8.0.0.
	————
	£49.0.0.

Although only eight years earlier the Irish Amateur Open Championship Perpetual Challenge Cup had been purchased for £50, it is inconceivable to imagine that the cost of the two magnificent trophies did not each exceed the monies subscribed and the cost must have been considerably augmented out of Union funds. The medals too were magnificent and whilst their modern counterparts are not so ornate, they are just as highly prized today as in the inaugural year.

The figure surmounting the lid of the Senior Cup is Frederick G. Tait (Royal and Ancient Golf Club) Amateur Champion 1896 and 1898. Runner-up 1893, 1894, 1895 and 1899.

The figure surmounting the lid of the Junior Cup is John Ball Jr (Royal Liverpool Golf Club), Amateur Champion 1888, 1890, 1892, 1894, 1899, 1902, 1909 and 1912. Runner-up 1887 and 1895. Open Champion 1890. Irish Amateur Open Champion 1893, 1894 and 1899.

The design of the first Irish Golf Clubs' Senior Challenge Cup Gold Medal presented to members of winning teams from 1900 to 1913. (Chapter 8)

THE IRISH GOLF CLUBS SENIOR CHALLENGE CUP TOURNAMENT

(Chapter 8 Appendix III)

Year	Winning Club	Year	Winning Club	Year	Winning Club
1900	Dublin University	1932	Portmarnock	1964	Shandon Park
1901	Royal Portrush	1933	Portmarnock	1965	Malahide
1902	Royal Portrush	1934	Portmarnock	1966	Shandon Park
1903	Royal Portrush	1935	Portmarnock	1967	Island
1904	Portmarnock	1936	Belvoir Park	1968	Shandon Park
1905	Malone	1937	Portmarnock	1969	Royal Dublin
1906	Portmarnock	1938	Portmarnock	1970	Clandeboye
1907	Portmarnock	1939	Cork	1971	Shandon Park
1908	Malone	1940	Portmarnock	1972	Shandon Park
1909	Malone	1941–5	No Tournament	1973	Shandon Park
1910	Dublin University	1946	Muskerry	1974	Co. Louth
1911	Dublin University	1947	Muskerry	1975	Cork
1912	Portmarnock	1948	Sutton	1976	Limerick
1913	Portmarnock	1949	Sutton	1977	Co. Louth
1914–18	No Tournament	1950	Sutton	1978	Shandon Park
1919	Portmarnock	1951	Malone	1979	Royal Portrush
1920	Milltown	1952	Belvoir Park	1980	Limerick
1921	Malone	1953	Muskerry	1981	Bangor
1922	Malone	1954	Malone	1982	Limerick
1923	Royal Portrush	1955	Malone	1983	Island
1924	Royal Dublin	1956	Sutton	1984	Bangor
1925	Royal Dublin	1957	Belvoir Park	1985	Clandeboye
1926	Hermitage	1958	Sutton	1986	Clandeboye
1927	Royal Dublin	1959	Lahinch	1987	Warrenpoint
1928	Portmarnock	1960	Shandon Park	1988	Portmarnock
1929	Royal Dublin	1961	Shandon Park	1989	Cork
1930	Portmarnock	1962	Shandon Park	1990	Warrenpoint
1931	Cork	1963	Sutton		

THE BARTON SHIELD FOURSOMES TOURNAMENT

(Chapter 10 Appendix IV)

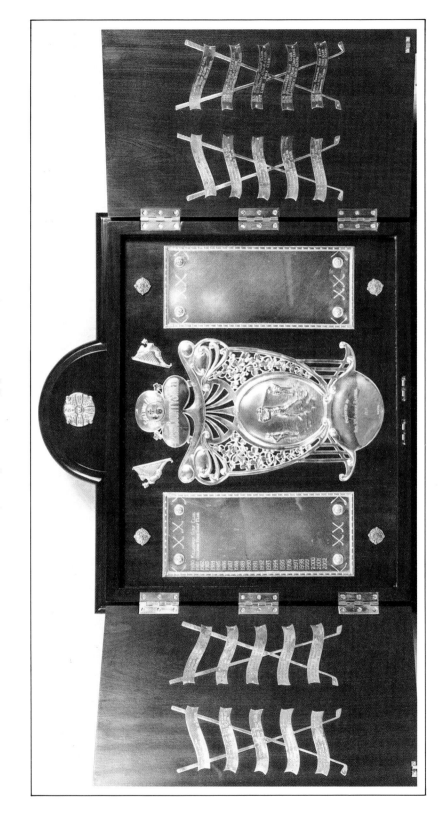

Year	Winning Club
1920	Portmarnock
1921	Malone
1922	Royal Portrush
1923	Holywood
1924	Royal Dublin
1925	Royal Dublin
1926	Queen's University
1927	Royal Co. Down
1928	Portmarnock
1929	Portmarnock
1930	Portmarnock
1931	Dublin University
1932	Portmarnock
1933	Monkstown
1934	Portmarnock
1935	Portmarnock
1936	Malone
1937	Cork
1938	Cork
1939	Portmarnock
1940	Portmarnock
1941–5	No Tournament
1946	Sutton
1947	Lahinch
1948	Royal Portrush
1949	Sutton
1950	Sutton
1951	Bangor
1952	Royal Belfast
1953	Muskerry
1954	Portmarnock
1955	Lahinch
1956	Portmarnock
1957	Galway
1958	Rathmore
1959	Athlone
1960	Rathmore
1961	Malone
1962	Clandeboye
1963	Shandon Park
1964	Rathmore
1965	Clandeboye
1966	Cork
1967	Limerick
1968	Royal Dublin
1969	Malone
1970	Shandon Park
1971	Malahide
1972	Galway
1973	Cork
1974	Woodbrook
1975	Shandon Park
1976	Limerick
1977	Royal Portrush
1978	Malahide
1979	Shandon Park
1980	Killarney
1981	Belvoir Park
1982	Malahide
1983	L'town & B'town
1984	Castletroy
1985	Shandon Park
1986	Woodbrook
1987	Warrenpoint
1988	Warrenpoint
1989	Hermitage
1990	Cork

THE IRISH GOLF CLUBS JUNIOR CHALLENGE CUP TOURNAMENT

(Chapter 8 Appendix III)

Year	Winning Club	Year	Winning Club	Year	Winning Club
1900	Portmarnock	1931	Dublin University	1963	Lahinch
1901	Ormeau	1932	Royal Dublin	1964	Portmarnock
1902	Portmarnock	1933	Portmarnock	1965	Fermoy
1903	North-West	1934	Knock	1966	Portmarnock
1904	Foxrock	1935	Hermitage	1967	Queen's University
1905	Foxrock	1936	UCD	1968	Knock
1906	Knock	1937	Cork	1969	Clandeboye
1907	Sutton	1938	Galway	1970	Newlands
1908	Knock	1939	Co. Sligo	1971	Co. Sligo
1909	Knock	1940	Rosslare	1972	Castletroy
1910	Helen's Bay	1941–5	No Tournament	1973	Portstewart
1911	Greenore	1946	Grange	1974	Sutton
1912	Milltown	1947	Ballymena	1975	Limerick
1913	Foxrock	1948	Rathmore	1976	Hermitage
1914	Foxrock	1949	Rathmore	1977	Limerick
1915–18	No Tournament	1950	Milltown	1978	Galway
1919	Royal Co. Down	1951	Milltown	1979	Limerick
1920	Royal Co. Down	1952	Shandon Park	1980	Westport
1921	Dunmurry	1953	Portmarnock	1981	Mallow
1922	Balmoral	1954	Muskerry	1982	Mullingar
1923	Malone	1955	Douglas	1983	Tullamore
1924	Hermitage	1956	Portmarnock	1984	Tramore
1925	Knock	1957	Galway	1985	Elm Park
1926	Cork	1958	Galway	1986	Galway
1927	Royal Dublin	1959	Mourne	1987	Downpatrick
1928	Bray	1960	Queen's University	1988	Limerick
1929	Killiney	1961	Lahinch	1989	Carrickfergus
1930	Douglas	1962	Muskerry	1990	Waterford

Collection of Gold Medals won by O.B. Webb and W.H. Webb (Royal Portrush Golf Club). (Chapter 34)

The officials charged with obtaining the two trophies are to be commended on their choice of design. The R & A advise that the figure adorning the Amateur Championship trophy is that of Old Tom Morris. The figure on the lid of the Senior Cup is that of Fred G. Tait (See Appendix IV, Section 4) and the one on the lid of the Junior Cup is that of John Ball, Jr.

One of the regulations prescribed that 'the Club named first in the draw shall have choice of ground unless one Club only has a full course of eighteen holes, in which case the match must be played on that course.' As a result of complaints from competing teams about the condition of some of the venues at which they were obliged to play, the Union amended this rule and made it obligatory that matches could only be played on links passed by a meeting of the Union as suitable for Inter-Club matches. At a meeting on 4 September 1900, the only links in that category were those of:

Leinster: Royal Dublin, Portmarnock, County Louth, Foxrock and Greenore;
Ulster: Royal Portrush, Royal County Down and North West;
Munster: Lahinch;
Connacht: Athlone.

Another of the conditions of each tournament was that 'the match should be decided by the number of holes won by each team.' This method of deciding team matches was the subject of constant discussion, with both Leinster and Munster golfers advocating individual wins or losses as in Championships, whilst Ulster golfers sought to retain the holes-won method. In 1907 the Union altered the rule to individual wins or losses, thus giving a balanced team a much greater chance of success against a team with just one or two outstanding players.

The ten Clubs whose links were declared suitable for both Club tournaments operated in that context until a meeting of the Union on 30 August 1904 when it was decided that the links of all Clubs declared to be Senior Clubs shall be considered suitable for all matches in the Senior Cup Competition.

In addition, the following Clubs were listed as having links suitable for the Junior Cup:

Ulster: Malone, Knock, Ormeau, Castlerock and Greenisland;
Leinster: The Island, Greystones, Carrickmines, Sutton, Malahide, Hermitage and Bray;
Connacht: Galway and County Sligo;
Munster: Cork.

This arrangement continued until 19 November 1913 when the Leinster Branch submitted a notice of motion — 'That in the Inter-Club Challenge Cup Competitions the distinction of Senior Clubs and Junior Clubs should be abolished and that the rules should be amended to allow a Club to enter a team in either or both.' The motion was passed and the rules are fundamentally the same today. The record of winning Clubs and teams in the Senior Cup and the Junior Cup are set out in Appendix IV (Sections 2 and 3).

Chapter 9

THE
DEVELOPMENT
OF GOLF
IN IRELAND

Period: 1901 to 1915

Having got off to such a heartening start in its first nine years, the Union increased its influence as more and more Clubs commenced activities. However, it was inevitable that as interest in the game grew and more 'greens' were opened for play, some of the earlier Clubs had, perforce, to close. This came about for various reasons but the most probable was the opening of a more challenging lay-out in the vicinity of an existing 'green' with the transfer of activity at the expense of the earlier location.

By 1915, 25 years after the historic meeting in Portrush, golf had started at 109 further venues. Whilst some of these are no longer in existence, they all share a place in the development of golf in Ireland:

1901   *Bantry (Co. Cork), A 1905; St Anne's Hill (Cork, Co. Cork); Waterville, A 1925.*

1902   *Athenry (originally County Galway), A 1929; Atlantic (Kilbrittain, Co. Cork); Cahir (Co. Tipperary); Kirkistown Castle, A 1903; Montrose (Donnybrook, Co. Dublin); Mountstewart (Co. Derry).*

1903   *Bangor, A 1903; Kenmare, A 1922; Killiney, A 1904; Maryboro (Queen's Co., now Co. Laois) A 1908.*

1904   *Ballymena, A 1908; Dundalk, A 1905; Fintona, A 1926; Holywood, A 1904; Newtownbarry (Co. Wexford); Roscommon, A 1915; Tuam, A 1907; Whitehead, A 1905; Wicklow, A 1906.*

1905   *Castlerea, A 1908; Dunmurry, A 1905; Hermitage (originally County Dublin), A 1906; Lisburn, A 1905; New Ross, A 1912; Rosslare, A 1908; Skerries, A 1908; Skibbereen (originally West Carbery, then Skibbereen and West Carbery), A 1931.*

1906   *Aghade (Tullow, Co. Carlow); Athy, A 1906; Castlecomer (Old) (Co. Kilkenny), A 1906; Dunfanaghy, A 1920; Durrow (Queen's County, now Co. Laois); Gorey (Co. Wexford), A 1911; Lisdoonvarna (Co. Clare); Mountbellew, A 1930; Royal Naval (originally Channel Fleet, then Atlantic Fleet) (Bere Island, Co. Cork).*

1907   *Borris, A 1908; Dervock (Livery Hill, Co. Fermanagh); Ennis, A 1910; Enniscorthy (Old) (Co. Wexford), A 1908; Ferbane and Moystown (King's Co., now Co. Offaly); Milltown, A 1907; Navan (Co. Meath), A 1908; Portumna, A*

1926; Queen's University (originally Queen's College, Belfast), A 1907; Scrabo, A 1908; Spa (Ballynahinch), A 1907; Valencia (originally Valencia Island) (Co. Kerry), A 1928.

1908   Ballyshannon (Co. Donegal), A 1910; Delgany, A 1908; Kilmashogue (Co. Dublin), A 1909; Milford (Co. Donegal), A 1910; Monkstown, A 1908; Riverside (Portmarnock, Co. Dublin), A 1908; Strabane, A 1910; Westport, A 1927.

1909   Charleville, A 1945; Douglas, A 1911; Dun Laoghaire (originally Kingstown), A 1910; Laytown & Bettystown, A 1909; Midleton (Co. Cork), A 1910; Mulrany (Co. Mayo); Portarlington, A 1911; Renvyle (Co. Galway); Stillorgan Park (Co. Dublin), A 1909; Thurles, A 1909.

1910   Ardcarne (Co. Leitrim); Athgarvan (Curragh, Co. Kildare), A 1912; Bagenalstown (Co. Carlow), A 1910; Ballina, A 1924; Carrick-on-Shannon, A 1910; Castlebar, A 1912; Castleknock (Co. Dublin); Derryvale (Co. Tipperary); Edenderry (originally Edenderry & District), A 1928; Grange, A 1911; Killahara (Co. Cork); Mitchelstown, A 1924; Omagh, A 1911; Robinhood (Fox & Geese, Co. Dublin).

1911   Ardee (originally South Louth), A 1911; Boyle, A 1924; Cliftonville, A 1911; Clonmel, A 1912; Clontarf, A 1912; Finglas (originally North Surburban) (Co. Dublin), A 1911; Glenariff (Co. Antrim), A 1912; Howth, A 1919; Markethill (Co. Antrim), A 1911.

1912   Carrickmacross (Co. Monaghan), A 1912; Cashel (Co. Tipperary); Castleblayney (Old) (Co. Monaghan), A 1923; City of Derry, A 1913; Kinsale, A 1924; Waterford, A 1912.

1913   Banbridge, A 1914; Castle, A 1913; Clones, A 1915; Dunmore (Co. Galway); Letterkenny, A 1913.

1914   Balmoral, A 1915; Fethard (Co. Tipperary); Newtownstewart, A 1918.

1915   Bessbrook (Co. Antrim), A 1915; Cullybrackey (Co. Antrim), A 1915; Inchydoney (Clonakilty, Co. Cork), A 1915.

Possibly the most radical reform in the administration of the Union during this period was the result of a decision made at a meeting on 14 June 1911. A committee comprising Mr Justice Barton (President), John L. Morrow (Honorary Secretary) and Hugh C. Kelly (Honorary Treasurer) together with George Combe, W. Campbell, Lloyd Campbell and H.M. Cairnes was appointed to draw up a new constitution to re-structure the Union in order to increase the Union's scope and interest in it by giving the Clubs a more direct say in the management of affairs in their own province.

The original charter of the Union in 1891 prescribed that each affiliated Club was entitled to send forward, depending on membership, up to three delegates to every meeting. By this time, 20 years on, 163 Clubs had become affiliated to the Union. With the growing popularity of golf and the increase in Clubs and Club membership, it became clear that it would be exceedingly difficult to conduct a meeting if affiliated Clubs sent forward their permitted number of delegates.

On April 1913 a new constitution was adopted which provided for a Central Council and four provincial Councils. Whilst the constitution has been updated since then this format has remained unchanged.

Another important decision was made by the Central Council at a meeting on 25 February 1914 which showed that the administrators were concerned with improving the standard of golf. The Council sanctioned a scheme, which came to be known as 'The Temporary Professional Scheme', whereby travelling professionals could provide tuition at smaller Clubs which did not have the services of a professional golfer. (See Chapter 12 for further information.)

Chapter 10

THE BARTON SHIELD FOURSOMES AND THE ALL-IRELAND COUNTY CHAMPIONSHIP

At a meeting of the Union on 24 February 1910 a new event was inaugurated. The President of the Union, the Honorable Mr Justice Barton, proposed the institution of an Inter-County Tournament and voiced the desire to present to the Union a trophy to be held by the winning County . Thus the Barton Shield came into existence. It is now the premier Inter-Club Foursomes Tournament in Ireland.

A sub-committee was appointed to draw up rules which were approved at a Council meeting held exactly one year later and are set out in Appendix V (Section 1). The format of the Tournament was teams of four playing foursomes matchplay off scratch, the full 18 holes to be played and holes up to decide.

Because there were a large number of Clubs in and around Belfast and Dublin, the sub-committee created two new counties in addition to the historic 32 counties of Ireland: the County of the City of Belfast being part of Belfast city within the municipal boundary, and the County of the City of Dublin being part of Dublin city within a radius of six miles from Nelson Pillar.

The first Inter-County Tournament was won by County Donegal in 1911. The team comprised J.B. Gillies, H.K. Mitchell and the brothers Ector M. and Lionel O. Munn. Lionel also achieved a unique double: having annexed the Irish Amateur Close Championship at Portrush earlier that year, he won the Irish Amateur Open Championship at Portmarnock immediately after the Inter-County Final and became the first man to be the holder of the two Championships in the same year.

In 1912, County Dublin was victorious and the County of the City of Dublin won in both 1913 and 1914, after which the Tournament was suspended because of the Great War. The County of the City of Dublin was again successful in 1919 and at a meeting of the Council on 20 November 1919, on the proposal of the Leinster Branch, it was agreed that because the number of players who could compete in this Tournament was limited, the competition did not get the support it deserved. Thus the scope should be broadened to an Inter-Club Tournament instead of an Inter-County event and run on the same lines as the Senior and Junior Cups. Portmarnock (whose team was H.A. Boyd, H.M. Cairnes, G. Moore and D.E. Soulby) was the first Club to win the new Barton Shield Tournament. The record of winning counties and teams and, from 1920 onwards, the winning Clubs and teams are set out in Appendix V (Section 2).

It was to be another 58 years before Mr Justice Dunbar Plunket Barton's original idea of an Inter-County contest was to be re-activated. The Province which, in 1920 had successfully advocated its discontinuance, now initiated its restoration in a somewhat different format.

At the February 1977 AGM of the Union the Leinster Branch submitted the following notice of motion: 'that an inter-county championship be inaugurated and that the proposed rules be considered.' As the motion had not earlier been submitted to the November 1976 Branch annual meetings for consideration, the Council had no alternative but to refer it back to the branches for their November 1977 AGMs. The secretariat was instructed to draw up conditions for the proposed championship and submit them to the branches with the Leinster motion.

The conditions of the original Inter-County Tournament only came to light during the research of this history. Had the Council been aware of the precedent regarding the two additional counties (the County of the City of Belfast and the County of the City of Dublin) it might well have followed it for this championship. There is, in fact, a greater reason for their re-introduction. In both areas there has been an extraordinary and welcome increase in the number of Clubs operating within the two boundaries. In addition, part of the City of Belfast is in Co. Antrim and part in Co. Down and there is a wealth of golfing talent in the 15 Clubs in Co. Antrim and 19 Clubs in Co. Down all of which are outside the municipal boundary of Belfast City.

The Leinster motion was approved unanimously at the branch AGMs and the Council adopted the recommendations and named the event 'The All-Ireland County Championship'. The conditions prescribed that teams would consist of five members, play would be by singles matchplay and all players would play off scratch. To ensure a big spread of players the eligibility condition was wide ranging and allowed that a player could be selected for that county provided he was born in, ordinarily resident in, of a member of an affiliated club in the county.

The provincial sections are under the management and control of the respective provincial branches, each of which is authorised to appoint a manager for each county who is empowered to select his team. The branch makes a draw and arranges dates and venues. The winning county in each province advances to the national final at a venue decided by the Central Council.

Messrs Johnnie Walker very generously agreed to sponsor the championship, which they continued to do up to 1987, and the provincial sections commenced in the latter part of

1979. The Union arranged with the committee of The Island Golf Club to host the national final at the commencement of the 1980 golfing season so that it would not interfere with the already extensive golfing calendar. The first national finalists were Down (all but one of whom, incidentally, were resident in and members of Clubs of Belfast City), Roscommon, Waterford and Wicklow. In the first semi-final Wicklow defeated Roscommon by 3 matches to 2, whilst in the second semi-final Waterford beat Down by 3½ matches to 1½. Wicklow then defeated Waterford by 3 matches to 2 to win the Championship. Wicklow won against the odds. Of the 20 players involved in the national final, 14 had represented their province in the senior interprovincials and seven of these had also represented Ireland in the home internationals. All five of the Down team were interprovincials with four of them internationals. Roscommon also had five interprovincials, two of whom had gained international honours. Waterford fielded three interprovincials of whom one was an international player. Wicklow, on the other hand, could only boast of one interprovincial player and he had been picked only once by his province and that had been many years earlier.

The most successful county to date has been Louth which won the Championship in 1982, 1983, 1984 and 1985. A record of winning counties and teams is set out in Appendix V (Section 3).

Chapter 11

THE CONSTITUTION OF THE UNION, THE CENTRAL COUNCIL AND PROVINCIAL BRANCHES

At the adjourned inaugural meeting in November 1891, a sub-committee had been appointed to draw up rules both for the Union and the Irish Amateur Open Championship. However, no progress appears to have been made towards defining the rules of the Union because at a meeting on 29 May 1900 a new sub-committee was appointed 'to find out from the minutes what were the duties of the Golfing Union of Ireland and to draw up a constitution and rules for future guidance.'

At its next meeting, on 4 September 1900, the Union formally approved the first constitution which embodied the resolutions passed at the 1891 meeting. Under the heading of delegates, the rule provided that 'every Club affiliated to the Union would be entitled to send to each meeting of the Union one delegate, and one extra delegate for every 150 members, or part thereof, over and above the first 150, provided always that no Club would be entitled to send more than three delegates.'

As the game increased in popularity, and more Clubs were opened for play and became affiliated, concern was expressed that if the majority of Clubs sent their full entitlement of delegates to Union meetings then numerical problems could arise. At the end of 1910, golf had been started in 201 other areas since Royal Belfast had been founded in 1881. Some of these were on private estates and were not open to membership, whilst some others did not survive the competition from neighbouring Clubs. An examination of the chapters on the Development of Golf in Ireland (2, 4 and 9) shows that 178 of these were members' Clubs and became affiliated to the Union. 134 of these Clubs are still in operation and continue to play their part in Union affairs.

By 14 June 1911, the provincial situation was: Connacht 15 Clubs, Leinster 53, Munster 34 and Ulster 53. The meeting on that date had before it this notice of motion: 'That it is desirable that the Golfing Union of Ireland be reorganised on the lines of the Irish Rugby Football Union so as to increase its scope and usefulness by allocating provincial matters to the provinces, and reserving the matters of national interest for the consideration of the general meetings of the Union, to be held as often as may be deemed necessary for the proper conduct of such business'. The motion was formally proposed by George Combe (Royal County Down). After lengthy discussions, at the request of Mr Combe, it was agreed to refer the matter for consideration and report to a committee consisting of Mr Justice Dunbar Plunket Barton (President – Chairman), Rev. John L. Morrow (Honorary Secretary), Messrs Hugh C. Kelly (Honorary Treasurer), G. Combe (Royal County Down), W. Campbell (County Sligo), H.M. Cairnes (Portmarnock) and Lloyd Campbell (Royal Portrush).

It is necessary to recount in some detail the lead up to the establishment of a Central Council and four provincial branches. At a meeting in Dublin on 23 January 1912, the Union considered the scheme submitted by the committee and it was referred back to the committee with the following expressions of opinion:

1. 'The concept of the Union being managed by a Central Council was accepted but not the numbers proposed for such Council.' (The scheme proposed that the officers of the Union, four provincial Secretaries, the Secretary of each affiliated Club and 34 other representatives appointed by the Senior Clubs would form the Council).
2. 'The majority of members were in favour of the principle of greater decentralisation and the appointment of four provincial Secretaries, but was against substituting Club officials for delegates.
3. 'In any scheme of decentralisation the governing body of the GUI should be smaller than that suggested in the scheme.'

A modified scheme was considered at a meeting in Belfast on 16 February 1912 and Messrs George Combe, John L. Morrow and Hugh C. Kelly were appointed to draft the new constitution. A printed draft was issued to all affiliated Clubs which provided, inter alia, that the Central Council would comprise the officers of the Union, Vice-Presidents, four provincial Secretaries and six delegates (two each from Ulster and Leinster and one each from Munster and Connacht). A special meeting in Belfast on 25 October 1912 approved the draft in principle except for the make-up of the Central Council. A further reprint which provided that there would be four Vice-Presidents with one each nominated by the four provinces and that the delegate representation would be doubled, was presented to a meeting in Dublin on 28 November 1912 and approved. It was decided that a final print would be issued to all Clubs and a formal notice of motion to approve the constitution would be tabled for a special general meeting in Dublin on 17 April 1913. The constitution as finally approved is set out in Appendix VI (Section 1).

The November meeting appointed Messrs J.L. Morrow, W.B. Fennell (new Honorary Secretary), G. Combe, W. Campbell, B.A. Morrison and G.T. Power (Portmarnock) as a committee to arrange for the first provincial meetings.

Unfortunately Leinster is the only province which can trace its records, while newspaper reports have been found regarding the Ulster and Connacht inaugural meetings. The Munster Branch has no knowledge of its inaugural meeting or its setting up. Despite this paucity of

The Barton Inter-Club Challenge Cup.

Open to all Leinster Clubs.
(Teams of ten. Foursomes match play.)

The Sir John Lumsden Memorial Cup.

Open to members of Leinster Clubs.
(54 holes stroke play.)

Leinster Branch Tournaments (continued)

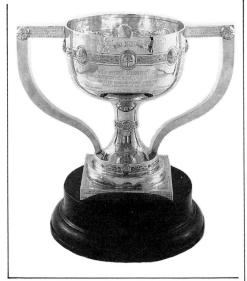

*(Each for teams of nine.
Singles match play.)*

The Guinness Metropolitan Trophy.

*Open to Leinster Clubs situated within the
metropolitan area
(18 miles from GPO, Dublin).*

*The Provincial Towns (Leinster) Challenge
Cup.*

*Open to Leinster Clubs situated outside the
metropolitan area.*

*The Bank of Ireland Leinster Seniors
Amateur Open Championship Cup.*

*(Open to players 55 years and over on
first day of Championship.
36 holes stroke play.)*

information, the Union minutes record the attendance at subsequent Council meetings of various provincial officers and delegates.

Leinster Branch

We are grateful to the Leinster Branch for providing us with the names of representatives of Clubs who attended the inaugural meeting held in the Metropole Hotel, Dublin, on 9 January 1913. (See Appendix VI, Section 20).

Beamish Morrison was re-elected as branch Chairman annually until 1930, when he became President of the Union. His successor was G.B. Butler (Castle). George Price was likewise a long serving officer of the branch and remained in office until 1926. His successor was Alan B. Kidd (Portmarnock).

The Barton Cup, an inter-Club 10-a-side foursomes tournament open to all Clubs in the province, was commenced in 1903. The original conditions were found in the *Irish Golfer* of 4 February, 1903, and are now with the Branch.

The first mention of Mr Justice Dunbar Plunket Barton in the minutes of meetings of the Union is when he, with the Hon. Thomas Sinclair DL and Sir Alexander Shaw DL were elected Vice-Presidents of the Union on 20 May 1902. Thomas Sinclair was the founder and first Captain of the Royal Belfast Golf Club in 1881. Alexander Shaw was the founder and first Captain of Lahinch Golf Club in 1892. He was also the donor of the replacement South of Ireland Amateur Open Championship trophy competed for annually at Lahinch since 1901. Plunket Barton was elected President of the Royal Dublin Golf Club in 1903 and continued until 1924. He was President of the Union from 1906 to 1925.

Plunket Barton presented the Cup for competition between the Leinster Golf Clubs and requested the greens committee of the Royal Dublin Golf Club to arrange details of the competition. The rules which were included in the report have not been radically altered and the tournament attracts over 90 per cent of the Clubs in the province. The record of winning Clubs and teams is set out in Appendix VI (Section 2).

At the second meeting of the Union held in Belfast on 25 March 1892 it was decided 'that the Royal Dublin Golf Club be invited to join the Union' and on 13 October 1893 John Lumsden was elected a Vice President of the Union. In 1926 the Leinster provincial Council decided to institute a tournament on handicap for single figure members of Leinster Clubs and named it The Sir John Lumsden Memorial Cup to commemorate the memory of the man who had done so much to popularise the game in the province. The Council invited Royal Dublin to house the first playing of the tournament and the first winner, J.G. Greene, was a member of that Club. The record of winners is set out in Appendix VI (Section 3).

The Provincial Towns Challenge Cup was instituted in 1932 for Leinster Clubs outside a radius of 18 miles from Dublin. When the Metropolitan Trophy Tournament was instituted in 1973, the Leinster Council defined the metropolitan area as 'a radius of 18 miles from the GPO in Dublin' and all Clubs outside that area were classified as provincial. Both competitions are for Club teams of nine players whose handicaps are 9 and over. Play is matchplay off scratch. At the last reckoning, 41 out of 46 eligible Clubs competed in the Towns Cup and 39 out of 46 eligible Clubs took part in the Metropolitan Trophy. The record of winning Clubs and teams in each of the tournaments is set out in Appendix VI (Section 4).

Ulster Branch Tournaments

The Belfast and District Cup and above the original Team Medal presented in 1903.

(Open to Ulster Clubs situated within 25 miles of Belfast City Hall. Teams of seven. Singles match play.)

The Ulster Cup.

(Open to all Ulster Clubs. Teams of seven. Singles match play.)

Milltown Golf Club had inaugurated an Open Mixed Foursomes Matchplay Handicap Tournament in 1929. Over the years, it had become extremely popular as both a golf and social week and it attracted large galleries. Between 1939 and 1967 it was dominated by Joe Carr who won it nine times. In the first three he was partnered by Ms Nicky Cunningham McIntyre (Sutton) and in the last six by his wife, Dor (Sutton). Milltown wished to upgrade the tournament to a scratch event and, on the Club's behalf, the Leinster Branch requested the Central Council to authorise it to adopt the title of East of Ireland Amateur Open Mixed Foursomes Championship. This was agreed, and the first playing of the restructured event was in 1974. Many members of the Club were not overjoyed with the new format as they could no longer compete in it and the event lost its social atmosphere. After nine years the Club asked the Leinster branch to change the format to a 54 hole medal foursomes event and to move it to the end of the season. The original Milltown Mixed was re-introduced at its June date. The record of winners of the Championship is set out in Appendix VI (Section 5).

In 1987 the Branch inaugurated the Leinster Seniors' (Golden Years) Championship which has already proved popular. The record of winners is set out in Appendix VI (Section 6).

The branch has always been most active in promoting Junior Golf in the province and events in this category are listed in Chapter 18.

Ulster Branch

Don McErvel (Ulster Branch) traced the inaugural meeting. Both the *Belfast Newsletter* and the *Northern Whig* carried a short report of the meeting which was held in the Grand Central Hotel, Belfast, on 10 January 1913. A large representation of golf Clubs in Ulster attended the meeting. The chair was taken by Henry Gregg (Royal Belfast). W.M. Davidson (Knock) was appointed first Honorary Secretary of the branch. The meeting also appointed Hugh Cunningham Kelly (Royal County Down), who was also a Vice-President of the Union, as a provincial delegate. The only other business recorded was the appointment of a match and handicapping committee to 'suggest rules and venues for the Senior, Junior, Belfast and District Cups and the Barton Shield.' With the exception of the Belfast and District Cup, the rules of the other Inter-Club tournaments had already been prescribed by the Union so the match and handicapping committee could only recommend venues for the Ulster sections of these events.

The record of Clubs and teams in the Belfast and District Cup is set out in Appendix VI (Section 7). This tournament started in 1903.[9] No specific rules came to light, but in April 1903, there was a six a side singles match between Helen's Bay and Greenisland in the Belfast and District League. Thereafter, matches between Greenisland, Ormeau, Malone, Royal Belfast, Helen's Bay and Knock took place.[10]

Having taken over the administration of the Belfast and District Cup, the Ulster Council turned its attention to introducing an Inter-Club Tournament in which all Clubs in the province could participate, and inaugurated the Ulster Cup in 1913. The conditions prescribed that each Club could enter a team of seven, all of whom must not only have a handicap of 12 and over, but must also be 30 years of age or over in the year of the Tournament. Play was to be singles matchplay off scratch on a home and away basis. A novel condition was that, in addition to a point for each match won, the accumulated number of

*The Bank of Ireland Ulster Seniors Amateur
Open Championship Cup.*

*(Open to players 55 years and over on first
day of Championship. 36 holes stroke play.)*

The Christie Flag (No Trophy).
*(Open to professional golfers attached to
Ulster Clubs, each playing with the leading
amateur in his Club. Where there is no
professional, a Club may enter a team
consisting of two category one handicap club
members. 18 holes fourball stroke play.)*

holes up at the conclusion of each match would be taken into account so that in the event of equal points at the end of the return series, the Club with the greatest number of holes up would win the tie. The record of winning Clubs is set out in Appendix VI (Section 8).

In 1939, Harry Christie, Chairman of the Ulster PGA presented a Flag Pennant for competition between teams comprising each Ulster Club professional and the holder of the Club Amateur Championship. Play was to be 36 holes medal play off handicap. The Ulster Council decided that this should become an annual event, and agreed to take over the organisation and administration of the Tournament in 1940. To enable more clubs to participate, the Council extended the eligibility to allow two Category One amateur members of a Club to represent that Club if it did not retain a professional. The format is now four ball strokeplay over 18 holes and play is off scratch. The record of winning teams and Clubs is set out in Appendix VI (Section 9).

Dr John Frazer, a member of Balmoral Golf Club, of which Fred Daly was the long time professional, presented a trophy to the Ulster Branch in 1973 to help promote Junior Golf in the province and requested that the trophy be named the Fred Daly Trophy. The Tournament is open to all Clubs in the province for Club teams of seven players all of whom must be under the age of 18 on 12 August in the year of the Tournament. The record of winning Clubs is set out in Appendix VI (Section 10). The branch also pursued a programme with other junior events, a list of which is included in Chapter 18. Their junior golf programme continues to be a priority.

Another recent addition to the branch calendar has been the introduction of an Ulster Seniors' (Golden Years) Championship. The record of winners appears in Appendix VI (Section 11).

Connacht Branch

Of the four provinces, Connacht has the smallest number of affiliated Clubs. From the foundation of Athlone in 1892 until the branch was formed in 1924[11], a total of 25 Clubs had commenced activities in Connacht of which 21 are still in operation. A further 16 Clubs opened since then of which four closed down and Connacht now has 33 Clubs under its jurisdiction. Unlike some of the more populated areas, golfers in Connacht usually have to travel long distances for a game away from their home Club and their enthusiasm for the game is shown by the support received in Union and branch tournaments.

The Connacht Shield was started in 1949. This is a foursomes matchplay tournament open to all Clubs in the province for teams of 10 players and the handicap limit is 19, subject to a maximum difference between any pair of 8. The record of winning Clubs is set out in Appendix VI (Section 12).

To commemorate the memory of its greatest golfer, the branch inaugurated The Cecil Ewing Shield in 1982. Each Club in the province is eligible to play. The format is teams of 10 foursomes matchplay for players on handicap of 18 and over at the end of the previous year. In addition, the combined handicaps of each pair shall not be less than 40 and all matches are played off scratch. The record of winning Clubs is set out in Appendix VI (Section 13).

Another commemorative tournament first played in 1988 is the Jack O'Sullivan Trophy, in memory of the man who served as Honorary Secretary of the branch for 25 years. Again,

Connacht Branch Tournaments

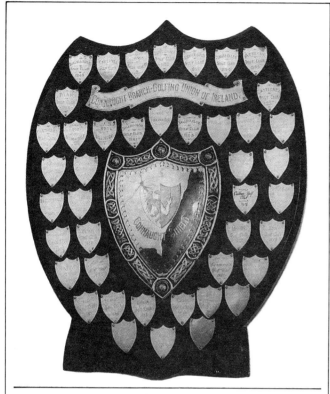

The Connacht Shield.

*(Open to all Connacht Clubs. Teams of ten.
Foursomes match play.)*

The Cecil Ewing Shield.

*(Open to all Connacht Clubs.
Teams of ten. Foursomes match play.)*

Connacht Branch Tournaments (continued)

The Jack O'Sullivan Trophy.

*(Open to all Connacht Clubs. Teams of ten.
Fourball match play.)*

*The Bank of Ireland Connacht Seniors'
Amateur Open Championship Cup.*

*Open to players 55 years and over on first
day of Championship. 36 holes stroke play.*

Munster Branch Tournaments

The Munster Country Clubs Cup.

*(Open to all Munster Clubs whose courses
are less than 18 holes. Teams of seven.
Singles match play.)*

The Bank of Ireland Munster Seniors'
Amateur Open Championship Cup.

*(Open to all players 55 years and over
on first day of Championship. 36 holes
stroke play.)*

the competition is for teams of 10 open to all Clubs in the province. All players must be 18 years or over on 1 January in the year of the tournament. Play is fourball matchplay off a handicap of 18 and under, with the maximum difference of 8 between any pair. The record of winning Clubs is set out in Appendix VI (Section 14).

In 1979 the Branch started the Connacht Seniors' (Golden Years) Championship. The format is 18 holes medal play. The record of winners is set out in Appendix VI (Section 15).

The branch also organises the Connacht Mixed Foursomes Strokeplay Championship which is also 18 holes medal play. The record of winners is set out in Appendix VI (Section 16).

At junior level, the branch is actively engaged in promoting this very important aspect of the game and events in this category are listed in Chapter 18.

Munster Branch

Cork Golf Club was founded in 1888 and was the first established Club in Munster. Between 1888 and 1913 (when the special meeting approved the new constitution) golf had been played at 55 Clubs in the province. Of these, 31 are still active and are affiliated to the Union. Perhaps the sub-committee of 28 November 1912 who arranged the first provincial meetings was responsible for the inauguration of the Leinster and Ulster Branches on 9 and 10 January respectively. There is no documentary evidence of the formation of the Munster Branch.

There is, however, a strong presumption that the committee also contacted Clubs in that province and that the Munster Branch was formed prior to the special meeting of 17 April 1913 as otherwise the attendance list recorded in the minute of that meeting could not have included the following names and classifications: E. O'S. Allen (Munster Secretary) and J.G. Crosbie (Munster delegate).

In 1932, Munster inaugurated the Munster Country Clubs Cup for which the branch provided a Perpetual Challenge Trophy. Originally the tournament was confined to Clubs in the province outside Cork city, having only a nine hole course. Each team member also had to be resident outside Cork city. The present conditions allow all Munster Clubs with less than 18 holes to enter and the residential qualification has been enlarged to include the entire country. The Tournament is for teams of seven with handicaps of 10 and over and play is singles matchplay off scratch. The record of winning Clubs is set out in Appendix VI (Section 17).

The branch also started the Munster Seniors' (Golden Years) Amateur Open Championship in 1989. The record of winners is set out in Appendix VI (Section 18).

As in the other provinces, the Junior Golf programme receives a high priority and the Munster junior events are listed in Chapter 0.

General

Originally it was recommended that each province should hold a meeting every three months to which every Club in the province was entitled, depending on membership, to send from one to three delegates. This was later changed to one branch annual meeting in each province, the affairs of each branch being administered by a provincial council comprising the branch officers and delegates elected by member Clubs at branch annual meetings.

The first yearbook in Union headquarters is that of 1927 and the constitution reproduced there shows that the main structure of the 1913 constitution is still intact, although by merging some of the rules their number was reduced from 13 to 10. However, the 1927 reproduction contains four new rules which were introduced during the intervening years.

The additional rules were rule III — property of the Union; rule VII — affiliated Clubs to be bound by the rules of the Union; rule XI — Yearbook; and rule XII — sub-committees. In this last rule, the composition of four sub-committees are listed, and with changing personnel these were updated in successive yearbooks.

No further change appears to have been considered necessary until the advent of the Malahide Golf Club case in 1947. This led to the only occasion in Union history when an affiliated Club was expelled for refusing to alter its constitution in order the comply with the constitution of the Union. The Union was compelled to take what might now be regarded as draconian action.

There are two separate and independent organisations controlling and administering amateur golf in Ireland. The Golfing Union of Ireland which was founded in 1891 and the Irish Ladies' Golf Union founded two years later. The two Unions have always enjoyed a most cordial relationship and have worked in close collaboration towards the promotion and advancement of amateur Golf in this country. The GUI controls and administers men's amateur golf, whilst the ILGU controls and administers ladies' amateur golf.

Every golf Club in Ireland was founded by a group of men amateur golfers to provide facilities for the ever-growing number of men taking to the game, and every Irish golf Club is affiliated to the GUI either on the application of the Club's founders or their successors in office.

The first constitution was approved in 1900. Neither that constitution nor the 1913 constitution which superceded it specifically prescribed that the GUI was legislating solely for men. This declaration was not considered necessary because it was accepted and confirmed by the founding of the ILGU which recorded that one of its objects was 'to promote and safeguard the interests of Irish women's golf.'

In the early days of both Unions the men ran the Clubs. Competition results around the turn of the century show that it was the wives, daughters and sisters of members of the Clubs who were playing. In fact Rhona Adair and the Hezlet sisters of Portrush did much to promote Ireland on the international golfing scene. Records are not available to show when the first ladies formed themselves into a ladies' branch within a Club, but this was a prerequisite before the ladies could apply for affiliation to the ILGU. Nor is there any certainty that the ladies who played over the various Irish courses paid a lower subscription than their male counterparts. This was and still is of no concern to either Union. Neither Union interferes with a Club's right to prescribe for different categories of member within the Club, nor the rate of subscription to be paid by members in these categories. However, at the beginning, each Club on affiliation paid to its respective Union an annual subscription based on the number of delegates the Club was entitled to send to meetings of its Union. Whilst both Unions now charge a per capita fee per Club member, the provision of delegate

The original clubhouse of Malahide Golf Club in use continuously since (circa) 1894.

Artist's impression of the clubhouse showing extensions. This remained the club's headquarters until 1990 when it moved to a new location at Beechwood, The Grange, Malahide where, in addition to constructing a new 27 hole lay-out, it built a new clubhouse (below) which was officially opened in 1990.

representation to meetings remains unchanged. The ILGU Annual General Meetings are attended by delegates from all member ladies' Clubs whilst the GUI changed its constitution in 1913 and Club delegates now attend provincial branch AGMs.

The Council met on 12 September 1930 and defined the term 'membership' on which subscriptions to the Union were payable. The minutes record that 'on and from 1 January 1931 the total "membership" on which subscriptions are payable comprises all classes of male members of the Club, including juvenile, country or out-lying members, honorary members and restricted members and associates having no vote.' This definition embraced every category of male member within every affiliated Club and clearly confirms that the GUI was legislating only for men's amateur golf. As further evidence of this assertion, there exists the Form of Application which was used at that time in which the Club had to state the total number of male members and indicate if there was a 'ladies' branch'. The Club was also required to undertake to be bound by the rules, regulations and bye-laws of the Union.

Time has not altered the pattern and it still operates today in all affiliated Clubs. Men administer the affairs of the Club, decide who may be elected to any of the categories of member within the Club and decide on the Club subscription to be paid by the different categories of member. The men collect and transmit the Union and provincial subscriptions to the GUI and the ILGU respectively. Had there been any change in this pattern since either Union or the various Clubs affiliated to them were founded, there would have been some reference to it, either in the records of the Unions or in the records of one or more of the affiliated Clubs.

Today most Club constitutions define the category containing the majority of men members as 'ordinary' or 'full' members and all ladies in the Club as 'lady associate' members. Invariably the largest group of ladies, usually those who play golf in the Club, pay a subscription ranging from one-third to one-half of the subscription payable by the ordinary members. Other lady associates pay a lower subscription.

Affiliation to either Union is voluntary and just like the men, so the lady associates, having formed a ladies' branch within the Club and having their own committees and AGM must apply to the ILGU for affiliation as a ladies' Club.

In 1938 the attention of the GUI Central Council was drawn to the case of ladies attending and voting at the annual general meetings of Curragh Golf Club. At that time the ladies' branch of the Club was affiliated to the ILGU.

At a meeting on 31 January 1938, the Council decided that rule 37 of the constitution of the Curragh Golf Club (which stated that the ladies were full members of the Club and entitled to vote at the general meetings of the Club) was not acceptable to the Golfing Union of Ireland as an approved rule for affiliation, and that the Curragh Golf Club be informed accordingly and be requested to amend it and to report amendments to the Leinster Branch. At the Council meeting on 12 December 1938 it was reported that the rules of the Curragh Golf Club had been amended as requested by the Union, and the Union Honorary Secretary indicated that he would obtain the constitutions of all affiliated Clubs to ascertain if their rules conformed with the requirements of the Union. However, because of the War this task was not completed until 1946. At a meeting on 28 March that year it was reported that the constitutions of all affiliated Clubs had been examined. Fifteen of them did not comply with the requirements of the Union; seven of these had amended their constitutions and another seven were in the process of doing so, but one Club, Malahide, had indicated that it would not alter its constitution.

The Council decided to inform the Club that it would be expelled from the Union if it did not amend its constitution and after correspondence the Club asked the Union to receive a delegation. A meeting of the Union's Standing Committee was convened on 22 June 1946 to meet five delegates from the Club. At the request of the Club it was agreed to appoint a sub-committee consisting of the Union Honorary Secretary, the Union solicitor and two members of the Club (one of whom was also a solicitor) to try and resolve the impasse. The media was taking a lively interest in the matter, and according to reports the problem was that although the Club had convened several special general meetings to change the constitution, 'the ladies insisted on their right, which had been there since the foundation of the Club close on 50 years ago, and they were supported in their views by a number of the "ordinary" members.'

At this point it should be mentioned that the ladies' branch of Malahide Golf Club had been affiliated to the Irish Ladies' Golf Union since 1911. Why was the GUI insisting on 'men only' at Club AGMs? All Clubs affiliated to the GUI have an input into its affairs and notices of motion or other proposals from a mixed AGM could not be accepted. Conversely the male members in a Club are not entitled to attend the AGM of the ladies' branch nor do they have any right to propose any changes in ILGU tournaments or its handicapping system.

As a result of the discussions of the four-member sub-committee, the following additional rules to the Union constitution were approved at a special general meeting on 29 November 1946:

XV. 'Any affiliated Club having rules, any of which are not in accordance with or are contrary to any ruling of the Central Council, or any affiliated Club which neglects or refuses to comply with any such ruling, may be expelled from the Union under rule VII.

XVI. 'No Irish Golf Club, the constitution of which, either expressly or by implication, confers on women the right to attend or vote at any annual or special general meeting of such Club shall be deemed to have a constitution approved by the Union under rule V.'

The Council decided to issue a special letter to all affiliated Clubs drawing their attention to the above additional rules in the constitution of the Union.

At the Annual General Meeting of the Council on 23 April 1947, it is recorded that a letter was read from Malahide Golf Club dated 3 April reporting that 'the proposals submitted to several general meetings of the Club for altering the Club rules to comply with the requirements of the Golfing Union of Ireland, in respect of the membership of women, has failed to meet with approval.'

The Council invoked the provisions of the constitution and expelled Malahide Golf Club from the Union. At the same meeting, instructions were given to inform Castle, Enniscrone and Warrenpoint Golf Clubs that immediate steps must be taken to alter their rules to conform with the rules of the Union in order to preserve their membership of it. The minutes of the next meeting on 28 November 1947 record that these three Clubs had changed their rules.

The repercussions of the Malahide expulsion were wide ranging, not only for the men members but for the ladies as well. The Leinster Branch had to re-draw all its Cups and Shields Tournaments and, at the request of some Leinster Clubs which sought guidance, issued a ruling regarding acceptance of entries in Club Open Competitions. The branch decided to issue the following press release:

'Entries for Open Competitions are limited to members of recognised Golf Clubs (in Ireland, of a Club affiliated to the Golfing Union of Ireland) and if the Open Competition is run by an affiliated Club no entry from the Malahide Club, either male or female, should be accepted. This ruling applies also to ladies' competitions and mixed competitions under the auspices of and run by an affiliated Club or any branch thereof.'

Writing in the *Irish Field*, J.P. Rooney stated: 'The only competitions in which the Malahide ladies can compete are the Irish Ladies' Championship and those held under the auspices of the executive or branches of the Irish Ladies' Golf Union. All other competitions are held by Clubs affiliated to the Golfing Union of Ireland, including the Irish Open Mixed Foursomes (Milltown), the Castle Ladies' Foursomes and the Dun Laoghaire Foursomes, and not by the ladies' branches, which are subject to the rules and regulations of the committees of the Clubs on whose course they are played. Thus the air had been cleared as far as the ladies of Malahide are concerned.' In another article, he expressed the hope that 'the lady members may realise the nature of the position in which they have placed the old Club — one of the oldest in the country — and that wiser counsels will prevail at the next meeting, and that the way will thus be paved for its re-admission to the Union. After all, the ladies of the Club have their own Union to look after their interests in golf.' The saga ended at the Annual General Meeting of the Union on 16 April 1948. The Honorary Secretary reported that the rules of Malahide Golf Club had been altered in accordance with the full requirements of the Union, and that an application for re-affiliation to the Union had been duly approved by the Leinster Branch.

Forty years later, in 1986, the Irish Ladies' Golf Union indicated that it considered the second rule incorporated in the GUI constitution on 19 November 1946 somewhat offensive to its members and the GUI removed it.

In clause 2 of the current constitution, under the heading of definitions and interpretations, a Golf Club is defined as follows:

'A "Golf Club" shall mean a Club, however constituted, which comprises:

(i)   An affiliated Golf Club, (affiliated to the Union) or
(ii)   an affiliated Ladies' Golf Club (affiliated to the ILGU), or
(iii)   An affiliated Club and an affiliated Ladies' Golf Club, or
(iv)   any one of (i), (ii) or (iii) above, together with other categories of membership of the "Golf Club" (e.g. Country, Five Day, Junior, etc.) and which complies with the rules of amateur status as approved by the Royal and Ancient Golf Club of St Andrews.

'An "Affiliated Golf Club" shall mean a group of male golfers who, having been formed into a Club, have the use of a particular course or links over which to play the game of golf, and which group shall have been admitted to membership of the Union.'

The constitution of the Irish Ladies' Golf Union states: 'Any Ladies' Golf Club having a designation and golfing green in Ireland shall be admissible into the Union, and every member or associate member of an affiliated Club shall be a member of the Union.'

The 1913 Constitution (Appendix VI Section 1) was superseded by a new Constitution in 1968 which was designed to legislate for modern administration requirements. Again, in 1990 the Central Council saw the need to update and modernise the 1968 Constitution. At a Special General Meeting on 4th January 1991 the Central Council adopted a new constitution to adminster its affairs from the commencement of its second hundred years and this constitution is reproduced in Appendix VI (Section 19).

Chapter 12

THE IRISH PROFESSIONAL GOLFERS' ASSOCIATION

The first recorded professional golfer engaged by an Irish Club was Alexander Day from Musselburgh, who was appointed greenkeeper and clubmaker at the Royal Belfast Golf Club in February 1889. A little more than a year later, the first recorded professional golf match took place between Day and Alexander Herd who had been appointed professional at the County Club, Portrush. The match was over 36 holes — 18 at Portrush and 18 at Holywood. Herd won at Portrush by returning 72 against Day's 82. Herd's drive on the 18th finished beyond the hole. The drive was subsequently measured and covered a distance of 280 yards. Herd was also successful at Holywood returning 83 to Day's 94. Herd, incidentally, had to wait 12 years before winning the Open Championship at Hoylake in 1902 in which, for the first time, he used the newly invented rubber-cored ball.

In February 1891 Jack Burns of Warwick took up the appointment of professional at County Down. In the meantime, Sandy Herd relinquished his appointment at the County Club and Charles Thompson was appointed as Club professional. Thompson laid out the North West golf links which was formally opened on 18 July 1891 and he also laid out Portsalon links later that year.

Royal Dublin Golf Club, Dollymount, was invited to host the third Irish Amateur Open Championship in 1894. The Club committee decided to provide their members and the golfing public with an added attraction and invited some cross-channel professionals to compete in a 36-hole stroke competition immediately after the Championship. The prize winners were:

George Duncan, Alexander Herd, Tom Ball and Harry Vardon at Rosapenna in 1896.

Alexander Herd putting on the 9th green in a match against Ben Sayers at Portrush in 1898.

Harry Vardon driving off the 1st tee at Portmarnock in the final of a professional match play tournament in which he defeated J.H. Taylor by 13 and 11.

Winner	Andrew Kilcardy (St Andrews)	76 78 154	1st Prize £15
2nd	Hugh Kilcardy (St Andrews)	78 78 156	2nd Prize £10
3rd	George Fulford (Royal Liverpool)	79 78 157	3rd Prize £5
4th	Robert Simpson (Aberdeen)	77 81 160	4th Prize £4.

The 1895 Irish Amateur Open was played at Portrush and, recognising the popularity of the professional tournament at Dollymount, the committee arranged a professional match-play event. There was an entry of 32 for a prize fund of £60, subscribed by the Portrush members. Whilst the field did not include John H. Taylor, the 1895 Open Champion, the cross-channel professionals attached some importance to the Irish tournament. Entries were received from Harry Vardon (Bury), Ben Sayers (North Berwick), Sandy Herd (Huddersfield), Willie Fernie (Troon) and the Kilcardy brothers of St Andrews. In the final, which was refereed by Thomas Gilroy, Herd beat Vardon by one hole. This was the first event of its kind in Ireland and the detailed results are set out in Appendix VII (Section 1).

As more and more people took to the game, many of the larger Clubs engaged the services of professional golfers whose duties were threefold: to take charge of the maintenance and upkeep of the course, the making of clubs and, possibly the most important of all, the imparting of their skills and knowledge of the game to Club members. Originally those appointed hailed from Scotland and one of the earliest records of an Irish-born professional is that of Michael Moran, attached to the Royal Dublin Club. Moran was born in a cottage in Curley's Yard between the present 3rd and 13th fairways on the Dollymount links, so it is true to say that he spent most of his life on North Bull Island. He is credited with contributing the word 'dyke' (one under par) to the Irish golfers' vocabulary and a measure of his skill was that he was Irish Professional Champion for five consecutive years from 1909 to 1913. He was killed in action in France during the First World War.

The Irish Professional Golfers' Association was set up and administered by the Union in 1911, and it was at the request of the Irish professionals that the Union had earlier inaugurated the Irish Professional Championship in 1907.

Interest in golf was increasing as more and more courses were opened for play, and many Club committees turned their minds to improving the standard of golf of their members and engaged 'resident' professionals. In 1906 a group of these professionals approached the Council with the request that the Golfing Union of Ireland should organise an Irish Professional Championship. The first of such annual events was played at Portrush on 20 and 21 May 1907 for which the prize fund was £24. All professionals living in Ireland for six months immediately preceding the Championship were eligible to play. The President of the Union, Mr Justice Dunbar Plunket Barton, Bart, presented a gold medal to be awarded to the winner in addition to the first prize of £10. From an entry of 24, James Edmundson, attached to the host Club, defeated B. Snowball (Portmarnock) by 2 and 1 to become the first Irish Professional Champion.

At a meeting of the Council on 14 June 1911, John L. Morrow, Honorary Secretary, reported that he had been invited to chair a meeting of Irish professionals at Portrush at which the Irish Professional Golfers' Association was formed for the promotion of professional golf and the establishment of a benevolent fund. The Association had requested the setting up of a joint committee of four professionals and four amateurs. The Association appointed as their members Tom Hood, James McKenna, A. Robertson and J. Aitken, and the Union appointed the President of the Union together with L. Stuart Anderson, F. Hoey and John L. Morrow as the amateur members of the committee.

It was agreed that the joint committee would draft a constitution and a scheme for a benevolent fund for submission to the two bodies. The constitution and rules are set out in Appendix VII (Section 2).

Reference has already been made to the Temporary Professional Scheme (see page 37). In essence the scheme was designed to provide tuition to the members of smaller Clubs many of which had not the finance to engage a 'resident' professional. By today's standards the monetary reward for the provision of this tuition seems almost derisory, but at that time it was regarded as a somewhat lucrative addition to a professional's other sources of income. The initial scheme provided that the professional would be paid £2 a week, Sundays excluded, and the tuition fees which would be retained by the Club would be not less than 1/- (5p) per hour. The Club paid the professional and the Union undertook to bear any deficit up to a maximum of £1 per week of engagement.

It was later decided to reduce the weekly fee to 30/- (£1.50) and the professional would be paid all tuition fees received in excess of that amount; should there be a deficit between the travelling expenses and the wages of the professional and the total of the fees received for tuition, such deficit would be borne equally between the Club and the Union. Because of the popularity of the scheme the Union was obliged to limit the number of weeks of tuition in a Club to six weeks in any one year to enable a greater number of Clubs to benefit, as demand exceeded the supply. Whilst the emoluments were increased to keep pace with rising standards of income, and the scheme remained available, it is no longer a practical proposition simply because the teaching professionals cannot be released by their Clubs in view of the demand for their services by their own Club members.

In 1929 the Association, at its request, was given the administration of its Championship. Whilst the Union continued to make an annual grant to the Championship fund, it did not supervise the organisation and conduct of the event.

In September 1965 the Council decided that the IPGA would be allowed to take over control of all its own affairs. A new constitution was ratified implementing this decision. At their first meeting as an independent organisation, the newly constituted Association passed the following resolution: 'the Central Council of the Irish Professional Golfers' Association wishes to thank the Golfing Union of Ireland for its invaluable assistance and co-operation since the inception of the Association and sincerely hopes that even greater co-operation (if this be possible) will ensue in the future.'

For many years individual members of the IPGA were also members of the Professional Golfers' Association and some years ago the Irish Association requested to become a full section of the PGA. Now all registered Irish professionals, both Club professionals and tournament players, are full members of the Professional Golfers' Association (Irish Region).

Chapter 13

THE
DEVELOPMENT
OF GOLF
IN IRELAND

Period: 1916 to 1940

The advent of World War 1 turned minds away from laying out new courses, and it is probable that the existing courses at the beginning of this period satisfied the immediate requirements of Irish golfers at that time. We also had domestic problems for most of the first decade of this era. Thus, there was a marked slowing down of new Clubs being established, over the ten years to 1925 only 29 new courses were opened:

1916   *Craig's Park (Co. Antrim), A 1916; Rossmore, A 1920.*

1918   *Claremorris, A 1920; Enniscrone, A 1931; Woodville (Co. Armagh) A 1918.*

1920   *Bunclody (Co. Wexford), A 1920; Cill Dara, A 1922; Kilrea, A 1920; Tandragee, A 1922.*

1921   *St Anne's, A 1923; Woodbrook, A 1921.*

1922   *Balla (Co. Mayo), A 1922; Coollattin (Old) (Co. Wicklow); Cuan (Co. Down), A 1922; Killua Castle (Co. Meath), A 1923; Royal Tara (originally Bellinter Park), A 1923; Swinford, A 1922.*

1923   *Ballyclare, A 1925; Dartry (Co. Monaghan), A 1926; Dungarvan, A 1924; Gort (originally Rockfield), A 1924.*

1924   *Ceann Sibeal (originally Dingle), A 1924; Loughrea, A 1924; Macroom, A 1924.*

1925   *Belmullet, A 1926; Clara (Co. Offaly), A 1925; Donabate, A 1928; Elm Park, A 1926; Enniscorthy, A 1925.*

The tempo of development accelerated by over one hundred and fifty per cent over the next ten years, during which time 42 new Clubs were established:

1926   *Carrickfergus, A 1926; Garvagh (Co. Derry), A 1926; Gweedore, A 1926, Irish Army (Co. Dublin), A 1927; Magherafelt (Co. Derry), A 1926; Newlands, A 1926; Ramelton (Co. Donegal), A 1926; Shandon Park, A 1926; Stamore (Collooney, Co. Sligo), A 1926; Tullow (Co. Carlow), A 1926.*

1927   *Arklow, A 1927; Belvoir Park, A 1928; Buncrana (Co. Donegal), A 1927; Carnalea, A 1927; Crosshaven (Co. Cork), A 1927; Doneraile, A 1927; Falcarragh (Co. Donegal), A 1927; Graiguenamanagh (Co. Kilkenny), A 1927; Lisnaskea (Co. Fermanagh), A 1927.*

1928	Baltinglass (originally St John's), A 1929; Cairndhu, A 1929; Headfort, A 1930.

1928   *Baltinglass (originally St John's), A 1929; Cairndhu, A 1929; Headfort, A 1930.*

1929   *Ballyhaunis, A 1929; Larne Town (Co. Antrim), A 1929; Mahee Island, A 1931; Mountrath, A 1932.*

1930   *Callan, A 1930; Castlemagarrett (Co. Mayo), A 1930; Heath, A 1931; Johnstown (Co. Kilkenny), A 1931; Narin & Portnoo, A 1933; Tantallon (Mount Charles, Co Donegal), A 1930.*

1931   *Rathdowney, A 1931; University College, Cork, A 1931; University College, Dublin, A 1931.*

1932   *Burtonport (originally Rosses) (Co. Donegal), A 1932; Downpatrick A 1932; Srandhill, A 1932.*

1933   *Clandeboye, A 1934.*

1934   *Kilrush, A 1934.*

1935   *Castlecomer, A 1936; Kilcroney (Co. Wicklow), A 1935.*

In the last five years of this quarter a further 17 Clubs were affiliated:

1936   *Courtown, A 1937; Glenarm (Co. Antrim), A 1936; Glengarriff, A 1936; Oldcastle (Co. Meath), A 1936.*

1937   *Ballaghadereen, A 1939; Carrigart (Co. Donegal), A 1937; Castletroy A 1938; Cushendall, A 1938.*

1939   *Carrick-on-Suir, A 1940; Lismore, A 1939; Newcastle West, A 1940; Tubbercurry (Old) (Co. Sligo), A 1939.*

1940   *Ballymote, A 1940; Dunmanway (Co. Cork), A 1940; Forrest Little (originally Corballis), A 1940; Monasterevin (Co. Kildare), A 1940; Tuam Commercial (Co. Galway), A 1940.*

Thus after half a century of existence, the Golfing Union of Ireland (whilst suffering the closure of a number of the smaller lay-outs) had under its administrative jurisdiction over 200 active Clubs spread throughout the length and breadth of the country.

Although getting off to a slow resumption in the period immediately following World War 1, activity and interest in the game grew at both administrative and competitive levels.

The Inter-County Barton Shield was changed to an Inter-Club Tournament and its popularity is now such that the majority of our affiliated Clubs enter each year.

On 14 February 1924 a conference initiated by the R & A was held at York to which representatives from the Irish, Welsh, Scottish Golf Unions and the recently founded English Golf Union were invited. The primary purpose of the conference was to set up a committee to act as advisers to the championship committee of the Royal and Ancient Golf Club of St Andrews. It was decided that the committee should have 14 members, taken from the four Unions based on the number of Clubs in each country. The committee comprised EGU–5, SGU–4, GUI–3 and WGU–2. The committee was originally named the Joint Advisory Committee (JAC); in 1932 the name was changed to the Joint Advisory Council.

In 1920 the Championship Committee of the R & A had decided that all players should be handicapped on a uniform basis and, with the co-operation of the Unions had fixed the scratch scores of nearly 800 courses. In May 1922 they fixed national handicaps, and an analysis of the results of the matches in the 1923 Amateur Championship at St Andrews shows that from a total of 208 matches played 88 per cent of the competitors were actually correctly handicapped. The R & A representative at the conference expressed the need for a uniform system of handicapping for all golfers.

The JAC introduced a standard scratch score and handicapping scheme which was adopted by the four Unions in 1925, and in 1932 arranged the first quadrangular international match between the four Unions, a series which will be discussed later. (See Chapter 15). They also established the Board of Greenkeeping Research which has played an important part in the improvement of golf courses. (See Chapter 26).

Another important happening during this era was the inauguration by our Union of the Open Championship of Ireland in 1926, and we will elaborate on the history of this event in the next chapter.

In addition, the method of the subvention by member Clubs to finance the Union was adjusted by the introduction of 'poll tax'. (See page 62).

Lionel O. Munn (North-West)

played for Ulster in the 1906 interprovincial matches. Irish Amateur Close Champion in 1908, 1911, 1913 and 1914, and was Irish Amateur Open Champion in 1909, 1910 and 1911. South of Ireland Amateur Open Champion 1911. Munn was a member of the County Donegal team which won the inaugural Barton Shield Inter County Foursomes Tournament 1911, and was an Irish international player in 1913. (Chapter 17)

THE OPEN CHAMPIONSHIP OF IRELAND

(Chapter 14 Appendix VII)

Winner's Gold Medal

Year	Venue	Winner and Club	Leading Amateur and Club
1927	Portmarnock	G. Duncan (Wentworth)	C.O. Hezlet (Royal Portrush)
1928	Newcastle	E.R. Whitcombe (Meyrick Park)	A.W. Briscoe (Castlerea)
			J.D. MacCormack (Hermitage) tie
1929	Portmarnock	A.B. Mitchell (Private)	C.O. Hezlet (Royal Portrush)
1930	Portrush	C.A. Whitcombe (Crew's Hill)	F.P. MacConnell (Royal Portrush)
			H.S. Sheals (Balmoral) tie
1931	Dollymount	E.W.H. Kenyon (West Lancs)	W.J. Gill (Sutton)
1932	Cork	A.H. Padgham (Royal Ashdown Forest)	J.D. MacCormack (Grange)
1933	Malone	E.W.H. Kenyon (West Lancs)	J. Burke (Lahinch)
1934	Portmarnock	S. Easterbrook (Knowle)	J.C. Brown (Waterford)
1935	Newcastle	E.R. Whitcombe (Meyrick Park)	J.C. Brown (Waterford)
1936	Dollymount	R.A.Whitcombe (Parkstone)	A.D. Locke (South Africa)
1937	Portrush	B. Gadd (West Cheshire)	J. Bruen Jr (Muskerry)
1938	Portmarnock	A.D. Locke (South Africa)	J. Bruen Jr (Muskerry)
1939	Newcastle	A. Lees (Dore and Totley)	J. Bruen Jr (Muskerry)
1940–45	No Championship		
1946	Portmarnock	F. Daly (Balmoral)	J.B. Carr (Sutton)
1947	Portrush	H. Bradshaw (Kilcroney)	S.M. McCready (Royal Portrush)
1948	Portmarnock	D.J. Rees (South Herts)	J.B. Carr (Sutton)
1949	Belvoir Park	H. Bradshaw (Kilcroney)	R. Patterson (Flackwell Heath)
1950	Dollymount	H.O. Pickworth (Australia)	J.B. Carr (Sutton)
1951	No Championship		
1952	No Championship		
1953	Belvoir Park	E. Brown (Unattached)	J.B. Carr (Sutton)

Championship discontinued

THE IRISH AMATEUR INTERPROVINCIAL CHAMPIONSHIP
(Chapter 17 Appendix IX)

Year	Winning Province	Year	Winning Province
1938	Munster	1972	Leinster
1939	Leinster	1973	Munster
1940–55	No Championship	1974	Munster
1956	Leinster, Munster and Ulster tied	1975	Ulster
1957	Munster and Ulster tied	1976	Leinster
1958	Ulster	1977	Ulster
1959	Ulster	1978	Ulster, Leinster and Munster Tied
1960	Ulster, Munster and Leinster Tied	1979	Ulster
1961	Ulster	1980	Munster
1962	Leinster	1981	Leinster
1963	Leinster	1982	Ulster
1964	Leinster	1983	Connacht
1965	Leinster	1984	Munster
1966	Leinster and Munster Tied	1985	Ulster
1967	Connacht	1986	Leinster
1968	Leinster	1987	Ulster
1969	Leinster	1988	Ulster
1970	Ulster	1989	Leinster
1971	Leinster	1990	Ulster

THE ALL-IRELAND COUNTY GOLF CHAMPIONSHIP

(Chapter 10 Appendix IV)

Year	Winning County
1911	Donegal
1912	Dublin
1913	City of Dublin
1914	City of Dublin
1915–18	No Tournament
1919	City of Dublin
1920	Original tournament converted to Inter-Club
1980	Wicklow
1981	Antrim
1982	Louth
1983	Louth
1984	Louth
1985	Louth
1986	Limerick
1987	Dublin
1988	Cork
1989	Roscommon
1990	Cork

The Canada Cup

Competed for annually in the International Golf Championship and Canada (now World) Cup matches.
(Chapter 19)

Chapter 14

THE
OPEN CHAMPIONSHIP
OF
IRELAND

The organisation of professional tournaments and exhibition matches by affiliated Clubs in various areas throughout the country has already been mentioned in Chapter 12.

As a result of one of the exhibition matches, the Open Championship of Ireland was born. In 1926 at the instigation of the Club Captain, Pierce F. Purcell (who 21 years later became President of the Union) the committee of Portmarnock Golf Club invited George Duncan of Wentworth and Abe Mitchell of St Alban's to come to Portmarnock for five days and play a series of exhibition matches. They were also to play with the Club professional, Willie Nolan, and with some of the members. Following the announcement of the impending visit, Douglas Golf Club in Cork and Malone Golf Club in Belfast issued invitations to the two professionals. In order not to disappoint the members of the two Clubs, Duncan intimated that he and Mitchell would do a mini-tour commencing in Cork and finishing in Belfast. At the last moment, Mitchell could not travel and his place was taken by Arthur Havers of Coombe Hill.

The pair visited Douglas on 26 September 1926 and then moved on to Portmarnock. Before they left for Malone, the Portmarnock committee hosted a dinner for their two visitors. Speaking at the dinner, George Duncan suggested the holding of an Open Championship at Portmarnock which, he assured his hosts, 'would have the support of 20 or 30 of the "Big Men" in the game in England and Scotland.'

The Portmarnock committee wrote to the Leinster Branch inviting the Union to hold an Open Championship over their links in 1927. The Leinster Branch decided to seek a special meeting of the Central Council. Under the constitution of the Union, such a meeting must be held at the request of two provincial branches, and Connacht supported Leinster. At a special meeting of the Central Council in December 1926 the invitation was considered, and on a split vote of 11 in favour to 7 against, it was decided to organise the first Open Championship of Ireland at Portmarnock in 1927, provided the Club guaranteed the Union against financial loss. Today such a requirement would be unheard of, but to understand the imposition of the guarantee condition it is necessary to explain the reason for the split vote at the special meeting. Whilst the seven members who did not wish the Union to embark on this project were no less anxious than their colleagues to foster and promote golf in Ireland, they were concerned with the financial implications of such a venture. Since its foundation, the Union had only imposed a rate of subscription on member Clubs geared to provide for the normal day-to-day administration expenses. There were no funds at the Union's disposal for an Open Championship.

In 1926 there were 176 Clubs affiliated to the Union. Subscriptions from these, based on delegate representation, amounted that year to £421.1s.0d. At the end of the financial year the accounts showed a surplus of £52 on the year's activities. The Union had no alternative other than to impose the guarantee condition. The Portmarnock committee gave the necessary assurance and the Union championship committee was instructed to proceed with the arrangements.

The Union invited Portmarnock to nominate four of its members to act on the championship committee and the Club named its Captain, Pierce F. Purcell; its Honorary Secretary, James Sheehan; H.M. Cairnes and William Fitzsimmons. As in the case of the Irish Amateur Open, 35 years earlier, the Union decided to contact the ruling authority for advice and guidance. Once again, the R & A was most supportive. The Union Council fully appreciated that even if it became the success everyone hoped for, the Irish Open could but be a pale shadow of the world's most prestigious Championship. The primary aim was to bring many of the leading professionals to our shores to display their skills in competitive golf for the benefit of Irish Club golfers.

The Council also consulted the Professional Golfers' Association and received much valuable advice. The 1927 Open Championship was scheduled for St Andrews on 13–15 July, and to avoid clashing with tournaments under its jurisdiction, the PGA recommended that the Irish Open be played in the week commencing Monday 15 August and intimated that it would assist by notifying its members and would also arrange for reduced travel fares.

Whilst the prize fund now provided by the R & A is a very important incentive to the large and representative field which the Open attracts, it is the prestige of winning the most important Championship in the world which transcends the monetary aspect. This has always been the case since William Park of Musselburgh won the first Open at Prestwick in 1860. For instance, it is said that when the American, Gene Sarazen, won the Open at Princes, Sandwich, in 1932 he was so delighted that he handed his prize money to his caddie!

In the 1927 Open Championship the prize fund was £500 divided into 15 prizes, with £75 for the winner down to £5 each for those attaining eleventh to fifteenth place. Whilst it was impossible to emulate the attraction and prestige of the Open, the Council considered it essential to provide a prize fund of £750 in the hope of persuading many of the named players to cross the Irish Sea. It was also very pleased to adopt the format and as many of the R & A conditions as possible. It was decided to award a gold medal to the winner, together with a first prize of £150. The other prizes to be awarded were: 2nd–£90;

This historic photograph hangs in the members' bar at Portmarnock, having been presented to the Club in 1944 by Gordon Ross, son of George Ross one of the founders of the Club and its first Captain. The photograph depicts a group on the 5th hole playing in the Captain's match on the day the links was officially opened in September 1894. The Captain, on extreme left, is watching John Petrie playing a stroke.

Following the extension of the links to 18 holes a new clubhouse (above) was officially opened on 28 March 1896. The competition to mark the occasion was won in Class 1 by W. Keating 90–15–75 and in Class 2 by H.L. Roper 104–24–80. W.C. Pickman (6) returned 79 and John Lumsden (6) returned 81.

The present clubhouse at Portmarnock.

3rd–£60; 4th–£50; 5th to 7th–£40 each; 8th and 9th–£35 each; 10th to 15th–£25 each and 16th to 18th–£20 each. In addition, *The Irish Times* and the *Irish Independent* both donated £100 for eight subsidiary prizes.

The PGA gave practical assistance and as a result 52 cross-channel and 3 American professionals entered. The Irish PGA was also active and 45 of its members entered. To this number was added 21 Irish and 4 cross-channel amateurs with handicaps of 1 and under, making up a field of 125 competitors. To give the amateurs an incentive, an inscribed silver plate was presented by John L. Morgan, a member of the host Club.

The PGA, as promised, arranged special travel facilities at reduced rates. In the week preceding the Championship, the PGA had a tournament at Blackpool and obtained the following terms:

1. Euston to Blackpool, Liverpool, Dublin returning to Euston: 1st Boat–3rd Rail 66s.9d.
2. Euston to Dublin return: 1st Boat–3rd Rail 65s.8d.
3. Blackpool to Dublin returning to Liverpool: 1st Boat–3rd Rail 30s.9d.
4. Liverpool to Dublin return: 1st Boat–3rd Rail 26s.9d.

The Irish railway companies also arranged to issue return tickets at single fare rate to all professional competitors.

Irish Clubs, particularly Portmarnock, were not found wanting as the necessary funds were made available to ensure the financial success of the Championship.

The Council was most gratified with not only the number but also the quality of the entry, which included six professionals who had won the Open, two of them on several occasions. Harry Vardon, who was no stranger to Ireland, was a six-times winner, a record which stands to this day; John H. Taylor had won on five occasions. In addition, Sandy Herd, Ted Ray, George Duncan and Arthur Havers had each recorded one victory. Two other competitors in the Championship that year subsequently joined the exclusive Club of 'Open' winners. Reggie Whitcombe and another player who at that time was still only 20 years old and came within a stroke of winning the first Open Championship of Ireland, and who, in a more altruistic crusade, succeeded in improving and elevating the status of the members of his chosen profession to the level it enjoys today. His name: Henry Cotton — a three times winner of the Open.

The Championship was scheduled for 16–18 August, with each competitor playing one round of 18 holes on each of the first two days. The leading 60 and all those who tied for 60th place qualified for two rounds of 18 holes on the final day.

The Championship began in wet and stormy conditions. Early in the day Henry Cotton (Langley Park) and Jack Smith (Wentworth) both came in with 73s to create a new course record for the lengthened course. However the host Club professional, Willie Nolan, later returned a 72 for a new course record and finished up leading the field. Also on the first day, one of the American entries, William Melhorn, had a hole-in-the one at the 7th, whilst Major Charles Hezlet took 9 at the 13th. At the end of the second day, during which the wind was even stronger, Henry Cotton led the field by returning a second 73 which was described as being near to perfection in the conditions. Sixty players, including six amateurs, qualified for the final two rounds with scores ranging from 146 to 185.

*George Duncan (Wentworth) the first Open
Champion of Ireland, Portmarnock 1927.*

In 1962 P.J. Carroll & Co. Ltd took over the organisation and
funding of the Irish Hospitals' Trust Tournament, which had
been inaugurated in 1958, and named it The Carroll's
International Tournament. Some years later Carroll's obtained
the permission of the Golfing Union of Ireland to use the title
'Open Championship of Ireland' for the duration of that
company's involvement in the event.

*Eric Brown (unattached) the last Open
Champion of Ireland, Belvoir Park 1953.
For financial reasons the Union discontinued
the Championship after 1953.*

'Golf in gale' was the headline reporting the final day's play. The report described unusual weather conditions, that the rain fell in torrents throughout the day, that the big catering marquee was lifted from its moorings and was torn to ribbons and that a full gale swept across the course. Perhaps the most expressive description of the problems affecting the players was made by one correspondent who said: 'The competitors found that direction was a thing to aim at rather than to achieve.'

In the third round only one player broke 80. Jack Smith, assistant to George Duncan at Wentworth, brought in a 77 to put him on 224 to lead Henry Cotton and Archie Compston of Wolverhampton by 8 strokes. As to the six former Open champions, Arthur Havers retired, George Duncan had 82, Harry Vardon and John Taylor each had 85, Sandy Herd 87 and Ted Ray 88.

In the final round, Smith returned 91 to finish on 315, Cotton had 81 for 313 whilst Compston scored 85 for 317. Once again, only one player broke 80: George Duncan, who had originally suggested the holding of this Championship, brought in 74 to finish on 312 to beat Henry Cotton by one stroke and win the Championship. In those days there was no such apparel as the waterproof golf jacket and pull-ups and for the final round 'Duncan played with brown paper inserted in layers inside his knickerbockers.' Ted Ray, commenting on Duncan's final round said it was 'one of the most wonderful rounds under the conditions which I know'; the American, William Melhorn said, 'It was the greatest round, under the circumstances, ever played in the history of golf.' Duncan himself said that his 74 was the best round he had ever played, even surpassing his final round of 69 at Sandwich in 1922 when he lost the Open by one stroke to Walter Hagen. He was also quick to give credit to his amateur playing partner, Charles Hezlet, who incidentally finished leading amateur, saying 'It was largely due to Major Hezlet that I stuck in. He told me that the others were not going well, and I began to feel like making a good round. He cheered me on and encouraged me to stick to it.' When considering Duncan's achievement, we must remember that he started the final round 14 strokes behind the leader. The detailed results of the Championship and the allocation of the prize fund are set out in Appendix VIII (Section 1).

The Union was gratified with the number of enthusiasts who, despite the atrocious weather, braved the elements to follow the matches. As a result, the gate receipts played no small part in ensuring that the inaugural Championship was also a financial success. In the final analysis the event showed a profit of £225.

Once again the Leinster Branch, under the Chairmanship of Dr Lorcan Sherlock, initiated the move to continue the Championship on an annual basis. As its notice of motion to the annual meeting of the Central Council held in Slieve Donard Hotel, Newcastle on 14 September, 1927 stated, 'It would if continued annually, materially improve the standard of golf in Ireland and [the Leinster Branch] urges the Golfing Union of Ireland to arrange its continuance as a yearly event, both in the interest of golf and of the country.' The Council approved the motion.

Royal County Down accepted the Union's invitation to house the second Championship, giving the same guarantee against loss. It was won by Ernest Whitcombe with 288, 25 strokes less than Duncan had taken the previous year. Archie Compston was second. The Championship showed a profit of £274. 5s. 4d. This profit was again made possible by gate receipts and generous donations from affiliated Clubs which readily responded to the Union's suggestion to donate the equivalent of one ordinary member's subscription to the championship fund.

Artist's impression of the County Down Clubhouse at Newcastle built at a cost of £2,200 and officially opened on 11 September 1897.

A rere view of the clubhouse with Slieve Donard in the background showing the new locker-room and bar extension added in 1965.

A further extension to mark the club's centenary was officially opened in 1990.

The front of the Royal County Down clubhouse which has remained unaltered since 1897.

Thereafter, the Championship was played annually (except from 1940 to 1945, because of the war) until 1950 when it was won, at Dollymount, by Ossie Pickworth of Australia. Norman von Nida, also of Australia and John Panton of Glenbervie were joint second. In the intervening years, other well known professionals won the Championship, including Abe Mitchell, Alf Padgham, Reggie Whitcombe, Bobby Locke, Arthur Lees and Dai Rees. The first Irishman to win was Fred Daly of Balmoral who, at Portmarnock in 1946, returned 288 to beat Bobby Locke by four strokes. Only one other Irishman won the Championship and he was victorious twice. Harry Bradshaw, when professional at Kilcroney, won at Portrush in 1947 beating Flory Van Donck by two strokes and at Belvoir Park in 1949 when he beat Bobby Locke also by two strokes, thus reversing positions when Locke had defeated him in a play-off for the Open Championship one week earlier.

In the 18 Championships played between 1927 and 1950, the Union availed of the following venues: Portmarnock on six occasions; Newcastle, Portrush and Dollymount on three occasions each and once each at Malone, Cork and Belvoir Park.

Whilst the first two events each showed a modest profit (mainly as a result of appeals to members' Clubs), the Council was concerned with the long-term financial structure. It readily accepted a proposal submitted by the championship committee 'to finance the Championship on a permanent basis by arranging for all affiliated Clubs to increase the annual subscription of each ordinary member by 1/- [now 5p] per annum and forward same to the Union Honorary Treasurer for the Open Championship of Ireland.' Thus was 'poll tax' introduced.

When the R & A announced that the 1951 Open Championship would be played at Portrush, the Council decided not to hold the Irish Championship that year. Incidently, this was the first and only time the world's most prestigious Championship was played in Ireland. At its Annual General Meeting on 29 November 1951, the Council took the opportunity of reviewing the future of the event, which had been losing money due to lack of spectator support in each of the post-war years. A proposal to hold the Championship every four years was referred to the branches for consideration by affiliated Clubs, and the standing committee was empowered to organise the Championship if the consensus was in favour. Belvoir Park was again selected as the venue and the prize fund was fixed at £3,000, of which the winner would receive £750. Not only was this the highest prize fund ever offered in these islands up to that time, but the winner's share was also the highest.

Eighty-four professionals and 12 amateurs competed, and Eric Brown, who at that time was not connected to any Club, led the field after the first round with a new course record of 66 which included a hole-in-one at the 196-yard 16th. Twenty-four competitors, including three amateurs, equalled or bettered the par of 73. On the second day, Brown held his lead with a 67; two other players, Peter Allis of Ferndown and Harry Weetman of Croham Hurst, equalled the course record established the previous day. The weather made its presence felt. There was a 20 minute cloudburst as the second round was nearing completion, and instructions were issued to the last four pairings to stop play. Anyone who knows Belvoir Park can visualise the rain cascading down the steep slope from the clubhouse level, which the members refer to as 'Coronary Hill', to and across the 18th green. One of the players, either because he knew he would not qualify or perhaps to get in out of the rain, disregarded the instructions and, as he was entitled to, played his approach to the 18th. He struck a good shot, his ball splashed down near the pin but was washed off the green and was never seen again. Thirty-seven professionals and two amateurs with scores of 149 and under qualified for the final 36 holes.

The Press reported that the Union was disappointed with the attendances on the first two days and appealed to golfers everywhere to support the Championship, as otherwise there would be a financial loss. In those days the 'leaders out last' format did not operate. In fact, this would have been impossible to implement, as two rounds were played on the final day and the same competitors played together in both rounds. It was an accepted practice that the organisers were allowed to select pairings and place them in the order of play which would avoid spectator congestion as the roping-off of fairways was only in vogue for the Open Championship. Volunteer stewards, usually members of neighbouring Clubs, helped with course control. Our two qualifying amateurs were drawn with prominent professionals: Joe Carr of Sutton with Bobby Locke and Norman Drew of Bangor with Peter Allis.

At the end of the third round, Brown with a 69 retained his lead but by only one stroke from Harry Weetman who had a 68; they were the only players to break 70 in that round. In the final round Peter Allis brought in a 67 whilst Max Faulkner (St George's Hill) returned 68; Sid Scott (Carlisle), Arthur Lees (Sunningdale) and Jimmy Adams (Royal Mid-Surrey) each scored 69. However, Brown's 70 was enough to secure him the Championship gold medal and first prize of £750. Weetman's closing 70 secured him second place on 273 with Allis third with 274. Joe Carr was leading amateur with 284 and was placed tenth. Brown's 272 was a record low score for the Championship. A feature of his play was his consistency at the 196-yard 16th. Having holed-in-one in the first round, he holed putts for twos in each of the second and third rounds and just missed holing a four-foot putt for yet another two in the final round. In his 67, Allis holed his second shot at the 396-yard second hole, and Jimmy Henderson (Warrenpoint) had seven birdies to card a 70.

Alas, the Union incurred a loss of £2,065 and the Council had to discontinue the Championship. A record of the venues, winners, runner-ups and leading amateurs is set out in Appendix VIII (Section 2).

Hospitals' Trust (1940) Limited, or as it was more commonly known, the Irish Hospitals' Sweepstakes, became involved in golf sponsorship in 1958. Its Chairman, Joseph McGrath, announced that the Trust would put up a purse of £5,000 'for a golf tournament to be held at Woodbrook during the Tostal period, with the primary object of stimulating the Irish tourist industry, by drawing attention to golfing facilities here as a major attraction.' The Tournament continued until 1962 when it was announced that P.J. Carroll & Co. Ltd would be taking it over and naming it The Carroll's International Tournament. In 1975, Carroll's approached the Union for permission to name the Tournament (which had been growing in international status each year) 'The Carroll's Irish Open Championship'. The Union acceded to the request. Since then, winners of world Classic events have sought to add the Championship to their list of successes.

In 1980, Carroll's introduced a most popular pre-Championship competition in the form of a pro-am. Every Club affiliated to the Union was invited to enter a team of three from the handicap categories — scratch to 7, 8 to 15 and 16 to 24. The four Provincial Councils arranged qualifying competitions and, based on the ratio of entries from Clubs in each province, the following number qualified: Leinster 8, Ulster 8, Munster 6 and Connacht 5. The 27 teams were joined by three further teams: the host Club, the Association of Golf Writers and the Irish Golf Writers' Association. A draw, at which an official of the Union was invited to participate, then took place to decide which team would play with one of the 30 leading professionals entered in the Championship. To get on the Club team and qualify for a chance to play with a leading professional became one of the most sought-after achievements in Club golf.

Woodbrook was the home of the Irish Hospitals' Tournament for the five years of its existence. With the exception of visiting Cork in 1965 and Royal Dublin in 1966, the Carroll's International Tournament was also played at Woodbrook from 1963 to 1974, as was also the first Carroll's Irish Open Championship in 1975. The Championship then moved north of the Liffey and Portmarnock was the venue for the next seven years. In 1983 Royal Dublin became the venue and the Championship remained there until 1985 when it formed part of the Club's centenary celebrations. In 1986 the Championship moved back to Portmarnock.

P.J. Carroll & Co. Ltd have been most generous sponsors of golf in this country, a fact which will be enlarged on in Chapter 34. In the context of the Championship, thanks is given to the sponsors and the Clubs which have housed the event for providing Irish golfers with such wonderful opportunities to see so many internationally acclaimed players in action, and for keeping Ireland in such a prominent position on the world golf scene.

Because the Royal and Ancient Golf Club accepted the Union's request, supported by the Committee of Portmarnock Golf Club, to play the 1991 Walker Cup matches in Ireland on the occasion of the GUI's centenary, the 1991 Irish Open Championship was transferred to Killarney to enable the Portmarnock links to be groomed for the prestigious World Amateur Golf event.

Chapter 15

THE AMATEUR INTERNATIONAL MATCHES

Portmarnock was the first golf Club to organise an international match between Ireland and Scotland. The match was played over the Portmarnock links on 6 March 1897. It was not, however, an international match as we regard such contests today; all of the 18 team members — nine a side — were members of Portmarnock Golf Club. The Scottish team, comprising players of Scottish birth now living in Ireland, was led by W.C. Pickman, who founded Portmarnock. Another member of his team was John Lumsden, the founder of the Dublin, now the Royal Dublin Golf Club. The Irish team won by 31 holes to 12, the matches all being played over the full 18 holes with holes won to decide.

A somewhat different type of international match was organised by the Union at Newcastle in 1900. The Honorary Secretaries of Clubs were asked to give the Union the names of any of their members with handicaps of six and under, playing in the Irish Amateur Open Championship, who would be willing to take part in an international match on 4 September 1900 preceding the Championship. Apparently the criteria this time was not place of birth but location of the Club from which the competitor entered the Championship, as W.C. Pickman played for Ireland.

The match resulted in Ireland defeating England by 27 holes to 24 and Scotland defeating Ireland by 40 holes to 9. Ireland managed to defeat England by 3 holes mainly because the Irish player won by 10 holes in the last match.

At this period Ireland was the only one of the three countries which had a constituted Union and an official handicapping system although various districts in Scotland and counties in England operated their own ones. On the Scottish team, nine of the twelve players had a handicap of plus 4. The English team was led by Harold H. Hilton playing off plus 7; also on its team was Sidney H. Fry playing off plus 4. These two players contested the final of the Championship and Hilton was victorious by 11 and 9. The best player on the Irish team had a handicap of scratch.

The Union continued these matches annually between the three countries until 1906. Up to 1905 the format was singles only over 18 holes with holes won to decide. In 1906, the present-day method of the match concluding when one player was more holes up than holes remaining was introduced. During these seven years, the number of players selected for each country varied from 12 to 24 a side.

For some reason which cannot be traced there were no internationals played in Ireland between 1907 and 1912. At Dollymount in 1913 an Ireland/Wales International was played. On this occasion the teams comprised ten players a side and the format then established — and continued by the four countries to the present time — was five foursomes and ten singles matches over 18 holes on the same day.

Harold Hilton, one of only three amateurs to win the Open Championship since its inception (he won at Muirfield in 1892 and at Hoylake in 1897) was a prominent member of the Royal Liverpool Golf Club. He represented England in the International matches in 1900 and 1901 and also won the Irish Championship in these two years. He also achieved a much more prestigious distinction during this period by winning the Amateur Championship at Sandwich in 1900 and at St Andrews in 1901. His Club had been instrumental in inaugurating the Amateur in 1885, and to him is given the credit for prompting it to follow the example of the Irish Union and inaugurate an International match prior to the Amateur.

In December 1901 the Royal Liverpool Golf Club gave notice to their fellow delegates on the Championship Committee that, on the occasion of the 1902 Amateur Championship on their links at Hoylake, they proposed to play an international match — Scotland v. England — on the Saturday preceding the Championship. They also gave notice that at the May meeting of the Championship Committee they would formally move that the match be played annually thereafter. The Club invited three Scottish and three English players to select the teams; ten a side, 36 holes singles to be decided by holes won. Scotland defeated England by 32 holes to 25.

At the annual meeting of delegates held during the Championship, the Royal Liverpool motion was approved. An amendment proposed by two Scottish delegates that consideration be given to including Ireland was ruled out of order by the Chairman. The five Clubs forming the Championship rota at that time were The Royal Liverpool, The Royal and Ancient, The Honourable Company of Edinburgh Golfers, The Royal St George's and Prestwick. They were instructed to form a committee to run the annual match. The committee retained the 36 holes singles format but reduced the teams to nine-a-side with each match played to a finish with matches won to count. In 1912 the committee reverted to ten-a-side and changed the format to foursomes throughout.

The 1914–18 war caused a curtailment of both Championships and the two series of international matches. In 1919 when the R & A took over the Amateur, they resuscitated the Scotland/England International Match and adopted the Irish/Welsh format of five foursomes and ten singles. Following the founding of the English Golf Union in 1924, the R & A invited that Union and the Scottish Union, which had been founded in 1920, to join the Championship Committee, and thereafter the two Unions selected the teams.

The 1913 Irish International Team.

Left to Right: standing: J.F. Jamieson, Ector Munn, A.H. Patterson, H.E. Reade, W.J. Carroll, J.D. MacCormack and J.L. Morrow (Honorary Secretary). Seated: H.A. Boyd, Lionel O. Munn, H.M. Cairnes (Captain) and A.B. Babington.

The 1925 Irish International Team.

Left to Right: standing: L.E.J. Werner, L.M. Callon, G. Waddell, R.M. McConnell and J.M. Marron. Seated: W.J. Carroll, J.L. Crabbe, C.O. Hezlet (Captain), H.M. Cairnes and G.N.C. Martin.

The Irish Championship was recommenced in 1919, but the International series was not renewed until 1923 when the Welsh Golfing Union invited Ireland to send a team to Southerndown to play a Welsh side and to compete in their Amateur Open Championship. Ireland next entered into a home or away series and played against teams representing Scotland, England, Wales and Midlands. In some years this necessitated two trips across the Channel.

In Chapter 13 on the SSS and handicapping scheme the York Conference which led to the formation of the JAC was mentioned. At the first annual meeting of that body in Liverpool on 28 January 1925, one of the Irish delegates, James Henderson, submitted a letter from Dr George Price, Honorary Secretary of the Golfing Union of Ireland expressing the hope that international matches might be arranged among the four Unions. Whilst the delegates expressed approval, the R & A was reluctant to discontinue the Scotland and England match which it had revived just six years earlier and the JAC was compelled to abandon the Irish proposal. For this reason, the Irish series was continued since the GUI was satisfied that playing against other countries at this level would not only improve Irish golfing standards but also help to re-activate the proposal for a four-country contest.

In 1931 the R & A decided to discontinue the pre-Amateur Championship match. The Irish series was quickly cancelled and the way was clear for the inauguration of the Quadrangular International Matches. The record of venues, Team Captains, and results of matches played up to 1931 is set in Appendix IX (Section 1).

The list of Irish international representatives from 1900 to 1931 is set out in Appendix IX (Section 2).

The JAC decided that the matches would comprise five foursomes and ten singles each played over 18 holes. They also accepted a proposal by the Welsh Golfing Union that no player who had played for any of the other countries on their international teams or in their Close Championships after 1 January 1929 would be eligible to compete. What prompted Wales to submit this particular wording? Charles Hezlet of Portrush was the Irish Close Champion in 1920. He was working in Wales for a Welsh company and this was apparently considered to be of sufficient qualification to select him to play for Wales against Midlands at Harlech a year before he was chosen to play for his native country. This instance of dual international representation on official teams is a unique record by any player. Also, Charles Hezlet was appointed Irish Team Captain ten times prior to 1932 and on six other occasions from 1948, another record which can never be equalled in this country now that the term of office of a Team Captain is limited to three years.

The first of the Quadrangular Internationals took place at Troon from Tuesday 2 to Friday 5 August 1932; Thursday 4 August was a 'rest' day. Scotland won the inaugural series by defeating the other three countries. As this was the first of the Quadrangular Internationals, the detailed results are set out in Appendix IX (Section 3.)

Almost without exception, the regulations for the conduct of the matches laid down by the JAC when the tournament was inaugurated have stood the test of time. The eligibility clause proposed by the Welsh Golfing Union has been streamlined. The number of players per country has been changed from ten with two travelling reserves to eleven from which the Captain nominates his five foursomes pairings and ten singles in order of play. Both foursomes and singles are 18 hole games, considered necessary because of the time factor.

The 1955 Irish International Team, winners of the Raymond Trophy at Royal Birkdale, England.

Left to Right: standing: G.F. Crosbie, J. Fitzgibbon, J.W. Hulme, W.J.J. Ferguson, P.J. Leyden, R.A. Fleury, J.B. Carr and L. McCarthy. Seated: J. Glover, J.R. Mahon, C. Ewing, W.J. Gill (Non-Playing Captain) and T. Craddock.

The 1983 Irish International Team, winners of the Raymond Trophy at Portmarnock.
Left to Right: standing: A.D. Pierse, T. Cleary, D.C. Long, T. Corridan, J.J. Carr, M. Burns, L. MacNamara and D. Rea O'Kelly (Honorary Secretary). Seated: M.F. Morris, G. McGimpsey, B. Edwards (Non-Playing Captain), A.J.C. Morrow and M.A. Gannon.

The Internationals are usually held at the end of the golfing season. A 'sudden death' decision in the foursomes could disrupt the strict timetable required to complete the singles which, with a similar condition, could make it impossible to finish the matches due to failing light. The host Union nominates the venue for the match in its own country and, whilst the JAC reserves the right of final decision regarding venue, it has never declined to accept the host Union's choice. Up to 1951 the winning country achieved only the 'honour and glory' of the victory.

Raymond H. Oppenheimer, who had an impressive record as an international player, is now best remembered as a dedicated administrator. His best performance in Ireland was at Dollymount in the 1928 Irish Amateur Open Championship when he reached the semi-final. He captained England in the Quadrangular Internationals and against France in the 1947 and 1948 seasons when England was unbeaten. He regularly attended all International matches and later, in 1962, he was elected President of the English Golf Union. As a measure of his enthusiasm and interest he presented a magnificent Perpetual Challenge Trophy to the JAC at Troon prior to the 1952 matches for annual competition between the four countries. The trophy was appropriately named 'The Raymond Trophy'.

Scotland had the honour of being the first winner of the trophy. It successfully defended the title at Killarney in 1953. England won at Porthcawl in 1954 and Ireland, under the captaincy of Willie Gill, won the trophy at Birkdale in 1955.

From 1932 the host Union, in addition to nominating the venue, was also afforded the right of deciding the rota of play. Whilst this was regarded as giving the host Union an advantage, the main reason was to help the Union in financing the matches by allowing it to arrange them so that they would attract the largest galleries on the local half-day and so enhance the 'gate'. The regulations prescribed 'that the Union entertaining the meeting shall make arrangements in connection with the organisation of the meeting and shall bear the costs thereof'.

The rota which was agreed in 1932 (Scotland, Ireland, England and Wales) remained unchanged until 1973. The matches were suspended from 1939 to 1946 because of the Second World War, but the rota was continued on resumption in 1947. The venues nominated by the GUI Central Council and accepted by the JAC were: 1933 Newcastle, 1937 Portmarnock, 1949 Portmarnock (chosen because the R & A had selected Portmarnock as the venue for the Amateur Championship scheduled to be played immediately after the Internationals), 1953 Killarney, 1957 Newcastle, 1961 Portmarnock, 1965 Portrush, 1969 Killarney and 1973 Newcastle.

In 1973, because of the unsettled situation in the North of Ireland, both the English and Scottish Unions advised CONGU that some members of their teams were reluctant to travel to Ireland. CONGU intimated that it would call a meeting of delegates to consider altering the rota. As the GUI did not wish to jeopardise the series, the Irish delegates were instructed to accept any proposed change. The new rota agreed was: 1973 England, 1974 Wales, 1975 Ireland, 1976 Scotland, and so on. For the 1975 match the GUI, with the full approval of the Ulster Branch, nominated Portmarnock. Ireland was again due to host the 1979 series and the GUI was unanimous in nominating Newcastle. Once more this venue was accepted by CONGU. Alas, the English Union again intimated that some of its players would not travel to this venue, but the Scottish and Welsh Unions assured the GUI that they would field teams. As a way out of the impasse, CONGU suggested that we might transfer the venue to Portmarnock. The standing committee first consulted the Ulster Provincial Council which expressed the view that even if it meant the cancellation of the 1979 matches, the venue already accepted by CONGU and by the Royal County Down Golf Club should not be changed; further, as three of the Unions were prepared to send teams to Newcastle, an Irish team should not be sent to compete at any other venue which CONGU might select even if such action might jeopardise the future of the Quadrangular International Matches. The other three Provincial Councils fully supported these views and CONGU was so informed. The 1979 series was cancelled.

As some of the younger players on the English and Scottish teams were anxious to obtain their first, and only, Amateur International 'cap' before turning professional that autumn, these two Unions arranged a mini International at Troon. On learning this, the Welsh Golfing Union immediately extended an invitation to Ireland to play a match at Porthcawl. This was readily accepted and the Welsh gesture is regarded as having been instrumental in saving the entire series from being abandoned.

At the ordinary general meeting that October, the GUI agreed that every effort should be made to re-establish the Quadrangular matches on the same basis as they had been played so successfully since 1932. It was decided to inform CONGU that Ireland would send a team to Royal Dornoch in 1980 and to Woodhall Spa in 1981. It was also recorded that arising out of the Newcastle cancellation, a bill for £4,000 had been received from the Slieve Donard Hotel for loss as the entire hotel had been block-booked for International week. The GUI paid the account and directed the delegates to acquaint CONGU of the payment. The other Unions agreed to reimburse the GUI each in a sum proportionate to the number of rooms booked in the hotel on behalf of that Union. The full series resumed in 1980 on the basis of the existing rota.

Subsequently, changes were made in the regulations, the first in prescribing a fixed rota of play and the second a method to ensure an outright winner. The rota is based on the previous year's results so that:

On day one:	in match 1:	the champion country plays the fourth placed country
	in match 2:	countries two and three meet.
On day two:	in match 1:	the winner of match 1 the previous day plays the loser of match 2
	in match 2:	the other two countries meet.
On the final day:		the countries which have not met shall play each other subject to the proviso that if two of the opposing countries are in contention for the championship, they shall go out in match 2.

To ensure that there would be an outright winner in the event of a tie at the end of the final day, the country with the greatest number of matchplay points (two for a win and one for a halved match) shall be the champion country. Finally, in the event of a tie at any stage of the tournament the higher placed country in the previous year shall have precedence.

The rota fixed by CONGU ensured that Ireland would be host in 1987 and the GUI broke new ground by selecting a links on the western seaboard as the venue. The teams and officials arrived in Lahinch where the Club committee had groomed the links to perfect condition.

As Eoghan O'Connell (Killarney) could not get time off from Wake Forrest University and as John McHenry (Douglas) had turned professional, regrettably the selectors had available only four of the six players who had won the European Amateur Golf Team Championship for Ireland some three months earlier: Neil Anderson (Shandon Park), Padraig Hogan (Elm Park), Liam MacNamara (Woodbrook) and Garth McGimpsey (Bangor). To this core were added the 1987 Close, East, North and South Champions: Eddie Power (Tramore), Paul Rayfus (Trim), Arthur Pierse (Tipperary) and Barry Reddan (County Louth). The remaining members of the team were Mark Gannon (County Louth), who had an impressive record as an international player and a winner of championships, Denis O'Sullivan (Cork) also an international player of experience and a former Close champion, and a new cap, Darren Clarke (Dungannon), a young player who had got through to the semi-final of both the Close and North Championships and who had won five out of six matches in helping Ulster to win the Junior Interprovincials at Baltray four months earlier.

Ireland faced England on the first day. Unfortunately, the weather was so bad that the morning foursomes had to be cancelled. In the afternoon singles Ireland won six matches to four. On the second day, the Irish foursomes success led Wales by four matches to one. Many would consider this an almost unbeatable lead; only another four wins out of ten singles were needed. However, remembering previous occasions when Wales had thwarted Irish efforts to win the Championship, many remained anxious — and justifiably so as it turned out. Wales fought back with such determination that five matches went to the 17th hole and four to the final green. In the end, Ireland won by just the odd match. Against Scotland on the third day, Ireland's foursomes pairings which were unchanged from the previous day, finished the morning session with an advantage of 4½ matches to ½. Despite the somewhat inclement weather, hundreds of Irish supporters excitedly followed each match in the afternoon hoping that at last the supreme honour of not only winning the International Championship, but, for the first time in the 56 years since the series was inaugurated, the mythical 'triple crown' might be secured. Scotland won the first two singles, Ireland won the next three requiring just a halved match for outright victory. The final result was 10½ matches to 4½ in Ireland's favour.

The jubilation both on the links and later in the clubhouse was unbounded. It was a wonderful moment to see the Irish Honorary Secretary, Des Rea O'Kelly, as Chairman of CONGU, presenting the Raymond Trophy to the Irish non-playing Captain, Eamon Curran, for whom acclaim cannot be too great. To each member of the team, all of whom played their part in the victory, congratulations and unstinted praise is given. Without denigrating their magnificent achievement, other captains had possibly more experienced players at their disposal in earlier Internationals without being able, as Eamon did, to mould and motivate his players into an unbeatable combination.

Under Eamon Curran's captaincy Ireland won the Cartier Trophy in the Quadrangular Bi-annual Continental Matches at Le Touquet against France (the host country), Germany and Sweden in 1986; the European Amateur Golf Team Championship at Murhof, Austria in June 1987 before culminating his three year term of office and achieving a hat-trick of wins with the International Championship and 'triple crown' at Lahinch.

George F. Crosbie (Cork), Irish non-playing Captain 1988–91 almost emulated the successes of his predecessor and enabled the Union to celebrate its centenary as holders of the Cartier Cup for the Quadrangular Continental Matches (see Chapter 31) and the Raymond Trophy for the Home International Championship and 'triple crown'.

*Desmond Rea O'Kelly (Honorary Secretary GUI), as Chairman of the Council of National Golf Unions',
presenting the Raymond Trophy to Eamon Curran, Irish Team Captain, following Ireland's victory in
the Home Internationals and the Triple Crown at Lahinch in 1987.*

The Welsh Golfing Union had nominated Conwy Golf Club in Caernarvonshire as the venue for the 1990 series as part of that Club's centenary celebrations. Serious set-backs to Ireland's hope of a success there followed the completion of the Irish Amateur Close Championship at County Louth Golf Club in August. The new champion, Darren Clarke (Dungannon), who would have been an automatic choice for the team, announced his decision to turn professional. Then Jim Carvill (Warrenpoint) who had been selected on the team announced that he was turning professional also. The Irish party set off for Conwy with what the media described as 'a sadly depleted team'.

Ireland was against Scotland on the opening day and having won 3 and halved 1 of the morning foursomes, was forced to substitute its eleventh player for one of the nominated players who had taken ill. Despite this further set-back, Ireland emerged the winner by 8 matches to 5 with 2 matches halved. On the same day England disposed of Wales by 8 matches to 2 with 4 matches halved.

On the second day, Ireland, having shared the foursomes, defeated Wales by 9 matches to 2 with 4 matches halved whilst Scotland defeated England by 9 matches to 5 with 1 match halved.

The rules which prescribe for an outright winner have been mentioned earlier and after the second day the position was:

INDIVIDUAL MATCHES

	won	halved	lost	points
Ireland	17	6	7	40
Scotland	14	3	13	31
England	13	5	12	31
Wales	5	8	17	18

Only Ireland, with two outright wins, could win the 'triple crown' but Ireland, Scotland or England could win the Championship and the Raymond Trophy.

Following intense calculations and computations an English official worked out that, providing Scotland did not defeat Wales by 10½ matches to 4½, England would retain the championship by beating Ireland by 10 matches to 5. A Scottish official stated that Scotland could win if it defeated Wales by 10 matches to 5 provided England beat Ireland by 9½ matches to 5½ as this would enable Scotland to tie with Ireland on points and, having been the higher ranking country at Ganton the previous year, Scotland would win the Championship. As far as Ireland was concerned its target was to beat England by 8 matches to 7 and take all the spoils.

Wales gave its answer to all these possibilities by defeating Scotland by 8 matches to 7 on the final day which left a straight contest between Ireland and England. After the morning foursomes England led by the odd match and in the afternoon singles, with 6 of the 10 matches completed, had extended this lead to 7 matches to 4. Ireland required 1½ matches for the championship and all 4 for the 'triple crown'. The next match was won by Ireland 'out in the country' with the Irish player getting 7 birdies. The championship was secured when the next Irish player won on the 17th. Tension became almost unbearable when the next match finished on the 18th green, also in Ireland's favour. In the last match the English player squared the match on the 17th and in what one of the Irish officials described as an electric atmosphere Ireland won the 'triple crown' when the Irish player

Peter Froggatt (left) and two of his sons, Mark (centre) and Keith (right) all members of Malone and Royal Portrush Golf Clubs.

When a member of Belvoir Park Golf Club, Peter represented Ireland in the Home Internationals at the Royal County Down links at Newcastle in 1957. The previous year he represented Ulster in the Interprovincial Championship and was again selected in 1957 and 1958. He won a Senior Cup gold medal in 1957 and a Barton Shield Gold medal in 1961.

A graduate of Dublin University (Trinity College), he was Vice-Chancellor of Queen's University, Belfast from 1976 to 1986 and was appointed pro-Chancellor of Dublin University in 1986.

Mark attended Cambridge University where he was elected Captain of the Golf Club for the season 1982–3. He won three 'Blues' (1980-81, 1981-2, 1982-3) and gained 5½ points out of a maximum of 6 thereby breaking the long-established record set by Cyril Tolley. The Ulster Youths' Champion in 1983, he was also a member of the Ulster team which visited Zimbabwe in 1985. In 1989 he won the President's Putter.

Keith attended Oxford University where he was first elected Honorary Secretary of the Golf Club for the 1989-90 season and he then emulated Mark by being elected Captain of the Golf Club in 1990-91. He won two 'Blues' gaining 2 points out of 4.

The records show that in the 102 years of these Varsity golf matches, there has been no other occasion when one brother was Captain of Cambridge and another brother was Captain of Oxford though not at the same time, and two Irishmen at that.

holed a 7 foot putt on the final green. Scenes reminiscent of Lahinch in 1987 followed. It should be mentioned that two of the Irish team had an unbeaten record. Padraig Harrington (Stackstown), playing his first International series at this level, won all his matches whilst Liam MacNamara, by sinking that putt in the last match finished with 5 wins and one halved match.

In the 47 series since the Home Internationals were inaugurated, England leads with 19 wins, Scotland is second with 18 whilst Ireland has achieved only 5 wins. Wales have yet to record their first win, although on many occasions, Wales has defeated one of the other countries so preventing that country obtaining outright victory.

Whilst Wales is the smallest and Ireland the second smallest of the four countries in golfing population, neither country claims this as a reason for its lack of success. The Welsh achievements have been 4 wins and 4 halved matches against Scotland, 2 wins and 2 halves against England and 7 wins and 2 halves against Ireland. As to the Irish record, 17 wins and 2 halves have been achieved against Scotland, 10 wins and 6 halves against England and 35 wins and 6 halves against Wales.

The record of venues, Team Captains and the result of matches played is set out in Appendix IX (Section 4). The list of Irish international representatives from 1932 to date is set out in Appendix IX (Section 5).

Chapter 16

THE
DEVELOPMENT
OF GOLF
IN IRELAND

Period: 1941 to 1958

The Second World War was taking place during the first five years of this period and, as in the 1914–18 conflict, minds were turned away from the development of golf. Between 1941 and 1945, only nine Clubs were established.

1941   Ballinamore, A 1941; Kilkee (West End) (Co. Clare), A 1941; Oughterard, A 1941.
1942   Garretstown (Co. Cork), A 1942; Royal College of Surgeons, A 1942.
1943   Garrycastle (Co. Westmeath), A 1943; Rush, A 1945.
1944   Edmondstown, A 1944.
1945   Balbriggan, A 1946.

Following the outbreak of war, the Union cancelled both the Irish Amateur Open Championship and the Open Championship of Ireland and these were not re-activated until 1946. As a result of a severe air raid in Ulster on 14 April 1941, the Leinster Branch proposed that the Union Cups and Shields Tournaments should not be held if Ulster Clubs were unable to compete. The standing committee unanimously accepted the proposal and decided to include also the Irish Amateur Close Championship. The decision was ratified by the Central Council. As with the other two Championships, these were not re-commenced until 1946. Arrangements were made to have all trophies returned to the Union for safe keeping in a bank strong room until the renewal of each event.

The Union also obtained exemption from the Compulsory Tillage Order for Clubs in the twenty-six counties. In the six counties the Northern Ireland Tillage Order required Clubs there either to arrange for tillage of certain areas or to graze additional land.

New golf balls became a rarity as manufacturing firms diverted to more urgent and vital pursuits. In January 1942 a committee was set up to investigate the problem of supplies of golf balls and black market activities. A year later, it reported to the Central Council that a visit had been made to the factory of the Irish Dunlop Company Limited in Cork to try and safeguard the interests of Irish golfers as much as possible. The firm had agreed to investigate the practicality of remoulding used golf balls. The Council decided 'that the limitation as to weight and size of a golf ball be waived for golf in Ireland during the war and/or for the present golf ball emergency'. The Dunlop Company produced remoulded golf balls somewhat larger than the standard ball and, whilst some of these did not fly too well, the majority proved satisfactory. Enthusiasts turned to a do-it-yourself exercise and repainted old balls to make them easier to find. The five minute rule became somewhat stretched in friendly fourballs as the recovery of a ball from a wayward shot assumed paramount importance. Inside the clubhouses, other restrictions had to be imposed. Whiskey was in short supply and many Clubs were compelled to introduce a rationing system of three bottles a day, one at 1.00 p.m., one at 6.00 p.m. and one at 9.00 p.m. Woe betide anyone who tried to jump the queue of Club regulars lining up for their allotted 'small one'.

At the end of 1943 the threat of invasion was receding and in response to a request from the Union the Department of Defence indicated that it had no objection to the removal of the concrete and metal obstructions which golf Clubs had been required to erect across open spaces. These obstructions, together with the remoulded and repainted balls, had become an accepted challenge to the golfers at that time.

During the next twelve years (1946–58) twelve more Clubs were opened:

1946   *Mourne, A 1946; Virginia, A 1946.*
1947   *Ballyliffin, A 1952; Rathmore, A 1948.*
1948   *Kilkeel, A 1952.*
1949   *Barleycove (Co. Cork), A 1949; Coollattin, A 1950.*
1950   *Belturbet, A 1951.*
1951   *Achill Island, A 1951; Buncrana Municipal, A 1951; Castleisland (Co. Kerry), A 1951.*
1958   *Ballybofey and Stranorlar, A 1959.*

In 1947, the Central Council decided to discontinue the assessment of Club subscriptions based on male membership and instead introduced an inclusive 'poll tax' of 2/- (equivalent to the present 20p) per male playing member in every Club.

In 1949 the Central Council decided that because of the increase in golfing activities since the war, the workload was becoming too onerous on the honorary officers and that a part-time paid Secretary should be appointed. It was decided that the appointee would be paid a commencing salary of £300 per annum out of which he would be required to provide and pay for office accommodation and staff. The Union would pay only vouched expenses (postage, printing and travelling on Union business). The Secretary's duties would include organising championships and tournaments, corresponding with Clubs, arranging meetings, hotel accommodation and travel, recording minutes and generally dealing with different administrative matters as they might arise. Following interviews, William A. Menton was appointed at the spring meeting of the Council on 29 March 1949 and remained General Secretary of the Union until his retirement, for health reasons, on 31 July 1983. Readers may be interested to learn of the then Council's interpretation of 'part time'. In the seven months following the appointment the golfing calendar read:

William A. Menton

Union General Secretary 1949–83
Union Historian 1984–90

May	The Amateur International Matches	Portmarnock
June	The Irish Cups and Shield National Finals	Galway
June	The Irish Amateur Close Championship	Galway
July	The Open Championship of Ireland	Belvoir Park
September	The Irish Amateur Open Championship	Killarney
November	The Central Council Annual General Meeting	Dublin

Interest in the game increased in 1949 when the R & A decided to cross the Irish Sea and stage the 54th Amateur Championship at Portmarnock. From a field of 204, and much to the delight of a large gallery of spectators, an Irishman, Max McCready, defeated an American, Willie Turnesa, by 2 and 1 in the 36 hole final. McCready was not the first Irish player to win the coveted trophy. Jimmy Bruen of Muskerry had been successful three years earlier at Royal Birkdale when he beat Robert Sweeney, also an American, by 4 and 3.

Other Irishmen to reach the final of this prestigious event up to that time were Charles Hezlet of Portrush, who lost to J.L.C. Jenkins by 3 and 2 at Sandwich in 1914; Lionel Munn of North West who lost to Robert Sweeney, also by 3 and 2, and also at Sandwich in 1937; whilst the following year Cecil Ewing of County Sligo was defeated by Charles Yates by 3 and 2 in the 1938 final at Troon.

Five years after McCreedy's success, Joe Carr of Sutton won the first of his three Amateur Championships when he got through by 2 holes against Harvie Ward of America at Hoylake in 1953. He was victorious again five years later when in 1958 he beat Alan Thirlwell of Gosforth by 3 and 2 at St Andrews. He won his third title at Portrush — the second occasion the R & A selected an Irish venue for the Amateur — when he beat Robert Cochran of America by 8 and 7. The nearest he got to winning his fourth Amateur occurred in the final at Troon in 1968 when he succumbed to the wizardry of Michael Bonallack who was winning the third of his five championships. Two years later, in 1970, the R & A again honoured Ireland by bringing the Amateur to Royal County Down, This time Michael Bonallack achieved his third successive win, and his fifth in all, when he beat W. Hyndman of the USA by 8 and 7 in the final. Michael has since turned his talents to the administration of the game and in the early 1980s took up the senior appointment at the home of golf and became Secretary of the Royal & Ancient Golf Club of St Andrews.

It was not until 1985 that another Irish player won golf's greatest amateur championship. At Royal Dornock, the northernmost of Scotland's championship links, Garth McGimpsey of Bangor defeated Graham Homewood of Ashford Manor by 8 and 7 to join the small but select band of Irishmen to win golf's coveted amateur trophy.

It is worth recording that in the same year Lilian Behan of Curragh Golf Club won the Ladies' Open Amateur Championship at Ganton. Thus two Irish players were holders of golf's most prestigious amateur trophies at the same time.

The success of Irish players in the Boys' Amateur Championship during the same era deserves mention. In 1936 Jimmy Bruen, then only 16 years of age, burst on the international golf scene when he defeated W. Innes of Lanark by 11 and 9 at Birkdale. Just before the outbreak of war, Joe Carr got to the semi-final in the 1939 Championship at Carnoustie where he was beaten by S.B. Williamson of Watsonians, the eventual winner, by 2 and 1.

Norman Drew of Clandeboye was defeated in the 1949 Championship at St Andrews by Harry MacAnspie of Bearsden Academy by 3 and 2, but in 1950 at Royal Lytham and

*A unique double – Garth McGimpsey (Bangor) 1985 Amateur Champion
and Lilian Behan (Curragh) 1985 Ladies' Amateur Champion.*

St Anne's John Glover of Knock defeated Ian Young at Strathaven by 2 and 1. After a distinguished international career John, like Michael Bonallack, turned his talents to the administrative side of golf and in 1981 was appointed Secretary of the Rules of Golf and the Rules of Amateur Status by the Royal & Ancient Golf Club of St Andrews. We waited nearly 30 years for the next Irish success when, at Barassie in 1979, Ronan Rafferty of Warrenpoint beat D. Ray of Long Ashton G.C. by 6 and 5. Then in 1986 Leslie Walker of Grange achieved Ireland's fourth success, winning by 5 and 4 from Graham King of Shotts Golf Club at Seaton Carew.

Club members also followed with interest the achievements of Irish professional golfers. The Irish triumvirate during this period was Fred Daly of Balmoral, Harry Bradshaw of Kilcroney and later appointed to Portmarnock and Christy O'Connor who was attached first to Galway, then Bundoran from where he moved to Killarney and finally, in 1959 he was appointed to Royal Dublin.

Fred Daly was the first and, up to this time, the only Irishman to win the Open Championship. He achieved this ultimate distinction at Hoylake in 1947. This was not a 'flash in the pan' for he was runner-up at Muirfield the following year, third at Troon in 1950, fourth in Portrush (the only occasion the R & A selected an Irish venue for the Open) in 1951 and third at Royal Lytham and St Anne's in 1952. He died in Belfast in 1990.

Harry Bradshaw tied with Bobby Locke in the 1949 Open at Sandwich but was beaten in the 36 hole play-off. At that time all competitors played two qualifying rounds of 18 holes on the Monday and Tuesday of Championship Week, and 140 of the field qualified to take part in the Championship proper. This consisted of a further four rounds of 18 holes over the next three days, one round on Wednesday, one on Thursday, with the leading 40 competitors then playing 36 holes on Friday.

Bradshaw returned 139 (67, 72) to lead the qualifiers. The qualifying scores were then discarded and the Championship comprised the next 72 holes. In the first round Bradshaw had a 68. In the second round he started with four 4s and then disaster struck. At the fifth he drove into the rough and when he reached his ball he found it inside a beer bottle, the neck and shoulder of which were broken off, and it had four sharp points sticking up. The bottle was standing and the ball had bounced into it. In those days there were no referees on the course as is the practice today, and in the pre-walkie talkie and golf cart era, players were reluctant to send their caddie in to the clubhouse to request an official to come out to give a ruling as this usually necessitated a long delay. As this specific situation was not then covered by the rules of golf under the unplayable ball or moveable obstruction rules, and to ensure that he would not incur the penalty of disqualification if he took relief, he felt he had no alternative other than to play the ball as it lay. With his 8 iron he smashed the bottle and sent the ball 30 yards. The hole, a par 4, cost him 6. The flying splintered glass added to his discomfiture and he said afterwards that it was six more holes before he got back his composure and was able to concentrate on his game. He returned a 77, his highest in the Championship. This enabled Bobby Locke, whose first two rounds were 69 and 76, to catch him going into the final day and left both of them joint ninth. They each had 68 for the third round and then 70 to finish in a tie. Had the two qualifying scores been taken into the reckoning Bradshaw would have won by a comfortable margin. The 'ball in the bottle', as the episode came to be known, led to the rules being changed at the next revision by the Rules of Golf Committee of the R & A. 'The Brad' died in Dublin in 1990.

Some years later the third of the trio, Christy O'Connor, started to make his presence felt and whilst he, like Bradshaw, never won the Open, he progressed from being joint 24th at Carnoustie in 1953, joint 20th at Birkdale in 1954, joint tenth at both St Andrews in 1955 and at Hoylake in 1956 to joint third at Royal Lytham and St Anne's in 1958. He finished fifth at Muirfield in 1959, third at Royal Birkdale in 1961 and sixth at Royal Lytham and St Anne's in 1963. His best performance, however, was at Royal Birkdale in 1965 where he gained second place, two shots behind Peter Thomson of Australia who was winning his fifth Open title.

We cannot leave these three great players without mentioning their more important international achievements. In the Ryder Cup, Daly played in four matches (1947–53), Bradshaw in three (1953–57) and O'Connor in a world record of ten matches between 1954 and 1973. In the Canada Cup, Daly played twice (1954–56), Bradshaw six times (1954–59) and O'Connor again achieved another world record with 14 appearances between 1956 and 1971.

These achievements were meritorious, for in addition to Locke and Thomson, other world-renowned golfers of the era competing in the Open were Henry Cotton, Roberto de Vincenzo, Ben Hogan, and 'the Big Three' of world golf, Gary Player, Arnold Palmer and Jack Nicklaus. Irish professionals were also successful on the British circuit and the victory in 1958 in Mexico by Bradshaw and O'Connor in the Canada Cup was another achievement which further helped to increase interest in golf in Ireland.

Despite the achievements of the leading Irish amateurs and professionals, it was still relatively easy to join a Club up to 1958. In fact, Clubs were so anxious to attract members that many of them dispensed with Club entry fees and annual subscriptions were small.

The outdoor and indoor staff of many of the affiliated Clubs sought permission from their Club committee to use the course at off periods. This permission was readily given and from these beginnings the Irish Artisan Golfers' Association came into being. The parent Club allowed its name to be used to prefix the Artisan Club for identification and the latter usually comprised the Club staff, former staff and others who, as youngsters, had caddied at the Club with a limit on total membership prescribed by the parent Club. Following an application for affiliation, the Union decided to amend its constitution and affiliated the IAGA as an associate member subject to the association submitting for approval a constitution which complied with the Union constitution and rules of golf. The IAGA constitution which, at their request, was drawn up by the Union Secretariat, was approved at the spring meeting of the Central Council on 27 March 1953. Whilst the constitution provided for an all-Ireland organisation somewhat similar to the GUI, to date the activities of the Association are confined to Clubs in and around Dublin city. The Union agreed to accept entries from members of the Association in the Irish Amateur Open and Close Championships provided the Association certified, on the entry form, that the entrant had a handicap within the limit prescribed for each championship. Fourteen IAGA members entered the 1954 Irish Amateur Open at Dollymount and one of them, Jimmy Kelly, reached the semi-final where he was defeated by Joe Carr (Sutton), the eventual winner. The handicaps of all members of the Association are now governed by the CONGU SSS and Handicapping Scheme.

By far the best known members of the Association were Tom Craddock and Paddy Caul, both of whom later became members of Malahide Golf Club. Tom's achievements appear in Chapter 36 on Irish Walker Cup players and Paddy's were:

East of Ireland Amateur Open Champion 1968
Leinster Interprovincial 1965, 1966, 1968
Irish International, Home Series 1968, 1969.

The Council decided to recommence the Interprovincial Series in 1956. Another major extension of Union activities occurred in 1957 when, on a proposal by the Leinster Branch, it was decided to investigate ways and means of improving the standard of golf in Ireland and particularly to review junior golf.

Chapter 17

THE AMATEUR INTERPROVINCIAL MATCHES

The town of Portrush has carved a special niche in the annals of Irish golf. The founding of the Union in Portrush's Great Northern Hotel in 1891 has already been recorded. In addition, both the Irish Amateur Open and Irish Amateur Close Championships were first played over the Portrush links in 1892 and 1893 respectively. In 1896, Portrush was again selected by the Union as the venue for the inaugural Interprovincial Match between teams representing Ulster and Leinster. When the Union made the decision, the Lahinch Golf Club delegate requested that a team representing Munster be included but, although an invitation was extended to that province, it could not muster a team; this was possibly because the venue was the most northern of the Championship links with its attendant travelling difficulties.

This match was played on Easter Tuesday, 7 April 1896 on the day before the Irish Amateur Close Championship. The teams were 20 a side with singles and foursomes and each match comprised 18 holes with the total of holes up to decide. Ulster won by a narrow margin. This match has been mentioned in Chapter 7 on the handicapping scheme and the detailed results are set out in Appendix X (Section 1).

In the years up to 1906 the series continued between the two provinces but comprised singles only and was played on the day prior to the Close Championship and at the same venue. Between 1896 and 1906, Leinster won eight times to Ulster's three. The list of interprovincial players and their records from 1896 to 1906 is set out in Appendix X (Section 2). In 1907 the Union decided to discontinue the series in favour of a Professional Championship.

We must also acknowledge another first in Portrush. In 1951 the Royal and Ancient Golf Club of St Andrews invited the Royal Portrush Golf Club to host the world's most prestigious Championship — the Open — over its links.

The Interprovincials were resuscitated briefly in 1938 in a somewhat different format. They survived for just two years and were suspended, as were other Union events, with the outbreak of the Second World War.

Following a proposal from the Munster Branch 'that Interprovincial Matches should be held for the purpose of aiding the selection committee in charge of International Matches' at a meeting on 13 December 1937, the Central Council decided 'that by way of experiment Interprovincial Matches [should] be held in August 1938, at a seaside course in the Dublin area, that teams [should] consist of ten a side, and that the venue and dates and eligibility basis be arranged by the standing committee. Selected players . . . to pay their own expenses.'

At a meeting on 31 January 1938, the standing committee decided 'that the Interprovincial Matches will be played at Portmarnock on 8 August 1938 and that provincial eligibility would be birth or permanent residence and also subject to international team's eligibility qualification; that the competition would be 36 holes strokeplay with the best seven returns from the ten players on each side to count.'

The eligibility conditions were more in line with modern interpretation and not the somewhat casual arrangement which operated for the 1896 to 1906 series when residence, even temporary, appears to have been the criterion. Both the 1938 and 1939 matches were played at Portmarnock with the format reduced from 36 to 18 holes in the second year. As this series was strokeplay and as only two years were involved, the detailed results are set out in Appendix X (Section 3) and the list of Interprovincial players for those two years is set out in Appendix X (Section 4).

Whilst the Championships and inter-club events were reactivated after the War, it was not until 1956 that the Interprovincials were resumed.

The Union decided to follow the format used in the Amateur International Matches, with foursomes each morning and singles each afternoon. Each team consisted of eight players with one reserve and whilst the Union would not accept responsibility for travelling expenses or caddies' fees, it did provide dinner and accommodation for four nights at a selected hotel together with luncheon each day in the clubhouse. Five of the 1938–39 players, Joe Brown (Waterford), Joe Carr (Sutton), Cecil Ewing (County Sligo), Billy Hulme (Warrenpoint) and Brennie Scannell (Woodbrook) survived the 17 year break. The 1956 match was played at Royal Dublin and resulted in a tie between Leinster, Munster and Ulster. The matches alternated between Royal Dublin and Portmarnock until 1961, when the Union decided to rotate the event around the four provinces and it also accepted responsibility for travelling and hotel expenses, meals and caddies' fees.

Two years later, the Council decided to award the former Irish Amateur Open Championship Cup as the interprovincial trophy and this necessitated considerable engraving. Supporting the trophy was a stepped 9" high circular wooden plinth on which had been fixed shields, each engraved with the year and name of the winner and his Club; this amounted to 56 shields in all. To ensure that the trophy would not lose its original historic identity, it was decided not to erase the engraving showing the title of the Amateur Championship, but to engrave its new identity as the interprovincial trophy on the other side of

The Bob Jones Award (Chapter 19)

THE IRISH SENIORS' AMATEUR OPEN CHAMPIONSHIP

(Chapter 24 Appendix XIV)

THE EWING CUP

Year	Venue	Winner and Club
1970	Lahinch	C. Ewing, Co. Sligo
1971	Rosslare	J. O'Sullivan, Athlone
1972	Co. Sligo	B.J. Scannell, Woodbrook
1973	Warrenpoint	J.W. Hulme, Warrenpoint
1974	Cork	P. Walsh, Roscrea
1975	Woodbrook	S.A. O'Connor, Athy
1976	Athlone	B.J. Scannell, Woodbrook
1977	Warrenpoint	D.B. Somers, L'town & B'town
1978	Limerick	D.P. Herlihy, Royal Dublin
1979	Royal Tara	P. Kelly, Coollattin
1980	Galway	G.N. Fogarty, Royal Dublin
1981	Bundoran	G.N. Fogarty, Royal Dublin
1982	Douglas	J. Murray, Bundoran
1983	Courtown	F. Sharpe, Royal Dublin
1984	Connemara	J. Boston, Royal Co. Down
1985	Royal Co. Down	J. Boston, Royal Co. Down
1986	Waterford	J.D. Coey, Clandeboye
1987	Castletroy	J. Murray, Bundoran
1988	Westport	B. Buckley, Grange
1989	Royal Belfast	B. McCrea, Royal Portrush
1990	Cork	C. Hartland, Huddersfield

THE IRISH SENIORS' AMATEUR OPEN CHAMPIONSHIP

(Chapter 24 Appendix XIV)

THE O'SULLIVAN OVER 60 SALVER

Year	Winner and Club
1972	C. Ewing, Co. Sligo
1973	S. Young, Clandeboye
1974	J. Warren, Muskerry
1975	R. Donnelly, Slade Valley
1976	J.W. Hulme, Warrenpoint
1977	B.J. Scannell, Woodbrook
1978	B.J. Scannell, Woodbrook
1979	B.J. Scannell, Woodbrook
1980	J.S. Ward, Galway
1981	J.P. Keegan, Newlands
1982	E. Curtin, Elm Park
1983	K. Garvey, Co. Louth
1984	J. Boston, Royal Co. Down
1985	J. Boston, Royal Co. Down
1986	J. Green, Rosslare
1987	J. Murray, Bundoran
1988	J. Fitzgibbon, Portmarnock
1989	H.B. Smyth, Ballymena
1990	J.D. Coey, Clandeboye

THE IRISH SENIORS' AMATEUR OPEN CHAMPIONSHIP

(Chapter 24 Appendix XIV)

THE McCANN OVER 65 ROSEBOWL

Year	Winner and Club		Year	Winner and Club
1979	G. Clancy, L'town & B'town		1985	E.Curtin, Elm Park
1980	M.J. Hennelly, Galway		1986	M. Cusack, Portmarnock
1981	R.M. Ryan, Thurles		1987	J.B. Carr, Sutton
1982	R.D. Lord, Cork		1988	M. Breen, L'town & B'town
1983	B.J. Scannell, Woodbrook		1989	H. Wray, Warrenpoint
1984	B. Lyden, Cork		1990	J. Fitzgibbon, Portmarnock

THE IRISH SENIORS' AMATEUR OPEN CHAMPIONSHIP

(Chapter 24 Appendix XIV)

THE OWENS OVER 70 CUP

Year	Winner and Club		
1984	G.H. Owens, Skerries	1987	J.J. Toner, Mourne
1985	J.J. Toner, Mourne	1988	B.J. Scannell, Woodbrook
1986	E. O'Carroll, Muskerry	1989	J. Keegan, Newlands
		1990	D. Killian, Athlone

THE PIERCE PURCELL SHIELD FOURSOMES TOURNAMENT

(Chapter 23 Appendix XIII)

Year	Winning Club				
1970	Massereene	1976	Roscommon	1984	Dublin & County
1971	Muskerry	1977	Killarney	1985	Adare Manor
1972	Cork	1978	Galway	1986	Kanturk
1973	Massereene	1979	Newlands	1987	Warrenpoint
1974	Galway	1980	Shannon	1988	Galway
1975	Ballybunion	1981	Warrenpoint	1989	Nenagh
		1982	Galway	1990	Oughterard
		1983	Warrenpoint		

THE JIMMY BRUEN FOURSOMES TOURNAMENT

(Chapter 28 Appendix XVI)

Year	Winning Club		1982	Stackstown		1987	Warrenpoint
1978	Stackstown		1983	Warrenpoint		1988	Clonmel
1979	Ballybunion		1984	Sutton		1989	Bangor
1980	Galway		1985	Clonmel		1990	to come
1981	Galway		1986	Castletroy			

THE IRISH GOLF CLUBS' MIXED FOURSOMES TOURNAMENT

(Chapter 29 Appendix XVIII)

THE CARROLL CUP

Year	Winning Club
1978	Donaghadee
1979	Birr
1980	Carrickfergus
1981	New Ross
1982	Sutton
1983	Holywood
1984	Co. Sligo
1985	Ennis
1986	Kirkistown Castle
1987	Co. Sligo
1988	Kilkenny
1989	Tralee
1990	Galway

the Cup and also to engrave the years with the names and Clubs of all Championship winners as a permanent record on the Cup itself. A new 5" high circular wooden plinth was made with a wide silver band to permit the engraving of the year and name of the winning province following each annual event. The Tournament was then titled 'The Interprovincial Championship' and each year the President of the Union presents the Cup to the winning captain who brings it to his home Club for display.

In 1978 the number on each team was increased to ten and the format became four foursomes and nine singles with matches played to a finish. In the same year, it was decided to reduce the event from three days to two and to play it immediately preceding the Close Championship and at the same venue. Heretofore, the host province had the right to decide the order of play, but the new format was based on the previous year's results so that on day one the winning province played the province which had been last, and province two played province three. On the second day the two first-day winners played for the Championship, whilst the two losers played for third place. This two-day idea was quickly discarded as it proved unpopular, and the Championship was restored to a three-day event with matches comprising 18 holes only and was moved away from the Close. It was also prescribed that in the event of a tie between two or more provinces, matches won would decide the event. If there was still a tie, 'holes up' would decide and if still tied the Championship would be shared, with the trophy being held by each province involved in the tie for an equal period during the following year.

To a certain extent, the need for deciding on an outright winner arose from the fact that at Portrush in 1978 there was a triple tie between Ulster, Munster and Leinster, the third occasion on which these three provinces had tied since the inception of the Tournament. On the two previous occasions, there had been no trophy to award but this time certain physical difficulties arose by having to move the trophy from one province to another (or in this case, two other provinces) during the year. The Union was reluctant to follow the regulations governing ties in the Amateur International matches where, if there is still a tie after holes won have been ascertained, the previous year's order of results decides the issue. On only three other occasions since 1956 has there been a tie, in 1957 between Munster and Ulster, in 1966 between Leinster and Munster and in 1988 between Leinster, Munster and Ulster which was the first time when the tie-breaking formula had to be used. An examination of results shows that of the 29 outright wins Leinster had 12, Ulster 11, Munster 4 and Connacht 2.

In racing parlance, the 1988 series at Portmarnock could be said to have 'gone down to the wire'. On day one, Ulster, the 1987 winners, defeated Connacht by 11 matches to 2, whilst Munster defeated Leinster by 10 matches to 3. The format prescribed that Ulster would oppose Leinster and that Munster would oppose Connacht on the second day. Ulster led Leinster by 3 matches to 1 in the morning foursomes, while Munster led Connacht by a similar margin. However, in the afternoon singles Leinster won 6 of the 9 matches to defeat Ulster by 7 to 6. In the meantime, Munster beat Connacht 8 matches to 5. Munster won on each of the first two days, and on the final day faced the holders, Ulster, for the Championship. Ulster with one win and a loss were facing a daunting task. Leinster also with a win and a loss could, by defeating Connacht, finish up with two wins. The stage was set for an exciting day's golf. Leinster was out first against Connacht, tied the foursomes and went on to win 6½ to Connacht's 2½ in the singles. Ulster went in to lunch leading Munster by 3 matches to 1, and in the afternoon after 8 matches the two sides were level with singles matches won; the final match was all square after 17 holes. Brian Patton won the 18th to give Ulster victory and an overall win by 8 matches to 5.

The position was then a tie between Leinster, Munster and Ulster. As a result, the matches won were taken into the reckoning. Ulster retained the title as it emerged with 25 matches to Munster's 23 and Leinster's 18½. Had John Morris of Munster, who was one hole to the good on the 17th tee against Patton, won his match, Ulster and Munster would have had 24 matches each and a check of the 'holes up' in all their matches would have enabled Munster to snatch victory.

As these matches form an important part in Club golf within the provinces, a list of Inter-provincial representatives, their Clubs and records are set out in Appendix X (Section 5).

Whilst the primary purpose of the interprovincials is to provide a proving ground from which the international selection committee can ascertain the best Irish players to represent Ireland at international level, it is also, for the majority of the players on the four teams, the ultimate goal of their golfing career: the honour of playing for their province. There is there-fore keen competition at the various provincial trials and other events used by the provincial selectors from which to decide on their best team. Ulster and Leinster have dominated the series possibly because numerically these two provinces have a greater number of courses and players. Connacht, by the same reckoning, is the weakest of the provinces and deserves all the support and congratulations for their enthusiastic approach to the annual matches.

Connacht have won the event only twice. The first in 1967 at County Sligo and again in 1983 at Connemara. Few present at County Sligo in 1967 will ever forget the unrestrained joy and emotion of the team non-playing Captain, Jack O'Sullivan (Athlone), when he was presented with the Interprovincial Championship Trophy by the President, Tommy O'Donnell. Jack had been a member of the Connacht team from 1956, when the series was resumed, to 1965 and was therefore in a better position than anyone else to assess the merit of this achievement. He was the long-serving Honorary Secretary of the Connacht Branch and it is appropriate to quote an extract from his 1967 annual report which sums up his feelings. 'Few ever thought it would happen but it did happen: Connacht won the Interprovincial Championship. The frustrations and disappointments of eleven years were wiped out and forgotten on the evening of the 26 August, when the Connacht flag was raised. To each member of the team I tender my sincere thanks and appreciation.' In his President's Review that year Tommy O'Donnell congratulating Connacht on their success said 'I have known Jack O'Sullivan for many years and when the final putt was sunk, giving Connacht the Championship outright, it was the first time I had ever seen Jack lost for words. He just couldn't believe it.'

This Chapter is devoted to what is popularly called the 'Senior' Interprovincials and the 'Junior' Interprovincials will be reviewed in Chapter 18 on Junior Golf.

In 1982 Ulster won the Championship at Portrush. The Union President, Fred Perry, presented the Trophy to the Ulster Captain, Frank McCarroll, who brought it in triumph to his home Club, City of Derry, for display. Tragically just one month later on 28 July the City of Derry clubhouse was completely destroyed by fire. On being acquainted of the loss of the Trophy the Union General Secretary requested the team Captain to make a search through the ashes to try and recover any part of the Trophy, which up to that time had been 90 years in existence. He hoped the Union would be able to preserve continuity by having any such pieces melted down and used with fresh silver to make a new Cup. A piece bearing the engraving 'ING UNION' was recovered, but the idea of using it in a new Trophy proved impracticable and the Union decided to provide a new Cup.

Fortunately one of the registered Golfing Societies was happy to come to the Union's assistance by providing an identical replica to replace the original Cup.

After a long and distinguished golfing career, Lionel Munn (North West) went to live in Killarney on his retirement. At an auction following his death in the late fifties, the replica of the Irish Amateur Open Championship Cup, which Munn had won at Royal Dublin in 1909, was purchased by Dr William O'Sullivan (President 1958-60). He presented it to the Clongowes Union Golfing Society which had been formed in 1919. Billy's reason for presenting the Cup was to commemorate the fact that both he and Commander George Crosbie (President 1938-42) had each also been Presidents of the Clongowes Union. The Cup was named the Crosbie/O'Sullivan Cup.

The minutes of the ordinary general meeting of the Central Council of 8 October 1982 record that the Union General Secretary, Bill Menton, the Life President of the Clongowes Union Golfing Society, advised the Council that his Society had an exact replica of the Championship Cup and, Billy O'Sullivan having agreed, would be happy to hand it over to the Union for the Interprovincial Championship. He only asked, in exchange, that the Union present his Society with a replacement Cup. The Council accepted the offer and thus the historic link with the original Cup was preserved.

We will conclude this Chapter by mentioning that the new Interprovincial Championship Cup is mounted on a two-tiered four-sided mahogany plinth with the recovered piece of the original trophy set into it; it also contains panels on which are engraved the years, names and Clubs of all winners of the Irish Amateur Open Championship and also the years and names of the winning provinces since 1938.

Chapter 18

JUNIOR GOLF

The concept that the game was only for the more mature citizen has changed dramatically over the last three or four decades. Fifty or so years ago young boys and girls who sought to play golf were barely tolerated by their elders and, for the most part, were regarded as somewhat of a nuisance. They were interfering with the serious business of the leisurely fourball of the more senior members of the Club. That is not to say that the undoubted talents of such young players as May Hezlet of Portrush, Jimmy Bruen of Muskerry or Joe Carr of Sutton were not recognised and fostered by their Clubs. May Hezlet, when only seventeen, won both the Ladies' Amateur and the Irish Ladies' Amateur Championships in successive weeks at Newcastle, Co. Down in 1899. Jimmy Bruen was just sixteen when he won the Boys' Amateur Championship at Birkdale in 1936 and, two years later playing No.1 in both foursomes and singles, he led the Britain and Ireland Walker Cup team in their first-ever victory over America. Joe Carr's first entry into the record books was when he won the inaugural East of Ireland Amateur Open Championship at Baltray in 1941 at the age of nineteen.

These and a few others were the exceptions. Mostly, juniors in a Club were few in number and usually allowed to play simply because their parents paid a family membership subscription. The juniors were afforded limited periods on the course. Even then they were obliged to give way to full members.

However, since the end of the Second World War attitudes have changed. Clubs began to introduce new categories of junior membership or to enlarge existing ones. The Union, for its part, then as now, did not impose on any Club a requirement to pay any poll tax or annual subscription to the Union in respect of any junior or university member in a Club.

In 1946, the Central Council discussed the inauguration of a Boys' Open Championship of Ireland but considered it impracticable at the time. However, in 1948 it was decided that each province could have a Boys' Championship provided the four events were uniform and on similar lines to the Boys' Amateur Championship run by the R & A. Leinster and Ulster inaugurated theirs in 1949 and Connacht and Munster followed in 1950. From these beginnings, the Union embarked on what has turned out to be the most fruitful advance in the development of golf in Ireland.

In 1957 investigation of ways and means of improving golf in Ireland resulted in a proposal to increase the poll tax by 50 per cent from 2/- (now 10p) to 3/- (now 15p) and to devote the additional revenue to fostering junior golf. There was universal approval of the proposal, and it was decided that half of these funds would be allocated to the branches in ratio to the amounts received from the Clubs in each province and that the remainder would be used by the Union for special coaching schemes for young players.

The additional 1/- on the poll tax brought in £1,240. Connacht had only 28 Clubs which, between them, had 1593 members on which poll tax was payable. To assist the province, the Council decided to allocate to it all the extra tax received from Connacht Clubs. This resulted in the province receiving £80. The other three provinces had £600 divided pro rata between them, leaving £560 available for the launch of the Union's programme.

A Junior Golf Committee was appointed to co-ordinate the work of the branches and was given full powers to arrange any tournaments it considered necessary. The committee was Tom Montgomery (Ulster) (Convenor), Dr Gerald Owens (Leinster), Ned Treacy (Munster) and Rev. Patrick O'Brien (Connacht).

Sir Henry Cotton, who died in December 1987, played a large part in helping to set up the Golf Foundation. In 1951 he had approached a number of public schools offering to give, free of charge, a lecture and demonstration to the pupils in an effort to encourage the inclusion of golf as part of the physical education curriculum. As a result, the Golf Foundation was born in 1952 with the primary aim of promoting and developing golf among young people.

The Golf Foundation obtains its funding from the R & A, the Golf Unions of England, Ireland, Scotland and Wales, the Ladies' and Irish Ladies' Golf Unions and other institutions and organisations, including golf ball and golf club interests. From the six schools which received tuition in 1952, the latest report records that the number is now upwards of 1500. Its main thrust is to introduce golf to schools and towards this end it will pay half the fees and travelling expenses of a professional golfer who gives up to 16 hours tuition in any one academic year. It is recommended that the number of pupils in a tuition group should not exceed 20. The Foundation will sanction tuition for a second group should this be requested.

The Golf Foundation is a good friend of golf in Ireland and its influence has been clearly shown, not only by the increase in the number of young people who have taken to the sport but, equally important, by the improvement in the standard of play. The Golf Foundation asked the Union to nominate an Irish representative to its committee who would act as a liaison officer between the two bodies. Dr Gerald H. Owens was nominated and the Golf Foundation later appointed him to its Executive Council. Through his efforts much progress has been made over the years in introducing the game both to boys and girls at schools throughout the country.

In reporting on the first full year of the junior golf programme to the 1960 Annual General Meeting, the President of the Union, David L. Baine, congratulated the committee on its enthusiasm and hard work. As a first step, provincial Junior Committees had been set up. Every Club had been contacted to ascertain the names and competition records of all players aged 25 and under with handicaps of six or less. From this information, the provincial Junior Committees had selected their best players for an interprovincial match at Baltray in July. This proved so informative that another similar match was played there in September. At both these series the Royal Portrush professional, P.G. Stevenson (Stevie), had been present and later submitted written reports on all players. In addition, a match had been arranged between an Irish international side and a junior selected side, again at Baltray, in both foursomes and singles. The juniors were defeated by 10 matches to 6 with two matches halved.

Various tournaments and inter-club matches were arranged throughout the provinces, always with professionals in attendance. Clinics were held and young players were urged to enter as many scratch cups in their area as possible to gain experience. As an indication of the interest and encouragement shown by the IPGA the Leinster Committee was permitted by that body to nominate young amateurs to play with a professional in the qualifying round of the Michael Moran Memorial Cup. Each branch had held its provincial Boys' Championship for which there had been a total entry of 242.

At the Junior Golf Committee's request, the Council ruled that persons under the age of 18 be classified as juveniles and those between 18 and 25 as juniors. This age limit of 25 was reduced to 22 in 1971 to coincide with R & A conditions of eligibility.

It was most heartening to all involved in junior golf when the Irish selectors picked five juniors for the 1961 Amateur International Matches at Portmarnock. These had been members of the junior side which played the international side at Rosses Point prior to the Close Championship. The juniors were David Sheahan (Grange) who won the Close, Brendan Edwards (Shandon Park), Jimmy Bowen (Cork), Michael Guerin (Killarney) and Brian Kissock (Bangor). In his report to the Council at the next Annual General Meeting, the team Captain, Cecil Ewing, was high in his praise of the young players. This applied particularly to David Sheahan, who, as the Close champion, led for Ireland. He had defeated the English and Welsh champions and had only gone down to the Scottish champion by 2 and 1.

Because of the increasing activities and workload, the Council enlarged the Union Junior Golf Committee and it now consists of the officers of the Union, two representatives from each province and the Golf Foundation representative.

Leinster inaugurated a Provincial Schools Championship in 1963, followed by Ulster in 1964 and Munster in 1967. In 1966, the Junior Golf Committee decided to inaugurate an Irish Schools Championship based on one school qualifying from each province for a national final. In its formative years this was held prior to the Leinster Boys' Championship and at the same venue. The Union provided a Perpetual Challenge Shield and medals for the four teams. Initially, to save travelling expenses for schools, it was agreed that any school near a provincial boundary could opt to play the qualifying competition at the selected venue in the adjoining province. This worked satisfactorily until a Leinster school won the Connacht qualifying section. As a result of vigorous objection from some Connacht schools, it was decided that in future a school can qualify only in its own province. Now, as then, there is no entry fee and the Union makes grants to the schools which qualify for the national final towards travelling and hotel expenses. It is true to say that this Championship engendered a new sport on the curriculum of many schools. The record of winners is set out in Appendix XI (Section 1).

Perhaps it was as a result of the Union's concern and efforts to develop junior golf that the construction of courses was undertaken by schools which had land available for this purpose. The first school to have its own course was Gormanston (Co. Meath), which was opened in 1961. Then followed Rockwell (Co. Tipperary) in 1964 and Clongowes (Co. Kildare) in 1966. St MacNissi's College, Garron Tower, (Co. Antrim) Club was formed in 1968, but having no land available it obtained playing facilities at both Cushendall and Ballycastle Golf Clubs. It is certain that many other Clubs would be more than willing to provide similar facilities to schools in their locality.

The Union, aware of the importance of this new departure from the usual practice of a group of enthusiasts getting together to form a golf Club, enlarged its constitution and introduced a new category of member to provide for the affiliation of College Clubs. The Union also decided that, as in the case of University golf Clubs, the annual subscription payable by College Clubs would be the nominal sum of £1, irrespective of the number of members in the Club. Students in these colleges were thus able to form Clubs, become affiliated to the Union and compete in Union and branch championships and tournaments.

Possibly due to its convenience to competitors from the other provinces, the Leinster Boys' Championship invariably attracted the largest number of entries. Dr Owens, the Leinster representative on the Junior Golf Committee, advocated the introduction of a Boys' Open Championship of Ireland. He indicated that, in an effort to launch the event, his branch would be prepared to discontinue their Championship so that the new one could be slotted in to the fixtures calendar in place of the Leinster event and played, for convenience, at a Leinster venue. The offer was accepted and the inaugural Championship was played at County Louth Golf Club in 1966. From an entry of 118, Michael Hanway (Sutton) beat Alister Rea (Downpatrick) at the 19th to become the first Irish Boys' Open Champion and he received the magnificent perpetual trophy from the Union President, Tom Brindley.

When it was decided to introduce the new event the Union General Secretary was charged with obtaining a suitable trophy. By chance he met Joe Kennedy, a long-serving delegate on the Leinster Provincial Council and member of both Hermitage and Portmarnock Golf Clubs. On hearing of the problem, Joe suggested that the trophy which had been awarded to the winning amateur in the now defunct Hermitage Amateur-cum-Professional Matchplay Foursomes would be suitable. This Tournament had been started by Hermitage in 1939. The first winners were Clifford McMullan (Knock) and Joe McCartney, the professional at Cliftonville. On another occasion Sammy Moore (Belvoir Park) had been successful, partnered by Fred Daly (Balmoral). In the other seven years of the competition, Joe Carr (Sutton) was the winning amateur. He was partnered six times by Harry Bradshaw who, when they won in 1940 and 1941, was attached to Delgany and for the remainder of this period was attached to Kilcroney. On the last occasion the competition was played, Joe won again, this time partnered by Christy Kane (Royal Dublin). Sutton Golf Club had almost become the permanent home of the trophy. On being approached by the Union to purchase the trophy, Patrick Doran, Hermitage Captain, indicated that his Club would make an outright gift of the Cup to the Union. This generous gesture is permanently acknowledged by an engraving on the Cup.

In 1967 the Championship was played at Royal Dublin and 64 entries were received. John Carey (Roscrea) defeated William O'Brien (Lahinch) by 4 and 3 to emerge the winner. It went back to Baltray in 1969 and from a field of 82, Mark Gannon of the home Club achieved the first of his many championship victories at all levels by beating Jimmy Brewer (Massereene) by 3 and 2 in the final.

Feeling that there was a void in the programme for juniors over 18, the committee decided to inaugurate the Youths' Amateur Open Championship of Ireland. The maximum age limit was fixed at under 22 on the last day of August in the year of the Championship and the format was 36 holes strokeplay. The inaugural event was played at Delgany in 1969, and the first winner was Declan Branigan of Laytown and Bettystown. Thereafter, the committee decided to discontinue the Boys' in favour of the Youths' which was extended to 72 holes with a handicap limit of 9. The Hermitage trophy became the Youths' trophy. Leinster revived its Boys' which, with the other Provincial Boys', has since been played annually. The record of winners, runners-up and venues of both the Irish Boys' and the Youths' is set out in Appendix XI (Sections 2 and 3).

The match against the international side which had been played annually since 1957 was discontinued and the Junior Interprovincials, with an age limit of 22, were extended on similar lines to the Senior Interprovincials.

In 1973 Barry Crymble (Malone and Royal County Down), an Ulster representative on the Junior Golf Committee, presented a perpetual challenge cup for the Junior Interprovincials. The record of winning provinces is engraved on the plinth.

With the co-operation of the R & A, an Irish Youth's Team played a Continent of Europe Youth's Team at the Royal Burgess Golf Club, Barnton, Scotland, in 1970. This was the first international match at junior level and Ireland won by 8 matches to 1 with 1 halved. The Irish team, under the captaincy of Tom Montgomery (Shandon Park) was M. Bloom (Edmondstown), J.C. Brewer (Massereene), J.E. Carey (Roscrea), R.J. Carr (Sutton), J. Coyne (Strabane), J. O'Grady (Fermoy), J.E. O'Leary (Foxrock), L.A. Owens (Portmarnock), D. Smyth (Laytown & Bettystown), H.B. Smyth (City of Derry) and V. Smyth (Laytown & Bettystown). The detailed results of the match are set out in Appendix XI (Section 4).

Two of the team, Roddy Carr and John O'Leary, were selected by the R & A for a team representing Britain and Ireland against the Continent of Europe at the same venue on the following day.

The junior golf programme got a further boost that year when three of that team won further awards. Mark Bloom, Roddy Carr and John O'Leary were selected on the six man Irish team against Germany at Dusseldorf and between them gained three points out of six matches in helping Ireland to win by 5½ matches to 3½. Mark had been runner-up at Grange to David Sheahan of the home Club who won his second Close Championship. Having been runner-up in the West of Ireland at Sligo, John went to Lahinch and won the South. Roddy emulated the achievement of his father Joe of 30 years earlier by winning his first Championship, the East, at Baltray. He was also runner-up in the North at Portrush. Roddy joined John, who had made his debut the previous year in the home internationals at Killarney, as a full international player for the matches at Royal Porthcawl. He then received the highest accolade in amateur team golf by being selected as a Walker Cup player. The Junior Golf Committee had every reason to be proud.

Patrick Doran (left), Captain, Hermitage Golf Club, presenting the Hermitage Perpetual Challenge Cup to Thomas P. Brindley, President GUI.

This cup was presented to Michael Hanway (Sutton) as winner of the Inaugural Boys' Amateur Open Championship of Ireland at Co. Louth Golf Club in 1966, to John Carey (Roscrea) winner at Royal Dublin Golf Club in 1967 and Mark Gannon (Co. Louth) winner at Co. Louth Golf Club in 1968. The Boys' Championship was then discontinued and replaced by the Youth Amateur Open Championship of Ireland with the Hermitage Cup becoming the Youths' Perpetual Challenge Cup.

In 1972, again with the willing co-operation of the R & A, a fixture was played which was to become an annual event. An Irish Boys' Team of six players travelled to Moortown, Leeds, to play a Welsh boys' team prior to the Boys' Amateur Championship at the same venue. The R & A arranged that the Irish/Welsh match would be played on the same day as a long-established English/Scottish annual match. It was the hope of the Junior Golf Committee that the introduction of this new match would eventually lead to the inauguration of a Boys' International series on similar lines as the 'home international matches'. The record of the junior international representatives against Wales from 1972 is set out in Appendix XI (Section 5).

Some years after the 1972 Irish/Welsh match, the Union received a bequest under the will of the late Dr J.D. MacCormack of all the memento trophies he had won playing in Irish championships. The Union decided to present one of these for the annual Ireland v. Wales match. The Welsh Union, anxious to be associated with the trophy, insisted on contributing to the refurbishing, engraving and mounting of the cup which is named 'The J.D. MacCormack Trophy'.

George McPartlin, Secretary Manager of the Golf Foundation, who had helped to foster the schools coaching scheme considered that a void existed in its programme. He advocated a Schools Golf Team Championship. As finance at that time was a very important consideration, he sought a sponsor. Following discussions Aer Lingus, the Irish national airline, agreed to underwrite the cost and the inaugural Aer Lingus Golf Foundation Schools Golf Team Championship was held in 1972. There was an entry of 112 schools made up of 68 English, 21 Scottish, 16 Irish and 7 Welsh. The regulations prescribed that each country would provide a national winner. The international final was played over the Ballybunion links and the first winner was Buckhaven High School, Scotland. Whilst there had been no precondition that the international final would be played each year at an Irish venue, this was the case during the 14 years Aer Lingus was associated with the event, except once. The international finals were played at Ballybunion in 1972, 1973, 1975 and 1983; at Portmarnock in 1974, 1976, 1980 and 1981 and once each at Connemara (1978), County Louth (1979), Carlow (1982), Lahinch (1984) and Waterville (1985). The only departure from an Irish venue was in 1977 when the final was played at Aer Lingus' own complex at Foxhills, England. Only one Irish school was successful in winning the Championship when St Facthna's High School, Skibbereen won at County Louth in 1979. Up to 1977, when the number of schools in the Championship reached 908, only schools in Britain and Ireland had competed. In 1978, 26 Swedish schools entered and this increased to 69 by 1984. Next, Denmark fielded 17 schools for the 1979 Championship and, like Sweden, has continued in the event ever since.

Financial considerations compelled Aer Lingus to relinquish its association with the Championship after 1985. However, as the Championship had proved so popular and had been supported by a very handsome financial contribution from the R & A, the Golf Foundation decided to widen its scope worldwide. Now, in addition to Sweden, Denmark and the four 'home' countries, schools in Australia, Canada, France, Iceland, India, New Zealand and Germany compete. This impressive number of participating countries is a lasting tribute to the foresight of the late Sir Henry Cotton and to all associated with the Golf Foundation. Here in Ireland, the entry increased from 16 to 143 schools and great credit is due to the Union and provincial Junior Golf Committees and all those connected with schools golf in this country.

Back in 1966, junior golf obtained another boost when juniors were selected to play on provincial teams against a Swedish junior touring team. Later, a junior team played and defeated the Swedish visitors. A novel feature of these five matches was that no Irish junior played in more than one match. Again in 1968, both Ulster and Leinster junior teams played matches against a junior Italian team.

Aer Lingus extended its interest in the promotion of junior golf with the introduction of a Youth's Club Championship. In its first year, 1974, Clubs from nine European countries participated. The format in Ireland was entry through each provincial branch and the Clubs which won through the provincial sections were County Sligo (Connacht); Sutton (Leinster); Limerick (Munster) and Belvoir Park (Ulster). In a knock-out national final at Edmondstown, Sutton emerged as the winner and later went on to win the international final and defeat the winning Clubs from the other eight countries at Portmarnock to become the first winner of the Aer Lingus Youths' Club Championship. During the lifetime of the event the international final was played at an Irish venue. Alas, as in the case of the Schools Team Championship, Aer Lingus relinquished their involvement in the Youths' Club event in 1985. The Union realised that the competition was exceedingly popular and gave young players an opportunity of gaining competitive experience and it decided to continue the event under the title of the Irish Club Youths' Championship and a perpetual challenge Cup was provided, with gold, silver and bronze medals awarded to the winners, runners-up and defeated national finalists. The Cup is another of J.D. MacCormack's memento trophies. The record of winning Clubs is set out in Appendix XI (Section 6).

The hopes and aspirations of the Junior Golf Committee were eventually realised when, in 1977, the Central Council acceded to its repeated requests that Ireland should enter a team in the European Amateur Junior Golf Team Championship. The response of the Irish juniors to this new challenge is dealt with in Chapter 30. Suffice it to say at this juncture that they emulated the achievements of the senior team.

Three years later, the European Golf Association inaugurated a European Amateur Boys' Golf Team Championship which will be dealt with also in Chapter 30.

In 1979 the Scottish Golf Union extended an invitation to the GUI to send a team of six youths to play a match against it prior to the Scottish Youths' Championship, and remain on and play in the Championship. The offer was accepted but the Irish players did not do too well in either event. The invitation was renewed and accepted in the following year, and in 1981 Ireland entertained a Scottish Youths' Team at Baltray. This has become an annual home-and-away fixture with the visiting team playing in the host country's Youth Championship. In 1988, having beaten Scotland at Ladybank, one of the Irish team, Paul McGinley of Grange, went on to win the Scottish Championship. The record of the youth international representatives against Scotland from 1979 is set out in Appendix XI (Section 7).

After 23 years the EGA decided that, with the increasing popularity of the Boys' Team Championship, there was no longer any necessity for a Youth Team Championship and the last of that annual series was played in 1984 at Hermitage Golf Club where Ireland emerged the winner. However, following requests from a number of member countries, including Ireland, the EGA agreed to reinstate the Youths' Team Championship on a biennial basis, and from 1990 it will be played in alternate years to the EAGTC.

Leinster Branch Junior Tournaments

The Gresham Hotel Cup for the Leinster
Youths' Amateur Open Championship.

*(Open to golfers under the age of 22 on
31 August of the year of the Championship.
Entry limit 60. 72 holes stroke play
off scratch.)*

Leinster Boys' Amateur Open Championship
Cup.

(Open to golfers under the age of 18.)

Leinster Boys' (under 15) Amateur Open
Championship Cup. (Played in conjunction
with the Leinster Boys' Amateur Open
Championship.)

The Joe Carr Trophy for the Leinster Juvenile Championship.

(Open to golfers under the age of 15.)

The Pepsi Shield for the Leinster Inter-Schools match play Tournament.

(Teams of 5 under 18 years of age.)

The aspirations of the Junior Golf Committee were realised again in 1985 when, at Royal Burgess Golf Club, Edinburgh, the R & A inaugurated a Boys' Home International Match for teams of eleven to compete annually for the Royal and Ancient Trophy.

Other individual and team events were inaugurated through the years. In an effort to indicate the tremendous strides made in the promotion and development of junior golf, the many championships and tournaments in which the younger golfers have been able to participate since the Union launched its junior golf programme from a small beginning in 1957 with an initial income of £1,240 are set out below.

INTERNATIONAL EVENTS

The European Amateur Junior (now Youth) Golf Team Championship
Teams of 6.   Under 22 years of age.

The European Amateur Boys' Golf Team Championship
Teams of 6.   Under 18 years of age.

The Boys' Home International Match
Teams of 11.   Under 18 years of age.

Ireland Youth's v. Scotland Youth's (The Standard Life Trophy)
Teams of 6.   Under 22 years of age.

Ireland Boys' v. Wales Boys' (MacCormack Cup)
Teams of 8.   Under 18 years of age.

Golf Foundation Team Championship for Schools
Teams of 3.   Under 18 years of age.

NATIONAL EVENTS

Youths' Amateur Open Championship of Ireland (Hermitage Cup)
Under 22 years of age.

Irish Boys' Amateur Close Championship (Bingham Cup)
Under 18 years of age. Group two (Union Cup) — under 16 years of age.

Junior Interprovincial Match (Crymble Cup)
Teams of 7.   Under 22 years of age.

Irish Club Youths' Team Championship (MacCormack Cup)
Teams of 3.   Under 22 years of age.

Irish Golf Clubs Junior Foursomes (Smurfit Trophy)
Teams of 4.   Under 18 years of age.

Irish Inter-Schools Golf Championship (Union Shield)
Teams of 5.   Under 20 years of age.

Ulster Branch Junior Tournaments

*The Charles O. Hezlet Memorial Cup for the Ulster Youths'
Amateur Open Championship.*

*(Open to golfers under the age of 22 on 31 August of the year of
the Championship. 18 holes stroke qualifying. 16 qualify for
match play.)*

The Fred Daly Trophy.

*(Open to members of all Ulster Clubs under
the age of 18. Teams of seven. Match play
singles off scratch, home and away.)*

PROVINCIAL EVENTS

Connacht Boys' Amateur Open Championship
    Over 15 and under 18 years of age.

Leinster Boys' Amateur Open Championship
    Over 15 and under 18 years of age.

Munster Boys' Amateur Open Championship
    Over 15 and under 18 years of age.

Ulster Boys' Amateur Open Championship
    Over 15 and under 18 years of age.

Leinster Youths' Amateur Open Championship (Gresham Hotel Cup)
    Under 22 years of age.

Munster Youths' Amateur Open championship
    Under 22 years of age.

Ulster Youths' Amateur Open Championship (Hezlet Cup)
    Under 22 years of age.

Connacht Youths' Amateur Open Championship
    Under 22 years of age.

The Fred Daly Ulster Clubs Trophy
    Teams of 7.   Under 18 years of age.

Connacht Junior Inter-Club Tournament
    Teams of 5.   Under 18 years of age.

Munster Inter-County Boys' Championship
    Teams of 6.   Over 15 and under 18 years of age.

Leinster Boys' Trophy
    Under 15 years of age.

Leinster Inter-Schools Tournament (Pepsi Shield)
    Teams of 5.   Under 18 years of age.

Leinster Juvenile Championship (Joe Carr Trophy)
    Under 15 years of age.

Chapter 19

THE DEVELOPMENT OF GOLF IN IRELAND

Period: 1959 to 1965

No Club was opened for play in 1959 and from 1960 to 1965 only nine Clubs commenced activities:

1960   *Donegal, A 1962.*
1961   *Gormanston, A 1962; Wexford, A 1965.*
1962   *Cahir Park, A 1969.*
1963   *Blacklion, A 1964.*
1964   *Nuremore, A 1965; Rockwell, A 1972.*
1965   *Clongowes, A 1969; Dromoland Castle (Old) (Co. Clare), A 1965.*

Notwithstanding the relatively small number of Clubs founded, this proved to be a period of massive expansion of the game in Ireland. The first of three events occurred in 1959 which started a sequence which led to golf becoming the most popular participant sport in this country.

The Dunlop Masters

In 1946 the Dunlop Sports Company inaugurated what came to be regarded as a Tournament of Champions. Participation was confined to home and overseas professional golfers on the PGA Order of Merit and the sponsor reserved the right to invite other players at its discretion. The field was limited to 40 players and was held at the end of the season. It was named 'The Dunlop Masters' and, except for the Open Championship, became one of the most prestigious events in these islands.

Two Irish professionals had won the Dunlop Masters on three occasions prior to 1959: Harry Bradshaw (Portmarnock) in 1953 at Sunningdale and in 1955 at Little Aston, and Christy O'Connor (when he was the professional attached to Bundoran) in 1956 at Prestwick. Following overtures from many Irish interests, the Dunlop Sports Company decided to hold the 1959 Dunlop Masters at Portmarnock.

It was many years since Irish golfers had had an opportunity of seeing leading professionals in action, and certainly not so many in the same place at the same time. This may have been one of the reasons why the attendances at Portmarnock exceeded those even at the Open Championship up to that time. Another, and possibly more realistic, reason was the generosity of the Irish Dunlop Company, who were extremely liberal in its issue of complimentary admission tickets and catering vouchers.

However, from a purist's point of view, many feel that the main reason why Irish golfers descended on Portmarnock in their tens of thousands — the official attendance for the four days was 27,000 — was because for the first time since 1930 there was a possibility of an amateur golfer beating the professionals in a golf event of international status.

Throughout the life of the Union, there have been golfers whose achievements have brought distinction and honour, not only to themselves and their Clubs, but in a wider sense, to their country.

Later in this history the achievements of these players will be recounted but here it is only necessary to refer to one such man whose example, extending over more than two score years of competitive golf, has been an inspiration to everyone who plays this great game.

Even in 1959 the name of Joe Carr, then 37 years of age and whose home Club was Sutton, was known in every golf Club throughout Ireland. In addition to his achievements in the Amateur Championship which have already been mentioned, he had also been successful in five Irish Championships a total of 23 times and played in the Amateur International matches for 13 consecutive years from 1947 and for Britain and Ireland in the Walker Cup matches on the seven biennial occasions prior to 1959 and in the Eisenhower Trophy matches in 1958.

His complete record will be detailed more specifically with those of other Irish Walker Cup players (see Chapter 36) and his record to this time is only given here to explain why the Dunlop Sports Company decided to invite this outstanding Irish amateur golfer to join the 40 leading home and overseas professionals in its Tournament of Champions on the first occasion the event was to be played in Ireland.

Portmarnock has been acknowledged by many internationally-renowned players and golf writers as being amongst the 12 best golf courses in the world. Measuring 6489 metres, it has a standard scratch score of 75 and a par of 73 (in 1959 the par was 74). A unique feature of the layout of the links is that not one of the 18 holes faces in precisely the same direction, and as it is open duneland it is always subject to the vagaries of the wind.

That Joe Carr accepted the challenge with relish was evident when he led the select field with an opening 69. Improving his score by one shot in the second round, he remained at the top of the leader board. A third round of 69 gave him a score of 206, an impressive 16 under par, and saw him going into the final round four shots clear of Christy O'Connor (by now attached to Royal Dublin) on 210 with Norman Drew (Bangor) a further two shots away on 212.

William Forshay, Chairman of the Award Committee of the United States Golf Association, presenting the Bobby Jones Plaque to Joe Carr. The award is made for distinguished sportsmanship in golf and this (1961) was the first occasion it had been won outside America.

Leading the field in each of the first three rounds in a prestigious professional tournament was certainly an achievement in itself, and this fired the imagination of the public who were enthralled at the possibility of an amateur winning the Masters. Alas, their amateur hero could not muster another 69 and was overtaken, and passed, by their professional hero, Christy O'Connor who, playing superb golf, returned an 8 under par 66 to win by four shots from Joe Carr, who with a par 74, tied for second place with Norman Drew who had a 68. For the record, the Dunlop Masters made a return visit to Ireland in 1965, when again at Portmarnock, Bernard Hunt (Hartsbourne) won with 283.

Thus was public awareness focused on golf in Ireland. It was indeed fitting and also a well–deserved tribute that two years later, in 1961, the United States Golf Association did Joe Carr the signal honour of selecting him to be the recipient of the Robert Tyre Jones Award for distinguished sportmanship in golf. This annual award was inaugurated in 1955 and Francis Ouimet became the first recipient. Joe Carr was the seventh winner and had the distinction of being the first non–American to be so honoured. Some of the most outstanding golfers in the world have since received the award. These include Gary Player (1966), Arnold Palmer (1971), Byron Nelson (1974), Jack Nicklaus (1975), Ben Hogan (1976) and Tom Watson (1986). Very few golfers throughout the world can be unaware of the famous Augusta National Golf course designed by the legendary Robert Tyre Jones which is the permanent home of his brain–child the American Masters Tournament.

Bobby Jones retired from competitive golf at the age of 28 whilst still an amateur, having achieved a unique 'grand slam' which is never likely to be equalled. In 1930 he won the four major Championships of the world, the Amateur Championship at St Andrews, the American Amateur Championship at Merion, the Open Championship at Hoylake and the American Open Championship at Interlakin.

To appreciate more fully Jones' tremendous dedication and skill at the game, it must be mentioned that in those days golf was looked on as a game for the more settled citizen. He must have been regarded as an 'infant prodigy' as he played in his first American Amateur Championship in 1916 when still only 14 years of age.

In his short but illustrious career, in addition to the grand slam, he won the American Open in 1923 (Inwood L.I.), 1926 (Scioto) and 1929 (Winged Foot, N.Y.); he won the American Amateur in 1924 (Merion), 1925 (Oakmont), 1927 (Minikahda) and 1928 (Brae Burn) and won the Open in 1926 (Royal Lytham and St Anne's) and 1927 (St Andrews).

The Canada Cup

The second outstanding event which popularised golf in Ireland at that time was the Canada Cup (since renamed The World Cup).

Henry Longhurst in an article on the history of the Canada Cup published in the 1960 souvenir programme wrote:

'The Canada Cup Tournament, and indeed the whole conception of golf as a means of fostering worldwide goodwill as against merely between two countries in such individual encounters as the Walker Cup match, owes its existence to one very fine man, the late John Jay Hopkins.'

Hopkins created the International Golf Association and decided its motto 'International Goodwill through Golf'. He presented a magnificent silver gilt perpetual trophy which he named 'The Canada Cup' for the Nations team event. He also presented a silver perpetual trophy for the individual team member who returned the best score in the four rounds of the medal tournament and named this 'The International Trophy'.

Credit must be given to Professor Pierce F. Purcell — 'The Prof.' — for the Canada Cup coming to Ireland. He went to Wentworth in 1956 ostensibly to see the Tournament but specifically to see John Jay Hopkins and invite him to bring the Canada Cup to Ireland. To a lesser mortal this would have been a daunting task but following discussion, Hopkins agreed to visit Portmarnock himself before making a decision. Having seen the links, he readily accepted the invitation. It must not be forgotten that this invitation was issued and accepted before Ireland won the Canada Cup in Mexico in 1958 and also before the successful Dunlop Masters at Portmarnock in 1959. It was unfortunate that Hopkins did not live to attend the Canada Cup in Ireland, as he died a few months after Wentworth.

In those days, competing in the Canada Cup was by invitation and to preserve this right the IGA invited the amateur administrative body in each country (and not that country's Professional Golfers' Association) to select the two players to represent the country in the Tournament.

As can be appreciated even at that time, this led to a degree of acrimony, particularly as one country, for a number of years, selected an amateur as one of its team of two. Nevertheless, the GUI adhered to the spirit of the invitation and always nominated Ireland's two best Irish professionals.

Ireland did not compete in the inaugural tournament in Montreal in 1953 (seven countries), but nominated the following players from 1954 until it itself insisted with the IGA that the Irish Professional Golfers' Association (IPGA) should be given the role of the Irish nominating body:

1954	Montreal	(25 countries)	H. Bradshaw and F. Daly	Joint 11th
1955	Washington D.C.	(25 countries)	H. Bradshaw and F. Daly	Eighth
1956	Wentworth	(29 countries)	H. Bradshaw and C. O'Connor	Joint 10th
1957	Tokyo	(30 countries)	H. Bradshaw and C. O'Connor	Bradshaw withdrew after 2 rounds because of illness.
1958	Mexico City	(29 countries)	H. Bradshaw and C. O'Connor	Winners
1959	Melbourne	(30 countries)	H. Bradshaw and C. O'Connor	Joint 12th
1960	Portmarnock	(30 countries)	C. O'Connor and N.V. Drew	Fourth

The hosting of the event involved considerable planning and organisation. To achieve this, the GUI set up a Tournament Organising Committee (TOC) with Dr William O'Sullivan, President of the GUI as Chairman. Pierce Purcell took on the arduous task of setting up the financial structure. He calculated that the Tournament could cost the GUI £30,000. At that time, one of the obligations of the host country was to discharge all hotel, travelling and catering costs of all members of the competing teams whilst in its country, in addition to all the expenses of organising the event which included the many expenses of links preparation, scoreboard, souvenir programme, receptions and official dinner.

It was decided to approach six national or multinational organisations and request them to guarantee the GUI against loss to a limit of £5,000 each. Even the Prof.'s prowess as a negotiator failed to persuade the first multinational firm approached. Nothing daunted, the Prof., next (and fortunately) set up a meeting with the Irish Dunlop Company. Now, instead of a 'six by one' situation, he asked Dunlop's to accept the responsibility of guaranteeing two units, namely, £10,000. Imagine the relief of all concerned when, with the approval of its parent Board, The Irish Dunlop Company agreed to take up any slack for the first £10,000, with Bord Fáilte being responsible for the next £5,000 and Dunlop's taking up any balance outstanding. In the event, the gate receipts and revenue from advertisements in the souvenir programme held Dunlop's financial commitment to less than £10,000, notwithstanding the fact that they had very generously agreed to the Golfing Union's suggestion that all monies from the sale of the 10,000 souvenir programmes be handed over to the Central Remedial Clinic in Dublin, whose founder, Lady Valerie Goulding, organised volunteer helpers to sell the programmes.

Having overcome the problem of finance, the TOC got down to the other enormous tasks of producing the souvenir programme, organising hotel accommodation, transport, press facilities (a large international Press Corps always attended) and, with the readily available co-operation of the Committee of Portmarnock Golf Club, the preparation of all the ancillary details in relation to the venue, such as the main and subsidiary scoreboards, telecommunications between each hole and the administration office, marshalling, catering facilities, practice facilities and, most important, the grooming of the links for this prestigious event. The Union was also indebted to Dublin County Council for widening and resurfacing the approach road from Portmarnock village to the Club boundary.

The IGA always invited the winners of the previous year to defend their title, so Kel Nagle and Peter Thomson, who had won the Canada Cup for Australia at Melbourne in 1959, received an invitation to come to Portmarnock. In addition, the IGA allowed the host country to nominate the members of the team whom they would wish to have representing America and South Africa. After consideration, the TOC requested the IGA to invite Ben Hogan and Sam Snead, the two legendary professionals who had won the Canada Cup for America at Wentworth in 1956, and the South African professionals Bobby Locke and Gary Player who had been runners-up to Hogan and Snead at Wentworth. Locke was no stranger to Portmarnock as he had won the gold medal there in the 1934 Open Championship of Ireland as leading amateur. On his return to Portmarnock four years later, this time as a professional, he won the same Championship. He had also won four Open Championships in 1949, 1950, 1952 and 1957, whilst Player, then only 24 years of age, was building up an impressive reputation worldwide having won the Open Championship at Muirfield in 1959. The thousands who flocked to Portmarnock on the first day of the Canada Cup saw him achieve a new course record with a nine under par 65.

In Ireland the Selection Committee, under the chairmanship of Dr William O'Sullivan, gave lengthy consideration to nominating Harry Bradshaw and Christy O'Connor, who had won the Canada Cup for Ireland in Mexico in 1958, particularly as Bradshaw was professional at Portmarnock. However, the results of the Dunlop Masters at Portmarnock the previous year had also to be considered. Finally, Christy O'Connor and Norman Drew were invited to represent Ireland.

The IGA advised that Ben Hogan had more or less retired from competitive golf and had declined the invitation. They strongly urged that Arnold Palmer be invited. He had

Pierce Purcell (Left) GUI President 1948–50, during his negotiations at Wentworth Golf Club in 1956, with John Jay Hopkins, founder of the International Golf Association, which resulted in the International Golf Championship and Canada Cup matches coming to Ireland.

Crowd scene at Portmarnock before the presentation of the Canada Cup and International Trophy in 1960.

been the top US money winner in 1958, the year he won his first US Masters. The Committee readily agreed and the stage was set for the greatest gathering of world class players ever to grace our shores. The format was 72 holes fourball strokeplay.

Snead and Palmer won the Tournament which was rated as one of the most successful and best organised Canada Cup matches ever staged. Flory Van Donck won the International Trophy for the best four round score. Ireland came fourth, just 10 strokes behind the winners.

During the Tournament, each player signed a parchment scroll which was presented to Dr William O'Sullivan 'in recognition of his warm hospitality and that of his associates'.

Radio Telefís Eireann

The third event which helped to popularise golf was the opening of an Irish television service. RTE began its television service on 31 December 1961.

Residents in most of Ulster as well as those along the east coast to just south of Dublin could pick up the BBC and UTV signals from the transmitters on Divis Mountain and Black Mountain. Programmes were mainly news and documentaries. Sports coverage was negligible and live outside broadcasting of golf was unknown.

Whilst this additional service was a bonus to viewers on the east coast, it was a welcome innovation to a great number of residents further inland and to the south and west, and at the beginning of 1963 approximately 40 per cent of householders had acquired a TV set.

In April 1963, RTE transmitted the first programme in the series called 'Shell's Wonderful World of Golf'. Seventeen programmes were screened over the next few years, and golfers and an ever–increasing number of other viewers were afforded the opportunity of seeing, not only world famous golf courses, but also golfing stars who were household names, many of whom had been in Ireland for the Canada Cup.

Irish viewers were particularly delighted to see two of the series played on Irish courses. Portmarnock was the venue for a match between Harry Bradshaw and Billy Casper of America. Casper was US Open Champion in 1959 and his record from then to the time of the match in Portmarnock was 12 wins on the US circuit and selection on the Ryder Cup team in 1961 and 1963. His Ryder Cup selection continued unbroken to 1973. The match, which consisted of 18 holes medal play, was won by Bradshaw by three strokes.

Killarney was the venue for the other match and the promoters took the unusual step of inviting the leading Irish amateur, Joe Carr, to take part. This created one or two problems as there was an attractive cash incentive for the players in each match of the series. The winner collected $5,000 and the other player $2,500. The R & A had to be approached for Carr to be permitted to play, and it authorised him to do so provided he received no money prize and the money would be handed over by the promoters direct to a charity of his choice. Carr nominated The Irish Professional Golfers' Association Benevolent Fund. His opponent was an American named Al Geiberger, who, whilst not as well known as Billy Casper, nevertheless had the distinction of returning the lowest ever score in a round in a major American tournament; he carded 59. Also, he had only turned professional in 1959 but later went on to become USPGA champion, gain Ryder Cup honours and finish second to Orville Moody in the 1969 American Open at Houston, Texas.

Sam Snead and Arnold Palmer (America) leaving the platform after being presented with the Canada Cup by Frank Pace, President IGA at Portmarnock 1960.

Flory Van Donck (Belgium) being presented with the International Trophy for best individual 72 hole score.

As at Portmarnock, a large gallery watched the match at Killarney, and although Carr had the edge with three holes to play, Geiberger managed to square the match on the 18th green. The trustees of the IPGA Benevolent Fund were delighted to receive $3,750 into their funds. Shell presented Carr with an engraved silver salver which likewise had to receive the imprimateur of the R & A.

And so, in addition to the thousands of Irish men and women who flocked to Portmarnock to see the Dunlop Masters and the Canada Cup, a much greater audience was introduced to golf through the medium of television.

Whilst the period under review witnessed a tremendous upsurge of interest in golf in this country, the leading Irish amateurs were still unable to make any great impact on our near neighbours England, Scotland and Wales in the annual home international matches. Lack of strength in depth had long been advanced as the reason, and whilst Ireland usually had the measure of Wales, Irish players invariably succumbed to England and Scotland. The Union decided to put this theory to the test and, at the same time, to broaden our horizons by going into Europe. In 1965 Ireland entered the European Amateur Golf Team Championship which was competed for biennially by teams of six players. The next Chapter will prove if the theory was correct.

Chapter 20

THE EUROPEAN AMATEUR GOLF TEAM CHAMPIONSHIP

The European Golf Association (EGA) was founded in November 1937 in Luxembourg. A small number of countries was represented. Like the majority of other sporting organisations, the EGA was obliged to suspend its activities during the 1939-45 war. Whilst it began to pick up the threads when things returned to normal, it was many years before it became anything other than an Association which co-ordinated open tournaments among member countries. In 1951 the Irish Council decided to join the EGA as it considered that membership would be beneficial to Irish golfers holidaying on the continent.

At the time of writing, there are 23 countries in the membership of the EGA and these have been divided into four geographical zones:

SCANDINAVIAN	CENTRAL	SOUTHERN	BRITAIN AND IRELAND
Denmark	Austria	France	England
Finland	Belgium	Greece	Ireland
Iceland	Czechoslovakia	Italy	Scotland
Norway	Germany	Portugal	Wales
Sweden	Holland	Spain	
	Hungary	Yugoslavia	
	Luxembourg		
	Switzerland		

The Association is administered by an Executive Committee which comprises a President, four other officers and one elected delegate from each zone. This Committee holds regular meetings each year, receives reports and approves the organising arrangements made by its Technical Committee whose functions include co-ordinating the various championships and tournaments with the host countries for that year. Following the conclusion of the competitive season there is an annual meeting of the General Assembly to which each member country is entitled to send two delegates.

In 1959 the EGA inaugurated a biennial European Amateur Golf Team Championship (EAGTC). The first Championship, which attracted entries from nine countries, was played at El Prat Golf Club, Barcelona, Spain and was won by Sweden. England was the first of the 'home' countries to compete which it did in 1961 at the Royal Club de Belgique, Brussels, Belgium. Sweden was again the winner. The third Championship, played at Falsterbo Golf Club, Sweden in 1963 saw England achieve its first victory.

The rota prescribed by the EGA meant that the fourth Championship was scheduled for the Britain and Ireland zone in 1965. The Irish Council decided to enter a team as did also Scotland and Wales. The Championship was played at the Royal St George's Golf Club, Sandwich, and from an entry of 17 countries, Ireland emerged the winner. Scotland was runner-up, England third and Wales fourth. The details of the Championship are set out in Appendix XII (Section 1).

Possibly because the four home countries had dominated the Championship at Sandwich, the format which operated up to that time was altered for the 1967 event. For Sandwich, each team comprised seven players. The format consisted of a 36 holes strokeplay qualifying competition over two days. Any six of each seven man team could play on either day. The aggregate of the four lowest scores returned by each country each day was that country's qualifying score. The countries, in order of qualification, were then divided into two flights of four each and three flights of three each. The three days matchplay was similar to that in the home international matches, with each country playing the other countries in its flight in three foursomes and six singles each over a maximum of 18 holes.

Following the qualifying tournament the first flight, from which only the winner could emerge was: 1st England, 2nd Ireland, 3rd Scotland and 4th Wales. At the end of the matchplay England, Ireland and Scotland had each won two and lost one. The rules of the Championship contained a condition which would ensure an outright winner in the event of a tie in the matchplay. The number of matches won, halved or lost was taken into the reckoning. The final tally was:

	Matches won	Matched halved	Matches lost
Ireland	14	6	7
Scotland	13	5	9
England	13	4	10

So Ireland won on its first entry into European Golf and by just the odd match.

Two years later and under a different format (teams of 6, one stroke qualifying round, flights of eight countries, a pre-set matchplay draw with matches played to a finish), Ireland successfully defended the Championship at Circola Golf Club, Turin, Italy.

The format was further altered in subsequent years by restoring the qualification tournament to two rounds of strokeplay and the Championship was extended to five days. The pre-set matchplay draw provides that on day one the qualifying countries play in the following order:

The 1965 Irish International Team, winners of the EAGTC at Sandwich, England.

*Left to Right: standing: M.J. Murphy (Irish EGA Representative), V. Nevin, T.P. Brindley
(President GUI), D.B. Sheahan, W.E. McCrea and W.A. Menton (General Secretary GUI).
Seated: R.M. Craigan, J.B. Carr, C. Ewing (Non-Playing Captain), T. Craddock and R.deL. Staunton.*

The 1967 Irish International Team, winners of the EAGTC at Turin, Italy.

Left to Right: T.E. O'Donnell (President GUI), V. Nevin, P.D. Flaherty, D.B. Sheahan, C. Ewing (Non-Playing Captain), J.B. Carr, T.W. Egan, T. Craddock and W.A. Menton (General Secretary GUI).

The 1983 Irish International Team, winners of the EAGTC at Chantilly, France.

Left to Right: standing: P. Walton, T. Cleary, G. McGimpsey and M.F. Morris. Seated: J.J. Carr, B. Edwards (Non-Playing Captain) and A.D. Pierse.

The 1987 Irish International Team winners of the EAGTC at Murhof, Austria.

Left to Right: standing: G. McGimpsey, L. MacNamara, G. O'Brien (President GUI), N. Anderson and P. Hogan. Seated: E. O'Connell, E. Curran (Non-Playing Captain) and J. McHenry.

2 v. 7
3 v. 6
4 v. 5
1 v. 8

On the final day the two countries competing for the Championship go out last.

We have already mentioned that Sweden won in 1959 and 1961. Since then no other country in mainland Europe has been successful. England have won on seven occasions; Ireland four times and Scotland three. Ireland has qualified for the first flight in every Championship except twice. At Penina, Portugal in 1973 it came 13th out of 18 countries and at the Hague Golf and Country Club, Holland in 1979 it came 12th out of 16 countries.

The other two wins were at Chantilly Golf Club, France in 1983 and at Murhof Golf Club, Austria in 1987.

The record of venues, team Captains, winning countries and Ireland's position in the order of merit are set out in Appendix XII (Section 2). The record of Ireland's International representatives is also set out in Appendix XII (Section 3).

On the administrative side, the Council decided to appoint only one representative to the EGA and it became the practice that he and the President in Office attended the meeting of the General Assembly each year. In 1965 the Council appointed Michael J. (Mixie) Murphy (Ballina) and he proved to be a dedicated representative of the Union, serving continuously for 21 years. During this period he was appointed a member of the Technical Committee in 1978, 1979 and 1980 and was elected to the Executive Committee for the years 1980 to 1984 inclusive. As appointee he attended each of the biennial EAGTCs from 1965 and the annual European Amateur Youth's Golf Team Championship (EAYGTC) from Ireland's entry in Oslo in 1980 until he retired in 1986. In 1979 the Council decided to appoint a second representative to the EGA and the Honorary Treasurer, David M. McAuley, was chosen and served until 1985. Patrick J. Foley, who was GUI President in 1967, was appointed to the Executive Committee in 1989 and he, with Declan Howley, are the current representatives. Another Irish appointee to the Technical Committee was Joseph B. Carr (Sutton) who served from 1981 to 1983.

Thus as golf became increasingly popular as a leisure sport at home, Irish players competing in international events have proved that their expertise on courses both at home and abroad is as good as that of competitors from other countries.

Chapter 21

THE
DEVELOPMENT
OF GOLF
IN IRELAND

Period: 1966 to 1975

Over the last 25 years the demand for golf has continued to grow as more and more people became attracted to the game as a leisure occupation. Clubs, particularly in the larger areas of population, have become full and most of them discontinued the long established 'waiting list' system. Many newcomers to the game were obliged to travel considerable distances to join Clubs in country areas. During the period under review 21 new Clubs were established:

1966   *Shannon, A 1968.*

1967   *Dunmore, A 1968.*

1968   *Garron Tower (St MacNissi's), A 1969; Mulrany, A 1972.*

1969   *University College, Galway, A 1969; University of Ulster (originally New University of Ulster), A 1970.*

1970   *Bright Castle, A 1979; East Cork, A 1971; Slade Valley, A 1971; Templemore, A 1975.*

1971   *Ballinascorney, A 1972; Dublin and County, A 1972; Kanturk, A 1975.*

1972   *Greenacres (Co. Dublin), A 1972.*

1973   *Beech Park, A 1973; Bodenstown, A 1973; Connemara, A 1973.*

1974   *Deerpark, A 1975; Parknasilla, A 1975.*

1975   *Bantry Park, A 1976; Stackstown, A 1976.*

Towards the end of this period there was a world recession and financial considerations became a major obstacle to the construction of new golf courses. However, with the increasing interest in the game, Clubs turned their attention to improving existing facilities by, where possible, extending the course from 9 to 18 holes, or, where this was not necessary or practical, by improving the layout of the course such as enlarging tees, tree planting programmes and watering and drainage schemes. Also with increased usage, the question of

ULSTER PROVINCIAL COUNCIL AND LEINSTER PROVINCIAL COUNCIL MATCH

(Chapter 11)

THE ALEXANDER CUP

Year	Winning Province
1972	Ulster
1973	Leinster
1974	Leinster
1975	Ulster
1976	Ulster
1977	Ulster
1978	Ulster
1979	Ulster
1980	Leinster
1981	Not played
1982	Ulster
1983	Leinster
1984	Leinster
1985	Ulster
1986	Ulster
1987	Ulster
1988	Ulster
1989	Leinster
1990	Leinster

THE SOUTH OF IRELAND AMATEUR OPEN CHAMPIONSHIP

(Chapter 33 Appendix XXII)

THE SHAW CUP

Year	Winner and Club	Year	Winner and Club
1895	G.S. Browning, Lahinch	1946	J. Burke, Lahinch
1896	B. O'Brien, Portsalon	1947	B. Slattery, Lahinch
1897	F. Ballingall, Blairgowrie	1948	J.B. Carr, Sutton
1898	F. Ballingall, Blairgowrie	1949	J.P. Carroll, Sutton
1899	J.R. Gardiner, Richmond	1950	M. Power, Muskerry
1900	F. Ballingall, Blairgowrie	1951	G. Gilligan, Limerick
1901	W. Dodd, Royal Liverpool	1952	M. Power, Muskerry
1902	W. Ballingall, Royal & Ancient	1953	P.J. Leyden, Lahinch
1903	J.B. Ballingall, Blairgowrie	1954	P. Bugler, Lahinch
1904	D. Foster, Frinton	1955	P.J. Leyden, Lahinch
1905	N. Castle, Chiswick	1956	P.J. Leyden, Lahinch
1906	Lord Glenawly, Royal Co. Down	1957	P.J. Leyden, Lahinch
1907	J.J. Hurley, Manrihaniesh	1958	J.C. Brown, Tramore
1908	A.R. Aitken, Prestwick	1959	G. Roberts, Southport & Ainsdale
1909	J.D. Little, Burnisland	1960	P. Sullivan, Kinsale
1910	G.R. Girdlestone, Oswestry	1961	M. Guerin, Killarney
1911	L.O. Munn, North-West	1962	M. Guerin, Killarney
1912	G.V.M. Boyd, Portmarnock	1963	M. Guerin, Killarney
1913	A.W. Murray, Purley Downs	1964	W.A. Kelleher, Douglas
1914-19	No Championship	1965	R.deL. Staunton, Castlerea
1920	E.C. Carter, Royal Portrush	1966	J.B. Carr, Sutton
1921	F. Murphy, Cork	1967	G.N. Fogarty, Royal Dublin
1922	No Championship	1968	J.D. Smyth, Lahinch
1923	F. Murphy, Cork	1969	J.B. Carr, Sutton
1924	J. Crabbe, Foxrock	1970	J.E. O'Leary, Foxrock
1925	M. Crowley, Portmarnock	1971	P. Mulcare, Woodbrook
1926	R. Simcox, Cork	1972	R.deL. Staunton, Castlerea
1927	R. Simcox, Cork	1973	M.A. Gannon, Co. Louth
1928	J. Burke, Lahinch	1974	D.C. Long, Shandon Park
1929	J. Burke, Lahinch	1975	B.P. Malone, Portmarnock
1930	J. Burke, Lahinch	1976	V. Nevin, Limerick
1931	J. Burke, Lahinch	1977	L. MacNamara, Woodbrook
1932	J.C. Brown, Tramore	1978	V. Nevin, Limerick
1933	J.C. Brown, Tramore	1979	P. O'Rourke, Kilkenny
1934	R.M. Saunders, Lahinch	1980	M. Burns, Tramore
1935	R.M. Saunders, Lahinch	1981	P. O'Rourke, Kilkenny
1936	T.F. Ryan, Tipperary	1982	M.F. Morris, Portmarnock
1937	M. O'Loughlin, Lahinch	1983	A.C.J. Morrow, Portmarnock
1938	M. O'Loughlin, Lahinch	1984	N.A. Anderson, Shandon Park
1939	J. Burke, Lahinch	1985	P. O'Rourke, Kilkenny
1940	P.F. Murray, Milltown	1986	J. McHenry, Douglas
1941	J. Burke, Lahinch	1987	B.V.M. Reddan, Co. Louth
1942	J. Burke, Lahinch	1988	M.A. Gannon, Co. Louth
1943	J. Burke, Lahinch	1989	S. Keenan, Galway
1944	J. Burke, Lahinch	1990	D. Clarke, Dungannon
1945	J. Burke, Lahinch		

THE WEST OF IRELAND AMATEUR OPEN CHAMPIONSHIP

(Chapter 33   Appendix   XXII)

THE COUNTY SLIGO CUP

Year	Winner and Club	Year	Winner and Club
1923	L.P. Vernon	1957	J.R. Mahon, Portmarnock
1924	J.L. Crabbe, Foxrock	1958	J.B. Carr, Sutton
1925	W.G. McConnell, Milltown	1959	W.J.J. Ferguson, Malone
1926	J.L. Crabbe, Foxrock	1960	J.B. Carr, Sutton
1927	N.G. McCallum, Troon	1961	J.B. Carr, Sutton
1928	A.W. Briscoe, Castlerea	1962	J.B. Carr, Sutton
1929	W.G. McConnell, Milltown	1963	R.M. Craigan, Malone
1930	C. Ewing, Co. Sligo	1964	B.P. Malone, Tullamore
1931	A.W. Briscoe, Castlerea	1965	R.M. Craigan, Malone
1932	C. Ewing, Co. Sligo	1966	J.B. Carr, Sutton
1933	J. Burke, Lahinch	1967	R.K.M. Pollin, Royal Belfast
1934	J. Burke, Lahinch	1968	D.A. Nelson, Royal Co. Down
1935	C. Ewing, Co. Sligo	1969	R.K.M. Pollin, Royal Belfast
1936	J. Burke, Lahinch	1970	J. McTear, Scotland
1937	J.F. McLoughlin, Royal Dublin	1971	R.J. Carr, Sutton
1938	J. Burke, Lahinch	1972	V. Nevin, Portmarnock
1939	C. Ewing, Co. Sligo	1973	H.B. Smyth, Royal Co. Down
1940	J. Burke, Lahinch	1974	M.A. Gannon, Co. Louth
1941	C. Ewing, Co. Sligo	1975	I.A. Elliott, Royal Portrush
1942	C. Ewing, Co. Sligo	1976	D. Branigan, Laytown & Bettystown
1943	C. Ewing, Co. Sligo	1977	T.B.C. Hoey, Shandon Park
1944	J. Burke, Lahinch	1978	B.V.M. Reddan, Co. Louth
1945	C. Ewing, Co. Sligo	1979	D.C. Long, Shandon Park
1946	J.B. Carr, Sutton	1980	A.D. Pierse, Tipperary
1947	J.B. Carr, Sutton	1981	D. Branigan, Laytown & Bettystown
1948	J.B. Carr, Sutton	1982	A.D. Pierse, Tipperary
1949	C. Ewing, Co. Sligo	1983	C. Glasgow, Donaghadee
1950	C. Ewing, Co. Sligo	1984	G. McGimpsey, Bangor
1951	J.B. Carr, Sutton	1985	J. Feeney, Chapel en Le Frith
1952	J.C. Brown, Tramore	1986	P. Rayfus, Trim
1953	J.B. Carr, Sutton	1987	N. McGrane, Greenore
1954	J.B. Carr, Sutton	1988	G. McGimpsey, Bangor
1955	W.I. Forsythe, Malone	1989	P. McInerney, Milltown
1956	J.B. Carr, Sutton	1990	N. Goulding, Portmarnock

THE NORTH OF IRELAND AMATEUR OPEN CHAMPIONSHIP

(Chapter 34 Appendix XXIII)

THE HARRIMAN CUP

Year	Winner and Club	Year	Winner and Club
1947	J. Fitzsimmons, Bushfoot	1969	M.J.C. Hoey, Shandon Park
1948	J. Fitzsimmons, Bushfoot	1970	J. Faith, Rathmore
1949	F. Webster, Portmarnock	1971	R.K.M. Pollin, Royal Belfast
1950	N.V Drew, Bangor	1972	J.L. Bamford, Royal Portrush
1951	W. Meharg, Castlerock	1973	B. Edwards, Shandon Park
1952	N.V Drew, Bangor	1974	B.J.S. Kissock, Bangor
1953	C. Knox, Royal Portrush	1975	J. Heggarty, Massereene
1954	J.L. Bamford Royal Portrush	1976	B.J.S. Kissock, Bangor
1955	R.McK. Fleury, Cork	1977	D.J.F. Young, Royal Portrush
1956	M. Edwards, Shandon Park	1978	G. McGimpsey, Bangor
1957	M. Edwards, Shandon Park	1979	T.B.C. Hoey, Shandon Park
1958	T.E. Dijon, Rathmore	1980	M. Malone, Belvoir Park
1959	J. Duncan, Shandon Park	1981	D.C. Long, Shandon Park
1960	W.H.E. Rainey, Shandon Park	1982	D.C. Long, Shandon Park
1961	J. Duncan, Shandon Park	1983	T.B.C. Hoey, Shandon Park
1962	J.F.D. Madeley, Royal Belfast	1984	G. McGimpsey, Bangor
1963	J.F.D. Madeley, Royal Belfast	1985	I.A. Elliott, Rathmore
1964	F. McCorry, Clandeboye	1986	D. Ballentine, Carrickfergus
1965	W.H.E. Rainey, Shandon Park	1987	A.D. Pierse, Tipperary
1966	B. Edwards, Shandon Park	1988	N.A. Anderson, Shandon Park
1967	W.R.A. Tennant, Cliftonville	1989	N.A. Anderson, Shandon Park
1968	M.J.C. Hoey, Shandon Park	1990	D. Clarke, Dungannon

To Our Host

Dr. William O'Sullivan

President
Golfing Union of Ireland
Who, by his sponsorship of the
Eighth International Golf Championship and
Canada Cup Matches
has attested for all the world his own and his countrymen's
belief in ideals of sportsmanship and international goodwill,
we present, in recognition of his warm hospitality and that of
his associates, this witness of our sincere appreciation.

President, International Golf Association

Argentina		Ireland	
Australia		Italy	
Belgium		Japan	
Brazil		Mexico	
Canada		New Zealand	
Central Africa		Peru	
Chile		Philippines	
China		Portugal	
Colombia		Scotland	
Denmark		South Africa	
Egypt		Spain	
England		Sweden	
France		Switzerland	
Germany		United States	
Holland		Wales	

The parchment memorial signed by the sixty Professionals who competed in
the International Golf Championship and Canada Cup matches at Portmarnock in 1960.

course maintenance became an important item of Club management. Committees engaged qualified Greenkeepers whose professional expertise improved the standard and quality of the courses under their management.

In addition to on-course improvements, practically every Club saw the necessity of enlarging and extending its clubhouse to provide additional locker room, bar and lounge facilities for its increasing membership and the growing demand for social amenities by its members.

The Union was not found wanting. One of the most serious problems facing a great number of Clubs which did not own the fee simple interest of its lands was the possibility of losing the course, without compensation, on the expiration of the lease or tenancy agreement under which it was permitted to operate. Clubs, particularly those on the perimeter of expanding cities and towns, were constantly unsure and, as a result, were reluctant to embark on any ambitious course or clubhouse improvement. When the Irish Government appointed a Landlord and Tenant Commission to review the then legislation the Union was quick to submit a case on behalf of all affiliated Clubs which did not own their own course. After many appearances before the Commission, the Union and other national sporting organisations which had also presented submissions were happy to learn that the Commission was advocating the following safeguards for sports clubs: where a lessee or tenant of any lands or buildings had been in continuous occupation of them for a period of 21 years for sports purposes the lessee or tenant would be entitled to obtain a new lease of them, subject to agreement regarding rent. In default of agreement the rent would be fixed by the Courts. The Government accepted the Commission's findings and the necessary legislation was enacted.

A Special Development Committee was set up in 1969 and this was a watershed in the affairs of Irish golf. Up to that time, when the Union faced a crisis it called on the Finance Committee to come up with proposals to overcome the problem. As often as not the Finance Committee's cure was to increase entry fees in championships, cups and shield inter-club tournaments, to reduce subsidies and grants and to reduce team numbers or cancel home or away matches.

At its first meeting the President, William J. Gill, said 'The aim of this Committee must be to look forward to and through the 1970s with the view to advancing still further the objects of the Union in the promotion and administration of the game of golf in Ireland and to foster it in every way'. At his invitation the branch representatives and the other officers of the Union submitted various propositions. Following an exchange of views, the President invited the branch representatives 'to go back to their Provincial Councils and discuss the whole problem in the broadest terms and see exactly what we wished to do and only then consider the financial implications and requirements for this purpose'. This was the first occasion, certainly for 50 years, that the financial aspect was demoted to being a secondary consideration.

The importance attached to this subject can be judged from the fact that, in addition to the initial meeting, the Committee held five further meetings over the following seven months and finally held a meeting with the Standing Committee in October 1969. During this period each Provincial Council also held many meetings to receive reports from and to instruct their representatives on the Committee.

At the 1970 Annual General Meeting the Central Council adopted the following ten recommendations of the Special Development Committee:

'1. that the Leinster Council, from funds obtained from the Leinster provincial levy ratified by the Central Council, should proceed with their Schemes which include:

(a) the inauguration of a professional scheme for outlying Clubs in the province.

(b) The provision of a coaching scheme.

(c) The subsidisation of part of the cost of an initial survey for the formation of a new or the extension of an existing Course.'

Leinster obtained permission from the Central Council to inaugurate a provincial levy as distinct from the poll tax payable by Clubs to the Union and the recommendation was regarded as a 'pilot scheme' which, if successful, could be introduced by the other provinces. Connacht commenced a provincial levy in 1971, Munster in 1972 and Ulster in 1974.

'2. That there is enough competitive golf for category 1 players and that no additional matches of senior international standard should be undertaken, except that in non-European Amateur Team Championship years one match either home or away may be played, and that the official party should consist of six players, a non–playing Captain and one official of the Union and that the Union should accept the invitation of the German Golf Federation in 1970.'

Since Ireland had been successful in winning the European Amateur Golf Team Championship on two successive occasions requests had been received from a number of continental countries for matches and the Committee was concerned that the leading Irish amateurs could not fit further representative fixtures into an already overcrowded calender. This decision led to the introduction of the quadrangular continental matches about which more later (see Chapter 22).

'3. That the Union should not enter a team in the European Amateur Junior Golf Team Championship at the present time.'

England, Scotland and Wales had indicated that as the standard of golf at this level in the 'home' countries was much higher than on the continent they were not entering this Championship because the constant winning of the event by one of the four home countries might ruin it. In addition, it was an annual championship and the expenses of sending a team would far outweigh the benefit achieved. A commitment to review the position in the next few years was agreed.

'4. That a new inter–Club competition open to all affiliated Clubs to be known as "The Pierce Purcell Shield" and consisting of teams of ten players be inaugurated. Play to be by foursomes with an individual minimum handicap of 12 and a minimum combined handicap of any pair of 27.'

A questionnaire issued to all affiliated Clubs had shown that they wished to add this type of tournament to the other inter–Club events. The tournament will be dealt with in more detail in Chapter 23.

'5. That pennants should, in future, be awarded to Clubs winning any of the Union cups and shields tournaments, and that any Club wishing to obtain pennants for any year prior to 1970 could do so at its own expense'.

Whilst a Club winning any of the inter–Club tournaments had custody of the trophy for display in its clubhouse until the final the following year, it had no permanent record of its achievement. This decision proved popular as practically every Club which had won any of the tournaments since their inception applied to Union headquarters for the appropriate pennant to display in the clubhouse. A few years later each provincial branch awarded a provincial pennant to each Club which represented the branch in the national finals.

'6. That after 1970 the Irish Amateur Close Championship be played in the month of May and that the qualifying rounds be played on Saturday and Sunday with the matchplay on Monday to Wednesday.'

The Close has already been dealt with in Chapter 6. At this time it was considered beneficial to those who failed to qualify for the matchplay stages to return home on Sunday night and so avoid losing time from business. In addition, the May date gave a better opportunity to the selectors to pick teams in European championship years. Also hotel accommodation was easier to obtain.

'7. That the Union continue to subsidise affiliated Clubs by paying 25 per cent of the current subscription to the Sports Turf Research Institute.'

This reversed a decision made at the previous Annual General Meeting for reasons of economy.

'8. That the 57 affiliated Clubs with a membership of less than 100 who have never been in membership be invited to join the Sports Turf Research Institute, provided they under-take to remain in membership for four years, and that the Union subsidise these Clubs by paying 50 per cent of the current subscription and the cost of an initial visit by an advisory officer of the Institute.'

Today there are only a dozen Clubs which have less than 100 members and most are on the Western seaboard in sparsely populated areas. Possibly, improvements to greens and fairways helped to attract more members to the others.

'9. That the Central Council should lay down conditions under which Clubs should be permitted to run open competitions sponsored from any source other than Clubs' funds and that in future any Club seeking to run such a competition must first obtain sanction and obtain a date from its Provincial Council and undertake to abide with the regulations of the Union.'

The Union as guardian of amateur golf in Ireland considered it necessary to lay down certain guidelines to protect this important aspect of its administration.

'10. That having examined the whole structure of the Union's finances, neither of the two notices of motion to increase the poll tax deferred from the last Annual Meeting should be approved at the present time.'

The notices of motion referred to had been submitted by Leinster and Connacht. Leinster sought a 100 per cent increase from 5/- to 10/- with 50 per cent of the increase being refunded to the branches in ratio to the amounts received from Clubs in each province. Connacht proposed that the poll tax should be 2½ per cent of Club subscriptions.

At the same meeting, the Council decided to inaugurate an Irish Seniors' Amateur Open Championship.

The decision not to increase the poll tax was short lived, as at the following Annual Meeting the Council considered the advisability of providing for future commitments including the European Amateur Golf Team Championship scheduled for Killarney in 1973 and the provision of office accommodation which up to that time was provided, together with staff, by the Union Secretary out of his salary. The Union decided to increase the poll tax from 5/- (25 pence) to 8/- (40 pence). Later that year the Union acquired 'Glencar', 81, Eglinton Road, Donnybrook, Dublin 4 which, following the formal opening by the Union President, Dr Gerald H. Owens, became Union headquarters.

Development continued. Firstly, in 1972, the Central Council approved a request from Leinster and Connacht to inaugurate an Inter–Club Mixed Foursomes Tournament between them which was extended to an All–Ireland event in 1978. Next, a decision of the Standing Committee that Ireland would join France, Germany and Sweden in an International Match in Killarney in 1972 was ratified by the Council. This was the forerunner of the Quadrangular International series between the four countries. In addition, the R & A sanctioned as official the Ireland v. Wales Boys' International prior to the Boys' Amateur Open Championship.

Headquarters of the Golfing Union of Ireland, 'Glencar House', 81 Eglinton Road, Donnybrook, Dublin 4.
(Chapter 21)

Chapter 22

THE QUADRANGULAR CONTINENTAL MATCHES

The winning of the fourth European Amateur Golf Team Championship at Sandwich in 1965 was the harbinger of Ireland's continental contacts. Early in 1966, the GUI received a request from the Swedish Golf Federation to allow it to send a team of six players and a Captain to make a tour of some of Ireland's Championship links and play a series of matches. In accepting the request the Council realised that this was an opportunity for as many players as possible (particularly the juniors) to obtain competitive experience in this first encounter with a continental side on Irish soil. It was agreed that Ireland would host five matches and the Council instructed that no Irish player could be selected for more than one match (foursomes and singles) against the visitors, with the provincial selectors nominating the provincial teams and the junior selectors nominating the junior team.

The first match was played at Portmarnock where Leinster was successful by 7 matches to 2. Next an Irish junior team won at County Louth by 6½ to 2½. These were Ireland's only victories as, at Royal County Down, Sweden defeated Ulster by 6 matches to 3. Next, Connacht, having led in the foursomes by the odd match at County Sligo, were beaten by a similar margin in the singles with a resultant halved match. In the final match at Lahinch Sweden scored another success by defeating Munster by 5 matches to 4. Following Ireland's retention of the European Championship at Turin in 1967, two other continental Federations asked the Council to receive visiting teams. The Council welcomed these requests and, in May 1968, Ireland played and defeated a German team by 8 matches to 1 at Portmarnock. Two months later the Italian Golf Federation sent a junior team and matches were arranged by the Junior Golf Committee for the visitors to play an Ulster junior team at Royal County Down and a Leinster junior team at Grange. The home sides were victorious by 4 and 3 and 5 and 4 respectively.

*The 1972 Irish International Team, winners of the Quadrangular
Continental Matches at Killarney.*

*Left to Right: standing: A. O'Connor, T.B.C. Hoey, T. Montgomery
(President GUI), P. Mulcare and M. Hanway. Seated: K. Stevenson,
W.J.J. Ferguson (Non-Playing Captain), R.M. Kane and V. Nevin.*

*The 1980 Irish International Team winners of the Cartier Trophy at
Portmarnock.*

*Left to Right: standing: P. Walton, M.A. Gannon, P. Mulcare,
M.F. Morris and R. Rafferty. Seated: A.D. Pierse, J.B. Carr (Non-Playing
Captain) and M.C. McAuley (President GUI).*

The 1986 Irish International Team, winners of the Cartier Trophy at Le Touquet, France.

Left to Right: standing: G. McGimpsey, D.F. O'Sullivan, J. McHenry and P. Hogan. Seated: N. Anderson, E. Curran (Non-Playing Captain) and L. MacNamara.

The 1988 Irish International Team, winners of the Cartier Trophy at Royal Portrush.

Left to Right: standing: P. Rayfus, B.T. Crymble (President GUI) and L. MacNamara. Seated: P. Hogan, G. McGimpsey, G.F. Crosbie (Non-Playing Captain), D.F. O'Sullivan and E. O'Connell.

Also in 1968, the R & A selected Portmarnock as the venue for the biennial match for the St Andrews Trophy between teams representing Britain and Ireland and the Continent of Europe. The Britain and Ireland team, under the captaincy of Cecil Ewing (County Sligo) had a comfortable win over the two days of competition by 20 matches to 10. There were two Irish players on this team, Joe Carr (Sutton) and Tom Craddock (Malahide), who between them gained 3 wins and 3 halves out of 7 matches. The juniors were in action against a Continent of Europe team that year at the Royal Burgess Golf Club, Edinburgh and won by 8½ matches to 2½.

In 1970 the German Golf Federation invited Ireland to send a team for a match in Cologne which Ireland won by 5½ matches to 3½. The Irish team remained on and played in the German Open Amateur Matchplay Championship in which Brian Hoey (Shandon Park) reached the final where he came up against J.G. Muller, the odds on favourite, and was beaten by 3 and 2.

An Irish team visited Germany again in 1974 and, at Hamburg, having first played in the German Amateur Open Strokeplay Championship, it was defeated in the match by 5½ to 3½. However, the Irish players acquitted themselves well in the Championship winning the Federal Republic of Germany Prize for the best three–man team return over the first two rounds. The winning team was P. Caul (Malahide), J. Purcell (Mullingar) and D.K. Corcoran (Royal Dublin). The other Irish three–man team was fourth. Paddy Caul finished third in the 72-hole Championship.

Whilst the foregoing matches were against individual continental teams at that time, they were not regarded as full international contests in the same category as the home internationals or the European Championships. Nevertheless the GUI considers that the players selected to represent Ireland in these matches deserve recognition and acknowledgment as Irish representatives who have gained international 'caps' and a record of all such players is set out in Appendix XIII (Section 1).

Two years earlier, in 1972, Ireland entertained three continental teams at Killarney in a competition which eventually became established as a biennial event in non-EAGTC years. Now known as the Quadrangular Continental Matches, the competition is between six-man teams representing France, Germany, Sweden and Ireland. Claude Cartier, when President of the French Golf Federation, presented a Perpetual Challenge Trophy. In the inaugural match at Killarney Ireland won all the matches, defeating Germany by 7½ matches to 1½, Sweden by 6 matches to 3 and France by 7 matches to 2. France beat both Sweden and Germany, and Sweden beat Germany.

The venues and order of merit in subsequent years were as follows:

1976 *Cologne, Germany*	*1 Sweden*	*2 France*	*3 Ireland*	*4 Germany*
1978 *Deauville, France*	*1 France*	*2 Sweden and Ireland tied*		*4 Germany*
1980 *Portmarnock, Ireland*	*1 Ireland*	*2 France*	*3 Sweden*	*4 Germany*
1982 *Halmsted, Sweden*	*1 Germany*	*2 France*	*3 Ireland*	*4 Sweden*
1984 *Bad Ems, Germany*	*1 Germany*	*2 France*	*3 Ireland*	*4 France*
1986 *Le Touquet, France*	*1 Ireland*	*2 Sweden*	*3 France*	*4 Germany*
1988 *Portrush, Ireland*	*1 Ireland*	*2 Sweden and France tied*		*4 Germany*
1990 *Ostersund, Sweden*	*1 Ireland*	*2 Sweden*	*3 Germany*	*4 France*

The record of the Irish international representatives in these matches is set out in Appendix XIII (Section 2).

Chapter 23

THE PIERCE PURCELL SHIELD

The three long established Inter–Club Tournaments (the Senior Cup, the Junior Cup and the Barton Shield) have been very successful. All three tournaments are played off scratch. Both the Senior Cup and Barton Shield teams are selected from the lowest handicapped members in each Club whilst the Junior Cup teams are selected from members of five handicap and upwards. Thus only a limited number of members in any Irish Club could gain a place on any of these teams each year.

One of the recommendations of the Special Development Committee which had been appointed by the Central Council at the 1969 Annual General Meeting was 'that a new competition to be known as "The Pierce Purcell Shield" be inaugurated consisting of teams of ten players, play to be by foursomes with an individual minimum handicap of 12 and a minimum combined handicap of 27.'

Professor Purcell has already been mentioned in Chapter 19 as the person who was instrumental in getting the Canada Cup for Ireland. The Prof. was an administrator of many talents. He had the unusual honour of being elected Captain of Portmarnock Golf Club on two separate occasions, the first in 1925 and again in 1937. Elected by the Union as an Irish international selector in 1936, he served in that capacity for 15 years. He was elected President of the Union for the years 1948 to 1950. In 1949, the Union appointed him as one of the representatives on the then British Golf Union's Joint Advisory Council. It was renamed at his instigation and is now known as the Council of National Golf Unions (CONGU) which, as we have mentioned, administers the amateur international golf matches and is responsible for the standard scratch score and handicapping scheme. The Prof. retired from CONGU in 1966. He was also appointed a member of the Championship Committee of the Royal and Ancient Golf Club of St Andrews for a five year term in 1950.

A civil engineer by profession, he was Dean of Engineering at the National University of Ireland, Dublin, for a great number of years and a member of the governing body of the university. He was an able and skillful negotiator; he was the representative appointed by the National University of Ireland to negotiate the purchase of the huge area of land on the outskirts of Dublin at Belfield, on which the magnificent university complex has since been built. Alas, his hope for a golf course there did not materialise. At the time of his death in 1967 he was President of Portmarnock Golf Club, a position to which he had been elected in 1959.

Although the Prof. had been involved with golf at the highest level, he always maintained that the backbone of the game was the middle and the high handicap members of affiliated Golf Clubs. It was fitting, therefore, that the Development Committee wished to name the new tournament in his memory. The Central Council accepted the recommendation and the tournament was inaugurated in 1970. The rules as approved by the Council are set out in Appendix XIV (Section 1).

Clubs took to the new tournament with enthusiasm: 135 Clubs entered in its first year. The format was similar to the other inter–Club tournaments and the national final was played at Portrush. Massereene defeated Howth by 3 matches to 2 in the first semi–final whilst Muskerry beat Galway by a similar margin in the other. Massereene went on to become the first Club to win the Shield by beating Muskerry in the final by 3½ matches to 1½.

The original concept of this Tournament was to provide a competition for Club members whose golfing ability was not of a standard sufficient to warrant selection on their Club teams for the Barton Shield, Senior Cup or Junior Cup Competitions. Many purists go so far as to maintain that this event was introduced for the more senior members who might otherwise never have the opportunity of representing their Club in competitive golf and regret that, in addition to prescribing a minimum handicap limit, the Union did not also prescribe a minimum age limit. As the Tournament gained in popularity and Clubs sought to win the Shield, the up–and–coming younger members of many Clubs were selected on teams. In 1970 a motion from Ulster 'that the minimum age limit for players in the Pierce Purcell Shield Tournament shall be 30 years' was supported by Connacht, opposed by Leinster and Munster, and was defeated by 10 votes to 8. Ulster submitted a similar motion three years later which was again defeated. In 1987 Ulster once again proposed the imposition of a minimum age limit. This time it proposed 'that no player under the age of 18 years on 1 January in the year of the Tournament may compete in the Pierce Purcell Shield.' The other three provinces accepted what some regarded as a minor concession to the original concept. The record of winning Clubs and teams is set out in Appendix XIV (Section 2).

Chapter 24

THE IRISH SENIORS' AMATEUR OPEN CHAMPIONSHIP

At the annual meeting of the Central Council in January 1970 it was decided to inaugurate this Championship for golfers who had reached the age of 55 by the first day of the Championship. The format was 36 holes medal play over two days. Cecil Ewing (County Sligo), then President–Elect, indicated that he would present a Perpetual Challenge Cup.

The first Championship, played at Lahinch later that year, attracted only 30 entries. It was won by Cecil Ewing who, having tied with Michael Power (Muskerry) after the allotted 36 holes, took just one hole to win the 'sudden–death' play–off and so become the first recipient of 'The Ewing Trophy'.

In an effort to increase the popularity of the Championship, the Council decided to reduce the age limit to 50 and over for the second Championship at Rosslare. There the entry was 37 and Jack O'Sullivan (Athlone) won. At that time, he was the long–time Honorary Secretary of the Connacht Branch and was regarded as the best scratch golfer in Ireland never to have been awarded an International cap. The age limit was restored to 55 and over in 1972 to keep it in line with other seniors' events.

In 1972 Dr William O'Sullivan (Killarney) presented 'The O'Sullivan Salver' to be awarded to the competitor over the age of 60 who returned the best 36 hole score. Seven years later, Myles McCann (Warrenpoint) presented 'The McCann Rosebowl' for the over 65s and in 1984 Dr Gerald Owens (Skerries) presented 'The Owens Cup' for the over 70s. Of these three donors, only Gerry Owens emulated Cecil Ewing by winning his Cup on the first occasion for which it was competed.

After its initial small entry, the Championship grew in popularity as many of the 'golden oldies', accompanied by their spouses, turned it into a social occasion which gave them the opportunity to renew friendships which had started when they had met in the Close or provincial Championships or in inter–Club matches. The social aspect proved exceedingly popular to such an extent that, in reply to a questionnaire sent to all entrants in the 1981 seniors, the consensus was in favour of an official reception being held in the clubhouse on the evening prior to the commencement of the Championship. It was also agreed that the entry fee should be increased by 100 per cent to provide for this social gathering. They agreed that the Championship be played on a Thursday and Friday instead of over a week-end. Many of the competitors were disappointed that the Council implemented only the last of these views.

The entries continued to increase and in 1986 over 200 were received. At the next Council meeting, it was suggested that the problem could be solved by extending the Championship over three days with the higher handicap players playing on day one with an agreed number qualifying for day three. The rest of the field would play on day two with two–thirds qualifying for day three. Unfortunately for many golden oldies, the majority of whom would be day one players, the low handicap seniors on the Council spoke against the proposal on the grounds that this was a Championship. The Council ruled against the extra day extension and fixed the limit of entries at 180. If the entries exceeded this figure there was a proviso that a ratio in each of four specified age groups would qualify on the lowest exact handicap. This latter proviso was discontinued the following year, and in 1988 the limit was still further reduced to 150 on lowest exact handicap. In 1990 the limit was restored to 180. Since its inauguration the Championship has rotated around the four provinces.

To date, only four of the winners of the Seniors' Championship had earlier recorded victories in other important Irish Championships. These are:

Cecil Ewing (County Sligo)	Irish Amateur Open (1948 and 1951)
	Irish Amateur Close (1948 and 1958)
	West (1930, 1932, 1935, 1939, 1941,
	1942, 1943, 1945, 1949 and 1950).
Brennie Scannell (Woodbrook)	East (1947, 1954 and 1955).
Billy Hulme (Warrenpoint)	East (1944).
Noel Fogarty (Royal Dublin)	East (1963 and 1967), South (1967).

A record of Championship, Over 60, Over 65, and Over 70 winners and venues is set out in Appendix XV.

Chapter 25

PUBLIC GOLF
IN
IRELAND

The origin of the game is shrouded in mystery. Undoubtedly the early exponents were the more affluent members of society. However, as the pioneers mostly played on common-ages or other open spaces, no class of citizen was precluded from following this leisure pastime. Thus public golf must be as old as the game itself.

In 1927 Fred Hawtree (golf course architect) and John H. Taylor (five times Open Champion) founded the National Association of Public Golf Courses. Affiliated to this Association are 98 Golf Clubs in England and Wales which enjoy playing facilities on public golf courses. Scottish public golf Clubs, of which there are 119, have no similar Association but the Scottish Golf Union have advised that the Clubs comply with the constitution of that Union.

The most famous public golf complex is at the home of golf where, under the jurisdiction and control of a Joint Links Committee representing the St Andrews Town Council and the Royal and Ancient Golf Club of St Andrews, there are at present five courses. The best known is the Old Course which is reputed to have been in play since the year 1400, some 350 years before the formation in 1754 of the Society of St Andrews, the precursor of the present Royal and Ancient Golf Club of St Andrews. The other courses are the New Course (1896), the Jubilee (1897), the Eden (1914) and the Balgrove (1972). A sixth course is under construction to meet the increasing demand for facilities.

The development of public golf in Ireland took much longer to materialise. The Honourable Christopher Gaisford St Lawrence, Earl of Howth, farmed extensively on his lands at Howth, Co. Dublin. In addition to tillage, he operated a dairy farm and when he decided to phase out the latter he surrounded Howth Castle and its renowned rhodo-dendron gardens with a number of golf facilities which he opened to the public in 1972. Now there is an 18 hole golf course measuring 6078 metres, a 9 hole course which is being extended to 18 holes, a par 3 course and a pitch and putt course. The complex, which was designed by Fred Hawtree, is known as Deerpark.

Corballis Golf Club had been founded in 1940 and its members played over a natural links amongst the sand dunes at Donabate, Co. Dublin. The links was in an area where a number of holiday chalets had been constructed. Despite defined 'rights of way' through the links to the adjoining beach, the members were constantly faced with the danger of children and adults taking short cuts across fairways at places which were blind to the players because of the nature of the terrain. In 1972 the Club acquired lands for the construction of an 18 hole course adjacent to Dublin Airport. With the move, the Club changed its name to Forrest Little. The Corballis links was acquired by Dublin County Council which retained it as a public golf course. The Council spent a considerable amount of money in making the 'rights of way' safe by building up the ground on the tee side of these paths in such a way that pedestrians could walk to the beach in safety, completely protected by high bank overhangs. The Council also secured the boundaries to prevent trespass.

In 1981 Dublin County Council and Cork City Corporation opened public golf courses at Ballyogan, Stepaside, Co. Dublin and Mahon Peninsula, Cork, respectively. Both courses were designed by Eddie Hackett who also supervised their construction by the respective local authorities. Gratitude is due to this golf course architect for his dedication and expertise over many years in not only designing new courses at various locations throughout Ireland, but in helping Club committees to extend and improve existing courses at a large number of affiliated Clubs. The Stepaside course is 9 holes, measuring 5848 metres and at the time of writing the second 9 holes are at the planning stage. Cork City Corporation originally opened a 12 hole course at Mahon Peninsula on the south side of Cork city and this has since been extended to a full 18 hole course measuring 4869 metres. The Union's involvement in both Stepaside and Mahon is dealt with later in this chapter.

In 1988 the Kilternan Hotel opened the fourth public golf course in the Dublin area adjoining the hotel at the foot of the Dublin Mountains. The course measures 4914 metres.

In the Belfast area, Whitehead Golf Club moved in 1975 to a new location at McCrea's Brae where there is now an 18 hole course. The old Whitehead course was taken over by Carrickfergus Urban District Council and, under the name of Bentra, was opened as a pub-lic golf course.

Castlereagh Urban District Council operates a 9 hole course measuring 5398 metres at Manns Corner, Gilnahirk, whilst Lisburn Urban District Council has a 5770 metres 9 hole course at Aberdelgy, Lambeg. These are modest indeed when one considers the huge following the game has had in this area since the Royal Belfast Golf Club commenced activities in 1881 but consideration is being given by these Councils to extend the facilities.

Over the years criticism has been levelled at the Union for not using its influence in persuading local authorities to include golf in their leisure amenity programmes. The saga of public golf in Ireland and the Union's efforts for the provision of this much needed facility may silence such criticism. Over a period of 85 years the subject had been raised by repre-sentatives of the Union on four occasions, the last three at the highest level of Government.

At a meeting of the Union on 3 March 1906 Henry J. Daly retired as Honorary Secretary and Reverend John L. Morrow was elected in his place. One of Morrow's first public pronouncements was to advocate the provision of public golf courses in the Dublin area. This was just 15 years after the Union had been founded, by which time 155 courses had been opened for play in various parts of Ireland. Happily, 110 of these courses are still in active use. The Honorary Secretary's concern appears to have arisen from the fact that only ten of the 155 courses served the requirements of the citizens of Dublin. John Lumsden, founder of the Dublin (now Royal Dublin) Golf Club was also keenly interested in the idea. Reverend Morrow's hopes and aspirations came to nothing and the subject did not surface again for another 20 years.

Next, the Public Golf Committee tried to have a course laid out at the far reaches of the Phoenix Park which, at 2300 acres, is the largest enclosed public park in Europe. Subject to the approval of the Government, a site was selected to the right of the Hibernian School and extended down to the road at the far end, with the Horse Gallops to the right. A deputation waited on Governor General Timothy Healy and also on the Minister for Finance, whose Department includes the Office of Public Works which manages the Phoenix Park. Following discussions, the Committee was invited to submit a layout. Unfortunately when the plan was submitted it was claimed that the proposed course cut across the established Horse Gallops used by the Army and could not be entertained.

Next, Mr Justice W.E. Wylie, the Land Judge, was appointed by the Government to chair a conference of all interested parties and the matters in dispute were adjusted to the mutual advantage of all concerned. Reverend J.L. Morrow was requested to submit another layout which was approved by the Minister's Department. It was reported that 'the next step will be to secure the necessary funds for the laying out of the course and getting it into some sort of playing order'.[12] In those days there was no sponsorship and as there were no Government or municipal funds available the project had to be abandoned.

The next mention of municipal or public golf appears in the Union minutes more than 30 years on. The minutes record that at the Annual General Meeting of the Central Council on 30 November 1961, the Leinster Branch sought and received support from the Council for the formation of a sub–committee by the branch with a view to approaching the authorities with regard to the provision of a municipal golf course. Intense activity followed, including meetings with Dublin Corporation and the Irish Pitch and Putt Union.

The minutes of the Annual General Meeting of the Central Council of 25 January 1968 record that the Leinster Branch Chairman reported that following consultation with the municipal authorities and with the Board of Works, his Committee had engaged the services of Fred Hawtree, who had visited the Phoenix Park and prepared a layout for an 18 hole course in a suitable area and the plan and report had been submitted to the authorities. He stated that the matter had been referred to the Minister for Finance who would have the final say and his Committee felt confident that this much–needed addition to golf amenities in the Dublin area would be provided.

A lengthy meeting look took place and the following were present: the Leinster Branch Special Sub–Committee, representatives of the Irish Pitch and Putt Union, Bórd Fáilte, the Minister for Finance and the Commissioners of Public Works.

The representatives of the last named indicated that they would present a report to the Commissioners. The Minister later advised the Leinster Branch that the Commissioners

The cover of the ninth EAGTC souvenir programme autographed by the Team Captains. (Chapter 34)

THE EAST OF IRELAND AMATEUR OPEN CHAMPIONSHIP

(Chapter 33 Appendix XXII)

THE LYONS CUP

(The Championship Cup)

Year	Winning Province	Year	Winning Province
1941	J.B. Carr, Sutton	1966	T. Craddock, Malahide
1942	K. Garvey, Co. Louth	1967	G.N. Fogarty, Royal Dublin
1943	J.B. Carr, Sutton	1968	P. Caul, Malahide
1944	J.W. Hulme, Warrenpoint	1969	J.B. Carr, Sutton
1945	J.B. Carr, Sutton	1970	R.J. Carr, Sutton
1946	J.B. Carr, Sutton	1971	P. Mulcare, Woodbrook
1947	B.J. Scannell, Woodbrook	1972	P. Mulcare, Woodbrook
1948	J.B. Carr, Sutton	1973	P. Mulcare, Woodbrook
1949	M. Ferguson, Dundalk	1974	H.B. Smyth, Royal Co. Down
1950	J.P. Carroll, Sutton	1975	A.C.J. Morrow, Portmarnock
1951	M. Power, Muskerry	1976	D. White, Tullamore
1952	N.V. Drew, Bangor	1977	T. Cleary, Fermoy
1953	J.P. Carroll, Sutton	1978	M.A. Gannon, Co. Louth
1954	B.J. Scannell, Woodbrook	1979	A.D. Pierse, Tipperary
1955	B.J. Scannell, Woodbrook	1980	P. Caul, Malahide
1956	J.B. Carr, Sutton	1981	D. Branigan, L'town & B'town
1957	J.B. Carr, Sutton	1982	M.F. Studds, The Island
1958	J.B. Carr, Sutton	1983	A.C.J. Morrow, Portmarnock
1959	T. Craddock, Malahide	1984	R.V.M. Reddan, Co. Louth
1960	J.B. Carr, Sutton	1985	F. Ronan, Co. Louth
1961	J.B. Carr, Sutton	1986	P.F. Hogan, Elm Park
1962	T.W. Egan, Monkstown	1987	P. Rayfus, Trim
1963	G.N. Fogarty, Royal Dublin	1988	G. McGimpsey, Bangor
1964	J.B. Carr, Sutton	1989	D. Clarke, Dungannon
1965	T. Craddock, Malahide	1990	D.F. O'Sullivan, Cork

THE EAST OF IRELAND AMATEUR OPEN CHAMPIONSHIP

(Chapter 34 Appendix XXIII)

THE CARBERY CUP

Year	Winner and Club	Year	Winner and Club
1948	J.P. Carroll (Sutton)	1969	J.J. O'Neill (Donabate)
1949	F.G. Moran (Clontarf)	1970	D.J. Smyth (Laytown & Bettystown)
1950	T.D. Hegarty (Mountbellew)	1971	M. Hanway (Sutton)
1951	G.A. Young (Kilrush)	1972	D. Branigan (Laytown & Bettystown)
1952	B.F. Smyth (Royal Dublin)	1973	R. McDonnell (Laytown & Bettystown)
1953	B.R. Overend (Castle)	1974	B.P. Malone (Portmarnock)
1954	O.M. Lochrin (Co. Louth)	1975	M. Burns (Tramore)
1955	J. O'Reilly (Newlands)	1976	F. Ronan (Co. Louth)
1956	D.C. Macaulay (Donabate)	1977	B. Reck (Lucan)
1957	B.J. Scannell (Woodbrook)	1978	A. Cosgrave (Woodbrook)
1958	J. O'Sullivan (Athlone)	1979	F. Ronan (Co. Louth)
1959	R.A. Howlett (Tramore)	1980	P.F. Hogan (Elm Park)
1960	M. McGuirk (Co. Louth)	1981	B.P. Malone (Elm Park)
1961	F. Gallagher (Co. Louth)	1982	S. McParland (Greenore)
1962	B.J. Scannell (Woodbrook)	1983	R. Rogers (The Island)
1963	B. Rogers (The Island)	1984	P. Lyons (Nenagh)
1964	B. Rogers (The Island)	1985	M. McGinley (Naas)
1965	J.M. Shiels (Foxrock)	1986	B. Rogers (The Island)
1966	G.L. McGuinness (Castle)	1987	T. Boylan (Naas)
1967	B. O'Beirne (Portmarnock)	1988	P. Gribben (Warrenpoint)
1968	H.N. McKeown (Cork)	1989	B. Kinsella (Skerries)
		1990	S. Moore (Royal Portrush)

THE EAST OF IRELAND AMATEUR OPEN CHAMPIONSHIP

(Chapter 33 Appendix XXII)

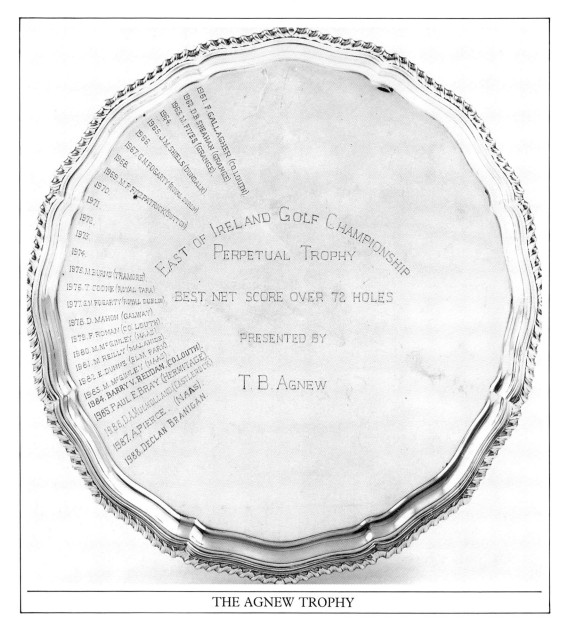

1961. F. GALLAGHER (CO. LOUTH)
1962. D.B. SHEAHAN (GRANGE)
1963. N. FIVES (DUNDALK)
1964.
1965. J.M. SHIELS (GRANGE)
1966.
1967. G.M. FOGARTY (ROYAL DUBLIN)
1968.
1969. M.F. FITZPATRICK (SUTTON)
1970.
1971.
1972.
1973.
1974.
1975. M. BURNS (TRAMORE)
1976. T. COONE (ROYAL TARA)
1977. G.M. FOGARTY (ROYAL DUBLIN)
1978. D. MAHON (GALWAY)
1979. F. RONAN (CO. LOUTH)
1980. M. McGINLEY (NAAS)
1981. M. REILLY (MALAHIDE)
1982. E. DUNNE (ELM PARK)
1983. M. McGINLEY (NAAS)
1984. BARRY V. REDDAN (HERMITAGE)
1985. PAUL E. BRAY (CASTLEROCK)
1986. D.A. MULHOLLAND (CO. LOUTH)
1987. A. PIERCE. (NAAS)
1988. DECLAN BRANIGAN

EAST OF IRELAND GOLF CHAMPIONSHIP
PERPETUAL TROPHY

BEST NET SCORE OVER 72 HOLES

PRESENTED BY

T. B. AGNEW

THE AGNEW TROPHY

Year	Winner and Club	Year	Winner and Club
1961	F. Gallagher (Co. Louth)	1976	T. Coone (Royal Tara)
1962	D.B. Sheahan (Grange)	1977	G.N. Fogarty (Royal Dublin)
1963	M. Fives (Grange)	1978	D. Mahon (Galway)
1964	F. Gallagher (Co. Louth)	1979	F. Ronan (Co. Louth)
1965	J.M. Shiels (Dundalk)	1980	M. McGinley (Naas)
1966	T. Craddock (Malahide)	1981	M. Reilly (Malahide)
1967	G.N. Fogarty (Royal Dublin)	1982	E. Dunne (Elm Park)
1968	R.N. Baker (Monkstown)	1983	M. McGinley (Naas)
1969	M.P. Fitzpatrick (Sutton)	1984	B.V.M. Reddan (Co. Louth)
1970	R.J. Carr (Sutton)	1985	P.E. Bray (Hermitage)
1971	M. Hanway (Sutton)	1986	D.A. Mulholland (Castlerock)
1972	P. Mulcare (Woodbrook)	1987	A. Pierce (Naas)
1973	S.L. Cooney (Milltown)	1988	D. Branigan (L'town & B'town)
1974	S. Rogers (The Island)	1989	B. Byrne (The Island)
1975	M. Burns (Tramore)	1990	B. Hobson (Malone)

THE QUADRANGULAR CONTINENTAL MATCHES

(Chapter 22 Appendix XII)

THE CARTIER CUP

Year	Venue	Winning Country
1972	Killarney, Ireland	Ireland
1976	Cologne, Germany	Sweden
1978	Deauville, France	France
1980	Portmarnock, Ireland	Ireland

Year	Venue	Winning Country
1982	Halmstad, Sweden	Germany
1984	Bad Ems, Germany	Germany
1986	Le Touquet, France	Ireland
1988	Portrush, Ireland	Ireland
1990	Ostersund, Sweden	Ireland

considered that closing off any portion of the Park would contravene the provisions of the Phoenix Park Act 1663, and he had no alternative other than to support their view and refused to sanction the proposal.

This raises some very important matters which should have been mentioned at the time although, in fairness, the Leinster Branch would not have been expected to have been aware of the first one:

1. Why were the findings of the Wylie Conference not referred to, particularly by the Board of Works which had been a party to the conference and must have had a complete file on the subject?

2. How could the Commissioners of Public Works seek to shelter behind the Phoenix Park Act when their predecessors in office had not done so at the Wylie Conference?

3. Furthermore, within the boundaries of the Phoenix Park there existed:

   (i) the former Governor General's official residence and now the official residence of the President of Ireland (Árus an Uachtaráin);
   (ii) the official residence of the Papal Nuncio (since transferred to Navan Road, Cabra);
   (iii) the official residence of the American Ambassador;
   (iv) the Garda Headquarters Training Depot;
   (v) the Zoological Gardens;
   (vi) the People's Gardens;
   (vii) the Ordnance Survey Office;
   all of which are enclosed by security fencing.
   (viii) Two cricket grounds;
   (ix) a polo ground (since disused);
   (x) numerous playing pitches used for Gaelic football, hurling, Association football, lacrosse, camogie and other field sports; all of which are either surrounded by boundary fencing or marked out.

4. The first golf course in the Dublin area had been laid out in the Park in 1885 by John Lumsden and Thomas Gilroy.

5. A private golf course had been laid out in the Governor General's grounds in the Vice-Regal Lodge by George Sayers (father of Ben Sayers) prior to 1902.

Perhaps a more realistic and enlightened view will be taken by the Commissioners should a further effort be made to allow the citizens of Dublin to enjoy more fully their public park.

Dublin Corporation was most sympathetic and the City Manager promised that should a suitable site be found he would make it available for a municipal golf course. Whilst the Minister had felt obliged to accept the advice of the Commissioners, he nevertheless arranged that when land at Chapelizod, on the south side of the Liffey and known as the Phoenix Park Extension was acquired, a feasibility study should be carried out to see if it could be utilised as a public golf course. Eddie Hackett was engaged but as a portion of the land was earmarked for the Western Approach Roadway this project proved also fruitless.

That was in the early 1970s and the subject of public golf remained dormant for another five years. When Don McErvel (Malone and Royal Portrush) was elected President of the

Union in 1976, he pledged to re–activate this whole question of public golf facilities. He approached members of the Northern Ireland Government in his native Belfast and sought a meeting with the Lord Mayor of Belfast. On every occasion when he represented the Union at a golf or other function he pressed for action by the municipal authorities, North and South. When attending the official opening of the new course and clubhouse of Donegal Golf Club at Murvagh in 1976, he met Mr Tom Fitzpatrick, the Republic's Minister for Agriculture, who said that he was so impressed with the President's oratory that he would set up a meeting in Dublin with one of his Ministerial colleagues and the Union. At the next meeting of the Standing Committee, the President reported on a meeting which he and the other officers of the Union had had with the Ministers in the Departments of Education, Local Government, Finance and Transport and Power. The President also reported on meetings which he had with different Ministries in Belfast and with Belfast Corporation. It was undoubtedly as a result of Don McErvel's efforts that Belfast now has public golf, and he must also be given credit for the breakthrough made in Dublin.

The Union officers were next asked to meet Mr John Bruton, the Parliamentary Secretary to the Minister for Education in Dublin. At that meeting the GUI President pointed out that clear evidence showed that public golf courses are profitable. He mentioned Deerpark in Howth and the very large number of successful public golf courses in England.

John Bruton then put it to the President that 'if these are all that profitable, why does the Union not start one on its own?' The President pointed out that the Union had no possibility of obtaining the land required at affordable prices to build even one public golf course. John Bruton then said 'If I can get the local authority to put up the land would the Union put up the money?' The President assured him that this would be done. This proved the breakthrough as the GUI were next invited to attend at the offices of Dublin County Council. The Union appointed the Honorary Secretary, Des Rea O'Kelly, as Convenor of a Public Golf Facilities Committee with power to co–opt. He first invited the President, Don McErvel, the former Honorary Secretary, Willie Gill and Dr Gerry Owens, who had been Leinster Branch Chairman when that branch sought to activate the construction of the Fred Hawtree layout in the Park, to form his initial Committee and to meet with Dublin County Council.

It transpired that the County Council owned an area of grassland adjoining its refuse tip at Ballyogan, Stepaside, which it would make available for development as a public golf course subject to satisfactory arrangements. The Facilities Committee decided to invite Eddie Hackett to conduct a feasibility study and he reported that the area would be suitable for a 9 hole course.

Negotiations resulted in agreement. Dublin County Council would retain ownership of the land and if the Union paid it £60,000, County Council staff would construct a 9 hole golf course to Eddie Hackett's design and under his supervision. In addition, when refuse tipping was completed at the adjoining Ballyogan site, the Council would cover the area with topsoil and landscape it to Eddie Hackett's requirements and, on its part, the Union would pay the County Council a further £84,000 towards the construction of the second 9 holes.

In exchange for its funding, which was not a loan but an outright payment, the County Council would pay annually to the Union a stated percentage of gross green fee income from Stepaside, as the course was to be known, for 25 years following the completion of the 18 hole course.

Officials of the Golfing Union of Ireland and officials of the Dublin County Council at the signing of the Agreement on 17 May 1978 under which, with funding provided by the Union, the County Council developed the first municipal public golf facility in Ireland.

The 1990 Irish International Team, winners of the Cartier Trophy at Ostersund, Sweden.
Left to Right: standing: J. Carvill, D. Clarke, H. Bennett (National Coach),
N. Goulding and P. McGinley.
Seated: G. McGimpsey, C.F. Crosbie (Non-Playing Captain),
G.D. Golden (President GUI) and L. MacNamara.
(Chapter 2)

The Central Council of the Union had been kept informed as the negotiations progressed. However, there were many members of the Council who were unhappy with the financial proposals on the grounds that even if the project became the success everyone hoped for, the Union would be placing financial constraints on its normal activities for too many years; if the project failed the Union would be at a complete loss of the investment. In addition, it was agreed that it would be some years before the first 9 holes would be open for play to engender green fees from which the Union would receive a percentage. Word of these problems must have got back to the County Council, as the Chairman, Councillor John Boland TD, intimated that as soon as the legal agreement was executed, the Council would pay the Union a stated percentage of gross green fee income from the Council's existing public golf course at Corballis for 25 years. Whilst this proposal did much to assuage the fears of those members of the GUI Council who had earlier expressed concern, it was the Honorary Secretary who, as Convenor of the Public Golf Facilities Committee, finally satisfied them regarding the advantages to be gained, not only by both sides, but also by the very large number of non–Club golfers who would wish to avail of the facility. He produced projections of anticipated income which showed a return of the Union's investment within 12 years. The legal agreement was signed on 17 May 1979. The popularity of the course was such that the Honorary Secretary's projections turned out to be conservative.

Shortly after negotiations commenced with Dublin County Council, an enquiry was received from Cork City Corporation. It too had lands and required funds to help develop a public golf course. The lands were at Mahon Peninsula and Eddie Hackett reported that the area would eventually accommodate 18 holes, of which 12 holes could be laid out immediately. Unlike Dublin County Council, Cork City Corporation was seeking a loan repayable without interest if stated instalments were paid within a fixed period. The Convenor agreed the final terms with Cork City Manager. A legal agreement was signed on 23 October 1979 under which the Union would lend £35,000 to Cork City Corporation for the development of the first 12 holes. No repayment was to be made for two years and no interest was payable on any outstanding capital for five years. After two years the Corporation would commence repaying the capital at the rate of 20 per cent of the gross green fee income, or more if it wished to discharge the loan sooner. In addition, because of the Union's participation, the Corporation agreed to pay an additional 5 per cent annually subject to review every ten years. The 12 holes were officially opened on 3 September 1980. A further £35,000 was lent to the Corporation to complete the last 6 holes. The full course is now in play, the first loan has been repaid and it is anticipated that the entire debt will be cleared within the time limit laid down.

At no time was it the intention of the Union to accumulate a profit from these investments. The Central Council anticipates that the provision of further public golf courses is a vital necessity and it has opened a special Public Golf Facilities Account. When its investments in the two courses have been recouped, any further income will be earmarked for the future development of additional public golf courses. Already Dublin County Council, which has developed a number of par 3 courses on the perimeter of the city, is talking about developing public golf courses at Blanchardstown, Tallaght and Clondalkin. Whilst the Union would be anxious for facilities to be made available at other centres in Ireland, each application from a local authority will be considered and each case will be decided on its merits.

Chapter 26

THE
DEVELOPMENT
OF GOLF
IN IRELAND

Period: 1976 to 1990

This period continued to be one of increasing activity with the introduction of new events to the golfing calendar.

In 1976 the Union was presented with a merit award by the retiring Honorary Secretary, Willie Gill, for competition in conjunction with the Close, and the four Provincial Championships which the Union named 'The Willie Gill Award'. (See Chapter 27.)

In 1977 the Union inaugurated two new tournaments and elevated another to all-Ireland status. At the instigation of the Connacht Branch an inter-Club Tournament for middle handicap players and named 'The Jimmy Bruen Shield' was introduced to fill the gap in the inter-Club team tournament programme and proved most popular. The Union also decided on the need for an inter-County Championship. This was a variation of an inter-County Tournament which had been started in 1911 and converted to an inter-Club event some years later. (See Chapter 10.) In 1972 both Connacht and Leinster had started an inter-Club Mixed Foursomes competition which the Union took over in 1977 and extended to an all-Ireland event.

On the international side, and also in 1977, Ireland made her first entry into Europe at junior level in the European Amateur Youth's Golf Team Championship, and three years later entered the newly established European Amateur Boys' Golf Team Championship.

Development of the game in Ireland continued. Despite the increasing costs of acquiring land and having a course designed and constructed, 29 new Clubs became affiliated to the Union, bringing the total of active Clubs to an all-time high of 274. These Clubs are:

1976   *Brown Trout, A 1984; Moyola Park, A 1977.*
1977   *Cabra Castle, A 1982; Old Conna (originally Dublin Sport), A 1977.*
1978   *Blainroe, A 1978.*
1980   *Clane, A 1980.*
1982   *Castleblayney, A 1984; Mahon, A 1982.*
1983   *Redcastle, A 1983.*
1984   *Beaverstown, A 1985; Frankfield, A 1984; Gilnahirk, A 1984; Silverwood (originally Craigavon), A 1984.*
1985   *Kilcock, A 1985, Knockanally, A 1985.*
1986   *Cruit Island, A 1986; Four Lakes, A 1986; Knockbracken, A 1986.*
1987   *Cobh, A 1987.*
1988   *Black Bush, A 1988; Hazel Grove, A 1988; Westmanstown, A 1988.*
1989   *Castletownbere, A 1989; European, A 1989; Lambeg, A 1989; Raffeen Creek, A 1989.*
1990   *Castlewarden, A 1990; Tubbercurry, A 1990; Tulfarris, A 1990.*

Many reasons are advanced for this sustained growth. Apart from additional leisure time, the main reason has been the impact of television. We have mentioned, in Chapter 19, the upsurge of interest in the early 1960s and the period between 1976 and the present day shows a marked increase in television coverage of international and tournament golf which portrays the increasing involvement of Irish players, both amateur and professional, in world golf.

The National Panel was introduced in 1978. The standard of play of our established players and many of our younger players improved dramatically. This was further enhanced when, in 1983, the Union appointed a National Coach. The lucrative professional career has enticed many of the younger amateurs to make the transition to professional golf. This has caused a considerable loss to the amateur game in this country, but nevertheless we wish them well, being happy in the knowledge that whatever successes they achieve is a credit to Ireland and to the Union which helped them in their formative years.

Chapter 13 briefly mentioned the setting up of the Joint Advisory Council in 1924 at the request of the R & A. An examination of the minute books shows that five years later at an annual meeting of the Council on 11 September 1929 it was reported that the JAC had decided 'to establish a Board of Research for Golf Greenkeeping in Great Britain and Ireland to be elected annually and that the control and management of research be vested in the JAC'. The title of the new organisation was The Board of Greenkeeping Research and its head-quarters were at St Ives Research Station, Bingley, Yorkshire. The Board engaged scientists and other professional staff who, in addition to commencing research programmes to study soils and grasses, offered advisory services on request to Clubs affiliated to the four home Unions. To help member Clubs avail of the service, the GUI paid a comprehensive annual subscription to the Institute. This entitled Irish Clubs to use the technical and practical ser-vices as often as desired and unlimited postal advice including examining and reporting on samples (soil, grasses, weeds, pests, diseases etc.) which was provided without extra charge. The GUI also organised periodic visits by an advisory officer from the Institute to groups of Clubs on payment of a fee which the Union also subsidised.

As the Institute gained in status other sporting organisations sought its services and in 1951 the JAC authorised the Board to extend the scope of its influence, to change its name to the Sports Turf Research Institute and embark on a much wider programme. Now, most of the field sports Unions and Associations are members and have representation on the Board of Management. With the change in emphasis the Board also adjusted its financial arrangements with the GUI. Instead of accepting a comprehensive annual subscription from the Union, the Board introduced an individual Club subscription which already operated in England, Scotland and Wales and was graded on 9, 18 and 27/36 hole courses. The Union advised all the Clubs of the new arrangement, exhorted them to continue supporting the work of the Institute and stated that it would contribute 25 per cent of the subscription payable by individual Clubs. It was arranged that a Club would forward to the Union 75 per cent of the subscription claimed and the Union would pay the full subscription to the Institute. The Board of Management comprises 24 members, over half of whom represent golf interests. The latest accounts show that the subscriptions received from golf Clubs are more than the total received from all other sports organisations.

As part of his business travels Jimmy Lenehan (Portmarnock) visited golf courses in various parts of America. Over there the title of the Head Greenkeeper is Course Superintendent. Jimmy took the opportunity of discussing the modern methods used by these Superintendents in course maintenance and upkeep and was shown the wide range of equipment available for this purpose. Here in Ireland on similar visits to our affiliated Clubs, he noted that few Head Greenkeepers had knowledge of these modern methods and most of the equipment in use was inadequate. Worse still, when the Head Greenkeeper retired there was usually no competent replacement on the existing staff. In Elm Park, Castle and Newlands, to mention three Clubs, he came across Head Greenkeepers who, through study and examination, had become certified qualified Greenkeepers. As a result, the greens and general condition of the courses under their care were the envy of many other Clubs. Jimmy approached the three Greenkeepers, Jim Byrne, Chris Nolan and Seamus Kelly and intimated that he was prepared to sponsor the setting up of an Association with the object of improving the standard of greenkeeping in Ireland. The advice and guidance of Dr Harry Spain (Elm Park), Deputy Secretary of the Department of Agriculture, was sought and between them the Irish Golf Greenkeepers' Association was established in 1974. The main aims of the Association are:

(1) to enhance the education and training of Greenkeepers and thereby bring direct benefits to golf Clubs and their members through improved course maintenance and development.
(2) To advance the status and improve the image of the professional Greenkeeper.
(3) To encourage Greenkeepers to play golf in order to improve their knowledge of the game and awareness of the needs of members.

In the following year, 1975, the Golf Foundation organised a Greenkeeping Conference as it became concerned at the number of Greenkeepers leaving golf to take up a more remunerative position with industrial firms which were developing sport complexes for their employees. The Standing Conference on Golf Greenkeeping was established with a Board comprising representatives from the four Home Unions, the R & A, the Golf Foundation, the Golf Development Council, the Greenkeepers' Association and the Golf Clubs' Secretaries Association. Its main aim was to encourage youths to take up greenkeeping as a career. A syllabus on greenkeeper training of the City and Guilds of London Institute, the recognised authority on this subject, was adopted.

The GUI Council appointed a committee with provincial representation which decided, as a first step, to issue a questionnaire to all Clubs seeking information regarding the number and competence of their ground staff. It was agreed that where a Club was satisfied with the technical and practical capabilities of its Head Greenkeeper, he could apply to the Standing

Conference Training Committee and become registered as a qualified Greenkeeper. By the end of 1980 a total of 98 Irish Greenkeepers had become registered through this facility. The next step was to arrange courses for trainees at a location in Ireland. The Council appointed Dr Harry Spain as Irish representative on the Standing Conference Training Committee. He advised that Dr Paul Cusack, Director of ACOT (Council for the Development of Agriculture), now Teagasc (the Agricultural and Food Development Authority), had been authorised to accept groups of 14 for specialised training courses in the National Botanic Gardens, Glasnevin, Dublin. Clubs were invited to enroll ground staff for a course which would extend over two years and comprise three 2 week block-release sessions each year after which the trainee would sit an examination set by the City and Guilds of London Institute for a certificate as a qualified Greenkeeper.

The scheme got off to a slow start but has since gained momentum as Clubs realise the benefits which accrue. As the game continues to increase in popularity, it is gratifying to see that more and more Clubs are investing, not only in their ground staff, but also in the modern equipment and machinery now available to ensure that courses are maintained to the standard which the members have come to require.

Also mindful of the necessity of improving clubhouses, members sanctioned proposals to extend and modernise their premises to provide additional and more comfortable facilities. In the early days clubhouses were used only as changing rooms. Today, these buildings with bar, catering and other attendant leisure activities have become a focal point in the social life of the members.

One might expect that after 100 years things would be slowing down. The contrary is the case in the Union and in the game in Ireland at all levels. Never has this leisure pastime been more vibrant and it is most heartening to everyone associated with the administration of golf in Ireland that it continues to grow in popularity and gives so much pleasure to young and old alike.

We can only record our gratitude to the pioneers who brought golf to Ireland and to those who, down the years, nurtured it to bring it to its present healthy state.

MERIT AWARDS

Illustrations throughout this history show the trophies presented to teams and individuals for achievements in national, provincial, inter-county and inter-Club championships and tournaments. It was only in the last 15 years that the idea of an individual merit award for consistent performances during the golfing season emerged and credit for this must be given to Willie Gill who was an outstanding player and administrator.

Willie was born in Sutton where he lived for most of his lifetime. He first joined Sutton Golf Club and became one of its leading players. He was a member of the 1928 Sutton team which won the Barton Cup. He was the leading amateur in the 1931 Open Championship of Ireland, played that year at the Royal Dublin Links, Dollymount. Also as a member of Sutton, he received his first international 'cap' in a match against Wales at the Royal Liverpool Golf Club, Hoylake, in the same year. At that time he was also a member of Portmarnock Golf Club and he was a member of both the Portmarnock Senior Cup and Barton Shield teams which won the two tournaments in 1930. Whilst he remained a member of Sutton all his life, he turned to Portmarnock for his competitive golf. In addition to 1930, he helped Portmarnock to win the Senior Cup on five subsequent occasions and the Barton Shield four other times up to 1940 after which both tournaments were suspended for five years because of the war. Although he was a regular competitor in the Close Championship, he never managed to reach the final stages. In fact, the only final of note in which he was involved was the 1940 West of Ireland in which he was defeated by John Burke. He was selected as a member of the Irish team to play in the inaugural Quadrangular International Matches at Troon in 1932 and continued to play in these matches for the next five years. In all, he played 24 times for Ireland winning 13 matches and halving one. He also won the Tailtean Games International Championship in 1932.

However, it is not as a player that he will be best remembered, but for his administrative qualities. First to recognise these was the committee of Portmarnock Golf Club where he was elected Honorary Secretary in 1942, an office he held up to 1953. He had the honour of being Captain of Portmarnock on two occasions; the first in 1944 during his period as Honorary Secretary and again in 1960 when the Club was host to the Canada (World) Cup. Eight years later he was elected President of Portmarnock, a position he held until his death in 1981.

On a wider scene, Willie guided the affairs of the Union for 27 years. His first association with the Union was when he was elected by the Leinster Branch as a delegate to the Central Council in 1946. At the 1949 AGM he was appointed Honorary Secretary of the Union. He served as Honorary secretary until 1976, with the exception of 1968 and 1969, when he was elected firstly President-Elect and then President of the Union.

A year before he was appointed Honorary Secretary, Willie had been elected an Irish International Selector, a position he retained until 1959. He was Irish Team Captain for the three years 1954 to 1956 and he had the honour, at the Royal Birkdale Golf Club in 1955, of being the first Irish Captain to accept the Raymond International Trophy on behalf of Ireland.

An example of Willie's concern for the affairs of the Union and his interest in it was shown in 1974. Because of failing health, he felt that he could no longer adequately fulfill his duties and he intimated to the Central Council his wish to retire. He suggested that to ensure a smooth transition and to maintain continuity, he would welcome the appointment of his successor as Joint Honorary Secretary for one year. When this was agreed he put forward the name of Desmond Rea O'Kelly (Howth) to fill this position. The Union has been most fortunate during the last four decades of its history in having two such efficient and dedicated officers occupying this premier position.

When he learned that the Council intended to make a presentation to him to mark his long service to Irish Golf (we had to ask him what form of memento he would like), he said that he did not want anything for himself. He intimated that he would be happy to accept some type of trophy which could be awarded in perpetuity on merit performances in the Championships. The Union considered what type of trophy would be appropriate and Ivan Dickson, then Secretary of the Leinster Branch, suggested that a trophy in the form of an open book would be in keeping with Willie's business of printer and publisher. Willie gave his Honorary Secretary's gold badge of office which was inserted at the base of the trophy and, at the 1976 AGM the incoming President, Don McErvel (Malone and Royal Portrush) presented the trophy to Willie who handed it back to the Union for annual competition.

With Willie's approval a merit table was drawn up which is included in the complete conditions set out in Appendix XVI (Section 1). A record of winners, their Clubs and points accumulated is set out in Appendix XVI (Section 2).

Possibly because the Union made a special presentation to Raymond Burns (Banbridge) who achieved the 'grand slam' by winning all four Provincial Boys' Open Championships in 1989, the Junior Golf Committee asked the Central Council to inaugurate merit awards at both youth and boy level. At the 1990 AGM, the Council approved the inauguration of the Joe Carr Award for the best performance by a youth in the Youths' Amateur Open Championship of Ireland and the four Provincial Youth Championships and the Tom

Montgomery Award for the best performance by a boy in the Irish Boys' Amateur Close Championship and the four Provincial Boys' Championships.

Joe Carr, whose achievements are recorded in Chapter 36 on Irish Walker Cup players, generously presented one of his replica trophies for his award.

Tom Montgomery was first elected as an Ulster Delegate to the Central Council in 1956. Four years later, he was elected Honorary Secretary of the Ulster Branch and in 1967 he became Ulster Chairman and a Vice-President of the Union. Having served as President-Elect in 1971, he was elected President of the Union in 1972. This was followed by his appointment, two years later, as a Trustee of the Union.

Running parallel to his Branch and Union activities was the prominent part he took in shaping and promoting junior golf affairs. When the Union initiated its programme for the promotion of junior golf, Tom, representing Ulster, together with Gerry Owens (Leinster), Ned Treacy (Munster) and Rev. Patrick O'Brien (Connacht) were elected the first Junior Golf Committee at the 1959 AGM, with Tom as Convenor. He was re-appointed Convenor for 22 successive years during which period he played a large part in the inauguration of international and interprovincial matches and Championships at both youth and boy level which are listed in the chapter on Junior Golf.

One of the highlights of Tom's term of office was when, as non-playing Captain, he led an Irish junior team to victory in the first Irish entry into Europe at that level in Oslo in 1977. He relinquished both his Chairmanship of junior golf and trusteeship of the Union in 1980.

The 1990 winner of the Joe Carr Award was R. Coughlan (Birr)–115 points and S. Quinlivan (Ballybunion)–135 points became the first winner of Tom Montgomery Award.

Chapter 28

THE
JIMMY BRUEN
SHIELD

The Connacht Branch submitted the following notice of motion to the 1977 AGM of the Central Council: 'that a competition on the lines of the Pierce Purcell Shield be inaugurated for golfers of 6 to 11 handicap. The combined handicaps to be not less than 16.' When moving the motion, Thomas Rogers (Roscommon), Chairman of the branch, suggested teams of ten.

Ulster was in favour; Munster expressed the view that it was worthy of consideration whilst Leinster was against it as the branch thought that the tournament would adversely affect the long established Barton Cup in Leinster. The Council decided to defer a decision until the October AGM to give Leinster time to reconsider the matter. At the AGM, Leinster intimated its acquiescence and the Tournament was inaugurated in 1978. The Connacht Branch was invited to name the tournament. 'The Jimmy Bruen Shield' was submitted and the Council accepted it. Jimmy's record will be discussed in Chapter 36 on Irish Walker Cup players.

The agreed format provides for teams of ten, play by foursomes, the minimum handicap eligibility is 6 and 17 is the minimum of the sum of combined handicaps. (It was increased to this figure with the introduction of the 1983 SSS and handicapping scheme.)

In the inaugural year, 151 Clubs entered teams. Gort, Stackstown, Monkstown and Warrenpoint won through in their respective provinces to the national final at Galway Golf Club where Stackstown became the first holder of the Shield. A record of winning Clubs and teams in the Jimmy Bruen Shield is set out in Appendix XVII.

There are now five inter-Club tournaments covering all ranges of handicap in member Clubs. Whilst the Union retains overall jurisdiction, each branch organises its provincial section and is required to advise Union headquarters of the name of the Club which will represent the province in the national finals. These finals are held over three days towards the end of the golfing season at a venue decided by the Central Council. The venue rotates around the four provinces. Interest is such that the venue must have adequate hotel accommodation as, apart from the 20 teams, reserves and each Team and Club Captain, there is always tremendous spectator support from members of the competing Clubs.

In addition to provincial and national pennants, the Union awards medals to each team member and reserve: gold to the winners, silver to the defeated finalists and bronze to the two defeated semi-finalists. A few years ago the Council also decided to present each national final Team Captain with a silver gilt Captain's badge. The inter-Club tournaments have become an integral part of competitive golf at all levels in Ireland.

Chapter 29

THE IRISH GOLF CLUBS' MIXED FOURSOMES CUP

In 1972 Connacht and Leinster inaugurated an Inter-Club Mixed Foursomes Tournament for which Independent Newspapers presented a trophy and prizes for the interprovincial final. Eighteen Clubs entered the Connacht section and 38 the Leinster section. Athlone defeated Mountbellew in the Connacht final and Tullamore won in Leinster by defeating Dun Laoghaire and went on to beat Athlone in the decider. Munster joined the other two provinces in 1974 and 29 Clubs took part in the Munster section that year.

The Tournament continued to grow in popularity and this prompted the Standing Committee to submit the recommendation to the 1977 AGM of the Central Council 'that if Ulster joined the other three provinces in competing in an All-Ireland Mixed Foursomes Tournament for Club teams, the control and management of the Tournament would be taken over by the Union and run on similar lines to the Cups and Shields Tournaments and a suitable Perpetual Challenge Trophy should be purchased.' Ulster agreed to participate and the Council implemented the recommendation. It was decided to award gold, silver and bronze brooches to the ladies and medals of similar content to the men as in the other Union inter-Club tournaments and also to purchase a perpetual challenge cup. Independent Newspapers were advised of the extension of the tournament to an all-Ireland event and invited to continue sponsorship on an increased scale, but the company declined to do so.

At the 1978 AGM, the Council approved the conditions of the re-structured event which prescribed that teams would consist of ten players, combined handicaps would be from a minimum of 18 to a maximum of 36, strokes allowance would be as on the men's Club card where the match is being played and men would drive off the first tee in all rounds. The Council also gratefully accepted the offer of sponsorship from P.J. Carroll and

Company, the generous sponsors of the Open Championship of Ireland for many years. The sponsorship included payment of the cost of the perpetual challenge cup and the annual payment of the cost of the brooches and medals for the national final. Carroll's were also anxious to host a buffet meal for all teams and officials in the clubhouse on the evening prior to the commencement of the national final. For the first two years the Union would not sanction this request. This was because the Union did not wish to create a precedent which it might be expected to follow in the other cups and shields national finals. However, as the mixed national final is held on a different weekend from them a problem would not arise and in 1980 at Royal Tara Golf Club the first buffet meal was provided. This was an enormous success. Firstly, Carroll's give the host Club a generous injection of funds and asks the Club to provide a buffet for up to 130 guests. In addition, and this adds enormously to the success of the national final, the four teams and their officials get to know each other at the function thus helping to ensure that the competition the following day is played, though keenly contested, in a most friendly and sporting manner.

The number of entries and provincial winners in the first year was: Connacht 24 (Ballina); Leinster 53 (Slade Valley); Munster 29 (Ennis) and Ulster 52 (Donaghadee). The national final was played at Royal Portrush Golf Club where both semi-finals were won by 3 matches to 2, Ennis beating Ballina and Donaghadee beating Slade Valley. In the final, Donaghadee beat Ennis by 4 matches to 1. An analysis of the results of the Cups and Shields winners show that this was the first occasion Donaghadee won a Union tournament. None of the other three finalists had ever won a Union tournament and Ennis had to wait until 1985 before it got its name on the Mixed Cup.

The record of winning Clubs and teams is set out in Appendix XVIII.

The Union decided that, as in the other inter-Club tournaments, 'freezing' of handicaps would operate. This 'freezing' was introduced to avoid the temptation of a player nursing his handicap to ensure eligibility throughout the extent of the tournament. Because of the limits prescribed on handicaps in the different tournaments, it ensured that a player would still be eligible to represent his Club irrespective of any adjustment in handicap during the playing of the various rounds. The Munster Branch advocated similar freezing of ladies' handicaps, but the Irish Ladies' Golf Union advised that under its regulations no player is entitled to compete in any competition on other than her current handicap.

As in the other inter-Club events, the Council fixed a rota for the national final: 1978 Ulster; 1979 Connacht; 1980 Leinster and 1981 Munster and so on. When fixing provincial rotas, the Council arranged that the Close, the Interprovincials, the Cups and Shields national finals and the Mixed national final would be allocated in such a manner that each province would have one of these events each year.

Whilst Clubs take the selection of teams for the inter-Club events most seriously with panels, trials, etc., the activity which takes place in matching suitable pairings for the Mixed creates enormous interest and camaraderie between the men's and ladies' sections within the Clubs. Over the years in the Cups and Shields national finals, the joys and the depressions of players who have won or lost their match is evident; but only in the Mixed national finals does the players' nervousness on the first tee show through and also the agony and ecstasy both during and after the matches. The supporters' Clubs are increasing in number each year in all the events.

Chapter 30

THE EUROPEAN AMATEUR YOUTHS' AND BOYS' GOLF TEAM CHAMPIONSHIPS

Following the inauguration of the adult EAGTC in 1959, the EGA turned its attention to a Championship for players under 22 years of age. The European Amateur Junior Golf Team Championship was commenced in 1960 and was played annually. In the late 1970s when the EGA was considering an under 18 boys' event, the EAJGTC became known as the European Amateur Youths' Golf Team Championship (EAYGTC) and it is by this title that it is hereafter referred.

In 1975, the Junior Golf Committee, to further its aims of improving the standard of golf of younger players, sought permission from the Central Council for Ireland to enter the EAYGTC. Because it was an annual event, the Council considered that the financial implications were too much and reluctantly turned down the proposal. The Junior Committee was nothing if not persistent. It put forward the case that competing against one another in internal events was not a satisfactory method of enabling young players, who would become the backbone of the adult international teams, to gain adequate competitive experience. The Council conceded the point.

The first Irish junior team with officials set out for the 17th EAYGTC at Oslo Golf Club in July 1977. To keep expenses to a minimum, all teams and officials were accommodated in the University of Oslo. The Norwegian Golf Federation and the Club committee deserve the highest commendation for the excellent arrangements and the condition of the course which had been under four feet of snow just four weeks earlier. The course is playable for only four or five months each year. A novel and expense-saving arrangement operates in Oslo Golf Club. Each hole is sponsored by a commercial concern (banks, insurance companies, etc.) with a plaque on each tee displaying the name of the sponsor. At the end

The 1977 Irish Youths' International Team at Oslo, Norway. Winners of Championship.

Left to Right: P.M. O'Boyle, S. Flanagan, B. McDaid, P.J. Foley (President GUI), T. Montgomery (Non-Playing Captain), P. O'Hagen, D.P. O'Connor and T. Corridan.

The 1979 Irish Youths' International Team at Marianske Lazne, Czechoslovakia. Winners of Championship.

Left to Right: B.J. Scannell (President GUI), J. Collins, P. Walton, B. McDaid, B.T. Crymble (Non-Playing Captain), R. Rafferty, R. Hanna and T. Corridan.

1984 Irish Youths' International Team at Hermitage. Winners of Championship.

Left to Right: standing: J. Morris, J. McHenry, E. O'Connell and J. Carvill. Seated: P. Murphy, W.J.J. Ferguson (President GUI), F.P. McDonnell (Non-Playing Captain) and J. Farrell.

of each financial year the Club auditors assess the total cost of course maintenance and reconstruction and simply divide the amount by the number of holes and each sponsor pays an equal amount.

At the conclusion of the 36-hole medal play Ireland qualified in fifth place in the first flight. Ireland's first match was against the host country, Norway. Having halved the foursomes, one match each, Ireland won four of the five singles, two of them at tie holes. This brought the Irish team up against the favourites, Sweden, whose qualifying score had been 20 strokes lower. Again Ireland halved the foursomes and, after some very exciting golf, won the singles by the odd match. In the final against France the Irish team made a disastrous start by losing both foursomes. However, the first two singles were won to draw level, then Ireland lost the third and won the fourth, both on the last green. Eventually Ireland won by 4 matches to 3 thus emulating the adult Irish international team by winning on her first entry in the Championship. The detailed results of the medal play rounds, order of qualification, matchplay results and final order of merit are set out in Appendix XIX (Section 1).

Ireland competed each year thereafter until 1984 when the EGA decided to terminate the Championship. During the eight years in which Ireland played, an impressive record was built up winning in Norway (1977), Czechoslovakia (1979), and Hermitage, Ireland (1984). Ireland was runner-up in Iceland (1981) having been third in Germany the previous year. The record of venues, Team Captains, winning countries and Ireland's position in the order of merit since our first entry is set out in Appendix XIX (Section 2). The record of Ireland's youths' international representatives is set out in Appendix XIX (Section 3).

The Junior Golf Committee requested the Central Council to instruct Ireland's EGA representatives to advocate the re-introduction of the EAYGTC. The matter was raised at the 1987 meeting of the General Assembly and, with the support of a number of other member countries, agreement was reached in 1989 to recommence the Championship in 1990 and play it in alternative years to the adult Team Championship, the EAGTC.

Possibly to persuade the EGA that there was a place for the youth event, a number of member countries (including Ireland) competed in what was termed a 'mini' series in Italy in 1988 where Sweden emerged the winner and in Belgium in 1989 where Spain won. Ireland came third in Italy and fifth in Belgium.

Ireland's EGA representatives were most supportive in discussions that the EGA should extend its activities by introducing another championship, this time for the under 18 age group. The EGA had presented two trophies of a similar style for its two higher age group championships and when the decision to inaugurate the Boys' Championship was made Gerald Micklem, who had been EGA President from 1967 to 1969, presented a perpetual silver salver for this event.

The regulations originally prescribed for teams of four players with, after flight qualification, two foursomes and three singles matchplay. This operated for the first two Championships in Spain (1980) and Italy (1981). For the third Championship in Germany, the teams were increased to five players and the matchplay format was altered to two foursomes and five singles. The number on each team was increased to six from 1985 onwards giving captains a wider choice in the deployment of their players and the regulations are now uniform in the three European Team Championships for male teams.

From an entry of nine countries in 1980, the number of competing countries has grown to 19 thus clearly vindicating the decision of the EGA to inaugurate this lower age event. Only Czechoslovakia, Hungary, Luxembourg and Yugoslavia of the 23 member countries have not, so far, competed. This could be attributed to the dual problems of some of the smaller golfing countries: scarcity of finance and lack of an adequate number of young players from which to select a team.

Ireland has entered a team each year since the Championship was inaugurated in 1980. This, together with the boys' home international matches, inaugurated by the R & A in 1985, gives younger players a tremendous incentive to improve their game and to achieve international honours. The record of venues, Team Captains and Ireland's position in the order of merit and Ireland's Boys International Representatives are set out in Appendix XIX (Section 4).

Chapter 31

THE IRISH INTERNATIONAL SELECTION COMMITTEE AND THE NATIONAL PANEL

Selection Committees, from Club to national level, are not held accountable for their actions when selecting teams. No minutes of their meetings are recorded. Following collective discussion, the team is announced. Not all such announcements meet with universal approval by members of the golfing public. Nevertheless, it is appreciated that the task of a Selection Committee is not an easy one, particularly when choosing the last few places — there is usually a number of players of equal ability. However, it is generally accepted that the final choice has been made only after the claims of all candidates have been carefully evaluated.

Today the Irish International Selection Committee consists of five members elected annually by the Central Council. The Council first elect a non-playing Captain, whose term of office is for a maximum of three years. The Captain is also Chairman and Convener of selectors. The Council then elect four other members. Over the years there have been suggestions that there should be one selector from each province but these have been rejected by the Council.

There is no evidence regarding the method of selection of Ireland's pre-1932 international teams. When the JAC agreed to Ireland's request to inaugurate an annual series between teams representing England, Ireland, Scotland and Wales, the GUI appointed a Selection Committee of nine to pick the Irish team. At that time and for the next few years the Committee included the officers in the Union. The records show that in 1937 the Committee numbered 13 persons, but from 1938 onwards the Committee was reduced to five and the officers of the Union were excluded.

Until 1947 the Captain was a member of the team, but it was then decided that a non-playing Captain would not only be more practical but would relieve the playing incumbent of additional pressures. Whilst there was no specific regulation, the Council's choice for non-playing Captain had always been a former international player. In a restructured constitution adopted by the Union in 1968, it was prescribed that when electing the Captain 'preference would be given to one who had been selected to represent Ireland as an international player.' This clear directive was implemented up to 1985 when the Council enlarged the scope of choice by prescribing that 'when making such appointment the Central Council shall give preference to one who had been selected to represent Ireland as a senior international player or his province as a senior interprovincial player.' Following this decision Eamon Curran (Woodbrook), a former Connacht interprovincial player, was elected Irish Team Captain.

A list of Irish international Team Captains from 1900 is set out in Appendix IX (Sections 1 and 4), and a record of Irish International Selection Committees since 1932 is set out in Appendix XX.

In his presidential review at the end of his term of office, Patrick J. Foley (Muskerry), sowed the seed for a more professional approach to improving Ireland's standing at international level. Before relinquishing office at the 1978 AGM, he presented this review to the Central Council: 'One cannot escape the responsibility of mentioning the unpalatable facts that see us lingering somewhat behind in the international playing league . . . in my view the time for action has come and a recommendation that would receive my benediction would see the immediate formation of a hand picked squad of players that, with an extended and closely supervised training regimen, would have, as their objective, the winning of the European title two years hence.' Pat's timely attention to the problem has since reaped a rich harvest.

The Council appointed a Panel Training Committee and directed each of the international and junior Selection Committees to nominate a panel of players and liaise with the PTC which drew up an action programme. The fitness and stamina required to go through seven successive days in which 11 rounds of golf are played (the number of rounds, including practice rounds, in the European Team Championships) became a priority. Towards this end Don Patterson, the Warrenpoint Golf Club professional at that time, was invited to The Island Golf Club to address the panel on aerobics and physical fitness training. In addition, a series of round robins was arranged prior to the commencement of the competitive golf season. These were at County Sligo (11/12 March), County Louth (8/9 April) and Carlow (29/30 April).

The introduction of panel training coincided with Larry McCarthy's last year as Irish Team Captain. In his final report on both the quadrangular continental matches and the home internationals, he intimated that the performance of the teams was a big improvement on the previous few years. Morale was high, keeness to win was very evident and all team members were very fit. He attributed this improvement to the National Panel programme.

Joseph B. Carr was appointed Irish Team Captain at the 1979 AGM and the action programme continued with round robins at Royal County Down (24/25 February), Carlow (10/11 March) and County Sligo (31 March/1 April). A tragedy occurred at Royal County Down when one of the selectors, Dermot Herlihy (Royal Dublin), playing in the last three-ball with two panel members, collapsed and died on the first fairway.

The weather conditions at the Carlow series were most unpleasant with intermittent sleet showers. Crouched under an umbrella at the back of the par 3 third hole the Union General Secretary was joined by the Captain. The weather was so bad that the players could not be recognised until they got to the green. The Secretary suggested to J.B. that round robins in these conditions were of little benefit either to the players or the selectors and would be much more fruitful if held in Spain. This observation must have set J.B. thinking. Following an equally inclement session at County Sligo, he started enquiries with his friend Gerald McMickian, the owner of the Sotogrande Golf Complex in Southern Spain. At the next meeting of the Council he broached the subject of a week in Spain instead of the three round robins at Irish venues. The Council agreed that, if the cost could be limited to not more than £1,000 above the cost of the 1979 round robins, it would sanction such a visit. Two main considerations made the trip viable: the team would bring their own Chef to provide meals for the entire party and the Sotogrande Management agreed to waive all green fees for the panel and selectors on the Las Aves (now Valderama) course designed by Trent Jones.

The trip proved an outstanding success. In his Captain's report to the Central Council J.B. said, 'It was a superb week where the panel played ten rounds of golf in six days, got to know one another intimately and became a team in every way. It also gave myself and my fellow selectors a chance to evaluate each player, their strengths, their weaknesses, their team spirit, etc.' What J.B. did not mention in his report were two other departures from previous sessions. To build up stamina, each panelist had to carry his own bag — no caddies, no trolleys — for all ten rounds over this difficult and undulating course measuring over 7000 yards. Possibly more importantly, he got rid of the 'them and us' barrier which seemed to exist between the players and officials by having discussion sessions between the panel, the selectors and Union officials at which everyone was invited to express views, voice complaints and ask questions. The whole week proved an enlightening experience.

The Council decided that this concentrated golf week in Spain was to be continued and, with some variations, it has become a fixture in the Irish golfing calendar. The first variation was the appointment of a professional golfer as a National Coach who, in addition to visiting various venues in Ireland to give tuition to selected groups, also went to Spain with the panel. The other variation occurred when the ownership of Sotogrande changed. Having ascertained the prohibitive amount of green fees which would have to be paid, the venue was moved firstly to another place in Spain and then to the Algarve in Portugal.

John Garner, appointed in 1983, was the first National Coach and his dedication to his duties proved itself in the successes which were to come. Sadly in 1987, for health reasons, he had to relinquish the post. David Jones was then appointed but, as his view of his duties did not coincide with those of the Union, he resigned. The present National Coach is Howard Bennett.

Brendan Edwards (Shandon Park) followed Joe Carr as Irish Team Captain. He was succeeded by Eamon Curran and the present Captain is George Crosbie (Cork).

To appreciate more fully the improvement in the standard at senior level, we must go back a few years prior to Pat Foley's Presidential review of 1977. At the 1975 European Amateur Golf Team Championship Ireland qualified for the first flight and finished seventh in the matchplay. Ireland finished third to Sweden and France in the 1976 Quadrangular

Continental Matches and again finished third to Scotland and England in the home internationals. In 1977 Ireland did not qualify for the first flight and were 12th out of 18 countries in the matchplay in the EAGTC. The Irish team was also beaten by Scotland, England and Wales in the home internationals and collected the 'wooden spoon'.

Ireland's record in these three international contests since then have been:

	EAGTC	*QCM*	*INTERNATIONALS*
1978		*Joint 2nd*	*3rd*
1979	*1st flight and 3rd*		*Lost to Wales (Mini)*
1980		*Winner*	*2nd*
1981	*1st flight and 5th*		*2nd*
1982		*3rd*	*3rd*
1983	*1st flight and Winner*		*Winner*
1984		*3rd*	*3rd*
1985	*1st flight and 6th*		*3rd*
1986		*Winner*	*2nd*
1987	*1st flight and Winner*		*Winner*
1988		*Winner*	*2nd*
1989	*1st flight and 3rd*		*2nd*
1990		*Winner*	*Winner*

This marked improvement in the standard of Irish golf validates the wisdom of the appointment of a National Coach and the introduction of panel training and coaching sessions which include a visit by the panel with the Coach to the Iberian Peninsula in the early part of the golfing season each year.

When Eamon Curran relinquished office at the end of the 1987 season, teams under his captaincy had not only achieved a unique treble but had also reached a goal which eluded successive Irish teams for 55 years. At Lahinch in 1987 Ireland won the 'triple crown' for the first time since the Home International Championship had been inaugurated in 1932 and, also for the first time, became holder of the three international trophies, the European Amateur Golf Team Championship Cup, the Cartier Cup for the Quadrangular Continental Matches and the Raymond Trophy for the Home International Championship.

George F. Crosbie was elected Irish Team Captain at the 1988 Annual General Meeting, and when he completed his term of office he had almost repeated the successes of his predecessor captaining teams which won the Cartier Cup in 1988 and again in 1990, coming third in the EAGTC in 1989 and winning the Raymond Trophy and the 'triple crown' in 1990. Although he had only two trophies to show at the end of his term he nevertheless achieved a superb treble.

Chapter 32

THE
BOYS'
HOME INTERNATIONAL
MATCHES

In Chapter 18 on junior golf the Boys' Amateur Championship was mentioned. This Championship was first played at the Royal Ascot Club in 1921 and each year thereafter at various venues, except from 1940 to 1945 when it was suspended because of the war. The Scotland and England Boys' International match started in 1923 and has always been played before the Championship. The introduction of the match at that time must have been un-official as the Scottish Golf Union had only been founded two years earlier and the English Golf Union did not come into existence until one year later. Jimmy Bruen (Muskerry) won the Championship in 1936 at Royal Birkdale, Norman Drew (Clandeboye) was runner-up at St Andrews in 1949, John Glover (Campbell College, Belfast) won at Royal Lytham and St Anne's in 1950, Ronan Rafferty (Warrenpoint) won at Kilmarnock, Barassie in 1979 and Leslie Walker (Grange) won at Seaton Carew in 1983.

It was only in 1949, some 27 years after it was started, that the R & A was invited to assume control and management of the Championship. In the 1920s, a Mr James G. Walker (not to be confused with Mr George H. Walker who presented the Walker Cup for the biennial match between Britain and Ireland and the USA) decided to present a Cup for a full international match between England and Scotland. The award of this Cup was dis-continued with the introduction of the home internationals in 1932. In 1958 agreement was reached to use the (James G.) Walker Cup for the annual boys' international match between England and Scotland. It has already been mentioned in Chapter 18, how the J.D. MacCormack Cup came to be played for in the annual international match between Ireland and Wales.

The Irish officials in charge of the teams at these annual matches had the support of their Welsh counterparts when advocating the introduction of a four country contest, and in

1985 the R & A decided to inaugurate the boys' home international matches and presented a trophy, to be known as the St Andrews Trophy, for annual competition. Time constraints necessitated that the new internationals be confined to two days. Conscious of the fact that the Walker and MacCormack Cups were being played for annually, the R & A prescribed that on the first day the existing matches between England and Scotland and between Ireland and Wales would continue as heretofore. On the second day, each winning country would play for the St Andrews Trophy. As in the full international series, teams comprised ten players a side and the format is five foursomes and ten singles over 18 holes.

The first match was played at the Royal Burgess Golf Club, Edinburgh. Ireland defeated Wales by 11½ matches to 3½ whilst England beat Scotland. On the second day, England led by 3 matches to 2 in the morning foursomes but Ireland succeeded in winning 5 and halving 1 match in the singles to tie and thus shared the inaugural Boys' Home Internationals and the St Andrew's Trophy. The following year at Seaton Carew, having again beaten Wales, this time by 8½ to 6½, Ireland faced Scotland on the second day and beat them also by 8½ to 6½ to win the Internationals.

The Central Council and the Junior Golf Committee are grateful to the R & A for its continued promotion of the game at all levels and are satisfied that this new competition will give younger players valuable competitive experience to assist them to progress to greater achievements at a higher level. The record of venues, Team Captains and the results of matches played is set out in Appendix XXI (Section 1). The list of Ireland's international representatives is set out in Appendix XXI (Section 2).

Chapter 33

THE PROVINCIAL CHAMPIONSHIPS

The South of Ireland Amateur Open Championship

According to the best information available, a group of enthusiastic members of Limerick Golf Club set out in 1892 to find new ground on which to pursue their golfing activities during the winter. They were led by Alexander Shaw (later to be knighted) and their travels took them along the Clare coast, through Ennistymon, to Lahinch. There they discovered sandhills and dunes ideal for their purposes between the town and the Liscannor river. Alexander Shaw engaged Old Tom Morris to lay out the original links to which many changes were made, firstly by John Gibson in 1907 and later by Dr Alister MacKenzie in 1927.

With the aim of promoting the popularity of their links, the Committee inaugurated the first Irish Provincial Championship in 1895. The timing of the event was very important. By having it during the week following the Irish Amateur Open Championship (held that year at Portrush), some cross-channel visitors who were competing in that event took part in the Provincial Championship also. The format was matchplay. Local knowledge proved too strong for the visitors as two Lahinch members contested the 36-hole final with Dr G.S. Browning beating W.F. McDonnell by 2 and 1.

The winner's handicap is unknown but the runner-up, playing off a handicap of 8, had also been runner-up in the pre-Championship medal competition returning 92-8-84. This was more than a year before George Combe introduced his handicapping scheme which has been dealt with in detail in Chapter 4. McDonnell's handicap appears to have gone up instead of down in the months following his near success in the inaugural 'South', and this is a good example of the necessity for a proper handicapping system. Some nine months after the 'South', it was reported that McDonnell won the Lahinch Monthly Medal playing off a handicap of 12. His score was 98-12-86. Later it was reported that he won the Shaw Cup (bogey competition) at Lahinch, playing off 8, returning 2 down. Next he won the Phelps Vase (matchplay) playing off 7. There is also a report of him winning a medal competition playing off 10.

In its second year the Championship was won by a Lahinch born competitor, B. O'Brien who entered from Portsalon. He played off scratch and beat a 7 handicap player, D.M. Wilson (Royal Dublin) by 9 and 7. The early grip on the 'South' by Irish players was quickly broken. Between 1897 and 1904 the last stage of the Championship was contested by British competitors, with the exception of 1902 when G.S. Browning was defeated in the final. Fred Ballingall (Glenalmond) beat J.R. Gardiner (Richmond) in the 1897 final; Ballingall then beat his brother Hugh (Blairgowrie) in 1898 and, after a lapse of one year when J.R. Gardiner won, succeeded in defeating T. Fullerton (Carnoustie) in the 1900 final to win the trophy outright. Sir Alexander Shaw then presented the Club with the magnificent perpetual challenge cup which has been competed for annually ever since except for the period of the First World War and 1922.

There are many stories of epic finals, mostly involving Lahinch's own John Burke who won the trophy 11 times with two sequences of four and six years thus creating a record. He won from 1928 to 1931 and from 1941 to 1946 with 1939 in between. The donor was very wise in prescribing that the Cup would be a perpetual award, for other multiple winners were: Paddy Leyden (Spanish Point) four times, Joe Brown (Tramore) three times, Michael Guerin (Killarney) three times and Joe Carr (Sutton) three times. The unluckiest runner-up was a long-standing and popular entrant in the Championship named Gregory Young (Kilrush) who finished in that unenviable position five times: 1965, 1966, 1968, 1970 and 1972. A record of winners and runners-up is set out in Appendix XXII (Section 1).

Anxious to retain the matchplay format, and at the same time accommodate as many entrants as possible, the committee decided to limit the entry to 192 and first to allocate a bye to the 64 lowest competitors into the second round. The remaining competitors would be drawn to compete in the first round in such a manner that each first round winner would be slotted in to play against one of the players who received a bye into the second round.

The original links laid out by Old Tom Morris extended along both sides of the roadway towards Liscannor. John Gibson, the professional at Westward Ho in Devonshire, was invited to re-design the links in 1907. He brought in more of the sandhills and dunes on the seaward side of the road. Alister MacKenzie later brought in more of the ground on the seaward side and the final result is the championship course we have today. Many years later, this enabled the Committee to develop a second 18 holes on the Castle side of the road. Only one hole of Old Tom's original lay-out remains. It is worth describing as it is possibly the most unique golf hole in Ireland if not further afield. The hole was originally the 4th and is now the 6th — The Dell. A blind par 3 hole might not be a novelty but the Dell is something different. Measuring 156 yards, the tee is at road level whilst the narrow elongated green (around which there is no fringe) is in a valley between four high sandhills and is completely blind from the tee. The tee shot must be played over the facing sandhill. There is a moveable white stone marker near the top of this sandhill which is adjusted to give the player the line to the pin. Immediately beyond the green is an equally high sandhill. If the tee shot carries beyond the stone marker and is short of the green, or if it carries the green, the ball may bounce down to the green. On the other hand, it may get caught which results in the player having an awkward and extremely difficult second. Over the years there have been many who maintain that it is not a proper golf hole and should be altered. Others, equally vehement, claim that it is the heart of Lahinch and should not be touched. This last legacy of Old Tom's craftsmanship is likely to continue as a novel and often frustrating test in a round of golf at Lahinch.

The Council selected Lahinch as the venue for the 1987 home internationals, the first time these matches were played on the West coast.

The West of Ireland Amateur Open Championship

It is uncertain whether County Sligo is the second or the third oldest golf Club in Connacht. Athlone, under its original name of Athlone Garrison Golf Club, was founded in 1892. Both Ballinasloe and County Sligo Golf Clubs were founded in 1894 but other than the year it is impossible to pinpoint which one preceded the other in origin. All three commenced as 9 hole courses with County Sligo the only one still occupying its original site at Rosses Point. In 1937 Ballinasloe moved to its third location, its present course at Rosgloss, where it now has 18 holes. The present course at Hodson Bay is also Athlone's third location, to which it moved in 1938 and where the layout is 18 holes.

It was George Combe who proposed the formation of County Sligo Golf Club[13] and he presented the Combe Cup for annual competition. As there was ample ground available, the committee decided to extend the links to 18 holes during the winter of 1906–07 to facilitate the ever-increasing membership as the Point was becoming a very popular holiday resort for enthusiastic golfers, particularly from the Dublin area.

Aware of the success of the 'South of Ireland', the County Sligo committee decided to inaugurate the second of Ireland's Provincial Championships. In 1923, the West of Ireland Amateur Open Championship was introduced. From Club funds the committee provided a perpetual challenge trophy and prescribed that the Championship would be matchplay over the Easter holiday period. From the outset the format and timing proved popular, as it enabled members and visitors alike to test their skills in what has come to be recognised as the opening event of the golfing season.

In 1926 the committee engaged the services of H.S. Colt, an outstanding golf course architect, who re-designed the 1907 layout to the Championship links of today. Under the shadow of Ben Bulben the links can be a very severe test of golf. It can be subject to the gale force winds and squalls sweeping in from the Atlantic Ocean. As against this it is a delight for the high handicap golfer (as well as the low man) to play the links in normal weather conditions.

Up to 1958 the Championship was matchplay throughout with a 36-hole final. Thereafter, as it grew in popularity, the Championship committee imposed not only a handicap limit but also a numerical limit. Easter is a moveable feast, so the numerical limit is adjusted to allow for the availability of daylight. Each competitor plays 18 holes medal play on the first and second day and the 64 leading qualifiers then compete by matchplay over the next three days.

For nearly 40 years, from 1928 to 1966, three Irish players dominated the 'West': Cecil Ewing, John Burke and Joe Carr. Between them, often one against the other, they contested the final on 39 occasions.

The GUI Council has asked the Club to host many tournaments, the Interprovincials, Cups and Shields national finals, and the Close which has been staged at Rosses Point eight times since 1931. The 'West' continues to thrive and in recent years the entry has been so large that it has become necessary to ballot out higher handicap entrants. A record of winners and runners-up is set out in Appendix XXII (Section 2).

The greatest honour in the Club's history is yet to come. It will be Ireland's turn to host the 1991 home international matches and the Central Council has nominated County Sligo as the venue in the centenary year of the GUI.

The East of Ireland Amateur Open Championship

The 'East', whose permanent home is County Louth Golf Club, is the third oldest of the Senior Provincial Championships. The inaugural event was played in 1941 and other than extending it from two days to three because of increased entries, it is the only one of the Championships to retain its original format of 72 holes medal play. The idea for such an event was the brainchild of Ms Josephine Carbery, who was a most active and dedicated Secretary of the County Louth Golf Club, a position to which she had been appointed in 1937. On her marriage in 1943 she became Josephine Connolly, a name which became more and more respected as the Championship grew in prestige. Josephine, as everyone came to call her, 'ran' the Championship from its inception until 1977 and the Club then handed its administration over to the Leinster Branch of the Union. The Club appointed a Championship Committee each year to oversee and control the event on which were representatives of the Leinster Branch. Josephine, as permanent Championship Secretary, took the entries, made the draw, made out all the score cards and personally welcomed every competitor when he reported at the office to check in.

County Louth was not her only interest in the golfing sphere; she served with distinction on the Irish Ladies' Golf Union and was elected President of it for the years 1971–73.

Very few Irish Clubs can claim the honour of having Presidents of both administrative organisations of amateur golf in Ireland. County Louth is one of this select number. Peter V. Lyons, a lifetime member of the Club and also a member of the East Championship Committee for 37 years was elected President of the Golfing Union of Ireland for the years 1975–76.

At a meeting of the Club Committee on 25 August 1939, the proposal to hold an East of Ireland Amateur Open Championship over 72 holes medal play was approved, and it was decided to approach the Leinster Branch for permission. Dr Lorcan Sherlock, Chairman of the Leinster Branch, advised the Committee that the Club did not have to seek permission for such a Championship as neither Lahinch nor County Sligo had sought such permission for the South and West Championships of Ireland. Josephine asked Peter Lyons if the Lyons family, all five of whom played golf at Baltray, would provide a trophy for the proposed Championship. The family readily agreed to donate a perpetual challenge cup in memory of their father.

By coincidence, the Central Council of the Union had been expressing concern at the growing practice of Clubs running open tournaments under the title of 'Championship' and, at a meeting on 5 April 1940 declared that 'no club shall be permitted to run a competition under the title of Championship, except a Club Championship which must be confined to individual members of the Club concerned'. This regulation still operates today. Because the South and West of Ireland Championships had been fixtures on the golfing calendar since 1895 and 1923 respectively, the two Clubs concerned were specifically excluded from this resolution. As a result of some behind-the-scenes activities, Dr Sherlock was able to announce at the Leinster Branch AGM on 16 November 1940 that the Union had granted permission to County Louth to hold the tournament under the title of Championship. Josephine recorded that the first entry she received for the inaugural Championship was from Alan B. Kidd, Honorary Secretary of the Union.

The links at Baltray proved a magnificent test for this Championship. As mentioned earlier in this history, the original lay-out was conceived by Thomas Gilroy in 1892. In 1938 the Club engaged the English golf course architects, Tom Simpson and Molly Gourlay, to carry out a major re-construction. Whilst the sequence of playing the holes has since been altered to enable greater supervision to be maintained, the only additional construction work to the Simpson/Gourlay design was the building of a new tee to the right hand side of the old 18th fairway. This is now the 1st tee and play is to the old 7th green, the 2nd is the old 8th, the 3rd the old 9th and the old 1st to 6th make up the first nine. The old 7th tee is now the 10th tee and play is to the old 18th green. Thereafter the 11th to 18th are the old 10th to 17th holes. The Championship course now measures 6728 yards and has a par of 72 and an SSS of 73. Before the advent of piped water on the links, only a perfectly executed shot would hold some of the elevated greens. Even today, a slack shot can be severely punished. This will help to explain why, in almost half a century, level fours have been achieved in the Championship only three times and a lower score than that on only five other occasions. The lowest 72 hole score was accomplished by Pat Mulcare of Woodbrook in 1971 when he won the first of his three successive championships. He returned 281.

Joe Carr of Sutton, then only 19 years of age, had the distinction of winning the inaugural Championship. By coincidence this was also his first championship success. He stamped his mark on the 'East' for between 1941 and 1969 he won the event twelve times and was runner-up twice. In addition to Carr and Mulcare, other multiple winners were Brennie Scannell (Woodbrook) and Tom Craddock (Malahide) each of whom won three times, whilst Billy Hulme (Warrenpoint), Jimmy Carroll (Sutton), Paddy Caul (Malahide) and Adrian Morrow (Portmarnock) each won twice. The host Club registered its first win in 1942 when Kevin Garvey was successful, but did not have another winner until 1978 when Mark Gannon brought in the winning score. He was joined by his clubmates Barry Reddan and Finbar Ronan, who won in 1984 and 1985 respectively.

In 1943 Josephine presented the 'Jo Carbery Cup' for the best nett four round score and some years later Tom Agnew (Belvoir Park) presented the 'Agnew Salver' for the best nett score in any single round.

Whit Sunday and Monday became the established days for the Championship (36 holes each day). As it grew in popularity, the Championship Committee tried unsuccessfully to reduce the number of entries to more manageable proportions by reducing the handicap limit to 3. Eventually it was decided to extend the Championship to three days and now each competitor plays 18 holes on both Saturday and Sunday. The 51 competitors who return the lowest total gross scores over the first 36 holes qualify for the final two rounds on Whit Monday.

Even with the extension to three days, the Championship still attracts more entries than the packed time sheet can facilitate. As a result, many of the competitors on the present handicap limit of 4 have to be balloted out and are placed on a waiting list. From a very early hour on the opening day many of the players on this list can be seen knocking balls around the practice ground hoping for a last minute call to the first tee to replace some other competitor who has been forced to pull out at the last moment.

Whilst the Youths' Amateur Open Championship of Ireland and the Leinster and Munster Youths' are decided over 72 holes medal play, no other 'strokeplay' championship commands such an enthusiastic interest from both competitors and spectators alike as the 'East'. The record of winners and runners-up is set out in Appendix XXII (Section 3), and also the winners of the Carbery Cup and the Agnew Salver.

The North of Ireland Amateur Open Championship

In 1947 the Council of the Royal Portrush Golf Club invited the Ulster Branch of the Union to inaugurate and administer the 'North' over their links and intimated that they would donate the Harriman Cup as a perpetual trophy.

The Harriman Cup had been presented to the Club in 1937 by H.M. Harriman who had won the American Amateur Championship in 1899. The Club used the trophy for the Ulster Scratch Singles played by 36 holes medal play at the Easter meeting. The competition was played on only four occasions between 1937 and 1946, having been suspended during the war.

As the established date of the West of Ireland was the Easter weekend, the Ulster Council decided to hold the new Championship during the Ulster holiday week associated with the 'Twelfth of July' thus avoiding a clash with the other three provincial championships. It also decided to have matchplay throughout with a 36 holes final. The first winner was J. Fitzsimmons who had played for Ireland at Royal Porthcawl in the last of the pre-war (1939–45) internationals. He was again selected on the Irish team in 1947 and 1948, probably as a result of winning the 'North' in those two years. Although his international record lists Royal Portrush as his Club, he entered the Championship from Bushfoot. In 1947 he defeated J.C. Kissock (Bangor) by 8 and 7 and in 1948 beat W.A. McNeill (Royal Belfast) by 10 and 9.

For 1949 the Ulster Council decided to break new ground and introduced a 72 hole medal play format. However, this did not prove popular and the event quickly reverted to matchplay. In 1949 F. Webster (Carlow) returned a somewhat high score of 311 but his was nevertheless the best score and he defeated the local player, Jackson Taggart, and W.A. McNeill (the 1948 runner-up), by one stroke.

The Championship had always been confined to the Dunluce (Championship) course but as it grew in popularity it became necessary to use the Valley course also. In 1953 competitors played 18 holes medal play over each course with the leading 8 qualifying for matchplay in a 36 hole final. Two years later, the event was played over four days for the first time, with 32 to qualify (over 36 holes) and an 18 hole final. Between 1955 and 1964 the final reverted to 36 holes.

The present format, introduced in 1964, is 36 holes qualifying (Dunluce and Valley) with 64 to qualify for matchplay, and an 18 hole final.

WILLIE GILL AWARD

(Chapter 27 Appendix XV)

Presented for the most consistent performance in the Irish Amateur Close Championship and the Four Provincial Championships.

Year	Winner and Club	Points
1976	D. Branigan, L'town & B'town	160
1977	L. MacNamara, Woodbrook	110
1978	M.F. Morris, Portmarnock	90
1979	M.A. Gannon, Co. Louth	95
1980	A.D. Pierse, Tipperary	90
1981	D. Branigan, L'town & B'town	160
1982	P. Walton, Malahide	90
1983	A.C.J. Morrow, Portmarnock	100
1984	G. McGimpsey, Bangor	100
1985	D. Branigan, L'town & B'town	95
1986	J. McHenry, Douglas	120
1987	P. Rayfus, Trim	95
1988	G. MacGimpsey, Bangor	180
1989	D. Clarke, Dungannon	125
1990	D. Clarke, Dungannon	160

AMATEUR INTERNATIONAL MATCHES

(Chapter 18 Appendix VIII)

THE RAYMOND TROPHY

Year	Venue	Winning Country	Year	Venue	Winning Country
1932	Troon	Scotland	1965	Portrush	England
1933	Newcastle	Scotland	1966	Porthcawl	England
1934	Porthcawl	Scotland	1967	Ganton	Scotland
1935	Lytham	Scotland, England and Ireland tied	1968	Gullane	England
			1969	Killarney	England
1936	Prestwick	Scotland	1970	Porthcawl	Scotland
1937	Portmarnock	Scotland	1971	Formby	Scotland
1938	Porthcawl	England	1972	Troon	Scotland and England tied
1939–46		No internationals held	1973	Lytham	England
1947	Hoylake	England	1974	Harlech	England
1948	Muirfield	England	1975	Portmarnock	Scotland
1949	Portmarnock	England	1976	Muirfield	Scotland
1950	Harlech	Ireland	1977	Hillside	England
1951	Lytham	Ireland and Scotland tied	1978	Ashburnham	England
1952	Troon	Scotland	1979	Matches cancelled. Ireland played Wales in friendly at Porthcawl.	Wales
1953	Killarney	Scotland			
1954	Porthcawl	England			
1955	Southport	Ireland	1980	Dornoch	England
1956	Muirfield	Scotland	1981	Woodhall Spa	Scotland
1957	Newcastle	England	1982	Porthcawl	Scotland and England tied
1958	Porthcawl	England	1983	Portmarnock	Ireland
1959	Lytham	England, Scotland and Ireland tied	1984	Troon	Scotland and England tied
			1985	Formby	England
1960	Turnberry	England	1986	Harlech	Scotland
1961	Portmarnock	Scotland	1987	Lahinch	Ireland
1962	Porthcawl	Scotland, England and Ireland tied	1988	Muirfield	England
			1989	Ganton	England
1963	Lytham	Scotland, England and Ireland tied	1990	Conway	Ireland
1964	Carnoustie	England			

The 1987 Irish international team at Lahinch — winners of the Raymond Trophy and the Triple Crown.

Left to Right: standing: G. McGimpsey, P. Rayfus, L. MacNamara, G. O'Brien (President GUI), N.A. Anderson, D. Clarke and P. Hogan. Seated: D.F. O'Sullivan, A.D. Pierse, E. Power, E. Curran (Non-Playing Captain), B. Reddan and M.A. Gannon. (Chapter 15)

*A unique treble. Eamon Curran, Irish Team Captain 1985 to 1987, with (left to right) the European
Amateur Golf Team Championship Cup, the Raymond Trophy and the Cartier Cup won by teams under his captaincy. (Chapter 31)*

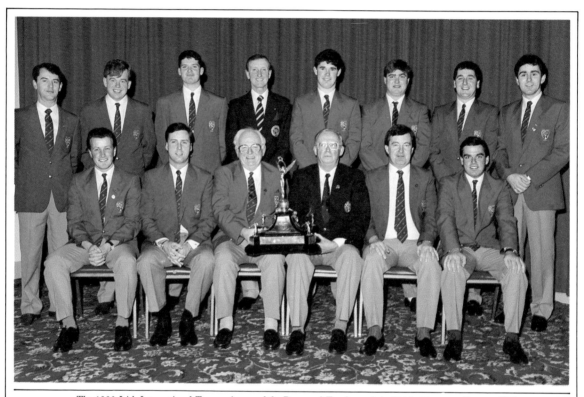

The 1990 Irish International Team, winners of the Raymond Trophy and the Triple Crown at Conwy, Wales.

*Left to Right: standing: M.A. Gannon, N.H. Anderson, G. McNeill, H. Bennett (National Coach),
P. Harrington, D. Errity, K. Kearney and J. Fanagan.
Seated: N. Goulding, G. McGimpsey, G.F. Crosbie (Non-Playing Captain), G.D. Golden (President
GUI), L. MacNamara and P. McGinley.*

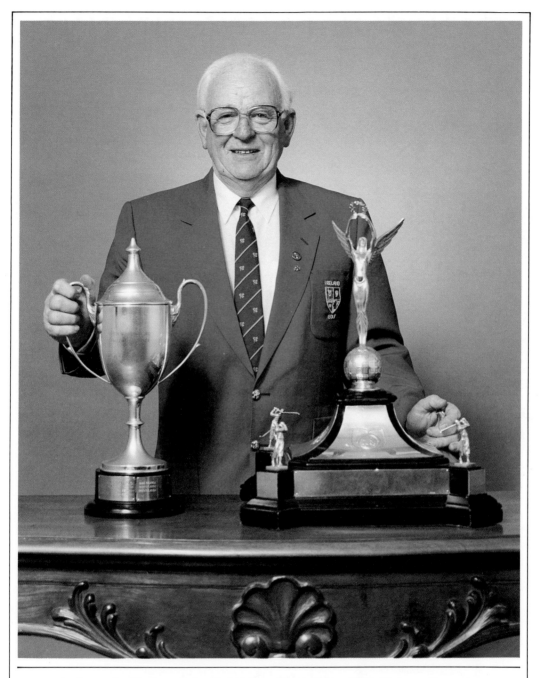

Another superb treble. George F. Crosbie, Irish Team Captain 1988 to 1991, with two trophies won by Irish teams under his captaincy.
The Cartier Cup for the Quadrangular Continental Matches won by Ireland at Portrush in 1988 and successfully defended at Ostersund, Sweden in 1990 and the Raymond Trophy for the Home International Championship won by Ireland at Conwy, Caernarvonshire, Wales in 1990 when Ireland won the Championship and the Triple Crown for the second time in four years. (Chapter 31)

THE JOE CARR AWARD

(Chapter 27)

Presented for the most consistent performance in the Youths' Amateur Open Championship of Ireland and the four Provincial Youths' Championships.

Year	Winner and Club	Points
1990	R. Coughlan, Birr	115

THE TOM MONTGOMERY AWARD

(Chapter 27)

Presented for the most consistent performance in the Irish Boys' Amateur Close Championship and the four Provincial Boys' Championships.

Year	Winner and Club	Points
1990	S. Quinlivan, Ballybunion	135

No competitor has ever won this Championship on more than two occasions. There have been 14 competitors who won twice, six of whom successfully defended the title. Ian Bamford holds the record for the longest period between wins. As a member of the home Club, he won in 1954. Eighteen years later, as a member of Warrenpoint Golf Club, he achieved his second success.

Only three Southern based players have won the 'North': Frank Webster (Carlow) in 1949, Bob Fleury (Monkstown) in 1955 and Arthur Pierse (Tipperary) in 1987. Unfortunately it is not a holiday period in the South, and perhaps this has a bearing on the ability to compete for many of these players. Those who have played over the years have been able to sample one of Ireland's finest championship links, aptly described by Ian Bamford in the History of the Royal Portrush Golf Club which he compiled for publication to mark the Club centenary in 1988.

The Club Council has always been most generous in making its facilities available for important events, the most famous of which were the Open Championship in 1951 which was won by Max Faulkner and the Amateur Championship in 1960, won by Joe Carr. Of the 57 playings of the now defunct Irish Open Amateur Championship, Portrush was the venue on 12 occasions. The Close has also been played there 12 times. The interprovincials and the national finals of the Cups and Shields have often been decided over the Dunluce course. All these have given its many visitors over the years an opportunity of enjoying this superb test of golf.

The record of winners and runners-up is set out in Appendix XXII (Section 4).

In Chapter 3 we mentioned the founding of the Union in Portrush. As part of the celebrations for its centenary the Union requested the Council of the Royal Portrush Golf Club to make the facilities of its Championship course and clubhouse available to the Union for a competition between teams representing the eight surviving Founder Clubs on 12 October 1991 exactly 100 years since the Union was founded. The Club Council readily agreed.

Chapter 34

UNION FINANCE AND SPONSORSHIP

Whilst the subject of finance was not considered at the inaugural meeting of the Union on 12 October 1891, it was one of the 14 proposals approved at the adjourned meeting on 13 November of that year. Each Club affiliated to the Union was required to subscribe one guinea (£1.05) for every delegate the Club was entitled to send to meetings of the Union.

The following delegate representation was decided:

Clubs with membership not exceeding 150:	one delegate
Clubs with membership exceeding 150 but not exceeding 300:	two delegates
Clubs with membership exceeding 300:	three delegates.

Regrettably there are no Union accounts or balance sheets available for the early years but the records show that by the time the 1913 constitution which set up a Central Council and four provincial branches was approved, 141 Clubs had become affiliated to the Union.

As the provincial branches had no source of income, it was decided at a meeting on 19 November 1913 to direct the Honorary Treasurer to forward to each provincial Honorary Secretary every year 'a sum of money calculated at the rate of five shillings [25p] for each guinea subscription received from Clubs in his province or such other sum as the Council may, from time to time, determine.'

During the 1914–18 war, the Council decided 'that in the case of Clubs whose grounds have been taken over for War purposes the Honorary Treasurer be authorised to suspend the payment of the annual subscription' and 'because of the suspension for the two Championships and the County Shield, Senior and Junior Cup Tournaments that all other Clubs only pay half subscription.' This latter decision was altered in 1916 to the effect that no annual subscription should be paid by any Club.

In January 1919 the Council recommenced activities and arranged dates and venues for the Championships and national finals of Union tournaments. The subscriptions payable by Clubs were increased at a meeting on 26 October 1921 to the following:

Clubs with membership not exceeding 60:	£1. 1s. 0d	(£1.05)
Clubs with membership between 61 and 100:	£1. 11s. 6d	(£1.58)
Clubs with membership between 101 and 150:	£2. 2s. 0d.	(£2.10)
Clubs with membership between 151 and 200:	£3. 3s. 0d.	(£3.15)
Clubs with membership between 201 and 250:	£4. 4s. 0d.	(£4.20)
Clubs with membership over 250:	£5. 5s. 0d.	(£5.25)

These subscriptions remained unchanged until the end of the Union's 1926 financial year when the audited accounts showed a deficit on the year of £40. 6s. 1d. (£40.30) and the balance sheet showed Union assets, including trophies, as £1,145. 18s. 9d. (£1,145.92).

In Chapter 14 it has been mentioned that whilst the Union was in favour of inaugurating the Open Championship of Ireland, it had not the funds to do so and Portmarnock Golf Club had guaranteed it against loss. In an effort to help raise the necessary funds the Union had suggested that each affiliated Club be requested to subscribe the equivalent of one ordinary member's subscription and, as a result, a small profit was made. The following year (1928) under a similar arrangement another surplus was achieved at Royal County Down.

At a meeting on 12 September 1928 although the Union accounts had shown a deficit, the Central Council decided that it would take over the future financing of the Championship and introduced a more equitable financial structure which would involve every ordinary Club member in Ireland on an equal basis. It prescribed that each affiliated Club should increase the annual subscription of each ordinary member by one shilling (5p) per annum and forward this each year to the Honorary Treasurer of the Union for the Championship. This scheme, originally known as the '1/- fund scheme' later came to be referred to as 'poll tax'. It eventually became the method by which the Union obtains its main income and is known now as the 'Annual Subscription'.

Also in 1928, the Union representatives on the Joint Advisory Council were authorised to guarantee the payment of £285 per annum for a period of five years (later extended by a further five years). This was the amount assessed by the JAC as Ireland's share to help fund the recently instituted Board of Greenkeeping Research. This necessitated adjusting the 1921 Club subscription rate to raise extra funds. However, matters did not work out as planned as many of the affiliated Clubs which up until then had only two categories of member (ordinary and lady associate) decided to introduce new categories (such as country, five day, overseas and others) all at reduced subscriptions. In those days it was quite a common practice for a golfer to be a member of three or more golf Clubs. The availability of the new categories, together with increases in rates for ordinary members meant that many players selected one Club for ordinary or full membership and transferred to country or five day in the others. As Union funding was based on ordinary membership only, this resulted in a decrease in income from both the Club subscription and the 1/- fund. Having incurred a loss in both the Union and the Championship accounts at the end of the 1930 financial year, the Central Council decided that 'on and from 1 January 1931 the total "membership" on which subscriptions are payable comprises all classes of male members of the Club including juvenile, five day, country or outlying members, honorary members and restricted members having no vote.' This classification was confined to categories of male members and did not include lady associate members over which the GUI has no jurisdiction. The ladies' section of Irish Clubs was then, as now, affiliated to the Irish Ladies' Golf Union. A year later the Council decided to exclude honorary and life members from the subscription grouping and to credit all income to a general purposes fund.

The Open Championship of Ireland was suspended following the outbreak of war in 1939. At a meeting on 13 December 1940 the Council decided 'to allocate a sum of £250 out of the £500 per annum which had been transferred to a special Open Championship account, and donate this for competition amongst Irish professionals in 1941, to be arranged in co-operation with the IPGA.' This amount was donated annually until the revival of the Open Championship of Ireland in 1946. Also at the 1940 meeting, the Council decided 'that the nett profit on the general account of the Golfing Union of Ireland for 1941 be re-funded in a proportional manner to each affiliated Club at the end of the financial year.' This decision was renewed annually until 1944, as the Union did not consider it desirable to accumulate funds at the expense of Clubs which were finding it difficult to survive with the many restrictions which had been placed upon them.

The next radical change in Union financing was made when the Central Council decided that as and from the end of the Union's 1948 financial year the annual Club subscription based on membership would be discontinued. The new method of funding which was decided increased the 1/- fund scheme to 2/- but relief from payment by certain categories was also provided. The decision was 'from January 1949 each affiliated Club shall pay to the Honorary Treasurer of the Union by way of annual subscription a sum calculated at 2/- per head on male members. "Male Members" comprise all classes of *playing* members except (1) honorary (2) junior members under 21 years of age and (3) university undergraduates. Members of more than one Club are liable to pay in each of the Clubs of which they are playing members. University Golf Clubs shall pay an annual subscription of one guinea and shall not be liable to the 2/- poll tax.' A directive issued with the decision stated that 'the Union desires to emphasise that while the collection of the poll tax is the liability of the Club, it is to be regarded as an individual and personal liability by all members of affiliated golf Clubs towards the cost of maintaining the Union and its Provincial Councils as the governing body of golf in Ireland.' The 2/- rate remained unchanged for the next ten years when, as we have seen in Chapter 18, the Council increased it by 1/- to fund its promotion of junior golf.

Ireland's successful trip to Sandwich for the European Amateur Golf Team Championship in 1965 cost the Union £251.12s. 5d. (c. £251.63). In anticipation of an Irish team travelling to Turin to defend the title in 1967, the Council voted to increase the annual subscription from 3/- (15p) to 5/- (25p).

The Union continued to expand its activities not only at national level but also at provincial level. At the 1969 AGM the Council authorised the Leinster Branch to introduce a provincial levy to enable it to embark on a development programme which included tuition at all levels of player in the province. At the same meeting, the Council decided to make what the Honorary Treasurer in his subsequent report described as 'a radical change in secretarial arrangements'. It decided to acquire its own premises and directly employ and pay the salaries of the staff. Since his appointment on a part time basis 20 years earlier, the provision of both office facilities and staffing had been the General Secretary's personal financial responsibility. In 1970 decimalisation arrived. At the 1971 AGM the subject of Ireland hosting the EAGTC in Killarney in 1973 and the provision of funds to purchase a suitable headquarters for the Union were considered and the annual subscription was increased from 5/- (25p) to 40 new pence.

A financial tragedy befell the Union's efforts to make the eighth EAGTC at Killarney in 1973 a credit to Irish golf and beneficial to Ireland. First of all it had been estimated that the cost of staging the Championship would be £25,000. Dr Billy O'Sullivan (President 1958–60), Chairman of the Killarney Club Organising Committee, approached his friend Jack Mulcahy who owned Waterville Golf Club and the Waterville Lake Hotel. He generously agreed to guarantee the Union against loss. The Championship Committee, under the Chairmanship of Mixie Murphy (President 1963–65), was aware that the main source of income would be derived from advertising revenue in the souvenir programme which it intended to publish. The GUI entered into a contract to obtain 10,000 programmes for £9,000 and engaged Bill Hodnett, a member of Dun Laoghaire Golf Club, to solicit advertisements. He did a first class job and by the time the EGA decided to change the venue from Ireland to Portugal, Bill had obtained £25,400 worth of advertisements. At the meeting of the General Assembly of the EGA in Luxembourg in November 1972, two member countries confirmed their decision that they would not be sending teams to Killarney because of the troubles in Northern Ireland. The EGA selected Portugal for the eighth Championship. However, at the request of the two Irish delegates (the GUI President, Tom Montgomery and Ireland's EGA representative, Mixie Murphy), the EGA agreed to play the ninth Championship at Killarney in 1975 irrespective of any withdrawals. Much work had been carried out both at Union headquarters and Killarney, the cost of which came to £8,000 for which Jack Mulcahy reimbursed the Union.

During 1974 Ireland felt the first effects of world recession and rising inflation. As a result of this Jack Mulcahy intimated that he could no longer assist the Union. Worse was to follow. The cost of the souvenir programme rose from £9,000 to £23,117. Bill Hodnett had to start again from scratch and could only obtain £16,796 worth of advertisements. The anticipated profit-making item went from a surplus of £16,400 to a deficit of £6,321. The cost of everything else went up also. Except for the fact that Ireland finished seventh, the 1975 Championship was an outstanding success from a golfing point of view. However, when the Honorary Treasurer completed the accounts the Union had incurred a loss of £26,343. As against this the GUI promoted the image of Ireland in every European country, and Killarney in particular was one of the areas which benefitted enormously.

In 1973 the Council had decided to consolidate the general purposes account, junior golf and international golf funds and in an effort to build up a reserve for the Championship increased the annual subscription from 40p to 50p. When the Killarney figures were finalised the Council had no alternative other than to raise the 50p to £1.

Despite the 1975 financial set-back and escalating costs, the Council continued with its programme of developing the game at all levels. Earlier, separate chapters have been devoted to Ireland's participation in the European Youths' and Boys' Championships and the Boys' Home Internationals. The formation of the National Panel, training sessions in Spain and Portugal and the appointment of a national coach have also been mentioned. All

The 1975 European Amateur Golf Team Championship Irish Tournament Organising Committee.

Left to Right: standing: W.A. Menton (General Secretary), P.J. Foley (Chairman, Munster), Gerald H. Owens (Honorary Vice-President), R. Barry (Honorary Secretary, Munster), P.F. Gaynor (Honorary Secretary, Leinster).

Seated: D.R. O'Kelly (Joint Honorary Secretary), D.M. McAuley (Honorary Treasurer), M.J. Murphy (Honorary Vice-President and Chairman TOC), P.V. Lyons (President), W.J. Gill (Honorary Vice-President and Joint Honorary Secretary).

Absent: W.M. O'Sullivan (Honorary Vice-President)

Killarney Golf and Fishing Club used a fishing lodge as its first clubhouse (the building on the left above).
The extension on right helped serve the needs of members and visitors when the course was 18 holes.
A later clubhouse built on the same site was used for a number of years until found inadequate for present
day activities over a 36 hole lay-out and was, in turn, extended and renovated to the present structure
below which was opened in 1989.

this expansion, which was introduced since 1976 and which has shown gratifying results, required finance. In addition, the cost of hosting the EAYGTC at Hermitage in 1984 had to be met. Between 1976 and 1987 the Council had to increase the annual subscription three times to its present level of £4.

In 1982 the Council voted to increase its annual contribution to the four branches from £3,300 to £24,820 to enable the Provincial Councils to develop coaching, junior golf and other activities, including administration within the provinces. The Council had to reduce this subvention by approximately £10,000 in 1985 because the general purposes account suffered a loss that year of £7,000. In his report to the Central Council the Honorary Treasurer pointed out that whilst the Union income had increased by only 8 per cent since 1982, the expenditure had risen by 42 per cent in the same period. At Union headquarters a new multiple photocopying machine was purchased as well as three computers and a fax machine to help meet the demand for greater efficiency. A new scoreboard with transport facilities was commissioned for Union events and it is available for use at provincial championships.

At this time the Union would have been completely lost but for some generous sponsorship. Had not the one-man sponsorship committee, Gerry O'Brien (President 1987–88), prevailed on a number of firms for assistance, the Union would have been forced to ask Irish golfers for even greater increases in the annual subscription. It is always a dangerous task to publish a list of assistance of this nature in case a benefactor might be overlooked at one time or another. Should such omission occur the Union can only extend its sincere apologies for the oversight. Before listing the sponsors for various events at the present time, reference must be made to some without whose help the Union could not have accomplished its goals: The Irish Dunlop Company guaranteed the Union against loss in the Canada Cup. From 1972, Aer Lingus financed two championships and its personnel attended the regional, national and international rounds at junior level, not only in the home countries but also in other parts of Europe. These were the Aer Lingus/Golf Foundation Schools' Golf Team Championship and the Aer Lingus Club Youth's Championship. Every international final, except one Schools' Championship, was played at venues in Ireland. The Union is satisfied that the initiative of Ireland's national airline resulted in many schools introducing golf and GUI member Clubs organising competitions for their younger members. When Aer Lingus withdrew its support for budgetary reasons, the Golf Foundation continued the schools event and the Union inaugurated its own Youths' Club Tournament. Jack Mulcahy guaranteed the Union against loss in the EAGTC in 1973.

The John Player Group provided the finance to enable the Union to print and distribute the 'Irish pilot' SSS and Handicapping scheme in 1971 to member Clubs in sufficient quantity to enable every Irish golfer to be supplied with a copy at no charge. When CONGU adopted a modified version of the scheme in 1973, the firm again provided the funds to repeat the earlier publication and distribution and also for a further revision in 1976.

P.J. Carroll & Co. Ltd, whose name is synonymous with golf in Ireland because of its promotion of the re-activated Open Championship of Ireland, stepped in when the John Player Group withdrew and printed and distributed two further SSS and Handicapping Scheme revisions in 1978 and 1983. The latest revision in 1989 was partially funded by Abbey Life, Allied Irish Finance and Glennon Craddock. Tara Publications printed and supplied the Union with 1,000 copies of the GUI Year Book, free of charge, each year from

1978 to 1989. Nissan (Datsun) Ireland Limited sponsored the Irish Amateur Close Championship from 1982 to 1984. Johnnie Walker sponsored the Inter-County Championship from 1980 to 1988. Standard Life Assurance Company sponsored the Ireland v. Scotland Youths' matches from 1979 to 1982. The First National Building Society sponsored the national finals of the Cups and Shields tournaments in 1986 and 1987. McDonalds' Hamburger Restaurants provided finance for the Irish Club Youths' Team Championship in 1986 and 1987. Stillorgan Bowl sponsored the Irish Schools' Championship in 1986 and 1987. The Northern Ireland Tourist Board sponsored the Quadrangular Continental Matches at Royal Portrush in 1988.

At the time of writing, the firms listed below sponsor, in whole or in part, the following Union events:

Amateur Interprovincial Matches	– Heineken Limited.
Cups and Shields National Finals	– Furstenberg.
Irish Amateur Close Championship	– Thomas Cook Travellers' Cheques.
Irish Boys' Amateur Close Championship	– Thomas Cook Travellers' Cheques.
Irish Golf Clubs Mixed Foursomes	– P.J. Carroll & Company Limited.
Irish international teams equipment	– Bank of Ireland Limited.
	– Dunlop Slazenger Ireland Limited.
	– Footjoy.
	– MacGregor Golf Ireland Limited.
	– O'Gorman's (Cork).
	– Titleist.
	– Two-Morrow Golf Limited.
Irish Junior Foursomes	– Smurfit Group Limited.
Irish Seniors' Amateur Open Championship	– Taylor Investment Group Limited.
Youths' Amateur Open Championship of Ireland	– Thomas Cook Travellers' Cheques.

Rank Xerox (Ireland) Limited provided copying equipment for the Championships and Tournaments.

The Union is also indebted to the R & A and to the Irish Sports Council — An Cospóir — for their very generous grants over a number of years towards the promotion of junior golf.

To all the above and to those who supported the Union over the last 20 years grateful thanks is expressed. Without question, their financial and material assistance has been a contributing factor in enabling the Union to continue with its original objects.

The names of donors of a number of cups and trophies have been mentioned before. These have been generously presented to the Union for annual competition. For all other events the Union provided the perpetual challenge trophies. The conditions of all the championships and tournaments now prescribe that all trophies, whether won by individuals or teams, are to be held by the Club of the winner until required for presentation at the conclusion of the particular event the following year. As early as the first Championship in 1892, a personal award was presented to the winner.

On the wall of the lounge in the Honorable Company of Edinburgh Golfers' clubhouse at Muirfield, Scotland, hangs a portrait of Alexander Stuart, the first Irish Amateur Open Champion. The Club also has the original gold medal presented to Stuart when he won the inaugural Championship at Portrush. The GUI is grateful to the Council of the Club for providing photographs of the portrait and medal. The Union is grateful also to William H. Webb (Royal County Down) for making available a set of medals won by his father and uncle in the early years of the Union which have been photographed for reproduction. One of the Webb medals is that of the original design of those presented to members of winning Senior Cup teams, which remained in use up to 1913. When the tournament was resumed after the 1914–18 war, a new design incorporating the crests of the four provinces of Ireland was introduced and this has become the standard design of all the inter-Club and inter-Schools team medals. Nine sets of team medals are awarded each year. Larger medals of a somewhat different design are awarded in the Irish Amateur Close Championship and the Youths' Amateur Open Championship of Ireland.

Gold medals are awarded to individual or team winners, silver medals to runners-up and bronze medals to the defeated semi-finalists. Some years ago the Council decided to provide any Club in the national final with an additional medal in each category to be awarded to the selected reserve on each team. Clubs can, and do, purchase additional medals from the Union to present to other Club members who played on the team in earlier rounds of the tournament. More recently it was decided to strike a special medal for presentation to each non-playing Captain of teams which reached the national finals. Each of these medals has the word 'Captain' on a scroll below it. In all, the Union presents 78 gold, 78 silver and 155 bronze medals each year.

Throughout this history, there are illustrations showing all Union cups and trophies, the portrait and medals mentioned above and all international trophies in events in which Irish teams compete. In addition, all cups and trophies awarded by the four provincial branches are likewise illustrated.

In conclusion, below are shown some Club entrance and green fee rates which operated in the early years. Fortunately, a copy of the 1897 Irish Golfers' Annual has been obtained from which the surviving eight of the founder Clubs have been selected, namely: 1. Ballycastle, 2. County (now Royal Portrush), 3. County Down (now Royal County Down), 4. Dungannon, 5. Killymoon, 6. Royal Belfast, 7. Portsalon and 8. North West.

	1.	2.	3.	4.	5.	6.	7.	8.
Entrance Fee	10/-	£5-5-0	£6-6-0	£1-1-0	None	£2-5-0	None	£1-1-0
Subscription	10/-	£1-1-0	£1-0-0	£1-1-0	£1-1-0	£2-2-0	10/6	£1-1-0
Green Fee:								
Daily		2/6	2/6	Free	Free			
Weekly	2/6	5/-	10/-	Free	Free	5/-	3/6	5/-
Monthly	7/6	10/-	£1-0-0	5/-	Free			15/-

The latest GUI Yearbook records the current green fees payable in these Clubs:

	1.	2.	3.	4.	5.	6.	7.	8
Daily	£10	£10	£30	n/a	£10	£14	n/a	£5
Sat. or Sun.	£14	£20	£35	n/a	£14	£16	n/a	£10

Some years ago when the question of increasing the Union subscription (then known as poll tax) was being considered, the Secretariat was instructed to ascertain the per capita rates paid by golfers is continental Clubs to their Unions or Associations and found that the GUI rates were infinitesimal compared with those on the continent. Those who go to continental locations on golfing holidays are aware also that the green fees now payable are three or four times higher than the highest Saturday or Sunday green fee listed above.

Chapter 35

THE
OFFICERS
OF
THE
UNION

At the inaugural meeting in Portrush on 12 October 1891 Captain James L. McCalmont J.P. (Captain of the Royal Belfast Golf Club) acted as Chairman. The first business of the meeting was to appoint Hugh Cunningham Kelly as Honorary Secretary pro. tem. Having passed a resolution to establish the Union, the meeting was adjourned to re-assemble in Belfast on a future date.

Hugh Kelly's temporary appointment to the office of Honorary Secretary lasted just 32 days. At the adjourned meeting in Belfast on 13 November W.H. Mann (Captain of the County Club, now Royal Portrush) was in the Chair and the following officers were elected:

> President: Lord Ranfurly
> Honorary Secretary: George Combe
> Honorary Treasurer: Hugh C. Kelly.

It would appear from the first minute book that during his 15 years as President, Lord Ranfurly did not take an active part in the affairs of the Union. He certainly never attended a meeting of the Union as the minutes record 16 different Chairmen at the 31 meetings held during his presidency. There have been 41 succeeding Presidents. They have taken their duties more diligently, chairing meetings of the Central Council and the Standing and other Committees, representing the Union at international events, attending championships and tournaments, presenting trophies and medals at events under the control and management of the Union and, at the invitation of many Club Captains, attending dinners and other social events as the senior officer of the GUI.

Union Presidents

Lord Ranfurly

1891–1906

D. Plunket Barton

1906–26

Hugh C. Kelly

1926–9

Beamish A. Morrison

1929–32

D. Wilson Smyth

1932–6

William Fitzsimmons

1936–8

George Crosbie

1938–42

Thomas P. Toher

1942–6

James Henderson

1946–8

Pierce F. Purcell

1948–50

Redmond Simcox

1950–52

William F. Neill

1952–4

Michael G. O'Malley

1954–6

Robert E. Davitt

1956–8

William M. O'Sullivan

1958–60

David L. Baine

1960–63

Michael J. Murphy

1963–5

Thomas P. Brindley

1965–7

Thomas E. O'Donnell

1967–8

H. Max Hadden

1968–9

William J. Gill

1969–70

Cecil Ewing

1970–71

Gerald H. Owens

1971–2

Thomas Montgomery

1972–3

Patrick J. McPolin

1973–4

Maurice De Lacy Staunton

1974–5

Peter V. Lyons

1975–6

John G. McErvel

1976–7

Patrick J. Foley

1977–8

Thomas J. Rogers

1978–9

Brendan J. Scannell

1979–80

Michael C. McAuley

1980–81

John P. McInerney

1981–2

Frederick W. Perry

1982–3

Michael P. Fitzpatrick

1983–4

William J.J. Ferguson

1984–5

Frank W. Bowen

1985–6

Michael J. Hennelly

1986–7

J. Gerard O'Brien

1987–8

Barry T. Crymble

1988–9

Joseph M. Quinlan

1989–90

Gerard D. Golden

1990–91

Mr Justice Dunbar Plunket Barton, Bart. was elected the second President of the Union at a meeting at Royal Portrush Golf Club on 4 September 1906. He remained in office for 20 years. In 1926, because his judicial duties necessitated his residing in London, he tendered his resignation and was succeeded by Hugh C. Kelly. On 9 September 1926, at the same meeting which dealt with the resignation and election, it was decided that the term of office of President be limited to two years with a proviso for re-election. Hugh Kelly was elected for a second term as were all subsequent Presidents until 1946 with the exception of William Fitzsimmons. He died in office in January 1938. The first six Presidents were alternatively from Ulster and Leinster covering the period 1891 to 1938. Commander George Crosbie was elected President in 1938 and became the first Munster based holder of this office. He was followed by Thomas P. Toher (Connacht). The Union minutes do not record any Council decision to introduce a provincial rota for the office of President, but it appears to have begun to operate with the election of Professor Pierce F. Purcell in 1948 and has become the established practice.

As the GUI constitution had not been updated in a major way since 1913, Tom Brindley, during his term as President (1965–66) proposed the introduction of a new constitution to keep pace with modern requirements. It was agreed that provision would be made for an additional officer, a President-Elect, and for reducing the term of office of the President to one year. The next President, Tommy O'Donnell, intimated that he would serve only one year if the Council agreed that Willie Gill, Honorary Secretary of the Union since 1949, would be elected the first President-Elect when the new constitution came into use. This was agreed and the established presidential rota was suspended for one year.

The Council also agreed to suspend the rota for the centenary year. Michael McAuley was President in 1980. He proposed that in 1990 the Central Council, and not a provincial branch, would nominate the President-Elect who would lead the Union into its second century the following year. At the 1990 AGM the Central Council elected Desmond Rea O'Kelly as President-Elect. Des had been Honorary Secretary since 1975. Both Willie and Des are most deserving of the honour as between them they guided the affairs of the Union for 41 years during which time there has been a phenomenal expansion of the game in Ireland and the status of the GUI has grown nationally and internationally.

Down the years each President has made his own contribution towards the advancement and continued well-being of the Union and has travelled to every part of Ireland in the fullfillment of his duties. Many have also travelled overseas enhancing the image of the GUI at international championships and conferences. Some holders of this office have been in the limelight more than others, in that important events or successes occurred during their term of office. We apologise to any President if we have omitted to include an important highlight during his term in the following list which extends from the first Home International match in 1932:

PRESIDENT	EVENT	YEAR
D. Wilson Smyth	Ireland joint winner of the home internationals at Royal Lytham and St Anne's.	1935
Pierce F. Purcell	The 54th Amateur Championship at Portmarnock.	1949
	Ireland won the home internationals at Harlech.	1950
Redmond Simcox	The 80th Open Championship at Royal Portrush.	1951
	Ireland joint winner of the home internationals at Royal Lytham and St Anne's.	1951
Michael G. O'Malley	Ireland won the home internationals at Royal Birkdale.	1955

PRESIDENT	EVENT	YEAR
William O'Sullivan	Ireland joint winner of the home internationals at Royal Lytham and St Anne's.	1959
	The GUI hosted the International Golf Association and organised the Canada Cup matches at Portmarnock.	1960
David L. Baine	Ireland joint winner of the home internationals at Royal Porthcawl.	1962
Michael J. Murphy	Ireland joint winner of the home internationals at Royal Lytham and St Anne's.	1963
Thomas P. Brindley	Ireland won the European Amateur Golf Team Championship at Royal St George's, Sandwich.	1965
Thomas E. O'Donnell	Ireland won the EAGTC at Turin, Italy.	1967
Cecil Ewing	The 75th Amateur Championship at Royal County Down.	1970
Thomas Montgomery	Ireland won the Quadrangular Continental Matches at Killarney.	1972
Patrick J. McPolin (for Maurice de L. Staunton)	Represented Ireland at the World Golf Conference at St Andrews.	1974
Peter V. Lyons	The GUI hosted the European Golf Association and organised the EAGTC at Killarney.	1975
Patrick J. Foley	Ireland won the European Amateur Youths' Golf Team Championship at Oslo, Norway.	1977
Brendan J. Scannell	Ireland won the EAYGTC at Marianske, Lazne, Czechoslovakia.	1979
Michael C. McAuley	Ireland won the QCM at Portmarnock.	1980
	Represented Ireland at the World Golf Conference at St Andrews.	1980
Michael P. Fitzpatrick	Ireland won the EAGTC at Chantilly, France.	1983
	The GUI was host to the Council of National Golf Unions and organised the home internationals at Portmarnock, which Ireland won.	1983
William J.J. Ferguson	The GUI hosted the EGA and organised the EAYGTC at Hermitage which Ireland won.	1984
Frank W. Bowen	Represented Ireland at the World Golf Conference at St Andrews.	1985
	Ireland joint winner of the inaugural Boys' home internationals at Royal Burgess.	1985
Michael J. Hennelly	Ireland won the QCM at Le Touquet, France.	1986
	Ireland won the Boys' home internationals at Seaton Carew.	1986
Gerard O'Brien	Ireland won the EAGTC at Murhof, Austria.	1987
	The GUI hosted the Council of National Golf Unions and organised the home internationals at Lahinch which Ireland won. In addition to winning the Raymond Trophy, Ireland also won the Triple Crown for the first time since the series was inaugurated in 1932.	1987
Barry T. Crymble	Ireland won the QCM at Royal Portrush.	1988
Joseph Quinlan	Represented Ireland at the World Golf Conference at St Andrews.	1989
Gerard D. Golden	Ireland won the QCM at Ostersund, Sweden.	1990
	Ireland won the home internationals and the 'triple crown' at Conwy, Wales.	1990

Not counting Hugh Kelly's brief and temporary appointment, there were only ten Honorary Secretaries during the first 100 years. George Combe (1891–98) was an energetic and dedicated Honorary Secretary, setting the pattern for his successors to this office. His first task was to organise the Irish Amateur Open Championship. He obtained guidance from the R & A which enabled him to draw up conditions for this Championship which commenced in 1892 and also the Close Championship which commenced in 1893. In 1895 he proposed the playing of inter-Club matches which progressed to the inauguration of the Senior and Junior Cups Tournaments in 1899. He also organised the first interprovincial matches between Ulster and Leinster at the County Club, Portrush on 7 April 1896 prior to the

Union Honorary Secretaries

George Combe

1891–9

Henry J. Daly

1899–1906

John L. Morrow

1906–21

George Price

1921–7

Alan B. Kidd

1927–48

John Roy

1948–9

William J. Gill

1949–68
1970–76

Thomas P. Brindley

1968–70

Desmond Rea O'Kelly

1975–90

J. Gerard O'Brien

1989–

Union Honorary Treasurers

Hugh C. Kelly

1891–1912

William B. Fennell

1912–30

Arthur H. Moody

1930–31

Charles S. Harden

1931–7

William F. Neill

1937–46

Frank J. Byrne

1946–8

Alfred S.G. Adams

1948–53

Hugh Stevenson

1953–68

Charles S. Adams

1968–74

David M. McAuley

1974–

Close Championship. However, what must be regarded as his greatest contribution to the development of the game in Ireland was the designing of the first universal handicapping scheme in 1896. This was used as a blueprint by the Joint Advisory Council when they introduced the standard scratch score and handicapping scheme for the four home Unions in 1924. It is no coincidence that the incumbent of the office of Honorary Secretary since 1975 has been very much involved in the latest revision of the SSS and Handicapping Scheme. At a meeting in the Imperial Hotel, Belfast on 10 March 1899 George Combe intimated that, for business reasons, he was compelled to relinquish the office and he proposed that the Union appoint a member of a southern Club as Honorary Secretary and this was unanimously agreed. The meeting also decided 'that in future the meetings, as far as possible, should be held alternatively in Dublin and Belfast'. Henry J. Daly, a member of County Louth Golf Club, was appointed to succeed George Combe who continued to show his interest by attending meetings of the Union as a delegate from County Down. The legacy left by George Combe has been adhered to by successive holders of this office. Reverend J.L. Morrow (1906–20) followed Henry Daly. The first mention of the name of J.L. Morrow is in the attendance list at a meeting in the Imperial Hotel, Belfast on 10 May 1899. Unfortunately the name of the Club of which he was a delegate is not entered after his name. A year later J.L. Morrow attended a meeting in the Metropole Hotel, Dublin, as a delegate for Lahinch. At Club level he will best be remembered as the founder of Clontarf Golf Club. Next there was George Price (1921–26). He was followed by Alan Kidd who held office for 20 years. The JAC had been formed in 1924 from which the Sports Turf Research Institute evolved. Alan Kidd was the Union's representative to the STRI and its Chairman for many years. We have earlier mentioned the long service of Willie Gill and Des Rea O'Kelly. Gerry O'Brien, having served his apprenticeship as Joint Honorary Secretary with Des Rea, was elected to the office at the 1990 AGM.

The talents of Hugh Kelly, our pro. tem. Honorary Secretary were recognised when at the adjourned meeting in 1891 he was given another portfolio, that of Honorary Treasurer. Since that time there have been ten holders of this important office. Hugh Kelly and his successor, William Fennell, served a total of 39 years. The Union has had a father and son looking after its finances, Fred Adams (1948–52) and Charles (1968–73). The present holder of this officer is David McAuley who was first elected in 1974. It is not possible to be certain whether the earlier Honorary Treasurers were Accountants by profession, but from 1948 onwards this has been the practice. The earlier Honorary Treasurers had a small number of Clubs to deal with from which funds were obtained, but the situation today is in the realm of big business, requiring not only professional expertise but constant vigilance.

Going back to the adjourned inaugural meeting of 13 November 1891 the first Honorary Treasurer was a member of an Ulster Club. All his successors in office have likewise been members of Ulster Clubs. The meeting of 10 March 1899 has been mentioned already. Since then the pattern has been to elect a member of a Leinster Club as Honorary Secretary.

Clause 19.1 of the GUI constitution prescribes that the President 'shall hold office for a period not exceeding one year'. The President-Elect 'shall hold office for a period not exceeding one year, and may be elected President of the Union on the termination of the office of his immediate predecessor'. The Honorary Secretary 'shall retire annually and shall be eligible for re-election'. The Honorary Treasurer 'shall retire annually and shall be eligible for re-election.'

Since the introduction of the 1913 constitution, the term of office of both the Honorary Secretary and the Honorary Treasurer has been an annual one. Should these officers wish to seek re-election their names must be submitted prior to the AGM. This procedure has been successful for an examination of the minutes discloses that it was only when the outgoing incumbent indicated that he did not wish to allow his name to go forward for re-election that the name of a new candidate was nominated. Another extraordinary vote of confidence by successive Councils is the fact that it has been the practice for the outgoing officer to nominate his successor. A list of all officers, showing date of election, is set out in Appendix XXIII.

Chapter 36

IRISH
WALKER CUP
PLAYERS

George H. Walker was educated at Stonyhurst, England before he went to an American university. He was President of the United States Golf Association when, in 1920, he led some members of the Executive of the USGA to St Andrews. The purpose of the visit was to confer with the R & A on the rules of Golf — a meeting which now takes place between the two bodies every four years. He became intrigued with the idea of an international match and on his return to America he put up The United States Golf Association International Challenge Cup. The trophy has since become universally known as The Walker Cup.

The first match was played in 1922 at Walker's home Club, the National Golf Links of America, on Long Island, New York. The format was four 36 holes foursomes, with eight 36 holes singles on the following day, between teams representing the United States of America and Britain and Ireland. The United States won the inaugural event by 8 matches to 4. St Andrews was the venue for the 1923 series and Garden City, New York the 1924 venue. Thereafter the two governing bodies decided that the matches would be played in alternate years.

In Chapter 13 the conference at York on 14 February 1924 was mentioned at which the Joint Advisory Council was formed. Following the conference, the R & A sought assistance from the four home Unions to fund the cost of sending a team of ten to compete in the Walker Cup matches in America, and asked the JAC to submit a panel of players from which the Walker Cup team could be selected. The GUI put forward the names of Major Charles O. Hezlet (Royal Portrush) and Dr John D. MacCormack (Hermitage) to the JAC to be included on the panel. The R & A selected Charles Hezlet for the 1924 series at Garden City and again in 1926 for the matches at St Andrews. J.D. MacCormack was also selected for the 1926 matches but he was a Medical Officer attached to the Department of Local Government and his superiors refused to grant him leave of absence to compete at St Andrews and so deprived him of one of the highest honours available to an amateur golfer. Such a bureaucratic approach would not occur today.

In the ten series of matches played between 1922 and 1938, the Britain and Ireland team achieved only one success, at St Andrews in 1938. The matches were suspended because of the war and were re-commenced in 1947, again at St Andrews. They have since continued in alternate years on each side of the Atlantic. Whilst the matches still extend over two days, the format was changed in 1963 from 36 holes foursomes on day one and 36 holes singles on day two, to 18 holes foursomes and 18 holes singles on each of the two days. This allows the Team Captains greater flexibility in nominating their order of play.

Since the Walker Cup was inaugurated, 32 matches have been played, 16 in America (each at a different venue) and 16 on this side of the Atlantic (eight at St Andrews; two each at Muirfield and Sandwich and one each at Birkdale, Turnberry, Hoylake and Sunningdale).

In response to a request from the Golfing Union of Ireland and strongly supported by the Committee of Portmarnock Golf Club, the R & A agreed to mark the GUI's centenary by playing the 1991 Walker Cup matches at Portmarnock.

With the inauguration of the home international matches in 1932 (which we have dealt with in Chapter 15), the R & A were in a position to assess the qualities of the leading amateurs in the four countries, and appointed its own Walker Cup Selection Committee. Probably by design, this Committee consists of one representative from each of the four home Unions with a Chairman nominated by the R & A. Whilst each Union is invited to submit the name of a candidate, the R & A reserves the sole right to decide to whom the invitation to serve on the Committee will be extended.

As to finance, each Union used to be advised of the contribution it was expected to make (based on the number of golfers in each country) and was asked to forward this amount to the R & A. However, the time came when the finances of the R & A were such that it could fund the matches itself and it indicated that contributions were no longer required. With the growing attendances at the Open Championship and revenue from other sources (such as T.V. etc.) the ruling authority has become a most generous benefactor and now provides the Unions and the Golf Foundation with grants to promote the game, particularly at Junior level.

The *R & A Championship Records* and the *Golfers' Handbook* provide some interesting facts. In the 70 years since the series was inaugurated, 172 American and 174 British and Irish players have attained Walker Cup honours. The record number of matches played is by Michael Bonallack with 25 and the American, Jay Segal comes a close second with 23. Segal has the highest points score of 31 with 14 matches won and 3 halved. Second in points is another American, William C. Campbell with 25; 11 matches won and 3 halved. Bill Campbell was Captain of the Royal and Ancient Golf Club in 1988.

Judged by points obtained, the performance of the British and Irish players has not been too flattering as the Americans have been defeated only once on their own territory (14 wins, 1 match halved and 1 lost). This superiority was also evident on this side of the Atlantic with 14 matches won and only 2 matches lost.

Nineteen Irish players have competed in 24 of the 32 matches. Ireland's greatest representation was in the 1949 series at Winged Foot, New Jersey and also in the 1951 series at St Andrews when we had four players on the team on each occasion: Cecil Ewing, Jimmy Bruen, Joe Carr and Max McCready.

The Irish players and their statistical records are:

Name	Club	Years	Played	Won	Halved	Lost	Points
Bruen, J.	Muskerry	1938-51	5	–	1	4	1
Burke, J.	Lahinch	1932	2	–	1	1	1
Carr, J.B.	Sutton	1947–67	20	5	1	14	11
Carr, R.J.	Sutton	1971	4	3	1	–	7
Craddock, T.	Malahide	1967–69	6	2	1	3	5
Drew, N.V.	Bangor	1953	1	–	–	1	–
Ewing, C.	County Sligo	1936–55	10	1	2	7	4
Hezlet, C.O.	Royal Portrush	1924–28	6	–	1	5	1
McCready, S.M.	Dunmurry	1949–51	3	–	–	3	–
McGimpsey, G.	Bangor	1985–89	4	1	2	1	4
McHenry, J.	Douglas	1987	4	2	–	2	4
Madeley, J.F.D.	Royal Belfast	1963	2	–	1	1	1
Martin, G.N.C.	Royal Portrush	1928	1	–	–	1	–
Mulcare, P.	Woodbrook	1975	3	2	–	1	4
O'Connell, E.	Killarney	1989	4	3	1	–	7
Pierse, A.D.	Tipperary	1983	3	–	1	2	1
Rafferty, R.	Warrenpoint	1981	4	2	–	2	4
Sheahan, D.B.	Grange	1963	4	2	–	2	4
Walton, P.	Malahide	1981–83	8	6	–	2	12

Hereunder are interesting facts about the above players. Their records are set out in Appendix XXIV.

Charles O. Hezlet (1924–28)

The Hezlets of Portrush were one of the most distinguished families in the history of the game in Ireland. An examination of the Captains' Boards reproduced in the history of the Royal Portrush Golf Club shows the esteem with which the family was held.

Charles Owen Hezlet was born in May 1891, some five months before the founding of the GUI. His father, Lieut. Col. R.J. Hezlet, was elected Captain of the Club in 1900 whilst his mother, Emily, had occupied the premier office in the Ladies' Branch in 1898–99. Charles was honoured with captaincy twice, from 1914 to 1920 and again from 1946 to 1948. He had four sisters: May, who won the Ladies' Amateur Championship in 1899, 1902 and 1907 and the Irish Ladies' Amateur Championship in 1899, 1904, 1905, 1906 and 1908. She was elected Lady Captain in 1905. Florence was runner-up to May in the 1907 Ladies' Amateur Championship and she was elected Lady Captain twice, in 1912 and again in 1924–25. The third sister, Violet, was also runner-up in the Ladies' Amateur Championship in 1911. Both Florence and Violet were each defeated finalists on three occasions for the Irish title. The fourth sister, Emmie, was elected Lady Captain in 1920–21.

Irish Walker Cup Players

Joseph B. Carr	Cecil Ewing	Charles O. Hezlet	James Bruen	John Burke
1947–67	1936–53	1924–8	1938–51	1932

G. Noel C. Martin

1928

S. Max McCready

1949–51

Norman V. Drew

1953

J.F. David Madeley

1963

David B. Sheahan

1963

Thomas Craddock

1967–9

Roderick J. Carr

1971

Patrick Mulcare

1973

Ronan Rafferty

1981

Philip Walton

1981–3

Arthur D. Pierse

1983

Garth McGimpsey

1985–9

John McHenry

1987

Eoghan O'Connell

1989

'C.O.H.' as he was known, won all the major trophies in his home Club:
   The Alexander Cup – 1906, 1910 and 1912.
   The President's Cup – 1908 and 1911.
   The Adair Shield – 1908, 1910, 1911, 1912, 1913, 1919, 1926, 1927, 1935 and 1936.
   The Richardson Cup – 1937 and 1949.

His Championship, international and other records are set out in Appendix XXIV (Section 1).

In addition to being a first-class player, he was also a capable administrator. He had the distinction of being appointed Irish Team Captain 16 times between 1923 and 1953. He was a member of the Central Council of the Union from 1946 until his death in 1965. Elected to the Irish Selection Committee in 1947, he served on it for seven years and was Chairman of selectors in all but the first year of that period. In 1948 he was appointed by the Union as a delegate to the JAC (now the Council of National Golf Unions) on which he served until 1954. He served on the Championship Committee of the R & A from 1948 to 1952, being Deputy Chairman in 1951 and Chairman in 1952. From 1949 to 1955 he was a member of the R & A Rules of Golf Committee, being Chairman from 1953 to 1955. He was also an Associate Member of the USGA Rules Committee. He was elected a member of the General Committee of the R & A for a term of three years.

It was due to his influence that the R & A decided to allocate the 80th Open Championship to Royal Portrush in 1951, the only occasion this prestigious Championship has been played in Ireland.[14] As a tribute to his memory, his daughter, Rosemary, presented one of his IAOC replica cups to the Ulster Branch of the Union to be known as the 'Hezlet Cup'. This is played for annually as the Ulster Youths' Amateur Open Championship trophy.

C.O.H. had a unique record which, because of clarification of the eligibility requirements, will never be equalled. He represented two countries in international matches. Whilst working in Wales in 1922 he was selected to play for it against Midlands. In the following year he was selected on two occasions for Ireland against Wales and Midlands. He served with distinction in the two World Wars. Twice mentioned in dispatches he was awarded the DSO and MC and rose to the rank of Lieutenant Colonel.

He died in Sussex, where he had gone to live, in 1965.

G. Noel C. Martin (1928)

Noel Martin was also born in 1891 in Portrush and, in the *History of Royal Portrush*[15] his name is linked with that of his contemporary, Charles Hezlet. Sir Edward Jones (Captain 1956–57), recounting what he saw in the final of the 1923 Victory Cup, describes them as golfing tritons who came literally from adjoining streets in Portrush. Noel won the match by 3 and 2 and it was the second occasion within two weeks that he had defeated his great rival of whom he had once said, 'If the big man could putt he'd be a world beater.'

Noel won the Irish Amateur Open Championship at Portmarnock in 1920. In the final of the same Championship at Newcastle in 1923 the two rivals met again. The *History of Royal County Down*[16] quotes an article on the match published in the *Belfast Newsletter* in which it described it as the best final ever seen in Irish Golf. The start was 3,3,3 (three birdies) with Noel winning the 1st and 3rd to be one up. The next birdie came at the 8th to put Noel 2 up. At the 9th C.O.H. was stymied, the same fate which had befallen him at the 6th. On this occasion, however, he lofted his ball over that of his opponent into the hole to reduce the deficit. The article states, 'this clever stroke was the most courageous of the day'. The second nine was almost a repeat of the first nine in that Noel got birdies at the 10th and 11th and C.O.H. replied with one at the 13th to reduce the deficit to 2 holes at which it remained for the rest of the round. Their better ball was 65 and the round was completed in two hours and sixteen minutes. Unfortunately the second 18 is not recorded in the history but Noel came out victorious by just one hole.

A man of the utmost integrity and a stickler for the rules, he conceded a hole in a championship because his caddie had inadvertently broken a rule of golf. Playing against Dr William O'Sullivan (Killarney) in the semi-final of the Irish Amateur Open at Killarney in 1949, he sliced his tee shot on the 17th on to the lake shore. His caddie, taking a short cut, went down off the tee on to the shore and, 'miles' from the ball picked up a piece of driftwood. Noel immediately conceded the hole as the shore was a hazard. At this time Noel was 58 years of age and it is a measure of his enthusiasm for the game that he was still competing at this level. He was beaten on the 18th and Billy went on to beat Brennie Scannell (Woodbrook), also on the 18th, in the final.

The Royal Portrush history records Noel as being Club Captain in 1949–50. It also contains a photograph of him, in his capacity of Club Captain, presenting Max Faulkner with the Open Championship Trophy at Portrush in July 1951. The reason for this anomaly arose because in those days the Club AGM did not take place until September. As Noel was a professional soldier (he rose to the rank of Brigadier General and was awarded both the DSO and the MC) he did not have much time to compete in Club events. This explains why the Club is only able to trace his success in two Club tournaments — the Town Cup in 1907 and the Victory Cup in 1923.[17]

Some years after he vacated the office of Club Captain Noel went to live in Greystones and joined Portmarnock. Eventually he retired to the Channel Islands where he died. His championship, international and other records are set out in Appendix XXIV (Section 2).

John Burke (1932)

John Burke was born in Lahinch in 1900. Whilst he played representative golf for some other Irish Golf Clubs, he entered from Lahinch in championships and international matches. Off the course he was regarded as an imaginative story teller as he would liberally embellish some of his reminiscences to suit his different audiences but on the course he was an opponent to be both respected and feared.

He had command of all the shots and, allied to his natural talent, his ability to disguise a stroke caused utter confusion to an unwitting opponent. John could take a wood or a long iron at a short hole, taking a full swing and appearing to strike the ball hard, yet the ball would only travel the short distance to the green. On other occasions he would take a 6 or 7 iron and hit it a very long way, without appearing to use much effort. He claimed that it was all a matter of timing but his opponents had another name for it. He was an expert at taking his driver and, from a close lie on the fairway, he would get home in two on a long par 5 hole. The golf writer, Bernard Darwin, rated him among the very best of the amateurs in the home countries in the years between the two World Wars and expressed regret that he did not compete overseas, reserving his finest efforts for his own country. Darwin also said, 'one of my greatest pleasures as a golf correspondent was to see Mr Burke of Ireland timing a driver off the fairway.'

His record in the South of Ireland Amateur Open Championship got him the name of King of the South. He won the Championship four times in succession from 1928 to 1931. He did not play in it again until 1939 — for the most extraordinary of reasons. Lahinch is a holiday resort and the local hoteliers rely heavily on golfers for most of their custom. They feared that as John appeared to be invincible in the most important event in the local calendar, many aspiring golfers would consider it a waste of effort and would not enter and so there would be a resultant loss to the local hotels. They asked John not to enter for some years and he acceded to their request.

As an alternative, he decided to turn his attention to a new conquest. He invaded Ewing Country and entered the West of Ireland Amateur Open Championship at County Sligo in 1933 and won. He successfully defended his title in 1934, was runner-up in 1935 and won again in 1936 and 1938. Over the following seven years he won twice and was runner-up twice.

Back in Lahinch, the 'South' continued to flourish so John entered again in 1939 and won. From 1941 to 1946 he again proved invincible, winning in six successive years. His hold on the trophy was eventually broken by his friend and Club-mate, Brud Slattery, the long serving Secretary to Lahinch Golf Club, who beat John in the 1947 final.

The East of Ireland Amateur Open Championship was inaugurated in 1941 and the following year John visited Baltray but had to be satisfied at being runner-up to the local member, Kevin Garvey, who returned one stroke less in the 72 hole event. John was runner-up again in 1943. He tied with Joe Carr in 1945 but was beaten by three strokes in the 36 hole play-off. He played again in 1946 and tied for runner-up.

His record in the Close is also impressive: eight wins (four in succession) and runner-up twice. His career as a leading amateur spanned 21 years and during that period many matches in which he was involved have been described as classics. Two of his most notable matches in Ireland, both against Joe (J.B.) Carr, come to mind.

In 1946, defending the 'South' for the sixth successive year, he came up against J.B. Carr in the final. J.B. was not only 20 years younger but had already won the 'West' and 'East' that year. The huge and sometimes partisan gallery was enthralled as Burke, the King, faced Carr in what turned out to be a marathon encounter which took 39 holes to resolve. The golf was of the highest standard. There was never more than one hole difference throughout with John covering the first eighteen in 69 to J.B.'s 70. In the afternoon the order was reversed with J.B. having 69 to John's 70 and the match finished all square. In the 'sudden death' playoff, the 37th and 38th were each halved in birdies and John, with a 3 at the 39th won the match.[18]

In the following year at Dollymount the two players met in the final of the Irish Amateur Open Championship. This time, John secured a commanding lead of five holes in the morning round but after lunch he found himself fighting a rear-guard action and he did not manage to win a single hole in the afternoon. The standard of play was very high: J.B. covered the opening nine in the afternoon in 33 strokes but only managed to win back one hole. He succeeded in reducing the deficit but ran out of holes and John won his first and only Irish

Amateur Open Championship by one hole. This was an unique double as earlier in the year John had won the Close. Only five golfers achieved this double: Lionel Munn (North West) in 1911, Jimmy Bruen in 1933, John in 1947, Cecil Ewing in 1948 and seven years later Joe Carr joined this exclusive hall of fame.

John played in one Walker Cup match, at Brookline, in 1932. Defeated in the foursomes on the first day by Francis Ouimet and G.T. Dunlap Jr, he faced Jack Westland (who had been runner-up in the American Amateur Championship the previous year) in the 36 holes singles on day two. Five down after the morning round, he showed his fighting spirit and by the time they reached the 34th John had reduced the deficit to three down with three to play. John proceeded to win the last three holes to square the match.

Lahinch honoured him with the captaincy of the Club in 1948. At that time his official handicap was plus 2. He won several Club trophies off handicaps ranging from plus 2 to plus 4, including the Golf Links Hotel Cup, the Shaw Cup and the Liscannor Cup. He also won a Captain's prize playing off plus 2.

At the age of 50 ill health reduced him to the role of spectator on the golf course, and he was only able to watch the 'South' from different vantage points whilst sitting in a car. Sadly he spent his last years in a wheelchair. He died in Limerick in 1974. His championship, international and other records are set out in Appendix XXIV (Section 3).

Cecil Ewing (1936–55)

Born in Rosses Point, Co. Sligo in July 1910 and christened Reginald Cecil, he was known (in golfing circles at any rate) as Cecil. It must be a record to have been in the final of the same major Championship 18 times over a period of 31 years. That was Cecil's record in the West of Ireland Amateur Open Championship and it comprised 11 wins and seven times runner-up. He played in his first final when he was only 17 years of age.

A member of County Sligo Golf Club from an early age, Cecil spent most of his life in the Sligo area. He had two great sporting loves. In addition to golf, he was an ardent and excellent shot. At the end of September each year he put away his golf clubs and spent the winter and spring game shooting. Unlike most players of his standard he never practised his golf. A week or so before the 'West' he would take out his clubs and play a few rounds over the Point. That was his only preparation at the start of the golfing season.

An extremely narrow stance became his normal address position, more by accident than design. He first won the 'West' in 1930 when still in his teens. He became hospitalised with a foot infection some time later. Up to that time he had a fairly wide stance and a full swing, but on his return to golf he found it painful to take a full pivot and transfer his weight. He decided to keep his feet close together, take a half swing and use his arms and shoulders. He discovered that he could hit the ball just as far, and more importantly, he could hit it much straighter than before. He wisely decided to adopt this new method.

An examination of his record shows that he helped Portmarnock Golf Club win the Senior Cup in four successive years from 1932 and in 1940, as well as the Barton Shield in 1935, 1939 and 1940. He was attached to an insurance company during these years which necessitated his taking up residence in Dublin, and he joined Portmarnock. In 1943 he joined an internationally renowned brewery firm and was appointed its representative for the Mayo area. He moved to Ballina where he remained until 1955. Then he was transferred to Sligo where he was appointed Manager in 1957.

Whilst he was a congenial companion off the course, he took his golf so seriously that he was considered a dour opponent. During his long career as one of Ireland's outstanding amateur golfers he had many memorable encounters with two other players of similar status, John Burke and Joe Carr. In seven Championship finals between Cecil and John, the latter held the edge by four wins to three. In eight finals between Cecil and Joe he was defeated on six occasions by the younger man. Joe became a welcome guest in the Ewing household when competing in the 'West', and although Joe came out the winner against Cecil in four 'West' finals this did not strain their friendship.

Cecil was the first Irish amateur to gain 50 international 'caps', but he had to stage a comeback to do so. Going to Newcastle for the 1957 Internationals, Cecil had already made 47 international appearances. Gerry Owens, the Irish non-playing Captain, picked Cecil for the matches against Scotland and Wales on the first two days. Cecil was not in robust health and lost his two foursomes and two singles matches. Gerry dropped a bombshell by omitting Cecil against England and many supporters were critical of the Captain for depriving Cecil of his half century. However, Gerry must be commended. He was a long time friend of Cecil's and had to make an agonising decision and decided to put his duty first. Cecil quietly left Newcastle after what most of those present thought was the end of his international career.

Such was his determination to achieve his goal of 50 caps that, over the next six months, Cecil went on a strict diet, shed some weight and got himself physically fit. He entered the 'West' the following Easter and got through to the final where he succumbed to Joe Carr who, two months later, went on to win the Amateur Championship (his second) at St Andrews.

The Close Championship was in Ballybunion that year and Cecil again went through the field to meet Gregory Young (Kilrush) in the final. In those days the Close extended over four days with one round on the first day, two rounds on each of the second and third days and a 36 hole final on the fourth day: a case of survival of the fittest. The morning round of the final finished all square but in the afternoon Cecil struck a devastating blow with birdie, eagle, birdie, eagle at four successive holes from the 7th to the 10th (now the 12th to the 15th) and won by 4 and 3. Gerry Owens, who was Chairman of selectors approached the winner after the trophy had been presented and congratulated him adding, 'When you are having your name engraved on the Cup put mine in brackets after it as you would never have won it if I had not dropped you last year'. Cecil replied, 'You can't drop me now'.

The following September Cecil achieved his ambition when he took part in the Internationals at Porthcawl and he then retired from international competitive golf.

He had not confined himself to home events, and competed in the Amateur Championship on a regular basis from 1935. His best performance was at Troon in 1938 when Charles Yates of Atlanta, USA, beat him by 3 and 2 in the 36 hole final. His last appearance was at St Andrews in 1950 where he lost to his fellow countryman, Max McCready, in the fourth round.

Whilst his Walker Cup career spanned 19 years, he only played in six matches during this period because they were suspended from 1938 to 1947. In addition, illness curtailed his golf in 1952 and the R & A invited him to become a Walker Cup selector. He acted in that capacity for the 1953 series but on his recovery he resigned as a selector and went on to gain further honour by being picked for the 1955 series.

When the Central Council decided to institute an Irish Seniors' Amateur Open Championship in 1970, Cecil presented a perpetual Challenge Cup as the Seniors' Trophy and to show that he had not lost his competitive skill he became its first winner at Lahinch.

Following his retirement from the international scene in 1958, Cecil turned his talents to administration. In 1959 he was elected an Irish international selector, an office he held for 11 years. He had also been a playing selector in 1949. The Connacht Branch nominated him as a delegate to the Central Council in 1961. He was elected Chairman of the Branch in 1964, and having been President-Elect in 1969, he was elected President of the Union in 1970.

The Central Council appointed him International Team Captain in 1960. During his ten year tenure in that office he captained 14 Irish teams. In 1965 the Council decided to enter the European Amateur Golf Team Championship which was being played that year at the Royal St George's Golf Club, Sandwich. He said afterwards that one of the proudest moments of his life was stepping forward at the head of his team to receive the European Trophy for Ireland from the President of the EGA. When Ireland retained the trophy in Turin two years later his team celebrated by pushing him into the Club swimming pool. He must have had some inkling of his team's intention as he gave the author his wrist watch to mind as soon as Tom Egan holed his putt on the final green to secure Ireland's victory.

His name is to be found on the major County Sligo perpetual trophies. As part of his come-back in 1957 he won the Captain's Prize by returning 68 off scratch. His Club honoured him on three occasions by appointing him Captain in 1940 and again in 1961 and President for 1970–72. He died in Rosses Point in 1973. His championship, international and other records are set out in Appendix XXIV (Section 4).

Jimmy Bruen (1938–51)

Jimmy Bruen was born in Belfast in 1920 but grew up in Cork. He first played golf whilst on a family holiday in Rosapenna, Co. Donegal, in 1931. His father got him a set of cut-down clubs and he became a juvenile member of Cork Golf Club where he spent most of his free time hitting balls. 'Because of a Cork Golf Club rule about juveniles, it was to Muskerry Golf Club that Jimmy turned for his first handicap of six. A few weeks and a few pieces of silver later he was down to scratch, his enormous strength and wonderful hands enabling him to swing a driver a fraction below 15 ounces with devastating effect.'[19] Although Jimmy was closely associated with Cork Golf Club during his entire life he always entered championships naming Muskerry as his Club, possibly because it was that Club which first handicapped him.

From his earliest years he had a looped swing. This meant that from the moment he started his backswing until he completed his follow-through, the clubhead was in continual motion. This enabled him to generate enormous speed at impact and he hit the ball huge distances. Harry Bradshaw, the long-time professional at Portmarnock, recounted that he played with Jimmy on a fairly regular basis over the championship course and witnessed him drive the 1st (394 yards), the 2nd (378 yards) and the 3rd (385 yards) on several occasions.

George Crosbie (Irish International 1952–57) describing what he refers to as 'Bruen power', relates that at Cork Golf Club Jimmy drove the uphill 1st (412 yards) once with a following wind and often drove the 6th (321 yards), the 8th (332 yards), the uphill 16th (274 yards) and regularly used a three wood to get to the green at both the 3rd (274 yards) and the 12th (268 yards).

In 1935, when still a student at Presentation College, Cork, he entered the Boys' Amateur Open Championship at the Royal Aberdeen Golf Club and was beaten in the second round. The following year he again competed in the Championship, this time at Royal Birkdale, and became the first Irish player to win an Open Championship run by the R & A. Next, at Ballybunion in 1937 he won the Irish Amateur Close Championship when he defeated John Burke by 3 and 2 in the 36 hole final. As a result of this victory he was awarded his first 'cap' to play for Ireland in the home internationals at Portmarnock the following September. As these matches clashed with the Boys' Championship he was unable to defend his title to that event.

In May 1938 three Irish players, Cecil Ewing, John Fitzsimmons and Jimmy, were included in a panel of 24 players for a Walker Cup trial at St Andrews. Jimmy had never seen the links before and returned 71 in each of the two pre-trial practice rounds. In the first match of the trial against two other players, he went round in 68 strokes equalling Bobby Jones' 1927 course record. The *Daily Telegraph* used all sorts of superlatives in reporting the match and described his superiority by stating, 'One of the longest hitters in the game, he played with a slight draw and reached the plateau green at the long fifth, 530 yards, with a drive and a three iron and then holed the 12 foot putt for an eagle.'

At the conclusion of the trials, Henry Cotton wrote, 'Fancy a 17-year-old doing 282 in four rounds here. I know what a stern course it is; long, difficult and tricky, but here was a mere boy playing it with a wise head and a technique which left everyone gasping. I have not known a player to do such scores no matter what his age. Bruen has set a standard for all players.'[20]

It was no surprise that Jimmy was selected on the Walker Cup side for the matches against the USA at the same venue later that year and at which the Britain and Ireland team gained its first ever win over the USA. Jimmy led the side in both foursomes and singles and George Crosbie states, 'Almost incredibly every one of the players, officials, writers and commentators of the time have always picked the Cork schoolboy as the inspiration behind the shock triumph'.[21] Henry Longhurst proclaimed before the match that the Americans were the greatest team ever assembled and that the other side would be fortunate to get even three points out of the 12 matches. After the match Longhurst reported that 'it was the psychological factor in the person of Bruen which had the effect of demonstrating to the other players on the side that the Old Course was not so difficult after all as this boy set an entirely new standard of golfing ability.'[22] The team Captain, John Beck, was even more direct in his recognition of Jimmy's historic role, saying, 'he gave the Americans an inferiority complex. They had heard of his phenomenal scoring on the Old Course even before they arrived and then they saw him continue to do these scores there.'

Such were the tributes showered on the Cork schoolboy. In the same year he successfully retained his Close Championship title and also brought off a double by winning the Irish Amateur Open Championship at Newcastle.

Defending his Close title for the second time at Rosses Point in 1939, he reached the fourth round where he met Gerry Owens (Skerries) whom he had beaten by one hole in the semi-final at Castle the previous year. This time Gerry was successful and went on to win the Championship. Writing about the match, George Crosbie says 'what the bare result does not record is that Bruen played the home nine holes off the Championship tees in only 32 shots — and that Owens covered that stretch in a superlative 28 strokes.'[23]

Unfortunately, the 1939–45 war brought international golf, the Amateur Championship, and both the Irish Amateur Open and Amateur Close Championships to a standstill.

The R & A re-activated the Amateur in 1946 and Jimmy went through the field and defeated Robert Sweeny, USA, by 4 and 3 in the 36 hole final. Then tragedy occurred in 1947. He loved practising and spent countless hours hitting balls. During one of these sessions he injured his right wrist and had to have it in plaster for two months. Unfortunately the cause remained a mystery and the injury never left him. Although he was obliged to scratch from the 1949 Amateur Championship at Portmarnock on medical advice, he was selected for the Walker Cup matches later that year. Selected again for the 1951 series at Birkdale, his wrist gave out during the foursomes on the first day and this effectively brought an end to his golfing career at international level.

In June 1963 the Close Championship was scheduled for Killarney. Jimmy, who spent a good portion of each summer in a mobile home parked near the old 5th green at Killarney, decided to enter — more as a tribute to the Club than anything else. The old flair was there and he reached the semi-final to come up against Joe Carr. Although they had both played against one another at Club level, this was the first time they had met in a Championship. Writing in *The Irish Times* after the match,[24] Paul MacWeeney wrote, 'All that could have been dreamed about in this match came true. The standard of play in an electric atmosphere was extraordinarily high and the strain of combat was intense. The better ball for the 18 holes was 65, ten better than par, and the sheer drama will never be forgotten by those who were there. Carr won on the 18th, Bruen conceding a two-foot putt with a smile and a handshake. Later he was to comment "I thoroughly enjoyed it and the better player won".' This was indeed a gracious tribute in defeat and it was the last Championship in which he competed.

He won the Cork Scratch Cup in four successive years, from 1938 to 1941, and the Club advises that his name is engraved on all the Club cups, not once but several times. Whilst the official handicap afforded to him by the Union was plus 4, for a number of years the Cork Golf Club made him play off a local handicap of plus 6 in Club events to try to equate his ability to that of other members.

On the administrative side he was elected an Irish international selector in 1959 and served in that capacity for four years. He was a member of the Central Council of the Union from 1960 to 1962. Cork Golf Club elected him Captain for two periods for 1943–44 and again for 1946–47. He also held the office of President of the Club for two periods, the first from 1960–62 and again in 1971 and 1972, the year in which he died.

His championship, international and other records are set out in Appendix XXIV (Section 5).

Joseph B. Carr (1947–67)

Joe Carr was born in Portmarnock in 1922. From his emergence on the golfing scene at the age of 19 when he won the inaugural East of Ireland Amateur Open Championship in 1941 until he defeated Rodney Foster (England) on the final day of the home internationals in Killarney in September 1969, he was the dominant figure in Irish amateur golf. The match in Killarney was his final appearance as a player of international golf. Earlier in 1969 he had repeated his initial Championship success by winning the 'East' for the twelfth time. That same year he also won the 'South' — for the third time. In the European Amateur Golf Team Championship at Hamburg some months earlier he gained three wins for Ireland out of five matches and, as in Killarney later, finished on a high note by winning his singles on the final day.

In the intervening years, J.B. competed in almost every championship of note and compiled such an impressive record of achievements that he was rightly regarded (especially by his golfing peers) as the greatest Irish amateur golfer ever to grace a fairway. His home Club was Sutton and the esteem in which he was held there is illustrated in a short history of the Club.[25]

The occasion commemorated the diamond jubilee of the Club which had been founded in 1896 by the Sutton Yacht and Boat Club, itself founded just two years earlier, in 1894. In the history, having mentioned two distinguished members, Mick Crowley and Willie Gill, who had earlier brought honour to the Club, the author states, 'Whatever ambitions the most optimistic had were sky rocketed when Joe Carr came forth with his fireworks. From that moment, Sutton took up a position in golf that was never thought possible. We now had a personal interest in every major competition and the thrill of seeing Joe bringing to us the most coveted of trophies. Whilst Joe is really Sutton's and has been a fine Captain of our Club for two years, he also belongs to every Irish golfer; even more, he belongs to every Irish man and woman from Antrim to Cork. Joe has reached the greatest heights in golf. He has played the top players of many lands and everywhere he is known as that great figure he is, a true sportsman. He has done honour to our country in his contests and, without doubt, he is our country's finest honorary ambassador. Though Joe has achieved much fame in golf, he has not allowed this to rob him of his modesty, charm and friendliness. He has gone from one success to another without these intruders affecting him in the least. He is well known for his readiness to dash off to support a golf match or some charity with no thought for the time and trouble involved.'

What was true in 1956 is still true today. In the record of achievements of Sutton members listed at the end of the Club history, J.B. is credited with winning 17 championships. Since 1956 he increased this number to a record 40 by the time he ceased his active international playing career.

Whilst his championship, international and other records are set out in Appendix XXIV (Section 6), the record of his 40 championship wins and other high placings is worthy of listing:

Championship	Win	Runner-up	Semi-Finalist
The Amateur	3	1	3
The Irish Amateur Open	4	4	—
The Irish Amateur Close	6	2	1
The West of Ireland Amateur Open	12	—	1
The East of Ireland Amateur Open	12	2	—
The South of Ireland Amateur Open	3	1	—
The American Amateur Open	—	—	1

J.B. also reached the quarter-finals of the Canadian Amateur Open Championship in 1957. He had the distinction of being leading amateur in two Open Championships, 1956 and 1958. He had achieved this ranking on four earlier occasions in the Open Championship of Ireland in 1946, 1948, 1950 and 1953 which was its final year.

A considerable number of publications which maintain records and statistics of championships throughout the world have been checked and these have failed to produce any other amateur golfer who has won 40 established championships during his career. It is known with certainty that, in Ireland, J.B. holds the record. John Burke comes second with 26 championship wins and Cecil Ewing comes third with 15.

The home internationals and the Irish Amateur Open Championship were both suspended between 1939 and 1946. During that period J.B. won the 'East' four times and the 'West' once. He also won the re-activated Irish Amateur Open in 1946 at Portrush, in the final defeating Alex Kyle who was a Scottish international, an amateur champion and a Walker Cup player. When the home internationals were renewed at Hoylake in 1947, J.B. was a member of the Irish team and so commenced his unbroken representation on Irish teams until the match in Killarney in 1969, another record, with 75 'caps' comprising 150 matches.

In 1965 Ireland entered the European Amateur Golf Team Championship at Sandwich. J.B. was a member of the winning team and again when Ireland won in Turin in 1967. He was also on the team in Hamburg in 1969 — a European total of 17 matches.

His Walker Cup career extended from 1947 to 1967 during which period he played 20 matches. In 1956, the R & A inaugurated a biennial match between Britain and Ireland and the Continent of Europe in alternate years to the Walker Cup. J.B. played in the 1956 and 1968 series.

The Amateur World Cup (Eisenhower Trophy) was inaugurated in 1956, also on a biennial basis, and J.B. was a member of the Britain and Ireland team in 1956 and 1960.

Whilst the winning of his first Amateur Championship at the Royal Liverpool Golf Club, Hoylake, in 1953 gave him his greatest thrill, it was his second win at St Andrews in 1958 which must have given him the greatest satisfaction. Like many other Irish players, J.B. hit the ball enormous distances. What became the strongest part of his game was his ability to play recovery shots from the seemingly impossible places where his tee shots finished.

In the 1950s two of the most knowledgeable and influential figures in golf were both former English international players: Raymond H. Oppenheimer (R.H.O.) and Gerald H. Micklem. Both were members of the R & A and were Walker Cup selectors. Gerald was also Walker Cup Captain at that time. In pursuance of their duties they were regular visitors to Ireland to attend championships here. Before the 1958 Amateur they were at Rosses Point for the 'West'. This is mentioned to help the reader to appreciate more fully these extracts from an article by Leonard Crawley entitled 'Invincible Carr wins again. Success of a player who learned to play all over again.' The article appeared in the 9 June edition of the *Daily Telegraph* immediately following the Amateur:

'Carr, who is 36, has been first choice and an inspiration to Britain and Ireland Walker Cup sides since the war and in the last three years he has done that which no other player of his immense stature has been prepared even to attempt. Realising, as he did, that his wonderful eye and natural ability, combined with a flaming competitive spirit, could no longer carry the crudest of methods, he decided to change and learn to play all over again.

'In the interim period his indomitable courage kept him his place in international golf, but even such great authorities as "the Emperor (R.H.O.) himself" whose occasional utterances are apt to be maddeningly correct, had stated after Minneapolis a year ago that "Joe" was going downhill and that he might make a useful selector and a good member of the Championship Committee in time to come.

'In time to come indeed, but not yet. Five weeks ago he met his Captain, Gerald Micklem, in the West of Ireland and with a twinkle in his eye he said, "Gerald I have it" and, like another great man, Wilfred Rhodes of immortal cricketing memory on another occasion, he added "I can keep 'em there."

'Carr's driving in the past has been spectacular, terrific, unbelievable, and yet, it has always given one a chance. I speak from experience. One up a tree here, another gone to ground there, the most famous of all the one which struck one of Her Majesty's engines bang on its puffing chimney. But now, as he said to Micklem the other day, he "can keep them there".

'He can hit them onto a pocket handkerchief all day long and to a range that will break all but the hearts of the greatest players.

'No championship in the last 30 years has been won so decisively from the tee, and no championship has been won by a finer character. An amateur to the core; no riches, no help, no sponsor, just live, love, work and play when you can.'

J.B. had bought a house beside the second green at Sutton Golf Club. With the Committee's permission, he had flood lights erected on his boundary and every night during the winter months he practised on the links. The author is aware personally that J.B. hit 300 balls a night and, to improve his driving, he had a torch fixed to a post 150 yards from the third tee with the beam pointing skywards so that he could see the trajectory of the ball as it passed through the beam. Such was his dedication and determination. Two years later he again won the Amateur, and a further eight years on he was defeated in the final by that great player, Michael Bonallack, who won five Amateurs altogether.

Before he ended his international playing career, the R & A honoured J.B. by appointing him Walker Cup Captain for the 1963 and 1965 series and also Captain for the Britain and Ireland team in the 1964 and 1966 Eisenhower Trophy matches. It has been mentioned already, in Chapter 19, that he received the Robert Tyre Jones Award in 1961. He had earlier been awarded the Golf Writers' Trophy in 1953 and he received the Walter Hagen Award in 1967.

He was a great Club member and between 1948 and 1963 he played number one on the Sutton team which won the Senior Cup on six occasions. He also led Sutton in winning the Barton Shield in 1946, 1949 and 1950.

On the administration side he served on the Central Council of the Union from 1949 to 1956 and was appointed an honorary delegate to the Council in 1978, a position he still holds.

The Council elected him International Team Captain and Chairman of selectors in 1979. During his three year term of office he introduced a new dimension to team training methods, which has been mentioned in Chapter 31 on the National Panel. The results on the international scene are a further tribute to J.B.'s initiative and foresight.

Samuel Maxwell McCready (1949–51)

Max McCready was first selected to play for Ireland at the Royal Liverpool Golf Club, Hoylake, in 1947 when the home international matches were resumed after the war. His home Club was recorded as Dunmurry. Born in Belfast in 1918, there is no record of his achievements until he won the RAF Championship in 1947. In the same year he was also selected as a reserve on the Walker Cup team for the matches at St Andrews. In 1948 he won the Jamaican Amateur Championship.

He entered from Sunningdale, where he had gone to live, for the 1949 Amateur Championship at Portmarnock. There he met and defeated the American, William P. Turnesa, by 2 and 1 in the 36 hole final to become the second Irish player to win this coveted trophy. A measure of the quality of his victory is that William Turnesa had won the Championship at Carnoustie in 1947 and had got to the semi-finals at Sandwich in 1948.

Max was selected for the Walker Cup matches at Winged Foot, New Jersey and again for the 1951 matches at Birkdale. He was a regular member of the Irish team for the home internationals from 1947 to 1954 during which time he played 28 matches, winning 14 and halving three. He was leading amateur in the 1947 Open Championship of Ireland.

His championship, international and other records, are set out in Appendix XXIV (Section 7).

Norman Vico Drew (1953)

Norman Drew was born in Belfast in 1932. His home Club was Bangor and he was one of the first of Ireland's younger golfers to gain competitive experience from the Union's programme of promoting Junior Golf. Norman won the inaugural Ulster Boys' Amateur Open Championship at Royal Belfast in 1949. He had to go beyond the allotted 36 holes in the final to do so, as John Glover (Knock) conceded victory to Norman only after 38 holes. John won the Ulster Boys' at Shandon Park the following year and he also emulated Jimmy Bruen by becoming the second Irish boy to win the Boys' Amateur Championship, which he did at Royal Lytham and St Anne's in 1950.

Norman quickly advanced to adult rank. Less than a year after his success in the Ulster Boys', he entered the North of Ireland Amateur Open Championship at the Royal Portrush Golf Club and defeated Jackson Taggart of the host Club in the final. From dormie two he birdied the 17th and 18th and won on the 19th.

1952 was his most successful year. He was involved in the final stages of the four provincial Championships. Runner-up in the West of Ireland at Easter, he won the East of Ireland at Whit, then won the North of Ireland in July and went on to be runner-up in the South of Ireland in August. He finished the championship season by winning the Irish Amateur Open Championship in September at Portrush. This surely established a unique record and Norman was still only 20 years old. The Irish selectors called on him for the home internationals at Troon where he achieved three wins and a halved match out of six appearances.

As 1953 was a Walker Cup year, the home internationals were scheduled for June instead of their usual time in September. It was Ireland's turn to host the matches and the Council nominated Killarney as the venue and decided to have the Irish Amateur Open Championship immediately following the Internationals there too. Norman was again selected for the Irish international team and won five and halved one out of six matches. Another member of the Irish team was the local resident, Dr Billy O'Sullivan, who won four and a half matches out of six. Billy had won the Irish Amateur Open when it had been played at Killarney four years earlier and everyone in the area made him favourite to repeat that success, but they reckoned without Norman, who defeated Billy by 4 and 3 in an exciting final. Norman went through the Home Internationals and the Championship in successive weeks without once losing a match, and this must surely be another record.

He was selected as a member of the Walker Cup team for the matches later that year at Kittansett, Massachusetts, and on his return home he announced that he was taking up professional golf as a career. His championship, international and other records are set out in Appendix XXIV (Section 8).

J. F. David Madeley (1963)

David Madeley was born in Belfast in 1938. His first Club was Royal Belfast from which he entered championships and tournaments. He later joined Royal County Down. The first trophy on which his name is engraved is the Ulster Boys' Amateur Open Championship which he won in 1955.

His performance when playing for Ulster in the 1959 interprovincial matches at Portmarnock brought him to the attention of the international selection Committee. He was picked to play for Ireland in September of that year at Royal Lytham and St Anne's where he achieved a rarely accomplished feat by winning all his six matches. He rightly regards this as his most vivid memory of international golf, particularly as it was his first taste of golf at this level. His interprovincial and international career progressed in tandem. With the exception of 1965, he played for Ulster and Ireland from 1959 to 1966.

David won the North of Ireland Amateur Open Championship in two successive years, 1963 and 1964. Before that he had been selected by the R & A on the 1962 Britain and Ireland team against the Continent of Europe team, and then in 1963 he was selected for the Walker Cup matches.

His lowest handicap was scratch and firstly he won the Royal Belfast Scratch Cup on six occasions between 1958 and 1966 and then won the Royal County Down Scratch Cup in 1972 and again in 1981. In 1964 and 1969 he helped Royal Belfast to win the Belfast and District Cup. His championship, international and other records are set out in Appendix XXIV (Section 9).

David B. Sheahan (1963)

Although David Sheahan was born in 1940 in Southsea, England, his parents were Irish and this qualified him to compete in the Irish Amateur Close Championship and he went on to represent Ireland at international level. The family moved back to Ireland soon after David was born. He decided to take up medicine as a career and became an undergraduate at University College, Dublin and a member of the UCD Golf Club. In 1962 he travelled to St Andrews and won the Boyd Quaich Trophy, a competition open to students of all universities in Britain and Ireland to commemorate two students who had been killed in World War Two.

David made his first impact on the Irish golfing scene when he was runner-up to John Duncan (Shandon Park) in the 1959 North of Ireland Amateur Open Championship at Portrush. This led to his selection on the Leinster team for the Interprovincial Championship and he remained a member of that team until 1965. By then a qualified doctor, pressure of work necessitated his having to advise the Leinster selectors that he would no longer be available for these matches.

Whilst still at university he joined Grange Golf Club and in 1961 he played number one for the Club in the Leinster section of the Senior Cup at Hermitage. He found himself drawn against the redoubtable J.B. Carr who was playing for Sutton. After ten holes David was four up but was eventually beaten by J.B. on the 21st. He recalls that he continued to play very good golf from the 11th onwards but J.B. played better and whittled his lead away. David says he learned a lot from this match particularly J.B.'s intense concentration and determination never to concede defeat.

Later that year David entered the Irish Amateur Close Championship at County Sligo and got through to the final where he met Joe Brown (Tramore). Early on the morning of the final a message was received to tell David that Grange was on its way. The caller (phoning from Kinnegad where the convoy had stopped for breakfast) was Philip Love, the benevolent landlord and patron of Grange Golf Club. On the previous evening Philip had organised more than 50 members to leave the Club in a fleet of cars at dawn and travel across country for the final to support their member. Just as the players and the referee were announced, Philip, followed by his Club members, walked up to the first tee and said, 'Mr Starter, you can commence the final; Grange has arrived.' David went on to win his first Close Championship by 5 and 4. In his speech at the presentation of the trophy (which incidentally Philip later filled with champagne) David acknowledged that the support and encouragement received from so many of his Club members had been a tremendous incentive to him. He got to the semi-final of the Close in 1962 and won again in 1966 and 1970.

His 1961 success at County Sligo signalled his call to international honours and his representation on the home international team terminated in 1970. He regards his most memorable match for Ireland as the foursomes, partnered by Bill McCrea, against Scotland at Portmarnock in 1967. They were three down with four to play, with Scotland on the green in one shot at the famous par 3 15th and Ireland in a greenside bunker off the tee. From this seemingly impossible situation Ireland won the last four holes for victory.

Undoubtedly his greatest achievement occurred in 1962 when he won the Jeyes Professional Tournament at Royal Dublin. David put together rounds of 69, 72, 72 and 69 to beat Denis Hutchinson (South Africa) by one shot. Also in the international field were

THE EUROPEAN AMATEUR GOLF TEAM CHAMPIONSHIP

(Chapter 20 Appendix XI)

Year	Venue	Winning Country
1959	Barcelona, Spain	Sweden
1961	Brussels, Belgium	Sweden
1963	Falsterbo, Sweden	England
1965	Sandwich, England	Ireland
1967	Turin, Italy	Ireland
1969	Hamburg, W. Germany	England
1971	Lausanne, Switzerland	England
1973	Penina, Portugal	England
1975	Killarney, Ireland	Scotland
1977	The Haagsche, Holland	Scotland
1979	Esbjerg, Denmark	England
1981	St Andrews, Scotland	England
1983	Chantilly, France	Ireland
1985	Halmstad, Sweden	Scotland
1987	Murhof, Austria	Ireland
1989	Porthcawl, Wales	England

THE EUROPEAN AMATEUR YOUTHS' GOLF TEAM CHAMPIONSHIP

(Chapter 30 Appendix XIX)

Year	Venue	Winning Country
1977	Oslo, Norway	Ireland
1978	Pals, Spain	France
1979	Marianske Lazne, Czechoslovakia	Ireland
1980	Dusseldorf, Germany	Sweden
1981	Reykjavik, Iceland	Spain
1982	Paris, France	Scotland
1983	No Championship	
1984	Dublin, Ireland	Ireland

Championship discontinued but recommenced in 1990 in alternative years to the EAGTC.

A mini series took place in 1988 and 1989.

1988	Turin, Italy	Sweden
1989	Limburg, Belgium	Spain

Championship recommenced.

1990	Turin, Italy	Italy

THE EUROPEAN AMATEUR BOYS' GOLF TEAM CHAMPIONSHIP

(Chapter 30 Appendix XIX)

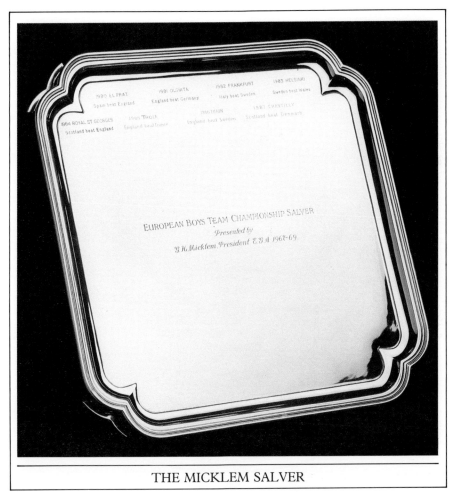

THE MICKLEM SALVER

Year	Venue	Winning Country
1980	Barcelona, Spain	Spain
1981	Rome, Italy	England
1982	Frankfurt, Germany	Italy
1983	Helsinki, Finland	Sweden
1984	Sandwich, England	Scotland
1985	Troia, Portugal	England
1986	Turin, Italy	England
1987	Chantilly, France	Scotland
1988	Renfrew, Scotland	France
1989	Lyckorna, Sweden	England
1990	Reykjavik, Iceland	Spain

THE YOUTHS' AMATUER OPEN CHAMPIONSHIP OF IRELAND

(Chapter 18 Appendix X)

THE HERMITAGE CUP

Inaugurated in 1966 as a Boys' Championship, it was changed to a Youths' Championship in 1969.

Year	Venue	Winner and Club
1966	Co. Louth	M. Hanway (Sutton)
1967	Royal Dublin	J. Carey (Roscrea)
1968	Co. Louth	M.A. Gannon (Co. Louth)
1969	Delgany	D. Branigan (L'town & B'town)
1970	Tullamore	L.A. Owens (Killiney)
1971	Athlone	M.A. Gannon (Co. Louth)
1972	Mullingar	M.A. Gannon (Co. Louth)
1973	Tullamore	J. Purcell (Mullingar)
1974	Athlone	S. Dunlop (Killarney)
1975	Mullingar	P. McNally (Edenderry)
1976	Tullamore	R. McCormack (Warrenpoint)

Year	Venue	Winner and Club
1977	Athlone	B. McDaid (Skibbereen)
1978	Thurles	T. Corridan (Ballybunion)
1979	Tullamore	R. Rafferty (Warrenpoint)
1980	Clandeboye	J. McHenry (Douglas)
1981	Westport	J. McHenry (Douglas)
1982	Mullingar	K. O'Donnell (Clandeboye)
1983	Cork	P. Murphy (Killarney)
1984	Bangor	J. Morris (Douglas)
1985	Co. Sligo	J. McHenry (Douglas)
1986	Carlow	J. Morris (Douglas)
1987	Killarney	C. Everett (Cambuslang, Scotland)
1988	Malone	P. McGinley (Grange)
1989	Athlone	A.W. Mathers (Elie, Scotland)
1990	Dundalk	D. Errity (Hermitage)

IRELAND YOUTHS' AND SCOTLAND YOUTHS' MATCH

(Chapter 18 Appendix X)

THE STANDARD LIFE TROPHY

Year	Venue	Winning Country
1980	Mussleburgh	Scotland
1981	Co. Louth	Scotland
1982	Leven	Scotland
1983	Cork	Scotland
1984	East Renfrewshire	Scotland
1985	Co. Sligo	Scotland and Ireland shared
1986	Cawder	Scotland
1987	Killarney	Scotland
1988	Ladybank	Ireland
1989	Athlone	Ireland and Scotland shared
1990	Stranraer	Ireland

IRELAND BOYS'
AND
WALES BOYS' MATCH
(Chapter 18)

THE MacCORMACK CUP

Year	Venue	Winning Country
1972	Moortown	Ireland
1973	Blairgowrie	Ireland
1974	Hoylake	Wales
1975	Bruntsfield	Wales
1976	Sunningdale	Wales
1977	Downfield	Ireland
1978	Seaton Carew	Wales
1979	Barassie	Ireland
1980	Formby	Wales
1981	Gullane	Ireland
1982	Burnham & Berrow	Wales
1983	Glenbervie	Ireland
1984	Porthcawl	Wales
1985	Barnton	Ireland
1986	Seaton Carew	Ireland
1987	Barassie	Wales
1988	Formby	Wales
1989	Nairn	Wales
1990	Huntstanton	Ireland

BOYS' HOME INTERNATIONAL MATCHES
Chapter 32 (Appendix XXII)

THE ST ANDREWS TROPHY

Year	Venue	Winning Country
1985	Royal Burgess, Scotland	England and Ireland tied
1986	Seaton Carew, England	Ireland
1987	Kilmarnock, Scotland	Scotland
1988	Formby, England	England
1989	Nairn, Scotland	England
1990	Hunstanton, England	Scotland

Bernard Hunt (Hartsbourne), Harry Weetman (Croham Hurst), Dai Rees (South Herts), Christy O'Connor (Royal Dublin) (all Ryder Cup Players), Ralph Moffat (Hearsall) and Paddy Skerritt (St Anne's). Ever afterwards, when lauding the merits of Grange Golf Club, Philip Love took great pleasure in saying, 'Grange is the only Club since the era of Bobby Jones which has an amateur member who beat the professionals.'

There is an interesting story relating to the final hole in David's last round, which may well be described as unsolicited advice. A prominent member of the host Club, Larry Gunning, affectionately known as 'The Lark' was in charge of communications and crowd control. On top of the clubhouse roof a hut had been constructed. This hut commanded a view of the links and the members had christened it 'The Lark's Nest' as it was from here that Larry operated. As the final round was drawing to a close, Larry took it upon himself to keep the large gallery at the 18th green informed over the public address system of the position of the matches coming up the dog-legged final hole. However, he did not appreciate that the wind carried his voice down the links. David's tee shot at the par 5 18th finished on the left-hand side of the fairway leaving him with a long second shot across the 'out of bounds' garden. Larry told the crowd where David's tee shot finished and mentioned that he was taking a wood for his shot to the green. He then expressed the view, still over the public address, that this was too much club and an iron would be a safer shot. He next advised the gallery that David had changed to an iron and described the flight of the ball to the green. David finished with a birdie and on leaving the green looked up at the Lark's Nest, waved and called up 'Thanks Larry'. It transpired later that David had changed from a 3 wood to a 4 iron.

In 1962 the R & A selected David for the Britain and Ireland team against the Continent of Europe team. He was again selected for the next match in 1964. He was selected for the 1963 Walker Cup matches at Turnberry where he won both his singles matches to record 2 wins out of 4. His other international appearances were on the 1965 and 1967 Irish team which firstly won and then successfully defended the European Amateur Golf Team Championship.

At Club level, he won the Club Championship on four occasions and the Love Cup in successive years, 1960 and 1961. His championship, international and other records are set out in Appendix XXIV (Section 10).

Thomas Craddock (1967–69)

Tom Craddock was the last winner of the defunct Irish Amateur Open Championship; he later gained Walker Cup selection. Born in 1931, his first 'Club' was the Irish Artisan Golfers' Association. It was because of the high standards set by players like Tom and his friend Paddy Caul (who also gained international honours) in their membership of the Association which led the Central Council to amend the constitution to enable the GUI to affiliate the IAGA as an associate member.

Tom became the first IAGA member to receive international recognition when he was selected to play for Ireland at Royal Birkdale in 1955. In all, he played for Ireland in 12 series from then until 1970. His appearances for Leinster in the interprovincials extended from 1956 to 1971, although he was not on the 1966 team.

At Irish Championship level he won the Irish Amateur Open in 1958, the Irish Amateur Close in 1959, the East of Ireland in 1959, 1965 and 1966; being runner-up in 1960 and 1963, runner-up in the West of Ireland in 1960 and runner-up in the Close in 1965.

The R & A selected him on the Britain and Ireland team against the Continent of Europe team in 1958, 1966 and 1968. His greatest honour was being selected as a Walker Cup player for two series, 1967 and 1969, in which he won two and halved one match out of six appearances.

His is a rare achievement. He was a member of the Irish teams the first time Ireland won two of the most prestigious trophies for which we compete, the Raymond Trophy in the home internationals in 1955 and, ten years later, the European Amateur Golf Team Championship Trophy in 1965.

Tom was selected on Ireland's EAGTC team for four successive matches from 1965 to 1971 and he regards his most memorable and exciting match as his singles on the final day at Sandwich in 1965 against Martin Christmas (England) who was a Walker Cup player in 1961 and 1963. Theirs was the last match out on the links and the winning of the Championship depended on the outcome. Tom's fellow team members and the Irish officials grew wildly excited when they learned that the match was all square on the 18th tee. What was not understood at the time was that a halved match would give England the Championship. Both tee shots finished in the left-hand rough but there was consternation in the Irish camp when it was discovered that Tom's ball had come to rest on a molehill. The most unperturbed person at the scene was Tom who drew Martin's attention to the lie of his ball and indicated that he was entitled to relief. Under a local rule made by the Championship Committee, relief could be provided from freshly formed molehills. Martin suggested that this was an old molehill from which relief was not obtainable. Tom decided to seek an official ruling which was made in his favour. Following the drop, Tom hit a good shot which finished 10 yards short of the green. In the meantime Martin had played from the rough down the fairway. As he was further away he had to play his approach first and put his third shot on the green ten feet from the pin. Next Tom played his chip, a shot which the Irish Captain, Cecil Ewing, was afraid to watch. Cecil asked other onlookers to tell him when the ball came to rest. He was relieved and delighted to hear that the ball was stone dead. Martin missed the putt and conceded the match.

In 1969 Tom won the Lytham Trophy, a tournament attended by the Walker Cup selectors and in which all leading amateurs in the home countries compete.

Tom became a member of Malahide Golf Club in 1958 and won the Club Scratch Cup and the Grand Hotel Cup on several occasions. Playing number one for the Club, he helped to win the Senior Cup in 1965 and the Barton Shield in 1971, 1978 and 1982. His lowest handicap was plus 3.

The Leinster Branch nominated him as an international selector and the Central Council elected him to that office for 1982. His championship, international and other records are set out in Appendix XXIV (Section 11).

Roderick J. Carr (1971)

When Roddy Carr was born in 1950 his father, J.B., had already many championships to his name. Growing up in the intense golfing atmosphere which existed in the Carr household must have been an invigorating experience. Roddy became a junior member of Sutton Golf Club. The Committee of Sutton must be praised for their long established promotion of Junior Golf down the years.

The first Championship Trophy to bear his name was the East of Ireland. In 1970 he tied with Ted Higgins (Cork) after the regulation 72 holes and then got a birdie to win the first tie hole in the 'sudden death' play-off. He was not yet 20 years old at the time and he recalls the immense pride he felt on bringing the trophy back to Sutton and handing it to his Club Captain, Bill Thompson, who restored it to the same position in the trophy cabinet where it had been displayed during the preceding 12 months, as his father had won it a year earlier.

Following this success, Roddy was selected firstly by Leinster to play in the Senior Inter-provincials at Portrush, then by the R & A on a Britain and Ireland youths' team against a Continent of Europe youths' team at the Royal Burgess Links, Barnton, and finally by the Irish selectors to play for Ireland in the home internationals at Portcawl.

He commenced the 1971 season by winning the West of Ireland at Rosses Point. The R & A invited the Union to send an Irish youths' team to Northamptonshire Country Club to play a Continent of Europe youths' team prior to the Youths' Amateur Championship at the same venue. Roddy was picked for the Irish team which won the ten singles contest by 6 matches to 4, Roddy being one of the winners. He and Mark Gannon (County Louth) were then selected by the R & A on the Britain and Ireland youths' team against the Continent of Europe youths' team and each gained maximum points in both foursomes and singles helping their side to win by 10 matches to 5. Roddy finished joint sixth in the Championship.

A seeded player in the 1971 Amateur Championship at Carnoustie, he was defeated in the quarter finals by Tom Kite of America, another seeded player who was on the American Walker Cup team. Kite had been runner-up in the 1970 American Amateur Championship and was also a member of the 1971 winning Eisenhower Trophy team. Most followers of the game are aware that Kite, who turned professional in 1972, became a leading player on the American professional circuit.

Roddy was picked for the Walker Cup team for the matches at St Andrews in 1971 where he was unbeaten with three wins and one halved match out of four. Britain and Ireland won the matches that year by 13 matches to 11. Roddy turned professional in 1971 but became reinstated as an amateur in 1983. His championship, international and other records are set out in Appendix XXIV (Section 12).

Patrick Mulcare (1975)

Ballybunion Golf Links is regarded by many knowledgeable golf writers as amongst the eight greatest natural links in the world. Three famous American professional golfers have acknowledged that it is a truly great links. Tom Watson has been a regular visitor there to tune up on his way to the Open Championship. More recently Byron Nelson and Jack Nicklaus have sampled the links. Nelson said, 'I wish I had discovered Ballybunion 50 years ago — it's a great, great links', and Nicklaus said, 'Ballybunion stands with the world's best courses and I want to come back and play it some more.'

It was in sight of this outstanding links that Pat Mulcare was born in 1945 and it was there that he learned the game which was to bring him international honours in later years.

Pat took up a position in Dublin and joined Woodbrook Golf Club from which he entered championships and tournaments. He attracted the attention of the Munster selectors and was a member of their Senior Interprovincial team for 12 years from 1967. The International Selection Committee picked him to play for Ireland in 1968 and he played in ten home international matches. He won the East of Ireland in three successive years: 1971, 1972 and 1973. In 1971 he also won the South of Ireland.

Pat played in six different series of international matches. In addition to the home international series, the Irish selectors picked him to represent Ireland in the Quadrangular Continental matches on three occasions and in the European Amateur Golf Team Championship once. The R & A selected him to play for Britain and Ireland against the Continent of Europe in 1971, and then came the ultimate honour of Walker Cup selection for the match at St Andrews in 1975. Three years later he was a member of the Continent of Europe team for the match against South America.

He says that his most exciting match was his Walker Cup singles against the American, Dick Siderowf, who had won the Amateur Championship at Porthcawl in 1973 and reached the semi-finals at Hoylake in 1974. (He became Amateur Champion again in 1976).

After a match of the highest quality, Pat and Dick came up the 18th all square. Both reached the green in two where Pat holed a 14 foot putt for a birdie to win by the narrowest of margins. His lowest handicap was plus one. His championship, international and other records are set out in Appendix XXIV (Section 13).

Ronan Rafferty (1981)

Whilst he cannot claim to have been the youngest player ever to win a championship, Ronan Rafferty holds the record for being the youngest to gain Walker Cup honours. To be precise, Ronan was 17 years and 227 days old when, in partnership with Philip Walton, he stood on the first tee in Cyprus Point, Pebble Beach, California in the opening foursomes against the Americans, Hal Sutton and Jay Segal in the 1981 Walker Cup matches. More about that later.

Born in Newry in 1964, he was educated in Abbey Christian Brothers' School, Newry, which he left in 1980. We do not know if it is another record but his mother, Marie, tells us that he became a juvenile member of Warrenpoint at the age of six. This was, no doubt, due to the influence and foresight of his father who was affectionately known as 'Doc'. Sadly 'Doc' died shortly before Ronan made his debut at the 1989 Ryder Cup matches at the Belfry.

Don Patterson, professional at Warrenpoint during Ronan's period of membership, was quick to realise the potential of this youngster and he became his coach and mentor.

Looking at his championship, international and other records which are set out in Appendix XXIV (Section 14), it can be seen that his progress from junior to adult rank was meteoric. In 1979, when still only 15, Ronan was a member of the Irish team which won the European Amateur Youths' Golf Team Championship at Marianske Lazne, Czechoslovakia; he also won the Youths' Amateur Open Championship of Ireland at Tullamore, the Ulster and the Munster Youths'. He then went to Barassie, Scotland, where, having played on the Irish Boys' team against the Welsh Boys', he proceeded to win the Boys' Amateur Championship, defeating D. Ray (Long Ashton) by 7 and 6 in the final. In the semi-final he had come up against his fellow countryman, Philip Walton, whom he beat by 2 and 1. The Irish selectors picked him to play in the home internationals which, that year, were scheduled for Royal County Down, Newcastle, which is 'down the road' from his home. Unfortunately the complete series was cancelled but the team travelled to Porthcawl to play Wales and Ronan got maximum points in his four matches. When the full series was restored in 1980, Ronan played at Royal Dornoch in Scotland and also at Woodhall Spa in the following year.

In 1980 he was selected to play in the inaugural European Amateur Boys' Golf Team Championship in Spain and this helped him to achieve another record as, having again been selected for the EAYGTC that year, he was picked for the EAGTC in 1981 and became the first Irish player to compete at all three levels of European Championships: the Boys', Youths' and Men's.

1980 also saw an impressive range of representative selection including the Irish junior and senior interprovincials. The Irish selectors called on Ronan to play in the quadrangular continental matches for the Cartier Trophy at Portmarnock. The R & A first selected him that year for the Britain and Ireland team against the Continent of Europe team at Sandwich and later as a member of the Britain and Ireland team for the World Cup (Eisenhower Trophy) match at Pinehurst, USA. The USA won that trophy and two members of their team were Hal Sutton, who returned the best four round total, and Jay Segal. In the 1981 Walker Cup matches at Cyprus Point, Ronan and Philip lost the first three holes playing against Sutton and Segal, but recovered so well that they were two up after 14. The 15th at Cyprus Point is a 139 yard par 3 hole along the edge of the Pacific Ocean and the tee shot has to carry across water to reach the green. Ronan drove and finished 15 yards short and Philip holed the chip to win the hole and make them dormie. The 16th has been described as the ultimate in water hazards and quite possibly the most beautiful golf hole in the world. The hole measures 233 yards and the carry is entirely across water to a green surrounded by four large bunkers and beyond which lies the Pacific Ocean. Philip drove and finished slightly to the left of the green. Not to be outdone, Ronan holed the chip to win the match.

Following the 1981 home internationals at Woodhall Spa, Ronan turned professional and became one of the new section of professional golfers, a tournament player. He achieved world renown in his chosen field leading the European order of merit in 1989.

Philip Walton (1981–83)

The first Irish golfer to become enrolled in an American university on a golf scholarship, Philip Walton was a student at the Oklahoma State University from 1981 to 1983. Born in Malahide, Co. Dublin in 1962, he attended St Andrew's School in Malahide and joined Malahide Golf Club as a juvenile member.

Having been defeated in the final of the 1977 Leinster Boys' Amateur Open Championship, he won the event in both 1978 and 1979. In 1977 he was also a member of the

Irish Boys' team for the annual match against the Welsh Boys' in which he gained maximum points. He was on the team again in 1978 and 1979.

His skills were in demand in 1979 by both the Junior and Senior Selection Committees. His record (which is set out in Appendix XXIV (Section 15)), shows that in 1979 he represented Ireland in the EAYGTC at Marianske Lazne, Czechoslovakia, and later in the men's international team match against Wales at Porthcawl. In the EAYGTC he returned the lowest score of all the competitors representing 15 nations in the 36 hole qualifying rounds and was presented with a magnificent Czechoslovakian cut glass vase by that country's Tourist Board. In the matchplay stages, Philip was unbeaten and so helped Ireland to win the Championship.

Another advance came in his golfing career in 1980. Not only did he play on both the junior and senior interprovincial teams for Leinster, but in the EAYGTC at Dusseldorf, the quadrangular matches at Portmarnock and the home international matches at Royal Dornoch. It was also the year when, at the Royal Troon Golf Club, he tied for the Youths' Amateur Open Championship but was beaten at the 2nd tie hole in the 'sudden death' play-off.

Further honours came his way in 1981 when he won the Spanish Amateur Open Championship on the first 'sudden death' tie hole at Torrquebrada and then won the Scottish Amateur Open Strokeplay Championship at Renfrew. But his greatest honour was being chosen by the R & A to represent Britain and Ireland in the 1981 Walker Cup matches at Cyprus Point. When recounting Ronan Rafferty's achievements in the previous section, the part Philip played in their first Walker Cup match against Hal Sutton and Jay Segal was mentioned. Philip agrees this was one of the most outstanding matches of his career.

In 1982 Philip won the Irish Amateur Close Championship at Woodbrook and this helped him to win the Willie Gill award. In the same year he again represented Ireland in the quadrangular continental matches at Halmstad, Sweden and the home international matches at Porthcawl. The R & A selected him on the Britain and Ireland team against the Continent of Europe. The following year he represented Ireland again in the EAGTC and the home internationals. Finally, the R & A selected him for the 1983 Walker Cup matches at Royal Liverpool Golf Club, Hoylake.

During most of this period Philip was attending the Oklahoma State University which limited his appearances in events on this side of the Atlantic except during holiday periods. Whilst in America he played in the American Amateur Championship in 1981 and was selected on the University team for the National Collegiate Athletic Association Championship in 1982 and 1983. This is the most important inter-university event in America. Oklahoma State University, with Philip ranked fifth on the team in both years, finished second in 1982 and won in 1983.

The match which he regards as his greatest achievement, even surpassing the foursomes win at Cyprus Point in the 1981 Walker Cup matches, was his singles against Jay Segal in the 1983 series at Hoylake. Philip won the first with a birdie and still held his one hole advantage when leaving the 8th green. Then Segal launched a blitz with six successive 3s from the 9th to the 14th recording birdie, birdie, par, birdie, par and eagle. Philip withstood the onslaught losing only two of the six holes to stand one down on the 15th tee. Segal failed to match Philip's pars on the 15th and 16th so Philip became one up again and by halving the 17th and 18th he won a memorable match the better ball of which was 64.

In all, Philip played in eight matches in the two series, 1981 and 1983, of which he won six gaining 12 points which was the largest number ever achieved by any of Ireland's Walker Cup players. He turned professional in 1983 and his greatest achievement in that capacity to date has been the winning of the French Open at Chantilly in 1990.

Arthur D'Arcy Pierse (1983)

Whilst Arthur Pierse is one of the relatively small number of players who have won three of Ireland's four provincial championships, he has never got to the final stages of the Close. This has not been for want of trying as he has been a regular entrant for this premier championship over a great number of years. In fact, he is such an enthusiastic supporter of the game that he travelled the length and breadth of the country to play in championships, scratch cups, and almost anything which offered a challenge.

Born in Tipperary in 1951, he spent most of his life there and became a member of the Club of the same name. He was selected on the Munster interprovincial team in 1974 and helped his province to win the Interprovincial Championship at Royal Dublin. Thereafter he was a member of the Munster team on nine further occasions up to 1988. He played for Ireland in the internationals at Hillside in 1976 and, with the exception of 1985, was a regular member of the team up to 1988. Arthur and Garth McGimpsey (Bangor) (see later in this chapter) are the only two Irish Walker Cup players who can boast of having also been members of a 'triple crown' winning team in the home internationals — the year 1987, the place Lahinch.

Having been runner-up in 1979, Arthur won the West of Ireland Championship in 1980 and again in 1982. In the 1979 final at Rosses Point he succumbed to David Long (Shandon Park) only at the 8th tie hole. He did not let this disappointment upset him as he went to Baltray later that year for the East of Ireland and having tied with Garth McGimpsey — they each scored a 4 under par 69 in the final round — Arthur won the 'sudden death' playoff at the first tie hole. Eight years later, in 1987, he won the 'North of Ireland' at Portrush.

He did not confine himself to domestic championships and entered the Amateur on three occasions. His most successful of these was at Porthcawl in 1980. He got to the semi-final where he was beaten by Duncan Evans (Leek) the eventual winner, by 2 and 1. This brought him to the attention of the R & A selectors and he was picked on the Britain and Ireland team for the match against the Continent of Europe team for the St Andrews Trophy match at Sandwich. He won 3 of his 4 matches.

Arthur was also picked for the Irish team for the 1981, 1983 and 1985 European Amateur Golf Team Championship and he was at Chantilly when Ireland won the Championship for the third time. Partnering John Carr (Sutton) against the second Scottish pair in the semi-final, they found themselves one down with two to play when they learned that the first Irish pair, Philip Walton and Garth McGimpsey, had been beaten by 2 and 1. John's tee shot on the 17th finished in a fairway bunker 170 yards from the green. Scotland got on the green in two, 12 feet from the hole. Arthur put his long bunker shot on the green and the hole was halved. On the 570 yard par 5 18th, Ireland finished in a greenside bunker in two and then got out and down in two to win the hole. Another birdie on the 19th was sufficient for

Ireland to win their match and at the end of the day the Irish won by the odd match and beat Spain in the final.

Arthur represented Ireland in 1980, 1982 and 1984 in the quadrangular continental matches and in 1983 he was selected on the Walker Cup team for the matches at the Royal Liverpool Golf Club, Hoylake. His lowest handicap was plus 1. His championship, international and other records are set out in Appendix XXIV (Section 16).

Garth McGimpsey (1985–89)

Garth McGimpsey, who was born in 1955, is only the fourth Irish golfer to win the Amateur Championship. In 1985, at the Royal Dornoch Golf Links in the north of Scotland, he added his name on the trophy to join Jimmy Bruen (Muskerry), Max McCready (Dunmurry) and Joe Carr (Sutton).

Garth came to prominence when he won the Irish Long Driving competition at Dun Laoghaire in 1977 with a drive of 320 yards. Three years later he also won the United Kingdom Long Driving competition at Little Aston.

Having won both the East of Ireland and the North of Ireland Championships in 1978, the Irish selectors picked him for the home internationals at Ashburnham, Wales. He has been on the team in successive years to date. Ulster selected him for their interprovincial side the following year and he has likewise been a regular member of that team since. He was selected to represent Ireland on Ireland's European Amateur Golf Team Championship side from 1981 to date.

The West of Ireland became the third provincial Championship for him to capture when he defeated Frank Gannon (County Louth) in the 1984 final at Rosses Point. In the same year, he again annexed the North of Ireland for the second time and these two events helped him to win the 1984 Willie Gill Award.

The R & A selected Garth for the Britain and Ireland team against the Continent of Europe team in 1984, 1986 and again in 1988. He was to receive even greater honours from the R & A. Firstly, he was selected to represent Britain and Ireland on their 1984 World Cup team for the Eisenhower Trophy and he was re-elected for the 1986 and 1988 teams. Britain and Ireland won the Eisenhower Trophy in 1988. Secondly, or concurrently, he was nominated as a member of the 1985 Walker Cup team. Whilst not wishing to appear critical of the Walker Cup selectors, surprise and disappointment were voiced from many sources when the 1987 Walker Cup team was announced and neither Garth nor Peter McEvoy were included. Peter McEvoy has been regarded as the best and most consistent English amateur since Michael Bonallack. Happily they were both re-selected for the 1989 team which won the series.

Garth had to wait until 1988 to win Ireland's premier event, the Irish Amateur Close Championship. At Portrush he defeated David Mulholland (Castletroy) in the final by 2 and 1. He was a member of the Irish QCM teams from 1984 to 1990 inclusive. In 1990 he helped Ireland to win the 'triple crown' for the second time, his second such achievement.

At Club level he helped Bangor to win the Belfast and District Cup in 1980, 1981 and 1983 and also the Irish Inter-Club Senior Cup in 1981 and 1984. He has cornered the

Bangor Club Championship since 1976 winning it nine times in the last 14 years. His lowest handicap was plus 2.4. His championship, international and other records are set out in Appendix XXIV (Section 17).

John McHenry (1987)

The second Irish player to avail of an American golf scholarship, John McHenry was born in Cork in 1964. He spent four years at the College of William and Mary in Williamsburg, Virginia. During his time there, from 1982 to 1986, he won both the Virginia Collegiate Title and the East Coast Athletic Conference Individual Title in 1986.

Unlike earlier Irish Walker Cup players, John was fortunate in being able to avail of the Union's expanding programme for the promotion of junior golf. At Boys' level he was a member of the Irish team which competed in the first European Amateur Boys' Golf Team Championship at El Prat, Spain, in 1980, where Ireland finished fourth out of nine countries. John and Ronan Rafferty, playing together in the foursomes, won their three matches. John and Ronan are Ireland's only two players who were later to gain Walker Cup honours and who have played at all three levels of European Amateur Golf Team Championships. In the adult event at Murhof Golf Club, Austria, John was a member of the winning Irish team.

1980 saw the first of John's three wins in the Youths' Amateur Open Championship of Ireland. He successfully defended his title in 1981 and his third victory came in 1984. The Munster Junior selectors picked him for the 1981 Junior Interprovincials at Portrush where he had maximum success by winning his four matches. This was a key factor in enabling Munster to win the Crymble Trophy. The Munster Senior selectors nominated him for the Senior Interprovincials at County Sligo later that year. The Junior selectors also picked him for the Youths' International against Scotland at County Louth Golf Club.

1986 was John's most successful year. He won the Irish Amateur Close Championship and the South of Ireland Amateur Open Championship and these two victories enabled him to win the Willie Gill Award. He finished the year by being called on again by the Irish selectors to play in the home internationals.

This, in turn, brought John to the attention of the Walker Cup selectors and he was picked to play in the 1987 contest at Sunningdale where he won two of his four matches.

He recalls his most exciting match as the singles on the final day of the 1984 European Amateur Youths' Golf Team Championship at Hermitage, Co. Dublin. Having qualified in the first flight, Ireland met Scotland on the first day and won by 5½ matches to 1½. In the semi-final the Irish team met and defeated Sweden by 4½ to 2½. Ireland's opponents in the final were Denmark and unfortunately both foursomes were lost. However, Ireland won the first two singles to level matters. John, playing number three, was four up with seven to play when it was learned that Ireland had won the fourth match and lost the fifth. John's opponent next produced a barrage of birdies and brought the match to the 18th all square. In the 'sudden death' the first four holes were halved in pars. Both players were on the par 5, 23rd hole in two. The Danish player putted first and charged his putt which ran five feet past the hole. John left his approach putt beside the hole and when his opponent missed the return putt, Ireland was victorious.

A member of Douglas Golf Club, he won the Club Scratch Cup in 1984. His lowest handicap was plus 1. His championship, international and other records are set out in Appendix XXIV (Section 18). He turned professional in 1987.

Eoghan O'Connell (1989)

Eoghan, the most recent of Ireland's Irish Walker Cup players, was born in Cork in 1968. When he was 12 years of age he was elected a juvenile member of Killarney Golf and Fishing Club and was given what quickly proved to be an over-generous handicap of 24. He almost won his first Championship when just 15, having led the qualifiers in the Munster Boys', and he was beaten by one hole in the final. He was also runner-up in the Leinster Boys', just one stroke behind the winner. Eoghan proved his ability in 1984, not only at Boys' but at Youths' and adult level. That year he won the Irish Boys' Close Championship at Mullingar, he finished third in the Youths' Amateur Open Championship of Ireland at Bangor, he was selected by both the Munster Junior and Senior selectors to represent the province firstly in the junior interprovincials at Thurles (where he gained maximum points) and then in the senior interprovincials at County Louth where he got 5½ points out of 6. In 1984 he also represented Ireland in four international matches. He was selected on the Boys' and Youths' teams against Wales and Scotland respectively and also on the teams for the European Amateur Boys' Golf Team Championship at the Royal St George's Golf Club, Sandwich, and for the European Amateur Youths' Golf Team Championship at Hermitage.

As he was still within the age limit, he was picked to represent Ireland in the inaugural Boys' International Matches at the Royal Burgess Golf Club, Edinburgh, in 1985 where Ireland tied with England for the R & A Trophy. Eoghan was unbeaten in his matches and the Senior selectors nominated him for the home internationals at Formby.

He took up a golf scholarship at Wake Forrest University, North Carolina, in May 1986. This restricted his competitive appearances on this side of the Atlantic except during the holidays. He was, however, able to play for Ireland at Murhof, Austria in 1987 in the European Amateur Golf Team Championship and, gaining maximum points, helped Ireland to win the Championship. Returning a second round 65 in the Open Championship at Muirfield, he missed the cut for the last stage of the Championship by 4 strokes. In 1988 he helped Ireland to win the quadrangular continental matches at Royal Portrush and went on to Portmarnock for the Open Championship of Ireland where he finished leading amateur, 15th overall. The R & A selected him for the St Andrews Trophy match against the Continent of Europe where he justified his selection by winning 3½ matches out of 4. With Peter McEvoy, Garth McGimpsey and Jim Milligan he represented Britain and Ireland in the World Cup when they won the Eisenhower Trophy at Ullva, Sweden.

In 1989 he played for Ireland in the EAGTC at Porthcawl, again winning 4 out of 6 matches. The R & A gave him the ultimate amateur honour by selecting him as a member of the Walker Cup team against America which Britain and Ireland won for the first time on American soil at Peach Tree.

He recalls his most exciting match as the final of the EAGTC in Murhof, Austria in 1987 when he played Peter McEvoy whom he defeated on the 14th at which stage he was six under par.

He established a reputation at Wake Forrest. In his first tournament in 1986 he won the Cardinal Intercollegiate and later the Guilford Invitational. In 1988 he was beaten in the final of the North/South Amateur Championship and came third in the Golf Digest Collegiate Invitational. In 1989 he led the qualifiers in the American Amateur at Merion returning 137 (68–69). A regular member of the Wake Forrest Senior team, he helped to win seven team events there and his lowest handicap was plus 3. He turned professional in 1990.

His championship, international and other records are set out in Appendix XXIV (Section 19).

The Staff at Union Headquarters.

Ms Cora Harris   Ivan E.R. Dickson   Mrs Pamela Carroll
(General Secretary)

Mrs Florence Greene   Mrs Betty Brophy

FOOTNOTES

1. This is authenticated by a scrapbook kept by David Ritchie's daughter.

2. We are grateful to Sutton Golf Club for this information.

3. J.P. Rooney: 'History of Irish Clubs,' *Irish Field*, 13 February 1926. His information must have been obtained from Sutton Golf Club because of its detail and photographs reproduced in the section dealing with the Club.

4. *Belfast Newsletter*, 1 November 1886.

5. *Golf*, 14 September 1894. Henry Gregg, William Henry Mann, George Combe, Thomas Dickson and Captain James McCalmont are listed in this article.

6. *Belfast Newsletter*.

7. R & A Championship Records.

8. Introduction to the Amateur Championship in the R & A Championship Records.

9. Some information on the Belfast and District Cup appears in the *Belfast Newsletter*. The first report of the Belfast and District League appears on 25 April 1903.

10. An interesting table was published in the *Belfast Newsletter* on 14 May 1903 under the heading 'Belfast and District Inter-Club Challenge Cup'. It lists matches played, won, drawn and lost between the six Clubs as at that date and below the table was printed 'the Cup may be seen in Mr Sharman D. Neill's window'. In subsequent editions up to 26 June 1903 further match results appeared. The final report on this tournament in that edition stated that Ormeau beat Greenisland by 5½ matches to ½. According to the records in Appendix VI, Section 7, the first Club to win the Cup was Ormeau. We have been happy to pass on the details to the Ulster Branch, which is satisfied that the Cup was donated by the Weir family who owned the silversmiths Sharman D. Neill.

11. The following report was discovered in the Belfast Newsletter of 8 October 1924 which was passed on to the Connacht Branch as it had no record of its origin. The article was headed 'Connacht Branch formed' and stated: 'Although the constitution of the Golfing Union of Ireland provided for the establishment of four provincial branches, a Connacht Branch has never been formed, but at a meeting at the Co. Sligo Golf Club, Rosses Point, last week this omission was rectified. The meeting was composed of representatives of Clubs in Connacht affiliated to the Union and was attended by Dr Price, Honorary Secretary of the Union, who explained the benefits that would accrue if the province had a Branch of its own. Amongst those present were:

    Co. Sligo: J.R. McCarthy (Captain), Major G.A. Benson, DSO, (Secretary) and A.P. Jackson; Ballina: W.S. Huggard; Carrick-on-Shannon: J. Ennis; Claremorris: Rev. G. R. Nixon; Roscommon: Gerald O'Connor.

    Mr Ennis will be remembered by many golfers in Ulster as a member of the Royal County Down Golf Club for which he frequently played in Club matches. The meeting unanimously decided to form a Branch of the Union in Connacht. Mr A.P. Jackson was nominated as the Branch's Vice-President and Major Benson was elected Honorary Secretary.'

12. *Irish Field*, 27 February 1926.

13. William H. Gibson: *Early Irish Golf*, Oakleaf Publications, Naas, Co. Kildare, Ireland, 1988.

14. This information was given by Charles Hezlet's daughter, Rosemary.

15. *History of Royal Portrush*, 1988.

16. *History of Royal County Down*, 1989.

17. This information was obtained from Ian Bamford, Club historian, Royal Portrush Golf Club.

18. We are grateful to the Austin 'Brud' Slattery for this information.

19. George Crosbie (Irish international 1953–57), writing in the *Cork Examiner*, 30 December 1986.

20. Ibid.

21. Ibid.

22. Ibid. *Cork Examiner*, 30 December 1986.

23. Ibid.

24. *The Irish Times*, June 1963.

25. A.G. Bogan's short history of Sutton Golf Club which appeared in the GUI Year Book, 1956.

PATRONS

The Golfing Union of Ireland wishes to place on record its gratitude to its many friends who subscribed most generously either personally, through their affiliated Clubs or through their business interests towards the cost of providing this official account of the development of golf in Ireland during the Union's first hundred years.

Personal

Charles Adams
David L. Baine
J.L. Bamford, BA. LLB.
Robert Barnett
The Barrett Family (Lahinch)
Richard Barry
Bobbie & Arthur Bell
Tony & Michael Black
William G. Black
John Boston
Colin G. Bristow
The Bruen Family
Jeremy J. Byrne (Ballybough)
Tony Campbell
Mrs Ronnie Canty (Cork)
Michael Carew (Elm Park GC)
Joe Carr
Denis V. Collins (Douglas GC)
P.J. Collins
Louis Copeland
George F. Crosbie
Barry T. Crymble FRCS
Eamon Curran
Jack Deignan (Elm Park GC)
W. Devlin
Ivan E.R. Dickson
J.J.B. Dowling
Tom Duggan (Kilkenny)
The Stanley Ferguson Families
W.J.J. Ferguson
John A. Fitzpatrick (Elm Park GC)
Michael P. Fitzpatrick
Jack Fives (Tivoli)
Richard B. Derek Flood FRCGP
Dr William Flynn
Patrick J. Foley
Noel Fox (Portmarnock)
John M. Frazer & Fred Daly OBE
Sir Peter Froggatt

John Gleeson (Limerick)
Gerard D. Golden
Paddy Governey (Carlow)
Tom Grealy
Buddy (John) Griffin (Limerick)
H. Max Hadden JP
Jack Harrington (Douglas GC)
Dr Brum Henderson
Gerald Hickey (Merrion V)
Eddie Higgins (MacGregor)
Declan J. Howley
Sean & Mary Hutch (Adare Manor GC)
Patrick Kearney
Rt Hon. Lord Lowry
Peter V. Lyons
Colm MacMahon (Sutton GC)
John MacNamara (Galway)
David M. McAuley
Miles V. McCann OBE
John McElderry
J.G. (Don) McErvel
Robert Henry (Hal) McGimpsey
Tim J. McHale (Lahinch)
The McHenry Family (Douglas)
John P. McInerney
Walter Magee
David L. Maxwell (Edmondstown GC)
William A. Menton
Batt Murphy (Professional) (Monkstown GC)
Mixie Murphy
Sean and John Murphy (Portmarnock GC)
Frank Murray (Malahide)
J. Gerard O'Brien
Liam O'Connell (Galway)
Pat O'Connell (Roscommon)
Eamon J. O'Connor
Vincent J. O'Connor
Desmond Rea O'Kelly
John F. O'Reilly

Padraic O'Rourke (Kilkenny)
Paddy O'Shea (Elm Park GC)
Phil O'Sullivan & Family
Dr William M. O'Sullivan
Dr Gerald H. Owens
Frederick W. Perry
Oliver Plunkett (Donnybrook)
Joseph M. Quinlan
Liam Reidy

Dr Harry Rice
Dr Michael J. Roberts (Limerick)
Thomas Rogers
Walter H. Skelton
Austin M. Slattery (Ennis)
Brud Slattery
C.H. Taylor (Lahinch)
W.H. Webb
John F. Wilton

The Connacht Provincial Council
The Leinster Provincial Council
The Munster Provincial Council
The Ulster Provincial Council

Affiliated Golf Clubs

Adare Manor
Ardee
Ardglass
Athlone
Ballinascorney
Ballybunion
Ballycastle
Bandon
Bangor
Belvoir Park
Cairndhu
Carlow
Carrickmines
Castle
Castlerock
Castletroy
City of Derry
Clandeboye
Clontarf
Coolattin
Cork
County Cavan
County Louth
County Sligo
Curragh
Delgany
Donabate
Donaghadee
Douglas
Dublin & County

Dundalk
Dungannon
Dun Laoghaire
East Cork
Elm Park
Forrest Little
Galway
Grange
Greenore
Greystones
Headfort
Hermitage
Holywood
Howth
The Island
Kilkenny
Killarney
Killiney
Killymoon
Kirkistown Castle
Knock
Lahinch
Laytown & Bettystown
Limerick
Lisburn
Lucan
Lurgan
Malahide
Massereene
Milltown

Monkstown
Mourne
Mullingar
Muskerry
Newlands
North West
Omagh
Portarlington
Portmarnock
Portsalon
Rathfarnham
Rathmore
The Royal Belfast
The Royal County Down
The Royal Dublin
The Royal Portrush
Royal Tara
Shandon Park
Shannon
St Anne's
Stackstown
Strandhill
Sutton
Trim
Tuam
Tullamore
Warrenpoint
Westport
Woodbrook
Youghal

JUNIOR INTERPROVINCIAL MATCHES

(Chapter 18)

THE CRYMBLE CUP

Year	Venue	Winner	Year	Venue	Winner
1961	Co. Louth	Ulster A	1976	Athlone	Munster
1962	Lahinch	Ulster	1977	Warrenpoint	Ulster
1963	Royal Portrush	Leinster	1978	Thurles	Munster
1964	Co. Sligo	Leinster	1979	Royal Tara	Ulster
1965	Co. Louth	Munster	1980	Co. Sligo	Leinster
1966	Little Island	Munster	1981	Royal Portrush	Munster
1967	Co. Louth	Leinster A	1982	Enniscrone	Munster
1968	Tullamore	Leinster	1983	Tullamore	Ulster
1969	Woodbrook	Leinster C & Munster A	1984	Thurles	Munster
1970	Grange	Leinster	1985	Clandeboye	Ulster
1971	Elm Park	Ulster	1986	Co. Sligo	Ulster
1972	Mullingar	Ulster	1987	Co. Louth	Ulster
1973	Athlone	Ulster	1988	Thurles	Ulster
1974	Thurles	Munster	1989	Massereene	Ulster
1975	Tullamore	Leinster	1990	Westport	Leinster

THE IRISH BOYS' AMATEUR CLOSE CHAMPIONSHIP

(Chapter 18)

THE BINGHAM CUP

Year	Venue	Winner and Club
1983	Curragh	J. Carvill, Warrenpoint
1984	Mullingar	E. O'Connell, Killarney
1985	Athlone	K. Kearney, Roscommon
1986	Royal Tara	D. Errity, Hermitage
1987	Warrenpoint	G. McNeill, Warrenpoint
1988	Birr	D. McGrane, Headfort
1989	Mullingar	D. Higgins, Waterville
1990	Kilkenny	R. Burns, Banbridge

IRISH JUNIOR BOYS' AMATEUR CLOSE CHAMPIONSHIP

(Chapter 18)

THE UNION CUP

Year	Venue	Winner and Club
1983	Curragh	J. Farrell, Carlow
1984	Mullingar	P. Gribben, Warrenpoint
1985	Athlone	P. Russell, Armagh
1986	Royal Tara	M. Sinclair, Knock
1987	Warrenpoint	G. Sproule, Co. Sligo
1988	Birr	G. Sproule, Co. Sligo
1989	Mullingar	S. McEnery, Ennis
1990	Kilkenny	D. Conway, Mallow

THE IRISH INTER-SCHOOLS GOLF CHAMPIONSHIP

(Chapter 18 Appendix X)

THE INTER-SCHOOLS SHIELD

Year	Venue	Winning School
1967	Royal Dublin	St Joseph's CBS, Drogheda
1968	Co. Louth	St Joseph's CBS, Drogheda
1969	Donabate	St Joseph's CBS, Drogheda
1970	Milltown	Regent House, Belfast
1971	Tullamore	St Joseph's CBS, Drogheda
1972	Edmondstown	Royal Belfast Academical Institution
1973	Birr	Rockwell College, Cashel
1974	Clontarf	Bangor Grammar School
1975	L'town & B'town	Rockwell College, Cashel
1976	Donabate	Belvedere College, Dublin
1977	Kilkenny	Blackrock College, Dublin
1978	Tullamore	Bangor Grammar School
1979	Athlone	Bangor Grammar School
1980	Headfort	Belcamp College, Dublin
1981	Donabate	CBC, Carlow
1982	Tullamore	St Patrick's High School
1983	Elm Park	Royal Belfast Academical Institution
1984	Mullingar	CBC, Cork
1985	Clontarf	Summerhill College, Sligo
1986	L'town & B'town	Summerhill College, Sligo
1987	Grange	Armagh College of Further Education
1988	Royal Tara	Summerhill College, Sligo
1989	Headfort	Kells Community
1990	Greystones	Coleraine Academical Institution

THE IRISH CLUBS YOUTHS' CHAMPIONSHIP

(Chapter 18 Appendix X)

THE MacCORMACK CUP

Year	Winning Club
1974	Sutton
1975	Sutton
1976	Royal Portrush
1977	Royal Dublin
1978	Galway
1979	Royal Portrush
1980	Castletroy
1981	The Island
1982	Warrenpoint
1983	Grange
1984	Ardglass
1985	Bantry Park
1986	Grange
1987	Grange
1988	Co. Sligo
1989	Warrenpoint
1990	Co. Sligo

IRISH GOLF CLUBS JUNIOR FOURSOMES TOURNAMENT

(Chapter 18)

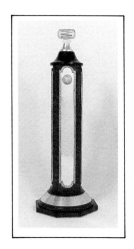

THE SMURFIT TROPHY

Year	Winning Club
1983	Galway
1984	Galway
1985	Dungarvan
1986	Sutton
1987	Warrenpoint
1988	Enniscorthy
1989	Royal Dublin
1990	Enniscrone

Business Interests

Aberdeen Arms Hotel (Lahinch)
Aer Lingus
AIB Group
Albatros Fertilisers Ltd (Galway)
Ballsbridge Motors
Bank of Ireland
Becketts Ltd (Cork)
Bord Gais Eireann
Brother International
P.J. Carroll & Co. plc
City Life Ltd (Cork)
Claddagh House Group (Dublin)
Coca-Cola Bottlers Ireland
Colorman Ltd (Dublin)
Colorprint Ltd (Sean A. Walshe)
Conway Kelleher Tobin (Cork)
Thomas Cook Financial Services
Coopers & Lybrand
Coopers Pitman-Moore
Cork Examiner Publications
Cork Licensed Vintners GS
Coyle Hamilton Ltd
Craft Cleaners
CRH plc
Deegan Auctioneering & Insurances (New Ross and Kilkenny)
Deloitte & Touche
Joe Duffy (Motors) Ltd (Dublin)
Dunlop Slazenger Ireland Ltd
Educational Building Society
Eirpage Ltd (Santry)
Electricity Supply Board
Electro Diesel (Ireland) Ltd (Ballyfermot)
Ever Ready Cars (Dublin)
FBD Insurance plc
Fitzpatrick's Shoes, Grafton Street
Friends Provident
Furstenberg
Gill & Macmillan Ltd
Goldcrop Ltd (Cork)
Goulding Chemicals Ltd
Grant Thornton (Dublin and Mullingar)
Grassland Fertilisers Ltd (Dublin)
P.J. Hegarty Ltd
Hibernian Insurance Co. Ltd

Hoechst Ireland Ltd
International Development Ireland Ltd
IRG plc (Newbridge)
Kalonil Drapery, Sports & Leisure Stores (New Ross) (Tom and Eamon Walsh)
Keanes' Jewellers (Cork)
Kilbride Consultants Ltd (Cork)
Laois Concrete Ltd
MacGregor Golf Ireland
McAuley Singleton
McCartan Turkington Breen & Co.
Magill Print (Ireland) Ltd (Dublin)
Mazda-Motor Distributors Ltd (Dublin)
S.S. Moore Ltd
Motorola Ireland Ltd (Santry)
National Irish Bank GS (Cork)
Nissan Ireland
Northern Bank Ltd (Belfast)
OCS Cleaning Services Ltd (Dublin)
Gay O'Driscoll (Dublin)
Quality Plastics Ltd (Cork)
Reinforced Earth Co. (Ireland) Ltd (Newbridge)
Roadstone Provinces Ltd
Sands Hotel (Portmarnock)
Scully Tyrell & Co. (Dublin)
Semperit (Sales) Ltd
Smurfit Packaging
Spawell Golf Centre (Templeogue)
Spring Grove Ireland Ltd (Cabinteely)
SystemAction Ltd (Dublin)
Toro Turf-care Equipment
Toyota Ireland Ltd
Trade Electric (Limerick) Ltd
TSB Bank Northern Ireland Ltd
Toyota Ireland Ltd
The Turf Club
Ulster Bank Ltd
United Beverages Group (Dublin)
United Drug plc
Walsh Maguire & O'Shea (Dublin)
Wellington Park Hotel
Wiggins Teape Ireland (Sales) Ltd
Burschi Wojner 'Wigoders' (Dublin)
J. Wood & Co. Ltd (Greystones)

APPENDICES

APPENDIX I

Section 1

Results of the first Irish Amateur Open Medal Competition held under the auspices of the Union at the Royal County Club, Portrush, on 7 September 1892

Player	Club	Gross	H/Cap	Nett
T. Stewart	Royal Dublin	101	24	77
E. McManus	Royal County	99	20	79
J. McKeown	Royal County	92	12	80
J. Dickson	Dungannon	98	18	80
G. Carter	Killymoon	105	24	81
C.W. Webb	Royal County	109	28	81
T. Dickson	Dungannon	90	7	83
J. Massey	Royal County	109	26	83
J. McMaster	—	103	20	83
A. Stuart	Hon. Co. of Ed. Golfers	79	+4	83
A. Dewar	Royal County	100	15	85
Jas. A. Patrick	Royal County	113	28	85
R.R. Gilroy	Royal County	90	4	86
R.W. Hutton	—	91	5	86
J.M. Dickson	Dungannon	103	16	87
C.M.D. Stuart	—	115	28	87
T. Gilroy	Royal County	84	+4	88
C.C. Scott	—	100	12	88
E.J. Maguire	County Down	104	15	89
W.H. Webb	Royal County	97	8	89
J.N.R. Pim	County Down	104	14	90
H. Adair	Royal County	99	8	91
J. Armstrong	—	106	15	91
R.A. Corry	Royal County	113	22	91
A. Dod	—	103	12	91
O.B. Webb	Royal County	119	28	91
S. Wilson	Royal Belfast	115	24	91
H. Bucknell	—	110	18	92
E.H. Clarke	Royal Belfast	108	16	92
N. Gilroy	Royal County	100	8	92
J. Patrick	Royal County	116	24	92
D. Anderson	Carnoustie	91	+2	93
J.S. Moreton	—	116	23	93
Major Alison	Royal Belfast	114	20	94
J.H. Andrew	Prestwick St Nicholas	90	+4	94
S.M. Fraser	—	114	20	94
J. Walker	—	106	12	94
J.S. Alexander	Royal County	109	14	95
Geo. Combe	County Down	102	7	95
F. Figgis	Royal Dublin	113	18	95
H.C. Kelly	Royal Belfast	118	22	96
W.J. MacGeagh	County Down	119	22	97
J. MacCormac	Royal Belfast	118	20	98
J.A. McDonald	Royal County	112	14	98
Dr Traill	Royal County	113	14	99
R. Woodside	Royal County	117	18	99
H. Johnston	Royal Belfast	106	6	100

The following also entered: Captain McCalmont, MP, John Ross, MP, L.C. Stuart, J.F. Moore, W.H. Shuter, S. Howard, C.J. Webb, E.D. Prothero, C.R. Topping, D. Moore, J.S. Smail, Wm. Tait, W.S. Gordon, Col. Knox, Cyril Plummer, W.H. McBolger, R. Reid, C.R. Forshaw, H.M. Borge, C. Randall, H.H. Brown, Dr Claxton and H.A. Macaulay.

APPENDIX I

Section 2

Results of the first Irish Amateur Open Championship, played at the Royal County Club, Portrush, on 8, 9 and 10 September 1892

Results of First Round

Dr D. Moore (Royal County)	beat	C.J. Webb (Royal County)
T.A. Dickson (County Down)	beat	J.S. Alexander (Royal County)
R. Keay (King James Vl Perth)	beat	C.B. Topping (Royal County)
C.L. Randall (Prestwick St Nicholas)	beat	W. Tait (Royal Musselburgh)
R.R. Gilroy (Royal County)	beat	C. Plummer (St George's Sandwich)
W.H. Webb (Royal County)	beat	W.J. MacGeagh (Royal County)
A. Stuart (Hon.Co.Ed. Golfers')	beat	W.H. Mann (Royal County)
H. Adair (Royal County)	beat	J.H. Pigot (Royal Dublin)
T. Gilroy (Royal County)	beat	R. Woodside (Royal County)
R. Dunsmore (Kings James Vl Perth)	beat	A.A. Taylor (King James Vl Perth)
G.M. Shaw (Royal Belfast)	beat	G. Combe (County Down)
D. Anderson (Carnoustie)	beat	E.D. Prothero (Troon)
H. Johnston (Royal Belfast)	beat	Capt. J. McCalmont, J.P. (Royal Belfast)
A. Jamison (King James VI Perth)	beat	E.J. Maguire (County Down)
J.H. Andrews (Prestwick St Nicholas)	beat	Major Alison (Royal County)
Jas. McKeown (Cambridge)	beat	C. Clare (Royal Wimbledon)

Results of Second Round

Dr D. Moore	beat	T.A. Dickson
R. Keay	beat	C.L. Randall
R.R. Gilroy	beat	W.H. Webb
A. Stuart	beat	H. Adair
T. Gilroy	beat	R. Dunsmore
D. Anderson	beat	G.M. Shaw
H. Johnston	beat	A. Jamison
J.H. Andrews	beat	Jas. McKeown

Results of Third Round

Dr D. Moore	beat	R. Keay	2 and 1
A. Stuart	beat	R.R. Gilroy	4 and 3
T. Gilroy	beat	D. Anderson	1 hole
J.H. Andrews	beat	H. Johnston	3 and 1

Results of Semi-Final

A. Stuart	beat	Dr D. Moore	3 and 2
J.H. Andrews	beat	T. Gilroy	1 hole

Result of Final

A. Stuart	beat	J.H. Andrews	1 hole

APPENDIX I

Section 3

Record of Winners of the Open Stroke Competition played preceding the Irish Amateur Open Championship

Date	Venue	Entry	Winner (Net)		Winner (Gross)	
1897	Dollymount		James Stephenson, Dublin University	74	O.W. Murray, St Andrews } Tie	80
					D.M. Wilson, Royal Dublin }	80
1898	Portrush		W.H. Boyd, Portmarnock	80	J.R. Gairdner	80
1899	Portmarnock		No Record			
1900	Newcastle		R. Hunter, Royal Portrush	77	Angus McDonald, Edinburgh Burgess	78
1901	Dollymount		H. Holden, Royal Liverpool } Tie	84	H.H. Hilton, Royal Liverpool	81
			A.P. Ross, Portmarnock }	84		
1902	Portrush		R. Hunter, Sr, Prestwick St Nicholas	77	S.H. Fry, Royal Mid-Surrey	76
1903	Portmarnock		J.F. Mitchell, Royal Musselburgh }	78		
			Cecil Boyd, Portmarnock } Tie	78	J.F. Mitchell, Royal Musselburgh	78
			E.B. Dillon, Cork }	78		
1904	Newcastle		R. Andrew, St Cuthbert }	79		
			E.A. Lassen, Lytham St Annes } Tie	79		
			H.C. 'Bruce' Malden }	79	D. Foster, Frinton-on-Sea	74
			R. Hunter, Prestwick St Nicholas }	79		
1905	Dollymount					
1906	Portrush		J. Livingstone, Royal Mid-Surrey } Tie	77	H.H. Barker, Huddersfield	73
			R.O.J. Dallymeyer, Bowden }	77		
1907	Portmarnock	142	J. Healing, Richmond	80	J. Healing, Richmond	79
1908	Newcastle		A.H. Craig, Fortwilliam	83	G.W. Crane, Sandwell Park } Tie	83
					A.D. La Touche, Royal Co. Down }	83

Date	Venue	Entry	Winner (Net)		Winner (Gross)	
1909	Dollymount		J.O. Little, Burntisland	76	J. Jameson, Portmarnock	84
1910	Portrush	120	A.B. Babington, Royal Dublin	79	L.O. Munn, North-West	77
1911	Portmarnock		L.O. Munn,. North-West	78	Clyde Pearse, Tasmania	79
1912	Newcastle		C.G. Manford, Edinburgh University	83	F. Carr, Handsworth	75
1913	Dollymount		C.H. West, Greystones	75	G. Lockhart, Prestwick St Nicholas } Tie	76
					F. Carr, Handsworth	76
1914–18			NO CHAMPIONSHIP			
1919	Portrush	131	F. O'Connor, Portmarnock	80	G.N.C. Martin, Royal Portrush } Tie	81
					E.S. Ulyat, Hunstanton	81
1920	Portmarnock		H.C. Pearson, Walton Heath	81	E.F. Carter, Royal Portrush	79
1921	Newcastle		P.T. Crymble, Royal Co. Down	76	W. Carroll, Dundalk	75
1922	Portrush		E.F. Spiller, North West	75	E.F. Carter, Royal Dublin	69
1923	Newcastle	104	D.J.O. Sinclair, Royal Co. Down	73	D.W. Smyth, Royal Co. Down	76
1924	Dollymount	94	H. Thrift, Milltown } Tie	75	T.W.G. Johnson, Royal Dublin	71
			D.J. Collins, Dublin University	75		
1925	Portrush	130	J.M. Mitchell, Queen's University	77	G. Waddell, Royal Portrush	76
1926	Portmarnock	101	R.M. McConnell, Royal Portrush	75	C.O. Hezlet, Royal Portrush	75
1927	Newcastle	114	H.M. Hadden, Cliftonville	74	H.S. Sheals, Balmoral	76
1928	Dollymount	103	T.M. Healy, Hermitage	77	G.S. Noon, Edinburgh Burgess	77
1929	Portrush	108	H.E. Bell, Portmarnock	71	W.F.C. Scott, Glasgow	72
1930	Portmarnock	130	T.M. Healy, Royal Dublin	74	M. Crowley, Portmarnock	73
1931	Newcastle	149	F.A. McMullen, Royal Co. Down } Tie	77	J. Burke, Lahinch	73
			R. Greene, Dublin University	77		
1932	Dollymount	82	J.F. McLoughlln, Royal Dublin	72	H.N.M. Fogg, Royal Liverpool } Tie	74
					A.F. de Forest, Addington	74
1933	Newcastle	122	R. Greene, Clontarf	71	E.B. Tipping, Royal Ashdown Fst } Tie	72
					G.A. Hill, Sandy Lodge	72
					J.R. Carr, Royal Co. Down	72
1934	Portmarnock	87	L. Crawley, Brancepeth Castle	72	J.R. Carr, Royal Co. Down } Tie	74
					W.J. Gill, Portmarnock	74
1935	Portrush	129	J.L. Crabbe, Foxrock	72	J. Burke, Lahinch	73
1936	Portmarnock	94	G.L. Sleath, Wallasey	74	W.S. McLeod, Ranfurly	75
1937	Dollymount		Cecil Ewing, Co. Sligo } Tie	75	W.S. McLeod, Ranfurly	72
			L.M. King-French, Hermitage	75		
1938	Newcastle		G.J. Moore, Beau Desert	75	J. Bruen Jr, Cork	70
			J.A.E. Johnston, Spa } Tie	75		
			H.F.C. Silcock, Royal Co. Down	75		
1939	Portmarnock	47	R.G. Duggan, Hermitage	73	Cecil Ewing, Co. Sligo	71
1940–45			NO CHAMPIONSHIP			
1946	Portrush	90	J. Taggart, Royal Portrush	73	J.B. Stevenson, Troon St Meddans	70
			T.E. Dijon, Royal Portrush } Tie	73		
			W.C.H. Gray, Troon	73		
1947	Dollymount	73	K.M. Hogan, Sutton	70	M. Power, Muskerry	73
1948	Newcastle	108	R.H. McInnally, Sutton } Tie	77	J.R. Mahon, Co. Sligo	75
			B. Herlihy, Portmarnock	77		
1949	Killarney	139	C.H. Beamish, Royal Portrush } Tie	77	M. Ferguson, Dundalk	75
			I.S. Dougal, Mortonhall	77		
1950	Rosses Point	80	G.P. O'Brien, Douglas } Tie	73	R.H. McInnally, Sutton	70
			P.J. Leydon, Spanish Point	73		
1951	Portmarnock	126	J. Caldwell, Portmarnock } Tie	72	J.B. Carr, Sutton	72
			T.M. Healy, Portmarnock	72		
1952	Portrush	74	C.A. Carroll, Dundalk	72	J.B. Carr, Sutton	68
1953	Killarney	95	W.J. Gill, Portmarnock	72	S.B. Hilliams, Longniddry	75
			R.M. Craigan, Malone } Tie	74		
			T. O'Sullivan, Ballybunion	74		
1954	Dollymount	102	B. Moylett, Ballina } Tie	69	W.J.J. Ferguson, Malone	69
			F.A. McCorry, Royal Portrush	69		
1955	Newcastle	170	W.N.M. Lawrence, Woking	72	J.R. Mahon, Portmarnock	74
1956	Portmarnock	160	F. Gallagher, Co. Louth	71	W.A. McNeill, Royal Belfast	72
1957	Portrush	130	F.A. McCorry, Royal Portrush	72	B.H.G. Chapman, Porters Park	72

APPENDIX I

Section 4

Record of Winners of the Irish Amateur Open Championship

Date	Venue	Entry	Winner and Club	Runner-up and Club
1892	Portrush	32	A. Stuart, Hon. Co. Edinburgh Golfers	J.H. Andrew, Prestwick St Nicholas
1893	Newcastle	35	J. Ball Jr, Royal Liverpool	L.S. Anderson, North Berwick
1894	Dollymount	37	J. Ball Jr, Royal Liverpool	D.L. Low, Moneybeath
1895	Portrush	64	W.B. Taylor, Carlton	J.M. Williamson, Musselburgh
1986	Newcastle	32	W.B. Taylor, Carlton	D. Anderson, Panmure
1897	Dollymount	38	H.H. Hilton, Royal Liverpool	L.S. Anderson, North Berwick
1898	Portrush	47	W.B. Taylor, Carlton	R.O. Dallmeyer, Bowden
1899	Portmarnock	42	J. Ball Jr, Royal Liverpool	J.M. Williamson, Musselburgh
1900	Newcastle	62	H.H. Hilton, Royal Liverpool	S.H. Fry, Royal Mid-Surrey
1901	Dollymount	41	H.H. Hilton, Royal Liverpool	P. Dowie, Edinburgh Burgess
1902	Portrush	96	H.H. Hilton, Royal Liverpool	W.H. Hamilton, Alban
1903	Portmarnock	87	Geo. Wilkie, Leven Thistle	H.A. Boyd, Portmarnock
1904	Newcastle	102	J.S. Worthington, Royal Mid-Surrey	J.F. Mitchell, Royal Musselburgh
1905	Dollymount	71	H.A. Boyd, Portmarnock	J.F. Mitchell, Royal Musselburgh
1906	Portrush	168	H.H. Barker, Huddersfield	J.S. Worthington, Royal Mid-Surrey
1907	Portmarnock	149	J. Douglas Brown, Murrayfield	S.H. Fry, Royal Mid-Surrey
1908	Newcastle	98	J.F. Mitchell, Royal Musselburgh	H.M. Cairnes, Portmarnock
1909	Dollymount	64	L.O. Munn, North West	R. Garson, Troon
1910	Portrush	154	L.O. Munn, North West	G. Lockhart, Prestwick St Nicholas
1911	Portmarnock	123	L.O. Munn, North West	Hon. M. Scott, Royal Melbourne
1912	Newcastle	98	Gordon Lockhart, Prestwick St Nicholas	P.G. Jenkins, Troon
1913	Dollymount	126	C.A. Palmer, Handsworth	L.A. Phillips, Newport
1914-18			NO CHAMPIONSHIP	
1919	Portrush	132	C. Bretherton, Handsworth	T.D. Armour, Lothian Burn
1920	Portmarnock	83	G.N.C. Martin, Royal Portrush	C.W. Robertson, Delgany
1921	Newcastle	72	D. Wilson Smyth, Royal Co. Down	J. Gorry, Co. Kildare
1922	Portrush	88	Alfred Lowe, Malone	Jas. Henderson, Royal Belfast
1923	Newcastle	104	G.N.C. Martin, Royal Portrush	C.O. Hezlet, Royal Portrush
1924	Dollymount	93	E.F. Spiller, North West	J.D. MacCormack, Hermitage
1925	Portrush	130	T.A. Torrance, Sandy Lodge	C.O. Hezlet, Royal Portrush
1926	Portmarnock	103	C.O. Hezlet, Royal Portrush	R.M. McConnell, Royal Portrush
1927	Newcastle	124	R.M. McConnell, Royel Portrush	D.E.B. Soulby, Fairhaven
1928	Dollymount	103	G.S. Noon, Edinburgh Burgess	E.F. Spiller, North-West
1929	Portrush	133	C.O. Hezlet, Royal Portrush	J.A. Lang, Erskine
1930	Portmarnock	139	William Sutton, Timperley	D.A. Fiddian, Stourbridge
1931	Newcastle	159	E.A. McRuvie, Leven Thistle	D.E.B. Soulby, Fortwilliam
1932	Dollymount	91	J. McLean, Hayston	J.C. Brown, Waterford
1933	Newcastle	.136	J. McLean, Hayston	E.W. Fiddian, Stourbridge
1934	Portmarnock	101	H. Thomson, Williamwood	H.G. Bentley, Birkdale
1935	Portrush	163	H. Thomson, Williamwood	J. McLean, Hayston
1936	Portmarnock	117	J.C. Brown, Waterford	W.M. O'Sullivan, Dooks
1937	Dollymount	93	J. Fitzsimmons, Bushfoot	R.A. McKinna, Gullane
1938	Newcastle	92	J. Bruen Jr, Cork	J.R. Mahon, Co. Sligo
1939	Portmarnock	—	*Championship cancelled*	
1940-45			NO CHAMPIONSHIP	
1946	Portrush	110	J.B. Carr, Sutton	A.T. Kyle, Sandmoor
1947	Dollymount	128	J. Burke, Limerick	J.B. Carr, Sutton
1948	Newcastle	121	Cecil Ewing, Co. Sligo	J.B. Carr, Sutton
1949	Killarney	170	W.M. O'Sullivan, Killarney	B.J. Scannell, Woodbrook
1950	Rosses Point	116	J.B. Carr, Sutton	Cecil Ewing, Co. Sligo
1951	Portmarnock	149	Cecil Ewing, Co. Sligo	J.B. Carr, Sutton
1952	Portrush	81	N.V. Drew, Bangor	C.H. Beamish, Royal Portrush
1953	Killarney	106	N.V. Drew, Bangor	W.M. O'Sullivan, Killarney
1954	Dollymount	142	J.B. Carr, Sutton	Cecil Ewing, Co. Sligo

1955	Newcastle	187	J.F. Fitzgibbon, Cork		J.W. Hulme, Warrenpoint		
1956	Portmarnock	90	J.B. Carr, Sutton		J.R. Mahon, Portmarnock		
1957	Portrush	149	J.L. Bamford, Royal Portrush		W. Meharg, Castlerock		
1958	Dollymount	138	T. Craddock, Malahide	294	J.W. Hulme, Warrenpoint J.B. Carr, Sutton	} Tie	295
1959	Newcastle	118	J. Duncan, Shandon Park	313	A.G. Gordan, Troon, St Meddans		318

APPENDIX II

Section 1

Results of the first Irish Amateur Close Championship, played at the Royal County Club, Portrush, on 26, 27 and 28 April 1893

RESULTS OF FIRST ROUND

Thomas Hughes (Royal County)	a bye	
George Combe (County Down)	beat	Henry Gregg (Royal Belfast)
William H. Webb (Royal County)	beat	James Woodside (Royal County)
Henry J. Daly (Royal Dublin)	a bye	
Thomas A. Dickson (County Down)	beat	James Young (County Down)
Hugh Adair (Killymoon)	beat	James S. Alexander (Royal County)
Hugh C. Kelly (Royal Belfast)	beat	George M. Shaw (County Down)
Arthur C. Gaussen (Killymoon)	a bye	

RESULTS OF SECOND ROUND

G. Combe	beat	T. Hughes
W.H. Webb	beat	H.J. Daly
T.A. Dickson	beat	H. Adair
A.C. Gaussen	beat	H.C. Kelly

RESULTS OF THIRD ROUND

G. Combe	beat	W.H. Webb
T.A. Dickson	beat	A.C. Gaussen

RESULT OF FINAL

Thomas A. Dickson (County Down)	beat	George Combe (County Down)	2 holes

APPENDIX II

Section 2

Record of Winners of the Irish Amateur Close Championship

Year	Venue	Entry	Winner and Club	Runner-up and Club	Result
1893	Portrush	12	T. Dickson, Co. Down	G. Combe, Co. Down	2 Holes
1894	Newcastle	22	R. Magill, Co. Down	T. Dickson, Co. Down	3 and 1
1895	Dollymount	28	W.H. Webb, Royal Portrush	Jas. Stevenson, Royal Dublin	10 and 9
1896	Portrush	28	J.S. Moore, Dublin University	H.A.S. Upton, Royal Dublin	8 and 7
1897	Newcastle	17	H.E. Reade, Royal Belfast	W.H. Webb, Royal Portrush	2 and 1
1898	Dollymount	26	W.H. Webb, Royal Portrush	J. Stewart Moore, Royal Portrush	9 and 8
1899	Portrush	26	H.E. Reade, Royal Belfast	J.P. Todd, Portmarnock	3 and 2
1900	Portmarnock	41	R.G.N. Henry, Portmarnock	J. McAvoy, Ormeau	4 and 3
1901	Newcastle	39	W.H. Boyd, Portmarnock	H.E. Reade, Royal Belfast	7 and 5
1902	Dollymount	31	F.B. Newett, Malone	R. Shaw, Dublin University	1 Hole
1903	Portrush	37	H.E. Reade, Royal Belfast	R.A. Campbell, Malahide	5 and 4
1904	Portmarnock	64	H.A. Boyd, Portmarnock	J.P. Todd, Portmarnock	4 and 2
1905	Newcastle	31	F.B. Newett, Malone	B. O'Brien, Malone	6 and 5
1906	Dollymount	42	H.A. Boyd, Portmarnock	H.M. Cairnes, Portmarnock	at 38th
1907	Portrush	40	H.M. Cairnes, Portmarnock	H.A. Boyd, Portmarnock	7 and 6
1908	Portmarnock	54	L.O. Munn, Dublin University	A.B. Babington, Royal Dublin	10 and 9
1909	Newcastle	34	A.H. Patterson, Dublin University	E.F. Spiller, Malone	at 37th
1910	Dollymount	44	J.F. Jameson, Malahide	L.O. Munn, North-West	2 and 1
1911	Portrush	34	L.O. Munn, North-West	H.A. Boyd, Portmarnock	7 and 6
1912	Castlerock	31	A.H. Craig, Fortwilliam	N. Halligan, Co. Louth	13 and 11
1913	Portmarnock	67	L.O. Munn, Royal Dublin	H.A. Boyd Portmarnock	6 and 5
1914	Hermitage	40	L.O. Munn, North-West	Earl Annesley, Royal Co. Down	10 and 8
1915–18			NO CHAMPIONSHIP		
1919	Portmarnock	65	E.F. Carter, Royal Portrush	W.G. McConnell, Portmarnock	9 and 7
1920	Castlerock	52	C.O. Hezlet, Royal Portrush	C.L. Crawford, Portstewart	12 and 11
1921	Portmarnock	53	E.F. Carter, Royal Dublin	G. Moore, Portmarnock	9 and 8
1922	Portrush	62	E.M. Munn, North-West	W.K. Tillie, Royal Portrush	3 and 1
1923	Milltown	62	J.D. MacCormack, Hermitage	L.E.J. Werner, Dublin University	3 and 1
1924	Newcastle	45	J.D. MacCormack, Hermitage	D.E.B. Soulby, Portmarnock	4 and 3
1925	Portmarnock	80	C.W. Robertson, Delgany	H.M. Cairnes, Portmarnock	4 and 2
1926	Portrush	35	A.C. Allison, Royal Portrush	O.W. Madden, Knock	4 and 3
1927	Cork	53	J.D. MacCormack, Hermitage	H.M. Cairnes, Portmarnock	at 37th
1928	Castlerock	67	D.E.B. Soulby, Fortwilliam	J.O. Wisdom, Dublin University	7 and 5
1929	Dollymount	74	D.E.B. Soulby, Fortwilliam	F.P. McConnell, Royal Portrush	4 and 3
1930	Lahinch	55	J. Burke, Lahinch	F.P. McConnell, Royal Portrush	6 and 5
1931	Rosses Point	54	J. Burke, Lahinch	F.P. McConnell, Royal Portrush	6 and 4
1932	Portrush	52	J. Burke, Lahinch	M. Crowley, Portmarnock	6 and 5
1933	Cork	61	J. Burke, Lahinch	C.J. McMullan, Knock	3 and 2
1934	Rosslare	63	J.C. Brown, Waterford	R.M. McConnell, Royal Portrush	6 and 5
1935	Galway	75	R.M. McConnell, Royal Portrush	J. Burke, Lahinch	2 and 1
1936	Castlerock	69	J. Burke, Newlands	R.M. McConnell, Royal Portrush	7 and 6
1937	Ballybunion	86	J. Bruen Jr, Muskerry	J. Burke, Lahinch	3 and 2
1938	Castle	86	J. Bruen Jr, Muskerry	R. Simcox, Cork	3 and 2
1939	Rosses Point	69	G.H. Owens, Skerries	R.M. McConnell, Royal Portrush	6 and 5
1940	Dollymount	49	J. Burke, Castletroy	W.M. O'Sullivan, Killarney	4 and 3
1941–5			NO CHAMPIONSHIP		
1946	Dollymount	106	J. Burke, Castletroy	C. Ewing, Co. Sligo	2 and 1
1947	Lahinch	67	J. Burke, Castletroy	J. Fitzsimmons, Bushfoot	2 Holes
1948	Portrush	73	C. Ewing, Co. Sligo	B.J. Scannell, Woodbrook	3 and 2
1949	Galway	74	J.P. Carroll, Sutton	T.P. Murphy, Elm Park	4 and 3
1950	Baltray	86	B. Herlihy, Portmarnock	B.C. McManus, Mourne	3 and 2
1951	Cork	126	M. Power, Muskerry	J.B. Carr, Sutton	3 and 2
1952	Craigivad	171	T.W. Egan, Monkstown	J.C. Brown, Tramore	at 41st

Year	Venue	Entry	Winner and Club	Runner-up and Club	Result
1953	Rosses Point	93	J. Malone, Portmarnock	M. Power, Muskerry	2 and 1
1954	Carlow	110	J.B. Carr, Sutton	W.I. Forsythe, Malone	3 and 2
1955	Lahinch	112	J.R. Mahon, Portmarnock	G.F. Crosbie, Cork	3 and 2
1956	Malone	133	A.G.H. Love, Knock	G.F. Crosbie, Cork	at 37th
1957	Galway	86	J.B. Carr, Sutton	G.F. Crosbie, Cork	2 Holes
1958	Ballybunion	100	C. Ewing, Co. Sligo	G.A. Young, Kilrush	4 and 3
1959	Portmarnock	108	T. Craddock, Malahide	J.B. Carr, Sutton	at 38th
1960	Portstewart	121	M. Edwards, Shandon Park	G.N. Fogarty, St Anne's	6 and 5
1961	Rosses Point	100	D. Sheahan, Grange & UCD	J.C. Brown, Tramore	5 and 4
1962	Baltray	140	M. Edwards, Shandon Park	J. Harrington, Adare Manor	at 42nd
1963	Killarney	144	J.B. Carr, Sutton	E.C. O'Brien, Tullamore & UCD	2 and 1
1964	Newcastle	172	J.B. Carr, Sutton	A. McDade, Bangor	6 and 5
1965	Rosses Point	131	J.B. Carr, Sutton	T. Craddock, Malahide	3 and 2
1966	Dollymount	186	D.B. Sheahan, Grange	J. Faith, Royal Portrush	3 and 2
1967	Lahinch	138	J.B. Carr, Sutton	P.D. Flaherty, Addington	1 Hole
1968	Portrush	179	M.D. O'Brien, New Ross	F.E. McCarroll, City of Derry	2 and 1
1969	Rosses Point	173	V. Nevin, Limerick	J.E. O'Leary, Foxrock	1 Hole
1970	Grange	242	D.B. Sheahan, Grange	M. Bloom, Edmondstown	2 Holes
1971	Ballybunion	141	R.M. Kane, Malahide	M.D. O'Brien, New Ross	4 and 3
1972	Newcastle	188	K. Stevenson, Banbridge	T.B.C. Hoey, Shandon Park	4 and 3
1973	Rosses Point	162	R.K.M. Pollin, Royal Belfast	R. de L. Staunton, Castlerea	1 Hole
1974	Portmarnock	302	R.M. Kane, Ealing	M.A. Gannon, Co. Louth	5 and 4
1975	Cork	192	M.D. O'Brien, New Ross	J.A. Byrne, Edmondstown	5 and 4
1976	Portrush	235	D. Branigan, Laytown & Bettystown	D.F. O'Sullivan, Cork	2 Holes
1977	Westport	209	M.A. Gannon, Co. Louth	J.A. Hayes, Hermitage	at 19th
1978	Carlow	192	M.F. Morris, Portmarnock	T. Cleary, Fermoy	2 Holes
1979	Ballybunion	202	J. Harrington, Adare Manor	M.A. Gannon, Co. Louth	2 and 1
1980	Newcastle	228	R. Rafferty, Warrenpoint	M.J. Bannon, Belvoir Park	8 and 7
1981	Rosses Point	196	D. Branigan, Laytown & Bettystown	E. McMenamin, Ballybofey	at 19th
1982	Woodbrook	229	P. Walton, Malahide	V. Smyth, Laytown & Bettystown	7 and 6
1983	Killarney	209	T. Corridan, Castletroy	E. Power, Tramore	2 Holes
1984	Malone	240	T.B.C. Hoey, Shandon Park	L. MacNamara, Woodbrook	at 20th
1985	Westport	198	D.F. O'Sullivan, Cork	D. Branigan, Laytown & Bettystown	1 Hole
1986	Dollymount	262	J. McHenry, Douglas	P. Rayfus, Trim	4 and 3
1987	Tramore	177	E. Power, Tramore	J.P. Fitzgerald, Co. Louth	2 Holes
1988	Portrush	222	G. McGimpsey, Bangor	D. Mulholland, Castlerock	2 and 1
1989	Rosses Point	189	P. McGinley, Grange	N. Goulding, Portmarnock	3 and 2
1990	Baltray	190	D. Clarke, Dungannon	P. Harrington, Stackstown	3 and 2

APPENDIX III

George Combe's Handicapping Scheme

The situation can best be explained by reproducing George Combe's circular letter issued to all affiliated Clubs in which he also set out his handicap system.

Handicaps at Golf

'The Interprovincial Match, last Easter at Portrush, plainly showed that there was a very considerable difference between the play of Northern and Southern golfers returning the same handicaps. In other words, the Ulster players were about on a par with the Leinster players, whose handicaps were some four strokes higher.

'Taking Royal Dublin as the leading Leinster Club, their 10 handicap men were as good as the Ulster men with 6. It was, and is, admitted that the Ulster scratch players were not as good as Scotch and English scratchmen.

'By scratchmen is meant the ordinary scratch player and not Messrs Tait, Ball, Hilton and Laidlay, who are in a class by themselves.

'Now, it was agreed that the handicaps of the Royal Dublin Club were as near as might be, on the same level as the Scotch and English handicaps and, in the face of this, I designed a system of handicapping which has already been taken up by my own Club, the County Down, and which I will now explain.

'Taking the list of members I raised their handicaps four all round. Then, according to the number of strokes received, I divided them into ten classes as follows, putting all players down on the centre figure in each class:

Class	Handicap				
0	+1	Scr.	and 1		
1	2	3	4		
2	5	6	7		
3	8	9	10		
4	11	12	13		
5	14	15	16		
6	17	18	19		
7	20	21	22		
8	23	24	25		
9	26	27	28	. . . 29	. . . 30

'As will be seen from the accompanying handicap lists, the numbers representing the classes give the number of strokes for 9 hole matchplay, and the lowest set of figures give medal handicaps. Having got all the players started out on the 0, 3, 6, 9, 12, 15, 18, 21, 24 and 27 marks, I then went over each class, putting the strong players down one stroke and the weak players up one, leaving the medium and doubtful players on the centre mark.

'I then submitted the list of members to Council. They went over it, and put any player who was palpably in a wrong class into that which suited him, and the list was then complete.

'The advantages claimed are as follows:

1. Simplicity and fairness;
2. Easy comparison of players;
3. Handicaps at a glance.

'The method of altering handicaps is as follows: The members of the handicapping committee have no hard and fast rule for reducing or raising a player's handicap, but their attention is attracted to any player by his winning a competition, or showing a marked improvement or falling off in his game. They can reduce or raise him one or two strokes in his own class or put him up or down a class according to requirements. Having all players in each class readily to hand, they can easily judge if a player is being put into a fair position with regard to other players in his own class.

'The County Down Club have adopted this system, thus bringing their handicaps into line with Royal Dublin and the leading Scotch and English Clubs. If Royal Portrush and Royal Belfast followed suit, the majority of the other Clubs in the Union will have no difficulty in arranging their handicaps on a basis got by taking the handicap of some of their reliable players from the larger Clubs and handicapping from these. As regards younger Clubs, having no members of a larger Club on whom to rely, it will be necessary for them to handicap at first on the par score system, 'til they can get the comparative merits of their players and then they will soon be able to come into line.

'The par score of a green may be reckoned as follows, and should represent the nett score of a player on his best form:

Holes up to 140 yards	3;
Holes from 140 to 300 or 350 yards, if good running ground	4;
Holes from 300 to 440 or 350 to 480 yards, if good run is obtainable	5;
Holes over 440 or 480 yards according to ground	6;

'In open competitions the home Clubs are not bound to put any player on the handicap which he returns, but should use this as a guide as to his probable position, and then see that he goes into his proper class with home Club members.

'It is absolutely impossible to make one handicap to cover all greens, as players are nearly sure to have a lower handicap on their home green; but I maintain that, with a good committee and the players arranged as per the accompanying sheet, the best results will be obtained, as it is almost always possible to find some one who knows a player's outside form, and if this knowledge cannot be obtained, the greatest good will be served by keeping any dark horse safe.

'Of course, I do not mean to say that the list submitted is absolutely correct, but any small errors will soon rectify themselves.

'Finally, I may add that it is the intention of the Golfing Union to institute a system of local sub-committees to look after the handicaps of Clubs in their district, and report on same to headquarters for the general benefit of Clubs belonging to the Union.

George Combe
Union Honorary Secretary
Golfing Union of Ireland'

The following Clubs had adopted Combe's handicapping scheme:

Royal Belfast, County Down, Ormeau, Greenisland,
Malone, Larne, Bundoran, Greenore, Armagh,
Portmarnock, Greencastle, Foxrock, Fortwilliam,
Warrenpoint, Dungannon and Roscrea.

The following Clubs approved of the scheme:

Royal Dublin, County Louth, Dublin University,
Knock, Massereene and North-West.

The handicapping list of County Down members referred to by George Combe is not traceable.

APPENDIX IV
Section 1

Irish Senior Golf Club Challenge Cup

Competition Rules

1. The Cup should be called 'The Irish Senior Golf Club Challenge Cup'.

2. The Competition shall be annual, and open to all Clubs affiliated to the Golfing Union, and shall be competed for under the St Andrews Rules.

3. The competing teams shall number 6 players each, full members, who must be resident in Ireland at least six months previous to the match, onus of proof resting with the players protested against.

4. While the players in each team may be changed, no individual shall play for more than one Club during the season, and he must be a member of the Club for which he proposes to compete at least six months previous to the match.

5. The names of the Clubs entered for the competition shall be placed in four lots according to their Provinces, and shall be drawn in the usual manner for Matchplay, all byes being in the first round.

6. The winning teams in the four Provinces to be placed by the Committee in one lot and drawn.

7. The Clubs which are in each instance first drawn in the ballot shall have choice of ground, unless one Club only has a full course of 18 holes, in which case the match must be played on such Course. In the event of two distant Clubs being drawn together, the Committee, on the application of either Club, may direct the match to be played upon any convenient Links.

8. In the event of one of the competing Clubs appealing that the ground selected is unfit for play, a Committee of Inspection shall investigate and decide the question; all expenses to be paid by the Club decided against.

9. In the Interprovincial rounds the Links shall be chosen by the Committee.

10. Any Club refusing or failing to play the Club against which it has been drawn within the time intimated to it, and without sufficient reason, shall be adjudged to have lost the match. When the Clubs are unable to agree as to the date on which to play the match, a date shall be fixed by the Committee, and if either Club refuse to play on such date, such Club shall be thrown out of the competition.

11. The match shall be decided by the number of holes won by each team, and in the event of a tie, each team shall play one extra hole and so on until the match is decided.

12. In the question of the interpretation of the Rules of the game, the decision of the Committee shall be final.

13. The Committee shall consist of two Delegates each from Ulster and Leinster and one each from Munster and Connacht — to be selected at a Meeting of the Golfing Union. Each member of the Committee to have power to appoint (in writing) a substitute when he cannot attend a Meeting personally. The Honorary Secretary and Treasurer of the Union to be members, and the Honorary Secretary Convenor of the Committee.

14. Medals or Badges shall be presented to the winning team.

15. The competing Clubs shall be requested to subscribe funds for the purchase of a Challenge Cup and shall pay £1 entry fee annually.

16. All matches must be played between 1st of March and 1st November.

17. In the case of absence of any Member of a team, his opponent shall be credited with nine holes.

18. Protest must be made in writing, and posted within 7 days after the match, to the Honorary Secretary of the Golfing Union, accompanied by 10/- deposit, to be forfeited to the Union if protest over-ruled.

Irish Junior Golf Club Challenge Cup

Competition Rules

1. The Cup shall be called 'The Irish Junior Golf Club Challenge Cup'.

2. The competition for the Cup shall be governed by the Rules of the Irish Senior Golf Club Challenge Cup, except as hereinafter altered.

3. The Committee may refuse to admit any Club whom they think should compete for the Senior Cup.

4. No player who has played in a team in the Senior Cup more than once, or in the Interprovincial Rounds, either as a member or as a substitute, shall be eligible to compete in a Junior team in the same season.

5. A Club entering a team for the Junior Cup shall send the names of the team and 3 substitutes with their handicaps to the Honorary Secretaries of the Golfing Union and the opposing Club at least 14 days before the match.

6. No team, whose aggregate handicaps are less than 60, shall be allowed to play in the Junior Cup Competition.

APPENDIX IV
Section 2

Record of Winning Clubs and Teams in the Senior Cup

1900 DUBLIN UNIVERSITY
H. Dodd
E.K. Figgis
E. Gibson
R.P. Meredith
C.S. Moore
A.C. Newett

1901 ROYAL PORTRUSH
D.J. Cameron
H.E. Reade
J.S. Reade
J.H. Richardson
O.B. Webb
W.H. Webb

1902 ROYAL PORTRUSH
D.J. Cameron
F.B. Newett
H.E. Reade
J.S. Reade
O.B. Webb
W.H. Webb

1903 ROYAL PORTRUSH
C.S. Moore
J.S. Moore
F.B. Newett
H.E. Reade
O.B. Webb
W.H. Webb

1904 PORT-MARNOCK
H.A. Boyd
H.M. Jackson
A.F. Dudgeon
G.W.F. Kelly
W.C. Pickman
J.P. Todd

1905 MALONE
R.J. Hewitt
J.L. Jackson
W. McMullan
F.B. Newett
B. O'Brien
E. Young

1906 PORT-MARNOCK
H.A. Boyd
H.M. Cairnes
R.G.N. Henry
G.W.F. Kelly
J.S. Matterson
W.C. Pickman

1907 PORT-MARNOCK
H.M. Cairnes
R.G.N. Henry
G.W.F. Kelly
W.C. Pickman
F.O. Stoker
J.P. Todd

1908 MALONE
R.J. Hewitt
J.L. Jackson
J.C. McClerry
F.B. Newett
B.O'Brien
S. Smiles
E.F. Spiller

1909 MALONE
C.F. Barker
J.D. Coates
R.J. Hewitt
J.L. Jackson
F.B. Newett
B.O'Brien
E.F. Spiller

1910 DUBLIN UNIVERSITY
R.M. Elvery
J. Henderson
T.W.G Johnstone
F.B. McCarter
W.H. McCarter
L.O. Munn
L. Sheil

1911 DUBLIN UNIVERSITY
W.St.J. Evans
A.K. Gildea
J. Henderson
T.W. Johnstone
F.B. McCarter
W.H. McCarter
L.O. Munn

1912 PORT-MARNOCK
H.M Cairnes
W.J. Carbery
F.E. Davies
W. O'Brien
B. Plunkett
J. Reid
E. Webb Smith

1913 PORT-MARNOCK
G. Beattie
H.A. Boyd
H.M. Cairnes
F.E. Davies
J.F. Jameson
A. Jeffcott
J. Reid

1914—18

No Tournament

1919 PORT-MARNOCK
G Beattie
H.A. Boyd
H.M. Cairnes
P. Hughes
J.F. Jameson
F. O'Connor
J. Reid

1920 MILLTOWN
A.B. Babington
E.F. Carter
W.G. McConnell
F.E. Davies
G. Ross
D.E.B. Soulby
H. Thrift

1921 MALONE
W.A. Barker
W.R. Knox
A. Lowe
C.J. Maguire
J.F. Stevenson
J.C. Timbey
A.E. Todd

1922 MALONE
W.A. Barker
W.R. Knox
A. Lowe
C.J. Maguire
J.F. Stevenson
J.C. Timbey
A.E. Todd

1923 ROYAL PORTRUSH
A.C. Allison
C.O. Hezlet
F.P. McConnell
R. McConnell
G.N.C. Martin
J.C. Mant Martin
H. Sparrow

1924 ROYAL DUBLIN
A.B. Babington
H.A. Boyd
J.F. Jameson
T.W. Johnstone
N. Manley
C.S. Wallis
H.S. Watson

1925 ROYAL DUBLIN
J.F. Jameson
J. Johnson
N. Manley
F. O'Connor
C.S. Wallis
J.D. Walsh
C.H. West

1926 HERMITAGE
T. Cormack
J. Gorry
C. Hames
J.D. MacCormack
J.J. McGowran
J. Nugent
J.S. Scott

1927 ROYAL DUBLIN
D.J. Collins
J. Fielding
J.G. Greene
N. Manley
T.C.K. Moore
F. O'Connor
C.H. West

1928 PORT-MARNOCK
H.A. Boyd
V.B. Carroll
M. Crowley
J.F. Jameson
J.D. MacCormack
W. O'Brien
C.W. Robertson

1929 ROYAL DUBLIN
D.J. Collins
T. Healy
E.L. Kidd
C.S. Wallis
H.S. Watson
E.D. Werner
C.H. West

1930 PORT-MARNOCK
H.E. Bell
H.M. Cairnes
W. Carroll
M. Crowley
W.J. Gill
J.F. Jameson
C.W. Robinson

1931 CORK
G. Crosbie
C.A. Murphy
R.St.J. Murphy
J.G. Musgrave
E. O'Flynn
W.R. Ogilvie
R. Simcox

1932 PORT-MARNOCK
H.E. Bell
H.M. Cairnes
W. Carroll
M. Crowley
C. Ewing
W.J. Gill

1933 PORT-MARNOCK
H.E. Bell
C.A. Carroll
W. Carroll
C. Ewing
W.J. Gill
J.D. MacCormack
P.F. Purcell

1934 PORT-MARNOCK
C.A. Carroll
C. Ewing
W.J. Gill
R. Greene
J.D. MacCormack

1935 PORT-MARNOCK
C.A. Carroll
C. Ewing
W.J. Gill
R. Greene
J.D. MacCormack

1936 BELVOIR PARK
A. Campbell
H.D. Connolly
R.J. Frizzell
J.F. Graham
J. McCaherty

1937 PORT-MARNOCK
C.A. Carroll
T.A. Healy
J.D. MacCormack
C.J. Mullan
G.H. Owens

1938 PORT-MARNOCK
W.J. Gill
R. Greene
T.A. Healy
T.D. Purcell
B.J. Scannell

1939 CORK
J. Bruen Jr
G. Crosbie
A.J. Dinan
J. Ronan
R. Simcox

1940 PORT-MARNOCK
C. Ewing
W.J. Gill
F.X. Kelly
D.P. Morris
J.F. Owens

1941-4
No Tournament

1946 MUSKERRY
M. Cronan
B.G. Dorgan
Rev. J. Hegarty
M.J. Hegarty
W. O'Sullivan
M. Power
J.H. Rice

1947 MUSKERRY
M. Cronan
Rev. J. Hegarty
L. McCarthy
E.P. O'Flynn
W. O'Sullivan
M. Power
J.H. Rice

1948 SUTTON
J.B. Carr
J.P. Carroll
M.P. Fitzpatrick
T.P. Fitzpatrick
R.H. McInnally

1949 SUTTON
J.B. Carr
J.P. Carroll
M. Fitzpatrick
T. Fitzpatrick
R.H. McInnally

1950 8UTTON
J.B. Carr
J.P. Carroll
M.P. Fitzpatrick
T.P. Fitzpatrick
R.H. McInnally

1951 MALONE
W.E. Dornan
W.J.J. Ferguson
R.J. Frizzell
R.L. Lowry
J.G. McErvel

1952 BELVOIR PARK
A.M.M.Boucher
A. Campbell
J.W. Graham
H.E. Irwin
J.P. McVeigh
A.R. Megaw
S.S. Moore
D.R. Young

1953 MUSKERRY
E.F. Casey
M.J. Hegarty
J.F. Lawlor
L. McCarthy
W. O'Sullivan
M. Power
J.H. Rice

1954 MALONE
R.M. Craigan
W.J.J. Ferguson
I. Forsythe
G.J. Irvine
J.G. McErvel

1955 MALONE
R.M. Craigan
W.J.J. Ferguson
G.J. Irvine
J.G. McErvel
I.A. Nesbitt

1956 SUTTON
J.B. Carr
E.A. Firth
M.P. Fitzpatrick
T.P. Fitzpatrick
J. Larkin

1957 BELVOIR PARK
T.B. Agnew
J. Cherry
P. Froggatt
J. McVeigh
D.R. Young

1958 SUTTON
J.B. Carr
J.P. Carroll
E.A. Firth
M. Fitzpatrick
T. Fitzpatrick

1959 LAHINCH
T. Ahern
P.J. Leydon
G. McGlennon
A. Skerritt
A.F. Slattery

1960 SHANDON PARK
J. Duncan
B. Edwards
M. Edwards
G.A. Heron
W.H.E. Rainey

1961 SHANDON PARK
J. Duncan
B. Edwards
M. Edwards
T.R.C. Hoey
W.H.E. Rainey

1962 SHANDON PARK
J. Duncan
B. Edwards
M. Edwards
G.A. Herron
W.H.E. Rainey

1963 SUTTON
J.B. Carr
J.P. Carroll
E.A. Firth
M.P. Fitzpatrick
T.P. Fitzpatrick

1964 SHANDON PARK
D.J. Crawford
J. Duncan
B. Edwards
M. Edwards
W.H.E. Rainey

1965 MALAHIDE
P. Caul
T. Craddock
S. Flanagan
J. Lawless
A. Murtagh

1966 SHANDON PARK
B. Edwards
M. Edwards
M.J.C. Hoey
T.B.C. Hoey
W.H.E. Rainey

1967 ISLAND
L. Kane
R.M. Kane
B. Moore
B. Rogers
P. Rogers

1968 SHANDON PARK
J. Boston
A. Brown
B. Edwards
T.B.C. Hoey
W.H.E. Rainey

1969 ROYAL DUBLIN
D.K. Corcoran
M.B. Costello
G.N. Fogarty
D.P. Herlihy
P.V. O'Neill

1970 CLANDE-BOYE
S.A.G. Cooley
J.H. Derby
R. Hutton
F.A. McCorry
B. Wilson

1971 SHANDON PARK
B. Edwards
D.P.W. Hoey
M.J.C. Hoey
T.B.C. Hoey
D.C. Long

1972 SHANDON PARK
C. Barr
B. Edwards
D.P.W. Hoey
M.J.C. Hoey
T.B.C. Hoey
D.C. Long

1973 SHANDON PARK
M.A. Brown
B. Edwards
M.J.C. Hoey
T.B.C. Hoey
D.C. Long

1974 CO. LOUTH
M.A. Gannon
A. Gormley
D. Levins
M. McGuirk
B.V.M. Reddan

1975 CORK
Match played 1976
R.N. Baker
L.D. Goulding
D. Kiely
N. Lehane
D.F. O'Sullivan

1976 LIMERICK
J. Harrington
M.G.I. Morris
V. Nevin
W. Rice
P. Walsh

1977 CO. LOUTH
F. Gannon
M.A. Gannon
D.P. McCann
M. McGuirk
B.V.M. Reddan

1978 SHANDON PARK
R. Beaney
B. Edwards
M.J.C. Hoey
T.B.C. Hoey
D.C. Long

1979 ROYAL PORTRUSH
J.C. Cross
J.R. Dickson
I.A. Elliott
G. McAleese
D.J.F. Young

1980 LIMERICK
J. Harrington
M.G.I. Morris
V. Nevin
W. Rice
P. Walsh

1981 BANGOR
B.J.S. Kissock
J.A. McDade
G. McGimpsey
B. Wilson
N.D. Woods

1982 LIMERICK
J. Carew
J. Fitzgerald
J.V. Lynch
V. Nevin
W. Rice

1983 ISLAND
R.M. Kane
B. Moore
B. Rogers
K. Rogers
A. Smith

1984 BANGOR
P. Barry
B.J.S. Kissock
A. McDade
G. McGimpsey
N. Woods

1985 CLANDE-BOYE
C. Glasgow
D. Jackson
G. Kerr
C. Murphy
E.T. Quiery

1986 CLANDE-BOYE
C. Glasgow
D. Jackson
G. Kerr
C. Murphy
E.T. Quiery

1987 WARREN-POINT
J. Carvill
P. Gribben
G. McNeill
D. Parr
K. Stevenson

1988 PORT-MARNOCK
D. Conway
N. Goulding
M.F. Morris
A.J.C. Morrow
D. Snow

1989 CORK
T. Cleary
P. Cowley
P. Lyons
D. O'Sullivan
M. Quirke

1990 WARRENPOINT
R. Burns
P. Gribben
G. McNeill
K. Stevenson
P. Trainor

APPENDIX IV
Section 3

Record of Winning Clubs and Teams in the Junior Cup

1900 PORT-MARNOCK
R.R. Boyd
W.J. Carbery
R.G.N. Henry
G.S. Kinahan
W.E. Rogers
W.H. Roper

1901 ORMEAU
H.W. Bailie
W.B. Fennell
J. McAvoy
H. McKeag
T.A. McKeag
P.E. Reade

1902 PORT-MARNOCK
C.A. Boyd
W.J. Carbery
P.J. Kiernan
G.S. Kinahan
W.G. Meldon
E. Webb-Smith

1903 NORTH WEST
A.B. Babington
F.G. Dickson
F.W. Lecky
J.H. McConnell
F.H. Millar
E.M. Munn

1904 FOXROCK
J.H. Barrington
C.W. Dunne
L. Martin
C.J. Rutherfoord
H.J. Synnott
J. Wilkinson Jr

1905 FOXROCK
G.W. Dunne
F. Fottrell
L. Martin
C. Rutherfoord
H.J. Synnott
J.Wilkinson Jr

1906 KNOCK
W.R. Forde
D. Gilchrist
P. Gilchrist
J.C. Taylor
J.E. Whyte
J.R. Whyte

1907 SUTTON
R.W. Louis
C.R. O'Dowd
G. Ross
J.S. Stuart
J.D. Walsh
C.H. Whyte

1908 KNOCK
W.N. Davidson
W. Fitchie
W.R. Forde
P. Gilchrist
S.H. Lowry
J.E. Whyte

1909 KNOCK
W.N. Davidson
W. Fitchie
R.H.T. Forde
W.R. Forde
S.H. Lowry
M.A. Trimble
J.R. Whyte

1910 HELEN'S BAY
A. Henderson
T.E. McConnell
J. Pyper
T.W. Pyper
W. Robinson
F.E. Ruddell
J.M. Scott

1911 GREENORE
V.B. Carroll
W.J. Carroll
W.E. Elkins
F.J. Horne
J.A. McArevey
J.M. Marron
C.W. Wilson

1912 MILLTOWN
P.J. Barry
E.C. Brady
T. Rae
T.A. Rae
W.G. Ryan
W.T. Sheppard
J.M. Staples

1913 FOXROCK
C.D. Considine
H.J. Considine
R.F.M. Crozier
Capt. Keith
H. O'Reilly
C.J. Rutherfoord
J. Wilkinson

1914 FOXROCK
H.J. Considine
T. Considine
W.R. Crawford
R.F.N.Crozier
J.G. Drury
A.H. Porter
J. Wilkinson

1915-18
No Tournament

1919 ROYAL CO. DOWN
L. Campbell
P.T. Crymble
E.S. Dashwood
G. Gilbert
J.R. Russell
R.W. Wilkinson
S.R. Wilson

1920 ROYAL CO. DOWN
P.T. Crymble
G.D. Gilbert
J.C. Gilbert Jr
W.O. Hume
J.S. Millar
R.W. Wilkinson
S.R. Wilson

1921 DUNMURRY
T.H. Graham
A.H. McBride
J. McGladdery
G. O'Kelly
R.B. Simms
H. Stevenson
A.E. Taylor

1922 BALMORAL
G. Brady
J. Dowling
S. Dugald
G. Greenfield
J. McAvoy
W. Scott
A.C. Young

1923 MALONE
W.M. Graham
J.W. Grant
A.W. Green
J. McCauchan
J.R. Russell
G.B. Walkington
G.T. Weir

1924 HERMITAGE
J.E. Dalton
J. Fielding
C. Hames
M. McDonald
P.F. O'Sullivan
J. Nugent
J. S. Scott

1925 KNOCK
W.M. Davidson
W. Fitchie
E. Graham
H. McGladdery
J.P. Scott
J.S. Sturgeon
W.F. Sturgeon

1926 CORK
G. Crosbie
A.J. Dinan
W.J. Hadden
D.J. Hegarty
A.St.J. Murphy
R. Murphy
W.R. Ogilvie

1927 ROYAL DUBLIN
C. Bailey
D.J. Collins
J.G . Green
T.L. Harrington
E.L. Kidd
G.T. Kingsmill-Moore
D. Pringle

1928 BRAY
W. Allen
P.K. Conway
C.W. Huet
R.N. Hunter
F.A. Kennedy
J.L. Morgan
A.N. Murphy

1929 KILLINEY
J.J. Carroll
T.M. Corbet
J.K. Mitchell
H.G . Moore
R.M. Saunders
G. Walker
H. Wright

1930 DOUGLAS
M.J. Henchy
D.P. McCarthy
V.M. Morrogh
J. Murphy
J.D. Musgrave
T.R. O'Regan
H. Whelan

1931 DUBLIN UNIVERSITY
W.B.J. Armstrong
A.H . Butler
R. Greene
L.C. Kole
R.J . McKeown
H.C.G. Silcock
G. H . Warren

1932 ROYAL DUBLIN
G. Downes
J.G. Greene
T. Lyons-Harrington
J.F. McLoughlin
R.H. Plews

1933 PORT-MARNOCK
P.A. Bell
D. Figgis
M. Hennigan
H.H. Maxwell
P.F. Purcell
J.A. Rogan
E. Spratt

1934 KNOCK
R.C. Davidson
W. McGaughey
T.P. Murphy
P.L. Shanks
W.H. Smyth

1935 HERMITAGE
M.J. Byrne
T. Cormack
J.E. D'Alton
J.P. Flynn
D.P. Morris

1936 UCD
P.F. Brennan
A.J. Elmes
J.F. Eustace
R.H. Ryan
B.J. Scannell

1937 CORK
D. McCarthy
C.F. Myerscough
J. O'Driscoll
J. Ronan
W.St Clair-Rice

1938 GALWAY
M. Garaghy
D. Kenny
J. O'Driscoll
C. O'Malley
J. Stewart

1939 CO. SLIGO
W.J. Fitzgerald
L. Howley
T.F. Jameson
T.L. Mahon
W. O'Connor

1940 ROSSLARE
J.E. Gibney
W.S. Kearney
C.P. Mahon
T.G. O'Connor
M. Veray
T.P. Walsh
R.C. Walsh

1941-5
No Tournament

1946 GRANGE
W.A. Bermingham
G.M. Bowers
R.E. Davitt
P. Keatley
D.H. Meredith

1947 BALLYMENA
W.N. Gaw
J.E. Lynn
G. MacManus
J.F. McAllister
R.O. Whyte

1948 RATHMORE
T. McMullan
A.E. Magee
J. Magee
N. Morrow
A. Taggart

1949 RATHMORE
T. McMullan
A.E. Magee
J. Magee
N. Morrow
A. Taggart

1950 MILLTOWN
C.J. Furlong
T.B. Hannin
J.G. Hickey
D.R. Roantree
T.A. Tierney

1951 MILLTOWN
C.J. Furlong
T.B. Hannin
J.A.O'Donoghue
D.R. Roantree
R.H. Ryan

1952 SHANDON PARK
J. Collins
M. Edwards
W. McCluskey
T. Paul
J. Robson

1953 PORT-MARNOCK
J.F. Bolger
T.M. Healy
D.V. Hickey
C.W.L. McCaw
S.J. Savage

1954 MUSKERRY
P.J. Ahern
B. Brennan
J.M. Glynn
B. Keniry
J.D. Murphy
D.A. O'Mahony

1955 DOUGLAS
J.J. Condon
P.J. Connolly
R. Daly
M. Gleeson
C.P.S. MacEnri
N. MacNamara
F. McSweeney

1956 PORT-MARNOCK
J.F. Eustace
F. Gallagher
C. Harnett
L.A. Moran
W.J. Phelan
D.L. Robinson

1957 GALWAY
S.F. Hosty
G. Molloy
P.M. O'Beirn
T. O'Connor
G. Smye

1958 GALWAY
S.F. Hosty
G. Molloy
P.M. O'Beirn
T. O'Connor
G. Smye

1959 MOURNE
J. Boden
P. McAteer
W.J. McCammon
C. McCormack
M. Murray

1960 QUEEN'S UNIVERSITY
J. Boyd
I. Dick
J. Jacques
B. Logan
C.M. Quinn

1961 LAHINCH
G. Barry
J. Keating
B. O'Brien
J. Smith
J. Wall

1962 MUSKERRY
B. Cantwell
A. Keary
P.A. Linehan
P. O'Donoghue
J. O'Shaughnessy

1963 LAHINCH
F. Lehane
J. O'Callaghan
M. Rush
B. Vaughan
J. Wall

1964 PORT-MARNOCK
M.A. Barry
F.V. Lahiffe
P.J. McAleese
P. O'Looney
J.K. O'Sullivan

1965 FERMOY
T. Cavanagh
W. Ennis
J. Morrison
P. O'Sullivan
J.F. Wright

1966 PORT-MARNOCK
R. Cuddy
J. Hanlon
J.M. Mahon
P. O'Looney
J.K.O'Sullivan

1967 QUEEN'S UNIVERSITY
J.V.W. Boyle
M.J. Malone
W.B. Montgomery
G. Partridge
B.D. Somers

1968 KNOCK
P. Bradley
R. McDowell
C. Patton
P.H. Stewart
P.J. Waddell

1969 CLANDEBOYE
J. Cleary
A. Gregg
J. McCrory
C. McCutcheon
E. Nightingale

1970 NEWLANDS
J. Buggy
P. Hanley
A. Keogh
P. McGovern
L. O'Brien

1971 CO. SLIGO
M. Cullen
K. Cunningham
S. O'Donovan
L. Parkinson
S. Peterson

1972 CASTLE-TROY
B. Begley
D. Houlihan
I. McGill
H. Mescall
D. Noonan
P. Ryan

1973 PORT-STEWART
P.V. Dijon
D. Griffen
M. Grant
R. Hemphill
V. McAuley

1974 SUTTON
J.J. Carr
D. Fitzpatrick
D.W.P. Heather
A. Levy
A. Williams

1975 LIMERICK
Match played 1976
J. Carew
G. Casey
J. Gleeson
M. Roberts
R. Smith

1976 HERMITAGE
F. King
D. Lee
A. McCarthy
J. McGill
O. O'Herlihy

1977 LIMERICK
J. Carew
N. McDonagh
M.F. Roberts
R. Smith
E. Tuite

1978 CLONMEL
B. McMahon
S. Moylan
M. Patterson
M. Slater
P. Wall

1979 LIMERICK
J. Carew
G. Casey
J. Gleeson
M.F. Roberts
E. Tuite

1980 WESTPORT
L. Gibbons
G.D. Golden
D. Joyce
T. Joyce
G. McAleer
P. O'Reilly

1981 MALLOW
B. Finn
J. Horgan
J. Howell
P. O'Callaghan
K. O'Keeffe

1982 MULLINGAR
M. Bagnall
P. Keegan
M. Quinn
J. Rickard
B. Timlin

1983 TULLAMORE
P. Cleary
P. Coen
S. Egan
C. Flanagan
S. Larkin

1984 TRAMORE
S. Kiely
K. Murray
F. O'Sullivan
M. O'Sullivan
A. Tracey

1985 ELM PARK
D. Bergin
M. Fives
B. Gilmore
S. Ryan
B. Whitaker

1986 GALWAY
T. Forde
N. Greaney
P. Hennelly
E. Lynch
D. Taylor

1987 DOWN-PATRICK
C. Coyle
L. Craig
E. Lynch
R. Madine
J.F. Moore

1988 LIMERICK	1989 CARRICK-FERGUS	1990 WATERFORD
J. Carew	B. McAtamney Jr	C. Carew
R. Cummins	B. McGahan	M. Foley
R. Egan	S. McLoughlin	T. Hanly
P. Power	T. Mulholland	J. O'Keeffe
P. Walsh	D. Stronge	C. Ryan

APPENDIX IV

Section 4

Freddie Tait

Freddie Tait was one of the leading amateurs at the end of the nineteenth century. A member of the R & A, he was a bronze medalist in the Amateur Championship for three years in succession, 1893–5. He won the Championship at Sandwich in 1896 and again at Hoylake in 1898. He was defeated in the 1899 final by John Ball Jr. This was his last Amateur, as he was killed in action in the Boer War in February 1900. He had played in the Open Championship from 1891 when it was held at St Andrews. He finished joint third at both Muirfield in 1896 and Hoylake in 1897, on each occasion being only three strokes behind the winner. In 1898 he came fifth, and in his last year he finished eighth. At St Andrews he had an impressive record, winning the Gold Medal in 1893; the Silver Cross, Royal Medal, Glennie Aggregate Medal and the Calcutta Cup in 1894; the Jubilee Vase and the Bombay Medal in 1895; the Silver Cross, Gold Medal and Glennie Medal in 1897; the Gold Medal in 1898 and the Silver Cross, Calcutta Cup, Royal Medal, Aggregate Medal and the Calcutta Cup in 1894; the Jubilee Vase and the Bombay Medal in 1895; the Silver Cross, Gold Medal and Glennie Medal in 1897; the Gold Medal in 1898 and the Silver Cross, Calcutta Cup, Royal Medal and the Glennie Medal in 1899. No evidence can be found of any visits by him to Ireland, but following his death the Golfing Union of Ireland opened a fund inviting subscriptions to a memorial to his memory. Subsequent developments are unknown, and the portrait of him in the Big Room in the R & A Clubhouse, painted posthumously from a photograph, may be this memorial.

APPENDIX V

Section 1

Inter-County Tournament (The Barton Shield)

1. That each County of Ireland shall be a unit with the following exceptions and additions:

   (a) Belfast City within the Municipal Boundary shall be a separate unit, known as the County of the City of Belfast.

(b) Dublin City within a radius of six miles from Nelson Pillar shall be a separate unit, known as the County of the City of Dublin.

2. That each of the foregoing 34 Counties shall be entitled to enter a team of players resident in Ireland for the Irish County Cup competition.

3. Golfers born or resident in the County, or full members of Golf Clubs, situated within the County, shall be qualified to play for the County.

4. Provincial Secretaries shall call on Senior Clubs in each County to take, in conjunction with other Clubs in the County, such steps as may be necessary to select a County Team and nominate its Captain.

5. That the Tournament shall be in the form of two foursomes, 18 hole heats holes up, and in case of a tie, the second match shall play an additional hole or holes to decide the tie.

6. Each Province shall play off by Counties to arrive at a Champion County of the Province; each Province to arrange time, place and Rules for their own Province.

7. The Semi-Finals and Final shall be played on the Friday preceding the Irish Amateur Open Championship and on the same Links as said Championship.

8. The Trophy shall be held by the Club in the County selected by the Captain of the winning County.

APPENDIX V
Section 2
Barton Shield Winners

1911 CO. DONEGAL
J.B. Giles
H.K. Mitchell
E.M. Munn
L.O. Munn

1912 CO. DUBLIN
R.M. Elvery
J.D. MacCormack
J. Reid
G. Ross

1913 COUNTY OF THE CITY OF DUBLIN
A.B. Babington
H.A. Boyd
F.E. Davies
D.N. Wilson

1914 COUNTY OF THE CITY OF DUBLIN
C. Barcroft
F.E. Davies
Hon. E. Gibson
H.B. Phillipson

1915–18
No Tournament

1919 COUNTY OF THE CITY OF DUBLIN
A.B. Babington
F.E. Davies
W.G. McConnell
G. Ross

1920 PORT-MARNOCK
H.A. Boyd
H.M. Cairnes
G. Moore
D.E.B. Soulby

1921 MALONE
W.R. Knox
A. Lowe
J.F. Stevenson
A.E. Todd

1922 ROYAL PORTRUSH
E.F. Carter
C.O. Hezlet
J.C. Mant-Martin
W.K. Tillie

1923 HOLYWOOD
C.L. Gaussen
W. Pyper
F.L. Small
M.J. Small

1924 ROYAL DUBLIN
A.B. Babington
T.W.G. Johnson
N. Manley
H.S. Watson

1925 ROYAL DUBLIN
N. Manley
F. O'Connor
C.S. Wallis
C.H. West

1926 QUEEN'S UNIVERSITY
A.C. Allison
F.P. McConnell
R.M. McConnell
A.L. Weir

1927 ROYAL CO. DOWN
J.R. Carr
J.B. Johnstone
W. Pollock
D. Wilson Smith

1928 PORT-MARNOCK
M. Crowley
J.F. Jameson
J.D. MacCormack
C.W. Robertson

1929 PORT-MARNOCK
H.E. Bell
M. Crowley
J.D. MacCormack
C.W. Robertson

1930 PORT-MARNOCK
H.E. Bell
W. Carroll
M. Crowley
W.J. Gill

1931 DUBLIN UNIVERSITY
R. Greene
J.D. Parsons
H.C.G. Silcock
J.O. Wisdom

1932 PORT-MARNOCK
H.E. Bell
H.M. Cairnes
M. Crowley
W.J. Gill

1933 MONKS-TOWN
S.H. McCarthy
C.A. Murphy
J.G. Musgrave
J.F. Nicholson

1934 PORT-MARNOCK
C.A. Carroll
W.J. Gill
R. Greene
J.D.MacCormack

1935 PORT-MARNOCK
C.A. Carroll
C. Ewing
W.J. Gill
J.D. MacCormack

1936 MALONE
J.R. Carr
H.S. Sheals
D. Wilson Smith
J.C. Timbey

1937 CORK
J. Bruen Jr
G. Crosbie
J. Kiely
S.H. McCarthy

1938 CORK
J. Bruen
A.J. Dinan
S.H. McCarthy
R. Simcox

1939 PORT-MARNOCK
C. Ewing
T.A. Healy
C.W. Robertson
B.J. Scannell

1940 PORT-MARNOCK
C. Ewing
W.J. Gill
D.P. Morris
J.F. Owens

1941–5
No Tournament

1946 SUTTON
J.B. Carr
M.P. Fitzpatrick
K.M. Hogan
R.H. McInnally

1947 LAHINCH
J. Burke
M. O'Loughlin
A.F. Slattery
D.J. Torrens

1948 ROYAL PORTRUSH
T.B. Agnew
T.E. Dijon
J. Neill
J. Taggart

1949 SUTTON
J.B. Carr
J.P. Carroll
M.P. Fitzpatrick
R.H. McInnally

1950 SUTTON
J.B. Carr
J.P. Carroll
M. Fitzpatrick
R.H. McInnally

1951 BANGOR
W.K. Brown
N.V. Drew
E.C. McQuade
R. Young

1952 ROYAL BELFAST
B.G. Corry
H.M. Hadden
M.C. McAuley
W.A. McNeill

1953 MUSKERRY
E.F. Casey
M.J. Hegarty
L. McCarthy
M. Power
J.H. Rice

1954 PORT-MARNOCK
B. Herlihy
J.R. Mahon
J. Malone
C.W. McCaw

1955 LAHINCH
P.J. Leyden
A. Skerritt
A.F. Slattery
G.A. Young

1956 PORT-MARNOCK
J. Caldwell
B. Herlihy
J.R. Mahon
D. Ryan

1957 GALWAY
J. Abernethy
P. Smyth
S. Ward
K. Wallace

1958 RATHMORE
M.C. Dijon
J. Faith
C. Knox
J.N. Meneely

1959 ATHLONE
P. Caulfield
P. Hughes
J. O'Sullivan
J. Solon

1960 RATHMORE
M.C. Dijon
T.E. Dijon
J. Faith
C. Knox

1961 MALONE
R.M. Craigan
W.J.J. Ferguson
P. Froggatt
J.G. McErvel

1962 CLANDE-BOYE
S.A.G. Cooley
J.H. Derby
F.A. McCorry
B. Wilson

1963 SHANDON PARK
J. Duncan
B. Edwards
M. Edwards
W.H.E. Rainey

1964 RATHMORE
M.C. Dijon
T.E. Dijon
J. Faith
C. Knox

1965 CLANDE-BOYE
S.A.G. Cooley
J.H. Derby
F.A. McCorry
B. Wilson

1966 CORK

J.E. Bowen
G.F. Crosbie
L.D. Goulding
E. Higgins

1967 LIMERICK

G. Geary
M.G.I. Morris
V. Nevin
W. Rice

1968 ROYAL DUBLIN

D.K. Corcoran
M.B. Costello
G.N. Fogarty
D.P. Herlihy

1969 MALONE

W.J.J. Ferguson
R.R. McClure
D.A. Nelson
D.J.F. Young

1970 SHANDON PARK

B. Edwards
D.P.W. Hoey
M.J.C. Hoey
T.B.C. Hoey

1971 MALAHIDE

P. Caul
M. Craddock
T. Craddock
R.M. Kane

1972 GALWAY

S.F. Hosty
M.A. Lynch
D. Mahon
T. O'Connor

1973 CORK

J.E. Bowen
E. Higgins
D. Kiely
H.N. Mackeown

1974 WOOD-BROOK

A.J. Heverin
D. Kennedy
L. MacNamara
P. Mulcare

1975 SHANDON PARK

B. Edwards
M.J.C. Hoey
T.B.C. Hoey
D.C. Long

1976 LIMERICK

J. Harrington
M.G.I. Morris
V. Nevin
W. Rice

1977 ROYAL PORTRUSH

B.J.S. Kissock
M. Patterson
J.C. Moss
D.J.F. Young

1978 MALAHIDE

P. Caul
T. Craddock
B. Sweeney
P. Walton

1979 SHANDON PARK

B. Edwards
M.J.C. Hoey
T.B.C. Hoey
D.C. Long

1980 KILLARNEY

S. Coyne
M. Guerin
J. Loughnane
A.D. Spring

1981 BELVOIR PARK

J.N. Browne
M.J. Malone
P.B. Malone
S.S. Moore

1982 MALAHIDE

P. Caul
J. Craddock
M. Craddock
T. Craddock

1983 L'TOWN & B'TOWN

D. Branigan
F. Flynn
R. Moore
V. Smyth

1984 CASTLE-TROY

B. Begley
T. Corridan
J. Kavanagh
G. McCormack

1985 SHANDON PARK

N. Anderson
T.B.C. Hoey
D.C. Long
B. Wilson

1986 WOOD-BROOK

J. Hughes
P. Lewis
L. MacNamara
G. O'Connor

1987 WARREN-POINT

J. Carvill
D. Parr
G. McNeill
K. Stevenson

1988 WARREN-POINT

P. Gribben
D. Parr
K. Stevenson
P. Trainor

1989 HERMIT-AGE

P. Bray
D. Errity
T. Heverin
T. Moran

1990 CORK

T. Cleary
P. Cowley
P. Lyons
D.F. O'Sullivan

APPENDIX V

Section 3

Record of winning counties and teams in the All-Ireland County Championship

1980 WICKLOW
E. Bradshaw
D. Clarke
T. Fitzpatrick
J. Hackman
R.J. Moran

1981 ANTRIM
I.A. Elliott
J.R. Dickson
J. Jones
G. McAleese
J. McAleese

1982 LOUTH
D. Branigan
M.A. Gannon
B.V.M. Reddan
P. Rogers
V. Smyth

1983 LOUTH
D. Branigan
F. Gannon
M.A. Gannon
P. Rogers
V. Smyth

1984 LOUTH
D. Branigan
F. Gannon
M.A. Gannon
B.V.M. Reddan
V. Smyth

1985 LOUTH
D. Branigan
F. Gannon
M.A. Gannon
B.V.M. Reddan
P. Rogers

1986 LIMERICK
B. Begley
J. Fitzgerald
J. Kavanagh
M.G.I. Morris
W. Rice

1987 DUBLIN
D.P.W. Heather
P. Hogan
A.C.J. Morrow
D. Quilligan
T. Smith

1988 CORK
N. Goulding
J. McKenna
J. Morris
D.F. O'Sullivan
M. Quirke

1989 ROSCOMMON
S. Heavey
K. Kearney
L. MacNamara
A. O'Shea
A. Wynne

1990 CORK
P. Cowley
F. Deasy
N. Goulding
P. Lyons
J. Morris Jr

APPENDIX VI

Section 1

Constitution and Rules (1913)

Name of Union

1. The name of the Union shall be 'The Golfing Union of Ireland'.

Object of Union

2. The object of the Union is the federation of the various Clubs, and the promotion of the game in every way in which this can be done better by the Union than by individual Clubs.

The Union shall be the authority to arrange:

1 – Open and Close Amateur and Close Professional Championships.
2 – Inter-Provincial Competitions.
3 – Inter-Club Challenge Cup Competitions.
4 – The Regulation of Handicaps.
5 – International Matches, and selection of Irish Teams.
6 – County Cup Tournament.

The Union accepts the Rules of Golf as authorised by the Royal & Ancient Club, St Andrews, and recognises the Rules Committee of said Club as the Court of Appeal.

Union Management

3. The Union shall be managed by a Council consisting of a President, four Vice-Presidents (one to be nominated by each Province), Hon. Secretary, Hon. Treasurer, four Provincial Secretaries, and twelve Delegates (Ulster and Leinster four each; Munster and Connacht two each), seven to form a quorum.

The Provincial Secretaries and Delegates shall be appointed annually by the Provincial Branches.

Honorary Officers

4. The Council shall from time to time, as required, elect the President and Vice-Presidents. The Hon. Secretary and Hon. Treasurer shall retire annually, but be eligible for re-election by the Council.

Provincial Management

5. A Branch of the Union shall be formed in each Province, with power to make Bye-Laws for its own management.

Delegates of the Clubs in Provinces

6. Every Club affiliated to the Union shall be entitled to send, to each Provincial Branch Meeting, one Delegate and one extra Delegate for every 150 Full Members, or part thereof,

over and above the first 150, provided always that no Club shall be entitled to send more than three Delegates.

Entrance Fee

7. Each Club shall pay an entrance fee of £1. ls. payable upon affiliation.

Subscriptions

8. The Annual Subscription for each Club shall be £1. ls. for each Delegate that the Club is entitled to send to a Provincial Branch Meeting; the Subscription shall become due on the first day of January each year, and if not paid to the Honorary Treasurer of the Union before the 1st January next ensuing, the Club shall cease to be a member of the Union. No Club shall send Delegates to any Meeting of the Union, or be allowed to take part in any competition promoted by the Union, unless the Annual Subscription for the current year shall have been paid.

Funds for Provincial Management

9. The Hon. Treasurer of the Union shall annually, in the month of February forward to each Provincial Secretary a sum of money calculated at the rate of 5/- for each £1. ls. subscription received from Clubs in his Province, or such other sum as the Council may from time to time determine, such money to be used for the management of the Provincial Branch.

Affiliation

10. A Club desirous of affiliation to the Union must obtain an Application Form from the Hon. Secretary of the Union, and return same filled in to the Secretary of the Province in which the Club is situated. This application shall be laid before the next ensuing Branch Meeting for consideration and election. If elected, the Provincial Secretary shall forward the approved form to the Honorary Secretary of the Union for registration.

Annual Meetings

11. The Hon. Secretary of the Union shall summon a Meeting of the Council in Dublin on the *3rd week November,* for receiving the Annual Report and Statement of Accounts; for electing the Honorary Secretary and Honorary Treasurer, making, revising or altering Rules, and transacting other business of the Union. Two weeks' notice of such Annual Meeting should be given to each Member of Council and shall be accompanied by the Report and Statement of Accounts duly audited by a Public Accountant, nominated by the Union Council.

No new Rule shall be made, nor shall any Rule be altered, unless with the assent of two-thirds of those present and voting at any Meeting of the Union Council. Seven shall form a quorum.

Notices of Motion and nomination of Officers of Council must be made by the Provincial Branches, through their Secretaries, to the Hon. Secretary of the Union, in writing, at least one month before the date of Meeting.

A statement of Provincial expenditure shall be sent to the Hon. Treasurer of the Union one month before the Annual Meeting.

A copy of the Report and Statement of Accounts shall be sent yearly to every Club affiliated to the Union before December 31st of that year.

Provincial Meetings

It is recommended that each Provincial Secretary should call a Meeting of the Delegates from the Clubs in his Province, every three months, say, *2nd week January, April, July and October*, or any other more convenient date during these months. The business arising from these Meetings shall go forward to the Union Council if necessary.

Special Meetings of the Union Council

12. May be called at the request of the Hon. Secretary or Hon. Treasurer of the Union, or of two Provincial Branches, stating business to be considered.

Officials' Expenses

13. The Union shall pay such expenses to Officials and Delegates as may seem right, to secure proper attendance of same at the Annual Council Meeting.

APPENDIX VI
Section 2
Barton Cup Winners

1905 BRAY
R.A. Anderson
Dr J. Bogan
S.R. Dillon
E.K. Figgis
F.A. Kennedy
M.McD. Bodkin
F. McCormack
H. Mason
R. Rice
L.R. Oswald Sealy
C. Triscott
Hon.Mr Justice Wright

1907 BRAY
R. Drew
C. Burnell
W. Deverill
E.K. Figgis
A. Fox
F. Kennedy
F. McCormack
J.H. Maher
P. Merier
R. Rice
W. Scott
L.R. Oswald Sealy

1908 CARLOW
P.A. Brown
A. Burden
Rev. P. Gorry
J.D. McCarthy
D.J. McGrath
R.J. Nicholson
J.J. O'Connell
W. O'Donnell
D. Ross
A.W. Storrar
A. Diggis La Touche
J.W. Weekes

1909 SUTTON
G.U. Cashel
V. Drennan
R.W. Lewis
A. MacNaughton
G. O'Dowd
J. Reid
G. Ross
J.D. Walsh

1910 MILLTOWN
P. Barry
W.J. Carberry
F.E. Davies
E.J. Donovan
H. Phillipson
E. Walsh
F.H. Wilson
G.M. Wilson

1911 ATHY
J.J. Bodley
E. Boylan
P. Downey
W. Hopkins
D. Hurley
S. O'Neill
A. Pennycook
D. Rice

1912 HERMITAGE
A. Clinch
J.D. MacCormack
J. Marron
B. O'Kelly
J.J. O'Neill
Rev. A. Ryan
R. Sheehy
G. Sterling
D. Sullivan
R. White

1913 FOXROCK
W. Bennett
C. Considine
H. Considine
T. Considine
F. Crozier
F. Fottrell
F. Home
B.T. O'Reilly
H. O'Reilly
A. Porter

1914 KILLINEY
S. Ashlin
A. Conan
J. Fuld
C. Goff
J. Lynch
J. Pim
R. Stewart
C. Walsh
H. Wright
R. Wright

1915–18

No Tournament

1919 KINGS-TOWN
R. McGovern
Capt. F. Mallet
Capt. J.M. Marrow
W. Mellon
G. Moore
R. Moore
T. Kingsmill-Moore
F. Ritchie
H. Taylor
R. Ward

1920 KINGS-TOWN
J. Birmingham
R. McGovern
Capt. F. Mallet
N. Manly
W. Mellon
G. Moore
R. Moore
C. Redhead
H.R. Sinclair
R. Ward

1921 CLONTARF
J. Aston
T. Carson
S. Dunseith
N. Fradley
P. Gore
C. Jamison
J. Kerr
R. Milne
T. Ryan
G. Sythes

1922 PORT-MARNOCK
G. Beattie
J. Brown
W. Charlton
G. Dawson
W. O'Brien
L. Plunkett
J. Reid
F. Sharpe
R. Grove White
R.J. White

1923 GRANGE
N. Clorke
J. Condon
J. Frewen
Dr W. Hooper
N. MacDougald
T. O'Brien
T. O'Keeffe
R. Tamplin
J. Trotter
S. Walker

1924 HERMITAGE
A. Conan
P. Conway
T. Cormack
J. Doyle
R. Feely
J. Fielding
C. Hames
C. Lee
J. Scott
W. Tunnell

1925 BRAY
F. Haughton
B. Howe
F.A. Kennedy
W. Meeke
J. Morgan
A. Murphy
D. O'Meara
J. Saul
C. Wallis
Capt. C. West

1926 CLONTARF
M. Ashbee
J. Aston
T. Carson
W. Cooper
T. Crowley
J. Healy
C. Jamison
J. Kerr
V. Lyons
P. Ryan

1927 HOWTH
J. Bourke
P. Hanlon
H. Healy
F. Kelly
D. McAsey
M. McMahon
J. Middleton
T. Murray
T. Phelan
T. Quane
J. Redmond
E. Stuart

1928 SUTTON
J. Coburn
J. Cuddy
G. Fitzgerald
T. Geary
W.J. Gill
A. Klingner
P. Maguire
W. Manico
P. Pentony
D. Sidford
G. Stanley
S. Wilson

1929 HOWTH
J. Bourke
W. Elford
C. Flanagan
H. Healy
F. Kelly
J. Kelly
J. Midleton
T. Phelan
T. Quane
J. Redmond

1930 MALAHIDE
A. Adams
T. Bailey
J. Connell
E. Crowley
W. Crowley
M. Duffy
L. Keane
P. Lawless
W. McCormack
J. McQueston
G. O'Neill
C. O'Shea

1931 PORT-MARNOCK
H. Bell
P. Bell
H. Boyd
M. Crowley
C. Ewing
D. Figgis
M. Hannigan
V. Hughes
J. Kelly
S. Lignell
J. O'Connor
C. Robertson
J. Rogan

1932 CLONTARF
M. Ashbee
W. Crozier
D. Finn
P. Gaffney
R. Greene
T. Healy
M. Kennedy
M. Knightly
D. Lynch
P. Lynch
J. Pierce
T. Pierce
P. Ryan
E. Verdon
R. White

1933 KILDARE
M. Clarson
S. Cullen
M. Gorry
T. Langan
D. McGuirke
R. Nix
M. Quinn
J. Rorke
P. Smith

1934 KILDARE
M. Clarson
S. Cullen
D. Gorry
M. Gorry
E. Kennedy
D. Lambe
J. Lawler
D. McGuirke
L. Malone
J. Rorke

1935 UNIVERSITY COLLEGE
P. Brennan
J.P. Byrne
J. Claffey
D. Cremin
D. Curran
A. Elmes
J.F. Eustace
D.A. Houlihan
J. Houlihan
H. Murphy
T.D. Purcell
R.H. Ryan

1936 CURRAGH
Rev. E. Carey, C.F.
Capt. P. Downes
Capt. T. Feely
Capt. J. Flynn
Comdt. T. Fox
Lt. W. Harrington
Capt. D. Kelly
Capt. M. McInerney
Comdt. M. O'Connor
T. O'Leary
Capt. T. O'Sullivan
Comdt. C. Stuart

1937 HERMITAGE
J.P. Byrne
T.P. Early
R. King-French
J. Howard
D. Kerr
J. McCrossan
T. Morris
P. Slavin
J. Toner
T. Wslsh

1938 CLONTARF
J. Barnwell
A. Byrne
J. Cregan
M. Fitzgerald
P. Heffron
P. Lynch
M. Martin
G. O'Neill
T. Prestage
R. Rice
P. Ryan
E. Verdon

1939 UNIVERSITY COLLEGE
N. Carroll
H. Counihan
R. Dempsey
M. Dyar
H.B. Linehan
D.J. Lynch
B. Murphy
M. O'Brien
T.D. Purcell
G. Ryan
B.J. Scannell

1940 CO. LOUTH
P. Gannon
K. Garvey
R. Jackson
J. Liddy
A. Maher
M. Matthews
M. Monahan
D. O'Kelly
M.V. Reddan
D. Sweeney

1941 CASTLE
J.S. Barrett
T. Commins
N. Fitzpatrick
J. Hollinger
E. Jeffares
F. Kelly
N.H. Lambert
W.A. Lawler
J. Lennon
R. Murray
N.C. Philip
W. Robbie
P.A. Sheehan
A.D. Smithwick

1942 CLONTARF
B. Cauldwell
G. Clancy
J. Fitzgerald
P. Heffron
K.I. Holland
S. MacMahon
S. McEvoy
M. Minogue
F. Moran
J. O'Reilly
P.T. Prestage
F. Quinn
R. Rice
J.A. Ryan
S.L. Tierney

1943 WOOD-BROOK
Rev. M.C. Brady
J.J. Doyle
B. Lynch
D. Lynch
M. McCarthy
J.A. McMahon
J. Moran
J.D. O'Reilly
P. Redmond
B.J. Scannell
K. Troy

1944 DUN LAOGHAIRE
E.A. Browett
J.P. Carroll
V. Connolly
E. Duke
L. Fitzgerald
D. Hogan
S. Jones
T. Lynch
J. Malone
J. O'Keeffe
J. St. J. Pike
M. Walsh

1945 CLONTARF

J. Belton
V. Clarke
H. Delaney
D. Fitzgerald
C. Garvey
R. Grogan
V. Herlihy
K.I. Holland
S. Kennedy
F. Moran
H. Murphy
T. Prestage
F. Quinn
R. Rice

1946 ROYAL DUBLIN

C. Armstrong
G. Clancy
F. Coghlan
K. Coghlan
J.R. Cummins
E. Drake
T. Gleeson
J. Green
T. Healy
J. Howard
W. Howley
J. Kearns
J. McLoughlin
J. Malley
J. Rogan
J. Stearn
C.H. West

1947 L'TOWN & B'TOWN

B. Anderson
J. Crotty
P. Delaney
P.F. Gray
P.J. Gray
O.M. Lochrin
P. Lynch
C. Murdock
J. Roche
D.B. Somers

1954 ST ANNE'S

H. Allen
H. Buckley
C. Byrne
P.J. Byrne
D. Collins
D. Derby
T. Kenny
J. Morgan
T. Mulhall
J. Plaistead
R. Rowlette
J. Sheeran

1955 NEWLANDS

W. Bergin
D. Brazil
S. Brennan
J. Burke
C. Coffey
J. Deveney
J. Drennan
P. Gallagher
J. Hughes
J. McDermott
R. Murray
A. O'Keefe
J. O'Reilly
W. Wynn

1956 DELGANY

F.M. Byrne
J. D'Arcy
E. Greene
R. Gregory
R.W. Harris
T. Hogan
T. McDonald
Rev. D. McDonald
M.T. Neary
P.E. Wallace

1948 ST ANNE'S

G. Agnew
K. Cahill
M. Carr
D. Collins
P. Cullinan
F. Kavanagh
J. Morgan
S. Mullan
W. O'Neill
L. O'Reilly
J. Sheeran
J. Tyson

1949 CLONTARF

J. Belton
A. Byrne
C. Byrne
V. Clarke
D. Dorgan
D. Fitzgerald
C. Garvey
V. Herlihy
C. Heron
F. McDevitt
T. McDonald
F. Moran
J. Moran
H. Murphy
F. Quinn

1950 PORT-ARLINGTON

J. Canning
T. Canning
P. Conran
R. Cotter
J. Daly
M. Finnegan
Sir G. Holden
J. Howling
T. Kirby
R. Russell
J. Scally

1957 HOWTH

C. Archer
E. Clarke
T. Connolly
M.S. Corcoran
M. Cronin
P.J. Donovan
D.M. Duff
A. Facey
P. Lordan
S. O'Briain
M. Reid
W. Walsh

1958 PORT-MARNOCK

C. Conroy
R.C. Cuddy
B. Ensor
J.A. Kelly
D. Lynch
C.W. McCaw
J. Maloney
J. O'Dwyer
S. Savage
B.R. Smith

1959 KILDARE

B. Gannon
A. Kelly
Fr R. Kelly
J. Kerin
D. McDermott
J. McDermott
L.J. Malone
M.J. Murray
J. O'Brien
N. Sheridan

1951 ROYAL DUBLIN

H. Brown
G. Clancy
C. Coghlan
J. Cummins
L. Gunning
D. Herlihy
V. Herlihy
J. Howard
W. Howley
J. Kearns
D. Magee
F. Moran
T. Murray
P. Patten
J. O'Hanlon
K. Troy
A. Quin

1952 CLONTARF

J. Belton
B. Bergin
C. Clarke
C. Garvey
D. McCarthy
F. Moran
J. Moran
H.E. Murphy
D. O'Halloran
T.P. O'Reilly

1953 KILKENNY

H. Byrne
D. Clohessy
J. Collins
W. Deegan
P. Deveney
Rev. J. Dunphy
M. Godwin
F. Harrison
J. Harte
C. Kenealy
P. Kennedy
T. Mahon
J. Mitchell
W. O'Connor
L. Reidy
J. Short

1960 MULLINGAR

R. Downes
M. Duffy
D. Feeney
M. Gavin
J. Graham
J. Healy
P. Hore
J.L. Lynch
P. McCartan
M. McKeogh
J. Murray
T. Shaw
D. Solon
Rev. R. Tehan

1961 DUNDALK

T. Byrne
D. Cassidy
J. Daly
M.C. Drey
W. Lambert
D. McArdle
V.G. Murphy
J.C. Parker
F. O'Callaghan
J.M. Shields

1962 RATH-FARNHAM

W. Bailey
M. Beggs
J.H. Brown
S. Livingston
J. Malone
N. Montgomery
S. Moran
W.G. Smyth
R. Stevens
W. Tector

1963 WICKLOW

I. Carroll
T. Delahunt
R. Fitzpatrick
S. Flanagan
J. Furlong
W. Hopkins
M. Howard
P. Kavanagh
P. Kavanagh Jr
P. Lawless
S. McGauley
D. Mooney
J. Murphy
J. Toner

1964 CO. LOUTH

S. Alcock
P. Dwyer
J. Dowd
B. Fogarty
F. Gannon
F. Gallagher
O.M. Lochrin
M. McGuirk
P. McGuirk
P. Maher
H.A. Murphy
E. O'Mahony
N. Owens
J. Ryle
P. Tiernan
U. Tully

1965 SKERRIES

J. Andrews
J. Bracken
C. Byrne
M. Carron
P. Grimes
B. Hoey
D. Kinsella
T.F. McDonald
W. Mulcahy
E.P. Owens
M. O'Hara
J. Ryan
M. Ryan
A. Webster
N. Weldon

1966 KILKENNY

J. Butler
J.B. Cleary
A. Duffin
T.M. Duggan
N. Godwin
K.M. Hunt
P.T. Kennedy
T.J. Mahon
W. O'Connor
K. O'Donovan
K. O'Neill
L. Reidy
T. Riordan
G. Stewart

1967 ROYAL DUBLIN

C.A. Byrne
M. Conway
D. Corcoran
M. Costello
P. Flanagan
G.N. Fogarty
T. Garvey
P.C. Haughey
M. Jordan
D.L. Mahon
K.C. Moore
F.G. Moran
K.L. Murray
J.J. O'Hanlon
P.V. O'Neill
J. Quill
P.J. Ryan
B.J. Sampson
F. Sharpe

1968 CLONTARF

T. Buggy
J.T. Clancy
D. Condon
M. Dalton
G. Devey
J. Dillon
E. Grumley
F. Kellett
A. Lally
J. Lawler
D. McCarthy
J. McClean
M. O'Donnell
J.V. O'Neill
M. O'Shea
S. O'Sullivan

1969 CARLOW

J.M. Carroll
M. P. Cunney
M.P. Donnelly
B.T. Doyle
Rev. Fr E. Dowling
P.J. Hyland
T. Jennings
T.J. Jordon
E. Kelly
J.R. Kelly
T.F. Leonard
T.L. McDonald
P. McEnroe
Rev. Fr T.J. McGrath
J. O'Boyle
Rev. Fr T. O'Donnell
J.F. Rush
J.J. Whitty

1970 HERMITAGE

E. Alford
T. Bishop
E. Browne
C. Cooke
P. Davey
J.B. Delaney
P. Dermody
M.M. McLoughlin
J. McMeara
B. Williams

1971 LUCAN

C. Burdon
P.J. Culligan
C.E. Fitzgerald
M. Gannon
B. Keely
T.J. Kelly
J. McLoughlin
T. Rogers
Rev. J.S.C. Stronge
E.M. Tully

1972 SUTTON

P. Bowen
F. Cassidy
R. Doherty
E.A. Firth
M.P. Fitzpatrick
P. O'Boyle
P. O'Reilly
C. Smith
J. Stafford
W.C. Thompson

1973 MOUNT-RATH

T. Brown
C. Carter
J. Carter
E. Doheny
J. Doheny
E. Kelly
T. Lalor
J. Mulhare
P. O'Flaherty
S. Reynolds

1974 BALTIN-GLASS

D. Bradshaw
M. Byrne
D. Kilcoyne
Rev.Fr.P.J. McDonnell
E. Mooney
T. Nolan
L Norton
L. O'Connell
D.R. Patterson
N. Scott

1975 LUCAN

I. Barr
K. Barr
K. Breslin
R. Conway
T. Conway
M. Curry
M. Gannon
A. McLoughlin
P. O'Reilly
E. Tully

1976 TULLAMORE

M. Bryant
V. Clarke
H. Cullen
L. Dolan
W. Galvin
T. Ledwidge
F. O'Brien
D. O'Connell
E. Vaughan
D. White

1977 KILKENNY

T. Deegan
D. DeLoughrey
G. DeLoughrey
T. Duggan
E. Goulding
J. Holohan
T. McDonald
D. Murphy
S. O'Neill
C. Rainey
G. Stewart

1978 CARLOW

L. Brennan
P. Callery
R. Carroll
F. Connolly
P. Dowling
H. Dunne
M. Kilbride
B. McCormack
J. McVeigh
R. Shannon

1979 ROYAL DUBLIN

M. Conway
P. Dermody
D. Downey
B. Fitzgerald
G. Fogarty
C. Freaney
M. Hanrahan
J. Hutchinson
J. McCullagh
M. Moore

1980 MALAHIDE

P. Caul
F. Coogan
J. Craddock
M. Craddock
T. Craddock
D. Feeney
P. Noonan
B. O'Toole
P. Power
M. Reilly

1981 DELGANY

M. Burke
A. Byrne
P. Fitzpatrick
P. Hautz
T. Jenkinson
W. Kennedy
A. May
D. O'Connor
M. O'Neill
J.J. Synnott

1982 SUTTON

D. Boylan
G. Carr
J. Carr
R. Doherty
M. Hanway
A. McWilliams
H. O'Neill
W.C. Thompson
B. Wallace
A. Williams

1983 SLADE VALLEY

B. Brophy
T. Browne
J. Cleere
P. Connolly
M. Daly
P. Joyce
E. Loughlin
N. Minogue
N. Mulvey
J. O'Grady
D. Quinn
A. Whelan

1984 DELGANY

E. Bradshaw
I. Byrne
D. Clarke
T. Conlon
T. Corcoran
M. Darcy
P. Hautz
T. Jenkinson
W. Kennedy
J. McDonald
L. May

1985 GREYSTONES

L. Behan
S. Cahill
E. Condren
0. Frawley
J. Hackman
D. Judge
P. McGrath
P. Mahon
L.T. O'Connor
L.V. O'Connor
P. O'Connor
T. Reid

1986 WICKLOW

K. Clarke
S. Dowling
B. Finlay
E. Harrington
B. Hickey
S. Hopkins
B. Murphy
B. Redmond
P. Roche
B Vickers

1987 SLADE VALLEY
T. Browne
P. Fitzpatrick
W. Fitzsimmons
C. Leonard
P. Maguire
J. O'Brien
J. O'Grady
D. Quinn
A. Whelan
B. Keenan

1988 LUCAN
K. Barr
P. Coakley
P. Dunne
T. Dunne
M. Eager
P. Fitzgerald
K. Moffat
P. Monoghan
B. Reck
E. Tully

1989 GRANGE
J. Bryan
C. Buckley
N. Caulwell
P. Cullen
V. Daly
S. Downer
C. McArdle
D. McCarthy
D. Sheahan
O. Treacy
P. Vince
P. Walsh
B. Williams

1990 BODENSTOWN
S. Farrell
J. Gray
M. Kelly
D. McClelland
J. McClelland
K. Mather
Padraic Mather
Paul Mather
P. Masterson
K. O'Flaherty

APPENDIX VI
Section 3
LUMSDEN CUP WINNERS

Year	Venue	Winner and Club
1926	Royal Dublin	J.G. Greene, Royal Dublin
1927		E.F. Kilduff, Milltown
1928		C.H. West, Greystones
1929		F.R. McLoughlin, Royal Dublin
1930		O.S. Barton, Hermitage
1931	Hermitage	R.A. Dwyer, Hermitage
1932		R. McConkey, Royal Dublin
1933		R. Greene, Clontarf
1934		G.H. Owens, Skerries
1935		E.F. Kilduff, Milltown
1936		K.J. Duggan, Hermitage
1937		G.H. Owens, Skerries
1938		F.X. Kelly, Howth
1939		J. Hanlon, Portmarnock
1940		T.D. Purcell, Killiney
1941	Hermitage	J.D.F. Lyons, Kilkenny
1942	Milltown	A. O'Mara, UCD
1943	Castle	G. Davis, Castle
1944	Grange	J. McDermott, Newlands
1945	Castle	V. Herlihy, Clontarf
1946	Woodbrook	L. King French, Portmarnock
1947	Hermitage	J.P. Cummins, Royal Dublin
1948	Newlands	W. Huet, Newlands
1949	Elm Park	M.J. Byrne, Hermitage
1950		Clontarf	J. Belton, Clontarf
1951	Royal Dublin	C. Harnett, Hermitage
1952	Milltown	D.V. Hickey, Milltown
1953	Hermitage	J.M. O'Donnell, Sutton
1954	Grange	J. McDermott, Newlands
1955	Dun Laoghaire	C. Byrne, St Anne's
1956	Royal Dublin	C. Byrne, St Anne's
1957	Woodbrook	P. Donnelly, Howth
1958	Portmarnock	R. Cuddy, Portmarnock
1959	Castle	O. McDermott, Elm Park
1960	Dun Laoghaire	F. Firth, Malahide
1961	Clontarf	P. Doyle, Clontarf
1962	Milltown	S. O'Hanlon, Foxrock
1963	Castle	J.J. Mooney, Donabate
1964	Hermitage	D.F. Rooney, Grange
1965	Grange	M. Fives, Grange
1966	Howth	B. Reck, Lucan
1967	Dun Laoghaire	J. McGill, Corballis
1968	Elm Park	J. Fagan, St Anne's
1969	Milltown	G. Lawlor, Lucan
1970	Royal Dublin	A. Gormley, Co. Louth
1971	Clontarf	V. Canavan, Royal Dublin
1972	Hermitage	A.J. Hayes, Hermitage
1973	Dun Laoghaire	E. O'Sullivan, Woodbrook
1974	Elm Park	P. Cowley, Sutton
1975	Hermitage	P. O'Reilly, Lucan
1976	Greystones	C. Walby, Arklow
1977	Edmondstown	F. Kavanagh, Edmondstown
1978	Clontarf	J. McClean, Clontarf
1979	Elm Park	G. Carr, Sutton
1980	Royal Dublin	T. Craddock, Malahide
1981	Woodbrook	J. Bryan, Grange
1982	Hermitage	C. Lee, Forrest Little
1983	Grange	C. Fitzgerald, Lucan
1984	Forrest Little	P. Darcy, Forrest Little
1985	Milltown	G. O'Connor, Naas
1986	Castle	D. Quilligan, Elm Park
1987	Newlands	R. Lennox, Slade Valley
1988	Dun Laoghaire	S. Hannon, Forrest Little
1989	Grange	S. Buckley, Grange
1990	Elm Park	C. Lee, Forrest Little

APPENDIX VI
Section 4
Provincial Towns Cup Winners

1932 KILKENNY
M. Barry
Rev. J.B. Byrne
K. Drea
M.J. Duffy
Rev. P. Dunphy
W. Murphy
Rev. J. O'Keeffe
N. O Keeffe
J.H. Todd

1933 KILKENNY
M.J. Crotty
K. Drea
M.J. Duffy
Rev. P. Dunphy
Rev. J. O'Keeffe
N. O'Keeffe
Rev. J. Ryan
J. Saunders
J.N. Todd

1934 TULLA-MORE
P. Acheson
P. Higgins
D.F. McCarthy
N. Mahon
J. Martin
M.D. Power
P.J. Sheehy
T. Smyth
N.J. Tippin

1935 KILKENNY

Dr M. Crotty
K. Drea
J. Enright
A. Lalor
J. McAllister
W. McGarry
J. Maloney
W. Murphy
J. Todd

1936 BELLINTER PARK

F. Hyland
Rev. J. Kilmartin
P. Lyons
A.J. Malone
J. Mathews
M. Mockler
Dr O'Dwyer
R. Seery
Rev. J. Whelan

1937 WATER-FORD

J. Brophy
D. Brown
E. Cassin
P. Grogan
G. Haddon
J. Hughes
J. McDonald
D.A. O'Dwyer
J. Phelan

1938 CO. LOUTH

J. Feran
P.J. Gannon
Rev. J. Kilmartin
J.F. Liddy
P.V. Lyons
J. McCombe
A. Maher
M. Matthews
R. Murdock

1939 CO. LOUTH

P. Gallagher
J.F. Liddy
R.J. Kelly-Lynch
P.V. Lyons
T. McCombe
A. Maher
M. Matthews
R. Murdock
P. O Kelly

1940 L'TOWN & B'TOWN

R.B. Davis
E. Delany
T.P. Delany
D. Drew
P. Gray
R. Hammond
P. Lynch
C. Murdock
F. O' Gogarty

1941 CO. LOUTH
Team names
not available

1942–4
No Tournament

1945 CO. LOUTH
Team names
not available

1946 CO. LOUTH

Team names
not available

1947 CO. LOUTH

Team names
not available

1948 L'TOWN & B'TOWN

J. Crotty
R. Deane
T.P. Delany
J. Gray
P. Gray
Peter Gray
A.T. Hoey
C.W. Murdock
J.O.P. Roche

1949 KILKENNY

W. Cleere
J. Collins
P. Devaney
J. Enright
J. Holmes
H. Latta
J. Mitchell
Rev. G. O'Sullivan
F. Wall

1950 KILKENNY

W. Cleere
P. Devaney
J. Enright
F. Harrison
J. Holmes
P. Kennedy
H. Latta
W. O'Connor
M. Teehan

1951 BELLINTER PARK

E. Breslin
K. Coates
T. Leonard
J. McCarthy
J. McConville
Rev. R. McGrath
W. Riddle
M. Saurin
R. Seery

1952 WICKLOW

L. Carroll
T. Delahunt
F. Fennell
K. Gleeson
G. Kent
J. McCarroll
N. McEachern
J. Toner
C. Walsh

1953 DUNDALK

E. Cleere
J. Daly
B. Duffy
F. Johnston
S. Gallaher
P. Martin
T. Martin
M. Spillane
E. Tuite

1954 DUNDALK

P. Breen
E. Cleere
J. Corr
B. Duffy
S. Gallagher
P. Jordan
Dr P. Murphy
M. Spillane
E. Tuite

1955 KILKENNY

D. Clohessy
P. Devaney
F. Harrison
D. Kelly
P. Kennedy
L. Reidy
T.J. Mahon
W. O'Connor
M. Teehan

1956 DUNDALK

E. Cleere
J. Corr
J. Daly
B. Duffy
S. Gallagher
B. Halpenny
W. Lambert
P. Martin
A. Murphy

1957 CO. LOUTH

J. Daly
J. Gannon
A.C. Graigie
R. Healy
P.V. Lyons
D. McQuillan
M. Matthews
D. Murphy
J. Sheridan

1958 CARLOW

M. Barry
W. Bramley
R. Carroll
Rev. N. Cullen
B. Dempsey
Rev. E. Dowling
T. Jackson
Rev. J. O'Leary
Rev. R. Prendergast
M. Ruddle
J. Scully

1959 KILKENNY

Rev. P. Bergin
P. Devaney
Rev. F. Grace
Rev. P. Grant
F. Harrison
R. Haughton
Dr E. Mitchell
K. O'Donovan
M. Teehan

1960 CARLOW

N. Bielenberg
W. Bramley
R. Carroll
B. Dempsey
P. Downey
J. Fitzgibbon
P. Hyland
T. Jackson
T. Mooney
Rev. R. Prendergast
P. Purcell
M. Ruddle

1961 DUNDALK

T. Byrne
M. Carroll
J. Daly
J. Dearey
M. Drea
B. Duffy
T. Gleeson
W. Lambert
R. Magnier
J. Moriarty
A. Murphy
V. Murphy
J. Packer

1962 DUNDALK

M. Carroll
J. Dearey
G. Duggan
M. Duggan
J.M. Logan
P.J. Lonergan
F.D. Melia
G. Norton
W. O'Shaughnessy

1963 BELLINTER PARK

D. Collier
N. Collier
J. Finnegan
Rev. Dr J. Flynn
Rev. Dr M. Kelly
V. Lyons
Rev. R. McGrath
J. Maguire
J. Marsh
M. Mohan
P. Randles
Rev. A. Rispin
Rev. P. Stewart
M. Tighe

1964 TULLA-MORE

N. Conroy
T. Doyle
P. Fahey
W.J. Hoctor
M. Hogan
D. Lumley
C. Mehigan
G. O'Brien
J. O'Connor

1965 ROSSLARE

L. Buckley
J. Gaynor
J. Hall
P. Hall
Rev. R. Kavanagh
C. McCarthy
D. McNamara
M. Mullins
J. Pettit
N. Quirke
W. Rahilly
E. Wheeler

1966 CURRAGH

Rev. G. Brophy
D. Butler
J. Butler
D. Byrne
J.P. Byrne
P. Dowling
H. McDwyer
D. McManus
C. Madison
L. Mitchell
M. O'Shea
P. Prendergast
E. Quigley
J.J. Quinn
J. Young

1967 CARLOW
J. Aughney
J. Flood
J. Jordan
B. Kennedy
R. McDarby
T. McDonald
T. Mooney
M. O'Dwyer
M. Whelan

1968 ROSSLARE
J. Breen
N. Corcoran
W. Davis
F. Eustace
P. Furlong
J. Green
P. Hall
M. Mullins
J.F. Pettit

1969 ROSSLARE
J. Breen
N. Casey
N. Corcoran
W. 'Davis
F. Eustace
P. Furlong
J. Green
P. Hall
M. Mullins
J.F. Pettit

1970 TULLA-MORE
E. Buggy
T. Ledwidge
D.A.B. Lumley
W. Lynam
C. O'Keeffe
B. Rossiter
Rev. J. Walsh
M. White
P. White

1971 KILKENNY
S. Caraway
P. Deegan
W.F. Deegan
P. Fennelly
J. Holohan
B. Kilbride
T. Murphy
K. O'Donovan
L. Renehan

1972 WATERFORD
T. Aspell
W. Carroll
P. Clohosey
E. Connolly
J. Flavin
M. Foley
A. Irish
R. Lucy
P. Power

1973 CARLOW
L. Bennan
G. Coen
T. Crotty
T. Jennings
P. Jordan
L. Lawler
O. McArdle
T. O'Shea
M. Whelan

1974 WATERFORD
T. Aspel
N. Brennan
G. Bryne
P. Freeman
A. Irish
M. O'Brien
J. O'Keeffe
A. Phelan
J. Phelan

1975 HEADFORT
T. Burns
E. Clarke
T. Clarke
M. Fitzpatrick
G. Grey
L. Hopkins
M. McLeavy
G. Renehan
A. Stanley

1976 CARLOW

R. Carroll
G. Coen
T. Crotty
J. Doran
P. Fletcher
J. Hutton
S. Kane
T. Mooney
D. O'Boyle

1977 ABBEYLEIX
H. Cole
E. Fennelly
J. Fennelly
J.J. Fennelly
C. Foley
K. Kelly
J. O'Brien
J. O'Halloran
P. Purcell

1978 ROYAL TARA
V. Byrne
T. Clynch
N. Collier
R. Creavin
J. Cullinane
P. Henshaw
T. McGovern
P. O'Brien
N. Shannon

1979 BIRR

D. Boyd
E. Garahy
B. Guinan
P. Keeley
T. Kenny
B. McGarry
M. McGarry
D. O'Brien
J. O'Meara
M. Spain

1980 TULLA-MORE
P. Burns
P. Carragher
P. Cloonan
H. Cullen
J. Flanagan
F. O'Brien
B. O'Hagan
M. White
L. Wyer

1981 TRIM
O. Cooney
G. Crolly
P. Darby
C. Dignam
F. Dignam
P. Hegarty
G. Nannery
M. Power
P. Walker

1982 DUNDALK
V. Conlon
L. Conneely
M. Crosby
P. Curran
G. Duggan
J. Dwyer
C. Kinney
B. McCooey
G. Rogers

1983 BORRIS
J. Doyle
M. Hanrahan
C. Hughes
B. Joyce
L. Kelly
S. Kelly
E. Lennon
M. Long
P. Murphy

1984 DUNDALK
T.J. Byrne
J. Culleton
P. Curran
J.P. Daly
J. Dwyer
P. McGuinness
P. Moriarty
D. O'Callaghan
M. Stewart

1985 BALTIN-GLASS
M. Byrne
P. Byrne
J. Hyland
P. Irwin
V. Kavanagh Jr
B. Kilcoyne
D. Lord
S. McDonagh
T. Nolan
D. Patterson
P. Walsh
J. Whelan

1986 ROYAL TARA
C. Bowers
B. Crookes
D. Foley
E. Guerin
L. Lynch
D. Murphy
P. O'Brien
M. O'Neill
N. Shannon

1987 HEADFORT
S. Bartley
E. Carolan
P. Dempsey
J. Garry
P. McCann
D. McGrane
D. McInerney

1988 CO. LOUTH
B. Breen
K. Byrne
C. Cassidy
T. Garry
O. Garvey
M. Kavanagh
J. Leonard
S. Martin
M. Murphy
P. McKenna
C. Walsh

1989 MULLINGAR
D. Bell
C. Connaughton
P. Eighan
C. Garry
T. Geraghty
J. Ryan
P. Taaffe
M. Talbot
T. Upton

1990 CALLAN
T. Donovan
B. Duggan
J. Fitzpatrick
M. Fitzpatrick
S. Horgan
J. Kirwan
J. O'Dwyer
J. Scriver
M. Shortall

Metropolitan Trophy Winners

1973 SUTTON

S. Carroll
F. Cassidy
P. Cowley
C. Moriarty
S. O'Byrne
S. O'Leary
H. O'Neill
P. O'Reilly
T. Smith

1974 HOWTH
J. Bryne
S. Cannon
J. Carberry
P. Fitzgerald
N. Harkin
N. Kelly
C. McMahon
J. O'Connell
P. Redmond

1975 SLADE VALLEY
J. Doyle
B. Hughes
J. Kavanagh
B. Kelly
P. Mulvey
J. O'Grady
M. Quinlan
P. Redmond
A. Tracy

1976 GREY-STONES
J. Burke
W. Doyle
M. Forde
L. Gaw
P. McGrath
L. O'Connor
L. Redmond
O. Spurling
F. Talbot

1977 FORREST LITTLE
C. Darcy
P. Kennedy
N. McGrath
C. McNamee
J. Marron
G. Rice
R. Stynes
H. Sheppard
P. Smith

1978 THE ISLAND
W. Donnelly
D. Fitzgerald
L. Harrison
W. Heather
J. Murnane
F. O'Brien
D. Rushe
S. Sludds
B. Walsh

1979 DONABATE
J. Blake
J. Caraher
M. Fearon
F. Fitzgerald
L. Hanway
H. Neville
B. O'Flaherty
E. Purcell
D. Singleton

1980 FORREST LITTLE
J. Byrne
B. Cooney
C. Darcy
P. Fortune
J. Hendley
P. Kennedy
J. Marron
K. O'Hara
M. O'Hara

1981 THE ISLAND
F. Cahill
P. Corkery
J. Cosgrave
M. Cronin
B. McDonnell
D. McSwiggan
W. Murphy
F. O'Brien
P. O'Dea

1982 NEWLANDS
C. Ahearne
H. Boyle
J. Dunne
A. Hade
L. Hanlon
W. Hughes
P. Kennedy
P. Mahon
F. O'Connor

1983 SUTTON
T. Bowen
S. Carroll
J. Cassidy
R. Doherty
E. Firth
D. Furlong
A. Higgins
A. McDonnell
A. McWilliams
S. O'Leary
E. O'Rourke
C. Smith
D. Twomey
D. Wallace

1984 LUCAN
R. Conway
T. Conway
O. Cumiskey
O. Dunne
T. Dunne
J. Finlay
T. Gough
B. Keeley
J. Thompson

1985 HOWTH
P. Fitzgerald
H. Flood
J. Foran
E. Golding
J. O'Connell
L. O'Reilly
P. Redmond
J. Richardson
G. Rooney

1986 DEER PARK
J. Brady
J. Fitzpatrick
J. Lynch
E. McCann
L. Magee
B. Martin
T. Monaghan
P. Nagle
J. Tierney

1987 HOWTH
J. Crookes
H. Flood
E. Golding
P. Keenan
T. McDonnell
D. McKenna
L. O'Reilly
P. Redmond
K. Walsh

1988 BALLINA-SCORNEY
P. Byrne
D. Doyle
O. Duff
M. Dunne
K. McConville
B. O'Brien
D. O'Connell
D. Owens
M. Wyse

1989 GREY-STONES
D. Ashe
L. Behan
M. Collins
L. D'Arcy
G. Kenny
S. Kinsella
B. Massey
P. Mahon
L. O'Connor
P. O'Connor
P. Pratt

1990 SLADE VALLEY
F. Casey
J. Cleere
B. Donnelly
P. Joyce
B. Keenan
P. Lynch
K. Maguire
P. Maguire
J. Mulvey
T. O'Toole
R. O'Sullivan

APPENDIX VI
Section 5

East of Ireland Amateur Open Mixed Foursomes Championship Winners

1974	B.P. Malone (Elm Park)	and	Ms V. Singleton (Donabate)
1975	D.P. Herlihy (Royal Dublin)	"	Mrs M.T. Moran (Donabate)
1976	B.P. Malone (Elm Park)	"	Ms V. Butler (Elm Park)
1977	A.J. Hayes (Hermitage)	"	Ms C. Nesbitt (Royal Portrush)
1978	A.J.C. Morrow (Co. Louth)	"	Ms R. Hegarty (Bandon)
1979	E. Dunne (Athlone)	"	Ms M. McKenna (Donabate)
1980	B. Whitaker (Elm Park)	"	Ms S. Gorman (Milltown)
1981	R.J. Moran (Woodenbridge)	"	Mrs T. O'Reilly (Donabate)
1982	M.K. Smyth (Milltown)	"	Ms B. Gleeson (Killarney)
1983	J.M. Gleeson (Milltown)	"	Ms C. Hourihane (Woodbrook)
1984	E. Dunne (Elm Park)	"	Ms M. McKenna (Donabate)
1985	M.A. Gannon (Co. Louth)	"	Ms S. O'Brien-Kenny (Grange)
1986	M.A. Gannon (Co. Louth)	"	Ms S. O'Brien-Kenny (Grange)
1987	P. Rayfus (Trim)	"	Ms M. McKenna (Donabate)
1988	A.J. Hayes (Co. Louth)	"	Mrs J. Barkman (Castletroy)
1989	P. Rayfus (Trim)	"	Ms M. McKenna (Donabate)
1990	L. MacNamara (Woodbrook)	"	Mrs M. MacNamara (Woodbrook)

APPENDIX VI
Section 6

Leinster Seniors' (Golden Years) Championship Winners and Runners-up

Year	Venue	Winner and Club	Score	Runner-up and Club	Score
1987	Clontarf	A. Foran, Howth	148	E. Curran, Woodbrook	149
1988	L'town & B'town	H. McQuillan, Royal Tara	148	M. Breen, L'town & B'town	150
1989	Clontarf	M. Hood, Grange	154	P. Dermody, Hermitage	155
1990	Kilkenny	D. O'Donoghue, Stackstown	153	P. O'Sullivan, Kinsale	156

APPENDIX VI

Section 7

Record of Winning Clubs and teams of the Belfast and District Cup

1903 ORMEAU
P.T. Crymble
W.B. Fenneli
J. McAvoy
H. McKeag
T.A. McKeag
C.W Patton

1904 ORMEAU
E. Everest
J. McAvoy
H. McKeag
T.A. McKeag
C.W. Patton
J.E. Wilson

1905 ORMEAU
P.T. Crymble
J. McAvoy
H. McKeag
T.A. McKeag
C.W. Patton
J.E. Wilson

1906 MALONE
C.F. Barker
E.L. Barker
R.J. Hewitt
F.B. Newett
E.F. Spiller

1907 MALONE
C.F. Barker
R.J. Hewitt
J.L. Jackson
F.B. Newett
B. O'Brien
S. Shiley
E.F. Spiller

1908 MALONE
C.F. Barker
R.J. Hewitt
J.L. Jackson
F.B. Newett
B. O'Brien
E.F. Spiller

1909 KNOCK
W.H. Davidson
W.R. Forde
P. Gilchrist
J.H.A. Peddie
M.A. Trimble
J .R. Whyte

1910 ORMEAU
J. Anderson
F. Curry
T.H. Graham
H. Hickey
T.A. McKeag
J . Mitchell
C.W. Patton
J.E. Wilson

1911 FORT-WILLIAM
J. Alexander
W. Barnett
J. Campbell
A.H. Craig
J. McCleery
R. Swanston

1912 FORT-WILLIAM
A. Alexander
J. Alexander
W. Barnett
J. Campbell
A.H. Craig
F. Keith
R. Swanson

1913 MALONE
J.D. Coates
C.C. Gotto
W.H. Graham
A. Lowe
J.S. Miller
H. Nicholson
B. O'Brien
J.E. Stevenson
H. Tweedie
C.B. Walkington

1914–18

No Tournament

1919 FORT-WILLIAM
J. Alexander
J. Campbell
J. McCleery
P. McDonald
W. Wallace
H.D. Stedman
A.E. Todd

1920 ORMEAU
J. Anderson
R.W. Barnett
C. Carroll
E. Currie
C.E. McConnell
G. Ross
E. Waddington

1921 MALONE
W.A. Barker
S.A. Bulloch
W.R. Knox
J.S. Lamont
A. Lowe
C.J. Maguire
J.F. Stevenson
J.C. Timbey

1922 MALONE
W.A. Barker
S.A. Bulloch
J.S. Lamont
A. Lowe
C.J. Maguire
J.F. Stevenson
J.C. Timbey
H.S. Tweedie

1923 MALONE
W.A. Barker
W.M. Graham
W.R. Knox
A. Lowe
A.C. Lowry
J.D. Stevenson
J.C. Timbey
A.E. Todd
H.S. Tweedie

1924 MALONE
W.A. Barker
J.C. Gilbert Jr
W.M. Graham
A.W. Green
W.R. Knox
A. Lowe
J.F. Stevenson
J.C. Timbey

1925 QUEEN'S UNIVERSITY
A.C. Allison
J.C. Gilbert
F.P. McConnell
R.H. McConnell
J.M. Mitchell
R.P. Smyth
A.L. Weir

1926 MALONE
J.R. Carr
W.R. Knox
A. Lowe
C.E. McConnell
J.F. Stevenson
J.C. Timbey
H.J. Titterington

1927 MALONE
J.R. Carr
W.O'B. Knox
A. Lowe
C.E. McConnell
J.F. Stevenson
D.W. Smyth
J.C. Timbey
H.J. Titterington
H.S. Tweedie

1928 MALONE
W.R. Knox
W.O'B. Knox
A. Lowe
C.E. McConnell
J.F. Stevenson
J.C. Timbey
H.J. Titterington
A.E. Todd
H.S. Tweedie

1929 BANGOR
F.J. Boyd
H. Clements
W.C. Drean
J. McAuley
B. Mullen
J.C. Nicholson
G.A. Simpson
J. Taylor

1930 BALMORAL
S. Dugald
J. Hudson
T.P. Livingston
E.H. Robertson
W.E. Scott
A.T. Sheals
H.S. Sheals

1931 BALMORAL
J. Hudson
T.P. Livingston
N.E. Scott
H. Sheals

1932 HOLYWOOD
H.B. Cochrane
S. Copeland
B.G. Corry
R.S. Graham
D.M. Kyle
N.J. Small
W.J. Thompson
P.T. Watson

1933 KNOCK
A. Campbell
C.J. McMullan
O.W. Madden
W.S. Morton
T.E. Murphy
R.M. Peddie
I.W. Seaton
H.R. Thompson

1934 KNOCK
A. Campbell
E.H.R. Colhoun
W. McCaughey
R.M. McConnell
C.J. McMullan
O.W. Madden
T.E. Murphy
R.M. Peddie
I.W. Seaton
J.H. Thompson

1935 HOLYWOOD
M.B. Cochran
B.G. Corry
R.S. Graham
H.M. Hadden
N.J. Small
W.J. Thompson
P.T. Watson

1936 BELVOIR PARK
T.B. Agnew
R.W. Barnett
A. Campbell
H.D. Connolly
R.J. Frizzell
J.F. Graham
R. McCaugherty
W.E. Scott

1937 BELVOIR PARK
T.B. Agnew
R.W. Barnett
J.N. Blair
A. Campbell
H.D. Connolly
R.J. Frizzell
J.F. Graham
J.S.S. Graham
J. McCaherty
W.E. Scott

1940–45

No Tournament

1948 BELVOIR PARK
T.B. Agnew
T.A. Blair
G. Brady
A. Campbell
J.W. Graham
J. McVeigh
A.R. Megaw
S.S. Moore
J.S. Spence

1951 SHANDON PARK
J. Boston
G.S. Cooke
D.J. Crawford
M. Edwards
R.C. Killops
H. McCluskey
E. McDowell
H. McKee
Q.W. Madden
T. Paul

1938 BANGOR
W.J. Brown
J. McAuley
H. Marshall
H. Martin
G.J. Stephenson
W.J. Stewart
W.J. Thompson
R. Young

1946 BELVOIR PARK
T.B. Agnew
R.W. Barnett
T.A. Blair
G. Brady
A. Campbell
G. McGladery
J. McVeigh
S.S. Moore
W.E. Scott
W.A. Wadsworth

1949 MALONE
A.S.G. Adams
W.E. Dornan
W.J.J. Ferguson
W.I. Forsythe
R.J. Frizzell
W. Hanna
G.J. Irvine
R.L. Lowry
J.G. McErvel
J.A. Peacocke

1952 MALONE
R.M. Craigan
W.E. Dornan
J.A. Dowling
J.H. Dowling
W.J.J. Ferguson
R.J. Frizzell
G.J. Irvine
R.L. Lowry
J.G. McErvel

1939 BELVOIR PARK
T.B. Agnew
R.W. Barnett
J.N. Blair
G. Brady
A. Campbell
H.S. Connolly
R.J. Frizzell
J.S.S. Graham
J. McCaherty
W.A. Wadsworth

1947 BELVOIR PARK
T.B. Agnew
T.A. Blair
G. Brady
A. Campbell
N.B. Lair
G. McGladery
A.R. Megaw
S.S. Moore
J.S. Spence
G. Thompson
W.A. Wadsworth

1950 MALONE
W.E. Dornan
J.A. Dowling
J.H. Dowling
W.J.J. Ferguson
R.J. Frizzell
R.L. Lowry
J.G. McErvel
J.A. Peacocke
W. Smyth

1953 BANGOR
G. Balher
W.K. Brown
N.V. Drew
J.G. Edwards
G.E. Gregory
A.H.G. Love
E.C. McDade
W. McMillan
J. Neill
G.J. Stephenson
R. Young

1954 SHANDON PARK
J. Boston
J. Collins
G.S. Cooke
D.J. Crawford
M. Edwards
R.C. Killops
H. McCluskey
T. Paul

1957 MALONE
J.H. Dowling
W.J.J. Ferguson
A.R. Humphreys
G.J. Irvine
R.L. Lowry
J.G. McErvel
I.A. Nesbitt

1960 SHANDON PARK
J. Boston
J. Duncan
B. Edwards
M. Edwards
G. Herron
T.B.C. Hoey
W.H.E. Rainey

1963 SHANDON PARK
R.S. Adamson
J. Boston
H.A. Brown
D. Crawford
J. Duncan
B. Edwards
M. Edwards
G. Herron
D.P.W. Hoey
S.D. Ingram
W.H.E. Rainey

1955 BELVOIR PARK
T.B. Agnew
N. Browne
D. Clark
I. Frazer
J.W. Grahame
J. Kennedy
J. Kirkwood
W. MacRory
J. McAnoy
N . McClughan
J. McVeigh
H. Marshall
A.R. Megaw
D. Young

1958 CLANDE-BOYE
J. Carlisle
S.A.G. Cooley
J. Elwood
V. McAuley
F.A. McCorry
J.N. Pyper
M.E. Quirey
D.F. Smith
S. Young

1961 SHANDON PARK
R.S. Adamson
J. Boston
J. Duncan
B. Edwards
M. Edwards
G. Herron
T.B.C. Hoey
I.O. Madden
W.H.E. Rainey

1964 ROYAL BELFAST
J. Ballagh
P. Copeland
W.I. Forsythe
R.B. Jordan
M.C. McAuley
I.H. McCaw
W. McKinney
R.A.D. McMillan
J.F.D. Madeley
R. Salisbury
W.R.A. Tennant

1956 SHANDON PARK
J. Boston
T. Caughey
G.S. Cooke
D. Crawford
J. Duncan
T.B.C. Hoey
H. McCluskey
O.W. Madden
W.H.E. Rainey

1959 SHANDON PARK
J. Boston
J. Collins
D. Crawford
J. Duncan
B. Edwards
G. Herron
T.B.C. Hoey
H. McCluskey
I.O. Madden
W.H.E. Rainey

1962 SHANDON PARK
R.S. Adamson
J. Boston
J. Duncan
B. Edwards
M. Edwards
G. Herron
W. McCluskey
I.O. Madden
T. Paul
W.H.E. Rainey

1965 CLANDE-BOYE
J. Benson
S.A.G. Cooley
J.H. Derby
R. Hutton
J.J. McAnoy
F.A. McCorry
J. McIlveen
M.E. Quirty
B. Wilson
F. Wilson

1966 FORT-WILLIAM
A. Black
S. Black
A.H. Bradley
H.S.E. Catherwood
M. Duffy
S. Johnson
D. Martin
R.A. Nesbitt
R.K.M. Pollin
B.G. Wallace

1967 SHANDON PARK
J. Boston
H.A. Brown
B. Edwards
M. Edwards
M.J.C. Hoey
T.B.C. Hoey
D.P.W. Hoey
W.H.E. Rainey

1968 SHANDON PARK
J. Boston
M.J.A. Brown
J. Duncan
B. Edwards
M. Edwards
D.P.W. Hoey
T.B.C. Hoey
W.H.E. Rainey

1969 ROYAL BELFAST
P.J. Buckley
C.P. Copeland
R.B. Jordan
T.R. Lennon
D. McAuley
J.F.D. Madeley
R.K.M. Pollin

1970 BANGOR
D.B. Blaikie
R. Ewart
B.J.S. Kissock
J.A. McDade
R.H. McGimpsey
C.R. Mullan
J.G. Neill
W.I.D. Sanderson
N.H. Timms
N.D. Woods

1971 BELVOIR PARK
T.S. Anderson
A.J. Boyd
J.N. Browne
M.G.I. Kerr
R.A. McAnoy
M.J. Malone
P.B. Malone
J.R. Murray
H.B. Smyth
D.R. Young

1972 KNOCK PARK
J.V.W. Boyle
J.P. Bradley
C. Desano
W.M. Hardy
J. McConvey
J.C. Moss
J.A.J. Spence
P.J. Waddell

1973 SHANDON
J. Boston
M.J.A. Brown
B. Edwards
D.P.W. Hoey
M.J.C. Hoey
G. Jenkins
D.C. Long
J.B. McAnoy
T. Osborne

1974 CLANDE-BOYE
B. Agnew
J. Benson
J.D. Coey
F. Coulter
J.H. Derby
T.G. Magee
B. Owen
B. Quiery
N. Russell
R. Uttley
P.J. Waddell
B. Wilson

1975 CLANDE-BOYE
J. Coey
S.A.G. Cooley
J.H. Derby
M. Lockhart
T.G. Magee
B. Owen
E.T. Quiery
A.C. Russell
P.J. Waddell
B. Wilson

1976 SHANDON PARK
R. Beaney
T. Dodds
B. Edwards
D.P.W. Hoey
M.J.C. Hoey
T.B.C. Hoey
R. Limmer
D.C. Long
A. Sinton

1977 SHANDON PARK
R. Beaney
A. Briggs
J. Boston
T. Dodds
B. Edwards
D.P.W. Hoey
D.C. Long
A. Sinton

1978 SHANDON PARK
N. Anderson
R. Beaney
A. Briggs
B. Edwards
D.P.W. Hoey
M.J.C. Hoey
T.B.C. Hoey
M. Jenkins
R. Limner
D.C. Long
P. Watson

1979 SHANDON PARK
N. Anderson
R. Beaney
T. Dodds
B. Edwards
D.P.W. Hoey
M.J.C. Hoey
T.B.C. Hoey
D.C. Long

1980 BANGOR
D.B. Blaikie
R.S. Irvine
B. Kearney
B.J.S. Kissock
M. McAuley
J.A. McDade
G. McGimpsey
W.A. Sanderson
E. Sterrett
B. Wilson
N.D. Woods

1981 BANGOR
D.B. Blaikie
P.A. Dawson
R.S. Irvine
B. Kearney
B.J.S. Kissock
J.A. McDade
G. McGimpsey
E. Sterrett
J. Whittle
B. Wilson
N.D. Woods

1984 CARRICK-FERGUS
D. Ballentine
B. McGahan
J. McIlwaine
S. McNally
O. O'Toole
P. Vizard
M. Montgomery

1987 LURGAN
G. Best
T. Cummins
T. Douglas
S. Guiseley
R. Nanna
M. Horan
I. McMurray
P. Magee
W. Turkington

1990 CLANDE-BOYE
K. Campbell
J. Fullerton
C. Glasgow
D. Jackson
G. Kerr
E.T. Quiery
N. Russell
W. Smith
M. Thompson
J. Verner

1982 BALLYMENA
J. Arthur
D. Cunning
F. Dawson
P. Grant
V. Greenwood
J. McAleese
C. McQuillan
D. Marcus
J.R. O'Hare
M.D.S. Rainey

1985 SHANDON
N. Anderson
R. Beaney
M.J.C. Hoey
T.B.C. Hoey
N. Jenkinson
D.C. Long
P. Purdy
B. Wilson

1988 SHANDON PARK
P. Acheson
N. Anderson
R. Beaney
I. Hall
T.B.C. Hoey
J. Laverty
D.C. Long
P. Purdy
B. Wilson

1983 BANGOR
P. Barry
D.B. Blaikie
R.S. Irvine
B.J.S. Kissock
M. McAuley
J.A. McDade
G. McGimpsey
G. Moore
B. Wilson
N.D. Woods

1986 LURGAN PARK
G. Best
T. Douglas
S. Guiseley
R. Hanna
M. Horan
I. McMurray
P. Magee
T.W. Turkington

1989 SHANDON PARK
N. Anderson
M. Curran
I. Hall
N. Jenkins
J. Laverty
G. Lynas
D.C. Long
P. Purdy
B. Wilson

APPENDIX VI

Section 8

Ulster Cup Winners

Year	Winner	Year	Winner
1913	Bangor	1930	Belvoir Park
1914–18	No Meeting	1931	Ormeau
1919	Bangor	1932	Fortwilliam
1920	Balmoral	1933	Shandon Park
1921	Greenisland	1934	Balmoral
1922	Malone	1935	Malone
1923	Knock	1936	Knock
1924	Bangor	1937	Shandon Park
1925	Knock	1938	Shandon Park
1926	Lisburn	1939	Malone
1927	Knock	1940	Knock
1928	Cliftonville	1941-5	No Meeting
1929	Larne	1946	Shandon Park

Year	Winner	Year	Winner
1947	Shandon Park	1970	Carnalea
1948	Carnalea	1971	Knock
1949	Carnalea	1972	Massereene
1950	Fortwilliam	1973	Scrabo
1951	Kirkistown Castle	1974	Cairndhu
1952	Shandon Park	1975	Kirkistown Castle
1953	Shandon Park	1976	Massereene
1954	Clandeboye	1977	Mourne
1955	Knock	1978	Ballyclare
1956	Ballymena	1979	Kirkistown Castle
1957	Clandeboye	1980	Balmoral
1958	Lisburn	1981	Scrabo
1959	Scrabo	1982	Dunmurry
1960	Carnalea	1983	Holywood
1961	Mourne	1984	Mourne
1962	Bangor	1985	Mourne
1963	Clandeboye	1986	Cliftonville
1964	Scrabo	1987	Letterkenny
1965	Carnalea	1988	Shandon Park
1966	Carnalea	1989	Castleblayney
1967	Holywood	1990	Ballymena
1968	Balmoral		
1969	Clandeboye		

APPENDIX VI

Section 9

Christie Flag Winners

Year	Winner	Runner-up
1940	C.C. Swann & F. Daly (City of Derry)	
1941	(Came under control of Ulster Branch)	
	C.C. Swann & F. Daly (City of Derry)	H. Tweedie & S. Fairweather (Malone)
1942	C.C. Swann & F. Daly (City of Derry)	J. Fitzsimons & P.G.Stevenson (Ryl Portrush)
1943	R.W. Barnett & E. Patterson (Donaghadee)	W.J. Thompson & J. McCartney (Holywood)
1944	S.S. Moore & P.G. Stevenson (Ryl Portrush)	S. Black & R. McCollum (Knock)
1945	W. Smyth & J. McLachan (Royal Co. Down)	H. Porter & F. Daly (Balmoral) ⎫ Tie R.W. Barnett & E. Patterson (Donaghadee) ⎭
1946	J.M. Neill & J. McCartney (Cliftonville)	W. Smyth & J. McLachan (Royal Co. Down)
1947	W. McCollum & H. Dickie (Knock)	J.M. Neill & J. McCartney (Cliftonville)
1948	S.S. Moore & J. McVeigh (Belvoir Park)	C.J.G. McErvel & J. McClean (Malone) ⎫ Tie W.A. Taylor & S. Black (Knock) ⎭
1949	J.M. Neill & J. McCartney (Cliftonville)	A. Megaw & S.S. Moore (Belvoir Park)
1950	J. Glover & S. Black (Knock)	J.M. Neill & J. McCartney (Cliftonville)
1951	G. Stevenson & J. Hamill (Bangor)	A. Megaw & H. Middleton (Belvoir Park)
1952	N.V. Drew & E.C. McDade (Bangor)	M. Edwards & C.K. Neill (Shandon Park)
1953	H. McIlree & G. Dodds (Knock)	J. Taggart & P.G. Stevenson (Ryl Portrush)
1954	J.A. McDowell & G. Herron (Donaghadee)	
1955	J. Dunwoodie & R.C. Killops (Shandon Park)	P.J. O' Donnell & J.B. Esler (Whitehead)
1956	W.R. Tennant & J. McCartney (Cliftonville)	J.G. Giffen & J.N. Hunter (Portstewart) ⎫ Tie R.E. McCandless & T. McAillister (C. Fergus) ⎭
1957	R.M. Craigan & J. McClean (Malone)	T.B.C. Hoey & B. Edwards (Shandon Park)
1958	R.M. Craigan & J. McClean (Malone)	W.R. Tennant & J. McCartney (Cliftonville)
1959	J. Kieran & R. Irvine (Holywood)	
1960	D. Duffy & A. Bacon (Rossmore)	
1961	H.M. Hadden & J.D.F. Madeley (Ryl Belfast)	
1962	J.H. Derby & W. Kerr (Clandeboye)	
1963	R.K.M. Pollin & B. Duffy (Fortwilliam)	

1964	R.M. Craigan & P. Leonard (Malone)	B. McCrea & R. Henry (Royal Portrush)
1965	J.F.D. Madeley & W.R. Tennant (Ryl Belfast)	
1966	J.W. Hulme & D. Patterson (Warrenpoint)	J.F.D. Madeley & W.R. Tennant (Ryl Belfast)
1967	J.W. Ritchie & D.A. Stevenson (Massereene)	J. Silcock & B. McGahan (Belvoir Park)
1968	J. Armstrong & R. Stevenson (Ryl Portrush)	G.R. Caldwell & T.R. Bell (City of Derry)
1969	B. Wilson & J. Henderson (Clandeboye)	W.J.J. Ferguson & J.B. Black (Malone)
1970	J. Spence & K. Hall (Knock)	B. Wilson & J. Henderson (Clandeboye)
1971	S.A.G. Cooley & J. Henderson (Clandeboye)	B.J. Kissock & K. Hall (Bangor)
1972	B. Blaikie & E. Jones (Bangor)	K. Stevenson & D. Patterson (Warrenpoint)
1973	S. McBurney & S.G. McGlure (Massereene)	B. Fleming & B.G. Cashell (Queen's Univ.)
1974	J. McAleese & I. Clarke (Ballymena)	J.F.D. Madeley & D. Carson (Ryl Belfast)
1975	S. McKillop & B. Thompson (Cushendall)	D. Jones & G. McGimpsey (Bangor)
1976	J. McAleese & I. Clarke (Ballymena)	R. Hanna & P. Leonard (Lurgan)
1977	J. Fisher & D. Robinson (Carnalea 'B')	R. Stevenson & B. McGahan (Carrickfergus)
1978	R. Stevenson & B. McGahan (Carrickfergus)	D. Patterson & R. Rafferty (Warrenpoint)
1979	W. Todd & P. Duffy (Co. Armagh)	L. Esdale & S. Irvine (Bangor)
1980	D.J.F. Young & M. Windebank (Ryl Portrush)	M. Kelly & M. Wolsley (Belvoir Park)
1981	S.J. King & G. McIlroy (Holywood)	I. Smyth & B. Fleming (Ballycastle)
1982	G. Parkhill & P. O'Donnell (Whitehead)	J. Smyth & T.J. Craig (Massereene)
1983	No match played	
1984	No match played	
1985	N.V. Drew & B. Wilson (Bangor)	E. Jones & J. Boston (Royal Co. Down)
1986	N.V. Drew & B. Wilson (Bangor)	K. Stevenson & K. Magennis (Banbridge)
1987	P. Hanna & A. O'Neill (Fortwilliam)	M. McGee & A. Robinson (Carnalea)
1988	M. McGee & A. Robinson (Carnalea)	K. Dorrian & C. Fitzsimons (Ardglass)
1989	D. Carson & R. McDowell (Royal Belfast)	P. Leonard & C. Conway (Killymoon)
1990	G. Drew & P. Brunton (Massereene)	N.V. Drew & G. McGimpsey (Bangor)

APPENDIX VI

Section 10

Fred Daly Trophy Winners

Year	Winner	Runner-up
1973	Donaghadee	Cairndhu
1974	Shandon Park	Donaghadee
1975	Warrenpoint	Massereene

Year	Winner	Runner-up
1976	Shandon Park	Lurgan
1977	Shandon Park	Royal Portrush
1978	Royal Portrush	Downpatrick
1979	Donaghadee	Clandeboye
1980	Clandeboye	Royal Portrush
1981	Ardglass	Portstewart
1982	Shandon Park	Cairndhu
1983	Warrenpoint	City of Derry
1984	Cairndhu	Warrenpoint
1985	Royal Portrush	Warrenpoint
1986	City of Derry	Carrickfergus
1987	Warrenpoint	Downpatrick
1988	Cairndhu	Clandeboye
1989	Downpatrick	Donaghadee
1990	City of Derry	Carrickfergus

APPENDIX VI

Section 11

Ulster Seniors' (Golden Years) Championship

Year	Venue	Winner and Club	Score	Runner-up and Club	Score
1988	Ryl Belfast	H.B. Smith, Ballymena (on 2nd best nett)	158	E. Henry, Kirkistown Castle	158
1989	Bangor	B. McCrea, Royal Portrush	151	S. McBurney, Massereene	157
1990	Shandon Park	J.P. Daly, Dundalk	153	S. McBurney, Massereene	154

APPENDIX VI
Section 12

Connacht Shield Winners

Year	Winner	Runner-up
1949	Ballinasloe	
1950	Castlerea	
1951	Ballinasloe	
1952	Portumna	
1953	Swinford	
1954	Mountbellew	
1955	Athlone	
1956	Tuam	
1957	Castlerea	
1958	Castlebar	
1959	Ballinasloe	
1960	Ballina	Roscommon
1961	Ballinasloe	Athlone
1962	Ballina	Swinford
1963	Ballinasloe	Carrick-on-Shannon
1964	Roscommon	Enniscrone
1965	Gort	Tuam
1966	Carrick-on-Shannon	Claremorris
1967	Ballinrobe	Tuam
1968	Stradhill	Ballyhaunis
1969	Ballinasloe	Strandhill
1970	Ballaghaderreen	Mountbellew
1971	Ballinasloe	Castlebar
1972	Castlebar	Roscommon
1973	Castlerea	Strandhill
1974	Athlone	Strandhill
1975	Strandhill	Tuam
1976	Galway	Connemara
1977	Athenry	Enniscrone
1978	Gort	Galway
1979	Co. Sligo	Westport
1980	Athlone	Galway
1981	Connemara	Enniscrone
1982	Ballinasloe	Loughrea
1983	Strandhill	Tuam
1984	Strandhill	Gort
1985	Galway	Ballinasloe
1986	Tuam	Westport
1987	Westport	Tuam
1988	Westport	Ballyhaunis
1989	Ballinrobe	Tuam
1990	Strandhill	Ballinasloe

APPENDIX VI
Section 13

Cecil Ewing Shield Winners

1982	Galway
1983	Tuam
1984	Co. Sligo
1985	Strandhill
1986	Strandhill
1987	Enniscrone
1988	Galway
1989	Athenry
1990	Mountbellow

APPENDIX VI
Section 14

Jack O'Sullivan Trophy Winners

1988	Galway
1989	Portumna
1990	Galway

APPENDIX VI
Section 15

Connacht Seniors' (Golden Years) Championship

Year	Venue	Winner and Club
1979		T. Larkin, Ballinasloe
1980		Rev. D. Killian, Athlone
1981		P. Fitzgerald, Tuam
1982		P. Fitzgerald, Tuam
1983		T. Larkin, Ballinasloe
1984		T. Larkin, Ballinasloe
1985		F. Rushe, Mountbellew
1986		J. Murray, Bundoran
1987		T. Collins, Athlone
1988		M. Hernon, Galway
1989	Athlone	J. Slattery, Ballinasloe
1990	Athlone	J.J. Byrne, Delgany

APPENDIX VI
Section 16

Connacht Mixed Foursomes Championship Winners

1984	
1985	
1986	P. O'Reilly & B. Hughes (Westport)
1987	W. O'Grady & A. Hyland (Ballinasloe)
1988	P. O'Reilly & B. Hughes (Westport)
1989	P. McGrath & G. Coyne (Mountbellew)
1990	B. Fleming & M. Costelloe (Mountbellew)

APPENDIX VI
Section 17

Munster Country Clubs Cup Winners

Year	Winner	Year	Winner
1932	Limerick	1963	Tipperary
1933	Limerick	1964	Mallow
1934	Kinsale	1965	Doneraile
1935	Midleton	1966	Charleville
1936	Inchydoney	1967	Charleville
1937	Mitchelstown	1968	Mitchelstown
1938	Adare Manor	1969	Fermoy
1939	Macroom	1970	Charleville
1940	Macroom	1971	Fermoy
1941	Midleton	1972	Kinsale
1942	Midleton	1973	Charleville
1943-6	No Tournament	1974	Kinsale
1947	Newcastlewest	1975	Tralee
1948	Macroom	1976	Charleville
1949	Ennis	1977	Macroom
1950	Bandon	1978	Tralee
1951	Dooks & Caragh	1979	Newcastlewest
1952	Tipperary	1980	Tralee
1953	Clonmel	1981	Glengarriff
1954	Macroom	1982	Kilkee
1955	Clonmel	1983	Tralee
1956	Charleville	1984	Kinsale
1957	Mallow	1985	Macroom
1958	Mallow	1986	Carrick-on-Suir
1959	Dooks & Caragh	1987	Dungarvan
1960	Newcastlewest	1988	Lismore
1961	Doneraile	1989	Doneraile
1962	Newcastlewest	1990	Adare Manor

APPENDIX VI
Section 18

Munster Seniors' (Golden Years) Championship

Year	Venue	Winner and Club	Score	Runner-up and Club	Score
1989	Dooks	P. O Sullivan, Kinsale	150	J. O Connell, Dooks	151
1990	Ennis	M. Kearce, Ennis	150	D. Culligan, Lahinch	152 (on last 18)

APPENDIX VI
Section 19

Constitution and Rules of the Golfing Union of Ireland

1.
Preliminary

1.1 Rules herein are indicated by consecutive numbers.

1.2 Clauses are indicated by consecutive numbers preceded by Rule numbers.

1.3 Sub-Clauses are indicated by consecutive numbers preceded by Clause numbers.

1.4 Sub-Sub-Clauses are indicated by consecutive numbers preceded by Sub-Clause numbers.

1.5 Cross reference of Rules, Clauses and Sub-Clauses herein referred to shall mean the Rules, Clauses and Sub-Clauses of these Rules.

2.
Name and Title

2.1 The name and title of the body constituted shall be 'The Golfing Union of Ireland'.

3.
Definitions and Interpretations

3.1 In this Constitution, in these Rules, in the Bye-Laws and in the Duties and Terms of Reference of Committees and Sub-Committees of the Union, unless the context otherwise requires:

   3.1.1 The 'Golfing Union of Ireland' hereinafter for brevity referred to as the 'Union' and founded in 1891 shall mean the National Administrative Authority for Mens' Amateur Golf in Ireland.

   3.1.2 The 'Irish Ladies' Golf Union' hereinafter for brevity referred to as the 'ILGU' and founded in 1893 shall mean the National Administrative Authority for Ladies' Amateur Golf in Ireland.

   3.1.3 The 'Professional Golfers' Association' (Irish Region) originally founded in 1911 by the Union at the request of the Professional Golfers of Ireland and then known as the Irish Professional Golfers' Association, shall mean the Governing Authority for Professional Golf in Ireland.

   3.1.4 The 'Central Council' shall mean the Central Council of the Union and where the word 'Council' appears without any qualification it shall mean that Council.

   3.1.5 The 'Provisional Branches' shall mean the Branches of the Union in each of the four Provinces of Ireland namely Connacht, Leinster, Munster and Ulster and where the word 'Branch' occurs it shall mean such one or all of the Provincial Branches as the context requires.

3.1.6   A 'Provincial Council' shall mean a Council constituted pursuant to the Provisions of Rule 16 hereof.

3.1.7   The 'Standing Committee' constituted under Rule 21 hereof shall mean that Committee of the Union appointed for the more convenient conduct of the affairs of the Union. It shall be answerable to the Central Council for all its actions.

3.1.8   All other Committees and Sub-Committees constituted under Rule 21 hereof shall be answerable to the Standing Committee except that the International Selection Committee and the Junior Selection Committee shall have authority to select such eligible players on representative teams as they in their absolute discretion shall think fit. (Vide Clauses 19.3 and 21.1)

3.1.9   A 'Golf Club' shall mean a Club, howsoever constituted which comprises:

    3.1.9.1 an Affiliated Golf Club (affiliated to the Union) or

    3.1.9.2 an Affiliated Ladies' Golf Club (affiliated to the ILGU) or

    3.1.9.3 an Affiliated Golf and an Affiliated Ladies' Golf Club or

    3.1.9.4 any one of Sub-Sub-Clauses 3.1.9.1, 3.1.9.2 or 3.1.9.3, together with other categories of membership of the 'Golf Club' (e.g. Country, Five Day, Junior etc.)

and which complies with the Rules of Amateur Status as approved by the Royal and Ancient Golf Club of St Andrews.

3.1.10 An 'Affiliated Golf Club' shall mean a group of male golfers who, having been formed into a Club, have the use of a particular course or links over which to play the game of golf, and which group shall have been admitted to Membership of the Union.

3.1.11 A 'University Club' shall mean a group of male golfers each of whom is a student member of the same Irish University (or in the case of an Irish University having constituent Colleges, a member of the same constituent College) and who shall have joined together to play golf subject to the Rules governing their association for this purpose (which Rules shall have been approved by the Council) and each of whom is a member in respect of whom the Union's Subscription has been paid or a University Member of a Golf Club which has control over his handicap, and which group shall have been admitted to Membership of the Union and hereafter unless the context so admits or requires, shall be construed as an Affiliated Golf Club.

3.1.12 A 'College Club' shall mean a group of male golfers each of whom is a student of a particular Irish School or Irish College who shall have joined together to play golf subject to Rules governing their association for this purpose (which Rules shall have been approved by the Council) and who are permitted by a Golf Club to play golf on its course or links whether generally or at particular times, or permitted to play on a course or links provided by the School or College of which they are students, subject to the Provision that in the case of a course or links provided by their School or College as aforesaid, such course or links shall have been approved by the Provincial Council concerned, and which group shall have been admitted to Membership of the Union.

Provided always that if any School or College is situate partly in one Province and partly in another Province or if any question shall arise as to the Province in which any particular School or College is situate, the matter shall be referred to the Standing Committee by any Branch or any interested party whereupon the Standing Committee shall decide which Branch shall be entitled to exercise the functions aforesaid in regard to the Association of students formed in the School or College in question, and hereafter unless the context so admits or requires, shall be construed as an Affiliated Golf Club. No School or College Club is entitled to allocate official handicaps.

3.1.13 A 'Club' shall mean an 'Affiliated Golf Club', 'University Club' and 'College Club' as defined by Sub-Clauses 3.1.10, 3.1.11 and 3.1.12.

3.1.14 A 'Voting Member' is a voting member of an Affiliated Club on whom the Union Subscription and Provincial Levy have been or are being paid.

3.1.15 'Associate' shall mean 'The Irish Artisans' Golf Association'.

3.1.16 A 'Golfing Society' shall mean a group of golfers whose objects are to promote social intercourse through golf competition amongst its Members and where the word 'Society' appears herein without any qualification it shall mean a 'Golfing Society'. (Vide Clause 13.1)

3.1.17 'Bye-Laws' shall mean the Bye-Laws of the Union. (Vide Clause 39.1)

4. *Objects and Recognition*

4.1 The objects of the Union shall be:

4.1.1 To promote and administer the game of mens' amateur golf in Ireland in accordance with the Rules of Golf as approved by the Royal and Ancient Golf Club of St Andrews.

4.1.2 To arrange

4.1.2.1 Championships
4.1.2.2 Inter-Club Competitions
4.1.2.3 School and College Matches
4.1.2.4 Inter Provincial and International Matches
4.1.2.5 Such other Tournaments as may be deemed appropriate from time to time

4.1.3 To co-operate with the Royal and Ancient Golf Club of St Andrews, the Council of National Golf Unions, other National Golf Unions, International Golf Associations and kindred bodies.

4.1.4 To secure a uniform standard of handicapping in accordance with the Standard Scratch Score and Handicapping Scheme as prescribed by the Council of National Golf Unions.

4.1.5 To provide to Clubs advice and assistance (other than financial) in all matters appertaining to golf.

4.1.6 Generally to promote and foster the game in every way.

4.2 The Union recognises the Irish Ladies' Golf Union as the corresponding Governing Authority for Ladies' Amateur Golf in Ireland.

4.3 The Union recognises the Professional Golfers' Association (Irish Region) as the Governing Authority for Professional Golf in Ireland.

5. *Establishment of Branches*

5.1 A Branch of the Union is established in each of the four Provinces of Ireland.

6. *Control and Management of the Union*

6.1 The business of the Union shall be controlled and managed by the Council.

7. *Control and Management of a Branch*

7.1 The business of a Branch shall be controlled and managed by its Provincial Council, and be subject to the terms of Rules 16, 17 and 18 of this Constitution.

8. *Trustees*

8.1 All property of the Union shall vest in three Trustees who shall be appointed by the Council and who shall deal with the property of the Union as directed by resolution of the Council.

8.2 Each Trustee shall be entitled to attend any meeting of the Council in his capacity as Trustee but in such capacity shall not have a vote.

8.3 Each Trustee shall be indemnified by the Union against losses and expenses which he may incur or for which he may become liable by reason of his acting as Trustee.

8.4 The Council shall have power by resolution to remove from such Office any Trustee if the Council in its absolute discretion considers it to be necessary or desirable in the interests of the Union to do so.

8.5 If a vacancy should occur in the number of Trustees by removal, resignation or death, the number of Trustees shall be restored to three at the next meeting of the Council.

9. *Finance*

9.1 The Bank Account shall be kept in the name of the Union in such Bank or Banks as the Council may from time to time determine.

9.2 All cheques shall be signed by the Honorary Treasurer and the Honorary Secretary except if either of those officers is absent for an extended period when the President shall be a co-signatory.

9.3 The Council shall have absolute discretion as to all investments of Union funds which shall stand in the names of the Trustees of the Union.

9.4 The Honorary Treasurer of the Union shall:

9.4.1   Keep full and detailed accounts, books and records showing the financial affairs, receipts and disbursements of the Union.

9.4.2   Pay all properly incurred expenses.

9.4.3   Prepare a budget for the ensuing year and submit same to the Finance Committee for consideration prior to submission to the Council.

9.4.4   Carry out such other duties as are set out in the Duties and Terms of Reference of the Finance Committee.

9.5 Each Club which is a member of the Union shall, on application, be supplied with a copy of the Report of the Honorary Treasurer of the Union and a copy of the Statement of Accounts of the Union.

9.6 The Financial Year of the Union shall be decided by the Council.

10.   *Membership and Entitlement*

10.1 Membership of the Union shall be open only to a group of male amateur golfers, not less than twenty-five in number, who having been formed into a club with rules governing their association:

10.1.1   Own, have a lease of, a tenancy agreement for or a legal licence to use land, situate in Ireland, on which the game of golf may be played. The course or links must be fit for play to a standard which warrants the allocation of an official Standard Scratch Score and be approved as such by the Provincial Council concerned. A Provincial Council may, in its absolute discretion, allocate an SSS appropriate to the condition of the course or links. Where the applicant club has permission in writing to use the course or links of another affiliated club or of a public or private golf facility the provisions of this clause may be deemed to have been satisfied.

10.1.2   Have the use of a particular clubhouse or premises which will be the official address of the club.

10.1.3   Have a constitution which prescribes, inter alia, that the club will:

10.1.3.1 Accept and comply with the Rules of Golf as approved by the Royal and Ancient Golf Club of St Andrews.

10.1.3.2 Accept and comply with the Rules of Amateur Status as approved by the Royal and Ancient Golf Club of St Andrews.

10.1.3.3 Hold an Annual General Meeting before a specified date each year at which only members entitled to vote and non-voting observers if permitted are in attendance and at which all the Officials and members of the General Committee in whole or in a specified proportion are elected annually from amongst the voting members to administer the affairs of the club for the ensuing year. (Vide: Sub-Clause 3.1.14)

10.1.3.4 Authorise such Officers and general committee to have and to exercise all the powers of the general body of members in the election of all categories of member prescribed by its constitution up to the limitation decided by members at annual general meeting and to accept for consideration for election on its merits any properly submitted application for membership received from any male amateur golfer to the category applied for provided there is a vacancy therein.

10.1.4 Accept and apply the Standard Scratch Score and Handicapping Scheme prescribed by the Council of National Golf Unions and such rules thereunder as may require to be implemented from time to time by the Golfing Union of Ireland.

10.1.5 Undertake in writing:

10.1.5.1 to be bound by the Constitution of the Union
10.1.5.2 to conform with the Bye-Laws of the Union
10.1.5.3 to conform with the Bye-Laws of its Provincial Branch.

10.2 Subject to above and to Rule 11 of this Constitution any such group may be admitted to membership of the Union and become an Affiliated Golf Club (Vide Sub-Clause 3.1.10) subject to the proviso that:

10.2.1 A club shall be disqualified from membership of the Union if an owner of a proprietary facility or a limited company formed by or on behalf of such owner of the lands on which the course or links has or is being constructed subsequently exercises any control over the affairs of the club contrary to the provisions of Sub-Clauses 10.1.3 to 10.1.5 inclusive.

10.3 Where the voting members of a club incorporate into a limited company to administer the affairs of such club and in which voting members only have an equal interest, such club shall be entitled to apply for or retain membership of the Union. (Vide: Sub-Clause 3.1.14)

10.4 An Affiliated Golf Club as defined by Sub-Clause 3.1.10 shall be the only club entitled to submit notices of motion or recommendations for consideration to an Annual Meeting of the Branch of its Province or to nominate the delegate or delegates from amongst its voting members to attend or vote at such Branch Annual Meeting. (Vide: Sub-Clause 3.1.14)

10.5 The Associate member shall consist of groups of male golfers each group of which is permitted by an affiliated golf club to play the game of golf at specified times over its course or links, and shall comply with the provisions of Sub-Sub-Clauses 10.1.5.1 and 10.1.5.2.

10.6 The Associate member shall not be entitled to representation on the Council or to take part in any of the control and management of the Union.

10.7 No club or the Associate member shall be permitted to make any amendments to its constitution which would be in conflict with the constitution of the Union.

10.8 All proposed alterations or amendments in the constitution of an affiliated club or the Associate member must be submitted to the Union for approval.

11.   *Admission to Membership*

11.1 Admission to membership of the Union as a club shall be conditional on the following:

    11.1.1 The applicant can only be a club as provided in Rule 10.

    11.1.2 The application for membership must have been considered and approved by a majority of the members of the club present and voting at a special general meeting convened for that purpose.

    11.1.3 The application must be on the form prescribed by the Bye-Laws of the Union which may be obtained from the Union or from a Provincial Branch Office.

    11.1.4 The completed form must be accompanied by:

        11.1.4.1 The appropriate fee fixed from time to time by the Council. (This fee will be returned if the application is not granted.)

        11.1.4.2 A copy of the constitution of the applicant.

        11.1.4.3 The completed and signed undertaking as prescribed in Sub-Clause 10.1.5. (Note: When applying for the form prescribed by Sub-Clause 11.1.3 the applicant should obtain advice on all aspects of the application.)

        11.1.4.4 A copy of the appropriate extract from the Minutes of the Special General Meeting held in compliance with Sub-Clause 11.1.2 signed by the Chairman thereat.

11.2 The documents and fee detailed in Sub-Clause 11.1.4 must be forwarded to the office of the Provincial Branch in whose Province the course or links the subject of the application is situate.

11.3 The Provincial Council of the Branch concerned shall:

    11.3.1 Forward the constitution to Union headquarters so that the Council can satisfy itself that the constitution complies with the Constitution of the Union.

    11.3.2 Appoint not less than two of its members to visit and inspect the course or links to ascertain if it warrants the allocation of a Standard Scratch Score.

11.4 On being satisfied that the application is in order and is not contrary to the best interests of another club having use of the same facilities and having received a favourable report from its inspection group and being advised that the constitution is acceptable to the Union, the Provincial Council shall notify the applicant that it is prepared to grant affiliation forthwith.

11.5 When affiliated a club:

    11.5.1 Shall be allocated a Standard Scratch Rating.

    11.5.2 May allot official handicaps to its members.

    11.5.3 May enter Union and Branch team events and its members may enter Union and Branch individual championships and tournaments and compete in open competitions run by other affiliated clubs.

11.6 The Council will formally ratify the decision of the Provincial Council at its next meeting and the club will be entered in the Union records as an Affiliated Golf Club.

11.7 If a Provincial Council rules that an applicant should not be admitted to membership it shall notify its decision in writing as soon as possible to the applicant which may appeal to the Council whereupon the matter shall be placed on the agenda for the next meeting of the Council for its consideration and the applicant shall be notified in writing of the time and place at which the meeting is to be held and shall be invited to send not more than three representatives to such meeting.

Having considered the report of the Provincial Council and such representations as shall have been made orally or in writing on behalf of the applicant, the Council shall either confirm the ruling of the Provincial Council or reverse such ruling and admit the applicant to membership subject, if the Council considers necessary, to such conditions as the Council may impose.

11.8 Any club applying for membership of the Union makes its application in the knowledge that it has no entitlement to membership and must accept that, if its application is refused by the Provincial Council, the outcome of the appeal to the Council is final.

11.9 Every applicant shall be furnished with a copy of the Constitution and Bye-Laws of the Union when being issued with the form of application for membership.

12. *Suspension or Termination of Membership*

12.1 Of an Affiliated Golf Club

12.1.1 In the case of infringement by a Club of any of the provisions of this Constitution or breach of any of the Rules or any of the Bye-Laws (including non-compliance with any of the provisions of Clause 10.1 (Sub-Clauses 10.1.1 to 10.1.4) hereof or breach of any undertaking given thereunder) such Club shall be liable to have its membership suspended for a stated period or have its membership terminated.

12.1.2 In the case of a Club which permits a breach of the Rules of Amateur Status as approved by the Royal and Ancient Golf Club of St Andrews to take place on its course or links or in its Clubhouse, the Club shall be held to have infringed the provisions of this Constitution and shall be liable to have its membership suspended for a stated period or to have its membership terminated.

12.1.3 Every allegation of such infringement committed or permitted by a Club which shall have been reported to the General Secretary of the Union shall be referred by him to the Provincial Council having control of the Club against which such allegation shall have been made. If such direction is given, the Provincial Council to which the matter has been referred shall, as soon as practicable, hold an enquiry into the allegation made having given reasonable notice to the club concerned of the time and place at which such enquiry shall be held, and shall give such Club every facility to appear and to be represented by not more than three representatives at such enquiry and shall afford every reasonable facility to such Club to refute the allegation made.

12.1.4 If, after holding such enquiry as aforesaid, the Provincial Council considers that the allegation is well founded it shall notify its finding in writing as soon as practicable to the Club concerned and shall submit its report to the Standing Committee and the Club concerned shall, as from the date of such notification, be suspended until the meeting of the Council held next after the expiration of one calendar month from the date of such notification as aforesaid. The report of the Provincial Council on such enquiry shall be placed on the Agenda of such meeting for consideration by the Council and the Club shall be notified in writing of the time and place at which such meeting is to be held and shall be invited to send not more than three representatives to such meeting.

12.1.5 Having considered the report of the Provincial Council and such representations as shall have been made orally or in writing on behalf of the Club, the Council shall either confirm or set aside the finding of the Provincial Council. If such finding is confirmed the Council may impose an additional period of suspension on the offending Club or permanently terminate such Club's membership as it shall consider appropriate in the circumstances.

12.1.6 Any Club whose membership is terminated shall forfeit all rights to any property of the Union.

12.2 Of the Associate Member

12.2.1 In the case of infringement by the Associate Member of any of the provisions of this Constitution or breach of any of the Rules or any of the Bye-Laws (including non-compliance with any of the provisions of Sub-Clauses 10.1.1 to 10.1.4 and Sub-Sub-Clauses 10.1.5.1 and 10.1.5.2 or breach of any undertaking given thereunder) the Associate Member shall be liable to have its Associate Membership suspended for a stated period or have its Associate Membership terminated.

12.2.2 If the Associate Member permits any breach of the Rules of Amateur Status as approved by the Royal and Ancient Golf Club of St Andrews the Associate Member shall be held to have infringed the provisions of this Constitution and shall be liable to have its membership suspended for a stated period or have its membership terminated.

12.2.3 Every allegation of such infringement or non-compliance or breach by the Associate Member which shall have been reported to the General Secretary of the Union shall be referred by him to the Standing Committee which Committee shall, as soon as practicable, hold an enquiry into the allegation made, having given reasonable notice to the Associate Member of the time and place at which such enquiry shall be held, and shall give the Associate Member every facility to appear and be represented by not more than three representatives at such enquiry and shall afford every reasonable facility to the Associate Member to refute the allegation made.

12.2.4 If, after holding such enquiry as aforesaid, the Standing Committee considers that the allegation is well founded, it shall notify its finding in writing as soon as practicable to the Associate Member which shall, as from the date of such notification, be suspended until the meeting of the Council held next after the expiration of one calendar month from the date of such notification as aforesaid, when the report of the Standing Committee on such enquiry shall be placed on the agenda of such meeting for consideration by the Council and the Associate Member shall be notified in writing of the time and place at which such meeting is to be held and shall be invited to send not more than three representatives to such meeting. Having considered the report of the Standing Committee and such representations as shall have been made orally or in writing on behalf of the Associate Member, the Council shall either confirm or set aside the finding of the Standing Committee, and if such finding is confirmed, may impose an additional period of suspension on the Associate Member or permanently terminate such Associate Membership as it shall consider appropriate in the circumstances.

13. *Golfing Societies*

13.1 The Union may accept golfing societies annually for registration which:

13.1.1 Comprise not less than fifteen members.

13.1.2 Complete the 'Application for Registration' form obtainable from the Union and which includes undertakings prescribed by the Constitution and the Bye-Laws of the Union.

13.2 No golfing society shall be eligible for or entitled to affiliation to the Union.

13.3 Male members of societies who are members of affiliated clubs shall, at all times, comply with the Standard Scratch Score and Handicapping Scheme as prescribed by the Council of National Golf Unions and any Regulations laid down by the Union in relation thereto.

13.4 At all times acceptance or refusal to grant facilities to societies, registered or otherwise, shall be the sole prerogative of the club concerned provided that such club conforms strictly with the Constitution and Bye-Laws of the Union.

13.5 It shall be the responsibility of any club granting facilities to any golfing society, registered or otherwise, to ensure that the provisions of this Rule and of Bye-Law 15 are strictly adhered to. Should any infringement be reported to a Provincial Council or to the Union that a club has not complied with this Clause the matter shall be dealt with under Rule 12 (Suspension or Termination or Membership)

13.6 Any golfing society which fails to adhere to its assurances and undertakings shall have its name immediately removed from the Union Society Register and Affiliated Clubs shall be notified accordingly.

14. *Union Subscriptions and Provincial Levies*

14.1 The amount of annual subscription payable to the Union by Affiliated Clubs, University Clubs, College Clubs, and the Associate Member shall be decided from time to time by the Council.

14.2 The amount of annual Levy payable to each Provincial Branch by Clubs in its Province shall be decided from time to time by each Branch at its Annual Branch Meeting.

14.3 The method of payment of the above subscription and levies and the penalty for delay or failure in paying same shall be as prescribed by the Bye-Laws.

15.   *Provincial Branches*

15.1 Each Branch shall be composed of the Clubs, as defined in Sub-Clause 3.1.13, in its Province. Each Club shall be entitled to delegate representation in its Branch in proportion to the number of members in respect of whom the Union Subscriptions and Provincial Levies have been paid as stated in its last annual return to the Union and according to the following scale:

15.1.1 up to 100 Members   One Delegate

15.1.2 from 101 to 200 Members   Two Delegates

15.1.3 from 201 to 400 Members   Three Delegates

15.1.4 401 Members and over   Four Delegates

15.2 No Club shall be entitled to more than four delegates.

15.3 A newly affiliated Club shall be entitled to delegate representation of one until such time as it can comply with the requirements of Clause 15.1 when the entitlement to the appropriate number of delegates shall apply.

15.4 Each University Club and College Club shall be entitled to delegate representation of one on the Branch exercising control over such University Club or College Club as the case may be.

15.5 The Associate Member shall not be entitled to delegate representation.

16.   *Provincial Councils*

16.1 The affairs of each Branch shall be administered by a Provincial Council which shall have control of each Club in its Province and be responsible to the Council for the supervision and control of the playing of the game of golf by the members of each Club in its Province.

16.2 The Officers of each Branch shall be the Chairman, the Hon. Secretary, the Hon. Treasurer and (if appointed) the Hon. Match and Handicapping Secretary of the Branch for the time being. The offices of Hon. Secretary and Hon. Treasurer may be held by the same person.

16.3 The Officers of each Branch, with the Immediate Past Chairman if eligible under the provisions of Sub-Clause 18.1.1, the Branch delegates to the Council and other elected members, including Honorary Delegates, elected under Clause 26.6 hereof, shall constitute the Provincial Council of the Branch.

16.4 A Provincial Council may appoint Sub-Committees for the more efficient discharge of business, but such Sub-Committees shall have no power to commit the Branch to any expenditure or liability without the direct authority of the Provincial Council previously obtained.

16.5 A Provincial Council shall have power by resolution to remove from office any Officer of the Branch or member of the Provincial Council or any member of any of its Sub-Committees if the Provincial Council, in its absolute discretion, considers it necessary or desirable in the interest of the Branch or the Union to do so.

16.6 If a vacancy shall occur by removal, resignation, death or any other cause, the Provincial Council may appoint a substitute to fill the vacancy until the next Annual or Extraordinary Branch General Meeting.

16.7 The Officers of a Branch may, as required, appoint a substitute for such of its Officers or Delegates to the Council as shall be unable to attend a Council Meeting.

16.8 At all meetings of a Provincial Council the Branch Chairman shall preside. In his absence an Officer of the Branch shall preside. Should none of these persons be present the meeting shall be abandoned.

16.9 Each Provincial Council shall have the right to:

16.9.1 Nominate an Honorary Delegate to the Council as provided for in Clause 26.3.

16.9.2 Elect Honorary Delegates to their Provincial Councils as provided for in Clause 26.6.

17. *Notification of Delegates to Branch Annual Meetings*

17.1 Each Club shall forward in writing to the Honorary Secretary of the Branch the names of its delegates prior to each Annual Meeting.

18. *Branch Meetings*

18.1 Each Branch shall hold a Branch Annual Meeting not later than 30 November in each year at which the following elections shall take place, and each Branch, by its Bye-Laws, shall prescribe the order of these elections:

18.1.1 A Branch Chairman who shall retire annually but shall be eligible for re-election. Unless he be elected to the office of President-Elect of the Union, each Chairman, on the expiration of his term of office, shall become, ex-officio, a member of the Provincial Council without voting rights, during the term of office of his immediate successor.

18.1.2 A Branch Honorary Secretary who shall retire annually, be eligible for re-election, act as Honorary Secretary to the Provincial Council and act as Honorary Treasurer unless the Provincial Council appoints a separate officer as Honorary Treasurer.

18.1.3 Such other Officer or Officers as the Branch by its Bye-Laws may prescribe.

18.1.4 Delegates to the Council as provided in Sub-Clause 19.1.6.

18.1.5 Ordinary members of the Provincial Council, the number and composition of which shall be prescribed by the Bye-Laws of the Branch.

18.1.6 An Honorary Auditor who shall retire annually but shall be eligible for re-election or the appointment of an Auditor who shall be eligible for reappointment.

18.2 At all meetings of the Branch the Branch Chairman shall preside. In his absence an Officer of the Branch shall preside. Should none of these persons be present the meeting shall be abandoned.

18.3 Each Branch shall, if required, hold such other Meetings as provided for in Clause 29.3.

18.4 Voting shall be in accordance with the appropriate provisions of Rule 24.

18.5 Notice of Branch Meetings shall be in accordance with the provisions of Rule 32.

19. *The Central Council*

19.1 The Council shall consist of:

19.1.1 The President of the Union, who shall be elected by the Council and shall hold office for a period not exceeding one year.

19.1.2 The President-Elect of the Union, who shall be elected by the Council and shall hold office for a period not exceeding one year and who may be elected President of the Union on the termination of the office of his immediate predecessor referred to in Sub-Clause 19.1.1.

19.1.3 The Honorary Secretary of the Union, who shall be elected by the Council and shall retire annually and shall be eligible for re-election. During his term of office he shall act as Honorary Secretary to the Council and shall submit a report to the Annual General Meeting.

19.1.4 The Honorary Treasurer of the Union, who shall be elected by the Council and shall retire annually but shall be eligible for re-election. During his term of office he shall carry out the duties prescribed in Rule 9 of this Constitution.

19.1.5 Subject to the requirements of Sub-Clause 19.1.6 the Chairman, Honorary Secretary or delegates elected by the Branch.

19.1.6 The total number of representatives from each Branch, inclusive of those named in Sub-Clause 16.2 will be:

Leinster	:	six
Ulster	:	six
Munster	:	five
Connacht	:	four

19.2 The Council shall appoint Auditors who shall retire annually and be eligible for re-appointment.

19.3 The Council may appoint Committees and Sub-Committees for the more efficient discharge of business, but such Committees shall have no power to commit the Union to any expenditure or liability without the direct authority of the Standing Committee previously obtained. (Vide sub-Clauses 3.1.8 and 21.1)

19.4 The Council shall employ a Secretary and such additional staff as it may deem necessary for the achievement of the objects of the Union.

19.5 The Council shall have power by resolution to remove from office any officer or delegate to the Council or any representative appointed by the Council or any member of any of its Committees or Sub-Committees if the Council in its absolute discretion considers it either necessary or desirable in the interest of the Union to do so.

19.6 If a vacancy should occur by resignation, removal or death the Provincial Council concerned shall nominate a replacement for election by the Central Council subject to the following provisos:

19.6.1 If the Office of the President becomes vacant it shall be filled by the President-Elect for the remainder of the year whilst he retains the office of President-Elect.

19.6.2 If the Office of President-Elect becomes vacant the Provincial Council concerned will nominate a replacement for election by the Council and the President-Elect thus appointed shall act in that capacity for the remainder of the year.

19.6.3 If the Office of Honorary Secretary or Honorary Treasurer becomes vacant the Standing Committee shall nominate an acting replacement who will serve in that capacity until the next Annual General Meeting of the Council.

19.7 At all meetings of the Council the President shall preside. In his absence the President-Elect shall preside. If neither the President nor the President-Elect is present an Officer of the Union shall preside. Should none of these persons be present the meeting shall be abandoned.

20. *Union Officers and Vice-Presidents*

20.1 The Officers of the Union shall be the President, the President-Elect, the Honorary Secretary and the Honorary Treasurer of the Union for the time being.

20.2 The Chairman of each Branch shall be a Vice-President of the Union.

21. *Committees and Sub-Committees*

21.1 The Standing, Finance, International Selection, Championship and Tournament, Junior Golf and such other Committees or Sub-Committees as shall be elected from time to time by the Council shall operate in compliance with the Duties and Terms of Reference of each Committee or Sub-Committee as set out in Appendix 1 (Vide Sub-Clauses 3.1.7, 3.1.8 and Clause 19.3).

22. *Representatives to Other Bodies*

22.1 The Council shall elect annually representatives to the undermentioned bodies as follows:

22.1.1 Council of National Golf Unions — two representatives from amongst those entitled to attend meetings of the Council. Maximum service in this capacity is eight years with the proviso that a two year overlap is maintained.

22.1.2 European Golf Association — one representative from amongst those entitled to attend meetings of the Council — except in a year when no representative is on the Executive Committee when there will be two representatives from amongst those entitled to attend meetings of the Council. Maximum service in this capacity is four years.

22.1.3 Sports Turf Research Institute — one representative. Maximum service in this capacity is four years.

22.1.4 Golf Foundation — one representative. Maximum service in this capacity is four years.

22.1.5 Greenkeeping Research Training Committee — one representative. Maximum service in this capacity is four years.

22.1.6 Council of National Golf Unions SSS & Handicapping Committee — two representatives one of whom shall be from amongst those entitled to attend meetings of the Council. Maximum service in this capacity is four years with the proviso that a two year overlap is maintained.

22.1.7 Such other Bodies as may come into being from time to time.

22.2 The above elections shall be in addition to the appointment of any member of the Union to Executive Office in any of the above mentioned Bodies.

22.3 If, for any reason whatsoever, any representative so appointed is unable to attend any Meeting of these organisations, the Honorary Secretary shall consult with the President regarding a Substitute.

22.4 Nominations of representatives to outside bodies or organisations involved in the promotion or administration of golf must have the approval of the Council subject to Rule 40.

23. *Eligibility for Election*

23.1 No person, unless he conforms with the 'Rules of Amateur Status' for the time being approved by the Royal and Ancient Golf Club of St Andrews and is a member for whom the Union and Provincial Subscriptions have been paid by the Club in the current year or is an Honorary Member of that Club shall be eligible to represent such Club at a Branch Meeting or to be elected a Branch Officer, a member of the Provincial Council, an Officer of the Union or a member of the Council.

If any question arises as to whether or not a person conforms with the said Rules the matter shall be referred to the Standing Committee whose decision thereon shall be final.

23.2 Captains

23.2.1 The Senior International Captain shall be elected annually by the Council at the Annual General Meeting and shall not serve in that capacity for more than three years.

When electing the Senior International Captain the Council shall give preference to a person who has been selected to represent Ireland as a Senior International player or his Province as a Senior Interprovincial player.

23.2.2 The Youths' Captain shall be elected annually by the Council at the Annual General Meeting and shall not serve in that capacity for more than three years.

He must be or have been a Category One Golfer.

23.2.3 The Boys' Captain shall be elected annually by the Council at the Annual General Meeting and shall not serve in that capacity for more than three years.

He must be or have been a Category One Golfer.

24.   *Voting Rights*

24.1 At Council Meetings

24.1.1 Only the Officers of the Union, Branch Chairmen and Branch Honorary Secretaries together with the Delegates of each Branch shall have a right to vote.

24.1.2 At the Annual General Meeting, on the election of the President the then Immediate Past President shall cease to have the right to vote and the candidate for the office of President-Elect shall not have the right to vote until elected to that Office.

24.2 At Branch Meetings

24.2.1 Every member of the Provincial Council and each duly appointed delegate of the Clubs in the Province shall have the right to vote.

24.2.2 Unless he be an outgoing member of a Provincial Council or a duly appointed delegate of a Club, a candidate for election shall not have a vote until after his election unless he is taking the place of a delegate of his own Club. An outgoing Officer or member of a Provincial Council shall not have a vote after the election of his successor unless he is taking the place of a delegate of his own Club elected in his stead at a Branch Meeting.

24.3 At Committee Meetings

24.3.1 At each meeting of the Standing Committee only the Officers of the Union, the Immediate Past President and the Chairman and Honorary Secretary of each Branch shall have the right to vote. A substitute representative for an Officer of the Union, a Branch Chairman or Honorary Secretary shall have the right to vote.

24.3.2 At each meeting of other Committees each member (including co-opted members) shall have the right to vote.

24.4 Except as provided in Rule 37 hereof where voting at elections is by secret ballot, the Chairman of each meeting of the Council or Branch Annual Meeting and at each Committee or Sub-Committee of the Union or Branch shall, in addition to his delib-erative vote, have and shall exercise the casting vote.

25. *Honorary Vice-Presidents*

25.1 Each Past President of the Union shall be an Honorary Vice-President and shall be entitled to attend all meetings of the Council at the expense of the Union, but shall not be entitled to vote in such capacity.

25.2 An Honorary Vice-President may be elected as a member of a Committee or Sub-Committee or as a representative of the Council and if so elected shall be entitled to vote at all meetings of the Committee, Sub-Committee or Body to which he has been elected and he shall be entitled to expenses as provide for in the Bye-Laws.

26. *Honorary Delegates*

26.1 Provided that the Immediate Past Chairman of a Provincial Council is not nominated for and elected to the office of President-Elect of the Union or does not hold some other Honorary Office on the Council, he shall be an Honorary Delegate to the Council, without voting power, and shall remain an Honorary Delegate until his successor in the office of Provincial Chairman shall cease to be such Chairman.

26.2 The Council shall have power to propose and elect, as an Honorary Delegate to the Council, without voting power, one person who, in its opinion, has given outstanding service to the administration of amateur golf in Ireland. Such Honorary Delegate shall hold office until the next Statutory meeting at which such election forms part of the Agenda.

26.3 The Standing Committee shall have power to elect as Honorary Delegates to the Council, without voting powers, not more than one person from each Province who, in its opinion, has given outstanding service to amateur golf in Ireland. Each person so elected must have been proposed by a Provincial Council and shall hold office until the next statutory meeting at which such election forms part of the Agenda.

26.4 An Honorary Delegate may attend any meeting of the Council.

26.5 An Honorary Delegate may be elected by the Council as a member of a Committee or Sub-Committee or as a representative of the Council and if so appointed shall be entitled to vote at all meetings of the Committee, Sub-Committee or Body to which he has been elected and he shall be entitled to expenses as provided for in the Bye-Laws.

26.6 Each Provincial Council shall have power to elect not more than six persons as Honorary Delegates to its Council without voting rights.

27. *Annual General Meeting of the Council*

27.1 The Council shall hold an Annual General Meeting not later than the last day of February in each year on a date to be fixed by the Officers of the Union to deal with the following business:

27.1.1 To receive

27.1.1.1 Minutes of the previous General Meeting and of Meetings of the Standing Committee and other Committees and Sub-Committees (except Selection Committees) held since the last General Meeting.

27.1.1.2 The President's Statement

27.1.1.3 The Honorary Secretary's Report

27.1.1.4 The Honorary Treasurer's Report and Statement of Accounts

27.1.1.5 The Annual Reports and Statements of Account of the Branches

27.1.1.6 Notices of Motion as provided in Rule 34

27.1.1.7 Reports and recommendations from Committees and Sub-Committees

27.1.1.8 Reports and/or Minutes of Bodies listed in Clause 22.1 and/or reports of Representatives thereto.

27.1.2 To elect

27.1.2.1 The President

27.1.2.2 The President-Elect

27.1.2.3 The Honorary Secretary

27.1.2.4 The Honorary Treasurer

27.1.2.5 The Senior International Team Captain (Vide Clause 23.2)

27.1.2.6 Four members to the Senior International Selection Committee

27.1.2.7 The Convenor of Junior Golf

27.1.2.8 The Youths' Team Captain (Vide Clause 23.2)

27.1.2.9 The Boys' Team Captain (Vide Clause 23.2)

27.1.2.10 One member from each Province as members of the Junior Selection Committee.

27.1.3 To appoint

27.2.3.1 Representatives as provided in Clause 22.1 hereof

27.1.3.2 Auditors

27.1.3.3 Committees and Sub-Committees as required.

27.2 All nominations for the foregoing elections or appointments must be made in writing to the General Secretary of the Union not less than twenty-eight days prior to the date of the Meeting.

27.3 Nominations may be made by a Provincial Council, by the Standing Committee or by two persons entitled to be present and vote at the Annual General Meeting.

27.4 To fix dates and venues for Union Events.

27.5 To consider and decide on:

27.5.1 Any proposed Notice of Motion to amend this Constitution or other notices of motion all of which must be made in writing to the General Secretary of the Union not less than twenty eight-days prior to the date of the meeting.

27.5.2 Any other relevant business submitted verbally by any member of the Council, or to defer it for further consideration by a future meeting.

27.5.3 Correspondence (if any).

28. *Ordinary General Meeting of the Council*

28.1 The Council may hold an Ordinary General Meeting not later than the last day of October in each year on a date to be fixed by the Officers of the Union to deal with the following business:

28.1.1 To receive

28.1.1.1 Minutes of the previous Annual General Meeting and of meetings of the Standing Committee and other Committees and Sub-Committees (except Selection Committee) held since the last Annual General Meeting.

28.1.1.2 A financial report from the Honorary Treasurer including a report on the forecast outcome of the current financial year and a budget for approval of the income and expenditure for the forthcoming financial year.

28.1.1.3 Notices of Motion as provided in Rule 34

28.1.1.4 Reports from Team Captains

28.1.1.5 Reports and/or Minutes of Bodies listed in Clause 22.1 and/or reports of Representatives thereto.

28.1.2 To consider and decide on

28.1.2.1 Points submitted by the Standing Committee, Provincial Councils, or other Committees or individual members of Council for discussion

28.1.2.2 Any Notice of Motion to amend this Constitution or other notice of motion all of which must be made in writing to the General Secretary of the Union not less than twenty-eight days prior to the date of the meeting.

28.1.2.3 Any other relevant business submitted verbally by any Member of the Council or to defer it for further consideration by a future meeting.

28.1.2.4 Correspondence (if any).

29. *Special General Meeting of the Council or of a Branch*

29.1 The Council or a Branch shall hold a Special General Meeting as required.

29.2 A special meeting of the Council may be called at the request of two Officers of the Union or at the request of any two Provincial Councils stating the business to be considered. Such meeting shall be convened in accordance with Clause 31.1.

29.3 Special meetings of a Branch may be called at the request of two Officers of the Branch or of a combination of clubs in the Province entitled to be represented by at least twenty-one delegates at a meeting of the Branch. Such meeting shall be convened in accordance with Clause 31.3.

29.4 At least three days notice shall be given of a Special Meeting. (Vide Clause 32.4)

29.5 The time and place at which such meeting is to be held shall be clearly stated on such notice and such notice shall also set forth the nature of the business proposed to be transacted thereat. This business only can be considered at such meeting.

30. *Attendance at Meetings*

30.1 The following persons only shall be entitled to attend meetings of the Council:

30.1.1 Officers of the Union

30.1.2 Trustees

30.1.3 Honorary Vice-Presidents

30.1.4 Representatives of Provincial Councils as specified in Sub-Clause 19.1.6

30.1.5 Candidates designate for Office on the Council

30.1.6 Honorary Delegates

30.1.7 General Secretary and Provincial Secretaries

30.1.8 Each person, Club or Associate member entitled by virtue of this Constitution and these Rules and Bye-Laws to appear, or to be heard, before the Council. In such cases, such person, Club or Associate Member or his or its representatives shall only be entitled to be present when the matter with which he or it is concerned is being enquired into.

31. *Convening of Meetings*

31.1 Each meeting of the Council and Standing Committee shall be convened by the President or Honorary Secretary.

Notice for such meetings shall be issued by the General Secretary or, in his absence, by such Officer as directed by the President or Honorary Secretary.

31.2 Each meeting of Union Sub-Committees shall be convened by the appointed Convenor, the President or the Honorary Secretary. Notice for such meetings (except meetings of Selection Committees) shall be issued by the General Secretary or, in his absence, by such Officer, by the relevant Convenor, the President or the Honorary Secretary.

Meetings of Selection Committees shall be convened by the Chairman appointed under Rule 21.

31.3 Each meeting of a Branch or Provincial Council shall be convened by the Branch Chairman.

Notice of such meeting shall be issued by the Branch Honorary Secretary or Secretary or other Branch Officer as directed by the Chairman.

31.4 Each meeting of a Branch Sub-Committee shall be convened by the relevant Convenor appointed under Branch Bye-Laws.

Notice for such meetings shall be issued by the Branch Honorary Secretary or Secretary or other Branch Officer as directed by the relevant Convenor.

32. *Notice of Council Meetings and Branch General Meetings*

32.1 Fourteen days notice shall be given to each person entitled to attend or be represented at each meeting of the Council and each Branch General Meeting and every such Notice shall be accompanied by the Agenda of the business to be transacted. Such notice shall clearly state the time at which and the place where such meeting is to be held.

32.2 If, however, in his opinion any business to be dealt with at a Special Meeting is urgent, the President of the Union or the Chairman of a Branch, as the case may be, may direct that less than fourteen days notice of a meeting be given but in no case shall less than three days notice be given.

33. *Quorum*

33.1 At each meeting of the Council nine persons, including an Officer present and entitled to vote, shall form a quorum.

33.2 At each meeting of a Branch eighteen persons present and entitled to vote, one of whom shall be an Officer of the Branch, and of the other seventeen at least one duly appointed delegate from five different Clubs in the Province shall form a quorum.

33.3 At each meeting of a Union Committee or Sub-Committee the quorum shall be as set out in the Duties and Terms of Reference.

34. *Notices of Motion*

34.1 Every motion to be proposed at a Council Meeting shall be proposed by the Standing Committee, a Provincial Council or by two persons entitled to be present and to vote at such Council Meeting and notice thereof must be given in writing so as to reach the General Secretary of the Union not less than twenty-eight days prior to such meeting.

34.2 Every motion to be proposed at a Branch Meeting shall be submitted by the Provincial Council of the Branch, a Club in that Branch or two persons entitled to be present and to vote at such Branch Meeting and the notice thereof must be given in writing so as to reach the Honorary Secretary or Secretary of the Branch not less than twenty-eight days prior to such meeting.

In order for the Notice of Motion to be considered each motion shall be proposed and seconded by two persons entitled to be present and to vote at such Branch Meeting.

34.3 Every motion to be proposed at a Branch Meeting which could be deemed to be of National relevance shall be circulated by the Provincial Council which received the motion to the other three Provincial Councils in time for inclusion on the Agenda for their Branch Annual Meetings.

35. *Notification of Branch Officers and Delegates and Requirements for Meetings of Council*

35.1 Each Branch Honorary Secretary or Secretary shall forward to the General Secretary of the Union not later than fourteen days after the Annual Meeting of Delegates:

35.1.1 The respective names and addresses of Branch Officers and Delegates to the Council

35.1.2 Details of all Notices of Motion being submitted by the Branch to the Council

35.1.3 A copy of the Annual Report of the Branch submitted to and passed at the Branch Annual Meeting

35.1.4 A copy of the Statement of Accounts of the Branch adopted at the Branch Annual Meeting.

35.2 Each Branch Honorary Secretary or Secretary shall forward to the General Secretary of the Union not later than twenty-eight days after the Branch Annual Meeting a copy of the Minutes of the Branch Annual Meeting and of each Special Meeting of the Branch held since the last Annual Meeting of the Council.

36. *Voting (Excepting Elections)*

36.1 Each decision at every meeting of the Council, Branch Annual Meeting, Provincial Council or any of their Committees or Sub-Committees shall be taken by a show of hands unless a poll is demanded or the Chairman of the Meeting shall otherwise direct, when the voting shall be by secret ballot and the Chairman shall appoint scrutineers from amongst those present.

36.2 A simple majority of those present using their franchise shall in all cases decide unless otherwise prescribed.

37. *Voting at Elections*

37.1 At all meetings of the Council, Branch Annual Meetings and Provincial Councils or at any meeting of their Committees or Sub-Committees the following voting procedure shall operate at elections:

37.1.1 One or more candidates for an equal number of vacancies.

The Chairman shall declare such candidate or candidates elected.

37.1.2 Two candidates for one vacancy.

Voting shall be by secret ballot and the candidate receiving the majority of votes of those present using their franchise shall be declared elected.

37.1.3 Three or more candidates for one vacancy.

Voting shall be by secret ballot and the candidate receiving the majority of votes of those present using their franchise shall be declared elected. Should no candidate receive such majority the candidate receiving the least number of votes shall be eliminated and a further ballot or ballots taken under the same conditions until only two candidates remain and a final ballot shall then be taken in compliance with Sub-Clause 37.1.2.

37.1.4 In all other cases where there are a greater number of candidates for election than there are vacancies to be filled voting shall be by secret ballot and the candidates receiving the greater number of votes to fill such vacancies shall be declared elected.

37.2 A simple majority shall, in all cases, decide unless otherwise prescribed.

37.3 The Chairman shall appoint not less than two persons attending the meeting to act as scrutineers.

37.4 Any voting paper containing a lesser number or a greater number of votes than there are vacancies to be filled shall be invalid.

37.5 In the event of a tie either for election or elimination there shall be a further secret ballot for those tieing in accordance with sub-Clause 37.1. If still a tie the matter shall be decided by lot.

37.6 Unless it is otherwise prescribed elections and co-options shall be effective until the next statutory meeting at which such elections form part of the Agenda.

38. *Alteration of Constitution or Rules*

38.1 To amend or add to any of the provisions hereof, either by way of addition, alteration, repeal or otherwise howsoever, the consent of at least two-thirds of the members of the Council present using their franchise shall be required.

38.2 Any motion to amend the Constitution must be proposed in accordance with Clause 34.1.

39. *Bye-Laws*

39.1 The Council shall have power from time to time to make such Bye-Laws as it considers necessary and to alter and repeal the same.

39.2 A Branch shall have power from time to time to make Bye-Laws governing the Clubs and their members in its Province but every such Bye-Law shall be subject to ratification by the Council.

40.

Decisions

40.1 Provided that it is not in contravention of a decision of Central Council, the President is empowered to make day by day decisions on matters which require urgent attention.

APPENDIX VI
Section 20

Details of Clubs represented at the inaugural meeting of the Leinster Branch, 9 January 1913

Bray — J.H. Maher and G. Price; Clontarf — I.J. Moore and Rev. J.L. Morrow; Dublin University — J.H. McCarter; Greenore — M. Mahon and W.C. Pickman; Greystones — J. Greenway; Hermitage — M.A. White; The Island — J.H. Barrington and J.R. Blood; Killiney — C. Andrews and J.M. Aston; Malahide — E. Manders; Milltown — F.E. Davies and E.J. Walsh; Portmarnock — B.A. Morrison, G.T. Power and J. Sheehan; Rathfarnham — J. Breaky; Royal Dublin — C. Barcroft, A.J. Crowe and J. Sealy; Skerries — J.A. Denning; Stillorgan Park — C. Haughton and A.B. Orr.

Rev. J.L. Morrow (Union Honorary Secretary) was invited to chair the meeting at which the following appointments were made:

Branch Chairman and Vice-President of the GUI: Beamish A. Morrison (Portmarnock); Branch Honorary Secretary: George Price (Bray); Provincial delegates to the Central Council: C. Barcroft (Royal Dublin), A. Digges (Carlow), A.B. Orr (Stillorgan Park) and E.J. Walsh (Milltown).

APPENDIX VII
Section 1

Results of the first Open Professional Tournament held in Ireland at the Royal County Club, Portrush on 12, 13 and 14 September 1895

RESULTS OF FIRST ROUND

G. Fulford (Hoylake)	beat	A. Brown (Dublin)	4 and 3
J. Logan (Portrush)	w.o.	David McEwan (Formby)	Scr.
Harry Vardon (Bury)	beat	Andrew Kilcardy (St Andrews)	5 and 4
Hugh Kilcardy (St Andrews)	beat	H. McGee (Portrush)	5 and 4
Ben Sayers (North Berwick)	beat	Jack White (Suffolk)	4 and 3
Hugh Henry (Portrush)	beat	A.C. Day (Belfast)	at 21st
W.H. Booth (Beckenham)	w.o.	P. McEwan (Formby)	Scr.
D. Brown (Malvern)	beat	H. Redman (Bradford)	3 and 2
David Herd (Bradford)	beat	J. Jones (Hoylake)	5 and 4
John Yonde (Hoylake)	beat	J. McGowan (Portrush)	3 and 2
P. Rainford (Hoylake)	beat	Chris Day (Greenisland)	2 and 1
J. McNeill (Portrush)	beat	J. Harvey (Portrush)	6 and 5
George Lowe (St Anne's)	w.o.	Douglas McEwan (Musselburgh)	Scr.
James McKenna (Lahinch)	beat	Samuel Jones (Fleetwood)	2 and 1
Alexander Herd (Huddersfield)	beat	William Toogood (Eltham)	5 and 4
William Fernie (Troon)	beat	P. Paxton (Tooting)	4 and 3

RESULTS OF SECOND ROUND

Fulford	beat	Logan	6 and 4
Vardon	beat	Kilcardy	5 and 3
Sayers	beat	Henry	Rtd
Brown	beat	Booth	2 and 1
D. Herd	beat	Yonde	Rtd
Rainford	beat	McNeill	2 and 1
Lowe	beat	McKenna	4 and 2
A. Herd	beat	Fernie	2 and 1

RESULTS OF THIRD ROUND

Vardon	beat	Fulford	2 and 1
Brown	beat	Sayers	1 hole
D. Herd	beat	Rainford	2 and 1
A. Herd	beat	Lowe	4 and 3

RESULTS OF SEMI-FINAL

Vardon	beat	Brown	2 holes
A. Herd	beat	D. Herd	4 and 3

RESULT OF FINAL

Herd	beat	Vardon	1 hole

(Referee: Thomas Gilroy)

APPENDIX VII
Section 2

The Irish Professional Golfers' Association

I. Constitution of Association

Name
1. The name of the Association shall be 'The Irish Professional Golfers' Association'.

Objects
2. The objects of the Association shall be the promotion of Professional play; the holding of Professional Meetings; the institution of a Benevolent Fund; the provision of an Agency to assist Professionals to obtain situations; and such other objects of a like nature as may be determined from time to time by the Association.

Members
3. Professional Golfers and Assistants in Ireland shall be eligible for election as members. The Association may elect Honorary Members as may be considered expedient, and these shall be eligible to vote and act on the management of the Association.

Management
4. The Association at its Annual Meeting shall elect a Captain, Honorary Treasurer, Honorary Secretary and a Committee of 8 (4 from Northern and 4 from Southern Clubs); half of each section shall be amateurs, approved of by the G.U.I. The President of the G.U.I. shall be President of the Association; the Vice-Presidents of the G.U.I. and such other prominent golfers as may be appointed by the Association shall be Vice-Presidents.

Annual General Meeting
5. The Association shall hold an Annual General Meeting in connection with the Irish Professional Championship. A fortnight's notice of the time, place and business to be transacted shall be given to each member. The business of the Annual Meeting shall be to elect the Officers and Committee, consider, and if approved, adopt the Committee's Annual Report and Statement of Accounts, and transact such business as may be necessary.

Special General Meetings
6. Special General Meetings shall be called, when necessary, by the Committee, or on a requisition signed by members representing five different Clubs, stating precisely the resolution to be proposed. The Secretary shall issue notices of any Special Meeting fourteen days previous to the Meeting, and no business save that set out in the notice, shall be transacted. All business decided at a Special Meeting shall be subject to confirmation at the Annual Meeting.

Quorum
7. At the Annual or Special General Meetings of the Association twelve shall form a Quorum. At the Meetings of the Committee three shall form a Quorum.

Election of Members
8. Honorary Members shall be elected by the Association; Ordinary Members by the Committee.

Subscriptions
9. The Annual Subscriptions for Professionals shall be 10s. per annum, and for Assistants, without a vote, 5s. The Secretary shall notify members of their election and thereafter when their subscriptions become due. In the case of a candidate for membership the first subscription must accompany the nomination paper. Subscriptions become payable on the 1st January in each year thereafter. Any member whose Annual Subscription is three months in arrear shall cease to be a member of the Association.

Life Members
10. Anyone interested in the Association (not being a Professional Golfer) may become a Life Member on payment of a donation of five guineas or an Annual Subscription of one guinea.

2. Benevolent Fund

1. The Fund shall be supported by Grants from the General Fund, by Special Donations and Annual Subscriptions.

2. All monies of the Fund shall be kept separate from the General Fund and Trustees shall be appointed.

3. The objects of the Fund shall be to relieve deserving members of the Association by:

   (a) Grants, temporary or permanent.

   (b) Assisting in cases of sickness, accident, death and interments.

   (c) Assisting, in pressing cases, to prevent the lapsing of Life, Accident or other Policies.

   (d) Providing, should funds ultimately permit, small annuities to the aged and incapacitated.

   (e) And allowances to Widows and Orphans.

4. The Fund shall be administered by a Committee elected ad hoc of which Committee the Captain, Secretary and Treasurer of the Association shall be *Ex-Officio* Members. Three shall form a Quorum. The Committee shall meet from time to time as occasion may require.

5. No member shall be eligible to receive assistance during the first year of his membership. All applications for relief must be made in writing.

6. Emergency cases, arising in intervals between Meetings of the Committee, may be dealt with temporarily by a Quorum of two but such action shall be forthwith reported to the Committee, and the sum so granted shall not exceed £2.

7. All cheques shall be signed by a member of the Committee, and countersigned by the Treasurer.

8. Accounts of the Fund shall be submitted annually to the members of the Association.

9. None of these Rules shall be altered, amended, rescinded or added to without the consent of at least two-thirds of those present at an Ordinary General Meeting or at a Special General Meeting called for the purpose.

10. All investments of monies of the Fund must be made in the names of the Trustees.

APPENDIX VIII

Section 1

The first Open Championship of Ireland, played at Portmarnock Golf Club on 17, 18 and 19 August 1927

COMPETITOR	CLUB	1st Rnd	2nd Rnd	3rd Rnd	4th Rnd	TOTAL	PRIZE FUND £
G. Duncan	Wentworth	76	80	82	74	312	
Winner of Gold Medal and first prize of:							150.
T.H. Cotton	Langley Park	73	73	86	81	313	90.
J. Smith	Wentworth	73	74	77	91	315	60.
A. Compston	Wolverhampton	75	75	82	85	317	50.
W. Nolan	Portmarnock	72	83	83	81	319	40.
E. Ray	Oxhey	75	77	88	80	320	40.
G. Murdock	Kilmarnock	76	78	80	86	320	40.
T. Barber	Cavendish	78	76	87	81	322	35.
J.H. Taylor	Royal Mid-Surrey	76	76	85	85	322	35.
M. O'Neill	Wrekin	79	80	83	81	323	25.
A.J. Young	Sonning	79	78	85	81	323	25.
E.R. Whitcombe	Mayrac Park	76	81	82	84	323	25.
C.A. Whitcombe	Crew's Hill	80	74	84	85	323	25.
W. Melhorn	USA	75	82	85	82	324	25.
H.C. Jolly	Foxgrove	77	80	85	83	325	22.10.0.
C. Sayner	Birkdale	74	77	84	90	325	22.10.0.
W.H. Davies	Prenton	81	82	81	82	326	20.
H. McNeill	Royal Portrush	81	76	86	84	327	6.13.4.
P.G. O'Connor	Woodbrook	77	75	89	86	327	6.13.4.
R. Vickers	Heswall	80	73	85	89	327	6.13.4.
							750. 0.0.

COMPETITOR	CLUB	1st Rnd	2nd Rnd	3rd Rnd	4th Rnd	TOTAL
Major C.O. Hezlet	Royal Portrush	77	79	85	87	328
Winner of Silver Plate as Leading Amateur.						
J. Hamill	Bangor	81	79	84	85	329
M. McDermot	Hermitage	80	81	90	79	330
S. Ball	Heaton Park	80	77	89	85	331
J. Sullivan	Bray	84	77	87	84	332
S. Fairweather	Malone	82	79	87	86	334
W.G. Oke	Fulwell	77	85	85	87	334
W.H. Ball	Lancaster	80	78	85	91	334
G. Falkender	Bramley	81	81	89	84	335
D. Murray	Skerries	79	80	89	87	335
L. Wallace	Royal Belfast	80	84	83	88	335
J. Ockenden	Hanger Hill	80	81	86	88	335
H. Large	Grange Park	78	83	86	88	335
A. Herd	Moor Park	78	80	87	90	335
C.W. Pope	Fortwilliam	79	85	89	83	336
H. Vardon	South Herts	83	80	85	88	336
J. O'Neill	Howth	83	77	87	89	336
A.J. Isherwood	Warrington	82	82	92	81	337
E.S. Douglas	Robinhood	81	79	92	85	337
H.C. Kinch	Woodcote Park	87	73	88	89	337
C.H. Corlett	Dorset	75	82	91	90	338
J. Bailey	Douglas	79	84	84	91	338
F. Smyth	Royal Dublin	76	85	86	91	338
J. Bond	Hillside	78	82	95	84	339
Mr R. McConnell	Royal Portrush	83	81	90	85	339
J. Sheridan	Unattached	83	77	93	86	339
P.H. Rodgers	Old St Anne's	78	83	89	89	339
E.T. Large	Keighley	80	81	91	88	340
Mr A. Lowe	Malone	80	84	94	86	344
D. Thwaites	Cork	84	81	93	88	346
Mr J. Gorry	Cill-Dara	84	80	91	93	348
Mr E.F. Kilduff	Milltown	78	86	104	99	367
L. Nabholtz	USA	77	81	91	Rtd	
L. Holland	Gerrard's Cross	80	81	90	Rtd	
Dr J.D. MacCormack	Hermitage	79	86	87	Rtd	
C. Gray	Willington	85	80	90	Rtd	
A. Robertson	Royal County Down	81	82	93	Rtd	
W. Bee	Leasmore	80	83	96	Rtd	
F. Lloyd	Rhos-on-Sea	82	83	97	Rtd	
A.G. Havers	Coombe Hill	80	82	Rtd		

NON-QUALIFIERS

COMPETITOR	CLUB	1st Rnd	2nd Rnd
W.B. Fenton	Haggs Castle	86	80
W. Large	Fulwood Park	85	81
T. Shannon	Milltown	84	82
H. Higgins	Muskerry	83	83
D. Mahony	Elm Park	86	81
P. O'Hare	Unattached	85	82
J. Gaffney	Lucan	82	85
J. Doran	Portmarnock	81	86
Mr C.H. West	Greystones	80	87
J. Martin	Newlands	86	82
J. Quinn	Clontarf	86	82
Mr A.W. Briscoe	Castlerea	85	83
Mr W.J. Carroll	Portmarnock	83	85
T. McGrath	Limerick	89	80
J. Mackie	Turnhouse	83	86
L. Skillen	Donaghadee	83	86
Mr N. Manley	Royal Dublin	82	87
Mr J.C. Timbey	Malone	82	87
Mr J.L. Crabbe	Foxrock	87	83
Mr C.W. Robertson	Portmarnock	86	84
W. Holley	Castle	85	85

COMPETITOR	CLUB	1st Rnd	2nd Rnd
E. Sinclair	Scotscraig	85	85
T. Travers	Dun Laoghaire	84	86
Mr J.O. Wisdom	Dublin University	83	87
P.P. Wynne	Chingford	83	87
J. Robson	Old Colyn	87	84
E. Bradshaw	Delgany	85	86
Mr H.M. Cairnes	Portmarnock	85	86
T. Trapp	Shirley Park	85	86
J. Redmond ·	USA	82	89
Mr F.P. McConnell	Royal Portrush	87	85
G.A. Pownall	Hindhead	83	89
J. Nugent	Malahide	89	84
A.E.J. Holton	Ladbrook Park	87	86
H.H. Fitzhugh	Knock	84	89
Mr C.A. Carroll	Dundalk	83	90
D. Higgins	Unattached	90	84
Mr D.Wilson Smyth	Malone	88	86
M. Bailey	Dundalk	85	89
P. Sawey	Carnalea	83	91
J. Barrett	Carrickmines	87	88
J. Murray	Unattached	87	88
T. Gaffney	Killiney	89	87
Major H.A. Boyd	Portmarnock	87	89
P. McKenna	Rathfarnham	87	89
T.E. Edgar	Newcastle United	87	90
W. McCavery	Royal County Down	87	90
Mr J.F. Stevenson	Malone	89	89
P. Neill	Foxrock	90	89
J. McKillop	Birr	91	89
Mr J.A. Neilan	Royal and Ancient	90	91
Mr W.A. Brown	Fortwilliam	90	92
W. Daly	Tralee	88	94
Mr W. Moran	Mid-Kent	91	92
Mr G.B. Kirway	Knott End and Fleetwood	88	98
Mr E.B. Tipping	Walton Heath	87	Rtd
W.E. MacNamara	Lahinch	89	Rtd
Mr C.S. Wallis	Bray	92	Rtd
W. Hanna	Rosslare	94	Rtd
G.R. Buckle	Edgbaston	Scr.	
R. Sheape	Perivale Park	Scr.	
J. McDowell	Turnberry	Scr.	
J. McCourt	County Sligo	Scr.	
A. Mitchell	Boxhill	Scr.	
T. Wilson	Little Hill	Scr.	

Subsidiary Prizes

Special 'Irish Times' prizes:

		£
1. Lowest score 1st round	W. Nolan (Portmarnock)	25
2. Lowest score 1st and 2nd rounds for age 45 and over	E. Ray (Oxhey)	25
3. Lowest score 3rd round	J. Smith (Wentworth)	25
4. Lowest score by Irish professional 1st and 2nd rounds	P.G. O'Connor (Woodbrook)	25

Special 'Irish Independent' Prizes:

1. Lowest score in any round	T.H. Cotton (Langley Park)	8.6.8.
	H.C. Kinch (Woodcote Park)	8.6.8.
	R. Vickers (Heswall)	8.6.8.
2. Lowest score 3rd and 4th rounds for age 45 and over	E. Ray (Oxhey)	25
3. Lowest score 4th round	G. Duncan (Westworth)	25
4. Lowest score by Irish professional 3rd and 4th rounds	W. Nolan (Portmarnock)	25

APPENDIX VIII
Section 2

Record of Venues, Winners, Runners-up and leading Amateurs in the Open Championship of Ireland

Date	Venue	Entry	Winner			Runner-up			Best Amateur	
1927	Portmarnock	126	Geo. Duncan			T. H. Cotton			C.O. Hezlet	
			Wentworth		312	Langley Park		313	Royal Portrush	328
1928	Newcastle	86	E.R. Whitcombe			A. Compston			A.W. Briscoe	
			Meyrick Park		288	Unattached		292	Castlerea	310
									J.D. MacCormack	
								Hermitage	310
			A. Mitchell						C.O. Hezlet	
			Private		309	Result of the play-off			Royal Portrush	316
			A. Compston			(1) A. Mitchell		150		
1929	Portmarnock	125	Coombe Hill		309	(2) A. Compston		152		
			Len Holland			(3) Len Holland		159		
			Gerrard's Cross		309					
1930	Portrush	80	C.A. Whitcombe			A. Mitchell			F.P. McConnell	
			Crews' Hill		289	Private		297	Royal Portrush	316
									H.S. Sheals	
									Balmoral	316
1931	Dollymount	131	E.W.H. Kenyon			W.H. Davies			W.J. Gill	
			West Lancs.		291	Wallasey		293	Sutton	302
1932	Cork	116	A.H. Padgham			W.H. Davies			J.D. MacCormack	
			Royal Ashdown Forest		283	Wallasey		284	Grange	295
1933	Malone	128	E.W.H. Kenyon			A.H. Padgham			J. Burke	
			West Lancs.		286	Royal Ashdown Forest		288	Lahinch	302
1934	Portmarnock	118	S. Easterbrook			W.H. Davies			J.C. Brown	
			Knowle		284	Wallasey		292	Waterford	294
1935	Newcastle	87	E.R. Whitcombe			R.A. Whitcombe			J.C. Brown	
			Meyrick Park (after tie)		292	Parkstone		292	Waterford	293
1936	Dollymount	134	R.A. Whitcombe			W.H. Davies			A.D. Locke	
			Parkstone		281	Wallasey		283	South Africa	287
1937	Portrush	109	Bert Gadd			Jas. Adams			J. Bruen Jr	
			West Cheshire		284	Royal Liverpool		285	Muskerry	292
1938	Portmarnock	111	A.D. Locke			T.H. Cotton			J. Bruen Jr	
			South Africa		292	Ashridge		293	Muskerry	304
1939	Newcastle	104	A. Lees			R.A. Whitcombe			J. Bruen Jr	
			Dore & Totley		287	Parkstone		289	Muskerry	296
1940–45	No Championship									
1946	Portmarnock	83	F. Daly			A.D. Locke			J.B. Carr	
			Balmoral		288	South Africa		292	Sutton	302
1947	Portrush	68	H. Bradshaw			F. Van Donck			S.M. McCready	
			Kilcroney		290	Belgium		292	Royal Portrush	309
1948	Portmarnock	123	Dai Rees	295		N.G. Von Nida			J.B. Carr	
			South Herts			Australia		297	Sutton	309
1949	Belvoir Park	107	H. Bradshaw			A.D. Locke			R. Pattinson	
			Kilcroney		286	South Africa		287	Flackwell Heath	306
1950	Dollymount	96	H.O. Pickworth			N.G. Von Nida			J.B. Carr	
			Australia		287	Australia		289	Sutton	292
						J. Panton				
						Glenbervie		289		
1951	No Championship									
1952	Belvoir Park	96	E. Browne			H. Weetman			J.B. Carr	
			Unattached		272	Croham Hurst		273	Sutton	284
1953	Championship Discontinued.									

APPENDIX IX

Section 1

Record of venues, Team Captains and results of Irish matches played from 1900 to 1931

Alphabetical code: (S) Singles only (A) 1 match halved (B) 2 matches halved (C) 3 matches halved

Unless otherwise stated, teams comprised 10 a side and matches were 5 Foursomes and 10 Singles.

Year	Venue	Captain	Code	Results of Matches
1900	Newcastle	H.E. Reade	S	Ireland lost to Scotland by 31 holes
	(12 a side)		S	Ireland beat England by 3 holes
1901	Dollymount	W.H. Boyd	S	Ireland lost to England by 32 holes
	(12 a side)		S	Ireland lost to Scotland by 18 holes
1902	Portrush	H.E. Reade	S	Ireland lost to Scotland by 3 holes
	(24 a side)		S	Ireland lost to England by 51 holes
1903	Portmarnock	H.M. Cairnes	S	Ireland lost to Scotland by 12 holes
	(18 a side)		S	Ireland lost to England by 4 holes
1904	Newcastle	H.M. Cairnes	S	Ireland lost to England by 12 holes
	(20 a side)		S	Ireland lost to Scotland by 12 holes
1905	Dollymount	H.M. Cairnes	S	Ireland beat Scotland by 41 holes
	(14 a side)		S	Ireland lost to England by 3 holes
1906	Portrush	H.A. Boyd	S A	Ireland 6 Scotland 17
	(24 a side)		S	Ireland 9 England 15
1913	Dollymount	H.M. Cairnes	C	Ireland 7 Wales 5
1923	Southerndown	C.O. Hezlet	S	Ireland 3 Midlands 6
	(9 a side)		S	Ireland 7 Wales 2
1924	Dollymount	J.F. Jamieson		Ireland 14 Wales 1
				Ireland 10 Midlands 5
1925	Hoylake	A. Lowe	A	Ireland and Wales 3 England 11
1925	Hollinwell	C.O. Hezlet		Ireland 7 Midlands 8
				Ireland 10 Wales 5
1926	No International Matches			
1927	Newcastle	C.O. Hezlet	A	Ireland 7 Scotland 7
1928	Troon	C.O. Hezlet		Ireland 4 Scotland 11
			A	Ireland 9 Wales 5
1928	Dollymount	R.M. McConnell	A	Ireland 7 England 7
				Ireland 7 Scotland 8
1929	Portrush	C.O. Hezlet		Ireland 7 Scotland 8
1929	Lytham	C.O. Hezlet	B	Ireland 5 England 8
1929	Harlech	C.O. Hezlet	B	Ireland 11 Wales 2
1929	St Andrews	G.N.C. Martin	A	Ireland 7 Scotland 7
1930	Dollymount	C.O. Hezlet	C	Ireland 9 Wales 3
1930	Portmarnock	C.O. Hezlet	C	Ireland 6 England 6
1931	Hoylake	C.O. Hezlet	A	Ireland 4 England 10
			B	Ireland 11 Wales 2
1931	Newcastle	D.W. Smyth	B	Ireland 6 Scotland 7

APPENDIX IX
Section 2

A record of all players who participated in the Home International Championship from 1900 to 1931

NAME	CLUB	YEARS
Allen, H.T.	Royal Co. Down	1904 (E)(S), 1906 (S)(E)
Allison, A.C.	Royal Portrush	1928 (E), 1929 (S)
Babington, A.B.	North West	1903 (E)(S), 1904 (E)(S), 1905 (E)(S), 1906 (E)(S), 1913 (W)
Barcroft, C.	Royal Dublin	1901 (E)(S), 1904 (S)(E)
Bell, H.E.	Portmarnock	1930 (W)
Boyd, H.A.	Portmarnock	1900 (S)(E), 1903 (E), 1904 (S)(E), 1905 (S)(E), 1906 (S)(E), 1913 (W), 1923 (M)(W)
Boyd, J.J.	Portmarnock	1903 (S)
Boyd, W.H.	Portmarnock	1900 (S)(E), 1901 (E)(S), 1902 (S)(E)
Brice, M.J.	Royal Co. Down	1900 (S)
Briscoe, A.W.	Castlerea	1928 (E), 1929 (S)(E)(W), 1930 (S)(W)(E), 1931 (E)(W)(S)
Burke, J.	Lahinch	1929 (E)(W), 1930 (S)(W)(E), 1931 (E)(W)(S)
Cairnes, H.M.	Portmarnock	1901 (E)(S), 1902 (E)(S), 1903 (S)(E), 1904 (S)(E), 1905 (E)(S), 1913 (W) 1925 (M)(W), 1927 (S)
Cameron, D.J.	Helen's Bay	1900 (S)(E)
Campbell, W.	Co. Sligo	1906 (S)(E)
Carr, J.R.	Royal Co. Down	1930 (W), 1931 (E)(W)
Carroll, C.A.	Greenore	1924 (W)(M)
Carroll, W.J.	Greenore	1913 (W), 1923 (M)(W), 1924 (W)(M), 1925 (E)(M)(W), 1929 (S)
Christie, D.M.	Royal Dublin	1901 (E)(S), 1905 (S)(E)
Clarke, G.S.	Royal Co. Down	1900 (S)(E) 1902 (S)(E) 1904 (S)(E)
Crabbe, J.L.	Foxrock	1925 (M)(W), 1927 (S), 1928 (S)
Crowley, M.	Portmarnock	1928 (E), 1929 (S)(E)(W), 1930 (S)(E), 1931 (E)(W)(S)
Crymble, P.T.	Ormeau	1902 (S)(E)
Cuming, F.E.	Royal Portrush	1906 (E)(S)
Davies, F.E.	Portmarnock	1906 (S)(E), 1923 (M)(W)
Dickson, F.G.	North West	1903 (E)(S), 1904 (E)(S), 1905 (S)(E), 1906 (5)
Dillon, E.B.	Cork	1902 (E)(S)
Dillon, W.H.	Royal Dublin	1903 (S)(E)
Dudgeon, A.F.	Royal Dublin	1903 (E)(S)
Elkins, W.E.	Greenore	1906 (S)(E)
Ffrench, W.	Rosslare	1929 (S)
Figgis, E.K.	Royal Dublin	1901 (E)(S)
Gibson, E.	Royal Dublin	1905 (E)(S)
Gill, W.J.	Sutton	1931 (W)
Glenawly, Vis,	Royal Co. Down	1902 (E)(S), 1904 (S)(E), 1906 (S)(E)
Goldfinch, J.H.	Royal Co. Down	1904 (E)(S), 1906 (E)(S)
Gore-Little, J.F.	East Brighton	1904 (E)(S)
Healy, T.M.	Royal Dublin	1931 (E)(S)
Henderson, J.	Royal Belfast	1923 (M)(W)
Henry, R.G.N.	Portmarnock	1903 (S)(E), 1905 (E)
Hezlett, C.O.	Royal Portrush	1923 (M)(W), 1925 (M)(W), 1927 (S), 1928 (S), 1929 (S)(E)(W), 1930 (S)(E), 1931 (E)(W)(S)
Hezlet, R.K.	Royal Portrush	1906 (S)(E)
Hogg, A.G.	Royal Portrush	1902 (S)(E)
Hunter, A.R.	Greenore	1904 (S)(E)
Hurley, J.J.	Machrinanish	1906 (E)(S)
Inglis, C.C.	Portmarnock	1901 (E)(S), 1903 (S)(E), 1904 (S)(E)
Inglis, J.J.	Portmarnock	1901 (E)(S), 1902 (E)(S)
Jamieson, J.F.	Portmarnock	1913 (W), 1924 (W)(M)
Jennings, T.	Cork	1902 (S)(E), 1903 (E)(S)
Johnston, T.W.G.	Royal Lytham & St Anne's	1929 (E)
Kelly, G.W.	Portmarnock	1903 (E)(S)
Kilduff, A.J.	Milltown	1928 (S)
Kilduff, E.F.	Milltown	1928 (S)
LaTouche, A.D.	Sutton	1904 (S)(E)
Long, G.B.	Royal Portrush	1906 (S)(E)
Lowe, A.	Malone	1924 (W)(M), 1925 (E), 1927 (S), 1928 (S)(E)
Lyttle, J.F.S.	Brighton	1902 (S)(E)
MacCormack, J.D.	Grange	1913 (W), 1924 (W)(M), 1927 (S), 1928 (S)(E)
MacGreagh, W.J.	Royal Co. Down	1902 (E)(S)
McConnell, F.P.	Royal Portrush	1929 (E)(W), 1930 (S)(W)(E), 1931 (E)(W)(S)
McConnell, R.M.	Royal Portrush	1924 (W)(M), 1925 (E)(M)(W), 1927 (S), 1928 (S)(E), 1929 (S)(W), 1930 (W)(E) 1931 (E)(W)(S)
McConnell, W.G.	Portmarnock	1925 (E)
McEvoy, J.	Ormeau	1900 (S)(E), 1902 (S)(E)
Manly, N.	Royal Dublin	1924 (W)(M), 1927 (S), 1928 (S)(E)
Marron, J.N.	Dun Laoghaire	1925 (M)(W)
Martin, G.N.C.	Royal Portrush	1923 (M)(W), 1925 (M)(W), 1928 (S) 1929 (S)(E)(W), 1930 (W)
Meldon, W.D.	Portmarnock	1900 (S)(E)
Meredith, R.P.	Royal Dublin	1901 (E)(S)
Moore, C.S.	Royal Dublin	1902 (S)(E), 1903 (S)(E), 1905 (S)(E)
Moore, G.J.	Beau Desert	1928 (E), 1929 (W)
Moore, J.S.	Royal Portrush	1903 (E)(S)
Morgan, D.	West Derby	1904 (E)
Morrissey, E.	Royal Co. Down	1904 (S)(E)

NAME	CLUB	YEARS
Munn, E.M.	North West	1913 (W), 1923 (M)(W), 1924 (W)(M)
Munn, L.O.	North West	1913 (W)
Newett, A.C.	Malone	1904 (E)(S)
Newett, F.B.	Malone	1900 (S)(E), 1902 (S)(E), 1904 (S)
O'Brien, B.	Greenisland	1902 (S)(E), 1906 (S)(E)
O'Donnell, T.F.	Greenore	1904 (S), 1905 (E)(S), 1906 (S)(E)
Parke, J.C.	Dublin University	1906 (S)(E)
Patterson, A.H.	Monkstown	1913 (W)
Pickman, W.C.	Portmarnock	1900 (S)(E), 1901 (E)(S), 1903 (S)(E) 1905 (E)(S), 1906 (E)(S)
Prentice, J.A.W.	Portobello	1903 (S)
Reade, H.E.	Royal Belfast	1900 (E), 1902 (E)(S), 1904 (E)(S) 1906 (S)(E), 1913 (W)
Reade, P.E.	Royal Belfast	1902 (E)(S)
Richardson, A.R.	North Hants	1906 (E)(S)
Richardson, J.H.	Royal Co. Down	1900 (S)(E)
Robertson, C.W.	Portmarnack	1930 (S)(W)
Ross, A.P.	Portmarnock	1903 (S)(E)
Royston, F.	Ormeau	1902 (E)
Saunderson, A.	Royal Dublin	1903 (E)(S), 1904 (E)(S)
Shaw, R.	Dublin University	1903 (E)
Sheals, H.S.	Balmoral	1929 (E)(W), 1930 (S)(E), 1931 (E)
Simcox, R.	Cork	1930 (S)(W), 1931 (E)(W)(S)
Smith, D.W.	Royal Co. Down	1923 (M)(W), 1927 (S), 1930 (W)(E), 1931 (S)

NAME	CLUB	YEARS
Soulby, D.E.	Fortwilliam	1929 (S)(E)(W), 1930 (S)(W)(E)
Sparrow, H.K.	Royal Portrush	1925 (M)(W)
Spiller, E.F.	North West	1924 (W)(M), 1928 (S)(E), 1929 (S)
Stevenson, J.F.	Malone	1923 (M)(W), 1924 (W)(M), 1925 (E), 1927 (S)
Stuart, C.E.	Royal Portrush	1902 (E)(S), 1904 (E)(S), 1905 (S)(E)
Stuart, F.A.K.	Royal Portrush	1902 (S)(E), 1905 (S)(E), 1906 (E)(S)
Timbey, J.C.	Malone	1927 (S), 1928 (S), 1931 (W)(S)
Tipping, E.B.	Glasgow University	1906 (S)(E)
Todd, J.P.	Portmarnock	1905 (E)(S)
Todd, W.F.	Portmarnock	1900 (S)(E), 1901 (E)(S), 1903 (E)(S)
Upton, A.J.	Royal Dublin	1902 (S)
Waddell, G.	Royal Portrush	1925 (M)(W)
Watson, P.M.	Royal Dublin	1901 (E)(S)
Webb, W.H.	Royal Portrush	1902 (E)(S)
Werner, L.E.J.	Royal Dublin	1925 (M)(W)
West, C.H.	Greystones	1928 (E)
White, J.N.	Knock	1902 (S)(E), 1906 (S)(E)
Wilson, C.W.	Greenore	1906 (S)(E)
Wilson, D.M.	Royal Dublin	1900 (S)(E), 1901 (E)(S), 1902 (E)(S), 1903 (S)(E), 1904 (E)(S), 1906 (S)(E)
Woodside, J.	Royal Belfast	1902 (E)(S)
Young, R.S.	Worsley	1906 (E)(S)

APPENDIX IX

Section 3

The first Quadrangular International Matches at Troon (Ayrshire) 2, 3 and 5 August 1932

England	v.		Ireland	
	Foursomes			
E.W. Fiddian (Stourbridge)			J. Burke (Lahinch)	
H.G. Bentley (Hesketh)	½		M. Crowley (Portmarnock)	½
L.G. Crawley (Brancepeth Castle)			J.D. MacCormack (Grange)	
A.S. Bradshaw (Stoke Poges) (4/3)	1		A.W. Briscoe (Castlerea)	0
S. Lunt (Moseley)			R. Simcox (Douglas)	
A.S. Newey (Moseley) (2/1)	1		H.S. Sheals (Malone)	0
C.D. Gray (Royal Mid-Surrey)			W.J. Gill (Portmarnock)	
R. Straker (Sunningdale) (3/2)	1		W.J. Carroll (Portmarnock)	0
E.R. Tipple (Addington Palace)			W.F. Ffrench (Rosslare)	
T.H. Bowman (Seacroft) (4/2)	1		C.H. West (Greystones)	0

England	v.	Ireland	
	Singles		
Fiddian (8/7)	1	Burke	0
Crawley (5/3)	1	Crowley	0
Bentley	0	MacCormack (1 hole)	1
Lunt (3/2)	1	Briscoe	0
Bradshaw	½	Simcox	½
Gray (2/1)	1	Sheals	0
Newey (4/2)	1	Gill	0
Straker (2/1)	1	Ffrench	0
Tipple (5/4)	1	Carroll	0
Bowman	0	West (3/2)	1

Result: England beat Ireland by 11 Matches to 2. 2 Matches halved.

Scotland	v.	Wales	
	Foursomes		
E.A. McRuvie (Leven Thistle)		H.R. Howell (Glamorgan)	
J.E. Dawson (Troon)	0	R.M. de Lloyd (Aberystwyth)(3/2)	1
S.L. McKinley (Alexandra)		A.D. Evans (Brecon)	
W. Tulloch (Cathkin Braes) (5/4)	1	F.R. Maliphant (Ashburnham)	0
R.B. Denholm (Bass Rock)		J.L. Black (Rhos-on-Sea)	
J. Nelson Smith(Earlsferry Thistle)	0	S.B. Roberts (Prestatyn) (2 holes)	1
J. Brock (Troon)		D.H. Lewis (Cardiff)	
D. McBride (Glasgow) (3/1)	1	J.E. Newman (Wrexham)	0
J.B. Stevenson (Troon St Meddans)		D. Hall (Bangor)	
A.J. Jamieson (Pollock) (6/4)	1	N.E. Jacob (Dinas Powis)	0
	Singles		
McRuvie	0	Howell (2/1)	1
McKinley (7/6)	1	De Lloyd	0
Jamieson	0	Black (2/1)	1
Tulloch	0	Evans (4/3)	1
Dawson (1 hole)	1	Roberts	0
Denholm (3/1)	1	Maliphant	0
Nelson Smith (5/4)	1	Lewis	0
Brock (2/1)	1	Hall	0
McBride	0	Jacob (4/3)	1
Stevenson (5/4)	1	Newman	0

Result: Scotland beat Wales by 9 matches to 6.

Scotland	v.	Ireland	
	Foursomes		
E. McRuvie		J. Burke	
J. E. Dawson (4/2)	1	R. Simcox	0
J. McLean (Hayston)		J. D. MacCormack	
J. Brock (2 holes)	1	A. W. Briscoe	0
S. L. McKinley		H. S. Sheals	
W. Tulloch (6/5)	1	H. E. Bell	0
R. B. Denholm		W. J. Gill	
J. Nelson Smith	0	C. H. West (2/1)	1
J. Wilson (Prestwick St Nicholas)		W. Carroll	
A. Jamieson (2/1)	1	W. F. Ffrench	0
	Singles		
McLean	0	Burke (1 hole)	1
McRuvie (1 hole)	1	MacCormack	0
Wilson	0	Briscoe (2 holes)	1
McKinley (7/5)	1	Simcox	0
Jamieson (1 hole)	1	Sheals	0
Tulloch (5/3)	1	Gill	0
Dawson (3/1)	1	Ffrench	0
Denholm (2/1)	1	West	0
Nelson Smith	0	Carroll (2/1)	1
Brock (2 holes)	1	Bell	0

Result: Scotland beat Ireland by 11 matches to 4.

England		v.	Wales	
		Foursomes		
E.W. Fiddian			H.R. Howell	
H.G. Bentley (4/3)	1		R.M. de Lloyd	0
L.G. Crawley			A.D. Evans	
A.S. Bradshaw (3/2)	1		F.R. Maliphant	0
S. Lunt			J.L. Black	
A.S. Newey	0		S.B. Roberts (1 hole)	1
C.D. Gray			N.E. Jacob	
R. Straker (1 hole)	1		T. Emerson (Radyr)	0
J.R. Smith(Royal Lytham & St Anne's)			D. Hall	
T.H. Bowman	½		R. Chapman (Newport)	½

	Singles		
Fiddian	0	Howell (2 holes)	1
Crawley (4/3)	1	de Lloyd	0
Bentley (3/1)	1	Black	0
Lunt (2 holes)	1	Evans	0
Bradshaw (3/2)	1	Roberts	0
Gray (3/2)	1	Maliphant	0
Newey	0	Jacob (4/3)	1
Straker (2 holes)	1	Hall	0
Bowman (3/1)	1	Chapman	0
Smith (1 hole)	1	Emerson	0

Result: England beat Wales by 11 matches to 3. 1 match halved.

Ireland		v.	Wales	
		Foursomes		
J. Burke			H.R. Howell	
R. Simcox (5/3)	1		R.M. de Lloyd	0
J.D. MacCormack			J.L. Black	
A.W. Briscoe (1 hole)	1		S.B. Roberts	0
W.J. Gill			A.D. Evans	
C.E. West (1 hole)	1		F.R. Maliphant	0
T.C. Nicholson (Queen's Univ.)			N.E. Jacob	
H.S. Sheals (2/1)	1		D.H. Lewis	0
W.F. Ffrench			D. Hall	
H.E. Bell	0		R. Chapman (3/2)	1

	Singles		
Burke	0	Howell (2/1)	1
MacCormack	0	Black (2/1)	1
Briscoe (5/4)	1	Evans	0
Simcox (3/2)	1	Roberts	0
Sheals	0	De Lloyd (3/2)	1
Gill	½	Jacobs	½
Ffrench (1 hole)	1	Maliphant	0
West (5/4)	1	Lewis	0
Bell (4/2)	1	Hall	0
Nicholson	0	Chapman (3/2)	1

Result: Ireland beat Wales by 9 matches to 5. 1 match halved.

Scotland		v.	England	
		Foursomes		
W. Tulloch			E. Fiddian	
S.L. McKinley	½		H.G. Bentley	½
E.A. McRuvie			W.L. Hartley (Chislehurst)	
J.E. Dawson (4/3)	1		L.G. Crawley	0
J. McLean			S: Lunt	
J. Brock	½		A.S. Newey	½
J. B. Stevenson			A.S. Bradshaw	
A. Jamieson	½		E.R. Tipple	½
R.B. Denholm			C.D. Gray	
J. Nelson Smith	0		R. Straker (2/1)	1

Scotland		v.	England	
		Singles		
McRuvie	½		Fiddian	½
McKinley	½		Hartley	½
McLean (1 hole)	1		Crawley	0
Tulloch	0		Bentley (4/3)	1
Jamieson	½		Lunt	··
Dawson (3/2)	1		Bradshaw	0
Denholm (2/1)	1		Gray	0
Brock	0		Newey (2/1)	1
Stevenson	0		Straker (5/4)	1
Nelson Smith (3/2)	1		Tipple	0

Result: Scotland beat England by 5 matches to 4. 6 matches halved.

SUMMARY OF RESULTS
Scotland beat Wales, beat Ireland, beat England;
England beat Ireland, beat Wales, lost to Scotland;
Ireland lost to England, lost to Scotland, beat Wales;
Wales lost to Scotland, lost to England, lost to Ireland.

APPENDIX IX

Section 4

Record of venues, Team Captains and results of Irish matches played from 1932 to 1990

Alphabetical code: (A) 1 match halved (B) 2 matches halved (C) 3 matches halved (D) 4 matches halved (E) 5 matches halved

Year	Venue	Captain	Code	Results of Matches			
1932	Troon	John Burke	B	Ireland	2	England	11
				Ireland	4	Scotland	11
			A	Ireland	9	Wales	5
1933	Newcastle	D. Wilson Smyth	E	Ireland	3	England	7
			B	Ireland	5	Scotland	8
				Ireland	11	Wales	4
1934	Porthcawl	John D. MacCormack	B	Ireland	11	England	4
			A	Ireland	4	Scotland	10
			B	Ireland	9	Wales	4
1935	Lytham	John D. MacCormack	C	Ireland	5	England	7
				Ireland	9	Scotland	6
			A	Ireland	11	Wales	3
1936	Prestwick	John D. MacCormack		Ireland	2	England	13
			B	Ireland	6	Scotland	7
			B	Ireland	10	Wales	3
1937	Portmarnock	John D. MacCormack		Ireland	7	England	8
			C	Ireland	4	Scotland	8
				Ireland	9	Wales	6
1938	Porthcawl	Redmond Simcox		Ireland	5	England	10
			A	Ireland	5	Scotland	9
				Ireland	9	Wales	6
1939–46	No International Matches						

Year	Venue	Captain	Code		Results of Matches		
1947	Liverpool	William O'Sullivan	D	Ireland	4	England	7
				Ireland	5	Scotland	10
			B	Ireland	11	Wales	2
1948	Muirfield	Charles O. Hezlet		Ireland	7	England	8
			A	Ireland	10	Scotland	4
			C	Ireland	11	Wales	1
1949	Portmarnock	Charles O. Hezlet	C	Ireland	9	Scotland	3
			A	Ireland	10	Wales	4
			B	Ireland	6	England	7
1950	Harlech	Charles O. Hezlet	C	Ireland	6	Scotland	6
			B	Ireland	9	Wales	4
				Ireland	8	England	7
1951	Lytham	Charles O. Hezlet	A	Ireland	8	Scotland	6
			B	Ireland	7	England	6
			C	Ireland	4	Wales	8
1952	Troon	Charles O. Hezlet	A	Ireland	7	England	7
			C	Ireland	6	Scotland	8
			A	Ireland	7	Wales	7
1953	Killarney	Charles O. Hezlet		Ireland	9	England	6
			A	Ireland	6	Wales	8
			C	Ireland	6	Scotland	6
1954	Porthcawl	William J. Gill	B	Ireland	8	Scotland	5
			D	Ireland	5	Wales	6
			A	Ireland	6	England	8
1955	Birkdale	William J. Gill	B	Ireland	8	Scotland	5
			A	Ireland	7	England	7
				Ireland	9	Wales	6
1956	Muirfield	William J. Gill		Ireland	4	England	11
			B	Ireland	6	Scotland	7
			B	Ireland	5	Wales	8
1957	Newcastle	Gerald H. Owens	A	Ireland	6	Wales	8
			B	Ireland	1	Scotland	12
			A	Ireland	4	England	10
1958	Porthcawl	Gerald H. Owens	A	Ireland	6	Scotland	8
			B	Ireland	5	England	8
				Ireland	7	Wales	8
1959	Lytham	Gerald H. Owens	B	Ireland	7	Wales	6
			A	Ireland	8	England	6
			E	Ireland	4	Scotland	6
1960	Turnberry	Cecil Ewing	B	Ireland	7	Scotland	6
				Ireland	7	England	8
				Ireland	12	Wales	3
1961	Portmarnock	Cecil Ewing	D	Ireland	6	England	5
				Ireland	11	Wales	4
			C	Ireland	2	Scotland	10
1962	Porthcawl	Cecil Ewing	A	Ireland	6	England	8
			A	Ireland	10	Wales	4
				Ireland	8	Scotland	7
1963	Lytham	Cecil Ewing		Ireland	10	Scotland	5
			C	Ireland	5	England	7
				Ireland	11	Wales	4
1964	Carnoustie	Cecil Ewing	C	Ireland	5	England	7
			B	Ireland	7	Scotland	6
				Ireland	10	Wales	5
1965	Portrush	Cecil Ewing	A	Ireland	9	Scotland	5
			A	Ireland	10	Wales	4
			A	Ireland	6	England	8
1966	Porthcawl	Cecil Ewing	A	Ireland	2	England	12
			A	Ireland	10	Scotland	4
			B	Ireland	8	Wales	5
1967	Ganton	Cecil Ewing	C	Ireland	5	Scotland	7
			A	Ireland	4	England	10
			A	Ireland	8	Wales	6
1968	Gullane	Cecil Ewing		Ireland	3	England	12
			B	Ireland	6	Scotland	7
				Ireland	9	Wales	6

The Golfing Union of Ireland

Year	Venue	Captain	Code	Results of Matches				
1969	Killarney	Cecil Ewing		Ireland	7	Scotland	8
			B	Ireland	7	Wales	6
			C	Ireland	6	England	6
1970	Porthcawl	William J.J. Ferguson		Ireland	5	Scotland	10
			A	Ireland	7	England	7
			B	Ireland	7	Wales	6
1971	Formby	William J.J. Ferguson	B	Ireland	2	England	11
			A	Ireland	6	Scotland	8
			A	Ireland	9	Wales	5
1972	Troon	William J.J. Ferguson	B	Ireland	6	England	7
			A	Ireland	6	Scotland	8
			B	Ireland	11	Wales	2
1973	Lytham	Brendan J. Scannell	E	Ireland	2	England	8
			A	Ireland	5	Scotland	9
			C	Ireland	9	Wales	3
1974	Harlech	Brendan J. Scannell	B	Ireland	3	England	10
			B	Ireland	5	Scotland	8
				Ireland	8	Wales	7
1975	Portmarnock	Brendan J. Scannell	A	Ireland	4	England	10
			B	Ireland	4	Scotland	9
			B	Ireland	8	Wales	5
1976	Muirfield	Laurence M. McCarthy	A	Ireland	4	England	10
			B	Ireland	4	Scotland	9
			B	Ireland	7	Wales	6
1977	Hillside	Laurence M. McCarthy	A	Ireland	6	England	8
			C	Ireland	2	Scotland	10
				Ireland	6	Wales	9
1978	Ashburnham	Laurence M. McCarthy	C	Ireland	5	England	7
			B	Ireland	7	Wales	6
			C	Ireland	6	Scotland	6
1979	Porthcawl	Joseph B. Carr	D	Ireland	15	Wales	17
1980	Dornoch	Joseph B. Carr	A	Ireland	7	England	7
				Ireland	9	Scotland	6
			A	Ireland	7	Wales	7
1981	Woodhall Spa	Joseph B. Carr	A	Ireland	10	Wales	4
				Ireland	8	England	7
				Ireland	6	Scotland	9
1982	Porthcawl	Brendan Edwards	A	Ireland	6	England	8
				Ireland	8	Scotland	7
			A	Ireland	7	Wales	7
1983	Portmarnock	Brendan Edwards	A	Ireland	7	England	7
			A	Ireland	9	Scotland	5
			A	Ireland	10	Wales	4
1984	Troon	Brendan Edwards	A	Ireland	7	Wales	7
				Ireland	5	Scotland	10
			E	Ireland	6	England	4
1985	Formby	Eamon Curran	A	Ireland	11	Scotland	3
			A	Ireland	5	Wales	9
			A	Ireland	5	England	9
1986	Harlech	Eamon Curran	A	Ireland	7	Wales	7
			A	Ireland	4	Scotland	10
				Ireland	8	England	7
1987	Lahinch	Eamon Curran		Ireland	6	England	4
				Ireland	8	Wales	7
			A	Ireland	10	Scotland	4
1988	Muirfield	George F. Crosbie		Ireland	9	Wales	6
				Ireland	10	Scotland	5
				Ireland	7	England	8
1989	Ganton	George F. Crosbie		Ireland	11	Wales	4
			A	Ireland	6	Scotland	8
				Ireland	7	England	8
1990	Conwy	George F. Crosbie	B	Ireland	8	Scotland	5
			D	Ireland	9	Wales	2
				Ireland	8	England	7

APPENDIX IX
Section 5

A record of all players who participated in the 'Home' International matches from 1932 to 1990

All players listed below whose names are prefixed by an asterisk also played in the pre-1932 International Matches series and their earlier recor.in Section 2 of this Appendix.

NAME	CLUB	YEARS	MATCHES	WON	DRAWN	LOST	POINTS
Anderson, N.H.	Shandon Park	1984–90	40	19	1	20	39
Baker, R.N.	Cork	1975	4	3	–	1	6
Bamford, J.L.	Royal Portrush	1954–6	10	3	–	7	6
Beamish, C.H.	Royal Portrush	1950–56	22	8	3	11	19
* Bell, H.E.	Portmarnock	1932	4	1	–	3	2
Bloom, M.	Edmondstown	1970	Selected but did not get a match				
Bowen, J.E.	Cork	1961–5	12	5	2	5	12
Branigan, D.	L'town & B'town	1975–6	37	11	5	21	27
* Briscoe, A.W.	Castlerea	1932–8	18	8	2	8	18
Brown, J.C.	Tramore	1933–53	52	19	3	30	41
Bruen, J.	Muskerry	1937–50	24	12	5	7	29
* Burke, J.	Lahinch	1932–49	58	23	9	26	55
Burns, I.M.	Tramore	1973–83	12	4	3	5	11
Carr, J.B.	Sutton	1947–69	138	78	10	50	166
Carr, J.J.	Sutton	1981–3	18	10	3	5	23
* Carr, J.R.	Royal Co. Down	1933	6	4	1	1	9
Carr, R.J.	Sutton	1970–71	12	3	2	7	8
Carroll, J.P.	Sutton	1948–62	28	14	3	11	31
* Carroll, W.J.	Greenore	1932	4	1	–	3	2
Carvill, J.	Warrenpoint	1989	6	3	–	3	6
Cashell, B.G.	Malone	1978	6	3	1	2	7
Caul, P.	Malahide	1968–75	39	19	4	16	42
Clarke, D.	Dungannon	1987–9	7	3	1	3	7
Cleary, T.	Fermoy	1976–86	41	16	8	17	40
Corcoran, D.K.	Royal Dublin	1972–3	10	4	3	3	11
Corridan, T.	Castletroy	1983–4	11	6	3	2	15
Craddock, T.	Malahide	1955–70	67	29	4	34	62
Craigan, R.M.	Malone	1963–5	18	13	1	4	27
Crosbie, G.F.	Cork	1953–7	24	7	2	15	16
* Crowley, M.	Portmarnock	1932	2	–	1	1	1
Dickson, J.R.	Holywood	1980	6	3	–	3	6
Dijon, M.C.	Rathmore	1958–60	16	4	3	9	11
Donnellan, B.	Dundalk	1952	2	–	–	2	0
Drew, N.V.	Bangor	1952–3	12	8	2	2	18
Duncan, J.	Shandon Park	1959–61	18	9	1	8	19
Dunne, E.	Athlone	1973–9	22	7	3	12	17
Edwards, B.	Shandon Park	1961–73	49	18	7	24	43
Edwards, M.	Shandon Park	1956–63	38	20	2	16	42
Egan, T.W.	Monkstown	1952–68	44	22	2	20	46
Elliott, I.A.	Royal Portrush	1975–8	18	8	2	8	18
Errity, D.	Hermitage	1990	6	3	2	1	8
Ewing, C.	Co. Sligo	1934–58	92	44	9	39	97
Faith, J.	Royal Portrush	1966	6	2	1	3	5
Fanagan, J.	Milltown	1989-90	12	7	–	5	14

NAME	CLUB	YEARS	MATCHES	WON	DRAWN	LOST	POINTS
Feeney, J.	Chapel-en-le-Frith	1985	Selected but did not get a match				
Ferguson, M.	Dundalk	1952	6	4	–	2	8
Ferguson, W.J.J.	Malone	1952–61	32	14	4	14	32
* French, W.F.	Rosslare	1932	6	1	–	5	2
Fitzgibbon, J.F.	Cork	1955–7	18	5	2	11	12
Fitzsimmons, J.	Royal Portrush	1938–48	16	6	3	7	15
Flaherty, J.A.	Langley Park	1934–7	24	8	4	12	20
Flaherty, P.D.	Addington	1965–7	10	5	2	3	12
Fleury, R.A.	Portmarnock	1974	4	1	–	3	2
Fleury, R.McK.	Monkstown	1955	Selected but did not get a match				
Fogarty, G.N.	Royal Dublin	1956–67	26	10	5	11	25
Froggatt, P.	Belvoir Park	1957	6	1	2	3	4
Gannon, M.A.	Co. Louth	1973–90	62	25	11	26	61
* Gill, W.J.	Sutton	1932–7	24	13	1	10	27
Glover, J.	Queen's University	1951–70	40	19	4	17	42
Goulding, N.	Portmarnock	1988–90	18	9	1	8	19
Graham, J.S.S.	Strandhill	1938–51	14	5	2	7	12
Greene, R.	Clontarf	1933	2	2	–	–	4
Guerin, M.	Killarney	1961–3	8	5	–	3	10
Hanway, M.	Sutton	1971–4	11	7	1	3	15
Harrington, J.A.	Adare Manor	1958–79	35	14	6	15	34
Harrington, P.	Stackstown	1990	6	6	–	–	12
Hayes, J.A.	Hermitage	1977	6	3	–	3	6
Heather, D.P.W.	Sutton	1976	6	2	–	4	4
Hegarty, T.D.	Royal Dublin	1951	4	–	1	3	1
Hegarty, J.	Massereene	1975	6	3	–	3	6
Herlihy, B.	Portmarnock	1950	6	2	–	4	4
Herlihy, D.P.	Royal Dublin	1961	Selected but did not get a match				
Heverin, A.J.	Woodbrook	1978	3	1	–	2	2
Higgins, E.	Cork	1966–70	10	2	–	8	4
Higgins, L.	Cork	1968–71	9	3	–	6	6
Hoey, T.B.C.	Royal Portrush	1970–84	28	14	2	12	30
Hogan, P.F.	Elm Park	1985–8	21	13	1	7	27
Howley, W.J.	Royal Dublin	1951	Selected but did not get a match				
Hulme, J.W.	Warrenpoint	1955–9	28	11	2	15	24
Humphries, A.R.	Malone	1957	2	1	–	1	2
Kane, R.M.	The Island	1965–79	44	16	5	23	37
Kearney, K.	Limerick	1988–90	18	6	4	8	16
Keenan, S.	Galway	1989	5	1	1	3	3
Kelleher, W.A.	Douglas	1962–4	17	10	2	5	22
Kelly, N.G.	Knock	1966	3	2	–	1	4
Kissock, B.J.S.	Bangor	1961–76	22	10	3	9	23
Lehane, N.	Cork	1976	3	2	–	1	4
Leyden, P.J.	Spanish Point	1950–59	20	8	2	10	18
Long, D.C.	Shandon Park	1973–84	42	23	6	13	52
Lyons, J.D.	Kilkenny	1954	2	–	–	2	0
Lyons, P.	Nenagh	1986	5	1	–	4	2
* MacCormack, J.D.	Grange	1932–7	36	16	3	17	35
Mackeown, H.N.	Cork	1973	6	1	3	2	5
MacNamara, L.G.	Woodbrook	1977–90	49	26	7	16	59
McCarroll, F.E.	City of Derry	1968–9	10	3	–	7	6
McCarthy, L.	Muskerry	1953–6	20	9	2	9	20
* McConnell, F.P.	Royal Portrush	1934	4	1	–	3	2
* McConnell, R.M.	Royal Portrush	1934–7	22	9	1	12	19
McCrea, W.E.	Walton Heath	1965–7	17	8	–	9	16
McCready, S.M.	Dunmurry	1947–54	28	14	3	11	31
McDaid, B.	Skibbereen	1979	3	–	–	3	0
McGimpsey, G.	Bangor	1978–90	71	35	11	25	81
McGinley, P.	Grange	1989–90	12	7	2	3	16
McGlennon, G.	Spanish Point	1958	2	1	–	1	2
McHenry, J.	Douglas	1985–6	12	6	–	6	12
McInnally, R.H.	Sutton	1949–51	12	7	–	5	14
McMenamin, E.	Ballybofey	1981–2	3	1	–	2	2

NAME	CLUB	YEARS	MATCHES	WON	DRAWN	LOST	POINTS
McMullan, C.J.	Knock	1933–5	19	10	3	6	23
McNeill, G.	Warrenpoint	1990	1	–	–	1	0
Madeley, J.F.D.	Royal Belfast	1959–66	42	26	1	15	53
Mahon, J.R.	Co. Sligo	1938–55	16	4	4	8	12
Malone, B.P.	Portmarnock	1959–75	30	13	2	15	28
Malone, J.	Portmarnock	1954	2	2	ç	–	4
Meharg, W.	Castlerock	1957	6	3	2	1	8
Morris, M.F.	Portmarnock	1978–84	32	16	5	11	37
Morrow, A.J.C.	Hermitage	1975–83	10	2	3	5	7
Mulcare, P.	Woodbrook	1968–80	44	11	6	27	28
Mulholland, D.	Castlerock	1988	5	3	1	1	7
* Munn, L.O.	North West	1936–7	12	4	2	6	10
Murphy, P.	Killarney	1984–6	15	6	1	8	13
Neill, J.M.	Cliftonville	1938–49	14	6	2	6	14
Nelson, D.A.	Malone	1968	Selected but did not get a match				
Nestor, J.M.	Milltown	1962–4	10	5	1	4	11
Nevin, V.	Ennis	1960–72	41	20	5	16	45
Nicholson, J.C.	Queen's University	1932	2	1	–	1	2
O'Boyle, P.M.	Royal Dublin	1977	Selected but did not get a match				
O'Brien, E.C.	Tullamore	1963	6	5	–	1	10
O'Brien, M.D.	New Ross	1968–77	44	9	4	31	22
O'Connell, E.	Killarney	1985	6	3	–	3	6
O'Connor, A.	Naas	1967–72	24	13	1	10	27
O'Leary, J.E.	Foxrock	1969–70	12	5	2	5	12
O'Neill, J.J.	Donabate	1968	3	1	–	2	2
O'Rourke, P.	Kilkenny	1980–85	24	9	3	12	21
O'Sullivan, D.F.	Cork	1976–87	19	7	2	10	16
O'Sullivan, W.M.	Killarney	1934–54	68	36	4	28	76
O'Sullivan, P.	Kinsale	1960	Selected but did not get a match				
Owens, G.H.	Skerries	1935–47	22	13	1	8	27
Pierse, A.D.	Tipperary	1976–88	63	26	9	28	61
Pollin, R.K.M.	Royal Belfast	1971	6	1	1	4	3
Power, E.	Tramore	1987–8	11	9	1	1	19
Power, M.	Muskerry	1947–54	38	18	2	18	38
Purcell, J.	Mullingar	1973	6	–	2	4	2
Rafferty, R.	Warrenpoint	1979–81	16	12	1	3	25
Rainey, W.H.E.	Shandon Park	1960–62	6	2	–	4	4
Rayfus, P.	Trim	1986–8	13	6	1	6	13
Rice, J.H.	Tralee	1947–52	12	5	2	5	12
Reddan, B.V.M.	Co. Louth	1987	5	2	2	1	6
Scannell, B.J.	Woodbrook	1947–54	32	14	5	13	33
Sheahan, D.B.	Grange	1961–70	44	21	3	20	45
* Sheals, H.S.	Balmoral	1932–3	12	3	1	8	7
* Simcox, R.	Cork	1932–8	32	14	4	14	32
Slattery, A.	Lahinch	1947–8	8	5	1	2	11
Sludds, M.F.	The Island	1982	6	2	2	2	6
Smyth, D.	L'town & B'town	1972–3	12	5	1	6	11
* Smyth, D.W.	Royal Co. Down	1933	4	2	–	2	4
Smyth, H.B.	Royal Co. Down	1974–8	24	13	2	9	28
Smyth, V.	L'town & B'town	1981–2	12	5	1	6	11
Staunton, R.de L.	Castlerea	1964–72	16	6	1	9	13
Stevenson, K.	Banbridge	1972	6	3	–	3	6
Taggart, J.	Royal Portrush	1953	4	1	–	3	2
Troy, K.	Royal Dublin	1951	Selected but did not get a match				
Walton, P.	Malahide	1979–81	16	9	–	7	18
Webster, F.	Carlow	1949	2	1	–	1	2
Welch, L.	Royal Dublin	1936	2	1	–	1	2
* West, C.H.	Greystones	1932	6	4	–	2	8
Young, D.J.F.	Malone	1969–77	14	4	1	9	9
Young, G.A.	Kilrush	1958	4	2	–	2	4

APPENDIX X
Section 1

The first Interprovincial match organised by the Golfing Union of Ireland, April 1896

LEINSTER	v.	ULSTER	
	Singles		
H.A.S. Upton (Royal Dublin)	lost to	R.R. Gilroy (Royal Portrush)	2 up
B. O'Brien (Dublin University)	beat	W.H. Webb (Shanes Park)	5 up
Jas. Stevenson (Royal Dublin)	beat	G. Combe (County Down)	2 up
J. Stewart-Moore (Royal Dublin)	beat	Jas Woodside (Ormeau)	6 up
W.D. Stewart (Portmarnock)	beat	Hugh Shaw (Royal Belfast)	2 up
R. Whyte (Dublin University)	lost to	J.S. Reade (Royal Belfast)	5 up
G.C. Green (Royal Dublin)	beat	George M. Shaw (Royal Belfast)	4 up
C.M. Barcroft (Royal Dublin)	lost to	T.A. Dickson (County Down)	5 up
J.H. Pigot (Royal Dublin)	lost to	Henry Gregg (County Down)	6 up
G.S.C. Maconcky (Royal Dublin)	lost to	Harold E. Reade (Royal Belfast)	4 up
J.H. Barrington (Royal Dublin)	lost to	John Woodside (Ballycastle)	3 up
D.M. Christie (Royal Dublin)	lost to	George S. Clarke (Royal Belfast)	2 up
G.C. May (Royal Dublin)	lost to	H. Richardson (Royal Portrush)	2 up
D.M. Wilson (Royal Dublin)	beat	A.D. Gaussen (Killymoon)	2 up
H.J. Daly (County Louth)	beat	R. Woodside (Royal Portrush)	10 up
J.P. Auld (Portmarnock)	beat	Dr. A. Traill (Royal Portrush)	2 up
A.S. Hussey (Malahide)	lost to	Norman Charley (Royal Belfast)	1 up
P.M. Watson (Royal Dublin)	beat	F.F. Figgis (Royal Belfast)	3 up
F.H. Orr (Royal Dublin)	halved with	W.L. Wheeler (County Down)	
T. Stewart (Royal Dublin)	lost to	C.W. Webb (Shanes Park)	2 up

Result: Leinster 37, Ulster 32. Leinster won by 5 holes.

	Foursomes		
Upton & O'Brien	halved with	Gilroy & W.H. Webb	
Stevenson & Stewart-Moore	beat	Combe & Jas. Woodside	4 up
Stewart & Whyte	lost to	Hugh Shaw & Jas. Reade	9 up
Green & Barcroft	beat	G.M. Shaw & Dickson	2 up
Pigot & Maconcky	lost to	Gregg & H. Reade	8 up
Barrington & Christie	halved with	John Woodside & Clark	
May & Wilson	lost to	Richardson & Gaussen	3 up
Daly & Auld	beat	R. Woodside & Traill	3 up
Hussey & Watson	beat	Charley & Figgis	5 up
Orr & Stewart	lost to	Wheeler & C.W. Webb	1 up

Result: Ulster 21, Leinster 14. Ulster won by 7 holes.
Combined Result: Ulster won by 2 holes.

APPENDIX X

Section 2

A record of all players who participated in official Interprovincial matches between 1896 and 1906

NAME	CLUB AND PROVINCE	YEARS	MATCHES	WON	DRAWN	LOST	POINTS
Auld, J.P.	Royal Dublin (Leinster)	1896–1900	4	2	1	1	2½
Barrington, A.B.	Dublin University (Leinster)	1901	1	1			
	North-West (Ulster)	1903–6	3		1	2	1½
Barcroft, C.M.	Royal Dublin (Leinster)	1896–1904	7	3		4	3
Barker, E.L.	Malone (Ulster)	1906	1	1			1
Barrington, J.H.	Royal Dublin (Leinster)	1896–1900	6	2	1	3	2½
Beard, C.T.	Foxrock (Leinster)	1902	1	1			1
Bennett, Col	County Down (Ulster)	1898	1	1			1
Boas, W.P.	Royal Belfast (Ulster)	1897–8	2		1	1	½
Boyd, H.A.	Portmarnock (Leinster)	1904–6	2	2			2
Boyd, R.	Portmarnock (Leinster)	1903	1	1			1
Boyd, W.H.	Portmarnock (Leinster)	1897–1906	8	5		3	5
Brady, J.	(Ulster)	1900	1			1	–
Brice, M.T.	Malone (Ulster)	1898–1900	3	3			3
Brier, W.T.	County Down (Ulster)	1901	1			1	–
Cairnes, H.M.	Portmarnock (Leinster)	1900–1906	5	2		3	2
Cairns, A.B.	County Louth (Leinster)	1899	1	1			1
Cameron, D.J.	Royal Portrush (Ulster)	1899–1903	4	2	1	1	2½
Campbell, L.	Greenisland (Ulster)	1897	1			1	–
Campbell, R.A.	Malahide (Leinster)	1898–1904	5	2	1	2	2½
Campbell, W.	(Leinster)	1901	1			1	–
Carden, H.	(Leinster	1901	1		1		–
Casement F.	Dublin University (Leinster)	1901	1		1		
	(Ulster)	1902–6	3	2		1	2½
Charley, M.	Royal Belfast (Ulster)	1896	2	1		1	1
Christie, D.M.	Royal Dublin (Leinster)	1896–1906	11	3	2	6	4
Clarke, G.S.	Royal Belfast (Ulster)	1896–1905	8	3	2	3	4
Coates, H.V.	County Down (Ulster)	1905	1	1			1
Combe, G.	County Down (Ulster)	1896–1901	5	2		3	2
Creery, J.T.		1903	1	1			1
Crymble, P.T.	Ormeau (Ulster)	1902–6	5	3		2	3
Daly, H.J.	County Louth (Leinster)	1896–1903	6	3	1	2	3½
Daniel, R.	Dungannon (Ulster)	1897	1			1	–
Dashwood, E.S.	Royal Portrush (Ulster)	1906	1			1	–
Dickson, F.G.	North West (Ulster)	1902–5	4	2		2	2
Dickson, T.W.	County Down (Ulster)	1896–1906	9	2	1	6	2½
Dillon, W.H.	Portmarnock (Leinster)	1901–4	4	2		2	2
Dodd, H.	Dublin University (Leinster)	1900	1	1			1
Dove, W.	County Louth (Leinster)	1905	1	1			1
Dudgeon, A.P.	Portmarnock (Leinster)	1904	1			1	–
Dunn, W.H.	Royal Dublin (Leinster)	1905	1			1	–
Dunne, G.W.	Foxrock (Leinster)	1903–6	3	2		1	2
Elliott, W.S.	Malahide (Leinster)	1898	1		1		½
Evans, S.	(Ulster)	1906	1			1	–
Fennell, W.B.	Greenisland (Ulster)	1897–1903	7	2		4	3
Figgis, A.L.	Greystones (Leinster)	1905	1	1			1
Figgis, E.K.	Greystones (Leinster)	1901–6	5	1		4	1
Figgis, F.F.	Royal Belfast (Ulster)	1896–1905	7	3		4	3
Forde, W.R.	Knock (Ulster)	1900–1906	3	2		1	2
Gaussen, A.D.	Killymoon (Ulster)	1896–7	3	1		2	1
Gibson, Hon. E	Royal Dublin (Leinster)	1896–1906	7	4	1	2	4½
Gillies, J. B	(Ulster)	1904	1			1	–
Gilroy, R. R	Royal Portrush (Ulster)	1896	2	1	1		1½

NAME	CLUB AND PROVINCE	YEARS	MATCHES	WON	DRAWN	LOST	POINTS
Goldfinch, Lt	County Down (Ulster)	1904–6	3			3	–
Gregg, H.	County Down (Ulster)	1896–7	3	2		1	2
Green, Maj	Royal Portrush (Ulster)	1906	1			1	–
Greene, G.C.	Royal Dublin (Leinster)	1896–1904	7	4	1	2	4½
Harden, C.S.	Malone (Ulster)	1901–4	2		2		1
Haskell, D.J.	County Down (Ulster)	1905	1			1	–
Henderson, J.	Royal Belfast (Ulster)	1900	1			1	–
Henry, R.G.N.	Portmarnock (Leinster)	1902–6	4	3		1	3
Henshaw, T.	Royal Dublin (Leinster)	1899–1906	7	3	1	3	3½
Hewitt, R.J.	Malone (Ulster)	1900–1905	4	1	1	2	1½
Hogg, A.G.	Royal Portrush (Ulster)	1899	1		1		½
Hunter, R.	Royal Portrush (Ulster)	1899	1	1			1
Hussey, A.S.	Malahide (Leinster)	1896–9	5	2		3	2
Inglis, C.C.	Portmarnock (Leinster)	1901–6	3	1	2		2
Inglis, J.J.	Portmarnock (Leinster)	1901–3	3		2	1	1
Jackson, J.L.	Malone (Ulster)	1905–6	2			2	–
Jones, B.	Royal Portrush (Ulster)	1904	1			1	–
Kelly, G.W.F.	Portmarnock (Leinster)	1903–6	4	1	2	1	2
Kelly, H.C.	County Down (Ulster)	1897	1			1	–
La Touche, A.D.	Sutton (Leinster)	1904–5	2	2			}
	Royal Portrush (Ulster)	1906	1	1			} 3
Leatham, C.A.B.	Portmarnock (Leinster)	1905	1			1	–
Livingston, W.L.	Royal Belfast (Ulster)	1897	1			1	–
Long, G.B.	Dublin University (Leinster)	1904	1			1	–
MacNaughton, S.	Portmarnock (Leinster)	1900	1	1			1
McAvoy, J.	Saintfield (Ulster)	1898–1905	7	4	1	2	4½
McClintock, J.G.	Royal Portrush (Ulster)	1903	1	1			1
McDaniel, C.	(Ulster)	1900	1			1	–
McDonald, J.R.	Dungannon (Ulster)	1897	1			1	–
McKeag, T.A.	Ormeau (Ulster)	1901–5	3	1	2		2
Maconcky, G.T.C.	Royal Dublin (Leinster)	1896	2			2	–
Magill, C.	Royal Dublin (Leinster)	1899	1		1		½
Maloney, W.D.	Royal Dublin (Leinster)	1900	1	1			1
Martin, L.	Royal Dublin (Leinster)	1903–5	2		1	1	½
Matterson, J.S.	Portmarnock (Leinster)	1906	1	1			1
May, G.C.	Royal Dublin (Leinster)	1896–9	5	1		4	1
Meldon, W.D.	Portmarnock (Leinster)	1900–1903	3	1		2	1
Meredith, R.P.	Dublin University (Leinster)	1899–1903	5	3		2	3
Molany, J.P.	Dublin University (Leinster)	1898	1			1	–
Moore, C.S.	Dublin University (Ulster)	1898–1904	5	3		2	}
	(Leinster)	1900–1901	2	2		1	} 5
Moore, J.	Royal Portrush (Ulster)	1903	1		1		½
Moore, J.S.	Royal Dublin (Leinster)	1896	2	2			2
Morgan, J.L.	Sutton (Leinster)	1904–5	2	1		1	1
Morrisson, H.	Royal Portrush (Ulster)	1900	1	1			1
Munn, L.O.	North West (Ulster)	1906	1		1		½
Newett, A.C.	Dublin University (Leinster)	1899–1901	2		1	1	}
	Royal Portrush (Ulster)	1902–6	3	2		1	} 2½
Newett, F.B.	County Down (Ulster)	1897–1906	10	4	1	5	4½
Newett, R.	County Down (Ulster)	1900	1			1	1
O'Brien, B.	Dublin University (Leinster)	1896	2	1	1		}
	Royal Belfast (Ulster)	1898–1906	5	2	2	1	} 4½
O'Donnell, J.F.	Greenore (Leinster)	1905–6	2	1		1	1
Orr, E.H.	Royal Dublin (Leinster)	1896–1903	6	2	1	3	2½
Owens, F.	Portmarnock (Leinster)	1906	1			1	–
Parke, J.C.	Dublin University (Ulster)	1900–1904	2		1	1	½
Parley, P.	County Down (Ulster)	1905	1			1	–
Patton, C.W.	Ormeau (Ulster)	1898–1902	3	2	1		2½
Pentland, G.H.	County Louth (Leinster)	1897–9	2			2	–
Pickman, W.C.	Portmarnock (Leinster)	1897–1906	6	4	1	1	4½
Pigot, J.H.	Royal Dublin (Leinster)	1896–1902	5	2		3	2
Reade, H.E	Royal Belfast (Ulster)	1896–1906	9	7		2	7
Reade, J.S.	Royal Belfast (Ulster)	1896–1902	6	4		2	4
Richardson, J.H.	Royal Portrush (Ulster)	1896–1901	6	3	1	2	3½
Ross, A.P.	Portmarnock (Leinster)	1901	1		1		½
Rutherford, C.J.	Foxrock (Leinster)	1905	1			1	–

NAME	CLUB AND PROVINCE	YEARS	MATCHES	WON	DRAWN	LOST	POINTS
Shaw, G.M.	Royal Belfast (Ulster)	1896–1906	5	2		3	2
Shaw, H.	Royal Belfast (Ulster)	1896–9	4	2		2	2
Shaw, J.R.	Greystones (Leinster)	1901–5	2	2			2
Shaw, R.A.	Dublin University (Leinster)	1902	1	1			1
Smyth, D.W.	County Down (Ulster)	1905–6	2	1		1	1
Steen, C.J.	County Down (Ulster)	1901	1	1			1
Steen, J.H.	County Down (Ulster)	1901	1		1		½
Stevenson, J.	Royal Dublin (Leinster)	1896–8	4	4			4
Stewart, T.	Royal Dublin (Leinster)	1896–7	3	1		2	1
Stewart, W.D.	Portmarnock (Leinster)	1896–1903	5	2		3	2
Synott, H.J.	Foxrock (Leinster)	1905	1	1			1
Todd, J.P.	Portmarnock (Leinster)	1898–1906	5	4		1	4
Todd, W.F.	Portmarnock (Leinster)	1897–1906	8	3	1	4	3½
Traill, A.	Royal Portrush (Ulster)	1896–1900	4	1		3 ⎫	
	Royal Dublin (Leinster)	1898–9	2	1		1 ⎬ 2	
Upton, H.A.S.	Royal Dublin (Leinster)	1896–1906	5		1	4	½
Walker, I.	Portmarnock (Leinster)	1900	1		1		½
Walkington, D.B.	Malone (Ulster)	1897–9	2	1	1		1½
Watson, P.M.	Royal Dublin (Leinster)	1896–1904	6	6		⎫	
	(Ulster)	1905	1			1 ⎬ 6	
Watson, T.	Royal Dublin (Leinster)	1898	1	1			1
Webb, C.W.	Shanes Park (Ulster)	1896	2	1		1 ⎫	
	Dublin University (Leinster)	1897–1901	4	3		1 ⎬ 4	
Webb, O.B.	Royal Portrush (Ulster)	1898–1904	6	5		1	5
Webb, W.H.	Shanes Park (Ulster)	1896–1904	8	1	2	5	2
Wellington, F.	Dublin University (Leinster)	1901	1	1			1
Wheeler, W.L.	County Down (Ulster)	1896	2	1	1		1½
Whyte, J.R.	Knock (Ulster)	1902–3	2	1		1	1
Whyte, R.	Dublin University (Leinster)	1896	2			2	–
Wilkie, J.	County Down (Ulster)	1905	1	1			1
Williams, H.	North West (Ulster)	1899	1			1	–
Wilkington, G.	Royal Dublin (Leinster)	1903	1			1	–
Wilson, C.W.	Armagh (Ulster)	1905	1			1	–
Wilson, D.M.	Royal Dublin (Leinster)	1896–1906	8	5		3	5
Wilson, W.	Royal Belfast (Ulster)	1897	1			1	–
Woodside, Jas.	Ormeau (Ulster)	1896–1901	7	1	2	4	2
Woodside, John	Ballycastle (Ulster)	1896–8	4	1	1	2	1½
Woodside, R.	Royal Portrush (Ulster)	1896	2			2	–
Young, E.	Malone (Ulster)	1897–1905	8	4		4	4

APPENDIX X

Section 3

The official Interprovincials were played at Portmarnock Golf Club in 1938 and 1939. The results were based on the best seven medal scores in each province.

At Portmarnock Golf Club, 15 August 1938

MUNSTER				LEINSTER			
J. Bruen (Muskerry)	70	73	143	G.H. Owens (Skerries)	77	78	155
J.C. Brown (Waterford)	80	72	152	W.J. Gill (Portmarnock)	79	80	159
J. Burke (Lahinch)	74	79	153	W.F. Ffrench (Rosslare)	77	82	159
Wm. O'Sullivan (Dooks)	80	77	157	T.A. Healy (Portmarnock)	82	78	160
R. Simcox (Cork)	84	79	163	M.F. Coghlan (Rosslare)	81	81	162
J. Beasley (Ballybunion)	77	87	164	B.J. Scannell (Woodbrook)	80	85	165
F.J. Hannan (Lahinch)	84	82	166	F.A. Lyons (Kilkenny)	84	83	167

A.J. Dinan (Cork)	84	83	167	J.B. Carr (Sutton)	82	86	168
D. Torrens (Lahinch)	83	85	168	C.A. Carroll (Dundalk)	86	83	169
S.H. McCarthy (Douglas)	84	Rtd		C.J. McMullan (Portmarnock)	81	89	170

<table>
<tr><td>Best 7 scores, 1,098</td><td>Best 7 scores, 1,127</td></tr>
</table>

CONNACHT

J.R. Mahon (Co.Sligo)	78	78	156
J.D. MacCormack (Grange)	80	77	157
A.W. Briscoe (Castlerea)	77	82	159
C. Ewing (Co. Sligo)	81	82	163
W.J. Howley (Co. Sligo)	81	83	164
D.P. Morris (Hermitage)	84	81	165
P. Lenihan (Galway)	84	89	173
J. O'Driscoll (Galway)	87	86	173
P. O'Flynn (Galway)	87	87	174
P. O'Beirn (Galway)	94	89	183

Best 7 scores, 1,137

ULSTER

J. Fitzsimmons (Bushfoot)	78	78	156
R.W. Barnett (Ryl.Co.Down)	80	82	162
H.M. Hadden (Holywood)	85	79	164
S.K. Neill (Whitehead)	84	82	166
J.M. Neill (Cliftonville)	86	82	168
H.P. Ritchie (Dunmurry)	83	85	168
F.P. McConnell (Ryl Portrush)	87	82	169
J. McAuley (Bangor)	79	91	170
R.J. Frizzell (Malone)	86	85	171
J. McKenna (North West)	89	85	174

Best 7 scores, 1,153

Result:
1st	Munster	1,098
2nd	Leinster	1,127
3rd	Connacht	1,137
4th	Ulster	1,153

At Portmarnock Golf Club, 2 September 1939

LEINSTER

T.A. Healy (Portmarnock)	76
R.G. Duggan (Hermitage)	77
W. Hewitt (Newlands)	78
W.J. Gill (Portmarnock)	80
G.H. Owens (Skerries)	80
T.D. Purcell (Killiney)	81
J.P. Byrne (Hermitage)	82
B.J. Scannell (Woodbrook)	82
J.F. McLaughlin (Royal Dublin)	85
R. McConkey (Royal Dublin)	N.R

Best 7 scores, 554

CONNACHT

C. Ewing (Co. Sligo)	71
J.R. Mahon (Co. Sligo)	76
W.J. Howley (Co. Sligo)	77
J. O'Driscoll (Galway)	82
A.W. Briscoe (Castlerea)	83
D.P. Morris (Hermitage)	84
P. O'Beirn (Galway)	84
P. Lenihan (Galway)	90
T.J. Conroy (Boyle)	91
P.J. O'Flynn (Galway)	N.R.

Best 7 scores, 557

MUNSTER

J. Burke (Lahinch)	74
J.C. Brown (Waterford)	75
J. Bruen (Muskerry)	78
J. Beasley (Ballybunion)	83
D. Torrens (Lahinch)	83
F.J. Hannan (Lahinch)	85
A. Slattery (Lahinch)	89
J. Keily (Muskerry)	90
Wm. O'Sullivan (Dooks)	90
G. Crosbie (Cork)	N.R

Best 7 scores, 567

ULSTER

J. McKenna (North West)	81
J.W. Hulme (Warrenpoint)	82
W.S. McMullan (Knock)	82
J.M. Neill (Cliftonville)	82
H.D. Connolly (Belvoir Pk.)	84
F.P. McConnell (Ryl Portrush)	85
W.J. McWilliams (Rossmore)	85
R.L.E. Lowry (Ryl Portrush)	86
G.A. Brady (Belvoir Park)	87
S.R. Sinclair (Ryl Belfast)	87

Best 7 scores, 581

Result:
1st	Leinster	554
2nd	Connacht	557
3rd	Munster	567
4th	Ulster	581

APPENDIX X
Section 4

A record of all players who participated in official Interprovincial matches in 1938 and 1939

Name	Club	Province	Year(s)	
Barnett, R.W.	Royal Co. Down	Ulster	1938	
Beasley, J.	Ballybunion	Munster	1938	1939
Brady, G.A.	Belvoir Park	Ulster		1939
Briscoe, A.W.	Castlerea	Connacht	1938	1939
Brown, J.C.	Waterford	Munster	1938	1939
Bruen, J.	Muskerry	Munster	1938	1939
Burke, J.	Lahinch	Munster	1938	1939
Byrne, J.P.	Hermitage	Leinster		1939
Carr, J.B.	Sutton	Leinster	1938	
Carroll, C.A.	Dundalk	Leinster	1938	
Coghlan, M.F.	Rosslare	Leinster	1938	
Conroy, T.J.	Boyle	Connacht		1939
Connolly, H.D.	Belvoir Park	Ulster		1939
Crosbie, Cdr. G.	Cork	Munster		1939
Dinan, A.J.	Cork	Munster	1938	
Duggan, R.G.	Hermitage	Leinster		1939
Ewing, C.	Co. Sligo	Connacht	1938	1939
Ffrench, W.F.	Rosslare	Leinster	1938	
Fitzsimmons, J.	Bushfoot	Ulster	1938	
Frizzell, R.J.	Malone	Ulster	1938	
Gill, W.J.	Portmarnock	Leinster	1938	1939
Hadden, H.M.	Holywood	Ulster	1938	
Hannan, F.J.	Lahinch	Munster	1938	1939
Healy, T.A.	Portmarnock	Leinster	1938	1939
Hewitt, W.	Newlands	Leinster		1939
Howley, W.J.	Co. Sligo	Connacht	1938	1939
Hulme, W.J.	Warrenpoint	Ulster		1939
Keily, J.	Muskerry	Munster		1939
Lenihan, P.	Galway	Connacht	1938	1939
Lowry, R.L.E.	Royal Portrush	Ulster		1939
Lyons, F.A.	Kilkenny	Leinster	1938	
MacCormack, J.D.	Grange	Connacht	1938	
McAuley, J.	Bangor	Ulster	1938	
McCarthy, S.H.	Douglas	Munster	1938	
McConkey, R.	Royal Dublin	Leinster	1939	
McConnell, F.P.	Royal Portrush	Ulster	1938	1939
McKenna, J.	North West	Ulster	1938	1939
McLaughlin, J.F.	Royal Dublin	Leinster		1939
McMullan, C.J.	Portmarnock	Leinster	1938	
McMullan, W.S.	Knock	Ulster		1939
McWilliams, W.J.	Rossmore	Ulster		1939
Mahon, J.R.	Co. Sligo	Connacht	1938	1939
Morris, D.P.	Hermitage	Connacht	1938	1939
Neill, J.M.	Cliftonville	Ulster	1938	1939
Neill, S.K.	Whitehead	Ulster	1938	
O'Beirn, P.M.	Galway	Connacht	1938	1939
O'Driscoll, J.	Galway	Connacht	1938	1939
O'Flynn, P.J.	Galway	Connacht	1938	1939
O'Sullivan, Wm.	Dooks	Munster	1938	1939
Owens, G.H.	Skerries	Leinster	1938	1939
Purcell, T.D.	Killiney	Leinster		1939
Ritchie, H.P	Dunmurry	Ulster	1938	
Scannell, B.J.	Woodbrook	Leinster	1938	1939

Simcox, R.	Cork	Munster	1938	
Sinclair, S.R.	Royal Belfast	Ulster		1939
Slattery, A.	Lahinch	Munster		1939
Torrens, D.	Lahinch	Munster	1938	1939

APPENDIX X
Section 5

A record of all players who participated in the Amateur Interprovincial Championship from 1956 to 1990

All players listed below whose names are prefixed by an asterisk also played in the pre-1956 Interprovincial Championship and their earlier records are included in Section 4 of Appendix IX.

NAME	CLUB & PROVINCE	YEAR(S)	MATCHES	WON	DRAWN	LOST	POINTS
Agnew, T.B.	Belvoir Park (Ulster)	1956	4	2	–	2	4
Anderson, N.H.	Shandon Park (Ulster)	1983–90	42	29	–	13	58
Armstrong, J.	Massereene (Ulster)	1972–3	10	5	1	4	11
Bailey, I.	Rathfarnham (Connacht)	1963	4	–	–	4	0
Baker, D.	Downpatrick (Ulster)	1985–90	27	10	–	17	20
Baker, R.N.	Cork (Munster)	1963–8	32	15	5	12	35
Ballentine, D.	Carrickfergus (Ulster)	1981–8	29	15	–	14	30
Bamford, J.L.	Royal Portrush (Ulster)	1957–72	7	3	–	4	6
Begley, B.	Castletroy (Munster)	1979–86	19	10	1	8	21
Bell, T.R.	City of Derry (Ulster)	1971–2	9	2	1	6	5
Bloom, M.	Edmondstown (Leinster)	1970	2	–	1	1	1
Bowen, J.E.	Cork (Munster)	1961–6	32	17	8	7	42
Bradley, A.J.	Co. Sligo (Connacht)	1978–9	7	1	1	5	3
Branigan, D.	L'town & B'town (Leinster)	1972–90	84	56	2	26	112
Bray, P.	Hermitage (Leinster)	1975	2	–	–	2	0
Brennan, S.	Co. Sligo (Connacht)	1960	4	–	–	4	0
*Brown, J.C.	Waterford (Munster)	1961	4	–	–	4	0
Burns, M.	Tramore (Munster)	1972–88	75	41	6	28	88
Butler, J.M.	Douglas (Munster)	1956	2	–	–	2	0
Butler, P.	Newlands (Leinster)	1985	3	2	–	1	4
Byrne, A.F.	Skerries (Leinster)	1956	6	1	1	4	3
Byrne, C.A.	St Anne's (Leinster)	1958	6	1	1	4	3
Byrne, T.	Wanstead (Leinster)	1959	4	1	1	2	3
Canavan, V.	Hermitage (Connacht)	1986	5	1	–	4	2
Carew, C.	Waterford (Leinster)	1986–90	19	10	1	8	21
*Carr, J.B.	Sutton (Leinster)	1956–70	44	29	6	9	64
Carr, J.J.	Sutton (Leinster)	1981–3	7	2	–	5	4
Carr, R.J.	Sutton (Leinster)	1970–71	11	4	2	5	10
Carroll, J.P.	Sutton (Leinster)	1956–62	14	8	4	2	20
Carvill, J.	Warrenpoint (Ulster)	1989–90	12	10	–	2	20
Cashell, B.G.	Portmarnock (Ulster)	1977–85	17	11	1	5	23
Caul, P.	Malahide (Leinster)	1965–77	62	38	6	18	82
Caulfield, D.	Galway (Connacht)	1984	3	1	–	2	2
Clarke, D.	Dungannon (Ulster)	1988–90	16	9	–	7	18
Clarke, G.	Royal Portrush (Ulster)	1988–90	12	7	–	5	14
Cleary, T.	Fermoy (Munster)	1976–90	69	37	3	29	77
Clynch, J.J.	L'town & B'town (Leinster)	1969–75	11	5	1	5	11
Collins, J.	Douglas (Munster)	1978–9	9	4	2	3	10

NAME	CLUB & PROVINCE	YEAR(S)	MATCHES	WON	DRAWN	LOST	POINTS
Connaughton, E.	Roscommon (Connacht)	1981	5	1	–	4	2
Connolly, P.	Galway (Connacht)	1958–61	18	5	–	13	10
Conway, D.J.	Portmarnock (Leinster)	1981	2	1	–	1	2
Conway, S.	Fermoy (Munster)	1969	5	3	1	1	7
Cooley, S.A.G.	Clandeboye (Ulster)	1958–71	34	16	5	13	37
Cooney, F.	Gort (Connacht)	1971–7	24	3	6	15	12
Corcoran, D.K.	Royal Dublin (Leinster)	1969–74	28	14	1	13	29
Corcoran, J.	Ballina (Connacht)	1978–84	23	7	1	15	15
Corridan, T.	Castletroy (Munster)	1977–90	33	15	–	18	30
Cotter, P.	Tuam (Connacht)	1964–7	13	3	1	9	7
Coughlan, R.	Birr (Leinster)	1990	5	1	–	4	2
Cowley, P.	Cork (Munster)	1990	4	4	–	–	8
Coyne, J.C.	Killarney (Connacht)	1969	5	1	1	3	3
Coyne, P.	Dun Laoghaire (Connacht)	1970–76	19	2	3	14	7
Craddock, M.	Malahide (Leinster)	1956–70	27	12	2	13	26
Craddock, T.	Malahide (Leinster)	1956–71	82	44	10	28	98
Craigan, R.M.	Malone (Ulster)	1957–66	50	26	7	17	59
Crosbie, G.F.	Cork (Munster)	1956–64	40	16	11	13	43
Cunningham, D.	Galway (Connacht)	1987–9	11	3	–	8	6
Curran, E.	Woodbrook (Connacht)	1968–71	19	2	1	16	5
Curran, T.	Tuam (Connacht)	1961–2	12	–	1	11	1
Deasy, F.	Cork (Munster)	1989	3	2	–	1	4
Devins, C.	Milltown (Connacht)	1966–77	34	8	3	23	19
Dickson, J.R.	Holywood (Ulster)	1977–83	33	18	1	14	37
Dijon, M.C.	Rathmore (Ulster)	1958–60	15	9	2	4	20
Doherty, F.	Co. Sligo (Connacht)	1965–7	12	2	2	8	6
Donnelly, P.	Queen's Univ. (Ulster)	1961	4	3	–	1	6
Duggan, T.M.	Kilkenny (Leinster)	1960–68	24	10	5	9	25
Duncan, J.	Shandon Park (Ulster)	1956–62	30	17	3	10	37
Dunne, E.	Athlone (Connacht)	1973–84	70	28	4	38	60
Edwards, B.	Shandon Park (Ulster)	1961–73	54	26	7	21	59
Edwards, M.	Royal Portrush (Ulster)	1956–63	40	21	7	12	49
Egan, P.	Athlone (Connacht)	1973–86	27	4	1	22	9
Egan, T.W.	Monkstown (Munster)	1956–69	72	36	10	26	82
Elliott, I.A.	Belvoir Park (Leinster/Ulster)	1969–86	83	40	5	38	85
Errity, D.	Hermitage (Leinster)	1989–90	12	10	–	2	20
*Ewing, C.	Co. Sligo (Connacht)	1958–63	14	3	2	9	8
Faith, J.	Royal Portrush (Ulster)	1965–70	24	10	2	12	22
Fanagan, J.	Milltown (Leinster)	1989–90	12	8	–	4	16
Farrell, J.	Carlow (Leinster)	1984	5	4	–	1	8
Ferguson, W.J.J.	Malone (Ulster)	1956–64	40	24	3	13	51
Firth, E.A.	Sutton (Leinster)	1956–61	16	7	1	8	15
Fitzgerald, J.G.	Limerick (Munster)	1983	6	3	–	3	6
Fitzgibbon, J.	Cork (Munster)	1956–8	18	4	5	9	13
Fitzpatrick, M.P.	Sutton (Leinster)	1956–7	12	6	2	4	14
Fitzsimons, C.	Ardglass (Ulster)	1986	5	2	–	3	4
Flaherty, P.D.	Addington (Connacht)	1964–9	30	12	2	16	26
Flanagan, K.	Co. Sligo (Connacht)	1988	4	–	–	4	0
Flanagan, S.	Co. Sligo (Connacht)	1966–78	78	27	9	42	63
Fleury, R.A.	Portmarnock (Munster)	1974–7	18	11	–	7	22
Fleury, R.McK.	Monkstown (Munster)	1956	4	1	2	1	4
Flynn, F.	L'town & B'town (Leinster)	1983	5	4	–	1	8
Forbes, G.	Newtownstewart (Ulster)	1989	3	1	–	2	2
Fogarty, G.N.	Royal Dublin (Leinster)	1956–70	65	29	7	29	65
Forde, T.	Co. Sligo (Connacht)	1988	5	1	–	4	2
Freyne, V.	Ballyhaunis (Connacht)	1981–3	6	1	–	5	2
Froggatt, P.	Belvoir Park (Ulster)	1956–8	16	10	2	4	22
Frost, B.	Castlerea (Connacht)	1987	2	–	–	2	0
Gallagher, F.	Co. Louth (Leinster)	1959–65	30	15	6	9	36
Gannon, F.	Co. Louth (Leinster)	1980–88	25	14	1	10	29
Gannon, M.A.	Co. Louth (Leinster)	1972–90	82	49	–	33	98
Gillen, D.	Co. Sligo (Connacht)	1960–67	25	5	3	17	13
Glasgow, C.E.	Clandeboye (Ulster)	1983–7	20	7	1	12	15

NAME	CLUB & PROVINCE	YEAR(S)	MATCHES	WON	DRAWN	LOST	POINTS
Glover, J.	Knock (Ulster)	1956–71	22	11	3	8	25
Glynn, F.	Tuam (Connacht)	1957–63	24	7	4	13	18
Golden, L.	Westport (Connacht)	1959–60	10	1	–	9	2
Goulding, M.	Portmarnock (Munster)	1988–90	12	7	–	5	14
Gribben, P.	Warrenpoint (Ulster)	1987	5	4	–	1	8
Guerin, M.	Killarney (Munster)	1960–82	48	24	5	19	53
Hamill, G.	Ardglass (Ulster)	1989–90	7	6	–	1	12
Hanna, R.A.	Lurgan (Ulster)	1987–8	6	4	–	2	8
Hanway, M.	Sutton (Leinster)	1967–75	30	17	–	13	34
Harnett, W.	Carlow (Leinster)	1959	4	2	–	2	4
Harrington, J.	Adare Manor (Munster)	1958–81	72	37	9	26	83
Harrington, P.	Stackstown (Leinster)	1990	5	3	–	2	6
Hayes, J.A.	Hermitage (Leinster)	1980	4	2	–	2	4
Hayes, N.	Castletroy (Munster)	1960	6	2	–	4	4
Heasley, R.	Lisburn (Ulster)	1989	3	1	–	2	2
Heather, D.P.	Sutton (Leinster)	1976–87	13	7	1	5	15
Heavey, S.	Castlerea (Connacht)	1986–90	24	6	–	18	12
Hegarty, T.D.	Royal Dublin (Connacht)	1956–7	12	4	2	6	10
Hegarty, R.J.	Massereene (Ulster)	1974	3	–	1	2	1
Hennessey, R.	Ennis (Munster)	1984	3	1	–	2	2
Herlihy, B.	Portmarnock (Leinster)	1957	6	2	1	3	5
Herlihy, D.P.	Royal Dublin (Leinster)	1961	6	4	–	2	8
Herron, G.A.	Rathmore (Ulster)	1955–9	11	3	2	6	8
Heverin, A.J.	Woodbrook (Leinster)	1976–8	17	11	1	5	23
Higgins, E.	Cork (Munster)	1965–73	48	27	3	18	57
Higgins, L.	Cork (Munster)	1968–71	24	13	4	7	30
Higgins, T.	Douglas (Munster)	1959–62	10	3	1	6	7
Hoey, M.J.C.	Shandon Park (Ulster)	1967–73	22	9	1	12	19
Hoey, T.B.C.	Shandon Park (Ulster)	1958–85	76	36	6	34	78
Hogan, A.	Carrick-on-Shannon (Connacht)	1979–85	15	3	–	12	6
Hogan, M.	Forrest Little (Connacht)	1989	2	–	–	2	0
Hogan, P.F.	Elm Park (Leinster)	1982–90	49	31	–	18	62
Holmes, A.W.	Massereene (Ulster)	1968	6	–	1	5	1
Hosty, S.F.	Galway (Connacht)	1957–78	85	19	10	56	48
Howlett, A.	Tramore (Munster)	1963	4	3	–	1	6
Howley, F.	Co. Sligo (Connacht)	1990	6	4	–	2	8
*Hulme, J.W.	Warrenpoint (Ulster)	1956–9	24	17	2	5	36
Humphries, A.R.	Malone (Ulster)	1956–7	10	6	1	3	13
Hutchinson, J.	Royal Dublin (Leinster)	1983–90	16	8	–	8	16
Hutton, R.	Clandeboye (Ulster)	1969	5	2	2	1	6
Hynes, J.C.	Greenore (Leinster)	1966	2	–	–	2	0
Jackson, D.	Scrabo (Ulster)	1969	5	2	–	3	4
Jamieson, J.M.	Royal Co. Down (Ulster)	1964–8	14	6	3	5	15
Jordan, M.	Royal Dublin (Leinster)	1960–65	10	6	–	4	12
Kane, P.	The Island (Leinster)	1963	2	1	–	1	2
Kane, R.M.	Malahide (Leinster)	1964–82	78	45	5	28	95
Kavanagh, J.	Castletroy (Munster)	1989–90	6	1	–	2	2
Keane, W.	Tuam (Connacht)	1966–8	7	1	1	5	3
Kearney, K.	Limerick/Portmarnock (Connacht)	1985–90	24	13	–	11	26
Keily, D.	Cork (Munster)	1974	2	2	–	–	4
Kelleher, W.A.	Douglas (Munster)	1962–6	30	15	5	10	35
Kelly, N.	Athlone (Connacht)	1990	5	–	–	5	0
Kelly, N.S.	Knock (Ulster)	1965–6	12	7	3	2	17
Kennedy, D.	Cork (Munster)	1967–73	15	8	1	6	17
Kenny, D.	Kilrush (Munster)	1980–87	35	21	–	14	42
Killeen, P.	Claremorris (Connacht)	1986–90	16	8	–	8	16
Kinsella, W.	Skerries (Leinster)	1960	6	1	2	3	4
Kissock, B.J.S.	Bangor (Ulster)	1961–87	60	34	7	19	75
Knox, C.	Royal Portrush (Ulster)	1957	4	3	–	1	6
Lehane, N.	Cork (Munster)	1976	6	1	3	2	5
Leyden, P.J.	Spanish Point (Munster)	1956–61	34	14	6	14	34
Long, D.C.	Shandon Park (Ulster)	1973–86	78	36	7	35	79
Lynch, J.V.	Limerick (Munster)	1972	4	1	1	2	3

NAME	CLUB & PROVINCE	YEAR(S)	MATCHES	WON	DRAWN	LOST	POINTS
Lynch, M.	Galway (Connacht)	1967–72	9	3	–	6	6
Lyons, P.	Cork (Munster)	1985–90	24	14	–	10	28
Macauley, D.C.	Donabate (Leinster)	1956–9	12	5	3	4	13
MacKeown, H.N.	Cork (Munster)	1972–6	27	14	1	12	29
MacNamara, J.	Woodbrook (Connacht)	1987–8	11	3	–	8	6
MacNamara, L.	Woodbrook (Connacht)	1974–90	99	32	4	63	68
McAleese, G.	Royal Portrush (Ulster)	1981	5	5	–	–	10
McAleese, J.A.	Ballymena (Ulster)	1965–76	32	19	3	10	41
McAleese, T.	UCD (Leinster)	1958–9	10	4	2	4	10
McCambridge, G.	Woodbrook (Leinster)	1958	2	2	–	–	4
McCarroll, C.A.	City of Derry (Ulster)	1984	6	2	–	4	4
McCarroll, F.E.	City of Derry (Ulster)	1965–71	33	17	2	14	36
McCarthy, L.	Muskerry (Munster)	1956–7	12	2	3	7	7
McCormack, C.H.	Castletroy (Munster)	1965–7	14	5	3	6	13
McCorry, F.A.	Clandeboye (Ulster)	1964	6	1	1	4	3
McCrea, W.E.	Walton Heath (Ulster)	1963–7	24	13	2	9	28
McDade, A.J.	Bangor (Ulster)	1964–80	15	6	2	7	14
McDaid, B.	Skibbereen (Munster)	1978–81	16	10	–	6	20
McDermott, S.F.	Athy (Leinster)	1966	5	4	–	1	8
McDonald, D.	Kilkenny (Leinster)	1982–7	25	15	–	10	30
McGimpsey, G.	Bangor (Ulster)	1979–90	68	49	–	19	98
McGinley, P.	Grange (Leinster)	1988	4	2	1	1	5
McGlennon, G.	Lahinch (Munster)	1958–9	12	6	–	6	12
McGrane, N.	Royal Dublin (Leinster)	1989	6	3	–	3	6
McGuirk, M.	Co. Louth (Leinster)	1961	4	–	–	4	0
McHenry, J.	Douglas (Munster)	1981–7	21	14	–	7	28
McInerney, P.	Lahinch (Munster)	1989	6	1	–	5	2
McKenna, J.	Muskerry (Munster)	1983	4	2	–	2	4
McKinney, H.	Dun Laoghaire (Connacht)	1983–6	17	6	1	10	13
McMenamin, E.	Ballybofey (Ulster)	1981–8	25	14	–	11	28
McNeill, G.	Warrenpoint (Ulster)	1989–90	12	10	–	2	20
McPartland, S.	Greenore (Leinster)	1985–7	15	8	–	7	16
McQuillan, H.	Royal Tara (Leinster)	1976	3	1	1	1	3
McSherry, S.	Co. Cavan (Connacht)	1985	4	–	–	4	0
Madeley, J.F.D.	Royal Belfast (Ulster)	1959–68	47	39	4	14	62
Mahon, D.	Galway (Connacht)	1968–85	84	21	7	56	49
Mahon, J.A.	Muskerry (Munster)	1957	6	3	–	3	6
Mahon, J.M.	Portmarnock (Leinster/Connacht)	1967–73	15	4	5	6	13
Malone, B.P.	Portmarnock (Leinster)	1959–81	100	55	9	36	119
Malone, M.J.	Belvoir Park (Ulster)	1981–2	6	3	–	3	6
Mannion, B.	Hearsall (Connacht)	1957	6	1	1	4	3
Mason, N.	Bodenstovn (Leinster)	1975–6	11	7	–	4	14
Meaney, S.	Castletroy (Munster)	1971	2	2	–	–	4
Meharg, W.	Castlerock (Ulster)	1956–7	12	7	2	3	16
Menealy, I.A.	Royal Portrush (Ulster)	1971	6	2	1	3	5
Mitchell, J.	Woodbrook (Connacht)	1988–90	16	5	–	11	10
Moore, B.	The Island (Leinster)	1977–9	14	7	1	6	15
Moore, G.	Royal Portrush (Ulster)	1985	3	1	–	2	2
Moore, R.	The Island (Leinster)	1983	3	1	–	2	2
Moran, A.	Claremorris (Connacht)	1989	3	1	–	2	2
Moran, R.J.	Woodenbridge (Leinster)	1979	4	2	–	2	4
Morris, D.	Tramore (Connacht)	1973	4	1	–	3	2
Morris, J. Jr	Douglas (Munster)	1986–90	16	9	–	7	18
Morris, M.F.	Portmarnock (Munster)	1972–85	63	32	3	28	67
Morris, M.G.I.	Limerick (Munster)	1969–83	45	21	4	20	46
Morris, P.	Douglas (Munster)	1986	5	1	–	4	2
Morrison, H.M.H.	Cliftonville (Ulster)	1958	4	4	–	–	8
Morrison, J.	Fermoy (Munster)	1968–70	15	6	2	7	14
Morrow, A.J.C.	Portmarnock (Leinster)	1982–9	29	13	1	15	27
Moss, J.C.	Royal Portrush (Ulster)	1970–76	16	4	–	12	8
Moylan, C.	Kilkenny (Leinster)	1975–9	7	4	–	3	8
Moylett, B.	Ballina (Connacht)	1956	4	–	–	4	0
Mulcare, P.	Woodbrook (Munster)	1967–80	72	38	6	28	82
Mullery, A.P.	Sutton (Connacht)	1956	6	2	–	4	4

NAME	CLUB & PROVINCE	YEAR(S)	MATCHES	WON	DRAWN	LOST	POINTS
Mulholland, D.	Castlerock (Ulster)	1988–90	11	5	–	6	10
Murphy, A.	Galway (Connacht)	1961–3	18	3	1	14	7
Murphy, C.	Clandeboye (Ulster)	1986–7	9	5	–	4	10
Murphy, J.	Dungarvan (Munster)	1987	3	1	–	2	2
Murphy, P.	Killarney (Munster)	1986–7	10	5	–	5	10
Murray, J.	Mullingar (Munster)	1957–61	12	7	1	4	15
Nelson, D.A.	Malone (Ulster)	1968	6	2	1	3	5
Nesbitt, I.A.	Malone (Ulster)	1960–61	10	6	3	1	15
Nestor, J.M.	Milltown (Leinster)	1962–6	24	16	3	5	35
Nevin, V.	Ennis (Munster)	1960–73	66	27	5	34	59
O'Beirne, B.	Swinford (Connacht)	1956–67	28	11	3	14	25
O'Boyle, P.	Athlone (Connacht)	1981–4	14	3	–	11	6
O'Boyle, P.M.	Royal Dublin (Leinster)	1975–8	22	14	–	8	28
O'Brien, E.	Limerick (Munster)	1956–7	12	8	1	3	17
O'Brien, E.C.	Tullamore (Leinster)	1963–4	8	4	2	2	10
O'Brien, M.D.	New Ross (Leinster)	1967–78	46	24	4	18	52
O'Connell, E.	Killarney (Munster)	1984–5	10	6	1	3	13
O'Connor, A.	Naas (Connacht)	1964–72	42	24	5	13	53
O'Connor, D.P.	Tramore (Munster)	1979–80	6	2	1	3	5
O'Connor, T.	Galway (Connacht)	1960–69	58	15	9	34	39
O'Donovan, S.	Co. Sligo (Connacht)	1983–6	20	7	–	13	14
O'Flaherty, P.D.	Clones (Connacht)	1967–70	13	2	2	9	6
O'Flynn, D.	Enniscrone (Connacht)	1990	5	1	–	4	2
O'Grady, D.	UCD (Leinster)	1958	6	2	–	4	4
O'Leary, J.E.	Foxrock (Leinster)	1968–70	18	12	1	5	25
O'Looney, P.	Connemara (Connacht)	1974–86	51	14	1	36	29
O'Neill, H.	Connemara (Connacht)	1987–9	17	3	1	14	7
O'Neill, J.J.	Donabate (Leinster)	1966–70	28	19	5	4	43
O'Rourke, P.	Kilkenny (Leinster)	1977–87	56	34	2	20	70
O'Shea, A.	Elm Park (Connacht)	1989–90	11	6	–	5	12
O'Sullivan, D.F.	Cork (Munster)	1971–90	77	38	2	37	78
O'Sullivan, G.	Tralee (Munster)	1988–9	10	4	–	6	8
O'Sullivan, J.	Athlone (Connacht)	1956–65	52	13	5	34	31
O'Sullivan, P.	Kinsale (Munster)	1961–82	28	14	5	9	33
O'Sullivan P.	Athlone (Connacht)	1980–82	10	2	–	8	4
Parkhill, G.	Castlerock (Ulster)	1983	6	4	–	2	8
Patterson, M.	Royal Portrush (Ulster)	1977–8	5	2	1	2	5
Patton, B.	Strabane (Ulster)	1986–9	18	12	–	6	24
Paul, S.	Tandragee (Ulster)	1990	6	1	–	5	2
Pierse, A.D.	Tipperary (Munster)	1974–90	69	38	2	29	78
Pollin, R.K.M.	Royal Belfast (Ulster)	1967–76	46	21	6	19	48
Power, E.	Tramore (Munster)	1986–90	22	12	–	10	24
Power, M.	Muskerry (Munster)	1957	6	3	2	1	8
Purcell, J.	Mullingar (Leinster)	1973–4	9	7	1	1	15
Quaid, M.C.	Galway (Connacht)	1979–90	22	5	1	16	11
Quigley, J.	Ballina (Connacht)	1956–9	20	5	3	12	13
Quinn, M.	Tuam (Connacht)	1961–4	18	–	2	16	2
Quirke, M.	Doneraile (Munster)	1987–8	8	4	–	4	8
Quirke, M.J.	Galway (Connacht)	1980	1	–	–	1	0
Rafferty, R.	Warrenpoint (Ulster)	1980	5	4	–	1	8
Rainey, W.H.E.	Shandon Park (Ulster)	1960–66	27	11	–	16	22
Rayfus, P.	Trim (Leinster)	1986–9	19	9	–	10	18
Reddan, B.V.M.	Co. Louth (Leinster)	1987–8	25	11	1	13	23
Rice, W.	Limerick (Munster)	1967–82	29	10	2	17	22
Ritchie, W.I.	Massereene (Ulster)	1969	4	2	–	2	4
Rogers, B.	The Island (Leinster)	1977–9	13	5	2	6	12
Rogers, P.	Dundalk (Leinster)	1982	5	2	–	3	4
Ronan, F.	Co. Louth (Leinster)	1979–88	19	10	–	9	20
Rooney, S.	Co. Sligo (Connacht)	1985–7	15	3	–	12	6
Ryan, D.	Portmarnock (Leinster)	1956–7	12	5	2	5	12
Ryan, P.A.	Milltown (Leinster)	1968	1	–	–	1	0

NAME	CLUB & PROVINCE	YEAR(S)	MATCHES	WON	DRAWN	LOST	POINTS
*Scannell, B.J.	Woodbrook (Leinster)	1956–62	16	8	4	4	20
Scott, P.	Galway (Connacht)	1984	3	1	–	2	2
Scott, R.	Royal Dublin (Connacht)	1981–2	11	2	–	9	4
Sheahan, D.B.	Grange (Leinster)	1959–76	49	22	8	19	52
Sheils, J.	Dundalk (Leinster)	1959	6	3	1	2	7
Shine, N.	Muskerry (Munster)	1978	6	1	1	4	3
Skerritt, A.	Lahinch (Munster)	1958–62	22	10	1	11	21
Skerritt, M.	Lahinch (Munster)	1962–5	18	9	3	6	21
Sludds, M.F.	The Island (Leinster)	1981–2	12	7	–	5	14
Smith, A.	The Island (Leinster)	1985	1	–	–	1	0
Smith, P.	Galway (Connacht)	1956–61	10	2	–	8	4
Smyth, D.	L'town & B'town (Leinster)	1971–3	14	9	1	4	19
Smyth, H.B.	City of Derry Royal Co. Down (Ulster)	1974–80	40	21	3	16	45
Smyth, J.D.	Lahinch (Munster)	1967–76	45	22	8	15	52
Smyth, V.J.	L'town & B'town (Leinster)	1970–84	35	27	–	8	54
Soden, P.P.	Co. Sligo (Connacht)	1971–81	21	10	1	10	21
Solon, J.	Athlone (Connacht)	1956–60	24	4	–	20	8
Spring, A.D.	Tralee (Munster)	1977–84	19	10	–	9	20
Staunton, H.deL.	Castlerea (Connacht)	1970	6	1	–	5	2
Staunton, R.deL.	Castlerea (Connacht)	1962–85	124	44	13	67	101
Stevenson, K.	Banbridge (Ulster)	1972–84	46	23	3	20	49
Stewart, C.	Royal Dublin (Leinster)	1961	2	2	–	–	4
Sweeney, B.	Skerries (Connacht)	1988–9	10	1	–	9	2
Taggart, J.	Royal Portrush (Ulster)	1962–3	12	6	4	2	16
Tennant, W.R.	Cliftonville (Ulster)	1960–67	8	5	1	2	11
Thomas, V.	Bootle (Connacht)	1962	6	1	–	5	2
Thompson, W.C.	Sutton (Connacht)	1977–80	16	4	–	12	8
Tinsley, W.G.	Bangor (Ulster)	1963	4	1	1	2	3
Troy, K.	Portmarnock (Leinster)	1957	6	3	2	1	8
Twohig, V.	Tullamore (Munster)	1982–3	10	5	–	5	10
Underwood, S.	Westport (Connacht)	1988	3	1	–	2	2
Walker, L.	Grange (Leinster)	1989–90	5	1	–	4	2
Wallace, K.	Galway (Connacht)	1956–60	30	7	2	21	16
Walsh, P.	Limerick (Munster)	1961	4	1	1	2	3
Walton, P.	Malahide (Leinster)	1980–81	12	7	–	5	14
Wilson, B.	Clandeboye (Ulster)	1965–85	55	28	12	15	68
Windebank, M.	Royal Portrush (Ulster)	1983	1	–	–	1	0
White, D.	Tullamore (Leinster)	1971	5	3	2	–	8
Wynne, A.	Carrick-on-Shannon (Connacht)	1983–4	9	2	–	7	4
Young, D.J.F.	Malone (Ulster)	1967–83	46	26	3	17	55
Young, G.A.	Kilrush (Munster)	1956–72	39	15	4	20	34

APPENDIX XI
Section 1

Record of Winners of the Irish Inter-Schools Golf Championship

YEAR	VENUE	WINNER
1967	Royal Dublin	St Joseph's CBS, Drogheda
1968	Co. Louth	St Joseph's CBS, Drogheda
1969	Donabate	St Joseph's CBS, Drogheda
1970	Milltown	Regent House, Belfast
1971	Tullamore	St Joseph's CBS, Drogheda
1972	Edmondstown	Royal Belfast Academical Inst.
1973	Birr	Rockwell College, Cashel
1974	Clontarf	Bangor Grammar School
1975	L'town & B'town	Rockwell College, Cashel
1976	Donabate	Belvedere College, Dublin
1977	Kilkenny	Blackrock College, Dublin
1978	Tullamore	Bangor Grammar School
1979	Athlone	Bangor Grammar School
1980	Headfort	Belcamp College, Dublin
1981	Donabate	CBC, Carlow
1982	Tullamore	St Patrick's High School
1983	Elm Park	Royal Belfast Academical Inst.
1984	Mullingar	CBC, Cork
1985	Clontarf	Summerhill College, Sligo
1986	L'town & B'town	Summerhill College, Sligo
1987	Grange	Armagh College of Further Educ.
1988	Royal Tara	Summerhill College, Sligo
1989	Headfort	Kells Community
1990	L'town & B'town	Coleraine Academical Institute

APPENDIX XI
Section 3

Record of Winners of Youths' Amateur Open Championship of Ireland

YEAR	VENUE	WINNER AND CLUB
1969	Delgany	D. Branigan (L'town & B'town)
1970	Tullamore	L.A. Owens (Killiney)
1971	Athlone	M.A. Gannon (Co. Louth)
1972	Mullingar	M.A. Gannon (Co. Louth)
1973	Tullamore	J. Purcell (Mullingar)
1974	Athlone	S. Dunlop (Killarney)
1975	Mullingar	P. McNally (Edenderry)
1976	Tullamore	R. McCormack (Warrenpoint)
1977	Athlone	B. McDaid (Skibbereen)
1978	Thurles	T. Corridan (Ballybunion)
1979	Tullamore	R. Rafferty (Warrenpoint)
1980	Clandeboye	J. McHenry (Douglas)
1981	Westport	J. McHenry (Douglas)
1982	Mullingar	K. O'Donnell (Clandeboye)
1983	Cork	P. Murphy (Killarney)
1984	Bangor	J. Morris (Douglas)
1985	Co. Sligo	J. McHenry (Douglas)
1986	Carlow	J. Morris (Douglas)
1987	Killarney	C. Everett (Scotland)
1988	Malone	P. McGinley (Grange)
1989	Athlone	A.W. Mathers (Elie, Scotland)
1990	Dundalk	D. Errity (Hermitage)

APPENDIX XI
Section 2

Record of Winners and Runners-up in the Boys' Amateur Open Championship of Ireland

YEAR	VENUE	WINNER	RUNNER-UP	RESULT
1966	Co. Louth	M. Hanway (Sutton)	A. Rea (Downpatrick)	19th
1967	Royal Dublin	J.R. Carey (Roscrea)	W. O'Brien (Lahinch)	4 and 3
1968	Co Louth	M.A. Gannon (Co. Louth)	J.C. Brewer (Massereene)	3 and 2

1969 Discontinued in favour of Youths' Amateur Open Championship of Ireland

APPENDIX XI

Section 4

Detailed results of the two Irish youth matches against the Continent of Europe at Royal Burgess Golf Club in 1970 and the Northamptonshire Country Club in 1971

1970

IRELAND	v.	CONTINENT OF EUROPE	
J.E. O'Leary (Foxrock)	halved with	B. Dassu (Italy)	
R.J. Carr (Sutton)	beat	R. Tava (Spain)	2 holes
J.E. Carey (Roscrea)	beat	O. Dahlgren (Sweden)	3 and 2
H.B. Smyth (City of Derry)	beat	H. Ortegren (Sweden)	4 and 3
J.C. Brewer (Massereene)	beat	C.H. Nilsson (Sweden)	5 and 4
L.A. Owens (Portmarnock)	beat	J.L. Noguer (Spain)	1 hole
J. O'Grady (Fermoy)	lost to	L. Sousa E. Melo (Portugal)	2 and 1
V. Smyth (L'town & B'town)	lost to	H. Heinrigs (Germany)	2 and 1
M. Bloom (Edmondstown)	beat	R. Darieumerlou (France)	1 hole
D. Smyth (L'town & B'town)	beat	J. Nielsen (Denmark)	3 and 2
J. Coyne (Strabane & U.C.D.)	beat	J. Gram Hagen (Denmark)	6 and 5

Ireland beat the Continent of Europe by 8 matches to 2 with 1 match halved.

1971

M.A. Gannon (Co. Louth)	beat	M. Tapia (France)	2 and 1
R.J. Carr (Sutton)	beat	T. Fortmann (Switzerland)	5 and 3
H.B. Smith (City of Derry)	beat	H.G. Heinrigs (Germany)	1 hole
J.C. Brewer (Massereene)	beat	J.L. Sousa E. Melo (Portugal)	1 hole
D. Smyth (Laytown & Bettystown)	beat	E. Donnestad (Norway)	1 hole
J. Turley (Portadown)	lost to	O. Carbonnelle (Belgium)	3 and 2
P.B. Malone (Belvoir Park)	lost to	J. Neilsen (Denmark)	5 and 4
R.A.F. Turnbull (Douglas)	beat	A. Trienen (Holland)	4 and 8
V.M. Ryan (Skerries)	lost to	Y. Mahain (Belgium)	6 and 4
J.R. Carey (Roscrea)	lost to	Y. Holfstetter (Switzerland)	3 and 2

Ireland beat the Continent of Europe by 6 matches to 4.

APPENDIX XI

Section 5

Record of Irish representatives in the Boys' International matches against Wales from 1972 to 1984

NAME	CLUB	YEAR(S)	MATCHES	WON	DRAWN	LOST	POINTS
P. Aherne	Malahide	1972	2	Match results unavailable			
N.H. Anderson	Shandon Park	1977–9	6	3	–	3	6
H. Boyd	Royal Portrush	1973	2	1	–	1	2
J. Brennan	Malone	1972	2	–	–	2	0
P. Brunton	Donaghadee	1980	2	–	–	2	0
W.J. Buckley	Ballybunion	1975	2	–	1	1	1
V. Buggy	Newlands	1977	2	1	1	–	3

NAME	CLUB	YEAR(S)	MATCHES	WON	DRAWN	LOST	POINTS
J. Carvill	Warrenpoint	1983	2	1	–	1	2
D. Casey	Skibbereen	1973	2	1	–	1	2
G. Clarke	Royal Portrush	1983	2	1	–	1	2
N. Coey	Clandeboye	1981	2	Match results unavailable			
T. Corridan	Ballybunion	1974–6	6	2	2	2	6
R. Culligan	Lahinch	1979–80	4	2	1	1	5
M. Curry	Castlecomer	1982–4	4	–	1	3	1
J. Doyle	Arklow	1973	2	1	–	1	2
M. Eaton	Clandeboye	1982	2	Match results unavailable			
J. Farrell	Carlow	1983–4	4	1	–	3	2
C. Fitzsimmons	Ardglass	1981	2	Match results unavailable			
K. Greene	Delgany	1978	2	1	–	1	2
P. Gribben	Warrenpoint	1984	2	1	–	1	2
G. Hamill	Ardglass	1980	2	2	–	–	4
R.A. Hanna	Lurgan	1977	1	–	–	1	0
D.P.W. Heather	Sutton	1974	2	–	–	2	0
B. Hobson	Malone	1978–9	4	1	–	3	2
A. Hogan	C. on-Shannon	1977	2	1	–	1	2
R. Houston	Cairndhu	1974	2	2	–	–	4
J. Hutchinson	Royal Dublin	1979	2	1	–	1	2
J. Jones	Whitehead	1977	2	1	1	–	3
M. Kavanagh	Kilkenny	1975	2	–	1	1	1
K. Kearney	Roscommon	1984	2	–	–	2	0
S. Keenan	Galway	1984	2	1	–	1	2
T. Kelliher	Killarney	1983	2	1	–	1	2
R. McCormack	Warrenpoint	1972	2	1	–	1	2
B. McDaid	Skibbereen	1977–80	6	1	–	5	2
K. McDaid	Skibbereen	1981	2	Match results unavailable			
P. McDonald	Carlow	1983	2	2	–	–	4
N. McGill	Castletroy	1978	2	1	–	1	2
G. McGimpsey	Bangor	1972	2	–	–	2	0
N. McGrane	Greenore	1980	2	1	1	–	3
J. McHenry	Douglas	1980	2	–	–	2	0
J. McHenry	Douglas	1981	2	Match results unavailable			
P. McInerney	Lahinch	1974	2	–	–	2	0
J. Mahony	Malahide	1975–6	4	–	–	4	0
P. Mitchel	Holywood	1981	2	Match results unavailable			
G. Moore	Royal Portrush	1984	2	–	1	1	1
J. Morris	Douglas	1982	2	Match results unavailable			
C. Moylan	Kilkenny	1973–4	4	3	–	1	6
P. Murphy	Killarney	1980	2	2	–	–	4
P. Murphy	Killarney	1981	2	Match results unavailable			
T. Murphy	Co. Sligo	1975	2	1	–	1	2
P.M. O'Boyle	Sutton	1973	2	1	1	–	3
E. O'Connell	Killarney	1984	2	1	–	1	2
D. O'Connor	Tramore	1977	2	1	–	1	2
G. O'Connor	Naas	1977–8	4	4	–	–	8
K. O'Donnell	Clandeboye	1981	2	Match results unavailable			
P. O'Hagen	Warrenpoint	1973–4	4	–	–	4	0
P. Orr	Royal Portrush	1975	2	–	–	2	0
P. Osborne	Shandon Park	1973	2	2	–	–	4
P. O'Sullivan	Athlone	1981	2	Match results unavailable			
J. Peden	Malone	1979	2	2	–	–	4
E. Power	Tramore	1982	2	Match results unavailable			
J. Purcell	Mullingar	1972	2	2	–	–	4
R. Rafferty	Warrenpoint	1978–9	4	2	–	2	4
S. Rooney	Co. Sligo	1980	2	1	–	1	2
K. Sheehen	Cork	1984	2	1	–	1	2
K. Sheridan	Curragh	1983	2	1	–	1	2
T. Sheehy	Skibbereen	1979	2	1	–	1	2
P. Trainor	Warrenpoint	1972	2	1	–	1	2
P. Walton	Malahide	1977–9	6	5	–	1	10

Record of venues, Team Captains and results

YEAR	VENUE	TEAM CAPTAIN	RESULT	
1972	Moortown, Leeds, England	H. Breffni O'Reilly	Ireland	5/4
1973	Blairgowrie, Scotland	H. Breffni O'Reilly	Ireland	5½/3½
1974	Royal Liverpool, England	H. Breffni O'Reilly	Wales	5/4
1975	Bruntsfield, Scotland	Frederick P. McDonnell	Wales	6½/2½
1976	Sunningdale, England	Patrick J. Foley	Wales	7½/1½
1977	Downfield, Scotland	Frederick P. McDonnell	Ireland	6½/5½
1978	Hartlepool, England	Frederick P. McDonnell	Ireland	8/4
1979	Barassie, Scotland	Frederick P. McDonnell	Ireland	9½/2½
1980	Formby, England	Frederick P. McDonnell	Wales	9½/2½
1981	Gullane, Scotland	Frederick P. McDonnell	Ireland	8/4
1982	Burnham, England	Joseph Quinlan	Wales	6½/5½
1983	Glenbervie, Scotland	Joseph Quinlan	Ireland	7/5
1984	Porthcawl, Wales	Joseph Quinlan	Wales	6½/5½

This annual match is now played as part of the Boys' 'Home' International matches for the R & A Trophy.

APPENDIX XI
Section 6

Record of winning Clubs and teams in the Irish Club Youths' Championship

1974 SUTTON

J. Carr
D. Fitzpatrick
D. Heather
P. O'Boyle

1975 SUTTON

J. Carr
D. Fitzpatrick
D. Heather

1976 ROYAL PORTRUSH

H. Boyd
D. Cameron
G. McAleese

1977 ROYAL DUBLIN
G. Fogarty
C. Herlihy
P.M. O'Boyle

1978 GALWAY
G. Kelly
J. Power
M. Quaid

1979 ROYAL PORTRUSH
P. Leckey
G. McAleese
M. Windebank

1980 CASTLE-TROY
T. Corridan
B. McDaid
N. McGill

1981 THE ISLAND
D. Rushe
M. Sludds
P. Walton

1982 WARREN-POINT
J. Carvill
R. Morgan
S. Rafferty

1983 GRANGE
D. O'Brien
B. Shaw
D. Walker

1984 ARDGLASS
M. Curran
C. Fitzsimons
G. Hamill

1985 BANTRY PARK
P. Buckley
D. Maguire
J. O'Reilly

1986 GRANGE
P. McGinley
B. Shaw
L. Walker

1987 GRANGE
P. McGinley
B. Shaw
L. Walker

1988 CO. SLIGO
F. Howley
S. Quirke
G. Sproule

1989 WARREN-POINT
E. Barr
P. Gribben
G. McNeill

1990 CO. SLIGO
F. Howley
N. Quirke
G. Sproule

APPENDIX XI
Section 7

Record of Irish representatives in the youth international matches against Scotland from 1979 to 1990

NAME	CLUB	YEAR(S)	MATCHES	WON	DRAWN	LOST	POINTS
N.H. Anderson	Shandon Park	1982–3	4	1	1	2	3
D.W. Ballentine	Portstewart	1981	2	1	–	1	2
J. Carvill	Warrenpoint	1984–5	4	1	1	2	3
D. Clarke	Dungannon	1987–8	4	1	1	2	3
P. Congden	Clontarf	1982	2	–	1	1	1
E. Connaughton	Roscommon	1981	2	1	1	–	3
J. Farrell	Carlow	1984–5	4	–	1	3	1
F. Flynn	L'town & B'town	1980	2	Match results unavailable			
N. Goulding	Portmarnock	1986	2	–	–	2	0
P. Grant	Ballymena	1983	2	–	–	2	0
P Gribben	Warrenpoint	1987–8	4	2	–	2	4
R.A. Hanna	Lurgan	1980	2	Match results unavailable			
P. Harrington	Stackstown	1990	2	1	–	1	2
R. Hennessy	Ennis	1982	2	1	–	1	2
F. Howley	Co. Sligo	1990	2	1	–	1	2
J. Hutchinson	Royal Dublin	1980	2	Match results unavailable			
J. Hutchinson	Royal Dublin	1982–3	4	1	1	2	3
K. Kearney	Roscommon	1987–8	4	1	2	1	4
S. Keenan	Galway	1986	2	–	–	2	0
B. McDaid	Skibbereen	1981	2	–	–	2	0
P. McGinley	Grange	1987–8	4	2	1	1	5
N. McGrane	Greenore	1982	2	–	–	2	0
J. McHenry	Douglas	1981–3	6	4	1	1	9
D. McInerney	Lahinch	1987	2	–	–	2	0
G. McNeill	Warrenpoint	1990	2	1	–	1	2
P. Mitchel	Holywood	1984	2	–	–	2	0
J.C. Morris	Douglas	1984–6	4	1	1	2	3
D. Mulholland	Castlerock	1986	2	2	–	–	4
P. Murphy	Killarney	1982–5	8	2	–	6	4
E. O'Connell	Killarney	1984–8	8	4	1	3	9
D. O'Connor	Tramore	1980	2	Match results unavailable			
K. O'Donnell	Clandeboye	1983	2	1	–	1	2
K. O'Flaherty	Cork	1990	2	1	1	–	3
H. O'Neill	Connemara	1988	2	1	1	–	3
P. O'Sullivan	Athlone	1980	2	Match results unavailable			
S. Paul	Tandragee	1990	2	–	–	2	0
E. Power	Tramore	1984–6	6	2	–	4	4
M. Sludds	The Island	1980	2	Match results unavailable			
M. Sludds	The Island	1981	2	–	1	1	1
L. Walker	Grange	1990	2	–	2	–	2
P. Walton	Malahide	1981	2	1	–	1	2

Record of venues, Team Captains and results

YEAR	VENUE	TEAM CAPTAIN	RESULT	
1980	Musselborough, Scotland	Barry T. Crymble	Scotland	7/2
1981	Co. Louth, Baltray, Ireland	Barry T. Crymble	Scotland	5½/3½
1982	Leven, Scotland	Frederick P. McDonnell	Scotland	7/2
1983	Cork, Ireland	Frederick P. McDonnell	Scotland	5½/3½
1984	East Renfrewshire, Scotland	Frederick P. McDonnell	Scotland	6/3
1985	Co. Sligo, Ireland	John V. Lynch	Scotland ⎱ Tie 4½/4½ Ireland ⎰	
1986	Cawder, Scotland	John V. Lynch	Scotland	7/2
1987	Killarney, Ireland	John V. Lynch	Scotland	7/2
1988	Ladybank, Scotland	Michael P. O'Donoghue	Ireland	7½/4½
1989	Athlone, Ireland	Michael P. O'Donoghue	Ireland ⎱ Tie 4½/4½ Scotland ⎰	
1990	Stranraer, Scotland	Michael P. O'Donoghue	Ireland	5/4

APPENDIX XII

Section 1

Results of the 1965 European Amateur Team Golf Championship at Royal St George's Golf Club, Sandwich, Kent on 23-27 June 1965

QUALIFYING ROUND 35 HOLES STROKEPLAY

First flight

1 England	597	
2 Ireland	599	
3 Scotland	603	
4 Wales	609	

Second flight

5 France	620
6 Sweden	631
7 Germany	631
8 Denmark	637

Third flight

9 Italy	638
10 Spain	643
11 Belgium	651

Fourth flight

12 Switzerland	673
13 Finland	673
14 Norway	675

Fifth flight

15 Portugal	679
16 Holland	681
17 Austria	698

Details of Ireland's qualifying scores

Player	1st Round	2nd Round
J.B. Carr (Sutton)	71	78
T. Craddock (Malahide)	76	74
R.M. Craigan (Malone)	88	74
W.E. McCrea (Walton Heath)	77	79
V. Nevin (Ennis)	76	73
R.de L. Staunton (Castlerea)	81	
D.B. Sheahan (Grange)		82

The leading 4 returns in each round counted for qualification

J.B. Carr (71) T. Craddock (76), W.E. McCrea (77), V. Nevin (76)	300
J.B. Carr (78) T. Craddock (74), R.M. Craigan (74), V. Nevin (73)	299
	599

MATCH PLAY

IRELAND		SCOTLAND	
FOURSOMES			
D.B. Sheahan & W.E. McCrea (2 and 1)	1	A.C. Sadler & C.W. Green	0
J.B. Carr & T. Craddock (5 and 3)	1	R.D.B.M. Shade & F.C. Black	0
B.M. Craigan & V. Nevin (3 and 2)	1	G.B. Cosh & A. J. Low	0
	3		0
SINGLES			
D.B. Sheahan	0	R.D.B.M. Shade (3 and 2)	1
J.B. Carr (4 and 3)	1	A.C. Sadler	0
T. Craddock (2 and 1)	1	G.B. Cosh	0
W.E. McCrea	½	A.J. Low	½
R.M. Craigan (4 and 3)	1	F.C. Black	0
V. Nevin	½	C.W. Green	½
	4		2

Ireland beat Scotland 6 Matches to 1 with 2 Matches Halved.

IRELAND			WALES	
	FOURSOMES			
D.B. Sheahan &			H.C. Squirrell &	
W.E. McCrea (7 and 5)	1		W.I. Tucker	0
J.B. Carr &			E.N. Davies &	
T. Craddock (1 hole)	1		J.L. Toye	0
R.M. Craigan &			J.L. Morgan &	
V. Nevin (1 hole)	1		J.K.D. Povall	0
	3			0

	SINGLES			
D.B. Sheahan	0		H.C. Squirrell (3 and 2)	1
J.B. Carr (4 and 3)	1		J.K.V. Povall	0
T. Craddock	½		W.I. Tucker	½
W.E. McCrea (6 and 4)	1		J.L. Morgan	0
R.M. Craigan	½		J.L. Toye	½
V. Nevin (4 and 3)	1		E.N. Davies	0
	4			2

Ireland beat Wales 6 Matches to 1 with 2 Matches Halved.

IRELAND			ENGLAND	
	FOURSOMES			
D.B. Sheahan &				
W.E. McCrea	½		R. Foster & C.A. Clark	½
J.B. Carr &			M.S.R. Lunt &	
T. Craddock (1 hole)	1		P.M. Townsend	0
B.M. Craigan & V. Nevin	½		M.F. Bonallack & G.J. Clark	½
	2			1

	SINGLES			
J.B. Carr	0		M.F. Bonallack (2 and 1)	1
D.B. Sheahan	0		R. Foster (4 and 2)	1
T. Craddock (1 hole)	1		M.J. Christmas	0
W.E. McCrea	0		G.J. Clark (1 hole)	1
R.M. Craigan	0		C.A. Clark (6 and 4)	1
V. Nevin	0		M.S.R. Lunt (4 and 2)	1
	1			5

England beat Ireland 5 Matches to 1 with 2 Matches Halved.

Summary of Results of First Flight

England beat Wales 6 Matches to 2 with 1 Match halved.
England lost to Scotland 2 Matches to 6 with 1 Match halved.
England beat Ireland 5 Matches to 2 with 2 Matches halved.
Ireland beat Wales 6 Matches to 1 with 2 Matches halved.
Ireland beat Scotland 6 Matches to 1 with 2 Matches halved.
Ireland lost to England 2 Matches to 5 with 2 Matches halved.
Scotland lost to Ireland 1 Match to 6 with 2 Matches halved.
Scotland beat England 6 Matches to 2 with 1 Match halved.
Scotland beat Wales 6 Matches to 1 with 2 Matches halved.
Wales lost to England 2 Matches to 6 with 1 Match halved.
Wales lost to Ireland 1 Match to 6 with 2 Matches halved.
Wales lost to Scotland 1 Match to 6 with 2 Matches halved.
As no country had outright wins against all other countries in the First Flight, the rules of the Championship provided that a decision be reached on matches won and the final result was: 1st Ireland 14 matches won, 6 matches halved, 7 matches lost. 2nd Scotland 13 matches won, 5 matches halved, 9 matches lost. 3rd England 13 matches won, 4 matches halved, 10 matches lost. 4th Wales 4 matches won, 5 matches halved, 18 matches lost. 5th France, 6th Sweden, 7th Germany, 8th Denmark, 9th Spain, 10th Belgium, 11th Italy, 12th Norway, 13th Switzerland, 14th Finland, 15th Holland, 16th Portugal, and 17th Austria.

APPENDIX XII

Section 2

YEAR	VENUE	IRISH CAPTAIN	WINNING COUNTRY	IRELAND'S POSITION	
1959	El Prat, Barcelona, Spain		Sweden		(9)
1961	Royal Club de Belgique, Brussels, Belgium		Sweden		(10)
1963	Falsterbo, Sweden		England		(14)
1965	The Royal St George's, Sandwich, England	Cecil Ewing	Ireland	First	(17)
1967	Cirola, Turin, Italy	Cecil Ewing	Ireland	First	(16)
1969	Hamburg Falkenstein, Germany	Cecil Ewing	England	Third	(18)
1971	Lausanne, Switzerland	William J. J. Ferguson	England	Fifth	(17)
1973	Penina, Portugal	Brendan J. Scannell	England	Thirteenth	(18)
1975	Killarney, Ireland	Brendan J. Scannell	Scotland	Seventh	(18)
1977	Haagsche, Holland	Laurence McCarthy	Scotland	Twelfth	(16)
1979	Esbjerg, Denmark	Joseph B. Carr	England	Second	(19)
1981	St Andrews, Scotland	Joseph B. Carr	England	Fifth	(19)
1983	Chantilly, France	Brendan Edwards	Ireland	First	(19)
1985	Halmstad, Sweden	Eamon Curran	Scotland	Sixth	(19)
1987	Murhof, Austria	Eamon Curran	Ireland	First	(19)
1989	Porthcawl, Wales	George F. Crosbie	England	Third	(20)

(The number in brackets in the right column indicates the number of competing countries)

APPENDIX XII
Section 3

A record of all players who participated in the European Amateur Golf Team Championship from 1965 to 1990

NAME	CLUB	YEAR(S)	MATCHES	WON	DRAWN	LOST	POINTS
Anderson, N.H.	Shandon Park	1985–9	13	5	2	6	12
Branigan, D.	L'town & B'town	1977–81	10	7	–	3	14
Carr, J.B.	Sutton	1965–9	17	13	–	4	26
Carr, J.J.	Sutton	1983	3	2	–	1	4
Carr, R.J.	Sutton	1971	6	4	–	2	8
Carvill, J.	Warrenpoint	1989	6	5	–	1	10
Clarke, D.	Dungannon	1989	3	1	–	2	2
Cleary, T.	Fermoy	1983	3	1	–	2	2
Corcoran, D.K.	Royal Dublin	1973	4	3	–	1	6
Craddock, T.	Malahide	1965–71	22	16	2	4	34
Craigan, R.M.	Malone	1965	6	3	2	1	8
Dickson, J.R.	Holywood	1977	4	3	–	1	6
Dunne, E.	Athlone	1975	1	–	–	1	0
Egan, T.W.	Monkstown	1967–9	10	4	–	6	8
Elliott, I.A.	Royal Portrush	1975	6	2	–	4	4
Feeney, J.	Chapel en Le Frith	1985	2	–	–	2	0
Flaherty, P.D.	Addington	1967–9	6	3	–	3	6
Gannon, M.A.	Co. Louth	1979–89	17	9	2	6	20
Harrington, J.	Adare Manor	1975	6	2	1	3	5
Hoey, T.B.C.	Shandon Park	1971–7	8	4	–	4	8
Hogan, P.F.	Elm Park	1987	1	–	–	1	0
Kane, R.M.	The Island	1971–9	10	4	–	6	8
Long, D.C.	Shandon Park	1979	6	2	1	3	5
Mackeown, H.N.	Cork	1973	3	3	–	–	6
MacNamara, L.	Woodbrook	1977–87	14	8	1	5	17
McCrea, W.E.	Walton Heath	1965	6	3	2	1	8
McGimpsey, G.	Bangor	1981–9	27	18	1	8	37
McHenry, J.	Douglas	1987	6	5	1	–	11
Malone, B.P.	Portmarnock	1971–5	7	4	–	3	8
Morris, M.F.	Portmarnock	1979–83	7	5	1	1	11
Mulcare, P.	Woodbrook	1975–9	10	3	–	7	6
Nevin, V.	Ennis	1965–73	14	7	2	5	16
O'Boyle, P.	Royal Dublin	1977	2	1	–	1	2
O'Brien, M.D.	New Ross	1971	5	3	–	2	6
O'Connell, E.	Killarney	1987–9	12	11	–	1	22
O'Leary, J.E.	Foxrock	1969	5	3	1	1	7
O'Sullivan, D.F.	Cork	1977	4	2	–	2	4
Pierse, A.D.	Tipperary	1981–5	18	8	2	8	18
Pollin, R.K.M.	Royal Belfast	1973	3	–	–	3	0
Rafferty, R.	Warrenpoint	1981	3	1	–	2	2
Sheehan, D.B.	Grange	1965–7	10	4	1	5	9
Smyth, D.	L'town & B'town	1973	4	2	–	2	4
Smyth, H.B.	Royal Co. Down	1975–9	7	4	1	2	9
Staunton, R.de L.	Castlerea	1965–73	2	1	–	1	2
Walton, P.	Malahide	1981–3	12	10	–	2	20

APPENDIX XIII

Section 1

Record of Irish representatives in friendly official matches against Sweden 1966 (five matches), Italy 1968 and Germany 1968, 1970 and 1974

An Ulster selected team (seven players) defeated Sweden by five matches to four but individual detailed results are not available.

NAME	CLUB	YEAR(S)	MATCHES	WON	DRAWN	LOST	POINTS
M. Bloom	Edmondstown	1970	2	–	–	2	0
A. Brown	Shandon Park	1968	2	Match results unavailable			
J.A. Bryan	Edmondstown	1966	2	1	1	–	3
J.B. Carr	Sutton	1968	2	2	–	–	4
R.J. Carr	Sutton	1970	2	2	–	–	4
P. Caul	Malahide	1974	2	1	–	1	2
R.M. Craigan	Malone	1966	2	–	1	1	1
D.K. Corcoran	Royal Dublin	1966–74	4	4	–	–	8
M. Craddock	Malahide	1966	2	1	–	1	2
T. Craddock	Malahide	1966–8	4	4	–	–	8
J. Derby	Clandeboye	1966	2	–	1	1	1
C. Devins	Co. Sligo	1966	2	1	–	1	2
B. Edwards	Shandon Park	1966–8	4	–	3	1	3
T.W. Egan	Monkstown	1968	2	2	–	–	4
I.A. Elliott	Delgany	1966	2	1	–	1	2
C. Ewing	Co. Sligo	1966	1	–	–	1	0
C.E. Fitzgerald	Lucan	1968	2	2	–	–	4
G.N. Fogarty	Royal Dublin	1968	2	2	–	–	4
F. Gannon	Co. Louth	1968	2	2	–	–	4
M.A. Gannon	Co. Louth	1974	2	–	–	2	0
D. Gillen	Co. Sligo	1966	2	1	–	1	2
L. Higgins	Cork	1966	2	1	–	1	2
T.B.C. Hoey	Shandon Park	1970	2	1	–	1	2
S.F. Hosty	Galway	1966	2	1	1	–	3
R.M. Kane	The Island	1974	2	1	1	–	3
N.S. Kelly	Knock	1966	2	1	–	1	2
G. McCormack	Castletroy	1966	2	–	1	1	1
T.P. McDonald	Skerries	1966	2	2	–	–	4
G. McGlennon	Lahinch	1966	2	–	1	1	1
K. McKeown	Lahinch	1966	2	2	–	–	4
J.F.D. Madeley	Royal Belfast	1966	2	1	–	1	2
J.M. Mahon	Portmarnock	1966	2	1	1	–	3
M.G.I. Morris	Limerick	1966	2	2	–	–	4
J. Morrison	Fermoy	1966	2	1	–	1	2
J.G. Moss	Knock	1968	2	Match results unavailable			
D. Nelson	Malone	1968	2	Match results unavailable			
M.D. O'Brien	New Ross	1970	2	2	–	–	4
A. O'Connor	Withington	1966	2	2	–	–	4
T. O'Connor	Galway	1966	2	1	–	1	2
J.E. O'Leary	Foxrock	1968–70	4	1	–	3	2
J. O'Sullivan	Athlone	1966	1	–	–	1	0
J. Purcell	Mullingar	1974	2	1	–	1	2
W. Rice	Limerick	1966	2	–	2	–	2
I.W. Ritchie	Massereene	1968	2	–	2	–	2
I.W. Ritchie	Massereene	1968	2	Match results unavailable			

NAME	CLUB	YEAR(S)	MATCHES	WON	DRAWN	LOST	POINTS
P.A. Ryan	Milltown	1968	2	1	–	1	2
D.B. Sheahan	Grange	1966–70	4	2	2	–	6
H.B. Smyth	City of Derry	1968	2	Match results unavailable			
H.B. Smyth	City of Derry	1974	2	–	–	2	–
J.D. Smyth	Lahinch	1968	2	1	1	–	2
R.de L.Staunton	Castlerea	1966	2	1	–	1	2
K. Stevenson	Banbridge	1968	2	Match results unavailable			
D.P. White	Tullamore	1968	1	1	–	–	2
B. Wilson	Clandeboye	1966	2	1	–	1	2
F. Wright	Muskerry	1966	2	1	–	1	2
D.J.F. Young	Malone	1968	2	Match results unavailable			

APPENDIX XIII

Section 2

Record of Irish representatives in the Quadrangular Continental Matches from 1972 to 1990

NAME	CLUB	YEAR(S)	MATCHES	WON	DRAWN	LOST	POINTS
N.H. Anderson	Shandon Park	1986	6	5		1	10
D. Branigan	L'town & B'town	1976–82	12	4	1	7	9
J.J. Carr	Sutton	1982	6	4	1	1	9
J. Carvill	Warrenpoint	1990	6	4	–	2	8
B.G. Cashell	Queen's Univ.	1978	6	1	2	3	4
D. Clarke	Dungannon	1990	6	5	–	1	10
T. Cleary	Fermoy	1976–84	12	3	1	8	7
I.A. Elliott	Belvoir Park	1978	6	1	1	4	3
M.A. Gannon	Co. Louth	1978–80	12	9	–	3	18
N. Goulding	Portmarnock	1990	6	3	–	3	6
D.P. Heather	Sutton	1976	6	1	2	3	4
A.J. Heverin	Woodbrook	1978	6	1	2	3	4
T.B. C. Hoey	Shandon Park	1972	6	2	3	1	7
P. Hogan	Elm Park	1986–8	12	5	1	6	11
R.M. Kane	The Island	1972	6	4	–	2	8
B.J. S. Kissock	Bangor	1978	6	2	–	4	4
N. Lehane	Cork	1972	6	–	3	3	3
D.C. Long	Shandon Park	1982	6	2	1	3	5
L. MacNamara	Woodbrook	1984–90	24	16	–	8	32
G. McGimpsey	Bangor	1984–90	24	18	–	6	36
P. McGinley	Grange	1990	6	3	–	3	6
J. McHenry	Douglas	1986	6	5	–	1	10
M.F. Morris	Portmarnock	1980–84	12	6	2	4	14
P. Mulcare	Woodbrook	1972–80	18	17	–	1	34
V. Nevin	Ennis	1972	6	5	1	–	11
M.D. O'Brien	New Ross	1976	6	1	–	5	2
E. O'Connell	Killarney	1988	6	5	–	1	10
A. O'Connor	Naas	1972	6	6	–	–	12
P. O'Rourke	Kilkenny	1984	6	2	1	3	5
D.J. O'Sullivan	Cork	1986–8	12	6	1	5	13
A.D. Pierse	Tipperary	1980–84	18	9	1	8	19
R. Rafferty	Warrenpoint	1980	6	4	–	2	8
P. Rayfus	Trim	1988	6	5	–	1	10
M. Sludds	The Island	1982	6	2	–	4	4
H.B. Smyth	City of Derry	1976	6	4	–	2	8
K. Stevenson	Bangor	1972	6	2	2	2	6
P. Walton	Malahide	1980–82	12	6	1	5	13

Record of venues, Team Captains and results

YEAR	VENUE	TEAM CAPTAIN	RESULT
1972	Killarney, İreland	William J.J. Ferguson	Ireland
1976	Cologne, Germany	Laurence M. McCarthy	Sweden
1978	Deauville, France	Laurence M. McCarthy	France
1980	Portmarnock, Ireland	Joseph B. Carr	Ireland
1982	Halmstad, Sweden	Brendan G. Edwards	Germany
1984	Bad Ems, Germany	Brendan G. Edwards	Germany
1986	Le Touquet, France	Eamon Curran	Ireland
1988	Royal Portrush, Ireland	George F. Crosbie	Ireland
1990	Ostersund, Sweden	George F. Crosbie	Ireland

APPENDIX XIV

Section 1

Rules of the Pierce Purcell Shield Tournament

1. The Shield shall be called the 'Pierce Purcell Shield'.

2. The Tournament is open to all Clubs affiliated to the Golfing Union of Ireland. Each Club shall be entitled to enter one team.

3. Each team shall consist of ten male members and play shall be by foursomes Medal Play or by foursomes Match Play.

4. (1) Each member of the team must be:

   (a) of Amateur Status as defined by the Royal and Ancient Golf Club of St Andrews:

   (b) the holder of an Official Handicap under the Council of National Golf Unions' Handicapping Scheme or similar standard:

   (c) a Member of the Club for which he is selected but an Honorary Member must have been, at some time, a fee paying member of the Club for a period of two years:

   (d) ordinarily resident in Ireland on and from the 31st day of March in the year of the Tournament. For the purpose of this Rule absence from Ireland on the relevant date for educational purposes, secondment, temporary employment or service with the Armed Forces shall not disqualify.

   (2) No player shall be eligible to compete in this Tournament whose playing handicap was less than twelve on the 1st day of January of the year of the Tournament. For the purpose of this Tournament handicap eligibility shall be deemed to be the playing handicap held by a player on the 1st day of January of the year of the Tournament provided that the combined playing handicap of each pair on that date shall not be less than twenty–seven.

(3) No player who is under eighteen years of age on 1st January of the year of the Tournament is eligible to compete.

5. All matches shall be played off scratch.

6. In all cases of doubt, eligibility shall be decided, in the Provincial Section by the Provincial Council of the Branch concerned, and in the National Section by the Tournament Committee.

7. The entrance fee payable shall be as decided from time to time by the Central Council of the Golfing Union of Ireland. Entry, accompanied by the fee, must be made with the authorised Official of the Province in which the Club is situate.

8. The Tournament is divided into two phases. Phase One will be the Provincial Section and Phase Two the National Section.

9. Each Club entered in the Tournament shall play the Provincial Section in its own Province. The winning Club shall represent the Province in the National Section.

10. Each Provincial Council shall have control of its Provincial Section and shall prescribe the regulations of play. It shall appoint a Tournament Committee which shall be responsible for the organisation and management of the Tournament and the decision of this Committee shall be final on all matters relating thereto.

11. The Tournament Committee appointed by the Central Council shall have control and management of the National Section which shall comprise Match Play Semi-Finals and final amongst the teams representing each Provincial Section and its decision on all questions or objections under these Rules in relation to the National Section shall be final. The Tournament Committee reserves the right to alter starting times.

12. Only persons appointed by the Tournament Committee shall be authorised to give a decision on any question or dispute arising during the course of play. Members of the Central Council or of a Provincial Council are the only persons eligible to be appointed for this purpose.

13. In all Match Play rounds of this Tournament, if a match is all square after 18 holes, the competitors shall immediately continue to play tie holes until a decision is reached unless an overall result on matches won has already decided the event.

14. The National Section shall be played at a venue and on a date to be fixed by the Central Council of the Union.

15. Any competitor who is not on the first teeing ground when his name is called, at or after the time fixed for his starting, will be liable to disqualification by the Starter, and his opponents shall be credited with the match.

16. Whilst the players on each team may be changed, no person shall play for more than one Club in this Tournament during the season.

17. (1) In the Provincial Section, the teams, in order of play, with the names of the substitutes, must be handed to the Official in charge of the Tournament in a sealed envelope not less than fifteen minutes before starting time.

(2) In the National Section the teams for the Semi–Finals, in order of play, with the names of substitutes, must be handed to the Union Official in charge in a sealed envelope not later than 16.00 hours on the day prior to the match and for the Final not more than thirty minutes after play in the Semi–Finals is completed.

(3) In all matches the team lists being handed in must show the handicap which each player and substitute held on the 1st day of January in the year of the Tournament.

18. Except in the case of sudden illness or other emergency which is considered by the Provincial Council or Tournament Committee to be sufficient justification, no alteration can be made in the list handed in, either in the matter of players or in the order of play.

19. Reserves taking the place of players after the team has been fixed shall be placed in the same position in the team as that occupied by the player who has taken ill or has been withdrawn. Alternatively a pair may be placed in the same position in the team as that occupied by the pair one of whom has taken ill or has been withdrawn.

20. It shall be obligatory for all competitors in the Tournament to play with a 1.68 golf ball which is named on the current list of conforming golf balls. (Penalty – 2 strokes or loss of hole for each hole on which the breach occurs.)

21. Each Branch shall advise the name of its Provincial winner to the General Secretary of the Union prior to the date of the National Section.

22. The winning Club in each Province shall be responsible for arranging accommodation for its team at the venue fixed for the National Section.

23. The Shield shall be held for the year by the winning Club. Gold Medals will be awarded to the members of the winning team, Silver Medals to the runners–up and Bronze Medals to the defeated semi–finalists. Non–playing Team Captains will be awarded a special medal.

24. Team Captains are permitted to give advice to their Teams during the course of play.

25. Team members are notified that they may be tested for the use of drugs which, if positive, will lead to automatic disqualification of the team concerned.

26. The winning Club in each Province will be presented with a Provincial Pennant and the Club which wins the Tournament will be presented with a National Pennant.

27. Any competitor who is currently disqualified from participation in all Union or Branch individual Championships cannot represent a Club on any Cup or Shield Team Event.

28. The penalty for breach of Rules 4, 16, 18, 19 or 27 shall be disqualification of the team.

APPENDIX XIV
Section 2

Record of winning Clubs and teams in the Pierce Purcell Shield

1970 MASSEREENE
D. Craig
E. Gaynor
G. Kelly
J. McConnell
T. McCullough
S. McHugh
R. Miller
R. Morrison
D. Rea
D. Thompson

1971 MUSKERRY
D. Bradley
P. Casey
T. Casey
F. Cronin
J. Grey
D. Healy
D.J. Murphy
T.C. Murphy
P. O'Regan
D. Quane
J.K. Quinlan
J. Taylor

1972 CORK
M. Costello
B. Hurley
N. Jennings
J. Madden
D. Moloney
W. Moloney
N. O'Connell
C. O'Mahoney
P. O'Sullivan
T. Owens
R. Payne
J.K.L. Sullivan

1973 BALLY-BUNION
F. Bennett
P.J. Byrne
R. Geaney
D. Gorman
M. Fitzgerald
J. Harman
D. Murphy
M. Noonan
F. O'Carroll
M. O'Shea

1974 GALWAY
J. Cawley
T. Fleming
P. Gibson
G. Kelly
T. Kelly
C. McCarrick
B. McDermott
E. O'Donnell
C. Tyrrell
M. Waters

1975 BALLY-BUNION
D. Burke
P. Kinlan
S. McCarthy
D. Murphy
M. Nagle
N. O'Brien
D.G. O'Connor
T. O'Keeffe
C. Stack
P. Taylor

1976 ROSCOMMON
L. Armstrong
P. Casey
V. Costello
B. Finn
B. Flanagan
J. Gilmore
P. Henry
T. McNally
D. O'Brien
D. Watts

1977 KILLARNEY
S. Counihan
S. Duggan
T. Healy
T.J. O'Connell
E. O'Connor
K. O'Connor
I. O'Leary
J. O'Riordan
J. O'Sullivan
D. Roche
N. Spillane
C. Stack

1978 MUSKERRY
K. Casey
J. Conway
F. Gannon
J. Gray
D. Hughes
D. Leahy
P.A. Lehane
J.J. Murphy
J. O'Brien
J. O'Connell

1979 NEWLANDS
C. Brannock
R. Caffrey
M. Deveney
Ml. Deveney
A. Donovan
C. Keenan
E. Nolan
A. Tolan
R. Ward
I. Whelan

1980 SHANNON
J. Begley
M. Carroll
M. Drysdale
C. Hackett
J. Larkin
J. Marnell
D. O'Brien
B. O'Gorman
J. Walsh
J. Woods

1981 WARREN-POINT
H. Byrne
B. Coffey
I. Kearney
P. Lynchehan
D. McCartan
D. McGivern
P. McGuigan
B. McKeown
R. Morgan
P. Ryan

1982 GALWAY
T. Carr
A. Carney
M. Corcoran
T. Donoghue
I. Flannery
S. Morris
B. Noone
T. O'Connor
N. Ruane
J. Sheil

1983 WARREN-POINT
H. Carr
M. Deegan
B. Doyle
P.J. Johnston
D. McCartan
J. McMahon
P. Magee
B. Reilly
J. Ryan
P. Ryan

1984 DUBLIN & COUNTY
T. Dent
G. Dowdall
L. Doyle
J. Duane
S. Fagan
T. Finegan
P. McEvoy
S. Minogue
M. Nulty
J. Reilly

1985 ADARE MANOR
M. Counihan
T. Griffin
L. Heffernan
T. Howard
L. McNamara
J. O'Connell
P. O'Sullivan
L. Purcell
M. Ryan
S. Ryan

1986 KANTURK
S. Buckley
B. Daly
D. Hannon
L. Harte
J. Kearney
D. Kiely
D. O'Leary
J. O'Leary
B. Riney
J. Tobin

1987 WARREN-POINT
P. Lynchehan
D. McCartan
P. McCartan
N. McDonnell
T. McLoughlin
B. Magee
B. Murphy Jr
J. Ryan
D. Robertson
J. Stewart

1988 GALWAY
A. Carney
T. Donoghue
P. Fahy
M. Greaney
T. Greene
K. Geraghty
B. Keane
B. McDermott
B. Noone
N. O'Shaughnessy

1989 NENAGH
C. Cavanagh
E. Cregan
W. Duff
J. Gleeson
T. Grace
G. Howard
J. McGrath
S. Minogue
N. O'Meara
B. O'Shea

1990 OUGHTER-ARD
K. Clancy
D. Conneely
J.J. Faherty
D. Healy
J. Healy
M. Lee
B. Lyden
D. McGrath
S. Mannion
J. Noone

APPENDIX XV

Irish Seniors' Amateur Open Championship

YEAR	ENTRY	VENUE	WINNER	OVER 60	OVER 65	OVER 70
1970	30	Lahinch	C. Ewing, Co. Sligo			
1971	37	Rosslare	J. O'Sullivan, Athlone			
1972	70	Co. Sligo	S.J. Scannell, Woodbrook	C. Ewing, Co. Sligo		
1973	49	Warrenpoint	J.W. Hulme, Warrenpoint	S. Young, Clandeboye		
1974	59	Cork	P. Walsh, Roscrea	J. Warren, Muskerry		
1975	79	Woodbrook	S.A. O'Connor, Athy	R. Donnelly, Slade Valley		
1976	91	Athlone	B.J. Scannell, Woodbrook	J.W. Hulme, Warrenpoint		
1977	74	Warrenpoint	D.B. Somers, L'town & B'town	B.J. Scannell, Woodbrook		
1978	111	Limerick	D.P. Herlihy, Ryl. Dublin	B.J. Scannell, Woodbrook		
1979	103	Royal Tara	P. Kelly, Coollattin	B.J. Scannell, Woodbrook	G. Clancy, L'town & B'town	
1980	80	Galway	G.N. Fogarty Ryl. Dublin	J.S. Ward, Galway	M.J. Hennelly, Galway	
1981	64	Bundoran	G.N. Fogarty, Ryl. Dublin	J.P. Keegan, Newlands	R.M. Ryan, Thurles	
1982	105	Douglas	J. Murray, Bundoran	E. Curtin, Elm Park	R.D. Lord, Cork	
1983	113	Courtown	F. Sharpe, Ryl. Dublin	K. Garvey, Co. Louth	B.J. Scannell, Woodbrook	
1984	142	Connemara	J. Boston, Ryl. Co.Down	J. Boston, Ryl. Co. Down	B. Lyden, Cork	G.H. Owens, Skerries
1985	181	Royal Co. Down	J. Boston, Ryl. Co.Down	J. Boston, Ryl. Co. Down	E. Curtin Elm Park	J.J. Toner, Mourne
1986	197	Waterford	J.D. Coey, Clandeboye	J. Green, Rosslare	M. Cusack, Portmarnock	E. O'Carroll, Musk
1987	229	Castletroy	J. Murray, Bundoran	J. Murray, Bundoran	J.B. Carr, Sutton	J.J. Toner, Mourne
1988	230	Westport	B. Buckley, Grange	J. Fitzgibbon, Portmarnock	M. Breen, L'town & B'town	B. Scannell, W'brook
1989	156	Royal Belfast	B. McCrea, Ryl. P'rush	H.B. Smyth, Ballymena	H. Wray, Warrenpoint	J. Keegan, N'lands
1990	290	Cork	C. Hartland, Huddersfield	J.D. Coey, Clandeboye	J. Fitzgibbon, Portmarnock	D. Killian, Athlone

APPENDIX XVI

Section 1

The Willie Gill Award Rules

This Award shall be competed for annually between competitors in the:

> West of Ireland Amateur Open Championship
> East of Ireland Amateur Open Championship
> North of Ireland Amateur Open Championship
> South of Ireland Amateur Open Championship
> Irish Amateur Close Championship

subject to the following conditions.

1. A player must have competed in one of the four Provincial Championships.

2. The Award shall be based on the following points system:

Match Play	Stroke Play	West	East	North	South	Close
Winner	1	50	50	50	50	60
Runner-Up	2	40	40	40	40	45
Defeated Semi-Finalists	3 & 4	30	30	30	30	35
Defeated Quarter-Finalist	5 to 8	20	20	20	20	25
Defeated in last 16	9 to 16	10	10	10	10	15

3. If two or more players tie for the Award the Winner shall be decided in the following sequence.

If one of the players is:

(a) The Irish Amateur Close Champion; *or if not*

(b) The Winner of three of the Provincial Championships; *or if not*

(c) The Winner of two of the Provincial Championships; *or if not*

(d) The Winner of one of the Provincial Championships he shall be the Winner of the Award.

Should two players still tie on (c) or (d) above then the players gaining the most points in the Irish Amateur Close Championship shall be the Winner of the Award.

In all other cases the player gaining the most points in the Irish Amateur Close Championship shall be the Winner of the Award.

Should there still be a tie the Award shall be shared for the year.

4. The Award shall be held by the Club from which the winner shall have entered in the Irish Amateur Close Championship or, if he did not compete in the Close Championship, the Club from which he shall have entered in the last event in which he was awarded points and shall be retained by that Club until the commencement of the Close Championship in the following year. Should the Award be shared, it shall be held by each of the Clubs concerned for an equal period. In the event of the Winner being a Member of the Irish Artisan Golfers' Association the Award shall be held by the Club to which his Section is attached or in the event of the Winner having entered from a Country outside Ireland, the Award shall be held by the Golfing Union of Ireland.

APPENDIX XVI
Section 2

Record of Winners, their Clubs and points accumulated in the Willie Gill Award

YEAR	WINNER AND CLUB	POINTS
1976	D. Branigan, L'town & B'town	160
1977	L. MacNamara, Woodbrook	110
1978	M.F. Morris, Portmarnock	90
1979	M.A. Gannon, Co. Louth	95
1980	A.D. Pierse, Tipperary	90
1981	D. Branigan, L'town & B'town	160
1982	P. Walton, Malahide	90
1983	A.C.J. Morrow, Portmarnock	100

YEAR	WINNER AND CLUB	POINTS
1984	G. McGimpsey, Bangor	100
1985	D. Branigan, L'town & B'town	95
1986	J. McHenry, Douglas	120
1987	P. Rayfus, Trim	95
1988	G. McGimpsey, Bangor	180
1989	D. Clarke, Dungannon	125
1990	D. Clarke, Dungannon	160

The Joe Carr Award

1990	R. Coughlan, Birr	155

The Tom Montgomery Award

1990	S. Quinlivan, Ballybunion	135

APPENDIX XVII

Record of winning Clubs and teams in the Jimmy Bruen Shield

1978 STACKS-TOWN	1979 BALLY-BUNION	1980 GALWAY	1984 SUTTON	1985 CLONMEL	1986 CASTLE-TROY	1990 ARDEE
A. Brown	M. Clarke	D. Boyce	J. Bowen	P. Dougan	P. Courtney	K. Cummins
M. Hynes	M. Coote	M. Breen	S. Carroll	M. Fahy	E. Haugh	G. Cromwell
J. Kavanagh	M. Fahy	W. Burke	E.A. Firth	P. McCarthy	M. Jones	B. Healy
D. McCormack	J. Galvin	P. Donnellan	M.P. Fitzpatrick	J. McMenamin	D. Leonard	P. Kelly
J. Moloughney	J. Griffin	M. Dowd	D.W.P. Heather	S. Moriarty	P. McDonnell	T. McDonald
J. Nealon	M. Henegan	J. Duggan	T. Higgins	J.E. Morrissey	M. Markham	D. Maguire
P. O'Connor	J. Molyneaux	B. McDermott	A. McWilliams	P. O'Connor	B. Moloney	T. Muldoon
T. O'Connor	M. Nagle	O. McDonagh	E. O'Rourke	T. O'Connor	P. Morrissey	G. O'Loughlin
T. O'Donoghue	R. O'Mahony	T. Noonan	B. Wallace	P. O'Dwyer	G. O'Mahoney	T. O'Rourke
P. Waters	S. Walshe	D. O'Shaughnessy	A. Williams	M. Patterson	M. Skehan	M. Rice

1981 GALWAY	1982 STACKS-TOWN	1983 WARREN-POINT	1987 WARREN-POINT	1988 CLONMEL	1989 BANGOR
D. Boyce	A. Brown	C. Blakley	G. Campbell	D. Dougan	M. Boyd
M. Breen	J. Doyle	H. Byrne	G. Durkin	M. Fahy	D. Cooke
W. Burke	J. Hennessy	R. Eyres	M. Hall	A. Fox	D. Cull
M. Dowd	J. Horgan	F. Fullen	P. McAteer	B. Keating	P. Davidson
W. Herterick	J. Kavanagh	G. McCartan	K. McCann	S. Moriarty	P. Feherty
C. Lennon	M. Keaty	K. Morgan	J. McMahon	S. Moylan	N. Lavelle
M. Molloy	P. Malone	R. Morgan	R. Prescot	S. Murphy	N. Porter
B. McDermott	P. O'Connor	L. Powell	S. Ryan	M. Patterson	B. Skelton
D. Shaughnessy	T. O'Connor	S. Ryan	E. Small	F. Smyth	J. Whittle
D. Staunton	D. Rickard	H. Wray	I. Wright	P. Wall	G. Yarr

APPENDIX XVIII

Record of winning Clubs and teams in the Irish Golf Clubs' Mixed Foursomes Cup

1978 DONAGHA-DEE
Joan Beatty
Gerald Bunting
Janet Campbell
Ethne Collett
Paul Cummings
Maureen Devlin
Enda McKibbin
John Nelson
Victor Stephens
Jack Stout

1979 BIRR
Francis Ashe
Josephine Butler
Michael Coughlan
Antoinette Enright
John Gilmartin
Donough Lampriere
Michael Lyons
Mary O'Gorman
Joe Slattery
Kay Slattery

1980 CARRICK-FERGUS
Margaret Boyle
Sheila Cobby
Denise Ervine
Elizabeth Hunter
Stanley Hutchinson
Sandra Lynn
Brian McGahan
James McIlwaine
Stephen McNally
Denis Stronge

1981 NEW ROSS
Kathy Dunphy
Anne English
Anne Fenlon
Edward Fenlon
Oliver J. Gough
Robert J. Howlett
Jean Murphy
Martin D. O'Brien
Vincent F. O'Reilly
Angela Treacy

1982 SUTTON
Tommy Bracken
John Carr
Eilis Gunning
Bernie Hourihan
Marie McMahon
Aidan McWilliams
Emer Mulvihill
Hugh O'Neill
William C. Thompson
Kay Thompson

1983 HOLY-WOOD
Norman Bennett
Eamon Carty
Ruth Croft
Joyce Fox
Cheryl Kelly
Cyril Kelly
Stephen King
Rosemary Orr
Patricia Russell
Alan Wigston

1984 CO. SLIGO
Sheila Crowley
Ken Cunningham
Declan Howley
Felicia Howley
Josephine McGonigle
Jimmy Mulligan
Anton Murphy
Irene O'Donovan
Stephen O'Donovan
Greta O'Reilly

1985 ENNIS
Noreen Doohan
Mary Fanning
Brian Gilligan
Noel Gilligan
Ray Hennessy
Bridget Hoey
Vera Madden
Des Mahon
Noel Pyne
Ann Roche

1986 KIRKIS-TOWN
Cynthia Allen
Jim Brown
Sennie McMaster
Alex McVea
Thompson Maginnis
Ronnie Millar
Sheila Shane
Sharon Smyth
Quennie Stewart
Sennie Thompson

1987 CO. SLIGO
Tom Crowley
Kieran Darling
Graine Demmel
Tom Forde
Felicia Howley
Irene O'Donovan
Greta O'Reilly
Patrick Neiland
Simon Rooney
Sheila Rooney

1988 KILKENNY
Brenda Burke
Brenda Crowley
Dick Daly
Eddie Guilfoyle
David McDonald
Joan Norris
Sean O'Neill
Padraic O'Rourke
Joan Spratt
Adrienne Walsh

1989 TRALEE
Veronica Blenerhasset
Anton Casey
Michael Coote
Eileen Corcoran
Donie Houlihan
Deirdre McElligott
Ann Morrissey
Moira O'Brien
Paddy O'Looney
Gerard O'Sullivan

1990 GALWAY
Michael Breen
Joe Corless
Noleen Hennelly
Tom Nolan

Jo Cawley
Pat Donnellan
Frances Kavanagh

Patricia Comer
Martin Greany
Ronnie Keenan

APPENDIX XIX

Section 1

Results of the European Amateur Youths' Golf Team Championship, Oslo 1977

QUALIFICATION ROUNDS

Country and Players' Names	1st Round Scores	5 Best Scores	2nd Round Scores	5 Best Scores	Total
AUSTRIA					
Kyrle	77	77	79	79	156
Laimer	82		77	77	159
Schwaiger	77	77	84	84	161
Lamberg	78	78	—		
Stolz	76	76	79	79	155
Prasthofer	80	80	79	79	159
Teams Total		388		398	786
BELGIUM					
De Doncker	83	83	80	80	163
Jamar	92		86		178
Goossens	86	86	78	78	164
Herman	79	79	78	78	157
Van Damme	85	85	83	83	168
Verplancke	80	80	84	84	164
Teams Total		413		403	816
DENMARK					
Frandsen	78	78	75	75	153
Gyrst	81	81	85		166
Holst	80	80	76	76	156
Isbrandtsen	80	80	76	76	156
Rasmussen	76	76	78	78	154
Jacobsen	83	76	76	76	159
Teams Total		395		381	776
FINLAND					
Alatalo	79	79	86		165
Altonen	81	81	86	86	167
Kuivasaari	81	81	84	84	165
Louhio	78	78	80	80	158
Sipponen	76	76	82	82	158
Utter	86		75	75	161
Teams Total		395		407	802
FRANCE					
Gayon	74	74	79		153
Planchin	76	76	77	77	153
Illouz	78	78	75	75	153
Farry	77	77	75	75	152
Perreau-Saussine	78		75	75	153
Raffray	75	75	77	77	152
Teams Total		380		379	759

Country and Players' Names	1st Round Scores	1st Round 5 Best Scores	2nd Round Scores	2nd Round 5 Best Scores	Total
GERMANY					
Born	79	79	82	82	161
Brugelmann	80	80	79	79	159
Flint	83	83	79	79	162
Grau	76	76	83		159
Rauth	76	76	73	73	149
Rolinck	91		82	82	173
Teams Total		394		395	789
ICELAND					
Svansson	83	83	85		168
Thorarensen	84	84	81	81	165
Petursson	80	80	83	83	163
Olafsson	76	76	78	78	154
Eyvindsson	75	75	81	81	156
Halldorsson	85		82	82	167
Teams Total		398		405	803
IRELAND					
Corridan	75	75	79	79	154
Flanagan	80	80	77	77	157
McDaid	77	77	77	77	154
O'Boyle	73	73	80	80	153
O'Connor	84		80	80	164
O'Hagan	76	76	80		156
Teams Total		381		393	774
ITALY					
Acutis	75	75	72	72	147
Betti	78	78	78	78	156
Mannelli	75	75	79	79	154
Candelli	76	76	75	75	151
Canessa	82		81		163
Durante	79	79	74	74	153
Teams Total		383		378	761
THE NETHERLANDS					
Swart	76	76	84	84	157
van Dam, G.	84		82	82	166
van Dam, B	81	81	77	77	158
Postma	77	77	88		165
Meyer	82	82	83	83	165
Nolte	79	79	82	82	161
Teams Total		395		408	803
NORWAY					
Bjerkholt	77	77	78	78	155
Hammer	74	74	74	74	148
Olav	81	81	77	77	158
Sviland	73	73	76	76	149
Underthun	81		79	79	160
Vinter	77	77	84		161
Teams Total		382		384	766
SPAIN					
Gabarda	76	76	81	81	157
Cortezo	78	78	83	83	161
Jimenez	83		78	78	161
Castillo	74	74	85		159
Vidaor	79	79	77	77	156
Trullenque	77	77	83	83	160
Teams Total		384		402	786
SWEDEN					
Andhagen	76	76	74	74	150
Lindwall	76	76	74	74	150
Nilsson	75	75	75	75	150
Stahle	80		76	76	156
Strand	73	73	80		153
Svedin	79	79	76	76	155
Teams Total		379		375	754
SWITZERLAND					
Bagnoud	78	78	75	75	153
Boillat	78	78	87		165
Borgeat	83		84	84	167
Frank	73	73	75	75	148
Kaeser	81	81	83	83	164
Rampone	81	81	84	84	165
Teams Total		391		401	792

RESULTS AFTER QUALIFICATION

Flight One		Flight Two	
1. SWEDEN	754	9. GERMANY	789
2. FRANCE	759	10. SWITZERLAND	792
3. ITALY	761	11. FINLAND	802
4. NORWAY	766	12. ICELAND	803
5. IRELAND	774	13. NETHERLANDS	803
6. DENMARK	776	14. BELGIUM	816
7. SPAIN	786		
8. AUSTRIA	786		

Flight One

Italy 4½; Denmark 2½

Foursomes

Acutis and Manelli	lost to	Isbrandtsen and Frandsen	2 holes
Betti and Gandelli	beat	Jacobsen and Rasmussen	4 and 3

Singles

Betti	beat	Rasmussen	4 and 3
Durante	halved with	Isbrandtsen	
Gandelli	lost to	Holst	3 and 2
Acutis	beat	Frandsen	4 and 3
Manelli	beat	Jacobsen	5 and 4

Norway 2; Ireland 5

Foursomes

Bjerkholt and Underthun	lost to	O'Boyle and Corridan	5 and 3
Sviland and Hammer	beat	O'Hagan and McDaid	6 and 4

Singles

Hammer	lost to	O'Hagan	at 21st
Bjerkholt	lost to	McDaid	at 19th
Underthun	lost to	Corridan	1 hole
Olav	lost to	Flanagan	3 and 2
Sviland	beat	O'Boyle	3 and 2

France 4; Spain 3

Foursomes

Planchin and Farry	beat	Gabarda and Castillo	4 and 3
Raffray and Gayon	lost to	Vidaor and Jimenez	1 hole

Singles

Planchin	beat	Castillo	4 and 3
Raffray	beat	Cortezo	4 and 3
Farry	lost to	Gabarda	1 hole
Illouz	lost to	Jimenez	4 and 3
Perreau-Saussine	beat	Vidaor	1 hole

Sweden 5; Austria 2

Foursomes

Stahle and Svedin	beat	Stolz and Lamberg	3 and 2
Andhagen and Strand	beat	Laimer and Kyrle	7 and 6

Singles

Lindvall	lost to	Prasthofer	1 hole
Nilsson	beat	Kyrle	4 and 3
Strand	beat	Laimer	1 hole
Stahle	beat	Schwaiger	5 and 4
Svedin	lost to	Stolz	2 and 1

Flight Two

Iceland 2; Netherlands 5

Foursomes

Thorarensen and Petursson	beat	B. van Dam and Swart	1 hole
Olafsson and Eyvindsson	lost to	G. van Dam and Meyer	2 and 1

Singles

Eyvindsson	lost to	Postma	1 hole
Svansson	lost to	Nolte	6 and 5
Thorarensen	lost to	G. van Dam	1 hole
Petursson	beat	Swart	3 and 2
Olafsson	lost to	B. van Dam	2 and 1

Finland 4; Belgium 3

Foursomes

Louhio and Sipponen	lost to	Goossens and Hermann	2 holes
Kuivasaari and Alatalo	beat	Verplancke and Van Damme	5 and 4

Singles

Louhio	beat	Verplancke	2 and 1
Sipponen	beat	De Doncker	2 and 1
Utter	lost to	Hermann	5 and 4
Kuivasaari	beat	Van Damme	3 and 2
Altonen	lost to	Goossens	3 and 1

Germany 5; Netherlands 2

Foursomes

Born and Routh	beat	Nolte and G. van Dam	1 hole
Brügelmann and Flint	beat	Swart and B. van Dam	2 and 1

Singles

Rauth	beat	Postma	4 and 2
Brüigelmann	lost to	Nolte	4 and 3
Rolinck	lost to	G. van Dam	1 hole
Grau	beat	Swart	2 holes
Flint	beat	B. van Dam	2 holes

Switzerland 3; Finland 4

Foursomes

Frank and Rampone	beat	Louhio and Sipponen	1 hole
Bagnoud and Borgeat	lost to	Kuivasaari and Alatalo	6 and 5

Singles

Kaeser	lost to	Alatalo	2 and 1
Boillat	lost to	Kuivasaari	4 and 3
Frank	lost to	Altonen	1 hole
Bagnoud	beat	Sipponen	4 and 3
Rampone	beat	Louhio	3 and 2

Iceland 4; Belgium 3

Foursomes

Olafsson and Eyvindsson	beat	Goossens and Herman	2 holes
Petursson and Thorarensen	lost to	Verplancke and De Doncker	2 holes

Singles

Olafsson	beat	Hermann	2 and 1
Thorarensen	lost to	Van Damme	4 and 3
Petursson	beat	De Doncker	1 up
Eyvindsson	beat	Verplancke	1 up
Halldorsson	lost to	Goossens	2 and 1

Flight One

Sweden 3; Ireland 4

Foursomes

Andhagen and Strand	beat	O'Boyle and Corridan	1 hole
Lindvall and Nilsson	lost to	O'Hagan and McDaid	1 hole

Singles

Svedin	lost to	O'Hagan	5 and 3
Andhagen	lost to	McDaid	2 and 1
Lindvall	lost to	Corridan	1 hole
Strand	beat	Flanagan	4 and 3
Stahle	beat	O'Boyle	3 and 2

France 4½; Italy 2½

Foursomes

Planchin and Farry	lost to	Manelli and Acutis	2 and 1
Perreau-Saussine and Raffray	lost to	Betti and Gandelli	at 20th

Singles

Planchin	beat	Betti	2 and 1
Raffray	beat	Durante	4 and 3
Gayon	beat	Gandelli	5 and 4
Farry	halved with	Acutis	
Perreau-Saussine	beat	Manelli	2 holes

Norway 5; Austria 2

Foursomes

Olav and Underthun	beat	Prasthofer and Schwaiger	1 up
Sviland and Hammer	beat	Laimer and Stolz	at 19th

Singles

Bjerkholt	beat	Lamberg	2 and 1
Vinter	lost to	Prasthofer	3 and 2
Underthun	lost to	Stolz	2 holes
Sviland	beat	Kyrle	4 and 2
Hammer	beat	Laimer	1 hole

Denmark 4; Spain 3

Foursomes

Gyrst and Holst	lost to	Gabarda and Cortezo	3 and 2
Isbrandtsen and Frandsen	beat	Vidaor and Jimenez	2 and 1

Single

Gyrst	lost to	Jimenez	1 hole
Isbrandten	beat	Trullenque	3 and 2
Holst	beat	Castillo	4 and 3
Frandsen	lost to	Vidaor	8 and 6
Rasmussen	beat	Gabarda	1 hole

Flight Two

Netherlands 1; Finland 6

Foursomes

Nolte and B. van Dam	lost to	Alatalo and Kuivasaari	2 holes
Postma and Swart	lost to	Louhio and Altonen	3 and 2

Singles

G. van Dam	lost to	Sipponen	3 and 1
Meyer	lost to	Utter	2 holes
Nolte	lost to	Alatalo	3 and 2
B. van Dam	beat	Altonen	1 hole
Postma	lost to	Louhio	7 and 6

Germany 5; Switzerland 2

Foursomes

Born and Rauth	lost to	Kaeser and Boillat	4 and 2
Brügelmann and Flint	beat	Frank and Rampone	at 19th

Singles

Rauth	beat	Ragnoud	5 and 4
Brügelmann	beat	Borgeat	at 19th
Grau	beat	Boillat	1 hole
Born	beat	Kaeser	1 hole
Flint	lost to	Frank	6 and 4

Flight One

Spain 4½ Austria 2½

Foursomes

Gabarda and Cortezo	beat	Stolz and Kyrle	3 and 2
Vidaor and Jimenez	beat	Prasthofer and Schwaiger	2 and 1

Singles

Jimenez	beat	Lamberg	5 and 4
Cortezo	lost to	Kyrle	1 hole
Castillo	halved with	Laimer	
Gabarda	beat	Schwaiger	6 and 5
Vidaor	lost to	Prasthofer	3 and 2

Norway 1½; Denmark 5½

Foursomes

Vinter and Bjerkholt	lost to	Jacobsen and Rasmussen	7 and 5
Hammer and Sviland	beat	Isbrandtsen and Frandsen	4 and 2

Singles

Bjerkholt	halved with	Gyrst	
Olav	lost to	Isbrandtsen	3 and 2
Underthun	lost to	Holst	6 and 4
Hammer	lost to	Rasmussen	3 and 2
Sviland	lost to	Jacobsen	6 and 5

Italy 4½; Sweden 2½

Foursomes

Betti and Gandelli	beat	Andhagen and Strand	2 and 1
Manelli and Acutis	lost to	Stahle and Svedin	1 hole

Singles

Acutis	halved with	Nilsson	
Betti	lost to	Andhagen	3 and 2
Canessa	beat	Strand	3 and 2
Mannelli	beat	Lindvall	3 and 2
Gandelli	beat	Stahle	2 and 1

Ireland 4; France 3

Foursomes

Corridan and Flanagan	lost to	Planchin and Farry	7 and 5
O'Hagan and McDaid	lost to	Illouz and Gayon	2 holes

Singles

O'Hagan	beat	Planchin	1 hole
McDaid	beat	Raffray	3 and 1
B. O'Boyle	lost to	Gayon	1 hole
Flanagan	beat	Farry	1 hole
Corridan	beat	Perreau-Saussine	2 and 1

Final Ranking

1. IRELAND
2. FRANCE
3. ITALY
4. SWEDEN
5. DENMARK
6. NORWAY
7. SPAIN
8. AUSTRIA
9. GERMANY
10. SWITZERLAND
11. FINLAND
12. NETHERLANDS
13. ICELAND
14. BELGIUM

APPENDIX XIX

Section 2

Record of venues, Team Captains, winning countries and Ireland's position in the order of merit in the EAYGTC since 1977

YEAR	VENUE	IRISH CAPTAIN	WINNING COUNTRY	IRELAND'S POSITION	
1977	Oslo, Norway	Tom Montgomery	Ireland	First	(14)
1978	Pals, Spain	Tom Rogers	France	Tenth	(14)
1979	Marianske Lazne, Czechoslovakia	Barry T. Crymble	Ireland	First	(15)
1980	Dusseldorf, Germany	Barry T. Crymble	Sweden	Third	(14)
1981	Reykjavik, Iceland	Barry T. Crymble	Spain	Second	(14)
1982	Paris, France	Frederick P. McDonnell	Scotland	Ninth	(14)
1983	No Championship				
1984	Hermitage, Ireland	Frederick P. McDonnell	Ireland	First	(17)

Championship discontinued but recommenced in 1990 in alternative years to the EAGTC.
(The number in brackets in the right column indicates the number of competing countries.)

A mini series took place in 1988, 1989 and 1990:

1988	Turin, Italy	Michael P. O'Donoghue	Sweden	Second	(8)
1989	Limburg, Belgium	Michael P. O'Donoghue	Spain	Fifth	(6)
1990	Turin, Italy	Michael P. O'Donoghue	Italy	Ninth	(16)

APPENDIX XIX

Section 3

Record of Irish representatives in the European Amateur Youths' Golf Team Championship from 1977 to 1984

NAME	CLUB	YEAR(S)	MATCHES	WON	DRAWN	LOST	POINTS
N.H. Anderson	Shandon Park	1982	4	4	–	–	8
D.W. Ballentine	Portstewart	1981	3	2	1	–	5
C. Carew	Waterford	1980–81	5	4	–	–	8
J. Carvill	Warrenpoint	1984	6	3	1	2	7
J. Collins	Monkstown	1978–9	7	3	1	3	7
P. Congden	Royal Dublin	1982	3	2	–	1	4
D. Conway	Dublin Univ.	1978	1	–	–	1	0
T. Corridan	Ballybunion	1977–9	11	6	1	4	13
J. Farrell	Carlow	1984	Played in Medal Qualifying Rounds				
S. Flanagan	Tullamore	1977	3	2	–	1	4
R.A. Hanna	Lurgan	1979	6	3	3	–	9
D.P. Heather	Sutton	1978	3	1	–	2	2
R. Hennessy	Ennis	1982	Played in Medal Qualifying Rounds				
A. Hogan	C. on-Shannon	1981	6	2	1	3	5

NAME	CLUB	YEAR(S)	MATCHES	WON	DRAWN	LOST	POINTS
J. Hutchinson	Royal Dublin	1982	1	1	–	–	2
J. Jones	Whitehead	1981	6	3	1	2	7
B. McDaid	Skibbereen	1977–80	19	10	1	8	21
N. McGrane	Greenore	1982	4	4	–	–	8
J. McHenry	Douglas	1980–84	17	10	1	6	21
P. Murphy	Killarney	1984	6	5	–	1	10
J. Morris	Douglas	1984	2	1	–	1	2
P.M. O'Boyle	Royal Dublin	1977	6	1	–	5	2
E. O'Connell	Killarney	1984	6	4	–	2	8
D.P. O'Connor	Tramore	1977	Played in Medal Qualifying Rounds				
K. O'Donnell	Clandeboye	1982	4	4	–	–	8
M. Quaid	Galway	1978	1	1	–	–	2
R. Rafferty	Warrenpoint	1979–80	11	9	–	2	18
M. Sludds	The Island	1980	2	1	–	1	2
P. Walton	Malahide	1979–81	18	12	1	5	25

The European Golf Association discontinued the Championship after the 1984 matches but, as a result of request from a number of member countries, decided to recommence the Championship in 1990 as a biennial tournament. During the interim period Ireland competed in a mini series in Turin, Italy (eight countries) in 1988 and in Limburg, Belgium (six countries) in 1989. The following is the record of Irish representatives who played in the two series:

NAME	CLUB	YEAR(S)	MATCHES	WON	DRAWN	LOST	POINTS
D. Clarke	Dungannon	1988	6	1	–	5	2
D. Cunningham	Galway	1989	1	–	–	1	0
D. Errity	Hermitage	1989	4	3	–	1	6
P. Gribben	Warrenpoint	1988	6	2	–	4	4
S. Hogan	Greystones	1988–9	5	2	–	3	4
K. Kearney	Limerick	1988	6	4	1	1	9
G. McNeill	Warrenpoint	1989	4	2	–	2	4
E. O'Connell	Killarney	1988	6	3	1	2	7
K. O'Flaherty	Cork	1989	4	2	–	2	4
H. O'Neill	Connemara	1988	2	–	–	2	0
P. Russell	Co. Armagh	1989	1	1	–	2	2

Record of Irish representatives in the re-instituted EAYGTC

NAME	CLUB	YEAR(S)	MATCHES	WON	DRAWN	LOST	POINTS
D. Basquill	Enniscrone	1990	2	1	–	1	2
P. Harrington	Stackstown	1990	6	4	–	2	8
N. Kelly	Athlone	1990	1	–	–	1	0
B. Kinsella	Skerries	1990	6	3	–	3	6
G. McNeill	Warrenpoint	1990	6	6	–	–	12
S. Paul	Tandragee	1990	6	5	–	1	10

APPENDIX XIX
Section 4

Record of venues, Team Captains, winning countries and Ireland's position in the order of merit in the EABGTC

YEAR	VENUE	TEAM CAPTAIN	WINNING COUNTRY	IRELAND'S POSITION	
1980	Barcelona, Spain	Frederick P. McDonnell	Spain	Fourth	(9)
1981	Rome, Italy	Frederick P. McDonnell	England	Fourth	(−)
1982	Frankfurt, Germany	Joseph Quinlan	Italy	Sixth	(15)
1983	Helsinki, Finland	Joseph Quinlan	Sweden	Ninth	(16)
1984	Sandwich, England	Joseph Quinlan	Scotland	Fifth	(13)
1985	Troia, Portugal	Michael P. O'Donoghue	England	Fourth	(18)
1986	Turin, Italy	Michael P. O'Donoghue	England	Fifth	(18)
1987	Chantilly, France	Michael P. O'Donoghue	Scotland	Sixth	(18)
1988	Renfrew, Scotland	John McKernan	France	Third	(18)
1989	Lyckorna, Sweden	John McKernan	England	Ninth	(18)
1990	Reykjavik, Iceland	John McKernan	Spain	Fourth	(16)

(The number in brackets in the right column indicates the number of competing countries.)

Record of Irish representatives in the European Amateur Boys' Golf Team Championship

NAME	CLUB	YEAR(S)	MATCHES	WON	DRAWN	LOST	POINTS
P. Acheson	Shandon Park	1987	6	2	–	4	4
R. Burns	Banbridge	1990	5	5	–	–	10
J. Carvill	Warrenpoint	1983	6	5	–	1	10
J.W.H. Clark	Cairndhu	1990	1	–	–	1	0
D. Clarke	Dungannon	1986	3	2	–	1	4
P.W. Clarke	Malone	1982	5	–	–	5	0
R. Coughlan	Birr	1990	5	4	–	1	8
R. Culligan	Lahinch	1980	3	1	–	2	2
D. Cunningham	Galway	1987–8	3	3	–	–	6
M. Curry	Castlecomer	1983–4	6	2	1	3	5
M. Eaton	Holywood	1982	5	1	–	4	2
D. Errity	Hermitage	1987	6	2	2	2	6
G. Fairweather	Lisburn	1982	5	1	–	4	2
J. Farrell	Carlow	1983–5	15	7	1	7	15
P. Gribben	Warrenpoint	1985–6	7	3	2	2	8
G. Hamill	Ardglass	1981	4	2	–	2	4
P. Harrington	Stackstown	1988–9	10	6	1	3	13
D. Higgins	Waterville	1990	3	1	–	2	2
S. Hogan	Greystones	1987	6	1	2	3	4
K. Kearney	Limerick	1984–6	16	7	–	9	14
T. Kelliher	Killarney	1983	6	2	2	2	6
N. Kelly	Athlone	1989	2	2	–	–	4
B. Kinsella	Skerries	1989	3	3	–	–	6
S. Kinsella	Skerries	1988	4	1	–	3	2
K. McDaid	Skibbereen	1981	6	4	–	2	8
J. McHenry	Douglas	1980–81	12	7	–	5	14
G. McNeill	Warrenpoint	1987–8	10	3	2	5	8
G. Moore	Royal Portrush	1985–6	12	5	1	6	11
J. Morris	Douglas	1982–3	12	7	–	5	14
G. Murphy	Kilkenny	1989–90	6	1	–	5	2

NAME	CLUB	YEAR(S)	MATCHES	WON	DRAWN	LOST	POINTS
P. Murphy	Killarney	1980–81	11	4	–	7	8
E. O'Connell	Killarney	1984–6	12	9	–	3	18
S. Paul	Tandragee	1988–9	7	4	1	2	9
E. Power	Tramore	1982	6	3	–	3	6
R. Rafferty	Warrenpoint	1980	6	5	–	1	10
P. Russell	Co. Armagh	1988	6	4	–	2	8
K. Sheehan	Cork	1984–5	9	5	1	3	11
K. Spillane	Douglas	1986	1	–	–	1	0
G. Sproule	Co. Sligo	1987–90	8	3	–	5	6
L. Walker	Grange	1987	4	–	–	4	0

APPENDIX XX

International Selection Committees appointed by the Central Council since the inauguration of the Quadrangular Matches in 1932

1932	1933	1934	1935
Butler, G.B.	Butler, G.B.	Cairnes, H.M.	Cairnes, H.M.
Cairnes, H.M.	Cairnes, H.M.	Harden, C.S.	Harden, C.S.
Davies, F.E.	Davies, F.E.	Henderson, J.	Henderson, J.
Harden, C.S.	Harden, C.S.	Kidd, A.B.	Kidd, A.B.
Henderson, J.	Henderson, J.	Musgrave, J.G.	Musgrave, J.G.
Kidd, A.B.	Kidd, A.B.	O'Flynn, P.	O'Flynn, P.
Morrison, B.A.	Musgrave, J.G.	Wilson-Smyth, D.	Wilson-Smyth, D.
O'Flynn, P.	O'Flynn, P.	Toher, T.P.	Toher, T.P.
Wilson-Smyth, D.	Wilson-Smyth, D.		

1936	1937	1938	1939
Cairnes, H.M.	Cairnes, H.M.	Costelloe, J.F	Costello, J.F.
Davidson, R.C.	Costelloe, J.F.	Davidson, R.C.	Davidson, R.C.
Harden, C.S.	Crosbie, G .	McConnell, R.M.	McConnell, R.M.
Kidd, A.B.	Dalton, J.E.	O'Flynn, P.	O'Flynn, P.
Musgrave, J.G.	Davidson, R.C.	Purcell, P.F.	Purcell, P.F.
O'Flynn, P.	Harden, C.S.		
Purcell, P.F.	Kidd, A.B.		
Toher, T.P.	McConnell, R.M.		
Wilson-Smyth, D.	Musgrave, J.G.		
	O'Flynn, P.		
	Purcell, P.F.		
	Toher, T.P.		
	Wilson-Smyth, D.		

1940	1941	1942	1943
Costelloe, J.F.	Costelloe, J.F.	Costelloe, J.F.	Costelloe, J.F.
Davidson, R.C.	Davidson, R.C.	Davidson, R.C.	Davidson, R.C.
McConnell, R.M.	McConnell, R.M.	McConnell, R.M.	McConnell, R.M.
O'Flynn, P.	O'Flynn, P.	O'Flynn, P.	O'Flynn, P.
Purcell, P.F.	Purcell, P.F.	Purcell, P.F.	Purcell, P.F.

1944	1945	1946	1947
Costelloe, J.F.	Costelloe, J.F.	Costelloe, J.F.	Costelloe, J.F.
Davidson, R.C.	Davidson, R.C.	Davidson, R.C.	Hezlet, Lt. Col. C.O.
McConnell, R.M.	MacCormack, Dr J.D.	MacCormack, Dr J.D.	McAuley, J.
O'Flynn, P.	McConnell, R.M.	McConnell, R.M.	O'Sullivan, Dr W.M.
Purcell, P.F.	O'Flynn, P.	O'Flynn, P.	Purcell, P.F.
	Purcell, P.F.	Purcell, P.F.	

1948	1949	1950	1951
Costelloe, J.F.	Ewing, C.	Gill, W.J.	Gill, W.J.
Gill, W.J.	Gill, W.J.	Hezlet, Lt. Col. C.O.	Hezlet, Lt. Col. C.O.
Hezlet, Lt. Col. C.O.	Hezlet, Lt. Col. C.O.	Owens, Dr G.H.	Knox, W.R.
O'Sullivan, Dr W.M.	O'Sullivan, Dr W.M.	Purcell, P.F.	Owens, Dr G.H.
Purcell, P.F.	Purcell, P.F.	Simcox, R.	Simcox, R.

1952	1953	1954	1955
Gill, W.J.	Gill, W.J.	Gill, W.J.	Gill, W.J.
Hezlet, Lt. Col. C.O.	Hadden, H.M.	Hadden, H.M.	Hadden, H.M.
Knox, W.R.	Knox, W.R.	Knox, W.R.	Knox, W.R.
Owens, Dr G.H.	Owens, Dr G.H.	Owens, Dr G.H.	Owens, Dr G.H.
Simcox, R.	Simcox, R.	Simcox, R.	Simcox, R.

1956	Baine, D.L.	1957	Gill, W.J.	1958	Gill, W.J.	1959	Bruen, J.
	Gill, W.J.		Hadden, H.M.		Hadden, H.M.		Ewing, C.
	Hadden, H.M.		O'Donnell, T.E.		O'Donnell, T.E.		Hadden, H.M.
	O'Donnell, T.E.		O'Sullivan, J.		O'Sullivan, J.		O'Sullivan, Dr W.M.
	Owens, Dr G.H.		Owens, Dr G.H.		Owens, Dr G.H.		Owens, Dr G.H.

1960	Bruen, J.	1961	Bruen, J.	1962	Bruen, J.	1963	Ewing, C.
	Ewing, C.		Ewing, C.		Ewing, C.		Hadden, H.M.
	Hadden, H.M.		Hadden, H.M.		Hadden, H.M.		Mahon, Dr J.R.
	O'Sullivan, Dr W.M.		O'Sullivan, Dr W.M.		O'Sullivan, Dr W.M.		O'Sullivan, Dr W.M.
	Owens, Dr G.H.		Owens, Dr G.H.		Owens, Dr G.H.		Owens, Dr G.H.

1964	Crosbie, G.F.	1965	Crosbie, G.F.	1966	Crosbie, G.F.	1967	Ewing, C.
	Ewing, C.		Ewing, C.		Ewing, C.		Ferguson, W.J.J.
	Hadden, H.M.		Ferguson, W.J.J .		Ferguson, W.J.J.		McPolin, P.J.
	Mahon, Dr J.R.		Mahon, Dr J.R.		Mahon, Dr J.R.		Mahon, Dr J.R.
	Owens, Dr G.H.		Montgomery, T.		Montgomery, T.		Montgomery, T.

1968	Ewing, C.	1969	Ewing, C.	1970	Ferguson, W.J.J.	1971	Ferguson, W.J.J.
	Ferguson, W.J.J.		Ferguson, W.J.J.		Fitzpatrick, M.P.		Fitzpatrick, M.P.
	McPolin, P.J.		McPolin, P.J		McPolin, P.J.		McPolin, P.J.
	Montgomery, T.		Montgomery, T.		O'Sullivan, J.		O'Sullivan, J.
	Scannell, B.J.		Scannell, B.J.		Scannell, B.J.		Scannell, B.J.

1972	Ferguson, W.J.J.	1973	Ferguson, W.J.J.	1974	Ferguson, W.J.J.	1975	Ferguson, W.J.J
	Fitzpatrick, M.P.		Fitzpatrick, M.P.		Fitzpatrick, M.P.		Hulme, J.W.
	McCarthy, L.M.		McCarthy, L.M.		McCarthy, L.M.		McCarthy, L.M.
	O'Sullivan, J.		O'Sullivan, J.		O'Sullivan, J.		O'Sullivan, J.
	Scannell, B.J.		Scannell, B.J.		Scannell, B.J.		Scannell, B.J.

1976	Ferguson, W.J.J.	1977	Ferguson, W.J.J.	1978	Bamford, J.L.	1979	Bamford, J.L.
	Hulme, J.W.		Hulme, J.W.		Ferguson, W.J.J.		Carr, J.B.
	McCarthy, L.M.		McCarthy, L.M.		Herlihy, D.P.		Ferguson, W.J.J. (Co-opted)
	O'Sullivan, J.		O'Sullivan, J.		McCarthy, L.M.		Herlihy, D.P. (Deceased)
	Scannell, B.J.		Scannell, B.J.		Scannell, B.J.		McCarthy, L.M.
							Rice, Dr J.H.

1980	Carr, J.B.	1981	Carr, J.B.	1982	Baker, R.N.	1983	Baker, R.N.
	Curran, E.		Curran, E.		Craddock, T.		Curran, E.
	Ferguson, W.J.J.		Edwards, B.		Curran, E.		Edwards, B.
	McCarthy, L.M.		McCarthy, L.M.		Edwards, B.		O'Brien, M.D.
	Rice, Dr J.H.		Rice, Dr J.H.		Rice, D.J.H.		Rice, Dr J.H.

1984	Baker, R.N.	1985	Baker, R.N.	1986	Bamford, J.L.	1987	Curran, E.
	Curran, E.		Curan, E.		Curran, E.		Crosbie, G.F.
	Edwards, B.		Edwards, B.		Edwards, B.		Edwards, B.
	O'Brien, M.D.		O'Brien, M.D.		O'Brien, M.D.		O'Brien, M.D.
	Rice, Dr J.H.		Rice, Dr J.H.		Staunton, R.de L.		Staunton, R.de L.

1988	Craddock, M.	1989	Craddock, M.	1990	Craddock, M.		
	Crosbie, G.F.		Crosbie, G.F.		Crosbie, G.F.		
	McCarroll, F.E.		McCarroll, F.E.		McCarroll, F.E.		
	O'Brien, M.D.		O'Brien, M.D.		O'Brien, M.D.		
	Staunton, R.de L.		Staunton, R.de L.		Staunton, R.de L.		

APPENDIX XXI

Section 1

Record of venues, Team Captains, winning countries and Ireland's position in the order of merit in the Boys' home international matches

YEAR	VENUE	TEAM CAPTAIN	WINNING COUNTRY	IRELAND'S POSITION
1985	Royal Burgess, Scotland	Michael P. O'Donoghue	Ireland England } Tie	Joint First
1986	Seaton Carew, England	Michael P. O'Donoghue	Ireland	First
1987	Kilmarnock, Scotland	Michael P. O'Donoghue	Scotland	Fourth
1988	Formby, England	John McKernan	England	Fourth
1989	Nairn, Scotland	John McKernan	England	Fourth
1990	Huntstanton, England	John McKernan	Scotland	Second

APPENDIX XXI

Section 2

Record of Irish representatives in the Boys' home internationals from 1985 to 1990

NAME	CLUB	YEAR(S)	MATCHES	WON	DRAWN	LOST	POINTS
P. Acheson	Shandon Park	1987	4	2	–	2	4
A. Adair	Fortwilliam	1990	4	1	–	3	2
C.J. Bell	Belvoir Park	1989	3	1	–	2	2
D. Butler	Galway	1986–7	8	2	–	6	4
R. Burns	Banbridge	1989–90	8	3	1	4	7
J.W.H. Clark	Cairndhu	1989	4	1	2	1	3
D. Clarke	Dungannon	1985	4	1	2	1	4
M. Coates	Sutton	1988	2	–	–	2	0
R. Conway	Portmarnock	1988	4	1	1	2	3
R. Coughlan	Birr	1989–90	8	2	1	5	5
D. Cunningham	Galway	1987	4	2	–	2	4
S. Dargan	Hermitage	1990	4	–	1	3	1
G. Deegan	Downpatrick	1989	2	1	–	1	2
D. Errity	Hermitage	1986–7	8	4	–	4	8
J. Farrell	Carlow	1985	4	3	–	1	6
B. Galway	Cairndhu	1988	2	–	1	1	1
D. Gilligan	Ennis	1985–6	8	2	–	5	6
P. Gribben	Warrenpoint	1985–6	8	5	1	2	11
P. Harrington	Stackstown	1987–9	11	4	1	6	9
D. Higgins	Waterville	1990	4	2	–	2	4
J. Hoey	Ennis	1987	2	–	–	2	0
S. Hogan	Greystones	1987–8	5	2	–	3	4

NAME	CLUB	YEAR(S)	MATCHES	WON	DRAWN	LOST	POINTS
R. Hunter	Whitehead	1987	3	–	–	3	0
R. Hutton	Ardglass	1986	4	2	1	1	5
K. Kearney	Roscommon	1985	4	2	–	2	4
N. Kelly	Athlone	1988	4	1	–	3	2
B. Kinsella	Skerries	1987–8	8	3	2	3	8
D. Kyle	Royal Belfast	1989	3	–	–	3	0
M. MacGuigan	Roscommon	1986	4	1	–	3	2
K. McLaughlin	City of Derry	1990	3	2	–	1	4
G. McNeill	Warrenpoint	1986–7	8	6	–	2	12
B. Meaney	Castle	1988	4	1	2	1	4
S. Moloney	Castletroy	1990	1	–	–	1	0
G. Moore	Royal Portrush	1985	4	3	1	–	7
G. Murphy	Kilkenny	1988–90	12	4	2	6	10
K. Nolan	Woodbrook	1990	4	1	1	2	3
E. O'Connell	Killarney	1985	4	3	1	–	7
B. O'Donovan	Youghal	1985	4	3	–	1	6
S. Parkhill	Castlerock	1989	4	1	–	3	2
S. Paul	Tandragee	1988	4	3	–	1	6
S. Quinlivan	Ballybunion	1990	4	–	–	4	0
M. Riseley	Killiney	1988	4	2	1	1	5
P. Russell	Co. Armagh	1986–7	8	2	–	6	4
K. Sheehan	Cork	1985–6	4	–	1	3	1
M. Sinclair	Knock	1989	4	–	2	2	2
G. Sproule	Co. Sligo	1989–90	8	1	1	6	3
D. Stenson	Sutton	1988	4	–	1	3	1
L. Walker	Grange	1985–6	8	4	–	4	8

APPENDIX XXII

Section 1

Record of winners and runners–up in the South of Ireland Amateur Open Championship

YEAR	WINNER AND CLUB	RUNNER–UP AND CLUB	RESULT
1895	G.S. Browning, Lahinch	W.F. McDonald, Limerick	2 and 1
1896	B. O'Brien, Portsalon	D.M. Wilson, Royal Dublin	9 and 7
1897	F. Ballingall, Blairgowrie	J.R. Gardiner, Richmond	2 and 1
1898	F. Ballingall, Blairgowrie	H.M. Ballingall, Blairgowrie	3 and 1
1899	J.R. Gardiner, Richmond	J. Livingstone, Edinburgh Burgess	6 and 5
1900	F. Ballingall, Blairgowrie	T. Fullerton, Troon	5 and 4
1901	W. Dodd, Royal Liverpool	S.H. Fry, Royal Mid–Surrey	2 and 1
1902	W. Ballingall, Royal & Ancient	G.S. Browning, Lahinch	2 and 1
1903	J.B. Ballingall, Blairgowrie	J.S. Worthington, Royal Mid–Surrey	2 and 1
1904	D. Foster, Frinton	H. Castle, Chiswick	1 hole
1905	H. Castle, Chiswick	A.C. Lincoln, South Herts	5 and 3
1906	Lord Glenawly, Royal Co. Down	A.E. Browning, Lahinch	10 and 8
1907	J.J. Hurley, Manrihaniesh	H.D. Gillies, Woking	4 and 2
1908	A.R. Aitken, Prestwick	Rev. P. Gannon, United Services	10 and 8
1909	J.D. Little, Burnisland	C. Taylor, Chislehurst	12 and 11
1910	G.R. Girdlestone, Oswestry	S.H. Fry, Mid Surrey	4 and 2
1911	L.O. Munn, North West	J.S. Kennedy, Turnberry	7 and 5
1912	G.V.M. Boyd, Portmarnock	T.S. Jennings, Cork	1 hole
1913	A.W. Murray, Purley Downs	T.S. Jennings, Cork	2 and 1
1914–19	No Championship		
1920	E.C. Carter, Royal Portrush	B.J. O'Brien, North West	10 and 9

YEAR	WINNER AND CLUB	RUNNER–UP AND CLUB	RESULT
1921	F. Murphy, Cork	D.D.B. Soulby, Portmarnock	1 Hole
1922	No Championship		
1923	F. Murphy, Cork	T.M. Healy, Royal Dublin	2 and 1
1924	J. Crabbe, Foxrock	W.G. McConnell, Royal Portrush	2 holes
1925	M. Crowley, Portmarnock	J. Crabbe, Foxrock	5 and 4
1926	R. Simcox, Cork	M. Crowley, Portmarnock	7 and 4
1927	R. Simcox, Cork	W.G. McConnell, Royal Portrush	2 and 1
1928	J. Burke, Lahinch	D.F. Sweeney, Galway	6 and 5
1929	J. Burke, Lahinch	D.F. Sweeney, Galway	8 and 5
1930	J. Burke, Lahinch	J.C. Brown, Tramore	6 and 5
1931	J. Burke, Lahinch	E. Dwyer, Cork	10 and 8
1932	J.C. Brown, Tramore	S.W. Martyn, Limerick	4 and 3
1933	J.C. Brown, Tramore	S.W. Martyn, Limerick	3 and 1
1934	R.M. Saunders, Lahinch	P.F. Murray, Milltown	3 and 1
1935	R.M. Saunders, Lahinch	M. Garrahey, Galway	4 and 2
1936	T.F. Ryan, Tipperary	R. Simcox, Cork	4 and 3
1937	M. O'Loughlin, Lahinch	D. Torrens, Lahinch	2 and 1
1938	M. O'Loughlin, Lahinch	R.M. Saunders, Lahinch	2 and 1
1939	J. Burke, Lahinch	T. Lenihan, Castle	6 and 4
1940	P.F. Murray, Milltown	J.A. English, Headford	8 and 7
1941	J. Burke, Lahinch	F. Hannon, Lahinch	9 and 8
1942	J. Burke, Lahinch	R. Garihy, Lahinch	8 and 7
1943	J. Burke, Lahinch	B. Slattery, Lahinch	1 hole
1944	J. Burke, Lahinch	J.C. Brown, Tramore	5 and 4
1945	J. Burke, Lahinch	C. Ewing, Co. Sligo	4 and 3
1946	J. Burke, Lahinch	J.B. Carr, Sutton	at 39th
1947	B. Slattery, Lahinch	J. Burke, Lahinch	6 and 5
1948	J.B. Carr, Sutton	J.P. Carroll, Sutton	3 and 2
1949	J.P. Carroll, Sutton	B. Slattery, Lahinch	1 hole
1950	M. Power, Muskerry	P.J. Leydon, Lahinch	12 and 10
1951	G. Gilligan, Limerick	T.W. Egan, Monkstown	5 and 3
1952	M. Power, Muskerry	N.V. Drew, Bangor	1 hole
1953	P.J. Leydon, Lahinch	M. Power, Muskerry	9 and 8
1954	P. Bugler, Lahinch	J.P. Mahon, Portmarnock	3 and 2
1955	P.J. Leydon, Lahinch	B. Slattery, Lahinch	4 and 3
1956	P.J. Leydon, Lahinch	M. Power, Muskerry	6 and 5
1957	P.J. Leydon, Lahinch	M. Power, Muskerry	8 and 7
1958	J.C. Brown, Tramore	G. McGlennon, Lahinch	5 and 4
1959	G. Roberts, Southport & Ainsdale	P. Donnelly, Queen's University	6 and 5
1960	P. Sullivan, Kinsale	P. Morrison, Oxford University	1 hole
1961	M. Guerin, Killarney	J.L. Bamford, Warrenpoint	7 and 6
1962	M. Guerin, Killarney	M. Skerritt, Lahinch	4 and 3
1963	M. Guerin, Killarney	D.B. Sheahan, Grange	2 and 1
1964	W.A. Kelleher, Douglas	J.M. Nestor, Milltown	2 and 1
1965	R.de L. Staunton, Castlerea	G.A. Young, Kilrush	5 and 3
1966	J.B. Carr, Sutton	G.A. Young, Kilrush	1 hole
1967	G.N. Fogarty, Royal Dublin	S. MacDonald, St Andrews	3 and 2
1968	J.D. Smyth, Lahinch	G.A. Young, Kilrush	3 and 2
1969	J.B. Carr, Sutton	G.N. Fogarty, Royal Dublin	2 and 1
1970	J.E. O'Leary, Foxrock	G.A. Young, Kilrush	1 hole
1971	P. Mulcare, Woodbrook	E. Higgins, Cork	1 hole
1972	R.de L. Staunton, Castlerea	G.A. Young, Kilrush	at 20th
1973	M.A. Gannon, Co. Louth	D.C. Long, Shandon Park	1 hole
1974	D.C. Long, Shandon Park	R.A. Fleury, Portmarnock	at 19th
1975	B.P. Malone, Portmarnock	M. Skerritt, Lahinch	2 holes
1976	V. Nevin, Limerick	P. Mulcare, Woodbrook	6 and 5
1977	L. MacNamara, Woodbrook	M.F. Morris, Portmarnock	4 and 3
1978	V. Nevin, Limerick	M. Guerin, Killarney	2 and 1
1979	P. O'Rourke, Kilkenny	T. Cleary, Fermoy	4 and 3
1980	M. Burns, Tramore	M.F. Morris, Portmarnock	4 and 3
1981	P. O'Rourke, Kilkenny	J.J. Carr, Sutton	2 and 1
1982	M.F. Morris, Portmarnock	C. McCarroll, City of Derry	1 hole
1983	A.C.J. Morrow, Portmarnock	M. Burns, Tramore	3 and 2
1984	N.H. Anderson, Shandon Park	M.F. Morris, Portmarnock	at 19th
1985	P. O'Rourke, Kilkenny	P. Lyons, Nenagh	3 and 2
1986	J. McHenry, Douglas	L. MacNamara, Woodbrook	3 and 2

YEAR	WINNER AND CLUB	RUNNER–UP AND CLUB	RESULT
1987	B.V.M. Reddan, Co. Louth	M.A. Gannon, Co. Louth	at 20th
1988	M.A. Gannon, Co. Louth	P.F. Hogan, Elm Park	3 and 2
1989	S. Keenan, Galway	J. Fanagan, Milltown	at 22nd
1990	D. Clarke, Dungannon	J. Carvill, Warrenpoint	4 and 3

APPENDIX XXII

Section 2

Record of winners and runners–up in the West of Ireland Amateur Open Championship

YEAR	WINNER AND CLUB	RUNNER–UP AND CLUB	RESULT
1923	L.P. Vernon	B.H. Cook	3 and 2
1924	J.L. Crabbe, Foxrock	W.G. McConnell, Milltown	3 and 2
1925	W.G. McConnell, Milltown	J.D. MacCormack, Hermitage	6 and 4
1926	J.L. Crabbe, Foxrock	W.G. McConnell, Milltown	3 and 2
1927	H.G. McCallum, Troon	A.W. Briscoe, Castlerea	4 and 3
1928	A.W. Briscoe, Castlerea	C. Ewing, Co. Sligo	1 hole
1929	W.G. McConnell, Milltown	E.P.J. O'Flynn, Galway	4 and 2
1930	C. Ewing, Co. Sligo	C. McMullan, Knock	4 and 3
1931	A.W. Briscoe, Castlerea	J. O'Mara	6 and 4
1932	C. Ewing, Co. Sligo	G. O'Connor, Roscommon	10 and 8
1933	J. Burke, Lahinch	C. O'Connor, Roscommon	13 and 12
1934	J. Burke, Lahinch	C. Ewing, Co. Sligo	3 and 1
1935	C. Ewing, Co. Sligo	J. Burke, Lahinch	3 and 1
1936	J. Burke, Lahinch	J.F. McLoughlin, Royal Dublin	11 and 10
1937	J.F. McLoughlin, Royal Dublin	C. Ewing, Co. Sligo	3 and 2
1938	J. Burke, Lahinch	M. Aherne, Boyle	8 and 7
1939	C. Ewing, Co. Sligo	J. Burke, Lahinch	3 and 1
1940	J. Burke, Lahinch	W.J. Gill, Portmarnock	4 and 3
1941	C. Ewing, Co. Sligo	J.F. McLoughlin, Royal Dublin	5 and 4
1942	C. Ewing, Co. Sligo	G.H. Owens, Skerries	4 and 3
1943	C. Ewing, Co. Sligo	L. Howley, Royal Dublin	10 and 8
1944	J. Burke, Lahinch	C. Ewing, Co. Sligo	3 and 2
1945	C. Ewing, Co. Sligo	J. Burke, Lahinch	4 and 3
1946	J.B. Carr, Sutton	B.J. Scannell, Woodbrook	11 and 9
1947	J.B. Carr, Sutton	C. Ewing, Co. Sligo	3 and 2
1948	J.B. Carr, Sutton	C. Ewing, Co. Sligo	5 and 4
1949	C. Ewing, Co. Sligo	F. Webster, Portmarnock	5 and 4
1950	C. Ewing, Co. Sligo	B. Slattery, Lahinch	1 hole
1951	J.B. Carr, Sutton	M. Ferguson, Dundalk	3 and 2
1952	J.C. Brown, Tramore	N.V. Drew, Bangor	2 and 1
1953	J.B. Carr, Sutton	R.H. McInnally, Sutton	1 hole
1954	J.B. Carr, Sutton	B.J. Scannell, Woodbrook	9 and 8
1955	W.I. Forsythe, Malone	T.D. Hegarty, Royal Dublin	2 and 1
1956	J.B. Carr, Sutton	C. Ewing, Co. Sligo	4 and 3
1957	J.R. Mahon, Portmarnock	J. Fitzgibbon, Cork	3 and 1
1958	J.B. Carr, Sutton	C. Ewing, Co. Sligo	4 and 3
1959	W.J.J. Ferguson, Malone	P.J. Leydon, Spanish Point	at 38th
1960	J.B. Carr, Sutton	T. Craddock, Malahide	at 19th
1961	J.B. Carr, Sutton	M. Edwards, Shandon Park	1 hole
1962	J.B. Carr, Sutton	B. O'Beirne, Portmarnock	7 and 5
1963	R.M. Craigan, Malone	T.M. Duggan, Kilkenny	1 hole
1964	B.P. Malone, Tullamore	W.A. Kelleher, Douglas	5 and 4
1965	R.M. Craigan, Malone	V. Nevin, Limerick	1 hole
1966	J.B. Carr, Sutton	R.de L. Staunton, Castlerea	2 and 1

YEAR	WINNER AND CLUB	RUNNER–UP AND CLUB	RESULT
1967	R.K.M. Pollin, Royal Belfast	A. O'Connor, Naas	1 hole
1968	D.A. Nelson, Royal Co. Down	J. Boston, Royal Co. Down	at 20th
1969	R.K.M. Pollin, Royal Belfast	M.J.C. Hoey, Shandon Park	1 hole
1970	J. McTear, Scotland	J.E. O'Leary, Foxrock	4 and 3
1971	R.J. Carr, Sutton	B.P. Malone, Portmarnock	1 hole
1972	V. Nevin, Portmarnock	B.P. Malone, Portmarnock	4 and 3
1973	H.B. Smyth, Royal Co. Down	V. Nevin, Limerick	2 and 1
1974	M.A. Gannon, Co. Louth	E. Dunne, Athlone	1 hole
1975	I.A. Elliott, Royal Portrush	D. Branigan, L'town & B'town	1 hole
1976	D. Branigan, L'town & B'town	T. Cleary, Fermoy	5 and 4
1977	T.B.C. Hoey, Shandon Park	L. MacNamara, Woodbrook	1 hole
1978	B.V.M. Reddan, Co. Louth	K. Stevenson, Banbridge	3 and 2
1979	D.C. Long, Shandon Park	A.D. Pierse, Tipperary	at 26th
1980	A.D. Pierse, Tipperary	P. Walton, Malahide	3 and 2
1981	D. Branigan, L'town & B'town	D. Conway, Portmarnock	7 and 5
1982	A.D. Pierse, Tipperary	M.J. Malone, Belvoir Park	3 and 1
1983	C. Glasgow, Donaghadee	G. McGimpsey, Bangor	2 and 1
1984	C. McGimpsey, Bangor	F. Gannon, Co. Louth	5 and 4
1985	J. Feeney, Chapel en Le Frith	G. Moore, Royal Portrush	1 hole
1986	P. Rayfus, Trim	E. McMenamin, Ballybofey	1 hole
1987	N. McGrane, Greenore	E. McMenamin, Ballybofey	1 hole
1988	G. McGimpsey, Bangor	C. Carew, Waterford	3 and 2
1989	P. McInerney, Milltown	K. Kearney, Limerick	2 and 1
1990	N. Goulding, Portmarnock	A.D. Pierse, Tipperary	3 and 2

APPENDIX XXII

Section 3

Record of winners and runners–up in the East of Ireland Amateur Open Championship

YEAR	WINNER AND CLUB	SCORE	RUNNER–UP AND CLUB	SCORE
1941	J.B. Carr, Sutton	301	K. Garvey, Co. Louth	305
1942	K. Garvey, Co. Louth	302	J. Burke, Lahinch	303
1943	J.B. Carr, Sutton	305	J. Burke, Lahinch	310
1944	J.W. Hulme, Warrenpoint	306	J.B. Carr, Sutton	314
1945	J.B. Carr, Sutton } Tie J. Burke, Lahinch	302	Result of Play–Off (1) J.B. Carr, Sutton (2) J. Burke, Lahinch	 154 157
1946	J.B. Carr, Sutton	316	J. Burke, Lahinch } Tie M. Ferguson, Dundalk	317 317
1947	B.J. Scannell, Woodbrook } Tie J.W. Hulme, Warrenpoint	321	Result of Play–Off (1) B.J. Scannell, Woodbrook (2) J.W. Hulme, Warrenpoint	 155 159
1948	J.B. Carr, Sutton	296	J.P. Carroll, Sutton	301
1949	M. Ferguson, Dundalk } Tie J.W. Hulme, Warrenpoint	305	Result of Play–Off (1) M. Ferguson, Dundalk (2) J.W. Hulme, Warrenpoint	 190 193
1950	J.P. Carroll, Sutton	311	K. Garvey, Co. Louth } Tie M. Ferguson, Dundalk	313 313
1951	M. Power, Muskerry	297	M. Ferguson, Dundalk	307
1952	N.V. Drew, Bangor	306	J.C. Brown, Tramore } Tie B.F. Smyth, Milltown	309 309
1953	J.P. Carroll, Sutton	303	B.J. Scannell, Woodbrook	304
1954	B.J. Scannell, Woodbrook	298	O.M. Lochrin, Co. Louth } Tie M. Power, Muskerry	300 300

YEAR	WINNER AND CLUBS	SCORE	RUNNER–UP AND CLUB	SCORE
1955	B.J. Scannell, Woodbrook	298	J. Caldwell, Portmarnock	312
1956	J.B. Carr, Sutton	300	D. Ryan, Portmarnock	310
1957	J.B. Carr, Sutton	287	G.N. Fogarty, Royal Dublin	292
1958	J.B. Carr, Sutton	288	J.W. Hulme, Warrenpoint	295
1959	T. Craddock, Malahide	294	J. Shiels, Foxrock	298
1960	J.B. Carr, Sutton	290	T. Craddock, Malahide	292
1961	J.B. Carr, Sutton	291	J. Murray, Mullingar } Tie	296
			E.A. Firth, Sutton	296
1962	T.W. Egan, Monkstown	290	B. Edwards, Shandon Park	291
1963	G.N. Fogarty, Royal Dublin	294	T. Craddock, Malahide	298
1964	J.B. Carr, Sutton	292	M. McGuirk, Co. Louth	293
1965	T. Craddock, Malahide	291	S.F. Hosty, Galway } Tie	295
			W.H. Rainey, Shandon Park	295
1966	T. Craddock, Malahide	288	J.B. Carr, Sutton	289
1967	C.N. Fogarty, Royal Dublin	293	M. Madeville, Dundalk	299
1968	P. Caul, Malahide	289	R.N. Baker, Cork	290
1969	J.B. Carr, Sutton	292	G.N. Fogarty, Royal Dublin } Tie	294
			J.J. O'Neill, Donabate	294
1970	R.J. Carr, Sutton	291	E. Higgins, Cork	291

R.J. Carr won on 'sudden death play–off'

YEAR	WINNER AND CLUBS	SCORE	RUNNER–UP AND CLUB	SCORE
1971	P. Mulcare, Woodbrook	281	R.J. Carr, Sutton } Tie	287
			D. White, Tullamore	287
1972	P. Mulcare, Woodbrook	292	J.C. Moss, Royal Portrush	293
1973	P. Mulcare, Woodbrook	291	S.L. Cooney, Milltown	292
1974	H.B. Smyth, Royal Co. Down	295	A.D. Pierse, Tipperary	298
1975	A.C.J. Morrow, Portmarnock	300	M.F. Morris, Portmarnock	303
1976	D. White, Tullamore	295	D. Branigan, L'town & B'town	296
1977	T. Cleary, Fermoy	299	M.A. Gannon, Co. Louth	299

T. Cleary won on 'sudden death play–off'

1978	M.A. Gannon, Co. Louth	295	H.B. Smyth, Royal Co. Down	300
1979	A.D. Pierse, Tipperary	288	G. McGimpsey, Bangor	288

A.D. Pierse won on 'sudden death play–off'

1980	P. Caul, Malahide	292	G. McGimpsey, Bangor	292

P. Caul won on 'sudden death play–off'

1981	D. Branigan, L'town & B'town	292	R.de L. Staunton, Castlerea	293
1982	M.F. Sludds, The Island	285	B. Rogers, The Island	291
1983	A.C.J. Morrow, Portmarnock	291	M.A. Gannon, Co. Louth	292
1984	R.V.M. Reddan, Co. Louth	293	M.A. Gannon, Co. Louth (on last 36)	299
1985	F. Ronan, Co. Louth	286	P.F. Hogan, Elm Park	294
1986	P.F. Hogan, Elm Park	291	E. Dunne, Elm Park	294
1987	P. Rayfus, Trim	297	T. Cleary, Fermoy (on last 5)	299
1988	C. McGimpsey, Bangor	283	P. Rayfus, Trim	291
1989	D. Clarke, Dungannon	285	A.D. Pierse, Tipperary	288
1990	D.F. O'Sullivan, Cork	291	G. McNeill, Warrenpoint	293

Record of winners of the Carbery Cup

1948	J.P. Carroll (Sutton)
1949	F.G. Moran (Clontarf)
1950	T.D. Hegarty (Mountbellew)
1951	G.A. Young (Kilrush)
1952	B.F. Smyth (Royal Dublin)
1953	B.R. Overend (Castle)
1954	O.M. Lochrin (Co. Louth)
1955	J. O'Reilly (Newlands)
1956	D.C. Macaulay (Donabate)
1957	B.J. Scannell (Woodbrook)
1958	J. O'Sullivan (Athlone)
1959	R.A. Howlett (Tramore)
1960	M. McGuirk (Co. Louth)
1961	F. Gallagher (Co. Louth)

1962	B.J. Scannell (Woodbrook)
1963	B. Rogers (Island)
1964	B. Rogers (Island)
1965	J.M. Shiels (Foxrock)
1966	G.L. McGuinness (Castle)
1967	B. O'Beirne (Portmarnock)
1968	H.N. McKeown (Cork)
1969	J.J. O'Neill (Donabate)
1970	D.J. Smyth (L'town & B'town)
1971	M. Hanway (Sutton)
1972	D. Branigan (L'town & B'town)
1973	R. McDonnell (L'town & B'town)
1974	B.P. Malone (Portmarnock)
1975	M. Burns (Tramore)
1976	F. Ronan (Co. Louth)
1977	B. Reck (Lucan)
1978	A. Cosgrave (Woodbrook)
1979	F. Ronan (Co. Louth)
1980	P.F. Hogan (Elm Park)
1981	B.P. Malone (Elm Park)

1982	S. McParland (Greenore)	1967	G.N. Fogarty (Royal Dublin)
1983	K. Rogers (Island)	1968	R.N. Baker (Monkstown)
1984	P. Lyons (Nenagh)	1969	M.P. Fitzpatrick (Sutton)
1985	M. McGinley (Naas)	1970	R.J. Carr (Sutton)
1986	B. Rogers (Island)	1971	M. Hanway (Sutton)
1987	T. Boylan (Naas)	1972	P. Mulcare (Woodbrook)
1988	P. Gribben (Warrenpoint)	1973	S.L. Cooney (Milltown)
1989	B. Kinsella (Skerries)	1974	S. Rogers (Island)
1990	S. Moore (Royal Portrush)	1975	M. Burns (Tramore)

Record of winners of the Agnew Salver

		1976	T. Coone (Royal Tara)
		1977	G.N. Fogarty (Royal Dublin)
		1978	D. Mahon (Galway)
		1979	F. Ronan (Co. Louth)
		1980	M. McGinley (Naas)
		1981	M. Reilly (Malahide)
1961	F. Gallagher (Co. Louth)	1982	E. Dunne (Elm Park)
1962	D.B. Sheahan (Grange)	1983	M. McGinley (Naas)
1963	M. Fives (Grange)	1984	B.V.M. Reddan (Co. Louth)
1964	F. Gallagher (Co. Louth)	1985	P.E. Bray (Hermitage)
1965	J.M. Shiels (Dundalk)	1986	D.A. Mulholland (Castlerock)
1966	T. Craddock (Malahide)	1987	A. Pierce (Naas)
		1988	D. Branigan (L'town & B'town)
		1989	B. Byrne (Island)
		1990	B. Hobson (Malone)

APPENDIX XXII

Section 4

Record of winners and runners–up in the North of Ireland Amateur Open Championship

YEAR	WINNER AND CLUB	SCORE	RUNNER–UP AND CLUB	SCORE	RESULT
1947	J. Fitzsimmons, Bushfoot		J.C. Kissock, Bangor		8 and 7
1948	J. Fitzsimmons, Bushfoot		W.A. McNeill		10 and 9
1949	F. Webster, Portmarnock	311	J. Taggart Royal Portrush } Tie	312	
			J.M. Neill, Cliftonville	312	
1950	N.V. Drew, Bangor		J. Taggart, Royal Portrush		at 19th
1951	W. Meharg, Castlerock		J. Glover, Knock		2 and 1
1952	N.V. Drew, Bangor		W. Meharg, Castlerock		2 and 1
1953	C. Knox, Royal Portrush		J.L. Bamford, Royal Portrush		2 and 1
1954	J.L. Bamford, Royal Portrush		J.P. Coulter, Scotland		6 and 5
1955	R.McK. Fleury, Cork		W.I. Forsythe, Malone		3 and 2
1956	M. Edwards, Shandon Park		M. Macauley, Malone		7 and 6
1957	M. Edwards, Shandon Park		C. Knox, Royal Portrush		7 and 6
1958	T.E. Dijon, Rathmore		S.A.C. Cooley, Clandeboye		5 and 3
1959	J. Duncan, Shandon Park		D.B. Sheahan, Grange		5 and 3
1960	W.H.E. Rainey, Shandon Park		M. Edwards, Shandon Park		3 and 2
1961	J. Duncan, Shandon Park		P. Donnelly, Queen's University		3 and 1
1962	J.F.D. Madeley, Royal Belfast		W.H.E. Rainey, Shandon Park		5 and 4
1963	J.F.D. Madeley, Royal Belfast		C. Muir, Greenisland		7 and 5
1964	F.A. McCorrty, Clandeboye		W.E. McCrea, Walton Heath		3 and 2
1965	W.H.A. Rainey, Shandon Park		N.S. Kelly, Knock		1 hole
1966	B. Edwards, Shandon Park		J. Faith, Rathmore		3 and 2
1967	W.R.A. Tennant, Cliftonville		J. Faith, Rathmore		3 and 2
1968	M.J.C. Hoey, Shandon Park		J.E. O'Leary, Foxrock		1 hole
1969	M.J.C. Hoey, Shandon Park		J. Faith, Rathmore		3 and 2
1970	J. Faith, Rathmore		R.J. Carr, Sutton		at 20th

The Golfing Union of Ireland

YEAR	WINNER AND CLUB	RUNNER–UP AND CLUB	RESULT
1971	R.K.M. Pollin, Royal Belfast	T.B.C. Hoey, Shandon Park	2 and 1
1972	J.L. Bamford, Royal Portrush	J. McAleese, Ballymena	5 and 4
1973	B. Edwards, Shandon Park	W.J.J. Ferguson, Malone	6 and 5
1974	B.J.S. Kissock, Bangor	W.J.C. Moss, Royal Portrush	1 hole
1975	J. Heggarty, Massereene	W.J.J. Ferguson, Malone	2 and 1
1976	B.J.S. Kissock, Bangor	M. Patterson, Royal Portrush	4 and 3
1977	D.J.F. Young, Royal Portrush	J.D. Coey, Clandeboye	5 and 4
1978	G. McGimpsey, Bangor	G. McGuckian, Rathmore	2 and 1
1979	T.B.C. Hoey, Shandon Park	J.A. McDade, Bangor	2 and 1
1980	M. Malone, Belvoir Park	M. Martin, Clandeboye	6 and 4
1981	D.C. Long, Shandon Park	B.J.S. Kissock, Bangor	1 hole
1982	D.C. Long, Shandon Park	D.J.F. Young, Royal Portrush	5 and 4
1983	T.B.C. Hoey, Shandon Park	I.A. Elliott, Rathmore	2 and 1
1984	G. McGimpsey, Bangor	D.C. Long, Shandon Park	6 and 5
1985	I.A. Elliott, Rathmore	B. Patton, Strabane	1 hole
1986	D.W. Ballentine, Carrickfergus	P. O'Donnell, Whitehead	5 and 3
1987	A.D. Pierse, Tipperary	R.A. Hanna, Lurgan	8 and 6
1988	N.H. Anderson, Shandon Park	B. Norgard, Denmark	4 and 3
1989	N.H. Anderson, Shandon Park	D. Baker, Downpatrick	3 and 2
1990	D. Clarke, Dungannon	P. McGinley, Grange	1 hole

APPENDIX XXIII

Officers of the Union

ELECTED AT MEETING	PRESIDENT	PRESIDENT-ELECT	HONORARY SECRETARY	HONORARY TREASURER
13 November, 1891	Lord Ranfurly		George Combe	Hugh C. Kelly
10 March, 1899			Henry J. Daly	
4 September, 1906	Sir D. Plunket Barton, Bart.		Rev. John L. Morrow BA DD	
9 September, 1912				William B. Fennell
26 October, 1921			George Price LLD	
8 September, 1926	Hugh C. Kelly			
14 September, 1927			Alan B. Kidd	
11 September, 1929	Beamish A. Morrison			
12 September, 1930				A.H. Moody
5 October, 1931				Charles S. Harden
14 November, 1932	D. Wilson Smyth, DL			
14 December, 1936	William G. Fitzsimmons			
13 December, 1937				William F. Neill
31 January, 1938	Commander George Crosbie			
23 January, 1942	Thomas P. Toher, MPSI			
28 March, 1946	James Henderson, DL			Francis J. Byrne
16 April, 1948	Prof. Pierce F. Purcell, MICE		Alfred S.G. Adams	
14 December, 1948			John Roy	
29 November, 1949			William J. Gill	
28 November, 1950	Redmond Simcox			
2 December, 1952	Sir William F. Neill, DL JP			
11 December, 1953				Hugh Stevenson
25 November, 1954	Prof. Michael G. O'Malley			
29 November, 1956	Dr Robert E. Davitt			
28 November, 1958	Dr William M. O'Sullivan			
24 November, 1960	David L. Baine, MBE			
10 January, 1963	Michael J. Murphy			
17 January, 1965	Thomas P. Brindley			
20 January, 1967	Thomas E. O'Donnell			
25 January, 1968	H. Max Hadden, JP	William J. Gill	Thomas P. Brindley	Charles H. Adams
24 January, 1969	William J. Gill	Cecil Ewing		

ELECTED AT MEETING	PRESIDENT	PRESIDENT-ELECT	HONORARY SECRETARY	HONORARY TREASURER
23 January, 1970	Cecil Ewing	Dr Gerald H. Owens LDS	William J. Gill	
29 January, 1971	Dr Gerald H. Owens, LDS	Thomas Montgomery		
28 January, 1972	Thomas Montgomery	Dr William M. O'Sullivan		
26 January, 1973	Patrick J. McPolìn	Maurice de Lacy Staunton		
25 January, 1974	Maurice de Lacy Staunton	Peter V. Lyons		David M. McAuley
17 January, 1975	Peter V. Lyons	John G. McErvel	Desmond Rea O'Kelly, FIEI	
13 February, 1976	John G. McErvel	Patrick J. Foley		
4 February, 1977	Patrick J. Foley	Thomas Rogers		
3 February, 1978	Thomas Rogers	Brendan J. Scannell		
2 February, 1979	Brendan J. Scannell	Michael C. McAuley		
1 February, 1980	Michael C. McAuley	John P. McInerney		
27 February, 1981	John P. McInerney	Frederick W. Perry		
5 February, 1982	Frederick W. Perry	Michael P. Fitzpatrick		
11 February, 1983	Michael P. Fitzpatrick	William J.J. Ferguson		
10 February, 1984	William J.J. Ferguson	Frank W. Bowen		
8 February, 1985	Frank W. Bowen	Michael J. Hennelly		
7 February, 1986	Michael J. Hennelly	J. Gerard O'Brien		
27 February, 1987	J. Gerard O'Brien	Barry T. Crymble, FRCS		
26 February, 1988	Barry T. Crymble, FRCS	Joseph Quinlan		
24 February, 1989	Joseph Quinlan	Gerard D. Golden	J. Gerard O'Brien	
23 February, 1990	Gerard D. Golden	Desmond Rea O'Kelly, FIEI		

APPENDIX XXIV
Section 1

Charles O. Hezlet (Royal Portrush)

Championships

Amateur:	Runner-up 1914
Irish Amateur Open:	Winner 1926, 1929
	Runner-up 1923, 1925
Irish Amateur Close:	Winner 1920
Welsh Amateur Open:	Runner-up 1923
Open Championship of Ireland:	Leading Amateur 1927, 1929
Surrey Amateur Open:	Winner 1928

International Matches

Walker Cup:	1924, 1926, 1928
Welsh Internationals:	1922
Home Internationals:	1923, 1924, 1925, 1927, 1928, 1929, 1930, 1931

Inter-Club Tournaments

Barton Shield Winner:	1922
Senior Cup Winner:	1923

Miscellaneous

St George's Vase, Sandwich:	Winner 1926
British Team in South Africa:	1927

Administrative

Irish International Team Captain:	1923, 1925, 1927, 1928, 1929(3), 1930(2), 1931, 1948, 1949, 1950, 1951, 1952, 1953
Irish International Selector:	1947, 1948, 1949, 1950, 1951, 1952, 1953
British Team Captain:	1952 (South Africa, Kenya, Rhodesia)
Club Captain:	Portrush 1914–20 and 1946–8
	West Hill 1927
	Crowborough Beacon 1957–8

APPENDIX XXIV
Section 2

G. Noel C. Martin (Royal Portrush)

Championships

Irish Amateur Open:	Winner 1920, 1923

International Matches

Walker Cup:	1928
Home Internationals:	1923, 1925, 1928, 1929, 1930

Administrative

Irish International Team Captain:	1930
Club Captain:	Royal Portrush 1949-50

APPENDIX XXIV
Section 3

John Burke (Lahinch)

Championships

Irish Amateur Open:	Winner 1947
Irish Amateur Close:	Winner 1930, 1931, 1932, 1933, 1936, 1940, 1946, 1947
	Runner-up 1935, 1937
South of Ireland:	Winner 1928, 1929, 1930, 1931, 1939, 1941, 1942, 1943, 1944, 1945, 1946
	Runner-up 1947
West of Ireland:	Winner 1933, 1934, 1936, 1938, 1940, 1944
	Runner-up 1935, 1939, 1945
East of Ireland:	Runner-up 1942, 1943, 1945, 1946
Open Championship of Ireland:	Leading Amateur 1933

International Matches

Walker Cup:	1932
Home Internationals:	1929, 1930, 1931, 1932, 1933, 1934, 1935, 1936, 1937, 1938, 1947, 1948, 1949

Interprovincial Matches

Senior Interprovincials:	1938, 1939

Administrative

Irish International Team Captain:	1932
Club Captain:	Lahinch 1948

APPENDIX XXIV

Section 4

Cecil Ewing (Co. Sligo)

Championships

Amateur:	Runner-up 1938
	Semi-Finalist 1936
Irish Amateur Open:	Winner 1948, 1951
	Runner-up 1950, 1954
Irish Amateur Close:	Winner 1948, 1958
	Runner-up 1946
West of Ireland:	Winner 1930, 1932, 1935, 1939, 1941, 1942, 1943, 1945, 1949, 1950
	Runner-up 1928, 1934, 1937, 1944, 1947, 1948, 1956, 1958
South of Ireland:	Runner-up 1945
Irish Seniors' Amateur Open:	Winner 1970
	Runner-up 1972

International Matches

Walker Cup:	1936, 1938, 1947, 1949, 1951, 1955
Home Internationals:	1934, 1935, 1936, 1937, 1938, 1947, 1948, 1949, 1950, 1951, 1953, 1954, 1955, 1956, 1957, 1958

Interprovincial Matches

Senior Interprovincials:	1938, 1939, 1958, 1959, 1963

Inter-Club Team Tournaments

Barton Shield Winner (Portmarnock):	1935, 1939, 1940
Senior Cup Winner (Portmarnock):	1932, 1933, 1934, 1935, 1940

Administrative

Irish International Selector:	1949, 1959, 1960, 1961, 1962, 1963, 1964, 1965, 1966, 1967, 1968, 1969.
Walker Cup Selector:	1952, 1953, 1954
Irish International Team Captain:	1960, 1961, 1962, 1963, 1964, 1965, 1966, 1967, 1968, 1969,
Club Captain:	Co. Sligo 1940 and 1961
GUI President:	1970

APPENDIX XXIV

Section 5

James Bruen (Muskerry)

Championships

Amateur:	Winner 1946
Irish Amateur Open:	Winner 1938
Irish Amateur Close:	Winner 1937, 1938
Open Championship:	Leading Amateur 1939
Open Championship of Ireland:	Leading Amateur 1937, 1938, 1939
Boys' Amateur Open:	Winner 1936

International Matches

Walker Cup:	1938, 1949, 1951
Home Internationals:	1937, 1938, 1939, 1950

Interprovincial Matches

Senior Interprovincials:	1938, 1939

Inter-Club Tournaments

Barton Shield Winner (Cork):	1937, 1938
Senior Cup Winner (Cork):	1939

Miscellaneous

St George's Challenge Cup:	Runner-up 1937
Prince of Wales Cup (Deal):	Runner-up 1937
Cork Scratch Cup:	Winner 1938, 1939, 1940, 1941

Administrative

Irish International Selector :	1959, 1960, 1961, 1962
Club Captain:	Cork 1943–4 and 1946–7
Club President:	Cork 1960–62 and 1971–2

APPENDIX XXIV

Section 6

Joseph B. Carr (Sutton)

Championships

Amateur:	Winner 1953, 1958, 1960
	Runner-up 1968
	Semi-finalist 1951, 1952, 1954
Irish Amateur Open:	Winner 1946, 1950, 1954, 1956
	Runner-up 1947, 1948, 1951, 1958
Irish Amateur Close:	Winner 1954, 1957, 1963, 1964, 1965, 1967
	Runner-up 1951, 1959

West of Ireland:	Winner 1946, 1947, 1948, 1951, 1953, 1954,1956, 1958, 1960, 1961, 1962, 1966
East of Ireland:	Winner 1941 1943, 1945, 1946, 1948, 1956, 1957, 1958, 1960, 1961, 1964, 1969
	Runner-up 1944 1966
South of Ireland:	Winner 1948, 1966, l969
	Runner-up 1946
Open Championship:	Leading Amateur 1956, 1958
Open Championship of Ireland:	Leading Amateur 1946, 1948, 1950, 1953
American Amateur Open:	Semi-finalist 1961
Canadian Amateur Open:	Quarter-finalist 1957
Boys' Amateur Open:	Semi-finalist 1939

International Matches

Walker Cup:	1947, 1949, 1951, 1953, 1955, 1957, 1959, 1961, 1963, 1967
Home Internationals:	1947, 1948, 1949, 1950, 1951, 1952, 1953, 1954, 1955, 1956, 1957, 1958, 1959, 1960, 1961, 1962, 1963, 1964, 1965, 1966, 1967, 1968, 1969
World Cup (Eisenhower Trophy):	1958, 1960
Britain & Ireland v. Continent of Europe:	1954, 1956, 1964, 1968
European Amateur Golf Team Championship:	1965, 1967, 1969
Quadrangular Continental:	1968

Interprovincial Matches

| Senior Interprovincials: | 1938, 1956, 1958, 1960, 1962, 1963, 1964, 1968, 1970 |

Inter-Club Team Tournaments

| Barton Shield Winner: | 1946, 1949, 1950, |
| Senior Cup Winner: | 1948, 1949, 1950, 1956, 1958, 1963 |

Miscellaneous

Birkdale Bowl:	Winner 1951
Golf Illustrated Golf Vase:	Winner 1951
	Runner-up 1949
An Tostal Golden Ball:	Winner l953
Gleneagles Saxone:	Winner 1955
Dunlop Masters:	Joint runner-up 1958
Berkshire Trophy:	Winner 1959
Formby Hare:	Winner 1962
Antlers Royal Mid Surrey:	Winner 1970
Golf Writers' Trophy Award:	1953
Bobby Jones Award:	1961
Walter Hagen Award:	1967

Administrative

Walker Cup Captain:	1963, 1965
World Cup (Eisenhower Trophy) Captain:	1964, 1966
Britain & Ireland Captain:	1964, 1966
Walker Cup Selector:	1979, 1980, 1981, 1982, 1983, 1984, 1985, 1986
Irish International Team Captain:	1979, 1980, 1981
Irish International Selector:	1979, 1980, 1981
Club Captain:	Sutton 1948, 1949, 1990

APPENDIX XXIV
Section 7

Samuel M. McCready (Dunmurry)

Championships

Amateur:	Winner 1949
R.A.F.:	Winner 1947
Jamaican Amateur:	Winner 1948
Open Championship of Ireland:	Leading Amateur 1947

International Matches

Walker Cup:	1949, 1951
	Reserve 1947
Home Internationals:	1947, 1949, 1950, 1952, 1954

APPENDIX XXIV
Section 8

Norman V. Drew (Bangor)

Championships

Irish Amateur Open:	Winner 1952, 1953
North of Ireland:	Winner 1950, 1952
East of Ireland:	Winner 1952
West of Ireland:	Runner-up 1952
South of Ireland:	Runner-up 1952
Boys' Amateur:	Runner-up 1949
Ulster Boys' Amateur Open:	Winner 1949

International Matches

| Walker Cup: | 1953 |
| Home Internationals: | 1952, 1953 |

Inter-Club Team Tournaments

| Barton Shield Winner: | 1951 |

Miscellaneous

| Turned Professional: | 1953 |

APPENDIX XXIV
Section 9

J.F. David Madeley (Royal Belfast and Royal Co. Down)

Championships
North of Ireland: Winner 1963, 1964

International Matches
Walker Cup: 1963
Home Internationals: 1959, 1960, 1961, 1962,
                                     1963, 1964, 1966
Britain & Ireland v.
   Continent of Europe: 1962

Interprovincial Matches
Senior Interprovincials: 1959, 1960, 1961, 1962,
                                     1963, 1964, 1966

Inter-Club Team Matches
Belfast and District Cup Winner: 1964, 1969

Miscellaneous
Royal Belfast Scratch Cup   Winner 1958 to 1966
                                     (six wins)
Royal County Down Scratch Cup   Winner 1973, 1981

APPENDIX XXIV
Section 10

David B. Sheahan (UCD and Grange)

Championships
Irish Amateur Close: Winner 1961, 1966, 1970
North of Ireland: Runner-up 1959
South of Ireland: Runner-up 1963

International Matches
Walker Cup: 1963
Home Internationals: 1961, 1962, 1963, 1964,
                                     1965, 1966, 1967, 1970
Britain & Ireland v.
   Continent of Europe: 1962, 1964
European Amateur Golf Team
   Championship: 1965, 1967

Interprovincial Matches
Senior Interprovincials: 1959, 1960, 1961, 1962,
                                     1963, 1964, 1965

Miscellaneous
Boyd Quaich: Winner 1962
Jeyes Professional Tournament: Winner 1962

APPENDIX XXIV
Section 11

Thomas Craddock (IAGA and Malahide)

Championships
Irish Amateur Open: Winner 1958
Irish Amateur Close: Winner 1959
                                     Runner-up 1965
East of Ireland: Winner 1959, 1965, 1966
                                     Runner-up 1960, 1963
West of Ireland: Runner-up 1960

International Matches
Walker Cup: 1967, 1969
Home Internationals: 1955, 1956, 1957, 1958,
                                     1959, 1960, 1965, 1966,
                                     1967, 1968, 1969, 1970
Britain & Ireland v.
   Continent of Europe: 1958, 1966, 1968,
European Amateur Golf Team
   Championship: 1965, 1967, 1969, 1971

Interprovincial Matches
Senior Interprovincials: 1956, 1957, 1958, 1959,
                                     1960, 1961, 1962, 1963,
                                     1964, 1965, 1967, 1968,
                                     1969, 1970, 1971

Inter-Club Team Tournaments
Barton Shield Winner: 1971, 1978, 1982,
Senior Cup Winner: 1965

Miscellaneous
Lytham Trophy: Winner 1969

Administrative
Irish International Selector: 1982

APPENDIX XXIV
Section 12

Roderick J. Carr (Sutton)

Championships

East of Ireland:	Winner 1970
West of Ireland:	Winner 1971
South African Open:	Leading Amateur 1971

International Matches

Walker Cup:	1971
Home Internationals:	1970, 1971
European Amateur Golf Team Championship:	1971
Irish Youths' v. Continent of Europe Youths':	1970
Britian & Ireland Youths' v. Continent of Europe Youths':	1970, 1971

Interprovincial Matches

Senior Interprovincials:	1970, 1971

Miscellaneous

Antlers Royal Mid-Surrey :	Winner 1970
Turnberry Pro-Am:	Winner 1970
Turned Professional:	1971
Reinstated to Amateur Status:	1983

APPENDIX XXIV
Section 13

Patrick Mulcare (Woodbrook)

Championships

East of Ireland:	Winner 1971, 1972, 1973
South of Ireland:	Winner 1971

International Matches

Walker Cup:	1975
Home Internationals:	1968, 1969, 1970, 1971, 1972, 1974, 1975, 1978, 1979, 1980
European Amateur Golf Team Championship:	1979
Britain & Ireland v. Continent of Europe:	1972
Quadrangular Continental:	1972, 1978, 1980
Continent of Europe v. South America	1978

Interprovincial Matches

Senior Interprovincials:	1967, 1968, 1969, 1970, 1971, 1972, 1973, 1974, 1975, 1977, 1978, 1980

APPENDIX XXIV
Section 14

Ronan Rafferty (Warrenpoint)

Championships

Amateur Championship:	Quarter-finalist 1980
Irish Amateur Close:	Winner 1980
Boys' Amateur:	Winner 1979
Youths' Amateur Open Championship of Ireland:	Winner 1979
Ulster Youths' Amateur Open:	Winner 1979
English Amateur Open Strokeplay:	Tied 1st 1980
Munster Youths' Amateur Open:	Runner-up 1980
Munster Boys' Amateur Open:	Winner 1979
	Runner-up 1978

International Matches

Walker Cup:	1981
Home Internationals:	1979, 1980, 1981
European Amateur Boys' Golf Team Championship:	1980
European Amateur Youths' Golf Team Championship:	1979, 1980
European Amateur Golf Team Championship:	1981
Ireland Boys' v. Wales Boys':	1979
Britain & Ireland Youths' v. Continent of Europe Youths':	1979
Britain & Ireland v. Continent of Europe:	1980
World Cup (Eisenhower Trophy):	1980
Quadrangular Continental:	1980

Interprovincial Matches

Junior Interprovincials:	1979, 1980
Senior Interprovincials:	1980

Miscellaneous

Turned Professional:	1981

APPENDIX XXIV
Section 15

Philip Walton (Malahide)

Championships

Irish Amateur Close:	Winner 1982
Spanish Amateur Open:	Winner 1981
Scottish Amateur Open Strokeplay:	Winner 1981
West of Ireland:	Runner-up 1980
Youths' Amateur:	Tied lst
	(beaten at 2nd tie hole)1980
Boys' Amateur:	Semi-finalist 1979
Youths' Amateur Open	
Championship of Ireland:	Runner-up 1980
Leinster Youths' Amateur Open:	Winner 1979
Leinster Boys' Amateur Open:	Winner 1978, 1979
	Runner-up 1977

International Matches

Walker Cup:	1981, 1983
Home Internationals:	1979, 1980, 1981, 1982,
	1983
European Amateur Youths'	
Golf Team Championship:	1979, 1980, 1981
European Amateur Golf Team	
Championship:	1981, 1983
Ireland Boys' v. Wales Boys':	1977, 1978, 1979
Britain & Ireland Youths' v.	
Continent of Europe Youths':	1980
Ireland Youths' v. Scotland Youths':	1981
Britain & Ireland v.	
Continent of Europe:	1982
Quadrangular Continental:	1980, 1982

Interprovincial Matches

Junior Interprovincials:	1979, 1980
Senior Interprovincials:	1980, 1981

Miscellaneous

Willie Gill Award:	1982
Turned Professional:	1983

APPENDIX XXIV
Section 16

Arthur Pierse (Tipperary)

Championships

Amateur:	Semi-finalist 1980,
East of Ireland:	Winner 1979
	Runner-up 1974
West of Ireland:	Winner 1980, 1982
	Runner-up 1979
North of Ireland:	Winner 1987

International Matches

Walker Cup:	1983
Home Internationals:	1976, 1977, 1978, 1979,
	1980, 1981, 1982, 1983,
	1984, 1985, 1987, 1988,
European Amateur Golf Team	
Championship:	1981, 1983, 1985
Britain & Ireland v.	
Continent of Europe:	1980, 1982,
Quadrangular Continental:	1980, 1982, 1984

Interprovincial Matches

Senior Interprovincials:	1974, 1975, 1977, 1978,
	1980, 1981, 1984, 1985,
	1987, 1988

Miscellaneous

Willie Gill Award:	1980

APPENDIX XXIV
Section 17

Garth McGimpsey (Bangor)

Championships

Amateur:	Winner, 1985
	Semi-finalist 1989
Irish Amateur Close:	Winner 1988
North of Ireland:	Winner 1978, 1984
West of Ireland:	Winner 1984, 1988
	Runner-up 1983
East of Ireland:	Winner 1988
	Runner-up 1979, 1980
Ulster Boys' Amateur Open:	Runner-up 1971

International Matches

Walker Cup:	1985, 1989
Home Internationals:	1978, 1979, 1980, 1981,
	1982, 1983, 1984, 1985,
	1986, 1987, 1988, 1989
European Amateur Golf Team	
Championship:	1981, 1983, 1985, 1987,
	1989
World Cup (Eisenhower Trophy):	1984, 1986, 1988
Britain & Ireland v.	
Continent of Europe:	1984, 1986, 1988
Quadrangular Continental:	1984, 1986, 1988

Interprovincial Matches

Senior Interprovincials:	1979, 1980, 1981, 1982,
	1983, 1984, 1985, 1986,
	1987, 1988, 1989

Inter-Club Team Tournaments

Senior Cup Winner:	1981, 1983
Belfast and District Cup Winner:	1980, 1981, 1983

Miscellaneous

Willie Gill Award:	1985
Bangor Club Championship:	1976, 1977, 1978, 1979,
	1982, 1984, 1986, 1987,
	1988

APPENDIX XXIV
Section 18

John McHenry (Douglas)

Championships

Irish Amateur Close:	Winner 1986
South of Ireland:	Winner 1986
Youths' Amateur Open	
Championship of Ireland:	Winner 1980, 1981, 1984
Connacht Youths' Amateur Open:	Winner 1980, 1983
Munster Boys' Amateur Open:	Runner-up 1981

International Matches

Walker Cup:	1987
Home Internationals:	1985, 1986
European Amateur Boys' Golf	
Team Championship:	1980, 1981
European Amateur Youths' Golf	
Team Championship:	1980, 1981, 1984
European Amateur Golf Team	
Championship:	1987
Ireland Youths' v. Scotland Youths':	1981

Interprovincial Matches

Junior Interprovincials:	1981
Senior Interprovincials:	1981, 1985, 1986, 1987

Miscellaneous

Willie Gill Award:	1986
Virginia Collegiate Title:	1986
East Coast (America) Athletic	
Conference Individual Title:	1986
Douglas Scratch Cup:	1984

APPENDIX XXIV
Section 19

Eoghan O'Connell (Killarney)

Championships

Irish Boys' Amateur Close:	Winner 1984
South of Ireland:	Semi-finalist 1986
Leinster Boys' Amateur Open:	Runner-up 1983
Munster Boys' Amateur Open:	Runner-up 1983
Munster Youths' Amateur Open:	Runner-up 1984
Open Championship of Ireland:	Leading Amateur 1989

International Matches

Walker Cup:	1989
Home Internationals:	1985
European Amateur Boys' Golf	
Team Championship:	1984, 1985
European Amateur Youths' Golf	
Team Championship:	1984
European Amateur Golf Team	
Championship:	1987
Quadrangular Continental:	1988
World Cup (Eisenhower Trophy):	1988
Ireland Boys' v. Wales Boys':	1984
Ireland Youths' v. Scotland Youths':	1984, 1985, 1987, 1988

Interprovincial Matches

Junior Interprovincials:	1984, 1985
Senior Interprovincials:	1984, 1985

Index — General

A

Adair, Hugh, 10, 12, 22, 28
Adair, Rhona, 66
Adams, A.S.G. (Fred), 215, 216
Adams, Charles S., 215, 216
Adams, Jimmy, 87
Agnew, Tom, 189
Aitken, J., 74
Alexander, John S., 10, 13, 22, 28
Alison, Major, 22
Allen, E. O'S., 65
Allis, Peter, 86–7
Anderson, D., 22
Anderson, L. Stuart, 75
Anderson, Neil H., 96, 140, 150
Andrews, J.A., 22, 24
Auchterlonie, Laurie, 35
Australian Golf Union, 40

B

Baillie, George L., 2, 3, 8, 35–6
Baine, David L., 116, 205, 211
Balfour Melville, L., 36
Ball, John Jr, 14
Ball, John III (later John Ball Jr), 13, 14, 22, 24, 36–7, 46, 47
Ball, Tom, 73
Ballingall, Fred, 186
Ballingall, Hugh, 186
Bamford, J.L. (Ian), 191
Barry, Richard, 196
Barton, Mr Justice Dunbar Plunket, Bart., 49, 50, 54, 57, 74, 203, 210
Beck, John, 231
Behan, Ms Lilian, 104, 105

Bennett, Howard, 181
Bingham, Dr John A., 125
Blackwell, Edward R.H., 24
Bloom, Mark, 118
Board of Greenkeeping Research (later The Sports Turf Research Institute) (STRI), 77, 145, 164–5, 193, 216
Boland, Councillor John TD, 162
Bonallack, Michael, 104, 219, 235, 246
Bond, F.S., 39
Bord Failte, 132, 158
Bowen, Frank W., 209, 211
Bowen, Jimmy, 116
Boyd, Henry A., 18, 26, 51
Boyd, R.R., 44
Bradshaw, Harry, 86, 106–7, 117, 128, 131, 132, 134, 230
Branigan, Declan, 118
Brewer, J.C., 118
Brindley, Thomas P., 119, 139, 205, 210, 211, 213
British Golf Unions' Joint Advisory Council (JAC) (later The Council of National Golf Unions) (CONGU), 39, 40, 77, 92, 94, 95, 96, 107, 152, 164, 179, 193, 198, 216, 218, 225
Brophy, Ms Betty, 250
Brown, Eric, 83, 86–7
Brown, Joe, 26, 110, 186, 238
Browning, Dr G.S., 185–6

Bruen, Jimmy, 26, 31, 40, 104, 114, 163, 170, 183, 220, 221, 238, 230, 231–2, 236, 246
Bruton, John, TD, 160
Burke, John, 31–2, 186–7, 220, 221, 226–7, 229, 231
Burns, Jack, 14, 72
Burns, Raymond, 168
Butler, G.B., 57
Byrne, Frank J., 214
Byrne, Jim, 165

C

Cairnes, H.M., 26, 49, 51, 54, 80
Cameron, H.J., 8
Campbell, Rev. Edward F., 12
Campbell, Lloyd, 49, 54
Campbell, W., 49, 54
Campbell, William C. (Bill), 219
Carberry, W.J., 44
Carey, John E., 118, 119
Carr, Ms Dor, 59
Carr, John J., 140, 245
Carr, Joseph B. (JB), 26, 31–2, 40, 59, 87, 104, 107, 110, 114, 117–18, 123, 126, 128, 129, 130, 134, 136, 139, 141, 149, 151, 168–9, 180–81, 186, 187, 189, 191, 220, 221, 227–8, 229, 232, 233–6, 238, 241, 246
Carr, Roddy J., 118, 220, 223, 241
Carrickfergus Urban District Council, 157
Carroll, Jimmy, 40, 189
Carroll, Ms Pamela, 250
Cartier, Claude, 151, 182

Carvill, Jim, 98, 176
Casper, Billy, 134
Castlereagh Urban District Council, 157
Caul, Paddy, 107, 151, 189, 239
Central Remedial Clinic, 132
Christie, Harry, 61
Christmas, Martin, 240
City and Guilds of London Institute, 165–6
Clarke, Darren, 96, 98
Cleary, T., 140
Cochran, Robert, 104
Collingwood, Richard A., 12
Collins, J., 175
Colt, H.S., 187
Combe, George, 8, 12, 13, 14, 15, 22, 23, 30, 35, 37, 38, 43, 49, 54, 185, 187, 202, 211, 212, 216
Commissioners of Public Works (Office of) (Board of Works), 158–9
Compston, Archie, 84
CONGU (see British Golf Unions' Joint Advisory Service) (JAC)
Connolly (nee Carbery) Ms Josephine, 188–9
Corcoran, D.K., 151
Cork City Corporation, 157, 162
Corridan, T., 175
Cotton, Sir Henry, 82, 84, 107, 115, 120, 231
Coughlan, R., 169
Coyne, J.C., 118
Craddock, Tom, 107, 139, 151, 189, 220, 222, 239, 240
Craig, George V., 12

Index — Links/Courses and Clubs

Published in Ireland by
Gill and Macmillan Ltd
Goldenbridge
Dublin 8
with associated companies in
Auckland, Delhi, Gaborone, Hamburg, Harare,
Hong Kong, Johannesburg, Kuala Lumpur, Lagos, London,
Manzini, Melbourne, Mexico City, Nairobi,
New York, Singapore, Tokyo
© William A. Menton, 1991
Design by The Unlimited Design Company, Dublin
Typesetting by Seton Music Graphics Ltd, Bantry, Co. Cork
Origination and Platemaking by Kulor Centre Ltd, Dublin
Printed by Criterion Press, Dublin

British Library Cataloguing in Publication Data
Menton, William A.
The Golfing Union of Ireland 1891–1991.
1. Great Britain. Ireland. Golf, history
I. Title
796.35209415

ISBN 0-7171-1855-X